perennials

perennials

The comprehensive guide to over 2700 plants

PROFESSOR MARSHALL CRAIGMYLE

Colin Gower Enterprises

Colin Gower Enterprises
Cordwainers
Caring Lane
Leeds
Maidstone
Kent
ME17 1TJ
United Kingdom

ISBN 0 681 37793 3

In fond memory of Marshall Craigmyle - 25th November 1923 to 1st July 2003.

Design, illustrations and layout by Hardlines Ltd, Charlbury, Oxford.
Reproduction by Hardlines Ltd, Charlbury, Oxford.

Printed and bound in China.

CONTENTS

INTRODUCTION

Plants are classified as annuals if they flower and die in one season, as biennials if they flower and die in their second year, and as perennials if they live and flower for three or more years. Despite the perennial connotation, not all perennials can be described as truly perennial in the sense of living forever, since some live for only a few years, but the great majority are long-lived given conditions of soil and climate which are to their liking. Perennials in nature grow in all climates from arctic through temperate and subtropical to tropical, and at all altitudes from sea level to alpine. Not surprisingly, therefore, they exhibit a wide range of hardiness, yet we expect to be able to grow them all in our gardens by manipulating the environment artificially to suit them; we are not always successful, however. I shall return to this later in the section on cultivation.

Perennials may retain their leaves over winter, and be evergreen; others may have leaves all year round if growing in warm climates but lose them if grown in cold climates. The great majority of perennials, however, lose their leaves in the autumn whatever the climate, and are classified as herbaceous or deciduous. Some types keep a few leaves over winter and are described as being semi-evergreen. There is no hard and fast rule as to why some are herbaceous and others evergreen, as both categories can usually be found in members of the same genus.

Perennials also vary in their root systems. Most are fibrous-rooted, but others have swollen underground stems in the form of a rhizome, a tuber, a corm or a bulb, in which energy is stored to help survive the winter. The subtle differences between these need not concern the average gardener inasmuch as it makes little or no difference as to their culture, but does come into play when the plants are to be propagated by division. Again I shall elaborate on this later, in the section on propagation of perennials by division.

Perennials may be classified as hardy or tender, but these terms are relative; what is hardy in one area may be tender in another, and so one must have some yardsticks to go by. The section on hardiness will give a full account of how to decide whether a plant is likely to be hardy in your garden, because every plant in this book has a hardiness rating to help you, and zone maps will also tell you the hardiness rating of your garden.

THE NAMING OF PLANTS

As far as nomenclature is concerned, this account applies to all classes of plants and not just to perennials. The plant world is classified into flowering plants (Angiospermae), cone-bearers (Gymnospermae), and ferns (Pteridophytae), and the flowering plants are sub classified into monocotyledons and dicotyledons depending on whether their seedlings have one or two leaflets. Beyond that plants are divided into families such as Primulaceae or Liliaceae. Within any given family are to be found genera such as the genus *Primula* or the genus *Lilium*, and the title of the genus is, by convention, placed in italics, and given a capital letter. Finally, within any given genus are to be found the species, which have a lot in common, can interbreed (hybridize) and often have a limited geographical range; examples of such are *Lilium longiflorum* (lily having long flowers) or *Primula sikkimensis*, (primula from Sikkim). The specific name is not given a capital letter, but is placed in italics; the name usually has some meaning with regard to the nature or the origin of the plant. So each and every plant has a label in the so-called binominal nomenclature such as *Bellis perennis* (perennial daisy), which is placed in italics and indicates its genus and species. Each genus in this book has the Family name in brackets in its Introduction, and the members of the genus have their names in binominal nomenclature alongside their picture.

Further subdivisions within a given species are indicated by "subsp." meaning "subspecies" or "var." meaning "variety," or "forma." meaning "form of" in that descending order, but none of these abbreviations are put in italics, so we can have plants with complex names such as *Allium carinatum* subsp. *pulchellum* forma. *album*, or *Agapanthus campanulatus* var. *albidus*. Hybrids are indicated by having "x" built into the name. Hybrids between two species (intergeneric hybrids) have the "x" before the name, such as *x Heucherella* (a hybrid between *Heuchera* and *Tiarella*) whereas hybrids between two species (interspecific hybrids) have the "x" between, such as *Sempervivum macedonicum x tectorum* (a cross between *S. macedonicum* and *S. tectorum*) The words "flore pleno" built into a plant name indicate that the flowers are double. Finally, cultivars are plants raised specifically, and accidentally or deliberately, for release to the gardening public, and given a specific name with which they may be identified, as for example, *Helenium* 'Rubinzwerg'A.G.M. The cultivar name is put in inverted commas, but not in italics. The letters A.G.M. listed after a plant name, as here, imply that the plant has been under trial at its Wisley garden by the Royal Horticultural Society for garden worthiness, has been decreed to be outstanding in that respect and has earned the Award of Garden Merit. Some cultivars have been patented by the raisers, and propagation for resale cannot be carried out without the permission of the breeder. Such plants carry the letters P.B.R., standing for Plant Breeders' Rights, after their name.

HARDINESS

Probably the most important consideration when acquiring any plant one hopes to grow in the open garden throughout the year is its degree of hardiness, and to know this is not the complete answer unless one also knows the hardiness rating of one's garden. This information is now available. The United States Department of Agriculture has subdivided North America into eleven Zones, from Zone 1 in the cold North to Zone 11 in the warm South, based on the annual average minimum temperature for that area, as follows:

Zone 1: Below −50°F (below −44°C)
Zone 2: −50° to −40°F (−44° to −37°C)
Zone 3: −40° to −30°F (−37° to −32°C)
Zone 4: −30° to −20°F (−32° to −27°C)
Zone 5: −20° to −10°F (−27° to −22°C)
Zone 6: −10° to 0°F (−22° to −16°C)
Zone 7: 0°F to +10°F (−16° to −10°C)
Zone 8: +10°F to +20°F (−10° to −5°C)
Zone 9: +20°F to +30°F (−5° to 0°C)
Zone 10: +30°F to +40°F (0° to +5°C)
Zone 11: Above +40°F (above +5°C)

Subsequently, maps with similar temperature zones have been made available for Western Europe, South Africa, Australia and New Zealand. Armed with this information, any gardener in any one of the above countries can readily find the rating for his garden.

Hardiness ratings for plants have now also become available, and every plant in this book has such a rating. So, if your garden is in, say, Zone 8, as is mine, you can assume that any plant with a rating between Zone 1 and Zone 8 will survive **average** winters, but not necessarily very severe winters, in your garden; plants of hardiness zones less than 8 will stand a better chance of surviving severe winters. However, it cannot be emphasized too strongly that survival over winter may depend equally on the soil condition the plants are growing in. I shall return to this later when dealing with cultivation.

Most gardens have microclimates, i.e. they have cold and warm corners, and a Zone 8 garden may have Zone 7 and Zone 9 parts, and so it is possible to grow Zone 9 plants, for example, in a warm corner in a Zone 8 garden; by the same token, cold corners should be planted up with plants from lower zones of hardiness. Otherwise, should one wish to grow plants from zones higher than the rating for your garden all year round in the open garden, one has to resort to some device to protect the plants during winter. For herbaceous plants, a deep mulch of compost will probably suffice, but a further problem may be that early growth in spring could be damaged by frosts, and so the emergent growths must be protected by a cloche or a pane of glass The way to over winter evergreen plants in the open ground is to cover them with a cloche or wrap them in fleece. A common practice to grow plants which are from a more highly-rated zone than that of one's garden (i.e. are tender) is to grow them in containers of size such that they can be lifted and grown under glass over winter; information on growing tender plants under glass is given throughout this book

PLANNING A PERENNIAL GARDEN

Herbaceous borders of grandiose proportions were the hallmark of English stately homes in the past. They were planted invariably in front of a high wall or tall evergreen hedge, and the result was that the plants grew away at an angle, gusts of wind would bounce over the wall and flatten the plants, so elaborate and time-consuming staking was necessary. This was overcome by planting perennials in herbaceous borders in the open or in island beds, as pioneered by the nurseryman Alan Bloom in his garden in Bressingham, Norfolk. Herbaceous borders or island beds sited in the open away from the shadow of high hedges, overhanging trees or tall buildings have the great advantages that the plants grow vertically, and hence staking is much less required. The bed, moreover, can be approached for maintenance reasons from all sides; if the bed is not too large, it eliminates the necessity of trampling through it, compacting the soil, which should be avoided at all costs.

Soil preparation is all-important in planning a garden for perennials, and drainage is the key factor. Most plants loathe waterlogged soil, unless they are bog or wetland plants. Any clay should be dug out two spits deep, all perennial weeds removed, and drainage in the form of coarse grit or clinker placed in the bottom. Replace the topsoil or compost or other suitable growing medium, with as much humus incorporated as possible, including substances which are slow to disintegrate such as bark chips, because the plants are likely to remain in position for many years; minimal attention, after all, is the main attraction of a perennial bed. A further spin-off of having good drainage and open soil is that plants survive wet and cold better in such circumstances.

Traditionally, perennials were grown in long herbaceous borders backed by a wall or hedge, as here in the National Trust garden at Sissinghurst, Kent.

Herbaceous borders growing in full sun do not have the problem of plants growing at an angle from shade.

The herbaceous borders in Inverewe garden, Wester Ross, Scotland, are traditional, and backed by a tall wall.

Key

Zone 1
Zone 2
Zone 3
Zone 4
Zone 5
Zone 6
Zone 7
Zone 8
Zone 9
Zone 10
Zone 11

Zonal Temperature Ranges

Zone 1: Below -50°F (Below -44°C)

Zone 2: -50° to -40°F (-44° to -37°C)

Zone 3: -40° to -30°F (-37° to -32°C)

Zone 4: -30° to -20°F (-32° to -27°C)

Zone 5: -20° to -10°F (-27° to -22°C)

Zone 6: -10° to 0°F (-22° to -16°C)

Zone 7: -0° to +10°F (-16° to -10°C)

Zone 8: +10° to +20°F (-10° to -5°C)

Zone 9: +20° to +32°F (-5° to -0°C)

Zone 10: +32° to +40°F (0° to +5°C)

Zone 11: Above +40°F (Above +5°C)

The use of island beds for perennials was introduced by Alan Bloom, in Bressingham, Diss, Norfolk.

A raised border of mixed perennials and dwarf shrubs at Chelsea, in 1979.

A raised bed, as in the author's garden in South Wales, allows planting on top and on the side walls.

RAISED BEDS

In areas of very heavy soil, it is possible to circumvent the labor of digging out the clay by creating raised beds. These have many advantages. The walls should be such that water can escape through, so dry stonewalling is ideal. The base of the raised bed should have a generous incorporation of coarse drainage covered by stone chippings. Raised beds have the advantage that plants can be grown on the side walls, thus effectively increasing the area of cultivation, and some plants such as Lewisias and *Erigeron karvinskianus* do particularly well, although there are many others from which to choose.

Raised beds can be filled with compost suited to the needs of the plants being grown; ericaceous plants can be grown if the bed contains acid compost, for example. Raised beds bring the plants nearer to one's senses of sight and smell and touch, and are very helpful in particular for the wheelchair-bound gardener, as he or she can do a lot of the routine maintenance such as weeding or dead-heading personally. I know from my handicapped friends that they derive great satisfaction from being able so to do. A stone path wide enough to take a wheelchair should be placed around the bed between it and the lawn. Trailing plants planted round the edges will fall over the wall and add to the number and selection of plants that may be grown. Another advantage of raised beds is that they can be filled with various types of compost such as very sharply-draining for those plants which grow in arid deserts in nature, or with ericaceous compost for those plants which demand this.

A scree garden in the author's garden. Such a bed allows for sharp drainage and weeds are kept to a minimum.

SCREE BEDS

A scree bed is very useful in wet gardens for ground-hugging or low-growing perennials such as alpines, which have a tendency to rot at the neck in cold wet ground, or for growing drought-tolerant plants, which do not require to be watered with any great regularity even during a dry spell. A listing of such plants will be found in the Appendix. A raised bed, preferably, can be filled with grit-enriched compost and then planted up with such plants, and then top-dressed with 2 in. (5 cm.) of alpine grit, which should be worked around and under the plants so that their foliage is not in contact with the soil, and the neck is surrounded on all sides by grit. Indeed alpine grit can be used as a top dressing in any bed to advantage in any garden, not just in wet regions. It has the additional advantages that it discourages slugs and snails, and weeds, and any weeds are easy to pull out. Large scree beds have become very fashionable, but have the disadvantage of being totally unsuitable for the wheelchair gardener; small scree beds, particularly if raised, are the ideal for them.

TROUGHS

A trough is nothing more than a scree garden in miniature and is best suited to dwarf plants, dwarf conifers and alpines. There should be ample drainage in the bottom, and open gritty compost must be used. Finally, a top-dressing of alpine grit is to be recommended. If raised on a plinth, the trough can be appreciated at close hand.

Fig 8: *A trough is a scree garden in miniature. Logan Botanic Garden, Wigtonshire, Scotland.*

Borders of flowering perennials should avoid color clashes, and the colors should blend, as here in Logan Botanic Garden, Wigtonshire.

Beds of a single species, such as Canna, *as here in Roath Park, Cardiff, are a popular way of growing perennials.*

CONTAINERS

Perennials may also be grown very successfully in containers, as their requirements can be met to the letter – for example, if filled with ericaceous compost, acid-lovers can be grown. I find containerization a very useful means of ensuring that the patio outside the French window is colorful all year round. Let me enlarge. Nerines, such as *Nerine bowdenii*, which flowers in October, flower best if pot bound, and so are ideal for a container, which can stand in an odd corner for eleven months, but brighten the patio during October when little else is in bloom. It goes without saying that the containers for this purpose should not be too heavy to carry around. So too, winter-flowering plants such as hellebores can be enjoyed at close quarters from the warmth of the house – and if they are perfumed, so much the better on a mild day when a window is open. Another group of perennials that can be grown in containers is those plants that are too tender to be left in the open all year round, in your garden. Many very desirable perennials such as Pelargoniums, Argyranthemums, Gazanias and Osteospermums if grown in containers will continue to flower when brought indoors into a conservatory or greenhouse at the first sign of frost. So, too, many tender perennials can be grown permanently in containers and over wintered under glass. In this book, all Zone 9 and 10 perennials, and even some from Zone 8, have instructions on their cultural requirements under glass.

Certain classes of perennials such a acid-lovers, and invasive plants, can be grown in containers as a device to meet their needs, or yours. I grow *Eomecon chionanthum* in a container, as it is so fiercely invasive, but has beautiful flowers and handsome foliage. Another invasive plant which should not be planted in the open garden but in a container is the handsome variegated ground elder, *Aegopodium podagraria* 'Variegata'. If you have very alkaline limy soil, then acid-lovers can be grown only if special beds are created with ericaceous compost, such as the raised beds mentioned above, and they do very well in containers of such compost. A container of dwarf heathers looks very attractive, for example.

Plants such as Nerine bowdenii, *which flower best when root bound, respond to cultivation in a container.*

BOG GARDENS.

Many moisture-loving plants such as *Astilbe*, *Primula japonica*, *Primula florindae*, and other Candelabrom primulas, *Iris pseudacorus*, *Iris foetidissima*, *Lysichiton*, and many others will grow happily in pond margins or in boggy ground, and if one does not have a naturally-occurring bog, one can be created by shallow excavation of a ground hollow, and top-dressing with compost.

PERENNIALS IN COMBINATION.

Nowadays it has become fashionable to incorporate grasses and sub shrubs into perennial borders, and these plants are covered comprehensively within these pages. Grasses, in particular, enhance any planting, as they add spires to what is otherwise rounded perennials – and many grasses have very handsome foliage, variegated in some instances, while some are evergreen. They have the effect of loosening-up the planting. Subshrubs such as *Fuchsia*, *Phygelius* and *Helianthemum* are very useful additions to mixed borders, as they are long-flowering and add

A bog garden allows for the cultivation of plants that relish moisture at their roots. Forde Abbey garden, Somerset

Plantings of perennials should ideally combine differing shapes and colors, as here at Hampton Court Palace garden.

At the Royal Horticultural Society garden, Wisley, borders are given over to members of the Monocotyledon family.

The white garden was fashionable at one time, as here in Sissinghurst, Kent.

vertical height. There are many hardy fuchsias in cultivation, despite the fact that there are many very tender forms. Ideally, beds and borders should be planted such that the outlines made by plants are of varied contours, such as rounded and spiky plants planted in combination, with the taller plants in the center and dwarf ones around the edges. Bulbous perennial can also be built successfully into beds, but many are spring-flowering, so the untidy gaps they leave have to be infilled with annuals or bedding plants; not that this is altogether a bad thing, but it is time-consuming. It is also important to plant colors which are compatible, and do not clash, next to one another—orange and pink for example. Beds of pastel–colored flowers are pleasing, and make for a restful atmosphere, whereas beds of hot colors such as oranges and red make a very pleasing impact. Blue and yellow plants make a very cheerful combination. It is important to plant up with plants having differing flowering seasons to provide all-season interest. Incorporation of foliage plants, many of which have insignificant flowers, is very desirable to create overall effect, and this is true especially if they are evergreen. A list of suitable plants will be found in the Appendix. Finally, the recommended practice is to plant in drifts of three, four, five or more to create the maximum effect. This, for me as a plantsman, is the least important consideration, since I'd rather have, say, three hundred different plants to enjoy than three of each of a hundred, and I do not think, personally, that it detracts from the overall effect too much if one grows single specimens.

It is also possible to ring the changes by planting up beds with plants of a single color or of a single genus. White gardens were fashionable at one time, but have fallen into disfavor. Beds of a single color, or of two or three harmonizing colors, can be very pleasing. In the Royal Horticultural Society garden at Wisley, there are beds composed exclusively of Monocotyledons. Beds of a single genus are fine for the enthusiast, but suffer from the great disadvantage that all bloom at the same time and the bed can be drab for much of the year unless planted up with plants having a long flowering season. The same holds true for seasonal beds, i.e. beds planted up with spring-flowering or summer-flowering or autumn-flowering plants. These are very attractive, but for a limited season.

It is very fashionable nowadays to combine flowering plants with foliage plants, some of which are non-flowering or have insignificant flowers. I have incorporated many such plants in this compendium, and I repeat that grasses and ferns are also covered comprehensively within these pages, as they are essential ingredients of the foliage bed. There are some foliage perennials which are also evergreen, such as *Heuchera* and *x Heucherella*, among others, (see Appendix Four) and it is possible to plant a bed with these, and thus overcome the main criticism of herbaceous beds and borders, which is that they are bleak and drab in winter. Foliage perennials and dwarf shrubs are used exclusively in bedding schemes in the Botanic garden in Funchal, Madeira. Containers are also enhanced by mixing flowering and foliage plants together.

ACQUIRING PERENNIALS

When deciding to create a garden of perennials that are to be grown in the open all year round, there are several major considerations to be kept in mind, and several of lesser importance. The major ones are hardiness, spread, degree of invasiveness, degree of self-seeding, and height, in that order. The hardiness question has been covered already, but nevertheless it may be sensible to buy plants that have been raised by local nurserymen, because such plants are likely to be hardy in your area without your having recourse to reference books. It may be, of course, that you will not be able to acquire all the plants you want locally, and then one has to cast around. Check out directories of garden centers to find out what plants they carry, or you can try on the internet search to track down a particularly elusive specimen.

Space is always at a premium. Plants such as *Gunnera manicata* that cover large areas are not for small gardens as they look entirely out of place, and do not repay one for the space they occupy. The spread for every plant in this book is given. It does not seem to make sense, again, to grow a few very large plants rather than larger numbers of smaller plants.

Degree of invasiveness is a very important factor in planning a perennial garden. Invasive plants will spread into neighboring plants, and these plants must, of necessity, be lifted to detach the invader, and replanted, but this is troublesome and fraught with the risk of losing plants. It is said that if one goes round any invasive plant with a spade once a year to divide the stolons this will suffice, but again there is no guarantee of success, and the last thing one should ever do is trample through one's beds to do any maintenance. If you must grow invasive plants, grow them in isolation from others, or in a container. Plants with invasive tendencies are highlighted in the book.

Plants which self-seed, such as grape hyacinths and bluebells in my garden, can give you as much trouble as their invasive cousins, as they self-seed into other plants, so again one is faced with the task of lifting and separating the two, with the same attendant risks. It is of course possible to dead-head such plants, but with the best will in the world, one misses a few, or has a few days away, and the damage is done. So, again, avoid such plants unless one has an odd corner where nothing will grow, and they can be tried there. All self-seeding perennials are noted in these pages.

Plants which require to be staked have less nuisance value than the others that have been discussed, but a nuisance they are nevertheless; it is very time consuming to tie them up with the old-fashioned string and cane method, and very expensive to surround them with modern green metal stakes – although, once bought, these can be used over and over again, and are easy and quick to install. Gardeners with exposed gardens know all about the problems with tall plants, and avoid them completely, so if you live in an exposed area, do the same. One further point on this topic; do not plant tall perennials in shade which will cause them to grow at an angle to the vertical, as this is a recipe for disaster. Plants that require to be staked are also noted in this book.

Some of us have allergy problems, and yet we continue to garden despite this drawback. All high-allergen plants are highlighted, as are those plants that are skin-irritant and cause urticaria, and both categories should be avoided by the allergic gardener. Nevertheless, it is possible to choose low allergen perennials if you are allergic, and such plants are noted in these pages.

The principal pest of my garden is the slug, and the remedies are so well known that I shall not enlarge on them here. Some genera such as *Hosta* are martyrs to the pests, and I surround mine with coarse grit, which acts as a considerable but not entirely foolproof deterrent.

The main disease of my perennials is powdery mildew, and some genera such as *Phlox paniculata* and *Monarda* and *Aster novi-belgii* just will not grow for me. Whilst there are remedial sprays available, I find that the best plan is to avoid such genera altogether. Plants that are mildew-prone are listed.

Here, in the National Trust garden at Sissinghurst, Kent, a border is devoted entirely to the genus Aquilegia.

Containers planted up with foliage plants, as here in the author's garden are an attractive feature in a garden.

CULTIVATION OF PERENNIALS

There are no special rules for having success with perennials other than the basic rules of good cultivation. However, it has to be borne in mind that perennials will be *in situ* for many, many years and so advance preparation as outlined earlier is vital to success. Some perennials do benefit from being lifted and divided and the healthy outer parts replanted every few years, and this gives one the chance to revitalize the soil as one does so; such plants are detailed in the book.

The beds should be mulched annually (when the ground is wet, or has been watered beforehand) with manure or garden compost, or universal compost, and great benefit ensues in the form of weed suppression, enhanced growth, and moisture preservation, so less watering is required.

Planting out can, with the advent of containerization, be done almost the year round, but ideally should be done in spring, so as to give the plants time to build up a root system before the winter. Autumn is also a suitable time to plant out, except perhaps in very cold climates. Planting out should be avoided if the soil is waterlogged, or frozen, or during hot weather.

Some perennials, such as Lupins, are tap-rooted, and resent disturbance once established; it is important to site these carefully at the outset, as they will die if one decides to move them thereafter. Such perennials are highlighted in the book.

Dead-heading should be done as soon as flowering is finished, since it prevents self-seeding, encourages repeat-flowering, and finally, stops the plant from devoting energy to seed production rather than building up reserves for the winter.

Staking is best done at an early stage by putting pea-sticks or metal hoops in position for the plant to grow through. Metal semi-circular supports are now readily available commercially, and a pair of these placed around a plant provides a quick and effective support.

Annual weeds are best controlled by hoeing, or mulching. Perennial weeds, such as couch grass, should be dug out at the earliest moment before they grow through the plants, otherwise it may be necessary to lift the plants to disentangle the weed. Spraying with weed-killer is not recommended unless one can be certain that no drifting onto plants occurs, as the weeds and plants may take some time to die, and then it is too late.

Watering has to be done in very hot weather, and should ideally be done in the evening, since most will be lost by evaporation if watering is done by day. A thorough soaking of small areas at a time is vastly superior to spraying a wide area superficially. The rationale of this is that repeated surface watering encourages plants to make surface roots at the expense of deep ones, and they become less tolerant of drought conditions. If your garden is very dry, then it is advisable to grow drought-tolerant plants, which in nature grow in hot, dry areas. All such plants are detailed in the book.

PROPAGATION OF PERENNIALS

There are the following means of increasing perennial plants: by seed, by division, by taking cuttings, by leaf cuttings, by layering, by air layering and by detaching rooted suckers. The methods of choice are given for each plant.

Propagation by seed

It is important at the outset to state that cultivars and hybrids (i.e. named varieties) do not come true from seed, and the progeny will be a mixed batch, with some resembling one parent, others like the second parent, and still others unlike either. There are very few exceptions to this rule, but *Geranium* 'Bill Wallis' is one such. On the other hand, species will come true from seed.

Seed of some species is best sown as soon as it is ripe, (i.e. in the autumn) whilst seed of others can be sown in autumn or the following spring. Some seed may not germinate for a year or two, and seed of others may germinate erratically. Seed of tender species will almost certainly require heat before it will germinate in cold climates, and the preferred temperature is given for each species.

Seed compost should be used, since it is sterilized. Small seed should be scattered on the surface, and larger seeds should be lightly covered. Some very large seeds, such as those of *Baptisia* or *Lupin,* may have to be chipped before sowing. The seedlings should never be allowed to dry out. Seed of tap-rooted plants should be sown in the proposed flowering site, for preference, but if sown in a container the seedlings should be moved on into their flowering positions at the earliest moment possible, to keep root disturbance to a minimum.

Foliage plants can be used exclusively to create effect, as here in the Botanic Garden of Madeira, in Funchal.

It is not uncommon for holders of National Collections to devote borders exclusively to their genus. The Michaelmas Daisy borders at the Paul Picton Garden.

Borders of one-color plants, such as the purple border at the National Trust Garden, Sissinghurst, are a favorite way of growing perennials.

Propagation by division

Perennials can have rootstocks of various types: fibrous, bulbous, tuberous, cormous or rhizomatous, and the division technique depends on the root form. Division must be done during the dormant period – spring is best, but autumn is also suitable.

Most perennials are fibrous-rooted, and they should be dug up, and if small divided by placing two hand forks back-to-back into the center of the plant and levering them apart. For larger plants, a pair of garden forks may be required, but the technique is similar. Replanting should be immediate, and the plants should not be allowed to dry out until established. Should immediate planting not be feasible, the plants should be stored wrapped in wet sacking until planted.

Tuberous and rhizomatous perennials have to be divided using a very sharp knife, and each division must have an 'eye' for it to take successfully. Should the divisions be very small, or if division was done in autumn, they are best grown on in the nursery conditions of a bed, or in pots in a cold frame or greenhouse, for a year or two until established.

Bulbous or cormous perennials are best increased by separating the offsets in the dormant season, (i.e. spring or autumn in most cases) and growing them on as for divisions until they are large enough to be planted out.

Propagation by taking cuttings

Cuttings can be taken of the leaves, stems, stem tips, roots, or basal shoots, of cultivars, hybrids, or species. The time of year ranges from early spring to midsummer – and even in winter for root cuttings. Bottom heat may be required. Details of the specific requirements of each genus are noted in the introductions relating to the genera.

Softwood and greenwood cuttings should be taken in the early morning in spring or early summer by severing below a node with a sharp knife, and removing the leaves from the lowest third. It should then be dipped in hormone rooting powder, inserted in standard cutting compost, and watered with a fungicide solution. It should then be rooted in a propagating case or a mist unit at 75 °F (24 °C). Any dead leaves should be removed at once. Water with fungicide solution weekly.

Basal stem cuttings are of new shoots, taken in spring. They should be taken when the new shoot is between 1-2in. (3-5 cm) high with a heel of older woody tissue at the base. Trim by removing leaves from lower third. Dip in rooting hormone and insert into standard cutting compost, and water with fungicide solution. Put in a cold frame or propagating case.

Hardwood cuttings are **leafless** shoots of current growth cut at the joint with old growth, taken with or without a heel, in early autumn to early winter. Trim to 6-9in. (15-22cm) long, with the cut just above a bud, or pair of buds, and the bottom cut just below a bud or pair of buds. It may be necessary to slit the stem base up to a height of 1/2 in. (1.5cm) in some cases. Dip the base into hormone rooting compound, and insert into gritty, compost in a trench or cold frame such that the top of the cutting is between 1-2 in. (2.5-5 cm) above the surface.

Stem-tip cuttings are from fast-growing, **non-flowering** shoots taken at any time between spring and autumn. They are taken just **above** a node, and are between 3-5 in. (8-12 cm) long. They should be taken in the early morning and trimmed to between 2-3 in. (5-8 cm) long in a horizontal cut just **below** a node, with the leaves removed from the lower third. Put them in a mist unit or a propagating chamber, and shade from hot sun. Any fallen leaves must be removed at once.

Root cuttings are taken when the plant is dormant, which in the majority of instances is during winter. The roots should be vigorous and 1/2 in. (1.5 cm) in diameter at a minimum, and the cutting taken horizontally from near the crown of the plant. Trim to 3-5 in. (8-12 cm) by making a slanting cut at the lower end, and removing all fibrous roots. Dust with fungicide. Insert thick roots vertically, and thin roots horizontally on the surface of standard rooting compost. Cover the thin roots with a thin layer of compost. Put in a cold frame or propagator. Do not water until rooting has taken place, as indicated by growth appearing.

Propagation by leaf cuttings

Leaf cuttings may be taken at any time of the year, and comprise healthy, mature leaves divided close to the base of the leaf-stalk. The leaves may be rooted entire, as for *Saintpaulia*, or halved across as for *Sreptocarpus,* or reduced to a small square as for *Begonia rex*. Insert whole leaves upright, with the blade in contact with the surface, half leaves cut surface down, and leaf squares flat on top of the compost, which should be very gritty. Put in a propagator at 75°F (24°C) in bright light but shaded from hot sun. Water with fungicide.

Propagation by layering

This technique is useful for plants whose stems will produce roots if damaged. The stem should be pegged to the ground while still attached.

Propagation from suckers

Stoloniferous plants have underground growths with roots, and all that is required is to detach these and grow them on.

Propagation by air-layering

Conservatory (i.e. tender) perennials can be increased in this way. Cut into an air stem and surround the area with damp sphagnum moss and enclose in a sleeve of plastic. When roots have formed, which may take a year or two, detach the layered plant and pot on.

A

ACAENA
ACANTHUS
ACHILLEA
ACHINENES
ACIPYLLA
ACONITUM
ACONUS
ACTAEA
ADENOPHORA
ADIANTUM
ADONIS
AECHMEA
AEGOPODUM
AEONIUM
AESCHYNANTHUS
AETHIONEMA
AGAPANTHUS
AGASTACHE
AGAVE
AGLAONEMA
AICHRYSON
AJANIA
AJUGA
ALBUCA
ALCEA
ALCHEMILLA
ALISMA
ALLIUM
ALOCASIA
ALOE
ALONSOA
ALOPECURUS
ALPINIA

ALSTROEMERIA
ALTHAEA
ALYSSUM
AMARYLLIS
AMICIA
AMPELOPSIS
AMSONIA
ANACYCLUS
ANAGALLIS
ANANAS
ANAPHALIS
ANCHUSA
ANEMONE
ANEMONELLA
ANEMONOPSIS
ANGELICA
ANGELONIA
ANIGOZANTHOS
ANISODONTEA
ANOMATHECA
ANTENNARIA
ANTHEMIS
ANTHERICUM
ANTHRISCUS
ANTHURIUM
ANTIRRHINUM

AQUILEGIA
ARABIS
ARCTOTHECA
ARCTOTIS
ARENARIA
ARGYRANTHEMUM
ARISAEMA
ARISARUM
ARISTEA
ARMERIA
ARMORACIA
ARTEMISIA
ARTHROPODIUM
ARUM
ARUNCUS
ARUNDO
ASARINA
ASARUM
ASCLEPIAS
ASPARAGUS
ASPHODELINE
ASPHODELUS
ASPIDISTRA
ASPLENIUM

ASTELIA
ASTER
ASTILBE
ASTRANTIA
ATHYRIUM
AUBRIETA
AURINIA
AZOLLA

A

ACAENA *(Rosaceae)*
Common names: Bidi-bidi; New Zealand burr

A genus of around 100 species of evergreen perennials and subshrubs, distributed in open habitats high in the mountains of the southern hemisphere. They are prostrate, mat-forming and root as they run so they can quickly make ground cover, but they can become scraggy over the years. They are cultivated for their foliage, the leaves being pinnate and ovate. The flowers are petal-less, inconspicuous, and in cylindrical spikes or globose heads. The fruits are enclosed in spiny burrs, which are very prickly, and can get caught up in the fur of household pets. Some species are invasive.

✔ Evergreen   ✔ Disease-free   ✘ Flowers insignificant
✔ Handsome foliage   ✔ Pest-free
✔ Attractive seed-heads

CULTIVATION
Grow in any soil that is well-drained, in sun or part shade. The rooting stems should be cut back to restrict plant size if space is at a premium.

PROPAGATION
Seed should be sown in an open frame in autumn. Plantlets can be separated from the main plant in spring or autumn. Softwood cuttings can be taken in late spring.

Acaena microphylla 'Kupferteppich'

Zone 6
Height: 2in. (5cm) Spread: 30in. (75cm)
Invasive

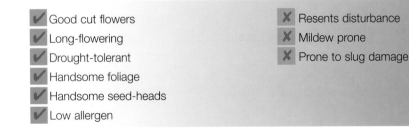

Acaena affinis

Zone 6
Height: 5in. (12cm) Spread: 3ft. (90cm)

Acaena caesiiglauca

Zone 6
Height: 5in. (12cm) Spread: 3ft. (90cm)
Invasive

ACANTHUS *(Acanthaceae)*
Common names: Bear's breeches

A genus of about 30 species of drought-tolerant perennials, which come from dry, stony sites in circum-Mediterranean countries. They are striking plants, with handsome foliage, and are thus good architectural plants. The leaves are usually basal, obovate, toothed or even spiny, and dark green in color. The flowers are tubular, two-lipped, and have spiny bracts. They are borne in upright, terminal racemes from summer to early autumn.

✔ Good cut flowers   ✘ Resents disturbance
✔ Long-flowering   ✘ Mildew prone
✔ Drought-tolerant   ✘ Prone to slug damage
✔ Handsome foliage
✔ Handsome seed-heads
✔ Low allergen

CULTIVATION
Grow in any soil that is well-drained, but they prefer deep, fertile loam, in sun or part shade.

PROPAGATION
Sow seed in a cold frame in spring. Division can be carried out in spring or autumn. Root cuttings may be taken in winter.

Acanthus dioscoridis var. *perringii*

Zone 8
Height: 16in. (40cm) Spread: 2ft. (60cm)

A

Acanthus hirsutus

Height: 14in. (35cm) Spread: 1ft. (30cm)

Acanthus hungaricus

Zone 8
Height: 4ft. (1.2m) Spread: 3ft. (90cm)
Needs staking/Invasive/Self-seeds

Acanthus mollis

Zone 6
Height: 5ft. (1.5m) Spread: 3ft. (90cm)
Needs staking/Invasive/Self-seeds

Acanthus mollis 'Pride of Morvan'

Zone 6
Height: 5ft. (1.5m) Spread: 3ft. (90cm)
Invasive/Self-seeds/Needs staking

Acanthus spinosus

Zone 6
Height: 4ft. (1.2m) Spread: 2ft. (60cm)
Needs staking/Invasive/Self-seeds

ACHILLEA *(Compositae)*

Common names: Yarrow; milfoil; sneezewort

A genus of around 80 species from temperate regions of the northern hemisphere. Species from mountainous regions are dwarf, whilst species from grassland and wasteland are tall. They have feathery foliage, with the exception of *A. ptarmica*, and may be herbaceous or evergreen. The flower heads are flat corymbs and appear in summer and autumn; they last a long time. *A. millefolium* and *A. ptarmica* are highly invasive weeds.

- ✓ Good cut flowers
- ✓ Good for drying for winter
- ✓ Handsome foliage
- ✓ Handsome seed-heads
- ✗ Mildew prone
- ✗ Need to lift & divide often

Achillea 'Coronation Gold' A.G.M.

Zone 6
Height: 30in. (75cm) Spread: 18in. (45cm)

CULTIVATION

Will grow in any well-drained soil, but prefers a deep moist well-drained soil in full sun; sharp drainage is necessary for silver-foliaged alpine species. They tend to die out in the center, so should be lifted and the healthy outer parts replanted every few years.

PROPAGATION

Seed may be sown in containers or *in situ* in spring. Division can be carried out in spring.

A

Achillea 'Credo' A.G.M.

Zone 6
Height: 4ft. (1.2m) Spread: 2ft. (60cm)
Needs staking

Achillea 'Fanal'

Zone 2
Height: 30in. (75cm) Spread: 2ft. (60cm)

Achillea filipendula
'Cloth of Gold' A.G.M.

Zone 3
Height: 5ft. (1.5m) Spread: 18in. (45cm)

Achillea filipendula 'Gold Plate' A.G.M.

Zone 3
Height: 4ft. (1.2m) Spread: 18in. (45cm)
Foliage aromatic/Needs staking

Achillea 'Forncett Candy'

Zone 6
Height: 3ft. (90cm) Spread: 18in.(45cm)

Achillea 'Huteri'

Zone 6
Height: 2ft. (60cm) Spread: 1ft. (30cm)

Achillea millefolium 'Cerise Queen'

Zone 2
Height and spread: 2ft. (60cm)
Aromatic foliage/Invasive

Achillea 'Moonshine' A.G.M.

Zone 7
Height and spread: 2ft. (60cm)

A

Achillea ptarmica 'Nana Compacta'

Zone 5
Height: 1ft. (30cm) Spread: 3ft. (90cm)
Invasive/Short-lived plant

Achillea ptarmica 'Stephanie Cohen'

Zone 5
Height: 30in. (75cm) Spread: 32in. (80 cm)
Invasive/Short-lived plant

Achillea 'Terracotta'

Zone 2
Height: 3ft. (90cm) Spread: 2ft. (60cm)

ACHIMENES *(Gesneriaceae)*

Common names: Cupid's bower; hot water plant

A genus of 25 species of rhizomatous perennials from subtropical forest in Central America and Mexico, which are winter-dormant. The leaves arise from a single stem and are ovate, dark green, hairy, toothed and fleshy. The flowers are salverform, and borne in cymes, or singly, from the leaf axils from summer to autumn. Many cultivars are in cultivation.

✔ Long-flowering	✘ Prone to aphid attack
✔ Handsome foliage	✘ Mildew prone

Achimenes 'Little Beauty'

Zone 10
Height: 10in. (25 cm) Spread: 1ft. (30cm)

CULTIVATION
Under glass, grow in loam-based or loam-free potting compost in bright filtered light, and with moderate humidity . Water sparingly as growth is starting in spring, freely during summer. Store in dry, frost-free conditions over winter.

Outside in very hot climates, grow in moist, well-drained, humus-rich soil in sun, or in part shade.

PROPAGATION
Rhizomes can be divided, or stem cuttings taken, in spring.

ACIPHYLLA *(Apiaceae)*

Common names: Bayonet plant; Speargrass

A genus of 40 species of evergreen perennials from alpine or lowland grasslands of New Zealand and Australia. They are dioecious, so plants of both sexes are required before flowering can take place, but this is not common in cool climates.

They form grassy clumps or rosettes of stiff, linear, flat, leathery leaves with terminal spines and spiny stipules. The flowers are borne in terminal panicles of several compound umbels of many very small greeny-yellow or white flowers surrounded by large spiny bracts.

✔ Long-flowering	✘ Resents disturbance
✔ Evergreen	✘ Prone to slug damage
✔ Handsome foliage	
✔ Architectural plants	

Aciphylla aurea

Zone 5
Height and spread: 3ft. (90cm)

CULTIVATION
Grow speargrass in full sun in moist, fertile, sharply-draining soil .

A

PROPAGATION

Seed should be sown in a cold frame as soon as it is ripe, and certainly within a year. The seedlings should be planted out in situ as soon as possible, as they resent disturbance.

Aciphylla glaucescens

Zone 8
Height and spread: 3ft. (90cm)

ACONITUM *(Ranunculaceae)*

Common names: Monkshood; Wolfbane; Aconite

A genus of about 100 species of highly poisonous biennials and perennials from hilly scrub, woodland or grassland across the northern hemisphere. They are tuberous, except for *A. lycotonum* subsp. *vulparia*, which is fibrous-rooted. The green leaves are kidney-shaped and palmate-lobed. The flower petals are nectarines, and hidden by a hood of sepals which provide the color. They are borne in tall racemes or panicles in mid- and late summer. Some species are twining.

✔ Good cut flowers	✖ All parts very poisonous	✖ Mildew prone
✔ Handsome foliage	✖ Foliage is skin-irritant	✖ Require staking
	✖ Need to lift & divide often	

Aconitum x cammarum 'Bicolor'
A.G.M.

Zone 3
Height: 4ft. (1.2m) Spread: 1ft. (30cm)

CULTIVATION

They will grow in almost any soil that is moist, fertile, humus-rich, and cool, in part shade or sun. Taller varieties require staking. They need to be lifted and divided every few years, but can be slow to establish.

PROPAGATION

Seed should be sown in a cold frame in spring. Divide in autumn or early winter

Aconitum septentrionale 'Ivorine'

Zone 5
Height: 3ft. (90cm) Spread: 18in. (45cm)

Aconitum lycotonum subsp.
vulparia

Zone 3
Height: 5ft. (1.5m) Spread: 1ft. (30cm)

Aconitum lycotonum subsp.
vulparia 'Albidus'

Zone 3
Height: 5ft. (1.5m) Spread: 1ft. (30cm)

A

Aconitum napellus

Zone 6
Height: 5ft. (1.5m) Spread: 1ft. (30cm)

Aconitum napellus subsp. *vulgare*
'Albidum'

Zone 6
Height: 5ft. (1.5m) Spread: 1ft. (30cm)

Aconitum 'Stainless Steel'

Zone 5
Height: 3ft. (90cm) Spread: 6in. (15cm)

ACORUS *(Acoraceae)*
Common names: None

A genus of just two species of marginal aquatic perennials, found across the northern hemisphere and in East Asia in particular. They are rhizomatous, and *A. calamus* is deciduous whereas *A.gramineus* is semi-evergreen. The leaves are strap-shaped, and sheathed. The insignificant flowers appear in summer. They are essentially foliage plants.

✔ Handsome foliage   ✘ Flowers insignificant
✔ Disease-free   ✘ Need to lift & divide often
✔ Pest-free

CULTIVATION
Grow *A. calamus* in a pool margin, or in very wet soil in full sun. *A. gramineus* should be grown in shallow water. They need to be lifted and divided every few years.

PROPAGATION
The rhizomes should be divided in spring.

Acorus gramineus 'Ogon'
Japanese rush

Zone 5
Height: 10in. (25 cm) Spread: 6in. (15cm)

A

ACTAEA *(Ranunculaceae)*
Common names: Baneberry

A genus of only eight species. They are rhizomatous, woodlanders from temperate regions of the northern hemisphere. The leaves are up to five-ternate, toothed and green. The flowers are white, in terminal fluffy, compact racemes, and are followed by highly poisonous berries, which are colored white or red. *Actaea simplex* is essentially a foliage plant.

✔ Has berries after flowering	✘ Flowers insignificant
✔ Handsome foliage	✘ Berries very poisonous
✔ Disease-free	
✔ Pest-free	

CULTIVATION
Grow in moist, humus-rich, fertile soil in part shade, or even deep in the case of *A. spicata*. Do not allow to dry out.

PROPAGATION
Sow seed in a cold frame in autumn. Division can be carried out in early spring.

Actaea rubra A.G.M.

Zone 3
Height: 18in. (45cm) Spread: 1ft. (30cm)

Actaea simplex 'Brunette' A.G.M.

Zone 4
Height: 2ft. (60cm) Spread: 18in. (45cm)

Actaea spicata

Zone 4
Height and spread: 18in. (45cm)

ADENOPHORA *(Campanulaceae)*
Common names: Ladybell

A genus of over 40 species of perennials from temperate grassland and woodland across Eurasia. They have fleshy roots, and resemble Campanulas in many respects. They have basal rounded leaves and small stem leaves, which may be entire or toothed, and are ovate or lance-shaped. The bell-shaped, pendent flowers are dark or pale blue, and borne in terminal racemes or panicles.

✘ Resents disturbance
✘ Handsome foliage

CULTIVATION
Grow in moist, light, humus-rich, well-drained soil in sun or part shade. They will not tolerate being divided.

PROPAGATION
Sow seed outdoors *in situ* or in containers as soon as is ripe, and plant the seedlings out when young in order not to damage the fragile roots. Cuttings of basal shoots can be rooted in spring.

Adenophora asiatica

Zone 5
Height: 1ft. (30cm) Spread: 6in. (15cm)

Adenophora potaninii

Zone 3
Height: 3ft. (90cm) Spread: 1ft. (30cm)

ADIANTUM (ADIANTACEAE)
Common names: Maidenhair fern

A genus of about 250 species of ferns, which may be deciduous, semi-evergreen or evergreen. Some are found in temperate regions of Eurasia, Australia and North America, mostly at woodland edges or stream sides. Others are found in subtropical and tropical regions of both South and North America. They are grown for their foliage especially, and for their purple-pink croziers. The fronds are up to five-pinnate, have rounded segments, and dark-colored stems. The sori are rounded and form on the margins of the divisions, and are covered by half-moon-shaped indusia.

CULTIVATION
Tropical species should be grown under glass in gritty, humus-rich, compost with added bark and limestone chippings. They should have no direct light in summer and filtered light in winter, when they should be watered sparingly. High humidity and good ventilation are desirable.

✔ Handsome foliage
✔ Disease-free
✔ Pest free

Temperate species should be grown in moist, fertile, well-drained soil in part shade. The soil should be alkaline for *A. capillus-veneris*.

PROPAGATION
Spores should be sown as soon as they are ripe, at 59°F (15°C) for temperate forms and at 70°F (21°C) for tropical varieties. Rhizomes can be divided in early spring. Some varieties form plantlets at the frond tips, and these can be detached and potted up.

Adiantum aleuticum A.G.M.

Zone 4
Height and spread: 30in. (75cm)

Adiantum aleuticum 'Subpumilum' A.G.M.

Zone 4
Height: 6in. (15cm) Spread: 1ft. (30cm)

A

Adiantum capillus veneris
(True Maidenhair fern)

Zone 8
Height: 1ft. (30cm) Spread: 18in. (45cm)

Adiantum pedatum

Zone 5
Height and spread: 16in. (40cm)

Adiantum raddianum
(Delta maidenhair fern)

Zone 10
Height: 2ft. (60cm) Spread: 32in. (80 cm)

ADONIS *(Ranunculaceae)*

Common names: None

A genus of 20 species of annuals and fully hardy perennials from alpine regions of Eurasia. The foliage is ferny. The flowers are solitary and terminal, yellow in perennials but red in annuals. They are of anemone form, and may be single or double.

✔ Handsome foliage	✘ All parts poisonous
	✘ Prone to slug damage
	✘ Resents disturbance

CULTIVATION

This is not easy. Grow Asiatic forms such as *A. amurensis* in moist, acid, humus-rich soil in full shade. Grow European forms such as *A. vernalis* in alkaline, fertile, well-drained soil in full sun. They resent division.

PROPAGATION

Seed should be sown in a cold frame in containers as soon as it is ripe.

Germination is erratic and slow, and seedlings slow to thrive.

Adonis amurensis

Zone 3
Height: 16in. (40cm) Spread: 1ft. (30cm)

Adonis vernalis

Zone 3
Height: 14in. (35cm) Spread: 18in. (45cm)

AECHMEA *(Bromeliaceae)*
Common names: Vase plant

A genus of 200 species of evergreen perennials, of which the majority are epiphytic, from Central and South America, Mexico and the West Indies. They are grown for both foliage and flowers. They have arching, strap-shaped leaves. The inflorescence is terminal, and the tubular flowers with triangular bracts are borne in summer and are long-lasting.

✔ Long-flowering
✔ Handsome foliage

CULTIVATION
Under glass, grow in epiphytic bromeliad compost, or grow epiphytically, in bright filtered light. Water freely during the growing season, ensuring that the central cup is full.

Outdoors, grow in moist, sharply-drained, humus-rich soil or epiphytically on a tree or branch or in bromeliad epiphytic compost, in sun or light shade. Water freely in the growing season, ensuring that the central vase is full of water at all times.

PROPAGATION
Offsets can be rooted in early summer.

Aechmea fasciata A.G.M.

Zone 9
Height: 20in. (50cm) Spread: 2ft. (60cm)

Aechmea nudicaulis A.G.M.

Zone 10
Height: 28in. (70 cm) Spread: 10in. (25 cm)

AEGOPODIUM *(Apiaceae)*
Common names: Ground elder

A genus of five species of highly invasive, rhizomatous perennials from Eurasian woodlands. Their leaves have three ovate leaflets, and the flowers are white and borne in umbels on branching stems.

✔ Handsome foliage   ✘ Invasive
✔ Disease-free
✔ Pest-free

CULTIVATION
Grow in any soil in part or full shade. Dead-head to prevent self-seeding and confine in a container to prevent spreading.

PROPAGATION
The rhizomes can be separated in spring or autumn

Aegopodium podagraria
'Variegatum'

Zone 2
Height: 2ft. (60cm) Spread: indefinite

A

AEONIUM *(Crassulaceae)*
Common names: None

A genus of 30 species of evergreen succulent perennials and subshrubs, from the Canary Islands, the Mediterranean region, the Cape Verde Islands and Madeira. The fleshy leaves are in rosettes at the ends of shoots. The many-petalled, star-shaped flowers are borne in the center of the rosette in terminal racemes, cymes or panicles in spring and summer.

✔ Evergreen   ✘ Prone to aphid attack
✔ Handsome foliage

CULTIVATION
Under glass, grow in cactus compost in filtered light. Water freely during the growing season, and allow to dry out almost completely between waterings. Keep dry when dormant.

Out of doors, grow in well-drained fertile soil in part shade.

PROPAGATION
Seed should be sown at 75°F (24°C) in spring. Cuttings of rosettes can be taken in early summer and planted up, once they have formed calluses, in gritty compost which is kept just moist, at 64°F (18°C).

Aeonium arboreum A.G.M.

Zone 9
Height and spread: 6ft. (2m)

Aeonium arboreum 'Atropurpureum' A.G.M.

Zone 9
Height and spread: 6ft. (2m)

Aeonium canariense

Zone 9
Height: 8in. (20cm) Spread: 20in. (50cm)

Aeonium cuneatum

Zone 9
Height: 6ft. (2m) Spread: 20in. (50cm)

Aeonium haworthii A.G.M.

Zone 9
Height and spread 2ft. (60cm)

Aeonium haworthii 'Variegatum'

Zone 9
Height and spread: 2ft. (60cm)

Aeonium rubrolineatum

Zone 9
Height: 8in. (20cm) Spread: 1ft. (30cm)

Aeonium 'Zwartkop' A.G.M.

Zone 9
Height: 2ft. (60cm) Spread: 1ft. (30cm)

AESCHYNANTHUS *(Gesneriaceae)*
Common names: Lipstick vine

A genus of 100 species of evergreen perennials, climbers, trailers and subshrubs from subtropical forest regions of Malaysia, Indonesia, New Guinea, Southern China and the Himalaya. Some are epiphytic. The leaves are fleshy, lance-shaped, and arranged in opposite pairs. The tubular flowers have prominent calyces and long, protruding, curved corollas, which may also be hooded, and are borne in the leaf axils, or in clusters or in terminal corymbs from summer to winter.

✔ Evergreen   ✘ Prone to aphids
✔ Handsome foliage

CULTIVATION
Under glass, grow in a mixture of three parts fibrous peat and one part sphagnum moss, in high humidity. Water freely during growth, but sparingly in winter.

Out of doors, grow in well-drained, humus-rich soil in part shade, or in sun if humidity is high.

PROPAGATION
Cuttings of fresh shoots may be taken in spring, and of semi-ripe shoots in summer, and rooted in a gritty compost.

Aeschynanthus lobbianus

Zone 10
Height: 8in. (20cm) Spread: 3ft. (90cm)

AETHIONEMA *(Brassicaceae)*
Common names: Stone cress

A genus of over 40 species of perennials, subshrubs, and annuals from open limestone sites in Turkey, Eastern Europe, and Western Asia. The leaves are fleshy, small and arranged in pairs or alternately. The flowers are small, four-petalled, and borne in dense terminal racemes from spring to early summer.

✔ Evergreen   ✘ Short-lived
✔ Disease-free   ✘ Prone to aphid attack

CULTIVATION
Grow in alkaline to neutral, well-drained, fertile soil in full sun.

PROPAGATION
Seed should be sown in a cold frame in spring. Softwood cuttings may be rooted in late spring or early summer.

Aethionema grandiflorum A.G.M.

Zone 7
Height and spread: 1ft. (30cm)

A

Aethionema schistosum

Zone 7
Height: 4in. (10 cm) Spread: 1ft. (30cm)

Aethionema 'Warley Rose' A.G.M.

Zone 7
Height and spread: 8in. (20cm)

Aethionema 'Warley Rose'

Zone 7
Height and spread: 8in. (20cm)

AGAPANTHUS *(Alliaceae)*

Common names: African blue lily

A genus of 10 species of herbaceous and evergreen perennials from southern Africa; the herbaceous species are found in moist, inland, grassland areas whilst the evergreen species occur in coastal regions. They form large clumps of broad, arching, strap-shaped, dark green leaves. The flower heads are umbels of many tubular/bell-shaped blue or white flowers. The umbels are classified as being:

1) rounded, where all the flowers are upright
2) intermediate, where the upper flowers are upright and the lower ones pendent
3) pendent, in which all the flowers are pendent.

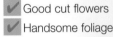

✔ Good cut flowers
✔ Handsome foliage
✔ Handsome seed-heads

✘ Prone to slug damage
✘ Resents disturbance

CULTIVATION
Grow in moist, well-drained, fertile soil in full sun. Water freely when in growth, and sparingly in winter. Protect against extreme cold or extreme wet in winter.

PROPAGATION
Seed should be sown when ripe, or in spring, at 59°F (15°C). Division can be carried out in spring, but they do not take kindly to transplantation.

Agapanthus 'Ben Hope'

Zone 7
Height: 4ft. (1.2m) Spread 2ft. (60cm)

Agapanthus 'Blue Imp'

Zone 7
Height: 1ft. (30cm) Spread: 8in. (20cm)

Agapanthus 'Bressingham Blue'

Zone 7
Height: 3ft. (90cm) Spread: 18in. (45cm)

Agapanthus campanulatus

Zone 7
Height: 4ft. (1.2m) Spread: 18in. (45cm)

Agapanthus campanulatus var. *albidus*

Zone 7
Height: 4ft. (1.2m) Spread: 18in. (45cm)

Agapanthus 'Lilliput'

Zone 7
Height and spread: 16in. (40cm)

Agapanthus praecox subsp. *orientalis*

Zone 7
Height: 3ft. (90cm) Spread: 2ft. (60cm)

Agapanthus praecox 'Vittatus'

Zone 7
Height: 3ft. (90cm) Spread: 2ft. (60cm)
Foliage variegated

Agapanthus 'Silver Moon'

Zone 7
Height: 3ft. (90cm) Spread: 2ft. (60cm)

AGASTACHE *(Lamiaceae)*

Common names: Hyssop

A genus of 30 species of short-lived, drought-tolerant perennials from dry habitats in Mexico, the U.S.A., China and Japan. The leaves are ovate or lance-shaped, gray-green, aromatic, and borne in opposite pairs. The tubular flowers are small, two-lipped, and borne in whorls on spikes from midsummer to autumn.

✔ Foliage aromatic

✔ Good cut flowers

✔ Drought-tolerant

✔ Attract butterflies

✖ Mildew prone

✖ Short-lived

CULTIVATION
Grow in fertile, well-drained soil in full sun.

PROPAGATION
Seed should be sown at 64°F (18°C) in early spring. Semi-ripe cuttings can be rooted in late summer, and overwintered under cover.

Agastache 'Firebird'

Zone 8
Height: 2ft. (60cm) Spread: 1ft. (30cm)

A

Agastache foeniculum

Zone 8
Height: 5ft. (1.5m) Spread: 1ft. (30cm)

Agastache mexicana

Zone 9
Height: 3ft. (90cm) Spread: 1ft. (30cm)

Agastache urticifolia 'Liquorice Blue'

Zone 8
Height: 4ft. (1.2m) Spread: 2ft. (60cm)
Foliage is skin-irritant

AGAVE *(Agavaceae)*
Common names: None

A genus of over 200 species of monocarpic or perennial, rosette-forming, drought-tolerant, evergreen succulents from desert regions of South and North America and the West Indies. The leaves are thick and fleshy, with marginal spines and a large terminal one. The flowers are short-tubed funnels, borne on leafless stems from the center of the rosette in racemes, panicles or umbels; the rosette dies after flowering in the majority of species, but offsets are formed.

- ✔ Evergreen
- ✔ Drought-tolerant
- ✔ Handsome foliage
- ✔ Disease-free
- ✘ Prone to scale insects

CULTIVATION
Under glass, grow in cactus compost in full light, and water freely during the growing season. Reduce watering in autumn, and keep dry in winter.

Out of doors, grow in very sharply-drained, fertile, slightly acid soil in full sun.

PROPAGATION
Seed should be sown at 70°F (21°C) in early spring. Offsets can be removed in spring or autumn, and potted up in gritty compost.

Agave americana 'Marginata'

Zone 9
Height: 6ft. (2m) Spread: 10ft. (3m)

Agave attenuata

Zone 9
Height: 6ft. (2m) Spread: 6ft. (2m)

Agave parviflora A.G.M.

Zone 9
Height: 6in. (15cm) Spread: 20in. (50cm)

Agave victoria-reginae A.G.M.

Zone 9
Height and spread: 20in. (50cm)

A

AGLAONEMA *(Araceae)*
Common names: None

A genus of 20 species of evergreen perennials from Asian tropical forests. The leaves are lance-shaped, and variegated in many species. The flowers are insignificant, spadices enclosed in greenish spathes, and borne sporadically.

✔ Evergreen   ✘ Flowers insignificant

CULTIVATION
Under glass, grow in sharply-draining, loam-based potting compost in high humidity in filtered light. Water with moderation at all times, and allow to dry out almost completely between waterings in winter.

Out of doors, grow in sharply-draining humus-rich, fertile soil in part shade.

PROPAGATION
Divide, or detach, basal rooted shoots, in spring.

Aglaonema 'Silver Queen' A.G.M.

Zone 10
Height and spread: 2ft. (60cm)

AICHRYSON *(Crassulaceae)*
Common names: None

A genus of 10 annual or perennial rosette-forming succulents from the Canary Islands, Madeira, and the Azores. The rosettes have alternate hairy fleshy leaves. The star-shaped red or yellow flowers are borne in cymes or panicles from late spring to summer.

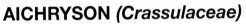

✔ Evergreen   ✘ Prone to aphids
✔ Handsome foliage

CULTIVATION
Under glass, grow in cactus, or loam-based potting compost with extra grit added, in full light or bright filtered light. Water with moderation at all times.

Out of doors, grow in fertile, well-drained soil in full sun.

PROPAGATION
Seed should be sown at 75°F (24°C) in spring. Offsets can be rooted in spring or early summer

Aichryson x domesticum
'Variegatum'

Zone 9
Height: 6in. (15cm) Spread: 16in. (40cm)

AJANIA *(Asteraceae)*
Common names: None

A genus of 30 species of perennials, subshrubs and shrubs from screes in Central and East Asia. The leaves are pinnatifid or lobed, and white-margined or woolly. The button-like yellow flowers lack ray florets and are borne in branched racemes or corymbs in summer and autumn. The plants have branching underground rhizomes.

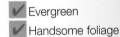

✔ Good cut flowers   ✘ Invasive
✔ Handsome foliage
✔ Attract butterflies
✔ Disease-free
✔ Pest-free

CULTIVATION
Grow in well-drained, poor soil in sun.

PROPAGATION
Seed should be sown in containers in a cold frame in spring. Basal cuttings can be taken in spring or summer. Runners can be divided in spring.

Ajania pacifica

Zone 6
Height: 1ft. (30cm) Spread: 3ft. (90 cm)

AJUGA *(Lamiaceae)*

Common names: Bugle

A genus of 40 species of annuals and evergreen or semi-evergreen perennials. The latter are rhizomatous, ground-coverers, and are found throughout Eurasia in shady locations. The ovate leaves are entire, sometimes toothed, and opposite; they are grown in many instances for their foliage, which may be dark-colored or silver-streaked or variegated. The tubular flowers are two-lipped, and borne in whorls from the axils of bracts, from spring to early summer. They are usually blue in color.

✔ Evergreen	✘ Mildew prone
✔ Low allergen	
✔ Attract butterflies	
✔ Handsome foliage	

CULTIVATION

Grow in moist soil in shade, or in sun as long as it is not too hot at mid-day, as the foliage can scorch in hot sun.

PROPAGATION

Separate rooted stems, or take softwood cuttings in early summer.

Ajuga pyramidalis (Pyramidal bugle)

Zone 6
Height: 10in. (25 cm) Spread: 2ft. (60cm)

Ajuga reptans 'Arctic Fox'

Zone 6
Height: 15 cm.(6 in) Spread: 3ft. (90cm)

Ajuga reptans 'Atropurpurea' A.G.M.

Zone 6
Height: 6in. (15cm) Spread: 3ft. (90cm)

Ajuga reptans 'Braunherz'

Zone 6
Height: 6in. (15cm) Spread: 3ft. (90cm)

Ajuga reptans 'Burgundy Glow'

Zone 6
Height: 6in. (15cm) Spread: 3ft. (90cm)

Ajuga reptans 'Ebony'

Zone 6
Height: 6in. (15cm) Spread: 3ft. (90cm)

Ajuga reptans 'Multicolor'

Zone 6
Height: 6in. (15cm) Spread: 3ft. (90cm)

Ajuga reptans 'Purple Brocade'

Zone 6
Height: 6in. (15cm) Spread: 3ft. (90cm)

Ajuga reptans 'Variegata'

Zone 6
Height: 6in. (15cm) Spread: 3ft. (90cm)

ALBUCA *(Liliaceae)*

Common names: None

A genus of 30 species of bulbous perennials found in grassland in Africa, and South Africa in particular, and the Middle East. The deep green leaves are basal and narrow linear, or lance-shaped. The flowers are open tubular, or bell-shaped, and borne in racemes; they are usually yellow or white, with a central stripe of green or red.

✔ Handsome foliage
✔ Disease-free
✔ Free of pests

CULTIVATION
Grow in well-drained, fertile soil in sun.

PROPAGATION
Seed should be sown at 64°F (18°C) as soon as ripe. Offsets can be removed in autumn.

Albuca altissima

Zone 9
Height: 18in. (45cm) Spread: 1ft. (30cm)

Albuca humilis

Zone 7
Height: 4in. (10 cm) Spread: 2in. (5cm)

A

ALCEA *(Malvaceae)*
Common names: Hollyhock

A genus of 60 species of short-lived perennials or biennials from stony and dry grassy habitats in temperate regions of Eurasia. The leaves are large, rounded and hairy. The flowers are borne on tall spikes over a long period in summer. They are short-stalked, funnel-shaped, brightly colored, and may be single or double. They are prone to Hollyhock rust, and rust-resistant strains should be introduced where it is a problem.

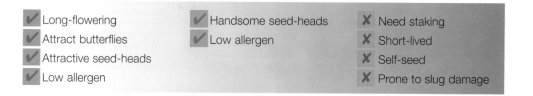

✔ Long-flowering   ✔ Handsome seed-heads   ✗ Need staking

✔ Attract butterflies   ✔ Low allergen   ✗ Short-lived

✔ Attractive seed-heads   ✗ Self-seed

✔ Low allergen   ✗ Prone to slug damage

CULTIVATION
Grow in well-drained soil in sun. They need to be staked and are susceptible to Hollyhock rust, but immune strains are now available.

PROPAGATION
Seed should be sown *in situ*, in midsummer.

Alcea rosea

Zone 3
Height: 6ft. (2m) Spread 2ft. (60cm)

Alcea rosea 'Alba'

Zone 3
Height: 10ft. (3m) Spread: 2ft. (60cm)

Alcea rosea 'Chater's double'

Zone 3
Height: 8ft. (2.5m) Spread: 2ft. (60cm)

Alcea rosea 'Indian Spring'

Zone 3
Height: 8ft. (2.5m) Spread: 2ft. (60cm)

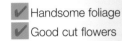

ALCHEMILLA *(Rosaceae)*
Common names: Lady's Mantle

A genus of 250 species of mostly rhizomatous perennials from woodland, grassland and rocky regions of temperate or even Arctic zones of the northern hemisphere. They occur also in mountainous regions of India, Sri Lanka, Java (Indonesia), and tropical Africa. The leaves are rounded, palmately-lobed or kidney-shaped, and covered in silky hairs; *A. mollis* is very attractive after rain. The green or yellow flowers are minute, and carried aloft of the foliage in much-branched cymes; they make excellent cut flowers and are much used in floral decoration.

✔ Handsome foliage	✘ Prone to slug damage
✔ Good cut flowers	✘ Self-seed

CULTIVATION
Grow in any moist, humus-rich soil in sun or shade. *A. mollis* should be dead-headed to prevent self-seeding.

PROPAGATION
Seed should be sown in containers in a cold frame in spring, and the seedlings transplanted whilst they are small. Division can be carried out in spring or autumn.

Alchemilla alpina (Mountain lady's mantle)

Height: 5in. (12cm) Spread: 20in. (50cm)
Flowers insignificant

Alchemilla mollis

Height: 2ft. (60cm) Spread: 3ft. (90cm)
Drought-tolerant

ALISMA *(Alismataceae)*
Common names: Water plantain

A genus of nine species of deciduous marginal aquatic perennials from temperate regions of the northern hemisphere, Australia and Southern Africa. They are rhizomatous, and the plantain-like leaves are borne in basal rosettes held above the water surface. The flowers are saucer-shaped, white or pink, and borne in umbel-like panicles above the foliage in mid to late summer.

✔ Good for drying for winter	✘ Self-seed
✔ Disease-free	
✔ Free of pests	

CULTIVATION
Grow in shallow water less than 1ft. (30cm) deep. Dead-head after flowering to prevent self-seeding.

PROPAGATION
Seed should be sown as soon as is ripe in seed trays half-submerged in water. The rhizomes may be divided in late spring.

Alisma plantago-aquatica

Zone 6
Height and spread: 30in. (75cm)

A

ALLIUM *(Liliaceae)*
Common names: Onion

A genus of 700 species of bulbous or rhizomatous perennials from hilly and dry areas of the northern hemisphere. The majority are deciduous. Some species have bulbils in the flower-heads, (*AA. carinatum, vineale* and *scordoprasum*, for example) and are to be avoided at all costs as garden plants, as they spread everywhere. Bulbous species to be avoided in gardens are *AA. canadense, ampeloprasum* var. *bulbiferum, paradoxum* and *roseum*. The leaves are strap-like, basal or stem, and, when crushed, emit a strong smell of garlic. The flower heads are umbels of few- or many-flowered cup- or bell-shaped flowers with tubular bases. The umbel may be upright or pendent.

✔ Good cut flowers	✔ Attractive seed-heads	✘ Bulbs are skin irritant
✔ Good for drying for winter	✔ Drought-tolerant	
✔ Attract bees		

CULTIVATION
Grow in well-drained fertile soil in sun. Bulbs should be planted 3-4in. (8-10cm) deep in autumn. Rhizomatous species should be planted in spring, with the rhizome just below the surface.

PROPAGATION
Seed should be sown when ripe in containers in the spring, and offsets can be removed from bulbous species in autumn. Rhizomatous species should be divided in spring.

Allium angulosum

Zone 5
Height and spread: 30in. (75cm)

Allium carinatum subsp. *pulchellum*

Zone 7
Height: 2ft. (60cm) Spread: 4in. (10 cm)

Allium cernuum

Zone 6
Height: 2ft. (60cm) Spread: 4in. (10 cm)

Allium christophii A.G.M.

Zone 5
Height: 2ft. (60cm) Spread: 8in. (20cm)

Allium flavum

Zone 7
Height: 16in. (40cm) Spread: 4in. (10 cm)

Allium giganteum

Zone 5
Height: 6ft. (2m) Spread: 8in. (20cm)

Allium 'Globemaster'

Zone 5
Height: 32in. (80 cm) Spread: 8in. (20cm)

Allium karataviense

Zone 4
Height: 10in. (25 cm) Spread 4in. (10 cm)

Allium moly

Zone 3
Height: 10in. (25 cm) Spread: 4in. (10 cm)

Allium nigrum

Zone 4
Height: 14in. (35cm) Spread: 3in. (8 cm)

Allium oreophilum

Zone 4
Height: 8in. (20cm) Spread: 2in. (5cm)

Allium 'Purple Sensation'

Zone 2
Height: 3ft. (90cm) Spread: 3in. (8 cm)

Allium schoenoprasum 'Forescate'
(Chives)

Zone 5
Height: 2ft. (60cm) Spread: 3in. (8 cm)
Culinary vegetable

Allium schubertii

Zone 5
Height: 2ft. (60cm) Spread: 8in. (20cm)

Allium senescens

Zone 5
Height: 2ft. (60cm) Spread: 2in. (5cm)

A

Allium sphaerocephalon
(Ballhead onion)

Zone 5
Height: 3ft. (90cm) Spread: 3in. (8cm)

Allium unifolium
(One-leaved onion)

Zone 4
Height: 10in. (25 cm) Spread: 2in. (5cm)

ALOCASIA *(Araceae)*

Common names: Elephant's ear

A genus of 70 species of large evergreen rhizomatous perennials from tropical forest and tropical damp shady or sunny sites in South East Asia. They are grown for their foliage. The leaves are large, peltate, arrow-shaped, heavily-veined and marked in black or purple. The flowers are relatively inconspicuous spathes, followed by red-orange fruits.

| ✔ Handsome foliage | ✘ All parts poisonous |
| | ✘ Sap skin-irritant |

CULTIVATION
Under glass, grow in a mixture of equal parts sand, loam and composted bark in filtered light, with high humidity and ample watering in the growing season. Water sparingly in winter

Out of doors, grow in moist, fertile, humus-rich soil in part shade.

PROPAGATION
Seed should be sown at 73°F (23°C) as soon as it is ripe. The rhizomes can be divided in spring. Stem cuttings can be rooted in early spring.

Alocasia callidora

Zone 10
Height: 12ft. (4m) Spread: 6ft. (2m)

Alocasia sanderiana (Kris plant)

Zone 10
Height and spread: 6ft. (2m)

A

ALOE *(Aloeaceae)*
Common names: None

A genus of 300 species of evergreen perennials from Arabia, Madagascar, the Cape Verde Islands, and southern Africa. The foliage is succulent, and in rosettes. The flowers are tubular or bell-shaped, and borne in terminal or axillary racemes or panicles. They can be invasive in warm gardens.

- ✔ Evergreen
- ✔ Handsome foliage
- ✔ Drought-tolerant
- ✔ Architectural plants
- ✔ Disease-free

CULTIVATION
Under glass, grow in sharply-draining potting compost in full light. Water moderately in summer, sparingly in winter.

Out of doors, grow in well-drained fertile soil in full sun.

PROPAGATION
Seed should be sown at 70ºF (21ºC) as soon as it is ripe. Rooted offsets can be separated in spring or early summer, and unrooted ones can be rooted in cactus potting compost.

Aloe aristata A.G.M.

Zone 9
Height: 5in. (12cm) Spread: indefinite
Invasive

Aloe ciliaris

Zone 9
Height: 15ft. (5m) Spread: 2ft. (60cm)

Aloe ferox

Zone 9
Height: 10ft. (3m) Spread: 5ft. (1.5 m)

Aloe tenuior

Zone 9
Height: 10ft. (3m) Spread: 2ft. (60cm)

Aloe variegata A.G.M.

Zone 9
Height: 8in. (20cm) Spread: indefinite
Invasive

Aloe vera A.G.M.

Zone 8
Height: 3ft. (90cm) Spread: indefinite
Invasive

A

A

ALONSOA *(Scrophulariaceae)*
Common names: Heartleaf mask flower

A genus of 12 species of evergreen perennials, subshrubs and shrubs from screes of subtropical and tropical western South America. The ovate, toothed, dark green leaves are arranged in opposite pairs. The red, orange or white flowers are asymmetrically two-lipped, spurred and borne in lax racemes from summer to autumn.

- ✔ Long-flowering
- ✔ Evergreen
- ✔ Good cut flowers

- ✘ Prone to aphid attack

CULTIVATION
Grow in any well-drained fertile soil in sun.

PROPAGATION
Seed should be sown at 64°F (18°C) in early spring. Semi-ripe cuttings can be rooted in late summer

Alonsoa warscewiczii A.G.M.

Zone 9
Height: 2ft. (60cm) Spread: 1ft. (30cm)

ALOPECURUS *(Poaceae)*
Common names: Foxtail grass

A genus of about 40 species of annual and perennial grasses from screes, rocky sites and grassland of the temperate northern hemisphere. They form tufted clumps of basal linear leaves, with terminal dense panicles of single-flowered spikes from spring to midsummer.

- ✔ Handsome foliage
- ✔ Attractive seed-heads
- ✔ Disease-free
- ✔ Free of pests

CULTIVATION
Grow in well-drained, fertile soil in sun or part shade.

PROPAGATION
Seed should be sown in a cold frame as soon as it is ripe. Divide in spring.

Alopecurus pratensis
'Aureovariegatus'

Zone 5
Height: 4ft. (1.2m) Spread: 2ft. (60cm)

ALPINIA *(Zingiberaceae)*
Common names: Ginger lily

A genus of 200 species of evergreen rhizomatous perennials from forest edges and open forest in Australia, China, India and south-east Asia. The rhizomes are ginger-scented. The leaves are lance-shaped, and the flowers narrow hooded bells enclosed in prominent bracts, in a raceme or panicle.

- ✔ Flowers perfumed
- ✔ Handsome foliage
- ✔ Disease-free
- ✔ Pest-free
- ✔ Architectural plants

CULTIVATION
Grow in moist, humus-rich soil in part shade.

PROPAGATION
Seed should be sown as soon as it is ripe at 68°F (20°C). Division of the rhizomes should be carried out in spring.

Alpinia zerumbet
(Shell ginger; porcelain lily)

Zone 10
Height: 10ft. (3m) Spread: 4ft. (1.2m)

A

Alpinia zerumbet
'Variegata'

Zone 10
Height: 10ft. (3m) Spread: 4ft. (1.2m)

ALSTROEMERIA *(Alstroemeriaceae)*

Common names: Peruvian lily

A genus of 50 species of perennials from grassland and screes of South America. They are tuberous, and spread fairly rapidly to form large clumps, so can become invasive if conditions are right. The tubers should be handled very carefully, and are best left undisturbed if possible. The leaves are linear or lance-shaped. Contact with the foliage may cause skin irritation. The flowers are funnel-shaped, and borne on compound terminal umbels over a long period in summer.

✔ Good cut flowers	✘ Prone to slug damage
✔ Long-flowering	✘ Need staking
✔ Attract bees	✘ Resents disturbance
	✘ Skin irritant
	✘ Highly allergenic

Alstroemeria aurea

Zone 7
Height: 3ft. (90cm) Spread: 18in. (45cm)
Requires staking

CULTIVATION

Under glass, the tubers should be planted 8in. (20cm) deep in late summer or early autumn in a mixture of equal parts loam, sharp sand and leaf mould. Water freely during growth, but sparingly in winter.

Out of doors, grow in moist, well-drained fertile soil in sun or part shade. Do not transplant.

PROPAGATION

Seed should be sown in small pots in a cold frame as soon as it is ripe. Plant seedlings out by the potful to minimize root disturbance. Division of established clumps should be carried out in early spring or autumn.

Alstroemeria
'Endless Love' (PBR)

Zone 7
Height: 1ft. (30cm) Spread: 18in. (45cm)

Alstroemeria Ligtu hybrid A.G.M.

Zone 7
Height: 3ft. (90cm) Spread: 18in. (45cm)
Requires staking

Alstroemeria
'Little Miss Isabel'

Zone 7
Height: 1ft. (30cm) Spread: 18in. (45cm)

Alstroemeria
'Little Miss Rosanna'

Zone 7
Height: 1ft. (30cm) Spread: 18in. (45cm)

Alstroemeria
'Little Miss Veronica'

Zone 7
Height: 1ft. (30cm) Spread: 18in. (45cm)

Alstroemeria
'Pink Dream' (PBR)

Zone 8
Height: 1ft. (30cm) Spread: 18in. (45cm)

Alstroemeria 'Polka'

Zone 7
Height: 2ft. (60cm) Spread: 18in. (45cm)
Variegated foliage

Alstroemeria
'Princess Angela' (PBR)

Zone 7
Height: 8in. (20cm) Spread: 1ft. (30cm)

Alstroemeria
'Princess Camilla' (PBR)

Zone 7
Height: 8in. (20cm) Spread: 1ft. (30cm)

Alstroemeria
'Princess Freckles'

Zone 7
Height: 8in. (20cm) Spread: 1ft. (30cm)

Alstroemeria
'Princess Paola'

Zone 7
Height: 8in. (20cm) Spread: 1ft. (30cm)

A

Alstroemeria
'Princess Stephanie'

Zone 7
Height: 8in. (20cm) Spread: 1ft. (30cm)

Alstroemeria
'Princess Zza Zza'

Zone 7
Height: 8in. (20cm) Spread: 1ft. (30cm)

Alstroemeria psittacina

Zone 7
Height: 3ft. (90cm) Spread: 18in. (45cm)

Alstroemeria psittacina
'Variiegata'

Zone 7
Height: 3ft. (90cm) Spread: 18in. (45cm)

Alstroemeria 'Queen Elizabeth the
Queen Mother' (PBR)

Zone 7
Height: 8in. (20cm) Spread: 1ft. (30cm)

Alstroemeria 'Red Beauty'

Zone 7
Height: 2ft. (60cm) Spread: 1ft. (30cm)
Variegated foliage

Alstroemeria
'Rose Frost'

Zone 7
Height and spread: 1ft. (30cm)

Alstroemeria
'Solent Wings'

Zone 7
Height: 3ft. (90cm) Spread: 18in. (45cm)

Alstroemeria
'Sovereign'

Zone 7
Height: 3ft. (90cm) Spread: 18in. (45cm)

Alstroemeria
'Sunburst' (PBR)

Zone 8
Height: 1ft. (30cm) Spread: 18in. (45cm)

Alstroemeria
'Sweet Love' (PBR)

Zone 8
Height: 1ft. (30cm) Spread: 18in. (45cm)

Alstroemeria
'White Apollo'

Zone 7
Height: 3ft. (90cm) Spread: 18in. (45cm)

Alstroemeria
'Xandra' (PBR)

Zone 8
Height: 1ft. (30cm) Spread: 18in. (45cm)

ALTHAEA (MALVACEAE)

Common names: Mallow

A genus of a dozen species of perennials and annuals from moist coastal areas across Western Europe to Central Asia. The leaves are ovate, lobed and dark green. The flowers are small, pink or bluish saucers borne on panicles from summer to autumn.

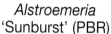

✔ Long-flowering   ✗ Needs to be staked

CULTIVATION
Grow in any soil in any position, but best results are obtained in well-drained, moist soil in sun.

PROPAGATION
Seed should be sown in midsummer, and the seedlings moved on in autumn when three true leaves have appeared.

Althaea cannabina

Zone 4
Height: 6ft. (2m) Spread: 30in. (75cm)
Flowers insignificant

A

Althaea officinalis
(Marsh mallow)

Zone 3
Height: 6ft. (2m) Spread: 5ft. (1.5m)

ALYSSUM *(Brassicaceae)*

Common names: None

A genus of 150 annuals and tuft-forming, drought-tolerant, aromatic, evergreen perennials from stony, open sites in Eurasia and North Africa. The leaves are gray-green, obovate, and alternate. The flowers are cruciform, white or yellow, and borne on corymb-like racemes in early summer.

✔ Foliage aromatic   ✘ Prone to aphids
✔ Evergreen
✔ Drought-tolerant
✔ Attracts butterflies
✔ Low allergen

CULTIVATION
Grow in sharply-draining, humus-rich soil in sun. Shear over lightly after flowering to keep compact.

PROPAGATION
Seed should be sown in a cold frame in spring or autumn. Green-wood cuttings can be rooted in early summer.

Alyssum montanum
'Berggold'

Zone 6
Height: 6in. (15cm) Spread: 2ft. (60cm)

Alyssum spinosum
'Roseum'

Height: 16in. (40cm) Spread: 20in. (50cm)

Alyssum wulfenianum

Zone 7
Height: 6in. (15cm) Spread: 20in. (50cm)

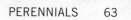

A

AMARYLLIS *(Amaryllidaceae)*
Common names: Belladonna lily

A genus of just one species of bulbous perennial from the stream sides and coastal hills of Western Cape, South Africa. It flowers in autumn, followed by the strap-shaped, green leaves. The flowers are funnel-shaped, perfumed, pink or white, and borne in umbels. All parts are poisonous, including the bulbs.

✔ Flowers perfumed   ✘ Prone to slug damage   ✘ Prone to aphid attack
✔ Good cut flowers   ✘ All parts poisonous

CULTIVATION
Under glass, grow in a mixture of equal parts of loam-based potting compost, leaf mould and sharp sand in full light. Water with moderation during growth, and keep dry and frost-free during dormancy.

Out of doors, plant bulbs just under the soil surface when dormant in spring or summer. Grow in well-drained fertile soil in sun. Protect foliage against frost.

PROPAGATION
Seed should be sown in containers at 61°F (16°C) as soon as it is ripe. Offsets can be removed in spring, and should be grown on under glass for a season or two before being planted out.

Amaryllis belladonna

Zone 9
Height: 2ft. (60cm) Spread: 4in. (10 cm)

AMICIA *(Papilionaceae)*
Common names: None

A genus of seven species of woody perennials from mountainous woodland and riverbanks of the Andes and Mexico. The foliage is handsome. The leaves are large, inversely heart-shaped, and with pale green stipules. The pea-like flowers are cream with purple keels, borne in autumn.

✔ Handsome foliage   ✘ Prone to slug damage

CULTIVATION
Grow in fertile, well-drained soil in sun. Protect against frost in winter. If cut down by frost, will regenerate from the base.

PROPAGATION
Seed should be sown at 64°F (18°C) in spring. Basal cuttings can be taken in late spring, and semi-ripe cuttings in summer.

Amicia zygomeris

Zone 9
Height: 6ft. (2m) Spread: 4ft. (1.2m)

AMPELOPSIS *(Vitaceae)*
Common names: None

A genus of 25 species of deciduous climbers and shrubs from woodland in North America and Asia. They are grown for their leaves, which are simple, palmate or pinnate, lobed or toothed, and color well in autumn. The flowers are small, green and insignificant, but are followed in the autumn by berries. If grown against a house, they can cause damage to tiles or gutters.

✔ Handsome foliage   ✔ Disease-free   ✘ Flowers insignificant
✔ Berries after flowering ✔ Free of pests

CULTIVATION
Under glass, grow in loam-based potting compost in bright filtered light. Water freely during growth, but sparingly in winter.

Out of doors, grow in moist, well-drained soil in sun for best fruiting. Prune in spring for size and shape.

PROPAGATION
Seed should be sown in a cold frame in spring or autumn. Divide in spring. Basal or softwood cuttings may be taken in early summer.

Ampelopsis glandulosa var. *brevipedunculata* 'Elegans'

Zone 9
Height: 10ft. (3m) Spread: 3ft. (90cm)

A

AMSONIA *(Apocynaceae)*
Common names: None

A genus of 20 species of perennials from light and heavy soils, in grassland or light woodland, in Turkey, Japan, south-east Europe and central and north-east United States. The small, alternate, matt-green leaves are elliptic or ovate. The flowers have five spreading blue petals, and are borne in panicles or cymes over a long period in spring and summer.

✔ Long-flowering
✔ Good cut flowers
✔ Disease-free
✔ Pest-free

✘ Sap skin-irritant

CULTIVATION
Grow in any well-drained, moist soil in sun.

PROPAGATION
Seed should be sown in a cold frame in spring or autumn. The clump can be divided in spring. Basal or softwood cuttings can be taken in early summer

Amsonia tabernaemontana

Zone 8
Height: 2ft. (60cm) Spread: 18in. (45cm)

ANACYCLUS *(Asteraceae)*
Common names: None

A genus of nine species of annuals and creeping perennials found on sandy and disturbed ground and stony slopes in the Mediterranean area. Their leaves are 2- or 3-pinnatisect, with finely-divided lobes. The daisy-like flowers are solitary or in pairs, and are borne on short stems in summer.

✔ Handsome foliage

✘ Prone to aphid attack
✘ Highly allergenic

CULTIVATION
Under glass, grow in an alpine house in a mix of equal parts loam and sharp grit, in full light.

Out of doors, grow in sharply-draining soil in sun. Protect against winter wet.

PROPAGATION
Seed should be sown in a cold frame in autumn. Softwood cuttings may be taken in spring or early summer

Anacyclus pyrethrum var.
depressus

Zone 6
Height: 2in. (5cm) Spread: 4in. (10 cm)

ANAGALLIS *(Primulaceae)*
Common names: Pimpernel

A genus of 20 species of annuals and evergreen perennials found on dry slopes, bogs, and open ground in western Europe and the Mediterranean. The leaves are mid-green, lance-shaped and stalkless. The deep blue flowers are solitary, bell- or saucer-shaped.

✔ Disease-free
✔ Pest-free

✘ Short-lived
✘ Prone to aphid attack

CULTIVATION
Grow in moist, well-drained, fertile soil in sun.

PROPAGATION
Seed should be sown in a cold frame in spring. Division can be carried out in spring.

Anagallis monellii A.G.M.

Zone 7
Height: 8in. (20cm) Spread: 16in. (40cm)

A

ANANAS *(Bromeliaceae)*

Common names: Pineapple

A genus of half a dozen species of evergreen, terrestrial, bromeliad perennials from South America. Their habitats vary from lowland to mountain, and from dry to wet. The spiny, lance-shaped leaves are in rosettes. The flowers are on stout stems, and are cone-like in dense terminal spikes; they are followed by edible fruits.

✔ Long-flowering	✔ Handsome foliage	✔ Pest-free
✔ Fruits edible	✔ Disease-free	

CULTIVATION
Under glass, grow in terrestrial bromeliad compost in full light, out of draughts, and in moderate humidity. Water freely in summer, reduce watering in autumn, and keep just moist at all other times.

Outside, grow in well-drained, humus-rich, fertile soil in sun.

PROPAGATION
Basal offsets should be rooted in early summer. The leafy rosette on top of the fruit may be detached, and after two days (by which time it will have formed a callus) rooted in just-moist sand/peat 50/50 mix at 70°F (21°C).

Ananas bracteatus
'Tricolor' A.G.M.

Zone 10
Height: 28in. (70 cm) Spread: 20in. (50cm)

Ananas comosus
'Variegatus'

Zone 10
Height: 3ft. (90cm) Spread: 20in. (50cm)

ANAPHALIS *(Asteraceae)*

Common names: Pearl everlasting

A genus of 100 species of perennials from moist woodland, dry screes, sunny riversides, and dry forests in the northern hemisphere. Some are evergreen. The foliage is white-woolly underneath, gray-green on top. The flowers are white-bracted, everlasting, domed corymbs.

✔ Good cut flowers	✘ Highly allergenic
✔ Good for drying for winter	
✔ Handsome foliage	
✔ Disease-free	
✔ Pest-free	

CULTIVATION
Grow in humus-rich fertile soil in sun or part shade.

PROPAGATION
Seed should be sown in a cold frame in spring. Division can also be undertaken in spring. Stem-tip or basal cuttings may be taken in spring or early summer.

A

Anaphalis triplinervis A.G.M.

Zone 5
Height: 3ft. (90cm) Spread: 2ft. (60cm)

Anaphalis triplinervis
'Sommerschnee' A.G.M.

Height: 3ft. (90cm) Spread: 2ft. (60cm)

ANCHUSA *(Boraginaceae)*

Common names: Italian alkanet; Italian bugloss

A genus of 35 species of annuals and short-lived perennials from sunny dry sites in the temperate northern hemisphere, and Africa. The leaves are alternate, linear to lance to elliptic, and hairy in some species. The flowers are usualy blue, and are tubular and borne on terminal and axillary cymes.

✔ Repeat-flowering
✔ Attract bees
✔ Low allergen
✔ Good cut flowers

✘ Short-lived
✘ Mildew prone

CULTIVATION
Grow in any well-drained, fertile moist soil in sun. They are remontant, and will produce a second flush of flowers if they are dead-headed soon after flowering. Cut back hard after flowering to promote basal growth over winter. They dislike too much winter wet. The tall varieties need to be staked.

PROPAGATION
Seed should be sown in a cold frame in spring. Basal cuttings can be rooted in spring, and root cuttings in winter.

Anchusa azurea

Zone 3
Height: 5ft. (1.5m) Spread: 2ft. (60cm)
Requires staking

Anchusa azurea
'Feltham Pride'

Zone 3
Height: 3ft. (90cm) Spread: 2ft. (60cm)

Anchusa azurea
'Loddon Royalist' A.G.M.

Zone 3
Height: 3ft. (90cm) Spread: 2ft. (60cm)

Anchusa azurea
'Opal'

Zone 3
Height: 3ft. (90cm) Spread: 2ft. (60cm)

A

ANEMONE *(Ranunculaceae)*
Common names: Windflower; Japanese anemone

A genus of 120 species from very diverse habitats across the northern hemisphere. Three categories of species are recognized:

1) Species that are found in alpine and woodland areas, and are spring-flowering.

2) Species that are tuberous/rhizomatous and occur in regions with hot, dry summers, and flower in spring and early summer.

3) Species that are found in moist grassland and woodland, and comprise tall, fibrous-rooted, herbaceous perennials that flower in late summer and autumn—this last group features largely here.

All anemones featured have been grouped according to the above classification. Anemones have large basal and small stem leaves. The basal leaves are rounded and lobed; the stem leaves are usually in a whorl below the flowers, which are shallow saucers, and can be solitary or in umbels or cymes. Some anemones are poisonous, others are invasive.

Anemone blanda A.G.M. (Group 1)

Zone 5
Height and spread: 6in. (15cm)
Poisonous

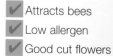 Attracts bees | ✗ Sap is skin-irritant
✔ Low allergen | ✗ Mildew prone
✔ Good cut flowers | ✗ Prone to slug damage

CULTIVATION
According to the three groups outlined above, plant in autumn and treat as follows:

Group 1: Alpine and woodland species should be grown in well-drained, humus-rich soil in sun or part shade respectively.

Group 2: Tuberous and rhizomatous species should be grown in light sandy soil in sun. They should have a dry winter dormancy, and even be lifted and overwintered in warm dry conditions.

Group 3: Tall herbaceous perennials should be grown in moist, humus-rich, fertile soil in sun or part shade.

PROPAGATION
Seed should be sown in a cold frame as soon as ripe; germination may be erratic, and slow. Autumn-flowering, fibrous-rooted types can be divided in spring or autumn. Rhizomatous types can be divided in spring or autumn; tuberous species should be separated in summer when dormant.

Anemone blanda 'White Splendour' A.G.M. (Group 1)

Zone 5
Height and spread: 6in. (15cm)
Poisonous

Anemone coronaria 'De Caen' (Group 2)

Zone 8
Height: 18in. (45cm) Spread: 6in. (15cm)

Anemone coronaria 'St Brigid' (Group 2)

Zone 8
Height: 18in. (45cm) Spread: 6in. (15cm)

Anemone coronaria 'Saint Peren' (Group 2)

Zone 8
Height: 18in. (45cm) Spread: 6in. (15cm)

A

Anemone cylindrica
(Group 3)

Zone 6
Height: 2ft. (60cm) Spread: 4in. (10 cm)

Anemone hupehensis 'Hadspen
Abundance' A.G.M. (Group 3)

Zone 6
Height: 3ft. (90cm) Spread: 18in. (45cm)
Long-flowering

Anemone hupehensis 'Prinz
Heinrich' A.G.M. (Dwarf Japanese
anemone) (Group 3)

Zone 6
Height: 3ft. (90cm) Spread: indefinite
Long-flowering/Invasive

Anemone x hybrida 'Andrea Atkinson'

Zone 6
Height: 4ft. (1.2m) Spread: indefinite
Invasive

Anemone x hybrida 'Elegans'
(Japanese anemone) (Group 3)

Zone 6
Height: 4ft. (1.2m) Spread: indefinite
Long-flowering/Invasive

Anemone x hybrida 'Honorine
Jobert' A.G.M.

Zone 6
Height: 4ft. (1.2m) Spread: indefinite
Invasive

Anemone x hybrida 'Margarete'
(Japanese anemone) (Group 3)

Zone 6
Height: 3ft. (90cm) Spread: indefinite
Long-flowering/Invasive

Anemone x hybrida 'Max Vogel'

Zone 6
Height: 4ft. (1.2m) Spread: indefinite
Invasive

Anemone x hybrida 'Pamina'
(Japanese anemone) (Group 3)

Zone 6
Height: 3ft. (90cm) Spread: indefinite
Long-flowering/Invasive

A

Anemone x hybrida 'Whirlwind'
(Japanese anemone) (Group 3)

Zone 6
Height: 3ft. (90cm) Spread: indefinite
Long-flowering/Invasive

Anemone x lesseri (Group 3)

Zone 3
Height: 16in. (40cm) Spread: 1ft. (30cm)

Anemone leveillei (Group 3)

Zone 6
Height: 2ft. (60cm) Spread: 1ft. (30cm)

Anemone multifida (Group 2)

Zone 2
Height: 1ft. (30cm) Spread: 6in. (15cm)
Long-flowering/Handsome foliage

Anemone nemorosa A.G.M. (Wood
anemone) (Group 1)

Zone 5
Height: 6in. (15cm) Spread: 1ft. (30cm)
Drought-tolerant/Poisonous

Anemone nemorosa
'Robinsoniana' A.G.M. (Group 1)

Zone 5
Height: 6in. (15cm) Spread: 1ft. (30cm)
Drought-tolerant/Poisonous

Anemone obtusiloba 'Sulphurea'
(Group 2)

Zone 5
Height: 2in. (5cm) Spread: 10in. (25 cm)

Anemone rivularis (Group 3)

Zone 7
Height: 3ft. (90cm) Spread: 1ft. (30cm)
Repeat-flowering

Anemone trifolia (Group 1)

Zone 6
Height: 6in. (15cm) Spread: 1ft. (30cm)

A

ANEMONELLA *(Ranunculaceae)*

Common names: Rue anemone

A genus of just one species of perennial from eastern North America. It is a woodlander, tuberous, clump-forming, and has ferny, dark bluish-green leaves. The flowers are white or pale pink cups, borne on slender stems in loose umbels from spring to early summer.

 Handsome foliage   ✗ Prone to slug damage

CULTIVATION

Grow in moist, humus-rich, very well-drained, fertile soil in part shade.

PROPAGATION

Seed should be sown in a cold frame as soon as is ripe. Division can be carried out in early spring

Anemonella thalictroides

Zone 4
Height: 4in. (10 cm) Spread: 1ft. (30cm)

Anemonella thalictroides
'Amelia'

Zone 4
Height: 4in. (10 cm) Spread: 1ft. (30cm)

Anemonella thalictroides
'Oscar Schoaff'

Zone 4
Height: 4in. (10 cm) Spread: 1ft. (30cm)

A

ANEMONOPSIS *(Ranunculaceae)*

Common names: None

A genus of only one species, *A. macrophylla*, which grows in mountain woodland in Japan. The leaves are glossy, triternate, toothed and lobed. The flowers are pendent cups of pale lilac color borne on loose racemes from mid- to late summer.

- ✔ Handsome foliage
- ✔ Handsome seed-heads
- ✔ Disease-free
- ✔ Pest-free

CULTIVATION

Grow in acid, moist, cool, humus-rich soil in part shade. They dislike cold drying winds, which cause leaf-curl.

PROPAGATION

Seed should be sown in a cold frame as soon as it is ripe, but germination is erratic. Division can be carried out in spring, taking care not to damage the fleshy thick roots.

Anemonopsis macrophylla

Zone 4
Height: 32in. (80 cm) Spread: 18in. (45cm)

ANGELICA *(Apiaceae)*

Common names: None

A genus of 50 species of herbaceous perennials, of which some are monocarpic. They are found in stream sides, fens, damp meadows and woodland in the temperate northern hemisphere. They are big, architectural plants. The leaves are tripinnate or triternate, diamond-shaped, and alternate. The flowers are small, red or white, and borne on tight umbels, followed by attractive seedheads of brown ribbed fruits. *A. archangelica* flowers in early to midsummer, and dies after flowering, but may flower a second year if dead-headed or prevented from flowering. *A. gigas* flowers from late summer to early autumn.

- ✔ Handsome seed-heads
- ✔ Architectural plants
- ✔ Culinary vegetable
- ✖ Resents disturbance
- ✖ Prone to slug damage
- ✖ Mildew prone
- ✖ Self-seed
- ✖ Highly allergenic

CULTIVATION

Grow in moist, deep humus-rich soil in part shade. Dead-head to prevent self-seeding.

PROPAGATION

Seed should be sown in a cold frame as soon as it is ripe, and the seedlings moved on as soon as possible as they do not transplant well.

Angelica archangelica

Zone 4
Height: 6ft. (2m) Spread: 3ft. (90cm)
Monocarpic

Angelica archangelica
'Corinne Tremaine'

Zone 4
Height: 6ft. (2m) Spread: 3ft. (90cm)
Variegated foliage/Monocarpic

Angelica gigas

Zone 4
Height: 6ft. (2m) Spread: 4ft. (1.2m)
Short-lived

A

ANGELONIA *(Scrophulariaceae)*
Common names: None

A genus of 30 species of subshrubs and evergreen perennials from wet savannah in subtropical and tropical South and Central America. The leaves are lance-shaped, and opposite. The flowers are two-lipped shallow cups with spreading lobes and are borne singly or in terminal racemes in summer.

✔ Long-flowering
✔ Evergreen

✖ Prone to aphids

CULTIVATION
Grow in moist, fertile, well-drained soil in sun.

PROPAGATION
Seed should be sown in spring at 75°F (24°C). Division can be carried out in spring. Softwood cuttings can be taken in spring

Angelonia gardneri

Zone 9
Height: 3ft. (90cm) Spread: 2ft. (60cm)

ANIGOZANTHOS *(Haemodoraceae)*
Common names: Kangaroo paw; cat's paw

A genus of 11 species of evergreen perennials from a range of habitats from dry woodland to wet swamps in south-west Australia. They are clump-forming, rhizomatous, and are good architectural plants. The leaves are lance- or strap-shaped, and in fans. The flowers are unusual, two-lipped, and tubular and said to resemble animal paws. They are borne in terminal racemes or panicles from spring to midsummer.

✔ Good cut flowers
✔ Evergreen

CULTIVATION
Grow in moist, well-drained humus-rich, gritty soil in sun and do not allow to dry out. They should be mulched in autumn to provide winter protection.

PROPAGATION
Seed should be sown at 64°F (18°C) as soon as is ripe. Division can be done in spring.

Anigozanthos flavidus

Zone 9
Height: 10ft. (3m) Spread: 32in. (80 cm)
Architectural plant

Anigozanthos kalbarriensis

Zone 9
Height: 30in. (75cm) Spread: 2ft. (60cm)

Anigozanthos manglesii A.G.M.

Zone 9
Height: 4ft. (1.2m) Spread: 2ft. (60cm)
Architectural plant

A

ANISODONTEA *(Malvaceae)*
Common names: None

A genus of 19 species of woody, evergreen perennials from a range of habitats in South Africa. The leaves are ovate or triangular, hairy, mid-green, and shallowly lobed. The flowers are single, pale pink, shallow cups, solitary or borne on racemes of two or three over a long period from summer to autumn.

✔ Drought-tolerant　　　　　　✘ Prone to aphid attack

✔ Long-flowering

✔ Evergreen

CULTIVATION
Under glass, grow in loam-based potting compost, in full light. Water freely in spring and summer, but sparingly in winter.

Out of doors, grow in fertile, well-drained soil in sun.

PROPAGATION
Seed should be sown at 64°F (18°C) in spring. Semi-ripe cuttings can be rooted in summer if given bottom heat.

Anisodontea capensis

Zone 9
Height: 3ft. (90cm) Spread: 32in. (80 cm)

Anisodontea malvastroides

Zone 9
Height: 3ft. (90cm) Spread: 30in. (75cm)

ANOMATHECA *(Iridaceae)*
Common names: None

A genus of six species of cormous perennials from high grassland in central and southern Africa. The leaves are broad, lance-shaped, and flat. The flowers are open, funnel- or trumpet-shaped, and borne on terminal racemes.

✔ Drought-tolerant

✔ Handsome seed-heads

✔ Disease-free

✔ Pest-free

CULTIVATION
Grow in gritty, well-drained soil in sun.

PROPAGATION
Seed should be sown at 61°F (16°C) in spring. Corms can be separated in spring.

Anomatheca laxa

Zone 8
Height: 1ft. (30cm) Spread: 2in. (5cm)

A

ANTENNARIA *(Asteraceae)*

Common names: Pussy-toes; Cat's ears

A genus of 45 species of semi-evergreen or evergreen perennials from open spaces in the northern hemisphere. They are mat-forming, and have basal rosettes of gray-green leaves with hairy undersides. The flowers are small, solitary or borne in corymbs, in late spring and early summer, and can be dried for winter decoration.

✔ Good for drying for winter
✔ Handsome foliage
✔ Disease-free
✔ Pest-free

CULTIVATION
Grow in any fertile soil in sun.

PROPAGATION
Seed should be sown in a cold frame in spring or autumn. Division can be carried out in spring.

Antennaria dioica

Zone 5
Height: 4in. (10 cm) Spread: 16in. (40cm)

ANTHEMIS *(Asteraceae)*

Common names: Chamomile; marguerite

A genus of some 100 species of mat- or clump-forming perennials from varied, but invariably sunny, habitats in North Africa, Europe, the Near East and the Caucasus. The foliage is aromatic, pinnatisect, hairy and filigree. The flowers are daisy-like, with white or yellow ray florets and yellow disc florets, and are borne over a long season from late spring to late summer.

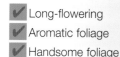

✔ Long-flowering   ✘ Prone to slug damage
✔ Aromatic foliage   ✘ Resents disturbance
✔ Handsome foliage   ✘ Mildew prone

CULTIVATION
Grow in very sharply-drained, humus-rich, open soil in sun. *AA. tinctoria* and *sancti-johannis* are short-lived, and their life can be extended by being sheared over after flowering to promote basal growth for overwintering, and to lessen the risk of powdery mildew. All dislike excessive wet.

PROPAGATION
Seed should be sown in a cold frame in spring. Division can be carried out in spring, but is not tolerated well. Basal cuttings can be rooted in spring.

Anthemis
'Grallagh Gold'

Zone 6
Height: 32in. (80 cm) Spread: 2ft. (60cm)

Anthemis marschalliana subsp.
biebersteiniana

Zone 7
Height: 18in. (45cm) Spread: 2ft. (60cm)

Anthemis punctata subsp.
cupaniana A.G.M. (Dog fennel)

Zone 6
Height: 1ft. (30cm) Spread: 3ft. (90cm)

Anthemis tinctoria
(Ox-eye chamomile)

Zone 6
Height and spread: 3ft. (90cm)

A

Anthemis tinctoria 'E.C.Buxton' (Ox-eye chamomile)

Zone 6
Height: 28in. (70 cm) Spread: 2ft. (60cm)

Anthemis tinctoria 'Sauce Hollandaise' (Ox eye chamomile)

Zone 6
Height and spread: 2ft. (60cm)

Anthemis tinctoria 'Wargrave' (Ox-eye)

Zone 6
Height and spread: 2ft. (60cm)

ANTHERICUM (ANTHERICACEAE)

Common names: St Bernard's lily

A genus of 50 species of clump-forming, rhizomatous perennials from scrubby hills in Turkey, Africa and Europe. The leaves are radical and linear. The flowers are small, lily-like, white, and borne on slender stems in panicles or racemes in spring and summer.

✔ Good cut flowers	✘ Self-seed
✔ Handsome seed-heads	✘ Prone to slug damage

CULTIVATION
Grow in any well-drained fertile soil in sun.

PROPAGATION
Seed should be sown in a cold frame in autumn or spring. Division can be carried out in spring.

Anthericum liliago

Zone 7
Height: 3ft. (90cm) Spread: 1ft. (30cm)

Anthericum liliago var. 'Major' A.G.M.

Zone 7
Height: 3ft. (90cm) Spread: 1ft. (30cm)

ANTHRISCUS *(Apiaceae)*

Common names: Chervil; cow parsley

A genus of a dozen species of annuals and perennials from wasteland, grassland and woodland in the temperate northern hemisphere. The leaves are 2- or 3-pinnate, and finely-divided. The flowers are tiny, and borne in many-flowered umbels.

✔ Handsome foliage   ✘ Prone to slug damage

CULTIVATION
Grow in any well-drained soil in sun or part shade. *A. sylvestris* must be dead-headed to prevent self-seeding.

PROPAGATION
Seed should be sown in a cold frame in autumn or spring.

Anthriscus sylvestris

Zone 7
Height: 3ft. (90cm) Spread: 1ft. (30cm)

Anthriscus sylvestris 'Ravenswing'

Zone 7
Height: 3ft. (90cm) Spread: 1ft. (30cm)

ANTHURIUM *(Araceae)*

Common names: Flamingo flower; Tail flower

A genus of up to 900 species of mainly epiphytic evergreen perennials from wet mountain forest in South and North America. The foliage is glossy, and the leaves large, palmately-lobed or entire. The highly-colored flat spathes and cylindrical spadices, which are usually pendent, are produced throughout the year, make excellent cut flowers and are followed by berries.

✔ Long-flowering
✔ Good cut flowers
✔ Have berries after flowering

CULTIVATION
Grow epiphytically in humus-rich, leaf-mould-rich, moist, fertile soil in full or part shade.

PROPAGATION
Seed should be sown at 81°F (27°C) as soon as it is ripe. Germination is very slow. Division can be carried out in winter. Offsets or stem cuttings can be rooted in spring.

Anthurium andreanum

Zone 10
Height: 2ft. (60cm) Spread: 1ft. (30cm)

ANTIRRHINUM *(Scrophulariaceae)*

Common names: Snapdragon

A genus of 40 species of annuals and perennials from stony and rocky sites in the U.S.A., Africa and Europe. The leaves are lance-shaped to ovate. The tubular flowers are two-lipped, the lower of which has a hairy palate, and are borne in terminal racemes from early summer to autumn.

✔ Good cut flowers
✔ Attractive seed-heads
✔ Attracts bees
✔ Repeat-flowering

✘ Self-seed
✘ Mildew prone
✘ Prone to slug damage

CULTIVATION
Grow in sharply-drained, fertile soil in sun. Dead-heading prevents self-seeding and encourages repeat-flowering.

PROPAGATION
Seed can be sown in summer, autumn or spring.

Antirrhinum braun-blanquettii
Zone 7
Height: 4ft. (1.2m) Spread: 18in. (45cm)
Foliage variegated

Antirrhinum hispanicum
Zone 7
Height: 8in. (20cm) Spread: 1ft. (30cm)

Antirrhinum majus
Floral Showers series
Zone 7
Height: 8in. (20cm) Spread: 1ft. (30cm)

Antirrhinum majus
Sonnet series
Zone 7
Height: 18in. (45cm) Spread: 10in. (25 cm)

Antirrhinum majus 'Taff's White'
Zone 7
Height and spread: 2ft. (60cm)
Variegated foliage

Antirrhinum molle
(Common snapdragon)
Zone 7
Height: 8in. (20cm) Spread: 1ft. (30cm)

A

AQUILEGIA *(Ranunculaceae)*
Common names: Columbine

A genus of 70 species of drought-tolerant perennials from various habitats, such as mountainous regions and woodland, across the temperate northern hemisphere. They are clump-forming and have foliage in basal rosettes. The leaves are deeply three-lobed, and commonly glaucous. The flowers are bell-shaped, and have colored tepals and spurred petals. They may be solitary or in branched stems. They bloom in late spring and early summer, and self-seed freely.

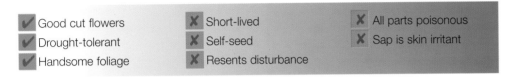

✔ Good cut flowers	✖ Short-lived	✖ All parts poisonous
✔ Drought-tolerant	✖ Self-seed	✖ Sap is skin irritant
✔ Handsome foliage	✖ Resents disturbance	

CULTIVATION
Grow in moist, well-drained, (or sharply-drained in the case of alpine species) fertile soil in sun or part shade. Dead-head to prevent self-seeding.

PROPAGATION
Seed should be sown in a cold frame as soon as it is ripe, or in spring. Named cultivars can be divided in spring, but they may not take very readily.

Aquilegia canadensis

Zone 3
Height: 3ft. (90cm) Spread: 1ft. (30cm)

Aquilegia
'Chaffinch' Songbird Series

Zone 3
Height: 2ft. (60cm) Spread: 18in. (45cm)

Aquilegia chrysantha
'Yellow Queen'

Zone 3
Height: 3ft. (90cm) Spread: 2ft. (60cm)

Aquilegia
'Goldfinch' Songbird Series

Zone 3
Height: 2ft. (60cm) Spread: 18in. (45cm)

Aquilegia
'Mellow Yellow'

Zone 3
Height: 8in. (20cm) Spread: 4in. (10 cm)

Aquilegia
Music Series A.G.M.

Zone 3
Height and spread: 18in. (45cm)

Aquilegia vulgaris

Zone 3
Height: 3ft. (90cm) Spread: 2ft. (60cm)

Aquilegia vulgaris var. *stellata*

Zone 3
Height: 3ft. (90cm) Spread: 2ft. (60cm)

Aquilegia vulgaris var. *stellata*
'Nora Barlow' A.G.M.

Zone 3
Height: 3ft. (90cm) Spread: 2ft. (60cm)

Aquilegia vulgaris Vervaeneana
Group 'Woodside White'

Zone 3
Height: 28in. (70 cm) Spread: 2ft. (60cm)

Aquilegia vulgaris
'William Guinness'

Zone 3
Height: 28in. (70 cm) Spread: 2ft. (60cm)

ARABIS *(Brassicaceae)*

Common names: Rock cress

A genus of 120 species of annuals and short-lived perennials, the majority of which are evergreen, from stony mountainous regions of Eurasia and North America. They are clump-forming or upright. The leaves are simple, hairy and toothed. The flowers are cruciform, purple or white, and borne in racemes. *A. caucasica* is invasive.

✔ Flowers perfumed	✘ Short-lived
✔ Attract butterflies	✘ Prone to aphid attack
✔ Handsome foliage	

CULTIVATION
Grow in any well-drained soil in sun. *A. blepharophylla* 'Fruhlingszauber' must be protected against excessive winter wet; it comes true from seed.

PROPAGATION
Seed should be sown in a cold frame in autumn. Softwood cuttings can be rooted in summer.

Arabis alpina
'Douler Angevine'

Zone 5
Height: 6in. (15cm) Spread: 20in. (50cm)

Arabis blepharophylla
'Fruhlingszauber' A.G.M.
Zone 7
Height: 4in. (10 cm) Spread: 8in. (20cm)
Comes true from seed

Arabis ferdinandi-coburgi
'Old Gold'

Zone 7
Height: 8in. (20cm) Spread: 1ft. (30cm)

Arabis procurrens
'Variegata' A.G.M.

Zone 5
Height: 3in. (8 cm) Spread: 8in. (20cm)

ARCTOTHECA *(Asteraceae)*

Common names: None

A genus of four species of perennials from open sandy regions of South Africa. They are low-growing, rosetted and rhizomatous, and form large plants eventually. The foliage may be white-woolly or green. The leaves are oblong and pinnatifid. The flowers appear in spring or early summer, and are yellow daisies with yellow discs, usually solitary, but two or three may be found on a single stem.

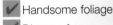

✔ Handsome foliage
✔ Disease-free
✔ Pest-free

Arctotheca calendula

Zone 9
Height: 20in. (50cm) Spread: indefinite
Invasive

CULTIVATION
Grow in any fertile, well-drained soil in sun.

PROPAGATION
Seed should be sown at 64°F (18°C) in spring; division can also be done then.

ARCTOTIS *(Asteraceae)*

Common names: African daisy

A genus of 50 species of annuals and perennials from stony, dry sites in South Africa. The foliage is in basal rosettes, and the leaves are elliptic or lance-shaped and glaucous or silvery-green. The flowers are solitary daisies, borne on long stems over a long period from midsummer to early autumn, but open only in sun. Modern hybrids are an improvement on species in this respect.

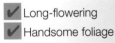 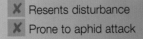

✔ Long-flowering   ✗ Resents disturbance
✔ Handsome foliage   ✗ Prone to aphid attack

Arctotis fastuosa
'Zulu Prince'

Zone 9
Height: 2ft. (60cm) Spread: 16in. (40cm)

CULTIVATION
Grow in gritty, well-drained soil in sun.

PROPAGATION
Seed should be sown at 64°F (18°C) in spring or autumn. Prick seedling out when small, to minimize root disturbance. Stem cuttings can be rooted at any time.

Arctotis x hybrida
'Flame' A.G.M.

Zone 9
Height: 2ft. (60cm) Spread: 1ft. (30cm)

Arctotis x hybrida

Zone 9
Height: 2ft. (60cm) Spread: 1ft. (30cm)

Arctotis x hybrida
'Mahogany'

Zone 9
Height: 2ft. (60cm) Spread: 1ft. (30cm)

Arctotis x hybrida
'Red Devil' A.G.M.

Zone 9
Height: 2ft. (60cm) Spread: 1ft. (30cm)

ARENARIA *(Caryophyllaceae)*

Common names: Sandwort

A genus of 160 species of annuals and perennials from temperate and arctic regions of the northern hemisphere. They are cushion-forming or low-growing, and may be evergreen, The leaves are in opposite pairs, and ovate or linear, green. The flowers may be solitary or in few-flowered cymes, and are five-petalled, usually white, and borne in late spring or early summer.

✔ Evergreen
✔ Handsome foliage
✔ Disease-free
✔ Pest-free

CULTIVATION
Grow in moist, well-drained, gritty soil in sun.

PROPAGATION
Seed should be sown in a cold frame in autumn. Division can be carried out in spring. Basal cuttings can be rooted in early summer.

Arenaria montana
A.G.M.

Zone 4
Height: 2in. (5cm) Spread: 1ft. (30cm)

A

ARGYRANTHEMUM *(Asteraceae)*
Common names: Marguerite

A genus of 25 species of evergreen subshrubs or perennials from Madeira and the Canary Islands. They are found in a variety of habitats from volcanic mountains to beaches. The leaves are alternate or opposite, entire or dissected, or lobed, and glaucous or green. The flowers are daisy-like, single, and in loose corymbs. They come in a range of colors, and may be double or anemone-centered. Flowering is over a long period from spring to autumn.

- ✔ Long-flowering
- ✔ Handsome foliage
- ✔ Evergreen
- ✔ Disease-free
- ✔ Pest-free

CULTIVATION
Under glass, grow in loam-based potting compost in full light. Water freely in growth, but sparingly in winter.

Out of doors, grow in well-drained, fertile soil in sun. Pinch the tip out when young to encourage bushiness. Dead-head to prolong flowering.

PROPAGATION
Greenwood cuttings should be rooted in spring, or cuttings of semi-ripe, non-flowering shoots in summer.

Argyranthemum frutescens

Zone 9
Height and spread: 28in. (70 cm)

Argyranthemum frutescens subsp. *canariae* A.G.M.

Zone 9
Height and spread: 2ft. (60cm)

Argyranthemum 'Jamaica Primrose' A.G.M.

Zone 9
Height and spread: 3ft. (90cm)

Argyranthemum maderense A.G.M.

Zone 9
Height: 1ft. (30cm) Spread: 20in. (50cm)

Argyranthemum 'Petite Pink' A.G.M.

Zone 9
Height and spread: 1ft. (30cm)

Argyranthemum 'Sugar Button'

Zone 9
Height and spread: 18in. (45cm)

A

Argyranthemum
'Summer Stars'

Zone 9
Height and spread: 16in. (40cm)

Argyranthemum
'Vancouver' A.G.M.

Zone 9
Height: 3ft. (90cm) Spread: 32in. (80 cm)

ARISAEMA *(Araceae)*

Common names: Jack in the pulpit

A genus of 150 species of tuberous or rhizomatous perennials from stony wasteland and moist woodland in China, Japan, the Himalayas and North America. They have palmately-lobed or palmate leaves The flowers are insignificant, and the plants are grown for their foliage and their attractive and unusually-colored spathes, followed by attractive seed-heads.

✔ Good cut flowers	✘ Prone to slug damage
✔ Attractive seed-heads	
✔ Handsome foliage	

CULTIVATION
They should be planted in winter or spring, 10in. (25 cm) deep in moist, well-drained, acid to neutral soil in part shade. They should be watered freely when in growth and kept just moist in winter.

PROPAGATION
Seed should be sown in a cold frame in spring. Offsets can be removed in late summer.

Arisaema amurense

Zone 6
Height: 18in. (45cm) Spread: 6in. (15cm)

Arisaema candidissimum

Zone 6
Height: 1ft. (30cm) Spread: 6in. (15cm)

Arisaema ciliatum

Zone 6
Height: 20in. (50cm) Spread: 6in. (15cm)

Arisaema ciliatun var. *liubaense*

Zone 6
Height: 18in. (45cm) Spread: 6in. (15cm)

A

Arisaema formosanum

Zone 5
Height: 1ft. (30cm) Spread: 18in. (45cm)

Arisaema sikokianum

Zone 5
Height: 20in. (50cm) Spread: 6in. (15cm)

Arisaema triphyllum

Zone 4
Height and spread: 1ft. (30cm)

ARISARUM *(Araceae)*
Common names: None

A genus of three species of tuberous or rhizomatous perennials from rocky wasteland and moist woodland in Europe. The densely-arranged leaves are arrow-shaped or ovate, and usually obscure the inflorescence, which takes the form of small hooded spathes enclosing spadices with minute flowers in winter or spring.

✔ Handsome foliage
✔ Disease-free
✔ Pest-free

CULTIVATION
Plant the tubers 3in. (8 cm) deep in autumn in moist, humus-rich soil in part shade.

PROPAGATION
Seed should be sown in a cold frame in spring . Division can be carried out in autumn or winter.

Arisarum proboscideum

Zone 7
Height: 8in. (20cm) Spread: indefinite
Invasive

Arisarum vulgare var. *typicum*

Zone 7
Height: 6in. (15cm) Spread: 4in. (10 cm)

A

ARISTEA *(Iridaceae)*
Common names: None

A genus of 50 species of evergreen, rhizomatous perennials from mountainous and coastal sites in South Africa, Madagascar and East Africa. The leaves are basal and stem-clasping, linear, green. The flowers are saucer-shaped, and in spikes with lateral clusters of flowers, each of which lasts but one day, in summer.

✔ Evergreen	✘ Resents disturbance
✔ Disease-free	
✔ Pest-free	

CULTIVATION
Grow in fertile, well-drained, humus-rich soil in sun. They dislike transplantation.

PROPAGATION
Seed should be sown at 61°F (16°C) in spring.

Aristea ecklonii

Zone 9
Height: 2ft. (60cm) Spread: 18in. (45cm)

Aristea major

Zone 8
Height: 5ft. (1.5m) Spread: 18in. (45cm)

ARMERIA *(Plumbaginaceae)*
Common names: Thrift; sea pink

A genus of 80 species of evergreen, hummock-forming perennials and subshrubs from the Pacific coasts of North and South America, Turkey, Europe and North Africa. The leaves are linear or strap-shaped, and in rosettes. The flowers are small, cup- or saucer-shaped, and in compact, many-flowered spherical heads, borne in summer.

✔ Evergreen
✔ Good for drying for winter
✔ Attract butterflies
✔ Disease-free
✔ Pest-free

Armeria maritima

Zone 4
Height and spread: 1ft. (30cm)

CULTIVATION
Grow in well-drained soil in an open spot in sun.

PROPAGATION
Seed should be sown in a cold frame in autumn or spring. Division can be done in early spring. Semi-ripe basal cuttings can be rooted in summer.

A

Armeria maritima
'Alba'

Zone 4
Height and spread: 1ft. (30cm)

Armeria maritima
'Vindictive' A.G.M.

Zone 4
Height: 6in. (15cm) Spread: 4in. (10 cm)

Armeria 'Nifty Thrifty'

Zone 4
Height: 6in. (15cm) Spread: 4in. (10 cm)
Variegated foliage

ARMORACIA *(Brassicaceae)*

Common names: Horseradish; red cole

A genus of three species of perennials from roadsides, wasteland and watersides in the eastern
U.S.A. and Eurasia. The leaves are basal, large, toothed, coarse, pinnatifid or simple. The flowers
are small, cruciform, and borne in terminal panicles or racemes, from late spring to late summer,
followed by oblong fruits. The roots of *A. rusticana* are used in cooking.

✔ Handsome foliage	✘ Sap is skin irritant
✔ Culinary vegetable	✘ Invasive
	✘ Flowers insignificant

CULTIVATION
Grow in moist, fertile, well-drained soil in sun. Ample water is important during the growing
season to prevent the roots from becoming woody.

PROPAGATION
Division should be done in winter; root cuttings can also be taken in winter.

Armoracia rusticana

Zone 4
Height: 3ft. (90cm) Spread: 2ft. (60cm)

Armoracia rusticana
'Variegata'

Zone 4
Height: 3ft. (90cm) Spread: 2ft. (60cm)

ARTEMISIA *(Asteraceae)*

Common names: Mugwort; wormwood; sagebrush

A genus of 300 species of annuals and evergreen shrubs and perennials from dry, open sites, mostly in the northern hemisphere, with a few from South Africa and South America. They are grown for their foliage effect, as the flowers are uninspiring, being small and white and in panicles or racemes, and may not appear at all. The foliage is universally handsome.

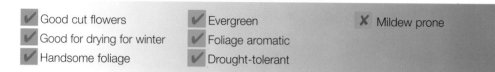

- ✔ Good cut flowers
- ✔ Good for drying for winter
- ✔ Handsome foliage
- ✔ Evergreen
- ✔ Foliage aromatic
- ✔ Drought-tolerant
- ✘ Mildew prone

CULTIVATION

Most species will grow in fertile, well-drained soil in sun. *A. lactiflora* requires a more moist, humus-rich soil. All artemisias dislike heavy, clay soil, and will die back and may be short-lived in such circumstances. Perennial species should be cut back to the ground in autumn.

PROPAGATION

Seed should be sown in a cold frame in autumn. Division of cultivars is necessary, and should be done in autumn or spring. Cultivars can also be perpetuated by taking heel or greenwood cuttings in early summer.

Artemisia arborescens
'Faith Raven'

Zone 8
Height: 3ft. (90cm) Spread: 5ft. (1.5m)

Artemisia lactiflora

Zone 4
Height: 5ft. (1.5m) Spread: 2ft. (60cm)
Prone to powdery mildew

Artemisia ludoviciana var. *latiloba*

Zone 5
Height: 4ft. (1.2m) Spread: 2ft. (60cm)

Artemisia ludoviciana 'Silver Queen' A.G.M.
Zone 5
Height: 30in. (75cm) Spread: 18in. (45cm)
Shy-flowering

Artemisia 'Powis Castle' A.G.M.

Zone 8
Height: 2ft. (60cm) Spread: 3ft. (90cm)
Does not flower

Artemisia schmidtiana
'Nana' A.G.M.

Zone 4
Height: 3in. (8 cm) Spread: 1ft. (30cm)

A

Artemisia stelleriana

Zone 3
Height: 1ft. (30cm) Spread: 18in. (45cm)

Artemisia stelleriana
'Boughton Silver'

Zone 3
Height: 6in. (15cm) Spread: 18in. (45cm)

Artemisia vulgaris 'Oriental Limelight'

Zone 3
Height: 2ft. (60cm) Spread: 1ft. (30cm)
Foliage variegated/Shy-flowering

ARTHROPODIUM *(Anthericaceae)*

Common names: None

A genus of a dozen species of herbaceous or evergreen perennials from open habitats in New Zealand and South Australia. The leaves are linear or lance-shaped. The flowers are small and borne in loose racemes or panicles in summer.

✔ Drought-tolerant   ✘ Prone to slug damage
✔ Handsome foliage

CULTIVATION
Grow in sharply-drained, fertile soil in sun.

PROPAGATION
Seed should be sown in a cold frame in autumn or spring. Division can be carried out in spring.

Arthropodium candidum
'Maculatum'

Zone 8
Height: 8in. (20cm) Spread: 4in. (10 cm)

Arthropodium cirrhatum

Zone 8
Height: 3ft. (90cm) Spread: 1ft. (30cm)
Evergreen

A

ARUM *(Araceae)*
Common names: Lords and Ladies; Cuckoo pint

A genus of 26 species of tuberous perennials from shaded habitats in south Europe, North Africa, west Asia, and the Himalayas. The leaves are arrow- or heart-shaped, and may be handsomely marked. The flowers are tiny, in spadices surrounded by large spathes, and are followed by spikes of berries. The flowers may be either unpleasantly or pleasantly scented.

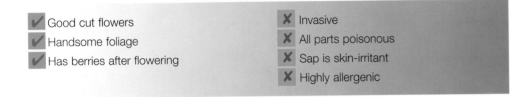

✔ Good cut flowers ✘ Invasive
✔ Handsome foliage ✘ All parts poisonous
✔ Has berries after flowering ✘ Sap is skin-irritant
✘ Highly allergenic

CULTIVATION
Tubers should be planted 6in. (15cm) deep in humus-rich, well-drained soil in sun or part shade.

PROPAGATION
Seed should be removed from the berries and sown in autumn in a cold frame. Tubers can be divided after flowering.

Arum italicum

Zone 6
Height: 1ft. (30cm) Spread: indefinite

Arum italicum subsp. *italicum*
'Marmoratum'

Zone 6
Height: 1ft. (30cm) Spread: indefinite

Arum maculatum
'Painted Lady' (Cuckoo pint)

Zone 7
Height: 10in. (25 cm) Spread: indefinite

ARUNCUS *(Rosaceae)*
Common names: None

A genus of four species of perennials from moist woodland across the northern hemisphere. Many are invasive. The pinnate leaves are toothed and boldly veined. The white or cream flowers are tiny, and borne in terminal panicles well above the foliage in early and midsummer.

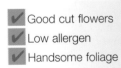

✔ Good cut flowers ✘ Self-seed
✔ Low allergen
✔ Handsome foliage

CULTIVATION
Grow in moist, humus-rich, fertile soil in sun or part shade. They should be dead-headed to prevent self-seeding.

PROPAGATION
Seed should be sown in a cold frame in spring or autumn. Division can be carried out in spring or autumn.

Aruncus aethusifolius

Zone 4
Height and spread: 16in. (40cm)

A

Aruncus dioicus A.G.M.

Zone 7
Height: 6ft. (2m) Spread: indefinite
Invasive

Aruncus dioicus 'Glasnevin'

Zone 7
Height: 6ft. (2m) Spread: indefinite
Invasive

Aruncus dioicus 'Kneiffii'

Zone 7
Height: 4ft. (1.2m) Spread: indefinite
Invasive

ARUNDO *(Poaceae)*
Common names: None

A genus of three species of evergreen, rhizomatous perennial grasses from river banks and ditches of the temperate northern hemisphere. The leaves are flat, linear, and borne on the thick stems and feathery flower spikes.

- ✔ Handsome foliage
- ✔ Evergreen
- ✔ Disease-free
- ✔ Pest-free

CULTIVATION
Grow in any soil, but preferably in moist soil in sun, and out of cold drying winds. Cut flower stems and foliage to the ground after flowering.

PROPAGATION
Seed should be sown in a cold frame in spring. Division can be carried out in spring or early summer. Sections of stems can be rooted in water at this time of year as well.

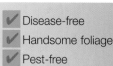

Arundo donax var. *versicolor*

Zone 7
Height: 6ft. (2m) Spread: 2ft. (60cm)

ASARINA *(Scrophulariaceae)*
Common names: None

A genus of just one species, *A. procumbens*, an evergreen, trailing perennial found amongst shady rocks in the Pyrenees mountains. The kidney-shaped leaves are glaucous, soft-sticky, and hairy. The snapdragon-like flowers are cream with yellow throats, and are found in the leaf-axils, and borne over a long period in summer.

- ✔ Long-flowering
- ✔ Evergreen
- ✔ Handsome foliage
- ✔ Drought-tolerant
- ✔ Disease-free
- ✔ Handsome foliage
- ✔ Pest-free
- ✖ Short-lived

CULTIVATION
Grow in sharply-drained, fertile soil in part shade, and preferably where it can trail over an overhang.

PROPAGATION
Seed should be sown at 61°F (16°C) in spring. Tip cuttings can be rooted in summer.

Asarina procumbens
(Wild ginger-snapdragon)

Zone 7
Height: 2in. (5cm) Spread: 2ft. (60cm)

A

ASARUM *(Arisrolochiaceae)*

Common names: None

A genus of 70 species of evergreen perennials from woodland in Eurasia and North America. They are rhizomatous, and the rhizomes smell of ginger. The leaves are large, glossy, usually marbled, and invariably conceal the pitcher-shaped flowers, which appear in spring and are mildly malodorous.

 Handsome foliage
 Evergreen

✗ Flowers malodorous
✗ Prone to slug damage

CULTIVATION
Grow in moist, acid to neutral, well-drained , humus-rich soil in part or full shade.

PROPAGATION
Seed should be sown in a cold frame as soon as it is ripe. Division can be done in early spring.

Asarum splendens

Zone 7
Height: 7in. (18cm) Spread: 8in. (20cm)

ASCLEPIAS *(Asclepiadaceae)*

Common names: Milkweed; silkweed

A genus of 119 species of herbaceous or evergreen perennials from either well-drained or marshy scrubland in temperate North America, tropical North and South America, and South Africa. The leaves are elliptic, ovate or lance-shaped, and they may be opposite, alternate or spirally-arranged. The flowers are small, and borne in umbel-like cymes, followed by seed-heads which split open to reveal rows of silky hairs.

✔ Evergreen
✔ Good cut flowers
✔ Attracts bees
✔ Good for drying for winter

✔ Attractive seed-heads
✔ Disease-free
✔ Pest-free

✗ Sap is skin irritant
✗ Resents disturbance

CULTIVATION
This depends on the habitat in nature. *A. incarnata* requires moist, humus-rich soil, whereas *A. tuberosa* and *A. syriaca* prefer well-drained soil. All like full sun. *A. syriaca* is very invasive.

PROPAGATION
Seed should be sown in a cold frame in early spring. Division can be carried out in spring. Basal cuttings may be rooted in spring.

Asclepias hallii

Zone 3
Height: 3ft. (90cm) Spread: 2ft. (60cm)

Asclepias incarnata

Zone 3
Height: 4ft. (1.2m) Spread: 2ft. (60cm)

Asclepias syriaca

Zone 3
Height: 6ft. (2m) Spread: indefinite
Invasive

Asclepias tuberosa

Zone 3
Height: 3ft. (90cm) Spread: 1ft. (30cm)
Drought-tolerant

ASPARAGUS *(Asparagaceae)*

Common names: Asparagus fern

A genus of 300 species of subshrubs, climbers and evergreen, tuberous perennials from coastal and sandy habitats in Eurasia and Africa. The foliage comprises scale-like true leaves and stems that resemble leaves. The pink or white flowers are borne singly or in racemes, and are followed by colorful berries.

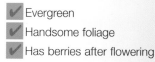

- ✔ Evergreen
- ✔ Handsome foliage
- ✔ Has berries after flowering

CULTIVATION
Grow in moist, well-drained soil in a sheltered corner in part shade.

PROPAGATION
Seed should be sown at 61°F (16°C) in autumn or spring. Division of tubers can be done in early spring.

Asparagus densiflorus

Zone 9
Height: 3ft. (90cm) Spread: 4ft. (1.2m)

ASPHODELINE *(Asphodelaceae)*

Common names: None

A genus of 20 species of perennials and biennials from stony meadows and dry slopes in sunny positions in the Mediterranean area, to Turkey and the Caucasus mountains. The leaves are basal and stem, narrow, grassy, and gray-green. The flowers are perfumed white or yellow stars, borne in unbranched stems in racemes.

- ✔ Flowers perfumed
- ✔ Low allergen
- ✔ Handsome foliage
- ✔ Drought-tolerant
- ✘ Self-seed
- ✘ Prone to aphid attack
- ✘ Prone to slug damage

CULTIVATION
Grow in well-drained, humus-rich, deep soil in sun. Dead-head to prevent self-seeding.

PROPAGATION
Seed should be sown in a cold frame in spring. Divide in autumn or spring so as to have two or three growing points on each division.

Asphodeline lutea

Zone 7
Height: 5ft. (1.5m) Spread: 1ft. (30cm)

ASPHODELUS *(Asphodelaceae)*

Common names: Asphodel

A genus of a dozen species of annuals and perennials found on scrubland, and open woodland in central Europe, and the Mediterranean area to the Himalayas. They are rhizomatous and clump-forming. The leaves are basal, linear and flat or cylindrical. The star-shaped flowers are white or pink, with dark central veins, and are surrounded by brown or white bracts.

- ✔ Good cut flowers
- ✔ Attractive seed-heads
- ✘ Self-seed
- ✘ Prone to aphid attack

CULTIVATION
Grow in fertile, well-drained, gritty soil in sun. Dead-head to prevent self-seeding.

PROPAGATION
Seed should be sown in a cold frame in spring, when division can also be carried out.

Asphodelus albus

Zone 6
Height: 3ft. (90cm) Spread: 1ft. (30cm)

A

Asphodelus ramosus

Zone7
Height: 5ft. (1.5m) Spread: 1ft. (30cm)

ASPIDISTRA *(Convallariaceae)*

Common names: None

A genus of 8 species of evergreen perennials from woodland in Japan, China and the Himalayas. They are rhizomatous. The leaves are glossy, leathery, elliptic, and pointed at the tip. The flowers are solitary, gray-white or purple, and borne at soil level almost hidden under the foliage. Pollination is by snails and slugs.

✔ Evergreen	✘ Flowers insignificant
✔ Handsome foliage	
✔ Disease-free	
✔ Pest-free	

CULTIVATION
Under glass, they are very tolerant of neglect and temperature swings. Grow in loam-based potting compost in bright filtered light. Water moderately in summer, sparingly in winter

Out of doors, grow in moist, well-drained, humus-rich, sandy soil in part or full shade.

PROPAGATION
Division in spring.

Aspidistra elatior
'Variegata' A.G.M.

Height and spread: 2ft. (60cm)

ASPLENIUM *(Aspleniaceae)*

Common names: Spleenwort; Hen & chicken fern; Bird's nest fern; Hart's tongue fern

A genus of 700 species of semi-evergreen or evergreen ferns, which can be terrestrial or epiphytic. They are found in various habitats on all the continents except Antarctica, are rhizomatous, and vary widely in their degree of hardiness. The rhizomes give rise to tufts of fronds. These can be entire, or pinnatifid or up to three-pinnate. The sori are in rows between the midrib and the frond edge. Some species are of bird's nest form i.e. the fronds overlap to form a cavity in which debris collects.

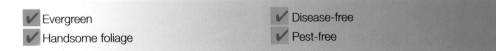

✔ Evergreen	✔ Disease-free
✔ Handsome foliage	✔ Pest-free

CULTIVATION
Grow in moist, humus-rich, gritty soil in part shade. The soil should be acid for the majority of species, but alkaline for *AA. scolopendron* and *trichomanes*.

PROPAGATION
Spores should be sown as soon as ripe at 59ºF (15ºC) for hardy species and at 70ºF (21ºC) for tender species. *A. bulbiferum* forms plantlets, which can be detached and potted up when they have three or four leaves. All hardy species may be divided in spring.

Asplenium bulbiferum
A.G.M. (Hen and chicken fern)

Zone 10
Height and spread: 4ft. (1.2m)

Asplenium nidus
A.G.M. (Bird's nest fern)

Zone 10
Height: 5ft. (1.5m) Spread: 3ft. (90cm)

Asplenium scolopendrium
A.G.M. (Hart's tongue fern)

Zone 5
Height: 28in. (70 cm) Spread: 2ft. (60cm)

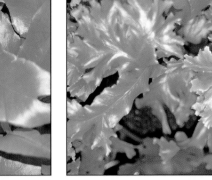

Asplenium scolopendrium
Cristatum Group

Zone 5
Height: 2ft. (60cm) Spread: 32in. (80 cm)

Asplenium scolopendrium
Undulatum Group

Zone 5
Height: 1ft. (30cm) Spread: 20in. (50cm)

Asplenium trichomanes
(Maidenhair spleenwort)

Zone 2
Height: 6in. (15cm) Spread: 8in. (20cm)

ASTELIA *(Asteliaceae)*
Common names: None

A genus of 25 species of evergreen perennials from boggy, peaty habitats in mountainous and alpine regions of Polynesia, Hawaii, Australasia, Falkland Islands, Mauritius, and New Guinea. They are rhizomatous and form large clumps of linear, arching leaves covered in silvery-white scales. The flowers are unisexual, small, with six reflexed or spreading tepals; they may be yellow, green, or brown, and are borne in panicles in spring or summer. They are followed by berries in female plants. They make excellent specimen plants.

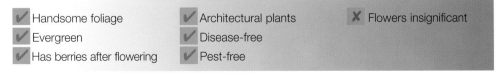

✔ Handsome foliage	✔ Architectural plants	✘ Flowers insignificant
✔ Evergreen	✔ Disease-free	
✔ Has berries after flowering	✔ Pest-free	

CULTIVATION
Grow in moist, fertile, humus-rich soil in sun or part shade.

PROPAGATION
Seed should be sown in a cold frame as soon as it is ripe. Division can be done in spring.

Astelia chatamica A.G.M.

Zone 9
Height: 4ft. (1.2m) Spread: 6ft. (2m)

A

Astelia nervosa
'Westland'

Zone 8
Height: 2ft. (60cm) Spread: 6ft. (2m)

ASTER *(Asteraceae)*
Common names: None

A genus of 250 species of annuals, subshrubs and perennials from both moist woodland and dry mountainous habitats across the northern hemisphere, and North America in particular; their hardiness and cultural needs therefore vary widely. The leaves are entire, lance-shaped, and can be either hairy or hairless. The flowers are daisies, with strap-shaped ray florets in a range of colors and tubular hermaphroditic disc florets, which are usually yellow.

✔ Good cut flowers
✔ Attract butterflies

✘ Prone to slug damage
✘ Need to lift & divide often
✘ Highly allergenic
✘ Prone to aphid attack

Aster alpinus
'Albus' (Group 2)

Zone 3
Height: 10in. (25 cm) Spread: 18in. (45cm)

CULTIVATION

According to the habitat in which the species grows in nature, cultivation is as follows by group, which is given under each entry;

Group 1: grow in moist, well-drained, fertile soil in sun or part shade.

Group 2: grow in sharply-drained soil in sun.

Group 3: grow in moist, fertile soil in part shade.

Most asters benefit from regular lifting and dividing every three years or so, and only young and vigorous shoots should be replanted. *A. novi-belgii* and its cultivars are excessively prone to powdery mildew. All make good cut flowers.

PROPAGATION

Seed should be sown in a cold frame in spring or autumn. Division or

Separation of runners is best done in spring, but in autumn otherwise. Basal cuttings of *AA. x frikartii*, *amellus* and *thomsonii* can be taken in spring.

Aster alpinus
'Happy End'

Zone 3
Height: 10in. (25 cm) Spread: 18in. (45cm)

A

Aster alpinus
'Trimix'

Zone 3
Height: 10in. (25 cm) Spread: 18in. (45cm)

Aster amellus
'King George' A.G.M. (Group 2)

Zone 5
Height and spread: 18in. (45cm)

Aster divaricatus
(Group 3)

Zone 4
Height and spread: 2ft. (60cm)

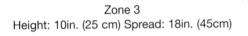

Aster ericoides
(Group 3)

Zone 3
Height: 3ft. (90cm) Spread: 16in. (40cm)

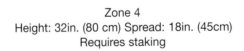

Aster x frikartii (Group 2)

Zone 4
Height: 32in. (80 cm) Spread: 18in. (45cm)
Requires staking

Aster x frikartii
'Flora's Delight'

Zone 4
Height: 20in. (50cm) Spread: 1ft. (30cm)

Aster x frikartii 'Monch' A.G.M.
(Group 2)
Zone 4
Height: 28in. (70 cm) Spread: 16in. (40cm)
Long-flowering

Aster lateriflorus
(Group 1)

Zone 3
Height and spread: 5ft. (1.5m)

Aster macrophyllus (Group 3)

Zone 3
Height: 3ft. (90cm) Spread: 28in. (70 cm)
Handsome foliage/Invasive

A

Aster novae-angliae 'Andenken an Alma Potschke' A.G.M. (Group 3)
Zone 2
Height: 4ft. (1.2m) Spread: 2ft. (60cm)
Needs staking

Aster novae-amgliae 'Lye End Beauty' (Group 3)

Zone 2
Height: 6ft. (2m) Spread: 32in. (80 cm)

Aster novi-belgii 'Jenny' (Group 1)

Zone 2
Height: 4ft. (1.2m) Spread: 3ft. (90cm)
Requires staking

Aster sedifolius 'Nanus' (Group 2)

Zone 6
Height: 18in. (45cm) Spread: 10in. (25 cm)

Aster thomsonii 'Nanus' (Group 3)

Zone 7
Height: 18in. (45cm) Spread: 10in. (25 cm)
Long-flowering

Aster tongolensis 'Berggarten' (Group 2)

Zone 8
Height and spread: 20in. (50cm)

Aster tongolensis var. *Wartburgen*

Zone 8
Height and spread: 20in. (50cm)

ASTILBE *(Saxifragaceae)*
Common names: None

A genus of a dozen species of perennials from moist sites in woodland, stream sides, and ravines in North America and south-east Asia. They are rhizomatous and clump-forming. The leaves are divided into up to five, toothed lobes. The flowers are tiny, but borne in often dense, tapering, plume-like panicles over a long period in summer and early autumn. The majority of Astilbes in cultivation are hybrids of complex parentage, and cannot be perpetuated from seed.

✔ Long-flowering	✔ Handsome foliage	✘ Need to lift & divide often
✔ Low allergen	✔ Attractive seed-heads	✘ Mildew prone
✔ Good for drying for winter		

CULTIVATION
Grow in wet or moist or boggy soil in sun. Do not allow to dry out in summer. Divide the rhizomes and replant every few years, in spring or autumn.

PROPAGATION
Divide in spring or autumn.

Astilbe x arendsii
'Feuer'

Zone 6
Height: 2ft. (60cm) Spread: 18in. (45cm)

Astilbe x arendsii
'Glut'

Zone 6
Height: 2ft. (60cm) Spread: 18in. (45cm)

Astilbe x arendsii
'Irrlicht'

Zone 6
Height and spread: 20in. (50cm)

Astilbe chinensis var. *pumila*
A.G.M.

Zone 5
Height: 10in. (25 cm) Spread: 8in. (20cm)

Astilbe chinensis var. *taquetii*
'Purpurlanze'

Zone 5
Height: 4ft. (1.2m) Spread: 3ft. (90cm)

Astilbe
'Jo Ophorst'

Zone 6
Height: 4ft. (1.2m) Spread: 2ft. (60cm)

Astilbe
'Red Sentinel'

Zone 5
Height: 3ft. (90cm) Spread: 20in. (50cm)

A

Astilbe
'Rheinland' A.G.M.

Zone 5
Height: 20in. (50cm) Spread: 18in. (45cm)

Astilbe
'Sprite' A.G.M.

Zone 7
Height: 20in. (50cm) Spread: 3ft. (90cm)

ASTRANTIA *(Apiaceae)*

Common names: Masterwort; Hattie's pincushion

A genus of around ten species of perennials from alpine meadows and woods across Eurasia. They are rosetted and clump-forming. The leaves are palmate or palmately-lobed. The flowers are five-petalled, and surrounded by a ruff of papery bracts; they are borne in sprays well above the foliage.

✔ Repeat-flowering	✔ Attracts bees	✘ Prone to slug damage
✔ Good cut flowers	✔ Attracts butterflies	✘ Mildew prone
✔ Good for drying for winter		✘ Self-seed

CULTIVATION
Grow in moist, humus-rich, fertile soil in sun or part shade, but *A. major* 'Sunningdale Variegated' must have full sun for maximal variegation to occur. Dead-head after flowering to prevent self-seeding and to encourage repeat-flowering.

PROPAGATION
Seed should be sown in a cold frame as soon as it is ripe. Division can be done in spring.

Astrantia major

Zone 6
Height: 3ft. (90cm) Spread: 18in. (45cm)

Astrantia major subsp. *involucrata*
'Shaggy' A.G.M.

Zone 6
Height: 3ft. (90cm) Spread: 18in. (45cm)

Astrantia major
'Hadspen Blood'

Zone 6
Height: 3ft. (90cm) Spread: 18in. (45cm)

Astrantia major
'Rubra'

Zone 6
Height: 3ft. (90cm) Spread: 18in. (45cm)

A

Astrantia major
'Roma' (PBR)

Zone 6
Height: 3ft. (90cm) Spread: 18in. (45cm)

Astrantia major
'Rosensinphonie'

Zone 6
Height: 3ft. (90cm) Spread: 18in. (45cm)

Astrantia major
'Ruby Wedding'

Zone 6
Height: 3ft. (90cm) Spread: 18in. (45cm)

Astrantia major 'Sunningdale
Variegated' A.G.M.

Zone 6
Height: 3ft. (90cm) Spread: 18in. (45cm)

Astrantia maxima

Zone 6
Height: 2ft. (60cm) Spread: 1ft. (30cm)

ATHYRIUM *(Athyriaceae)*
Common names: Lady fern

A genus of 180 species of rhizomatous, terrestrial, deciduous ferns found in moist forest or woodland in tropical and temperate regions of the globe. The fronds are usually pinnatifid or pinnate, but some are simple. Sori are found in two rows, and covered by indusia.

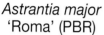

✔ Handsome foliage
✔ Disease-free
✔ Pest-free

CULTIVATION
Grow in moist, acid to neutral, fertile, humus-rich soil in shade in a sheltered corner.

PROPAGATION
Spores should be sown as soon as ripe, and at 61°F (16°C) for hardy forms and at 70°F (21°C) for tender ones. Division can be effected in spring.

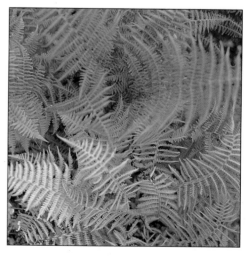

Athyrium filix-femina A.G.M.

Zone 5
Height: 4ft. (1.2m) Spread: 3ft. (90cm)

A

Athyrium filx-femina
'Minutissimum'

Zone 5
Height: 1ft. (30cm) Spread: 16in. (40cm)

Athyrium nipponicum var. *pictum*
A.G.M.
Zone 4
Height: 1ft. (30cm) Spread: indefinite
Invasive

AUBRIETA *(Brassicaceae)*

Common names: Aubretia

A genus of a dozen species of evergreen, low-growing perennials from scree, and coniferous woodland in Eurasia. The leaves are oblong or obovate, toothed or entire, and hairy. The cruciform flowers are borne freely in few-flowered racemes in spring.

✔ Evergreen
✔ Attracts butterflies
✔ Handsome foliage

✘ Prone to aphid attack

CULTIVATION
Grow in well-drained, alkaline or neutral soil in sun. They should be trimmed over after flowering to retain compactness.

PROPAGATION
Seed should be sown in a cold frame in spring or autumn. Softwood cuttings can be taken in early summer or semi-ripe cuttings in mid-summer. They do not tolerate division well.

Aubrieta
'Argenteovariegata' A.G.M.

Zone 7
Height: 2in. (5cm) Spread: 30in. (75cm)

Aubrieta
'Aureovariegata' A.G.M.

Zone 7
Height: 2in. (5cm) Spread: 30in. (75cm)

Aubrieta
'Downer's Variegated'

Zone 7
Height: 2in. (5cm) Spread: 30in. (75cm)

Aubrieta
'Red Carpet'

Zone 7
Height: 2in. (5cm) Spread: 30in. (75cm)

AURINIA *(Brassicaceae)*

Common names: Golden tuft

A genus of seven species of woody, evergreen perennials and clump-forming biennials from screes and mountains in Turkey, Russia and southern and central Europe. The leaves are obovate, toothed, hairy, gray-green and in rosettes. The flowers are yellow, and borne in dense panicles in late spring and early summer.

✔ Evergreen ✗ Prone to aphid attack

✔ Handsome foliage

✔ Attracts butterflies

CULTIVATION

Grow in well-drained, fertile soil in sun. .Trim over after flowering to retain compactness.

PROPAGATION

Seed should be sown in a cold frame in autumn, or take softwood cuttings in early summer.

Aurinia saxatilis
A.G.M.

Zone 3
Height: 10in. (25 cm) Spread: 16in. (40cm)

Aurinia saxatilis
'Variegata'

Zone 3
Height: 10in. (25 cm) Spread: 16in. (40cm)

AZOLLA *(Azollaceae)*

Common names: Fairy moss; mosquito plant

A genus of eight species of aquatic floating ferns found everywhere in the world. They have floating rhizomes with pink roots, which give rise to two-lobed, scaly fronds of pale green that turn red or brown in autumn. They are very highly invasive, and help keep algae to a minimum by covering the surface of the water and shutting out the light. It is illegal to release them into the wild in some countries.

✔ Handsome foliage ✗ Invasive

✔ Disease-free ✗ Eaten by waterfowl

✔ Pest-free

CULTIVATION

Scatter plants on the water surface; they grow in sun or shade. They fall to the bottom in winter in cold climates, only to resurface in spring.

PROPAGATION

Scatter plant segments on the water surface in spring.

Azolla filiculoides

Zone 7
Height: 1in. (2.5 cm) Spread: indefinite
Invasive

B

BACOPA
BALLOTA
BAPTISIA
BEGONIA
BELAMCANDA
BELLIS
BELLIUM
BERGENIA
BESCHORNERIA
BIDENS
BILLBERGIA
BLECHNUM
BLETILLA
BORAGO
BOYKINIA
BRIMEURA
BRUNNERA
BRUNSVIGIA
BUGLOSSOIDES
BULBINE
BULBINELLA
BUPHTHALMUM
BUPLEURUM
BUTOMUS

B

BACOPA *(Scrophulariaceae)*

Common names: Water hyssop

A genus of 56 species of aquatic or semi-aquatic perennials from Australia, Africa, U.S.A. and Asia. They are creeping and mat-forming. The leaves are spoon-shaped, with a dentate apex. The flowers are small, five-petalled, pink or white, and appear in summer.

 Invasive

CULTIVATION
Grow in shallow water or pond margins, in sun.

PROPAGATION
Division should be done in spring.

Bacopa monnieri

Zone 8
Height: 4in. (10 cm) Spread: indefinite

BALLOTA *(Lamiaceae)*

Common names: None

A genus of over 30 species of perennials and evergreen subshrubs found in waste places in the Mediterranean, and Eurasia, The leaves are aromatic, ovate or heart-shaped, toothed or scalloped, and arranged opposite. The flowers are two-lipped, white or pale green, and found in whorls in the leaf-axils of terminal shoots. The two plants illustrated are subshrubs.

- ✔ Aromatic foliage
- ✔ Drought-tolerant
- ✔ Handsome foliage
- ✔ Evergreen
- ✔ Disease-free
- ✔ Pest-free

CULTIVATION
Grow in sharply-drained, poor, sandy soil in sun. Cut back in summer to maintain compactness.

PROPAGATION
Perennials should be divided in spring. Softwood or semi-ripe cuttings of subshrubs should be taken in early summer.

Ballota
'All Hallows Green'

Zone 8
Height: 2ft. (60cm) Spread: 30in. (75cm)

Ballota pseudodictamnus
A.G.M.

Zone 8
Height: 20in. (50cm) Spread: 2ft. (60cm)

B

BAPTISIA *(Papilionaceae)*

Common names: Wild indigo

A genus of over 20 species of perennials found in dry grasslands and woodlands in the eastern U.S.A. They have fully-divided tripalmate leaves. The flowers are pea-like, and borne in terminal or axillary racemes, on tall stems well above the foliage in early summer, and are followed by inflated seed pods.

✔ Good cut flowers	✔ Low allergen	✘ Short-lived
✔ Good for drying for winter	✔ Disease-free	✘ Resents disturbance
✔ Handsome seed-heads	✔ Pest-free	✘ Need staking

Baptisia australis
A.G.M.

Zone 5
Height: 5ft. (1.5m) Spread: 2ft. (60cm)

CULTIVATION
Grow in sharply-draining soil in sun.

PROPAGATION
Seed should be sown in a cold frame as soon as it is ripe. Division can be done in early spring, but is not well tolerated.

BEGONIA *(Begoniaceae)*

Common names: None

A large genus of 900 species, including a few annuals, climbers, evergreen shrubs, succulents and epiphytes, although by far the majority are perennials, which may be evergreen or herbaceous. They occur in a widespread band of 15 degrees either side of the Equator, so are tropical or subtropical. They may be fibrous-rooted, tuberous or rhizomatous, and may be grown for their foliage or their flowers, which are bisexual and borne in terminal or axillary racemes or cymes.

| ✔ Handsome foliage | ✘ Mildew prone |
| ✔ Long-flowering | |

Begonias can be classified as follows; each entry has its classification indicated in brackets:

Cane-stemmed (C) These are Brazilian for the greater part, are fibrous-rooted and grown for their foliage and flowers. They bloom from early spring to summer. The foliage is generally very handsome.

CULTIVATION
Grow in well-drained, humus-rich acid or neutral soil in part shade. Do not over-water or they will drop their leaves. They should be cut back to 2 to 4 buds from the base in spring.

PROPAGATION
Take tip, stem or leaf cuttings in spring.

Rex–cultorum (R) rhizomatous evergreen perennials derived from crosses of *B. rex* and other species and are essentially foliage plants, as the flowers are inconspicuous.

CULTIVATION
Grow in well-drained humus-rich acid to neutral soil in sun.

PROPAGATION
Sow seed, divide rhizomes, or take leaf cuttings in spring.

Rhizomatous (RH) These are mostly evergreen perennials grown for their foliage. The flowers are small and borne in winter or early spring. They derive from *B. bowerae* and *B. imperialis* crosses.

CULTIVATION
Grow in well-drained, humus-rich acid to neutral soil in part shade.

PROPAGATION
Sow seed, divide rhizomes, or take leaf cuttings in spring.

Begonia albopicta (C)

Zone 10
Height: 3ft. (90cm) Spread: 1ft. (30cm)
Drought-tolerant

Begonia 'Beatrice Hadrell' (RH)

Zone 10
Height and spread: 8in. (20cm)
Drought-tolerant

B

Semperflorens (S) These are bushy, evergreen, fibrous-rooted perennials derived from crosses between, among others, *B. cucullata* and *B. schmidtiana*. They are compact, and grown for foliage and flowers, borne throughout summer.

CULTIVATION
Grow in well-drained humus-rich, acid or neutral soil in part shade.

PROPAGATION
Sow seed or take basal cuttings in spring.

Shrubby (SH) These are, nevertheless, perennials. They are evergreen, and may be succulent. They are grown for their foliage, as the flowers are usually small.

CULTIVATION
Grow in well-drained humus-rich, acid to neutral soil in part shade. Nip out the growing tip twice each season to promote compactness.

PROPAGATION
Sow seed, or take stem, leaf or tip cuttings in spring.

Tuberous (T) This group includes begonias sold as Pendulas, Multifloras and Tuberhybridas. They are tuberous, winter-dormant perennials grown for their flowers and foliage. They may be pendent or upright, have succulent stems, and glossy leaves. They are derived from complex crosses of Andean begonias such as *veitchii*, *gracilis* and *pearcei*. The only hardy begonia, *B. grandis evansiana*—is in this category.

CULTIVATION
Plant tubers in spring in well-drained, humus-rich, acid to neutral soil in sun. Remove the small female flowers to prolong flowering. Lift tubers in autumn, and dust with fungicide and store at 45°F (7°C).

PROPAGATION
Sow seed, or take basal, or side-shoot stem cuttings in spring.

Winter-flowering (W) These are low-growing, evergreen perennials grown for their foliage and flowers. They have succulent stems and include Lorraine, Christmas, Cheimantha, Elatior and Rieger groups. They bloom from late autumn to early spring.

CULTIVATION
Under glass, grow in well-drained, humus-rich acid to neutral soil in bright light and mid-day shade. Good ventilation is important. Water moderately during growth, but sparingly in winter.

Out of doors, grow in neutral to acid, well-drained, humus-rich, fertile soil in good light but not direct sun, or in part shade.

PROPAGATION
Basal cuttings in spring.

Begonia
'Benitochiba' (R)

Zone 10
Height: 10in. (25 cm) Spread: 1ft. (30cm)

Begonia
'Captain Nemo' (RH)

Zone 10
Height: 10in. (25 cm) Spread: 1ft. (30cm)

Begonia
'Cleopatra' A.G.M. (RH)

Zone 10
Height: 10in. (25 cm) Spread: 1ft. (30cm)

Begonia fuchsioides var. *miniata*
'Rosea' (SH)

Zone 10
Height: 18in. (45cm) Spread: 1ft. (30cm)

Begonia grandis subsp. *evansiana*
(T) (Evans' Begonia)
Zone 8
Height: 32in. (80 cm) Spread: 1ft. (30cm)
Self-seeds

B

Begonia maculata
A.G.M. (C)

Zone 10
Height: 4ft. (1.2m) Spread: 2ft. (60cm)

Begonia manicata
'Aureomaculata Crispa' (RH)

Zone 10
Height: 2ft. (60cm) Spread: 14in. (35cm)

Begonia
'Marmaduke' A.G.M. (RH)

Zone 10
Height: 4in. (10 cm) Spread: 1ft. (30cm)

Begonia
'Marmalade' (RH)

Zone 10
Height: 4in. (10 cm) Spread: 1ft. (30cm)

Begonia masoniana
A.G.M. (RH)

Zone 10
Height: 20in. (50cm) Spread: 18in. (45cm)

Begonia metallica
A.G.M. (SH)

Zone 10
Height: 3ft. (90cm) Spread: 2ft. (60cm)

Begonia
'Midnight Magic' (RH)

Zone 10
Height: 4in. (10 cm) Spread: 1ft. (30cm)

Begonia
Non-stop Series A.G.M. (T)

Zone 10
Height and spread: 1ft. (30cm)

Begonia
'Queen Olympus'

Zone 10
Height: 4in. (10 cm) Spread: 1ft. (30cm)

B

Begonia rex (R)

Zone 10
Height: 10in. (25 cm) Spread: 1ft. (30cm)

Begonia rex
'Pink Champagne' (R)

Zone 10
Height: 10in. (25 cm) Spread: 1ft. (30cm)

Begonia semperflorens
Cocktail Series A.G.M.

Zone 10
Height and spread: 1ft. (30cm)

Begonia semperflorens
Cultorum Group (S) (Wax begonia)

Zone 10
Height: 4in. (10 cm) Spread: 1ft. (30cm)

Begonia sutherlandii
A.G.M. (T)

Zone 10
Height: 1ft. (30cm) Spread: 18in. (45cm)

Begonia
'Thrush'

Zone 10
Height: 4in. (10 cm) Spread: 10in. (25 cm)

Begonia
'Tiger Paws' A.G.M. (RH)

Zone 10
Height: 1ft. (30cm) Spread: 18in. (45cm)

Begonia tuberhybrida
Non-stop Series (T)

Zone 10
Height and spread: 1ft. (30cm)

Begonia venosa (W)

Zone 10
Height: 3ft. (90cm) Spread: 2ft. (60cm)

B

BELAMCANDA *(Iridaceae)*
Common names: Blackberry lily

A genus of just two species of rhizomatous perennials from coastal sandy meadows and grassland in India, China, Japan and Russia. They are short-lived. The leaves are sword-shaped, and in fans. The 6-tepalled, open flowers are orange with maroon spots, are borne in succession in summer, and are followed by handsome seed-heads.

✔ Long-flowering

✔ Good cut flowers

✔ Handsome seed-heads

✔ Disease-free

✔ Pest-free

✘ Short-lived

Belamcanda chinensis

Height: 3ft. (90cm) Spread: 8in. (20cm)

CULTIVATION
Grow in moist, well-drained, humus-rich soil in sun or part shade. Do not allow to dry out.

PROPAGATION
Seed should be sown in a cold frame in spring. Division can be done in spring.

BELLIS *(Asteraceae)*
Common names: Common daisy; English daisy

A genus of 15 species of evergreen carpeting perennials, from grassland in Turkey and Europe. They have rosettes of spoon-shaped, dark green leaves. The flowers are either solitary, single, semi-double or double daisies, in pink, white or red.

✔ Long-flowering

✔ Evergreen

✔ Good cut flowers

✔ Good for drying for winter

✔ Disease-free

✔ Pest-free

✘ Self-seed

CULTIVATION
Grow in any soil in sun or part shade. Dead-head to prevent self-seeding.

PROPAGATION
Seed should be sown in spring. Division can be done in spring or autumn.

Bellis perennis
Roggli Series

Zone 4
Height and spread: 8in. (20cm)

Bellis perennis
Pomponette Series A.G.M.

Zone 4
Height and spread: 8in. (20cm)

BELLIUM *(Asteraceae)*

Common names: None

A genus of only three species of annual and perennial daisies from sunny habitats in southern Europe. The leaves are fleshy and elliptic, or spoon-shaped. The flowers are solitary white single daisies with yellow discs, borne in summer.

 Handsome foliage

CULTIVATION
Grow in sharply-drained fertile soil in sun.

PROPAGATION
Seed should be sown in a cold frame in spring.

Bellium crassifolium canescens

Zone 8
Height: 6in. (15cm) Spread: 8in. (20cm)

BERGENIA *(Saxifagaceae)*

Common names: Elephants' ears

A genus of eight species of evergreen perennials from moorland, meadowland and woodland of East and Central Asia. They are clump-forming, rhizomatous, and grown for foliage and flowers. The leaves are large, leathery, glossy, and in rosettes. The flowers are funnel- or bell-shaped in panicle-like cymes, and are borne in early spring.

✔ Evergreen   ✔ Low allergen   ✘ Prone to slug damage
✔ Handsome foliage   ✔ Leaves good for cutting   ✘ Need to lift & divide often
✔ Good cut flowers

CULTIVATION
Grow in moist, humus-rich, well-drained soil in sun or part shade. Division should be carried out every few years as the clumps deteriorate.

PROPAGATION
Seed should be sown in spring, but the hybrids will not come true. Division should be carried out in spring.

Bergenia cordifolia

Zone 3
Height: 2ft. (60cm) Spread: 32in. (80 cm)

Bergenia
'Silberlicht' A.G.M.

Zone 3
Height: 18in. (45cm) Spread: 2ft. (60cm)

Bergenia
'Sunningdale'

Zone 3
Height: 18in. (45cm) Spread: 2ft. (60cm)

BESCHORNERIA *(Agavaceae)*

Common names: None

A genus of seven species of perennial succulents found in semi-arid regions of Mexico. Their leaves are lance-shaped or linear, glaucous, keeled, and have fine teeth along the edge. The yellow flowers are tubular, with red bracts and are borne in panicles or racemes in late spring and summer.

✔ Handsome foliage

✔ Disease-free

✔ Architectural plants

CULTIVATION
Under glass, grow in cactus compost in full light. Water with moderation during growth, but sparingly in winter.

Out of doors, grow in sharply-draining, humus-rich soil in sun.

PROPAGATION
Seed should be sown at 70°F (21°C) in early spring,when offsets may also be rooted.

Beschorneria yuccoides
A.G.M.

Zone 9
Height: 5ft. (1.5m) Spread: 4ft. (1.2m)

BIDENS *(Asteraceae)*

Common names: Beggar ticks

A genus of 200 species of annuals, shrubs and perennials from wasteland, and grassland in Eurasia, Australia and tropical and temperate America. The leaves are pinnate, or simple, opposite, spreading or erect. The flowers may be solitary or in cymes, and borne from spring to winter in warm sites.

✔ Long-flowering

✔ Disease-free

✔ Pest-free

CULTIVATION
Grow in moist, well-drained,fertile soil in sun.

PROPAGATION
Seed should be sown at 64°F (18°C) in spring. Division can be done in spring. Stem cuttings can be rooted in spring or autumn.

Bidens ferulifolia
A.G.M.

Zone 8
Height: 1ft. (30cm) Spread: indefinite

Bidens heterophylla

Zone 8
Height: 3ft. (90cm) Spread: 4ft. (1.2m)

B

BILLBERGIA *(Bromeliaceae)*
Common names: Friendship plant; Queen's tears

A genus of 60 species of evergreen perennials. They are rhizomatous or suckering, mainly epiphytic, and rosette-forming. They are found in Mexico, and Central and South America in forest, woodland or scrubland. The leaves are linear, and arching. The flowers are tubular, short-lived, and borne in racemes or panicles.

✔ Evergreen	✘ Invasive
✔ Handsome foliage	

CULTIVATION
Under glass, grow epiphytically on a tree branch or in epiphytic bromeliad compost in indirect, bright light. The central funnel should be kept full of water.

Out of doors, grow epiphytically on a tree branch, or in sharply-drained, humus-rich, loamy soil in part shade.

PROPAGATION
Seed should be sown as soon as ripe at 81°F (27°C). Offsets can be rooted in summer.

Billbergia nutans
'Variegata'

Zone 9
Height: 20in. (50cm) Spread: indefinite

BLECHNUM *(Blechnaceae)*
Common names: Hard fern

A genus of probably 200 species of ferns, mostly evergreen, from acid, moist, sites in both tropical and temperate regions of the world. They are rhizomatous, some of which are stoloniferous, and terrestrial. The fronds are leathery, and pinnate or pinnatifid, and in rosettes. The sori are deployed in two rows along the midrib of the frond, or its segments. Some species are invasive.

✔ Evergreen
✔ Handsome foliage
✔ Disease-free
✔ Pest-free

CULTIVATION
Grow in acid, moist, humus-rich soil in deep or part shade. High humidity is important for success.

PROPAGATION
Spores should be sown in late summer Only *BB. penna-marina* and *spicant* respond well to division, and this should be done in spring.

Blechnum chilense A.G.M.

Zone 8
Height: 6ft. (2m) Spread: indefinite
Invasive

Blechnum spicant
A.G.M.

Zone 5
Height: 20in. (50cm) Spread: 2ft. (60cm)

Blechnum tabulare
A.G.M.

Zone 8
Height: 3ft. (90cm) Spread: 4ft. (1.2m)

B

BLETILLA *(Orchidaceae)*
Common names: None

A genus of 10 species of terrestrial, deciduous orchids from temperate regions of Japan, China and Taiwan. They are rhizomatous, and the rhizomes give rise to pseudobulbs. The leaves are obovate or linear, and folded. The flowers are bell-shaped, and borne on terminal racemes from spring to early summer.

✔ Good cut flowers   ✘ Prone to aphid attack
✔ Handsome foliage

CULTIVATION
Grow in moist, well-drained, humus-rich, soil, in sun, but not at mid-day.

PROPAGATION
Division in early spring.

Bletilla striata

Zone 7
Height and spread: 2ft. (60cm)

Bletilla striata 'Albostriata'

Zone 7
Height and spread: 2ft. (60cm)
Foliage variegated

BORAGO *(Boraginaceae)*
Common names: None

A genus of three species. One is the well-known annual borage, *Borago officinalis*. The only perennial is *B. pygmaea*, from rocky areas in Sardinia and Corsica. It blooms from early summer to early autumn. The lance-shaped leaves are rough and hairy.

✔ Handsome foliage   ✘ Short-lived
✔ Long-flowering   ✘ Mildew prone
✔ Drought-tolerant

CULTIVATION
Grow in moist soil in part shade.

PROPAGATION
Seed should be sown in situ in spring. Division can also be done in spring.

Borago pygmaea

Zone 7
Height and spread: 2ft. (60cm)

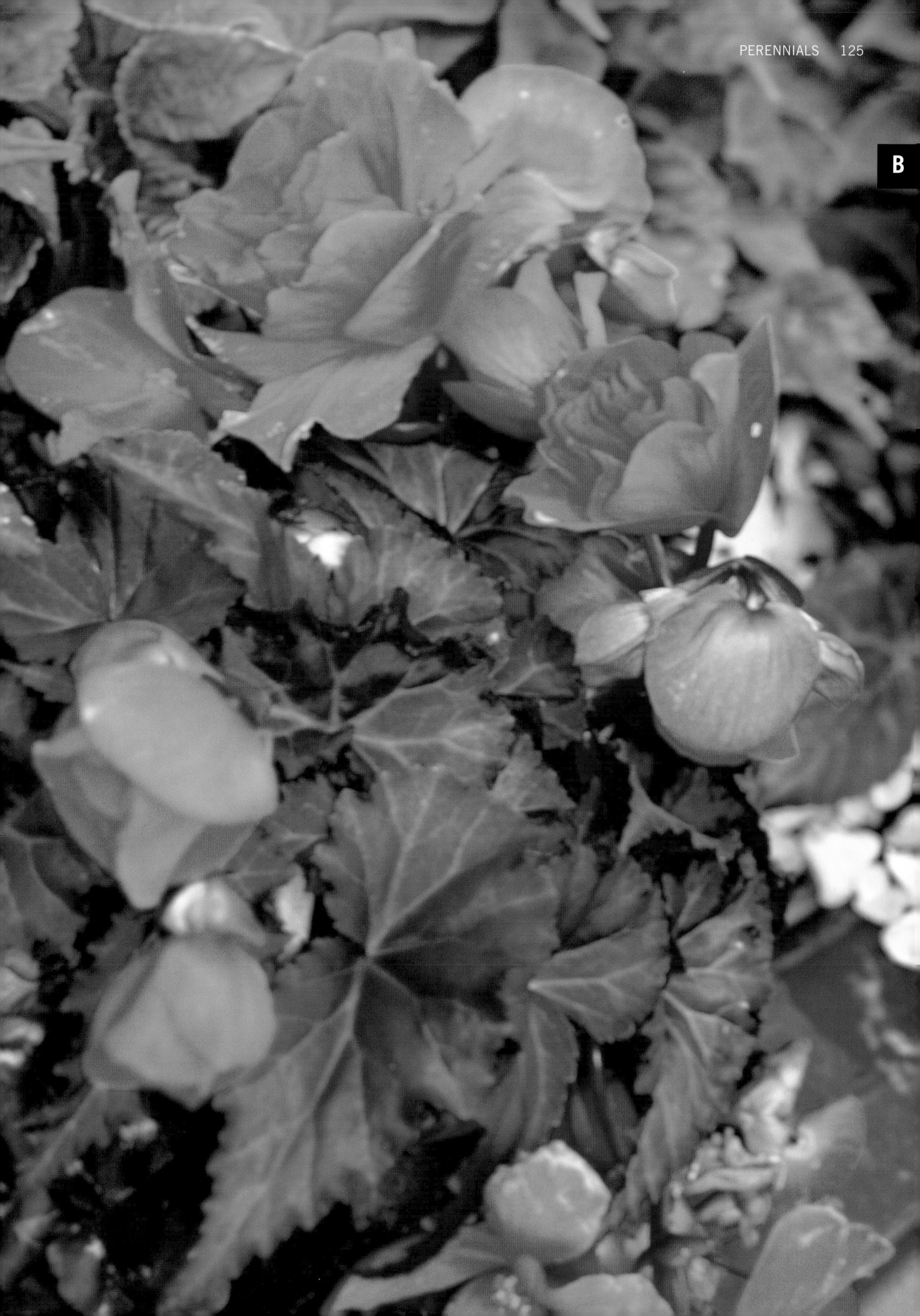

B

BOYKINIA *(Saxifragaceae)*
Common names: None
A genus of ten species of rhizomatous perennials from mountains and moist woodlands in North America and Japan. The bright green leaves are basal and stem, rounded or kidney-shaped. The flowers are small, white or red, and borne in lax panicles.

✔ Handsome foliage
✔ Disease-free
✔ Pest-free
✖ Flowers insignificant

CULTIVATION
Grow in acid, moist, humus-rich soil in part shade.

PROPAGATION
Seed should be sown in a cold frame as soon as it is ripe. Division can be done in spring.

Boykinia rotundifolia

Zone 8
Height: 2ft. (60cm) Spread: 18in. (45cm)

BRIMEURA *(Hyacinthaceae)*
Common names: None
A genus of but two species of bulbous perennials that grow in maquis or meadows in south-eastern Europe. They are grown for their tall-stemmed flower heads, in racemes, of bell-shaped, bluebell-like flowers in spring. The leaves are linear, channeled, and bright green.

✔ Handsome foliage
✔ Disease-free
✔ Pest-free

CULTIVATION
The bulbs should be planted 2in. (5cm) deep in autumn in well-drained, humus-rich soil in sun or part shade; does well under shrubs.

PROPAGATION
Seed should be sown in a cold frame as soon as it is ripe. Division can be done in summer.

Brimeura amethystina

Zone 5
Height: 8in. (20cm) Spread: 2in. (5cm)

BRUNNERA *(Boraginaceae)*
Common names: None
A genus of three species of perennials that grow in woodland in eastern Europe and western Asia. They are rhizomatous, and have handsome foliage. The leaves are ovate, hairy and rough, and the basal ones are ovate whereas the stem leaves are lance-shaped. The flowers resemble those of forget-me–nots; they are white or blue and borne in panicles in mid and late spring.

✔ Repeat-flowering   ✔ Handsome foliage   ✖ Self-seed
✔ Good cut flowers   ✔ Disease-free
✔ Low allergen   ✔ Pest-free

CULTIVATION
Grow in moist, humus-rich, well-drained soil in part shade. Dead-head to prevent self-seeding, and to encourage repeat-flowering.

PROPAGATION
Seed should be sown in a cold frame in early spring. Division is required for named varieties, and this should be done in spring.

Brunnera macrophylla
A.G.M.

Zone 3
Height and spread: 2ft. (60cm)

Brunnera macrophylla
'Dawson's White'

Zone 3
Height and spread: 2ft. (60cm)

Brunnera macrophylla
'Gordano Gold'

Zone 3
Height and spread: 2ft. (60cm)

Brunnera macrophylla
'Hadspen Cream' A.G.M.

Zone 3
Height and spread: 2ft. (60cm)

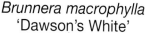

Brunnera macrophylla
'Jack Frost'

Zone 3
Height and spread: 2ft. (60cm)

BRUNSVIGIA *(Amaryllidaceae)*

Common names: None

A genus of 20 species of bulbous perennials from grassy places in South Africa. They are grown for their showy, funnel-shaped flowers, which are borne, in terminal umbels in autumn. The leaves are basal and strap-shaped, and appear with, or after, the flowers.

✔ Handsome foliage   ✘ Prone to aphid attack

CULTIVATION

Under glass, plant bulbs with their necks just above the soil in autumn in loam-based potting compost in full light. Water freely whilst in growth, but keep dry in winter. Keep frost-free over winter.

Out of doors, grow in very sharply-drained soil in sun.

PROPAGATION

Seed should be sown as soon as it is ripe at 70°F (21°C) in very open compost. Bulbils can be detached in late summer whilst plants are dormant.

Brunsvigia subacaulis

Zone 9
Height: 18in. (45cm) Spread: 8in. (20cm)

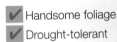

BUGLOSSOIDES *(Boraginaceae)*

Common names: None

A genus of some 15 species of annuals, perennials and subshrubs from Eurasia and North Africa. They may be upright or decumbent, and the latter are tip-rooting, and therefore make good ground cover. The leaves are lance-shaped, hairy, rough and dark green. The flowers are smallish, salvers, borne in terminal cymes.

✔ Drought-tolerant   ✘ Invasive
✔ Disease-free
✔ Pest-free

CULTIVATION
Grow in limy, well-drained fertile soil in sun, but with shade at mid-day.

PROPAGATION
Perennials should be divided in early spring.

Buglossoides purpurocaerulea

Zone 6
Height: 2ft. (60cm) Spread: indefinite

BULBINE *(Asphodelaceae)*

Common names: None

A genus of 30 species of perennials found in dry grassland of Australia and South and East Africa. Some are succulent, some not. They may be tuberous or rhizomatous. The leaves are in rosettes, linear and blue-green. The flowers are star-shaped, and borne in dense terminal racemes in spring or summer.

✔ Handsome foliage   ✔ Disease-free
✔ Drought-tolerant   ✔ Pest-free

CULTIVATION
Under glass, grow in gritty, loam-based potting compost, in full light and good ventilation. Water freely during summer but keep dry in winter.

Out of doors; grow in sharply-drained soil in sun.

PROPAGATION
Seed should be sown at 64°F (18°C) in spring, when division can also be carried out.

Bulbine alooides

Zone 9
Height: 1ft. (30cm) Spread: 6in. (15cm)

BULBINELLA *(Asphodelaceae)*

Common names: None

A genus of 20 species of perennials from grassy places in New Zealand and South Africa. They have fleshy roots and grassy foliage. The flowers are yellow stars in dense racemes from spring to summer.

✔ Good cut flowers
✔ Disease-free
✔ Pest-free

CULTIVATION
Grow in acid to neutral, well-drained soil in sun or part shade.

PROPAGATION
Seed should be sown in a cold frame as soon as it is ripe. Division should be done in autumn.

Bulbinella hookeri

Zone 8
Height: 2ft. (60cm) Spread: 1ft. (30cm)

BUPHTHALMUM *(Asteraceae)*

Common names: Willowleaf ox eye

A genus of two species of perennials from meadows and open woodland in Eurasia. The leaves are willow-like, obovate or lance-shaped, and dark green. The flowers are yellow single, solitary daisies borne for a long season from early summer to autumn.

✔ Good cut flowers
✔ Long-flowering
✔ Disease-free
✔ Pest-free

CULTIVATION
Grow in poorish, well-drained soil in sun.

PROPAGATION
Seed should be sown in a cold frame in spring, when division can also be carried out.

Buphthalmum salicifolium

Zone 4
Height: 2ft. (60cm) Spread: 18in. (45cm)

BUPLEURUM *(Apiaceae)*

Common names: Thorow-wax

A genus of 100 species of annuals, perennials and shrubs from scrubland and moist habitats in Southern Africa and the northern hemisphere. The leaves vary, but are simple, alternate and often conspicuously veined. The green or yellow flowers are star-shaped, surrounded by leafy bracts, and borne in umbels.

✔ Long-flowering
✔ Good cut flowers
✔ Drought-tolerant
✔ Disease-free
✔ Pest-free

✘ Self-seed

CULTIVATION
Grow in any well-drained soil in sun. They should be dead-headed to prevent self-seeding.

PROPAGATION
Seed should be sown in a cold frame in spring., when division can also be carried out.

Bupleurum falcatum

Zone 3
Height: 3ft. (90cm) Spread: 2ft. (60cm)
Short-lived

Bupleurum fruticosum
(Shrubby hare's ear)
Zone 7
Height: 6ft. (2m) Spread: 9ft. (3m)
Handsome foliage/Architectural plant

BUTOMUS *(Butomaceae)*

Common names: Flowering rush

A genus of just one species of aquatic, rhizomatous perennial, which is widely distributed over Eurasia. The leaves are long, radical, twisted and green, turning brown in autumn. The flowers are cup-shaped, fragrant, pink, and borne in flat umbels in late summer.

Butomus umbellatus A.G.M.

Zone 5
Height: 4ft. (1.2m) Spread: 18in. (45cm)

✔ Flowers perfumed

✘ Need to lift & divide often
✘ Prone to aphid attack

CULTIVATION
Grow in mud or shallow water less than 10in. (25 cm) deep, in sun. If grown in a container, divide and repot often.

PROPAGATION
Seed should be sown in moist soil in a half-submerged seed tray. The rhizomes can be divided when dormant in early spring.

B

C

CACALIA
CALADIUM
CALAMAGROSTIS
CALAMINTHA
CALANDRINIA
CALANTHE
CALATHEA
CALCEOLARIA
CALLIRHOE
CALLISIA
CALTHA
CAMASSIA
CAMPANULA
CANNA
CARDAMINE
CARDIOCRINUM
CAREX
CARLINA
CATANANCHE
CATHARANTHUS
CAUTLEYA
CEDRONELLA
CELMISIA
CELOSIA
CENTAUREA
CENTAURIUM
CENTRANTHUS
CEPHALARIA
CERASTIUM
CHAEROPHYLLUM

CHAMAEMELUM
CHELIDONIUM
CHELONE
CHIASTOPHYLLUM
CHIRITA
CHLOROPHYTUM
CHRYSANTHEMUM
CHRYSOGONUM
CHUSQUEA
CICERBITA
CICHORIUM
CIMICIFUGA
CIRCAEA
CIRSIUM
CLAYTONIA
CLEMATIS
CLINTONIA
CLIVIA
CODONOPSIS
COLCHICUM
COMMELINA
CONVALLARIA
CONVOLVULUS

COREOPSIS
CORIARIA
CORNUS
CORTADERIA
CORTUSA
CORYDALIS
COSMOS
CRAMBE
COTULA
COTYLEDON
CRASPEDIA
CRASSULA
CREPIS
CRINUM
CROCOSMIA
CROCUS
CRYPTANTHUS
CTENANTHE
CUPHEA
CYCLAMEN
CYCLAMEN
CYMBOPOGON

CYNARA
CYNOGLOSSUM
CYPELLA
CYPRIPEDIUM
CYRTANTHUS

C

CACALIA *(Asteraceae)*
Common names: None

A genus of five species of perennials from open sunny habitats in south Europe and Asia Minor. The pale green leaves are kidney-shaped, with glabrous undersides. The flowers are small and pink, and in flattish corymbs.

✔ Handsome foliage	✘ Flowers insignificant

CULTIVATION
Grow in well-drained fertile soil in sun.

PROPAGATION
Seed should be sown in a cold frame in spring.

Cacalia glabra

Zone 6
Height: 32in. (80 cm) Spread: 18in. (45 cm)

CALADIUM *(Araceae)*
Common names: None

A genus of seven species of tuberous perennials from margins of woodland in tropical South America. They are grown for their foliage. The leaves are arrow-shaped, and variegated in white, or pink or red, or all three. Spathes with green flowers and green-white spadices are followed by white berries.

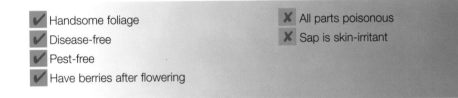

✔ Handsome foliage	✘ All parts poisonous
✔ Disease-free	✘ Sap is skin-irritant
✔ Pest-free	
✔ Have berries after flowering	

CULTIVATION
Under glass, pot tubers up in spring and grow in loamless potting compost in bright filtered light, in high humidity at 70°F (21°C). Water freely in summer, reduce watering in autumn and keep dry in winter at 61°F (16°C).

Out of doors, plant tubers in spring in acid, moist, humus-rich well-drained soil in part shade. High humidity and ample watering are important during the growing season. The tubers should be kept almost dry in winter.

PROPAGATION
The tubers should be divided in spring, and the cut edges dusted with fungicide.

Caladium bicolor 'Candidum'

Zone 10
Height: 1ft. (30cm) Spread: 8in. (20cm)

*Caladium bicolor
'Mrs. W.B.Haldeman'*

Zone 10
Height: 1ft. (30cm) Spread: 8in. (20cm)

CALAMAGROSTIS *(Poaceae)*

Common names: Reed grass; Smallweed

A genus of 250 species of rhizomatous perennial grasses from damp woodland or marshland of the temperate northern hemisphere. They are clump-forming and the leaves are linear, channeled or flat. The inflorescence is dense, and borne in branching panicles.

- ✔ Good for drying for winter
- ✔ Architectural plants
- ✔ Handsome foliage
- ✔ Disease-free
- ✔ Pest-free

CULTIVATION
Grow in moist, humus-rich soil in part shade.

PROPAGATION
Division can be carried out in spring.

Calamagrostis x acutiflora
'Overdam' (Feather reed grass)

Zone 7
Height and spread: 4ft. (1.2m)

CALAMINTHA *(Lamiaceae)*

Common names: None

A genus of eight species of perennials, some of which are short-lived, from scrubland, grassy meadows and woodland of the temperate northern hemisphere. They have aromatic foliage and may be rhizomatous or fibrous-rooted. The leaves are oblong or ovate, and usually toothed.

The flowers are two-lipped, tubular, pink, blue or white in color, and borne in axillary cymes in summer.

- ✔ Foliage aromatic
- ✔ Long-flowering
- ✔ Attracts butterflies

- ✘ Mildew prone

CULTIVATION
Grow in moist, humus-rich, well-drained soil in sun or part shade.

PROPAGATION
Seed can be sown, and division carried out, in spring

Calamintha grandiflora
'Variegata'

Zone 5
Height and spread: 18in. (45 cm)

Calamintha nepeta

Zone 6
Height: 18in. (45 cm) Spread: 32in. (80 cm)
Short-lived

Calamintha nepeta subsp.
glandulosa 'White Cloud'
Zone 6
Height: 18in. (45 cm) Spread: 32in. (80 cm)
Short-lived

C

CALANDRINIA *(Portulacaceae)*
Common names: None

A genus of 150 species of annuals and perennials, of which a few are succulent, from open dry hot habitats in North, Central, and South America and Australia. The perennials are evergreen, short-lived, and clump-forming. The leaves are alternate, narrow, elliptic, and fleshy. The flowers are single, red, pink or white in color, and borne on long stems. They may be solitary or borne in panicles or racemes.

 Evergreen

✗ Short-lived
✗ Prone to slug damage

CULTIVATION
Grow in acid to neutral, sharply-drained, humus-rich soil in sun.

PROPAGATION
Seed should be sown at 64°F (18°C) in spring or autumn. Stem cuttings can be taken in spring.

Calandrinia grandiflora

Zone 7
Height: 3ft. (90cm) Spread: 18in. (45 cm)

CALANTHE *(Orchidaceae)*
Common names: None

A genus of 150 species of orchids from Madagascar, Polynesia and Asia. They grow at all heights from sea level to 10,000ft. (3000 m), and in a variety of habitats in woodland or open amongst shady rocks. They may be terrestrial or epiphytic, herbaceous or evergreen and they have corm-like pseudo-bulbs. The leaves are in basal clusters, and are folded, oblong, and dark green. The spurred, three-lobed flowers are in erect dense racemes. They may be spring-, summer- or winter-flowering.

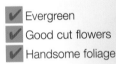 Evergreen
✔ Good cut flowers
✔ Handsome foliage

✗ Prone to slug damage

CULTIVATION
Grow in gritty, well-drained, humus-rich soil in a sheltered corner in part shade.

PROPAGATION
Division should be carried out in early spring as new growth is seen.

Calanthe discolor

Zone 8
Height and spread: 8in. (20cm)

Calanthe tricarnata

Zone 8
Height and spread: 20in. (50cm)

CALATHEA *(Marantaceae)*
Common names: Cathedral windows; peacock plant

A genus of 300 species of rhizomatous perennials from humid areas such as tropical forest in the West Indies, and South and Central America. They do not flower well in cultivation, but are grown for their handsome foliage. The leaves are ovate, shiny, pale and dark green in attractive patterns. The flowers are borne in summer and are tubular, with prominent upper and lower lips, and surrounded by sheathed bracts.

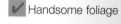 Handsome foliage

✖ Shy-flowering
✖ Prone to aphid attack

CULTIVATION
Under glass, grow in loam-free or loam-based potting compost, in filtered light, in high humidity, out of draughts, and in an even temperature. Water freely in summer, sparingly in winter. Pot on in spring.

Out of doors, grow in moist, humus-rich, well-drained soil in sun or part shade.

PROPAGATION
Division can be done in late spring.

Calathea crocata
A.G.M.

Zone 9
Height: 8in. (20cm) Spread: 1ft. (30cm)

Calathea lancifolia
A.G.M.

Zone 9
Height: 30in. (75cm) Spread: 2ft. (60cm)

Calathea majestica A.G.M.

Zone 9
Height: 6ft. (2m) Spread: 3ft. (90cm)
Architectural plant

Calathea makoyana
A.G.M.

Zone 9
Height: 18in. (45 cm) Spread: 9in. (22cm)

Calathea
'Rosa Star'

Zone 9
Height: 10in. (25 cm) Spread: 9in. (22cm)

Calathea roseopicta
A.G.M.

Zone 9
Height: 10in. (25 cm) Spread: 6in. (15cm)

Calathea
'Trio'

Zone 9
Height: 1ft. (30cm) Spread: 10in. (25 cm)

C

CALCEOLARIA *(Scrophulariaceae)*
Common names: Slipperflower; Slipperwort

A genus of 300 species of annuals, perennials, biennials and shrubs from very varied habitats, such as dry lowland to high alpine, and in temperate and tropical regions. They are found in Central and South America, Mexico and the Falkland Islands. Their leaves are varied, but opposite, and in rosettes. The flowers are described as being 'slipper-like' since they are two-lipped, with a small upper lip and an inflated, pouched, lower one. They are borne over a long season in summer.

 Evergreen   ✔ Long-flowering   ✗ Prone to slug damage

CULTIVATION

Under glass, grow in loam-based potting compost, in good ventilation and bright filtered light. Water freely during growth, but sparingly in winter.

Out of doors, grow lowland species in acid to neutral, fertile, gritty soil in cool conditions if they are to flower freely, and in sun or part shade. Alpine species such as *C. polyrhiza* require sharply-drained soil in part shade, and protection against winter wet—an alpine house is ideal.

PROPAGATION

Seed should be sown in a cold frame in early spring or autumn. Division can also be done in spring. Rosettes can be rooted in early summer.

Calceolaria biflora

Zone 6
Height and spread: 8in. (20cm)

Calceolaria integrifolia
A.G.M.

Zone 9
Height: 3ft. (90cm) Spread: 1ft. (30cm)

Calceolaria
'John Innes'

Zone 9
Height: 1ft. (30cm) Spread: 6in. (15cm)

Calceolaria polyrhiza

Zone 9
Height: 3in. (8 cm) Spread: 8in. (20cm)

Calceolaria
'Sunset Red'

Zone 9
Height: 1ft. (30cm) Spread: 6in. (15cm)

Calceolaria tenella

Zone 9
Height: 3in. (8 cm) Spread: 8in. (20cm)

C

CALLIRHOE *(Malvaceae)*
Common names: Poppy mallow

A genus of eight species of annuals and perennials from grassland in Mexico and the U.S.A. The leaves are deeply lobed palmately. The perennials are tap-rooted, and so do not transplant well. The flowers are open, shallow, cups, mallow-like, and borne singly or in racemes.

✔ Trouble-free　　　　　　　　✘ Resents disturbance

CULTIVATION
Grow in sharply-drained, humus-rich soil in sun. They dislike winter wet.

PROPAGATION
Seed should be sown *in situ* in early spring. Softwood cuttings can be rooted in early summer.

Callirhoe triangulata
(Clustered poppy mallow)

Zone 4
Height: 3ft. (90cm) Spread: 1ft. (30cm)

CALLISIA *(Commelinaceae)*
Common names: None

A genus, closely related to Tradescantia, of 20 species of creeping, evergreen perennials from forest margins in south-eastern U.S.A., and tropical South and North America. Their foliage is succulent, oval, pointed, and alternate. The flowers have three petals and three sepals, and are borne in pairs on stemless cymes or panicles from autumn to winter.

✔ Evergreen　　　　　　　　　✔ Disease-free
✔ Handsome foliage　　　　　　✔ Pest-free

CULTIVATION
Under glass, grow in sharply-draining, potting compost in indirect or bright filtered light. Water moderately during growth, and sparingly in winter.

Out of doors, grow in sharply-draining soil in part shade.

PROPAGATION
Tip cuttings can be taken in spring. Root in shade.

Callisia elegans
A.G.M.

Zone 10
Height: 6in. (15cm) Spread: 3ft. (90cm)

CALTHA *(Ranunculaceae)*
Common names: Marsh marigold

A genus of 10 species of marginal aquatic perennials from cold or temperate areas of the northern hemisphere. They have heart- or kidney-shaped leaves, which form dense clumps after flowering. The flowers are waxy, single or double, and usually yellow, but sometimes white. They are borne in corymbs.

✔ Good cut flowers　　　　　　✘ Mildew prone
✔ Handsome foliage　　　　　　✘ Highly allergenic

CULTIVATION
Grow in a planting basket in shallow water, or mud, or boggy soil at the water's edge or in a very damp bed in full sun.

PROPAGATION
Seed should be sown as soon as it is ripe in very wet compost, in a shady position. Division can be carried out in early spring or late summer.

Caltha palustris
A.G.M.

Zone 3
Height and spread: 18in. (45 cm)

C

Caltha palustris barthei

Zone 3
Height and spread: 10in. (25 cm)

Caltha palustris
'Flore Pleno' A.G.M.

Zone 3
Height and spread: 10in. (25 cm)

CAMASSIA *(Hyacinthaceae)*
Common names: Quamash

A genus of half a dozen species of bulbous perennials from wet meadows in North America. The leaves are narrow, linear, channeled and basal. The flowers are star-shaped, and borne in terminal racemes on leafless stems for a short period only in spring or summer.

✔ Bulbs edible
✔ Good cut flowers
✔ Low allergen
✔ Attracts bees
✔ Disease-free
✔ Pest-free

✘ Need to lift & divide often
✘ Short flowering season

CULTIVATION
Grow in moist, sharply-drained, humus-rich soil in sun or part shade.

PROPAGATION
Seed should be sown as soon as it is ripe in a cold frame Offsets can be detached during the summer dormancy.

Camassia leichtlinii subsp.
leichtlinii A.G.M.

Zone 3
Height: 4ft. (1.2m) Spread: 4in. (10 cm)

Camassia leichtlinii
'Semiplena'

Zone 3
Height: 4ft. (1.2m) Spread: 4in. (10 cm)

Camassia quamash

Zone 5
Height: 3ft. (90cm) Spread: 4in. (10 cm)

C

CAMPANULA *(Campanulaceae)*
Common names: Bellflower

A big, and very variable, genus of 300 species of annuals, biennials and perennials from a very diverse set of habitats from high alpine scree to lowland meadow, woodland and grassland. They occur across the temperate northern hemisphere, but especially in Turkey and southern Europe. Some of the perennials are evergreen. They are easy, accommodating plants and bloom over an extended season from late spring to late summer; some are remontant, i.e. they will flower a second time if dead-headed. Their cultural requirements vary, reflecting their range of habitat. The leaves are toothed or entire, alternate, green. The flowers may be tubular, bell-, cup-, saucer- or star-shaped, and may be solitary or borne in racemes or panicles or spikes. Some (*CC. pulla, glomerata, takesimana* and *persicifolia*) are very highly invasive, and the last also seeds everywhere, (as do also *CC. lactiflora* and *latifolia*) so these three should be deadheaded. Some need to be staked and some are short-lived. The high alpine species are difficult to cultivate, and are not dealt with here.

Campanula barbata

Zone 6
Height: 1ft. (30cm) Spread: 8in. (20cm)
Short-lived

 Attracts bees
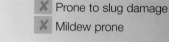 Low allergen

✖ Prone to slug damage
✖ Mildew prone

CULTIVATION
All the hardy herbaceous perennials included here require moist, alkaline, well-drained soil in sun or in part shade, where their color will be better preserved, except *C. pyramidalis*, which prefers dry soil and full sun, and *C. trachelium*, which prefers dry soil and part shade.

PROPAGATION
Seed should be sown in a cold frame in spring. Division can be done in spring or autumn. Basal cuttings can be taken in spring.

Campanula 'Burghaltii' A.G.M.

Zone 7
Height: 2ft. (60cm) Spread: 1ft. (30cm)
Long-flowering/Short-lived

Campanula carpatica
A.G.M. (Carpathian bellflower)
Zone 3
Height: 8in. (20cm) Spread: 2ft. (60cm)
Long-flowering

Campanula carpatica 'Blaue Clips'

Zone 3
Height and spread: 1ft. (30cm)
Long –flowering

Campanula carpatica
'Weisse Clips'
Zone 3
Height and spread: 1ft. (30cm)
Long-flowering

Campanula cochleariifolia
A.G.M.

Zone 6
Height: 4in. (10 cm) Spread: 1ft. (30cm)

C

Campanula 'Elizabeth'

Zone 7
Height and spread: 16in. (40cm)
Repeat-flowering

Campanula garganica
'Dickson's Gold'
Zone 5
Height: 2in. (5cm) Spread: 1ft. (30cm)
Handsome foliage

Campanula glomerata 'Superba'
(Clustered bellflower)
Zone 2
Height: 2ft. (60cm) Spread: indefinite
Repeat-flowering/Invasive/Needs staking

Campanula glomerata var. 'Alba'

Zone 2
Height: 2ft. (60cm) Spread: indefinite
Repeat-flowering/Invasive/Needs staking

Campanula incurva
'Alba'

Zone 8
Height and spread: 1ft. (30cm)

Campanula 'Kent Belle'

Zone 3
Height: 30in. (75cm) Spread: 1ft. (30cm)
Requires staking

Campanula lactiflora

Zone 5
Height: 5ft. (1.5m) Spread: 2ft. (60cm)

Campanula lactiflora 'Loddon
Anna' A.G.M. (Milky bellflower)
Zone 5
Height: 3ft. (90cm) Spread: 2ft. (60cm)
Repeat-flowering/Resents disturbance
Self-seeds

Campanula lactiflora
'Pritchard's Variety' A.G.M.
Zone 5
Height: 30in. (75cm) Spread: 2ft. (60cm)
Repeat-flowering/Resents disturbance
Self-seeds

C

Campanula lactifolia 'Alba'

Zone 3
Height: 4ft. (1.2m) Spread: 2ft. (60cm)
Self-seeds/Requires staking

Campanula latiloba
'Hidcote Amethyst' A.G.M.
Zone 3
Height: 3ft. (90cm) Spread: 18in. (45 cm)
Repeat-flowering

Campanula persicifolia
'Alba' (Peach-leaved bellflower)
Zone 3
Height: 3ft. (90cm) Spread: 18in. (45 cm)
Evergreen/Repeat-flowering/
Requires staking/Invasive/Need to lift &
divide often/Self-seeds

Campanula persicifolia 'Blue Bloomers'
Zone 3
Height: 3ft. (90cm) Spread: 1ft. (30cm)
Evergreen/Repeat-flowering/Need to lift &
divide often/Requires staking

Campanula persicifolia 'Chettle Charm'
Zone 3
Height: 3ft. (90cm) Spread: 1ft. (30cm)
Evergreen/Repeat-flowering/Requires
staking/Need to lift & divide often

Campanula persicifolia
'Telham Beauty'
Zone 3
Height: 3ft. (90cm) Spread: 1ft. (30cm)
Evergreen/Repeat-flowering/Need to lift &
divide often/Self-seeds

Campanula pulla

Zone 6
Height: 8in. (20cm) Spread: 1ft. (30cm)
Invasive/Need to lift & divide often/Short-lived

Campanula pyramidalis

Zone 8
Height: 6ft. (2m) Spread: indefinite
Repeat-flowering/Invasive/Need to lift &
divide often/Short-lived

Campanula rotundifolia

Zone 3
Height: 1ft. (30cm) Spread: indefinite
Repeat-flowering/Invasive

Campanula takesimana

Zone 7
Height: 32in. (80 cm) Spread: indefinite
Repeat-flowering/Invasive

Campanula trachelium

Zone 3
Height: 3ft. (90cm) Spread: 1ft. (30cm)
Self-seeds

CANNA (*Cannaceae*)
Common names: Indian shot plant

A genus of 50 species of rhizomatous herbaceous perennials from moist forest clearings and margins in tropical South and North America, and Asia. They are grown for both foliage and flowers. The leaves are large, paddle-shaped, and veined pinnately. The flowers are asymmetric, tubular, with three petals and three stamens, and borne in pairs in panicles or racemes over a long period from midsummer to autumn. A large number of hybrids are in cultivation, many with brightly-colored flowers or very handsome leaves, or both.

✔ Long-flowering
✔ Good cut flowers
✔ Handsome foliage

✘ Prone to slug damage

CULTIVATION
Under glass, grow in loamless potting compost in full light, with shade in hot sun. Water freely during the growing season. Dry off in winter.

Out of doors, grow in fertile soil in a warm corner in sun. Dead-head to prolong flowering. In very cold regions, it is best to lift the rhizomes and store in a warm dry place over winter. They should then be planted out when all danger of frost is past.

PROPAGATION
Seed should be sown at 70°F (21°C) in spring or autumn, but hybrids must be propagated by division of the rhizomes in early spring. In doing so, ensure that each piece has a prominent eye, and water sparingly at first.

Canna
'Assault'

Zone 8
Height: 6ft. (2m) Spread: 20in. (50cm)

Canna
'Australia'

Zone 8
Height: 6ft. (2m) Spread: 2ft. (60cm)

Canna
'Champion'

Zone 8
Height: 4ft. (1.2m) Spread: 20in. (50cm)

Canna
'Durban'

Zone 8
Height: 4ft. (1.2m) Spread: 2ft. (60cm)

Canna
'En Avant'

Zone 8
Height: 5ft. (1.5m) Spread: 2ft. (60cm)

Canna
'Fatamorgana'

Zone 8
Height: 4ft. (1.2m) Spread: 2ft. (60cm)

Canna
'Fireside'

Zone 8
Height: 4ft. (1.2m) Spread: 20in. (50cm)

Canna
'Hercule'

Zone 8
Height: 4ft. (1.2m) Spread: 2ft. (60cm)

Canna indica

Zone 8
Height: 6ft. (2m) Spread: 2ft. (60cm)

Canna
'Rosemond Coles'

Zone 8
Height: 4ft. (1.2m) Spread: 20in. (50cm)

Canna
'Striata'

Zone 8
Height: 5ft. (1.5m) Spread: 2ft. (60cm)

Canna
'Stuttgart'

Zone 8
Height: 6ft. (2m) Spread: 2ft. (60cm)

Canna
'Taroudant'

Zone 8
Height: 4ft. (1.2m) Spread: 2ft. (60cm)

Canna
'Verdi'

Zone 8
Height: 4ft. (1.2m) Spread: 2ft. (60cm)

CARDAMINE *(Brassicaceae)*

Common names: Bittercress

A genus of 150 species of annuals and perennials from damp, cool, shady habitats all over the world, but principally in the northern hemisphere. They may be rhizomatous or fibrous-rooted and may be invasive. The leaves are pinnate, palmate or simple. The flowers are four-petalled, and borne in racemes or panicles, in late spring; they are variously colored.

X Prone to aphid attack

X Invasive

CULTIVATION
Grow in any moist, humus-rich soil in part or full shade.

PROPAGATION
Seed should be sown in cold frame in spring or autumn. They can be divided in spring or after flowering. *C. pratensis* can form plantlets in the leaf axils, and these can be grown on.

Cardamine bulbifera

Zone 6
Height: 28in. (70 cm) Spread: 8in. (20cm)

Cardamine pentaphyllos

Zone 6
Height: 2ft. (60cm) Spread: 1ft. (30cm)
Invasive

Cardamine pratensis 'Flore Pleno'
A.G.M. (Lady's smock)
Zone 4
Height: 8in. (20cm) Spread: 1ft. (30cm)
Invasive

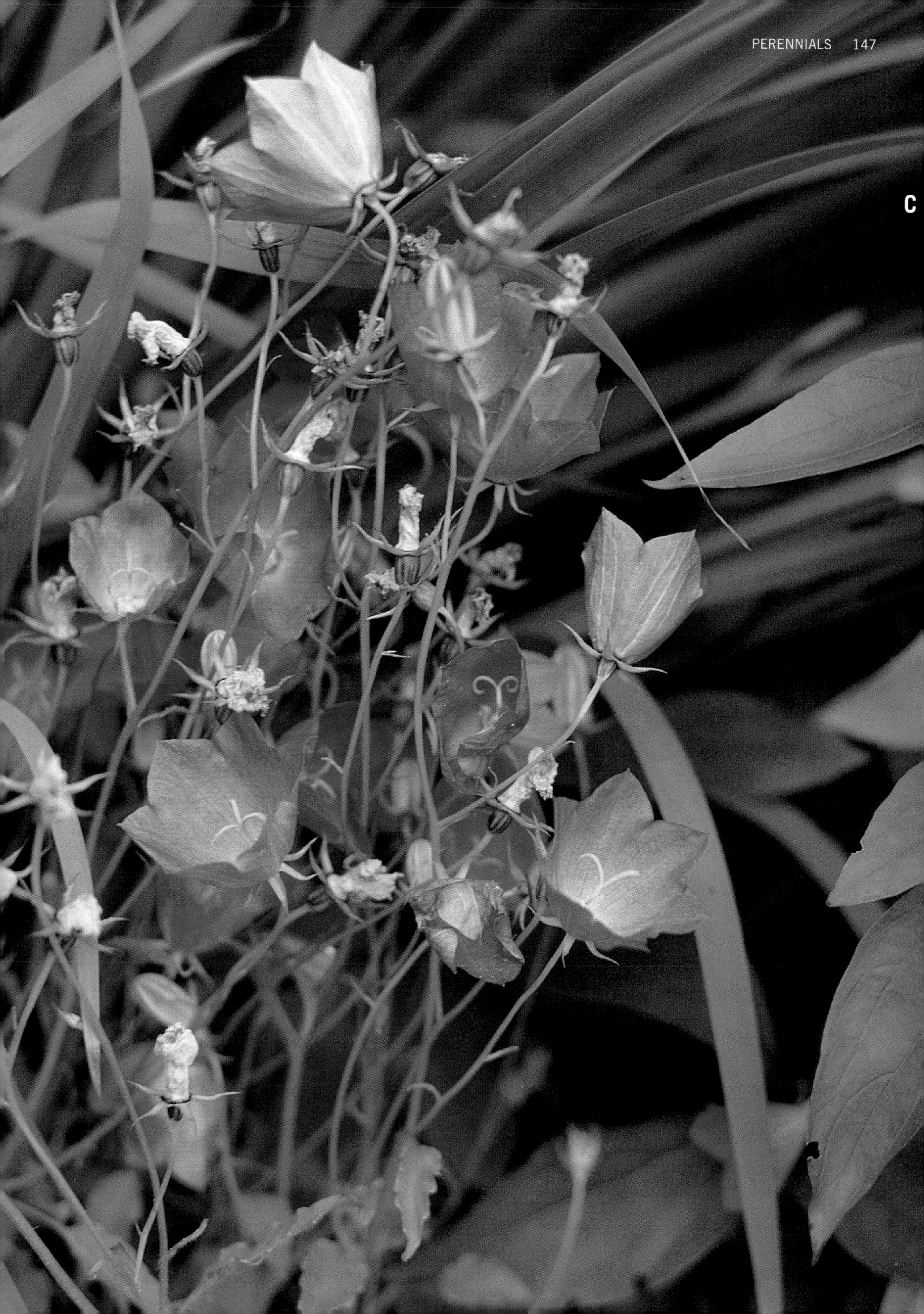

C

CARDIOCRINUM *(Liliaceae)*
Common names: Giant lily

A genus of three species of bulbous perennials found in forests and wasteland in China, Japan and the Himalayas. They are monocarpic, i.e. they die after flowering, but they do not do so for several years and leave behind plenty of bulblets. The leaves are large, veined, and heart-shaped. The flowers are trumpet-shaped, large, and appear in summer, followed by handsome seed-heads.

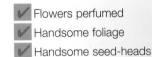

✔ Flowers perfumed	✔ Architectural plants	✘ Prone to slug damage
✔ Handsome foliage		
✔ Handsome seed-heads		

CULTIVATION
The bulbs should be planted just under the soil surface in autumn in moist, humus-rich, fertile, well-drained soil in a cool spot in part shade. Do not allow to dry out in summer and do not over water at any time.

PROPAGATION
Seed should be sown in a cold frame as soon as it is ripe; it takes at least seven years for seedling to flower. Separation of bulbils can be done after flowering; these take four years to flower.

Cardiocrinum giganteum
A.G.M.

Zone 7
Height: 12ft. (4m) Spread: 18in. (45 cm)

CAREX *(Cypereceae)*
Common names: Sedge

A genus of 1,500 species of perennials from boggy, damp sites in temperate, arctic and high-altitude tropical zones across the world. They may be evergreen or herbaceous, rhizomatous or clump-forming. The leaves are grass-like, linear, and may be variegated. The inflorescence is also grass-like, and in panicles on short spikes.

✔ Handsome foliage	✘ Highly allergenic
	✘ Prone to aphid attack

CULTIVATION
Requirements vary according to the habitat. *CC. buchananii, comans* and *testacea* need moist soil in sun or part shade; avoid extremes of wet or drought. *CC. conica* and *oshimensis* need moist, well-drained soil in sun or part shade. *CC. elata, pendula* and *siderosticha* need moist or wet soil in sun or part shade. *CC. morrowi* and *phyllocepala* need moist soil in sun or part shade.

PROPAGATION
Seed of species from Eurasia and the New World should be sown in autumn and exposed to winter cold. Seed of New Zealand species should be sown at 55°F (13°C) in early spring. Division can be carried out between late spring and early summer.

Carex buchananii
A.G.M. (New Zealand)
Zone 7
Height: 30in. (75cm) Spread: 3ft. (90cm)
Evergreen

Carex comans (New Zealand)

Zone 7
Height: 16in. (40cm) Spread: 30in. (75cm)
Evergreen/Invasive

Carex comans
'Frosted Curls' (New Zealand)
Zone 7
Height: 2ft. (60cm) Spread: 18in. (45 cm)
Evergreen

Carex conica 'Snowline'

Zone 7
Height: 6in. (15cm) Spread: 10in. (25 cm)
Evergreen

C

Carex elata
'Aurea' A.G.M. (Europe)

Zone 7
Height: 28in. (70 cm) Spread: 18in. (45 cm)

Carex morrowi
'Fisher's Form' (Japan)
Zone 5
Height: 20in. (50cm) Spread: 1ft. (30cm)
Evergreen

Carex oshimensis
'Evergold' (Japan)
Zone 5
Height: 1ft. (30cm) Spread: 14in. (35cm)
Evergreen

Carex pendula
(Weeping sedge) (Europe)
Zone 8
Height and Spread: 5ft. (1.5m)
Evergreen

Carex phyllocepala
'Sparkler'

Zone 5
Height and spread: 3ft. (90cm)

Carex siderosticha
'Shima-nishiki' (Japan)

Zone 8
Height: 6in. (15cm) Spread: 1ft. (30cm)

Carex siderosticha
'Variegata' (Japan)

Zone 8
Height: 1ft. (30cm) Spread: 16in. (40cm)

Carex
'Silver Sceptre'

Zone 7
Height: 10in. (25 cm) Spread: 1ft. (30cm)

Carex testacea (New Zealand)

Zone 7
Height and spread: 5ft. (1.5m)
Evergreen

C

CARLINA *(Asteraceae)*

Common names: None

A genus of 28 species of annuals and short-lived perennials from wasteland across Eurasia. The leaves are entire to pinnatisect, spiny and in basal rosettes. The flowers are 'everlasting' composed as they are of papery, spiny bracts. They are stemless, and solitary or in cymes.

✔ Good for drying for winter   ✖ Short-lived
✔ Handsome foliage
✔ Disease-free
✔ Pest-free

CULTIVATION
Grow in poor, well-drained soil in sun. They resent waterlogging.

PROPAGATION
Seed should be sown *in situ* or in a cold frame in autumn.

Carlina acaulis

Zone 4
Height: 4in. (10 cm) Spread: 10in. (25 cm)

CATANANCHE *(Asteraceae)*

Common names: Cupid's dart

A genus of five species of annuals and short-lived perennials from dry regions of the Mediterranean area. The leaves are linear to inversely-lance-shaped, and gray-green. The flowers are solitary, single, and have ray florets in blue, yellow or white, and silvery-white bracts. *C caerulea* flowers most freely in its second year and is therefore best treated as a biennial; it is very short-lived in wet soil or clay.

✔ Long-flowering   ✖ Short-lived
✔ Good cut flowers   ✖ Prone to slug damage
✔ Good for drying for winter   ✖ Resents disturbance
✔ Drought-tolerant   ✖ Mildew prone
✔ Handsome seed-heads   ✖ Highly allergenic

CULTIVATION
Grow in any soil that is not waterlogged in sun.

PROPAGATION
Seed should be sown in a cold frame or in situ in spring. Division can be done in spring, but is not tolerated well.

Catananche caerulea
(Blue Cupid's dart)

Zone 7
Height: 3ft. (90cm) Spread: 1ft. (30cm)

Catananche caerulea
'Alba' A.G.M.

Zone 7
Height: 3ft. (90cm) Spread: 1ft. (30cm)

C

CATHARANTHUS (*Apocynaceae*)

Common names: Madagascar periwinkle

A genus of just eight species of annuals and perennials from scrubland and forest edges in Madagascar. They have entire, simple leaves. The flowers are single, and solitary or in cymes, and borne from spring to summer.

✔ Long-flowering	✘ All parts poisonous
✔ Evergreen	
✔ Disease-free	
✔ Pest-free	

CULTIVATION
Under glass, grow in loam-based potting compost in full light and good ventilation; water with moderation during growth, but sparingly in winter.

Out of doors, grow in well-drained, fertile soil in sun. Protect against winter wet and cold.

PROPAGATION
Seed should be sown at 64°F (18°C) in early spring. Softwood cuttings can be taken in late spring and semi-ripe cuttings in summer.

Catharanthus roseus

Zone 10
Height and spread: 2ft. (60cm)

Catharanthus roseus 'Variegatus'

Zone 10
Height and spread: 2ft. (60cm)

CAUTLEYA (*Zingiberaceae*)

Common names: None

A genus of five species of rhizomatous perennials from grassy and shrubby ravines in the Himalayas. Their leaves are two-ranked, and oblong or lance-shaped. The flowers are complex, two-lipped, yellow with red sepals and bracts, borne in spiky racemes in late summer.

✔ Handsome foliage	✘ Prone to slug damage

CULTIVATION
Plant the rhizomes 6in. (15cm) deep in spring in moist, humus-rich soil in part shade. Do not allow to dry out in summer.

PROPAGATION
Seed should be sown at 64°F (18°C) in early spring. Division can be done in late spring as first growth appears

Cautleya gracilis

Zone 8
Height: 18in. (45 cm) Spread: 10in. (25 cm)

Cautleya spicata

Zone 8
Height: 2ft. (60cm) Spread: 18in. (45 cm)

Cautleya spicata 'Robusta'

Zone 8
Height: 2ft. (60cm) Spread: 18in. (45 cm)

CEDRONELLA *(Lamiaceae)*
Common names: None

A monospecific genus of one species, *C. canariensis*, which grows on rocky, sunny slopes in the Canary Islands. The leaves are aromatic, alternate, and tripalmate, and are used in herb tea and pot-pourri. The flowers are two-lipped, pink, white or lilac, in whorls in summer.

✔ Foliage aromatic	✘ Require staking
✔ Drought-tolerant	
✔ Disease-free	
✔ Pest-free	

Cedronella canariensis

Zone 9
Height: 3ft. (90cm) Spread: 2ft. (60cm)

CULTIVATION
Under glass, grow in loam-based potting compost in full light. Water with moderation during growth, but sparingly during winter.

Out of doors, grow in well-drained soil in sun.

PROPAGATION
Seed should be sown at 64°F (18°C) in early spring. Softwood cuttings can be rooted in late spring.

CELMISIA *(Asteraceae)*
Common names: None

A genus of 60 species of free-flowering, evergreen perennials and subshrubs from New Zealand and Australia. They are grown for their rosettes of silky, silvery foliage and daisy flowers. The leaves are lance-shaped, and glaucous or silver, and the undersides can be similar in some species. The single or semi-double, solitary flowers have white ray florets and yellow disc florets, and appear in early summer. Some species require protection against winter wet, and so are best suited to alpine house treatment.

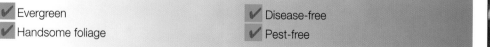

✔ Evergreen	✔ Disease-free
✔ Handsome foliage	✔ Pest-free

Celmisia allanii

Zone 7
Height: and spread: 10in. (25 cm)

CULTIVATION
They thrive only in cool moist situations. In hot gardens, mist-spray during hot spells in summer. Grow in acid to neutral, moist, well-drained soil in sun.

PROPAGATION
Seed should be sown as soon as it is ripe in a cold frame in early spring; germination is erratic. Division can be done in spring. Rosettes can be detached and rooted in spring.

C

Celmisia coriacea

Zone 7
Height: 2ft. (60cm) Spread: 1ft. (30cm)

Celmisia gracilenta

Zone 7
Height: 8in. (20cm) Spread: 10in. (25 cm)

Celmisia hookeri

Zone 7
Height: 1ft. (30cm) Spread: 2ft. (60cm)

Celmisia incana

Zone 7
Height: 6in. (15cm) Spread: 8in. (20cm)

Celmisia semicordata

Zone 7
Height: 20in. (50cm) Spread: 1ft. (30cm)

Celmisia spectabilis

Zone 7
Height and spread: 1ft. (30cm)

CELOSIA *(Amaranthaceae)*

Common names: Cockscomb

A genus of 60 species of annuals, perennials and shrubs found in dry slopes, scrubland and stony soil in tropical and subtropical Africa, Asia and the Americas. Their leaves are oval or lance-shaped, simple or lobed, and alternate. The tiny flowers are borne in plume-like, terminal pyramidal cymes all summer. They are often grown as annuals in cold gardens.

✔ Good cut flowers

✔ Good for drying for winter

✔ Long-flowering

✘ Prone to aphid attack

Celosia argentea
'Fairy Fountains'

Zone 9
Height: 2ft. (60cm) Spread: 18in. (45 cm)

CULTIVATION

Under glass, grow in loam-based potting compost, with full ventilation, and in bright filtered light. Water with moderation, but do not allow to dry out.

Out of doors, grow in moist, well-drained soil in a sheltered corner in sun. Do not allow to dry out.

PROPAGATION

Seed should be sown at 64°F (18°C) in spring.

CENTAUREA *(Asteraceae)*
Common names: Knapweed; Hardheads

A genus of 450 species of annuals, biennials, subshrubs and perennials from a range of essentially dry habitats at various altitudes in Eurasia, North America and Australia. Their leaves are simple, and pinnatifid or pinnatisect, and silvery in some species. The flowers are complex, being hemi-spherical or spherical and having tubular, deeply-lobed florets and an involucre of overlapping bracts with spiny black or white tips in summer.

C

✔ Handsome foliage	✖ Mildew prone
✔ Good cut flowers	✖ Highly allergenic
✔ Attracts bees	
✔ Attracts butterflies	

CULTIVATION
Grow in any soil that is moist but not waterlogged, and in sun or part shade. Some are drought-tolerant.

PROPAGATION
Seed should be sown in a cold frame in spring, but in autumn in the instance of *C. montana*. Divide in autumn or spring.

Centaurea argentea

Zone 8
Height: 20in. (50cm) Spread: 1ft. (30cm)

Centaurea bella

Zone 6
Height: 1ft. (30cm) Spread: 18in. (45 cm)

Centaurea dealbata 'Steenbergii'

Zone 3
Height and spread: 2ft. (60cm)

Centaurea hypoleuca 'John Coutts'

Zone 5
Height: 2ft. (60cm) Spread: 18in. (45 cm)
Flowers perfumed

Centaurea macrocephala

Zone 3
Height: 6ft. (2m) Spread: 2ft. (60cm)
Good for drying for winter/Needs staking

Centaurea montana (Mountain blue)

Zone 3
Height: 18in. (45 cm) Spread: 2ft. (60cm)
Repeat-flowering/Self-seeds

Centaurea montana 'Alba' (White mountain blue)

Zone 3
Height: 18in. (45 cm) Spread: 2ft. (60cm)
Repeat-flowering/Self-seeds

Centaurea montana
'Carnea' (Pink mountain blue)
Zone 3
Height: 18in. (45 cm) Spread: 2ft. (60cm)
Repeat-flowering/Self-seeds

Centaurea montana 'Gold Bullion'
Zone 3
Height: 18in. (45 cm) Spread: 2ft. (60cm)
Repeat-flowering

CENTAURIUM *(Gentianaceae)*
Common names: Centaury

A genus of 30 species of annuals, short-lived perennials and biennials from seaside habitats in Eurasia, north Africa, Chile, Australia and the U.S.A. The leaves are in basal rosettes or clumps, obovate, and gray-green. The flowers are salverform or shallow bell-shaped, and borne in flat-topped cymes from early to late summer.

✔ Long-flowering

✘ Short-lived
✘ Prone to slug damage

CULTIVATION
Grow in moist, well-drained soil in sun or part shade.

PROPAGATION
Seed should be sown in a cold frame as soon as it is ripe. Division can be done in spring.

Centaurium erythraea

Zone 8
Height: 3in. (8 cm) Spread: 2in. (5cm)

CENTRANTHUS *(Valerianaceae)*
Common names: Valerian

A genus of a dozen species of annuals and perennials from dry slopes in southerin Europe, North Africa and south-west Asia. There is only one in general cultivation—*C. ruber*. It has fleshy, ovate or lance-shaped glaucous leaves. The flowers are small, funnel-shaped, but borne in dense cymes all summer.

✔ Drought-tolerant
✔ Long-flowering
✔ Good cut flowers
✔ Attracts butterflies
✔ Trouble-free

✘ Self-seeds
✘ Resents disturbance

CULTIVATION
Grow in light, chalky, well-drained soil in sun or part shade. Dead-head after flowering to prevent self-seeding.

PROPAGATION
Seed should be sown in a cold frame in spring. Division can be done in spring, but is not tolerated well.

Centranthus ruber
(Red Valerian)

Zone 7
Height and spread: 3ft. (90cm)

C

Centranthus ruber
'Albus' (White Valerian)

Zone 7
Height and spread: 3ft. (90cm)

CEPHALARIA *(Dipsacaceae)*

Common names: Giant scabious

A genus of 65 species of annuals and perennials from Eurasia and Africa. They are found in lowland meadows and mountain pastures. Their green leaves are opposite, toothed, pinnate or pinnatisect. The scabious-like flowers are terminal and borne in stiff, branched, spikes. They are usually yellow, and have an involucre of stiff bracts.

✔ Architectural plants	✘ Require staking
✔ Good cut flowers	✘ Self-seeds
✔ Attracts butterflies	✘ Resents disturbance
✔ Disease-free	
✔ Pest-free	

Cephalaria gigantea

Zone 7
Height: 6ft. (2m) Spread: 32in. (80 cm)

CULTIVATION
Grow in moist, fertile, well-drained soil in sun or part shade.

PROPAGATION
Seed should be sown in a cold frame in early spring. Division can be done also in spring, but is not tolerated well.

CERASTIUM *(Caryophyllaceae)*

Common names: Snow-in-summer

A genus of 100 annuals and perennials from arctic and temperate regions of North America and Europe. They are low-growing, and many are invasive weeds. The leaves are entire, opposite and simple. The flowers are small, star-shaped, and borne singly or in cymes.

✔ Evergreen	✘ Invasive
✔ Long-flowering	
✔ Handsome foliage	
✔ Disease-free	
✔ Pest-free	

Cerastium tomentosum

Zone 4
Height: 3in. (8 cm) Spread: indefinite

CULTIVATION
Grow in any well-drained soil in sun.

PROPAGATION
Seed should be sown in a cold frame in autumn. Division should be carried out in spring. Stem-tip cuttings can be rooted in summer.

CHAEROPHYLLUM *(Apiaceae)*
Common names: None

A genus of 35 species of annuals, biennials and perennials from open woods and meadows of the temperate northern hemisphere. They are tap-rooted, and therefore do not transplant well. The foliage is ferny, and green. The flowers are small, and borne in compound umbels in late spring or early summer. Will repeat-flower if dead-headed.

✔ Repeat-flowering	✘ Prone to slug damage
✔ Foliage aromatic	✘ Mildew prone
✔ Good cut flowers	✘ Poisonous
	✘ Resents disturbance

CULTIVATION
Grow in moist, fertile, soil in sun or part shade.

PROPAGATION
Seed should be sown in a cold frame as soon as it is ripe, or next spring.

Chaerophyllum hirsutum 'Roseum'

Zone 6
Height: 2ft. (60cm) Spread: 1ft. (30cm)

CHAMAEMELUM *(Asteraceae)*
Common names: Chamomile

A genus of four species of annuals and perennials from grassland and wasteland across Europe. The leaves are aromatic, feathery, and alternate. The flowers are daisies with white ray florets and yellow disc florets. *C. nobile* can be used to make a garden seat or a lawn if cut back repeatedly, and trodden down.

✔ Foliage aromatic	✘ Invasive
✔ Handsome foliage	✘ Highly allergenic
✔ Disease-free	✘ Foliage is skin-irritant
✔ Pest-free	

CULTIVATION
Grow in well-drained light soil in sun.

PROPAGATION
Seed should be sown in situ in spring.

Chamaemelum nobile 'Flore Pleno' (Double Roman chamomile)

Zone 4
Height: 1ft. (30cm) Spread: indefinite

CHELIDONIUM *(Papaveraceae)*
Common names: Greater celandine

A genus of just one species. It is found in scrubland, waste ground and woodland in Eurasia and is short-lived. The leaves are deeply pinnatifid or pinnatisect. The flowers are yellow and poppy-like, single or double, and borne in umbels in summer.

✔ Handsome foliage	✘ Sap is skin-irritant
✔ Disease-free	✘ Self-seeds
✔ Pest-free	✘ Short-lived
	✘ All parts poisonous
	✘ Highly allergenic

CULTIVATION
Grow in any soil in any site. It is an excellent woodlander. Dead-head to prevent self-seeding.

PROPAGATION
Seed should be sown *in situ* in spring.

Chelidonium majus

Zone 6
Height: 2ft. (60cm) Spread: 8in. (20cm)

Chelidonium majus 'Flore Pleno'

Zone 6
Height: 2ft. (60cm) Spread: 8in. (20cm)

CHELONE *(Scrophulariaceae)*
Common names: Turtlehead

A genus of half a dozen species of perennials from moist sites in prairies, woodland and mountains of North America. The foliage is in opposite pairs of lance-shaped, toothed, smooth leaves. The flowers are tubular, two-lipped, and the lower lip is bearded inside. They are borne in dense terminal racemes in late summer and early autumn.

✔ Flowers weather-resistant ✘ Prone to slug damage
✔ Good cut flowers ✘ Mildew prone

CULTIVATION
Grow in moist, wet or boggy, deep, fertile soil in sun or part shade.

PROPAGATION
Seed should be sown in a cold frame in early spring. Division can be done in spring. Soft tip cuttings can be rooted in late spring/early summer.

Chelone glabra

Zone 3
Height: 3ft. (90cm) Spread: 18in. (45 cm)

Chelone obliqua (Rose turtlehead)

Zone 3
Height: 2ft. (60cm) Spread: 1ft. (30cm)

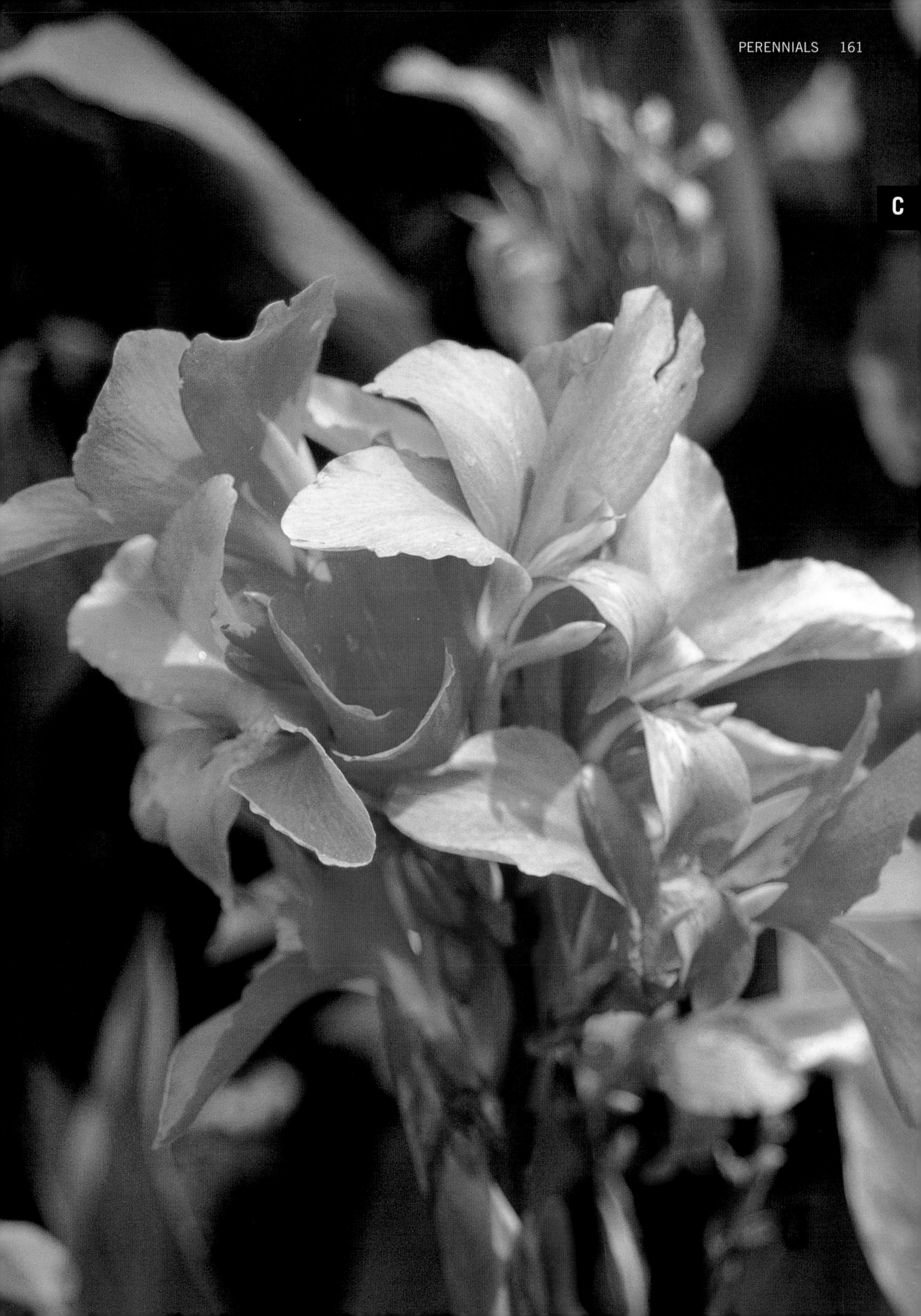

CHIASTOPHYLLUM *(Crassulaceae)*

Common names: None

A genus of just one species of rhizomatous, evergreen, perennial from shady mountain regions of the Caucasus. The green leaves are ovate, fleshy, and succulent. The flowers are small, yellow, bells in arching pendent racemes borne in spring to summer.

✔ Evergreen   ✘ Prone to slug damage

CULTIVATION
Grow in moist, well-drained soil in part shade.

PROPAGATION
Seed should be sown in a cold frame in autumn. Sideshoot cuttings can be rooted in summer.

Chiastophyllum oppositifolium
A.G.M.

Zone 7
Height: 8in. (20cm) Spread: 6in. (15cm)

Chiastophyllum oppositifolium
'Jim's Pride'
Zone 7
Height: 8in. (20cm) Spread: 6in. (15cm)
Variegated foliage

CHIRITA *(Gesneriaceae)*

Common names: None

A genus of 100 species of annuals and evergreen perennials found in semi-shady damp sites in tropical Asia. Their leaves are bristly-hairy, or downy, and opposite. The flowers are tubular, and either solitary or borne in clusters from the leaf axils, appearing in summer and autumn.

✔ Evergreen

CULTIVATION
Under glass, grow in loam-free potting compost in bright filtered light, with good ventilation and high humidity. Water with moderation during growth, and sparingly in winter.

Out of doors, grow in humus-rich, well-drained soil in part shade.

PROPAGATION
Seed should be sown at 75°F (24°C) in early spring.

Chirita heterotricha

Zone 10
Height: 4in. (10 cm) Spread: 1ft. (30cm)

CHLOROPHYTUM *(Anthericaceae)*

Common names: None

A genus of 240 species of rhizomatous, clump-forming evergreen perennials from various habitats in South and West Africa. The leaves are basal, linear, and arching. The flowers are inconspicuous, and are borne on arching panicles or racemes in summer. They are tolerant of wide ranges of conditions.

✔ Handsome foliage　　　　　　✘ Flowers insignificant

✔ Disease-free

✔ Pest-free

CULTIVATION
Under glass, grow in loam-based potting compost in bright indirect to full light, with shade from sun. Water freely in growth, and with moderation at all other times.

Out of doors, grow in any soil in sun or part shade. Water freely in summer, sparingly at other times.

PROPAGATION
Seed should be sown at 68°F (20°C) in spring. Plantlets that form on the leaves can be detached and rooted from spring to autumn.

Chlorophytum comosum 'Vittatum'

Zone 10
Height: 8in. (20cm) Spread: 1ft. (30cm)

CHRYSANTHEMUM *(Asteraceae)*

Common names: None

A genus of 20 species of annuals and herbaceous perennials; the latter hail from China, Japan, northern and central Russia, and the Arctic. The dark geen leaves are aromatic, ovate or lance-shaped, deeply-lobed, or pinnatisect. The flowers are single or double; the ray come in many colors, but the disc florets are invariably yellow.

✔ Foliage aromatic　　　　　　✘ Prone to slug damage

✔ Good cut flowers　　　　　　✘ Mildew prone

✔ Handsome foliage　　　　　　✘ Poisonous

✔ Attractive seed-heads　　　　✘ Prone to aphid attack

✔ Handsome seed-heads

✔ Low allergen

CULTIVATION
Grow in moist, well-drained, fertile soil in sun.

PROPAGATION
Seed should be sown in a cold frame in autumn. Division can be carried out in spring or autumn.

Chrysanthemum weyrichii

Zone 4
Height: 1ft. (30cm) Spread: 18in. (45 cm)

Chrysanthemum yezoense
A.G.M.

Zone 3
Height: 1ft. (30cm) Spread: 18in. (45 cm)

C

CHRYSOGONUM *(Asteraceae)*

Common names: None

A genus of but a single species of evergreen, rhizomatous perennial, from rich woodland in the eastern U.S.A. It spreads by leafy runners and makes excellent ground cover. The ovate or heart-shaped leaves are hairy and opposite. The yellow flowers are solitary, single, star-shaped, and borne on branched stems from early spring to late summer.

✔ Long-flowering
✔ Evergreen
✔ Disease-free
✔ Pest-free

CULTIVATION
Grow in moist, well-drained, humus-rich soil in sun or part shade.

PROPAGATION
Seed should be sown in a cold frame as soon as it is ripe. The runners can be separated, or division can be done in spring or autumn.

Chrysogonum virginianum
(Goldenstar)

Zone 5
Height and spread: 8in. (20cm)

CHUSQUEA *(Poaceae)*

Common names: None

A genus of 100 species of evergreen bamboos found in high woodland from Chile and Mexico. They have smooth, cylindrical, glossy canes with three primary branches. The green leaves are linear, oval or pointed. They make good specimen or architectural plants.

✔ Handsome foliage   ✘ Prone to slug damage
✔ Architectural plants

CULTIVATION
Grow in moist, humus-rich, well-drained soil in a sheltered corner in sun or part shade.

PROPAGATION
Seed should be sown at 64°F (18°C) in spring. Division can be done in spring; each division must have a root and a stem.

Chusquea culeou
A.G.M.

Zone 7
Height: 20ft. (6m) Spread: 8ft. (2.5m)

CICERBITA *(Asteraceae)*

Common names: Sow thistle

A genus of 20 species of perennials found in a wide range of habitats from mountain to lowland in the northern hemisphere. The leaves are basal and stem, green and pinnatifid or pinnatisect. The flowers are star-shaped, blue, lilac, pink, or yellow in color, and borne on panicles from midsummer to early autumn.

✘ Self-seeds
✘ Mildew prone

CULTIVATION
Grow in acid to neutral, moist, humus-rich soil in sun or part shade. They should be dead-headed to prevent self-seeding.

PROPAGATION
Seed should be sown in a cold frame in early spring, when they can also be divided.

Cicerbita plumieri

Zone 5
Height: 4ft. (1.2m) Spread: 18in. (45 cm)

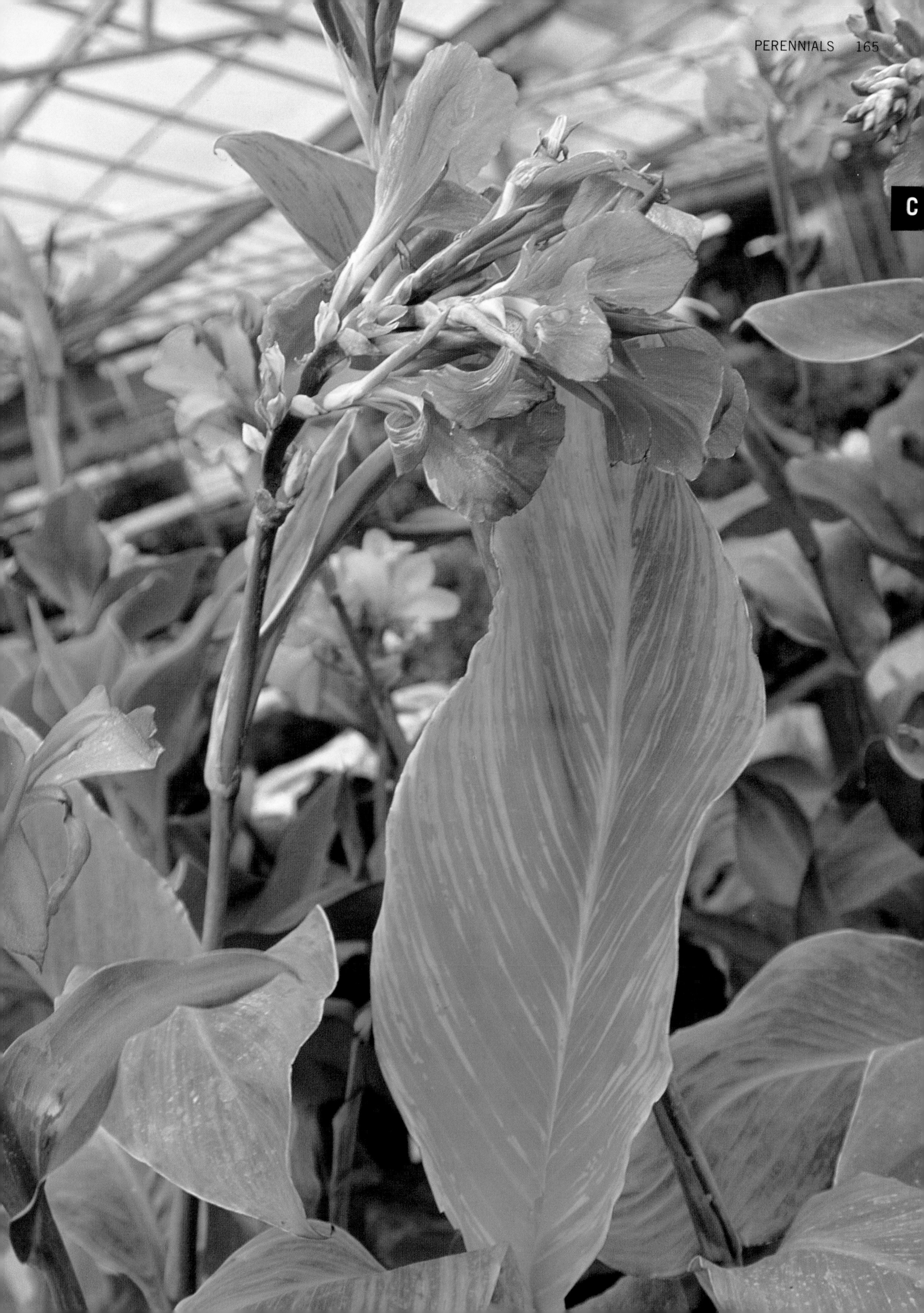

C

CICHORIUM *(Asteraceae)*
Common names: Chicory

A genus of some eight species of annuals and perennials from sunny, dry locations in Eurasia, the Mediterranean area, and Ethiopia. The leaves are basal, large, inverse lance–shaped and toothed; contact with them can cause skin irritation. The flowers are single, star-shaped, blue, white or pink in color, and borne on branched stems in summer. They close by mid-day.

✔ Good for drying for winter
✔ Culinary vegetable

✘ Prone to slug damage
✘ Resents disturbance
✘ Mildew prone
✘ Skin irritant
✘ Flowers close by mid-day

CULTIVATION
Grow in well-drained, fertile soil in sun.

PROPAGATION
Seed should be sown in a cold frame in early spring.

Cichorium intybus

Zone 3
Height: 4ft. (1.2m) Spread: 2ft. (60cm)

CIMICIFUGA *(Ranunculaceae)*
Common names: Bugbane; cohosh

A genus of 18 species of perennials from various moist, shady habitats in the temperate northern hemisphere. The green leaves are up to three-ternate, alternate, and toothed. The white or cream flowers are small, but crowded onto racemes or panicles like bottle-brushes; they are borne in summer and followed by handsome seed-heads. The flowers of some species are unpleasantly scented. Although tallish, they need to be staked only in exposed areas.

✔ Handsome foliage
✔ Handsome seed-heads
✔ Trouble-free

CULTIVATION
Grow in moist, humus-rich soil in part shade.

PROPAGATION
Seed should be sown in a cold frame as soon as it is ripe. Germination will occur the next season. Divide in spring.

Cimicifuga racemosa A.G.M.

Zone 4
Height: 6ft. (2m) Spread: 2ft. (60cm)
Flowers malodorous

Cimicifuga simplex

Zone 5
Height: 4ft. (1.2m) Spread: 2ft. (60cm)

Cimicifuga simplex var. *simplex* 'Atropurpurea'

Zone 5
Height: 4ft. (1.2m) Spread: 2ft. (60cm)

CIRCAEA *(Onagraceae)*

Common names: Enchanter's nightshade

A genus of seven rhizomatous perennials from across the northern hemisphere. They have alternate, ovoid, stem leaves. The flowers are small, pink, and in simple or branched racemes, and open at dawn.

| ✔ Handsome foliage | ✘ Invasive |
| | ✘ Flowers insignificant |

CULTIVATION
Grow in any soil that is not waterlogged.

PROPAGATION
Seed should be sown in a cold frame in spring.

Circaea lutetiana
'Caveat Emptor'

Zone 5
Height: 1ft. (30cm) Spread: indefinite

CIRSIUM *(Asteraceae)*

Common names: None

A genus of 200 species of biennials and perennials from various habitats at low and high altitudes, in the temperate northern hemisphere. The leaves are elliptic or lance-shaped, spiny, fiercely so in some species, and entire or pinnatifid. The flowers are tubular, and borne in tight heads. They may be invasive.

✔ Good cut flowers	✘ Require staking
✔ Handsome foliage	✘ Self-seeds
	✘ Mildew prone

CULTIVATION
Grow in moist, well-drained soil in sun. Dead-heading prevents self-seeding.

PROPAGATION
Seed should be sown in a cold frame in spring. Division can be carried out any time between autumn and spring.

Cirsium helenioides

Zone 5
Height: 5ft. (1.5m) Spread: 2ft. (60cm)

Cirsium rivulare
'Atropurpureum' (Plume thistle)

Zone 5
Height: 4ft. (1.2m) Spread: 2ft. (60cm)

Cirsium spinosissimum

Zone 5
Height: 4ft. (1.2m) Spread: 28in. (70 cm)

CLAYTONIA *(Portulacaceae)*
Common names: Purslane; Spring Beauty

A genus of 15 species of annuals and short-lived, succulent perennials from mountainous scree in western North America and Australia. They may be evergreen or herbaceous, and some are short-lived. The leaves are spoon-shaped, fleshy, basal in rosettes, and stem. The flowers are smallish, bowl- or cup-shaped, white or pink in color, and borne in terminal racemes in summer.

✔ Drought-tolerant	✘ Short-lived
✔ Handsome foliage	✘ Resents disturbance
✔ Trouble-free	

CULTIVATION
Grow in sharply-drained, humus-rich soil in sun. Protect against winter wet.

PROPAGATION
Seed should be sown in a cold frame in autumn.

Claytonia megarhiza

Zone 4
Height: 2in. (5cm) Spread: 6in. (15cm)

Claytonia virginica

Zone 6
Height: 1ft. (30cm) Spread: 8in. (20cm)

CLEMATIS *(Ranunculaceae)*
Common names: Old man's beard; Travellers' joy

A genus of 200 species of climbers, trailing or scandent shrubs, and herbaceous perennials. The perennials are woody and are widespread in occurrence in both hemispheres. They carry flowers from midsummer to autumn on the current year's shoots. The leaves are heart-shaped or ovate, entire or toothed, and dark green. The flowers are single or semi-double, bell- or saucer-shaped or tubular. Some have perfumed flowers. Clematis are classified as:

Group 1: Early-flowering species, including *CC. montana*, *macropetala* and *alpina* and their cultivars.

Group 2: Early and midseason large-flowered cultivars.

Group 3: Late-flowering species, late-flowering large-flowered cultivars, and herbaceous species and cultivars.

✔ Good cut flowers	✘ Sap is skin-irritant
✔ Attracts bees	✘ Require staking
✔ Handsome seed-heads	✘ Prone to aphid attack
✔ Low allergen	✘ Prone to Clematis wilt

Clematis 'Comptess de Bouchard'
A.G.M. (Group 2)

Zone 4
Height: 10ft. (3m) Spread: 3ft. (90cm)

CULTIVATION

Plant climbers with the root ball some 3in. (8 cm) below the soil surface, to minimize the risk of clematis wilt, in well-drained, humus-rich, fertile soil in full sun, but with the roots and the base of the plant in shade. They may require support.

Pruning requirements are:

Group 1: prune after flowering by shortening stems to fit available space.

Group 2: trim all stems back in spring to a strong bud.

Group 3: cut back previous year's growth to a strong pair of buds.

PROPAGATION

Seed of species should be sown in as soon as it is ripe in a cold frame. Cultivars or species can be divided, or basal cuttings can be taken, in spring.

Clematis
'Countess of Lovelace' (Group 2)
Zone 6
Height: 10ft. (3m) Spread: 3ft. (90cm)
Climber

Clematis 'Dr. Ruppel' A.G.M.
Zone 4
Height: 8ft. (2.5m) Spread: 3ft. (90cm)
Long-flowering

Clematis 'Etoile Violette' A.G.M.
(Group 3)
Zone 5
Height: 15ft. (5m) Spread: 5ft. (1.5m)
Climber

Clematis x eriostemon
'Hendersonii (Group 3)
Zone 4
Height: 15ft. (5m) Spread: 3ft. (90cm)
Flowers perfumed/Climber

Clematis 'Fireworks' (Group 2)
Zone 5
Height: 12ft. (4m) Spread: 18in. (45 cm)
Climber

Clematis florida var. *sieboldiana*
(Group 2)
Zone 4
Height: 8ft. (2.5m) Spread: 3ft. (90cm)
Climber

Clematis heracleifolia (Group 3)
Zone 3
Height: 3ft. (90cm) Spread: 4ft. (1.2m)
Flowers perfumed

Clematis heracleifolia var. *davidiana*
(Group 3)
Zone 3
Height: 3ft. (90cm) Spread: 4ft. (1.2m)
Flowers perfumed

C

Clematis integrifolia
(Group 3)

Zone 3
Height: and spread: 2ft. (60cm)

Clematis integrifolia
'Rosea' A.G.M. (Group 3)

Zone 3
Height and spread: 2ft. (60cm)

Clematis x jouiniana
(Group 3)

Zone 4
Height: 12ft. (4m) Spread: 4ft. (1.2m)

Clematis 'Minuet' A.G.M. (Group 3)

Zone 6
Height: 10ft. (3m) Spread: 3ft. (90cm)
Climber

Clematis montana var. *rubens*
A.G.M. (Group 1)
Zone 6
Height: 30ft. (10m) Spread: 6ft. (2m)
Climber

Clematis
'Nellie Moser' A.G.M. (Group 2)
Zone 4
Height: 10ft. (3m) Spread: 3ft. (90cm)
Climber

Clematis
'Princess of Wales' (Group 2)
Zone 4
Height: 6ft. (2m) Spread: 3ft. (90cm)
Long-flowering/Climber

Clematis
'Richard Pennell' A.G.M. (Group 2)
Zone 3
Height: 10ft. (3m) Spread: 3ft. (90cm)
Climber

C

Clematis
'Rouge Cardinal' (Group 3)
Zone 4
Height: 10ft. (3m) Spread: 3ft. (90cm)
Climber

Clematis
'Sir Trevor Lawrence' (Group 3)
Zone 5
Height: 10ft. (3m) Spread: 3ft. (90cm)
Climber

Clematis vitcella
'Purpurea Plena Elegans' (Group 3)
Zone 6
Height: 10ft. (3m) Spread: 3ft. (90cm)
Climber

CLINTONIA *(Convallariaceae)*

Common names: None

A genus of five species of rhizomatous woodland perennials from North America, the Himalayas, and East Asia. They form herbaceous clumps of glossy, entire, elliptic green leaves. The flowers are bell- or star-shaped, and borne on stiff stems in umbels, followed by fleshy berries.

✔ Handsome foliage
✔ Have berries after flowering

✖ Prone to slug damage

CULTIVATION
Grow in acid to neutral, humus-rich, leafy soil in part or full shade.

PROPAGATION
Seed should be sown in a cold frame in autumn. They can be divided in spring, but are slow to recover.

Clintonia andrewsiana

Zone 8
Height: 2ft. (60cm) Spread: 10in. (25 cm)

Clintonia umbellulata
(Speckled wood lily)

Zone 4
Height: 1ft. (30cm) Spread: 6in. (15cm)

CLIVIA *(Amaryllidaceae)*
Common names: None

A genus of four species of evergreen perennials from lowland woodland in South Africa. They have bulb-like bases. Their leaves are basal, shiny, lance-shaped, and dark green. The flowers are trumpet-shaped, in umbels atop stout stems. The picture of *C. nobilis* was taken in thick mountain mist in South Africa.

✔ Evergreen   ✘ Resents disturbance
✔ Handsome foliage

CULTIVATION
Under glass, grow in sharply-draining, loam-based potting compost in indirect light or bright filtered light. Water copiously in the growing season, and sparingly at all other times.

Out of doors, grow in well-drained, humus-rich, fertile soil in part shade. They resent disturbance, and flower freely only if their root run is restricted.

PROPAGATION
Seed should be sown at 70°F (21°C) as soon as it is ripe.

Clivia miniata A.G.M.

Zone 10
Height: 18in. (45 cm) Spread: 1ft. (30cm)

Clivia nobilis

Zone 10
Height: 16in. (40cm) Spread: 1ft. (30cm)

CODONOPSIS *(Campanulaceae)*
Common names: None

A genus of 30 species of herbaceous perennials from alpine scrubland and rocky hilly slopes, from the Himalayas to Japan. They are scandent or twining. The leaves are ovate or lance-shaped or oblong, and opposite or alternate. The flowers are nodding, solitary and bell-shaped, and handsomely marked internally.

✔ Good cut flowers   ✘ Prone to slug damage

CULTIVATION
Grow in moist, well-drained, humus-rich soil in sun or part shade and where they can scramble up through other plants. Support in the form of twigs provides an alternative.

PROPAGATION
Seed should be sown in a cold frame in autumn or spring.

Codonopsis clematidea

Zone 4
Height and spread: 2ft. (60cm)

COLCHICUM *(Colchicaceae)*

Common names: Meadow saffron; Autumn crocus

A genus of 45 species of cormous perennials from mountainous meadows and rocky hillsides in North Africa, China, India and Eurasia. The leaves appear with or after the flowers, and are basal, linear, elliptic or lance-shaped, and pleated or ribbed. The flowers are goblet-shaped, with long perianth tubes, and can appear in spring, summer, autumn or winter depending on the species. Some have fragrant flowers.

✔ Attracts bees

✘ All parts poisonous
✘ Skin irritant
✘ Prone to slug damage

CULTIVATION
Plant the corms of the larger species, such as are included here, 4in. (10 cm) deep amongst deciduous shrubs in well-drained, fertile, humus-rich soil. They like a dry dormant season.

PROPAGATION
Separate the corms during the dormant season. Seed should be sown in a cold frame as soon as it is ripe.

Colchicum autumnale

Zone 5
Height: 6in. (15cm) Spread: 3in. (8 cm)

Colchicum bivonae

Zone 6
Height: 6in. (15cm) Spread: 4in. (10 cm)

Colchicum byzantium A.G.M.

Zone 6
Height: 5in. (12cm) Spread: 4in. (10 cm)

COMMELINA *(Commelinaceae)*

Common names: Day flower; Widow's tears

A genus of 100 species of annuals and perennials from forests in subtropical and tropical areas of North, Central, and South America, Asia and southern Africa. The perennials may be tuberous or fibrous-rooted and root at the leaf-nodes as they spread, and so make excellent ground cover. The leaves are lance-shaped or linear, and alternate. The flowers are saucer-shaped and enclosed in bracts; they are borne on one-sided cymes in late summer and autumn.

✔ Long-flowering
✔ Drought-tolerant
✔ Handsome foliage

✔ Attractive seed-heads
✔ Handsome seed-heads
✔ Low allergen

✘ Invasive
✘ Prone to slug damage

CULTIVATION
Grow in well-drained, fertile soil in a sheltered corner in sun or part shade.

PROPAGATION
Seed should be sown at 64°F (18°C) in spring, when division can also be done.

Commelina coelestis 'Mexican dayflower'

Zone 8
Height: 3ft. (90cm) Spread: 18in. (45 cm)

CONVALLARIA *(Convallariaceae)*

Common names: Lily of the valley

A genus of one species of rhizomatous perennial occurring in scrub, alpine grassland or woodland in the temperate northern hemisphere, It has basal, ovate, leaves. The bell-shaped flowers are pendent, white, perfumed, and borne in arching racemes in late spring.

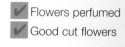

- ✔ Flowers perfumed
- ✔ Good cut flowers
- ✘ Invasive
- ✘ Self-seeds
- ✘ Seeds poisonous

Convallaria majalis

Zone 3
Height: 10in. (25 cm) Spread: 18in. (45 cm)

CULTIVATION
Grow in moist, fertile, humus-rich soil in full or part shade.

PROPAGATION
Seed should be sown, after having had the flesh removed, in a cold frame as soon as it is ripe. The rhizomes can be separated in autumn; they should not be allowed to dry out until established.

Convallaria majalis 'Albostriata'

Zone 3
Height: 10in. (25 cm) Spread: 18in. (45 cm)
Foliage variegated

Convallaria majalis var. *rosea*

Zone 3
Height: 8in. (20cm) Spread: 1ft. (30cm)

Convallaria majalis
'Vic Pawlowski's Gold'
Zone 3
Height: 8in. (20cm) Spread: 18in. (45 cm)
Foliage variegated

CONVOLVULUS *(Convolvulaceae)*

Common names: Bindweed

A genus of 250 species of annuals, perennials, and shrubs from various habitats in temperate and tropical regions of the world. They have oblong or ovate, entire leaves. The flowers are trumpet- or funnel-shaped, and are in clusters or solitary. Some species may be invasive.

- ✔ Drought-tolerant
- ✔ Disease-free
- ✔ Pest-free

CULTIVATION
Grow in sharply-drained, fertile soil in sun. *C sabatius* has to be protected against winter wet and cold. *C. tricolor* is grown usually as an annual in cold climates.

PROPAGATION
Seed should be sown at 64°F (18°C) in spring. Divide in spring.

Convolvulus althaeoides

Zone 8
Height: 6in. (15cm) Spread: indefinite
Invasive

Convolvulus sabatius
A.G.M.

Zone 8
Height: 6in. (15cm) Spread: 20in. (50cm)

Convolvulus tricolor
Zone 8
Height and spread: 1ft. (30cm)
Low allergen/Short-lived/
Resents disturbance

COREOPSIS *(Asteraceae)*

Common names: Tickseed

A genus of 100 annuals and perennials from woodland and prairie in North America, Mexico and South America. The leaves may be entire, palmate or pinnate. The flowers are yellow daisies borne on tall upright stems. They are sometimes short-lived, and are often grown as annuals.

✔ Repeat-flowering	✘ Prone to slug damage
✔ Good cut flowers	✘ Need to lift & divide often
✔ Attracts bees	✘ Highly allergenic
✔ Attracts butterflies	

CULTIVATION
Grow in well-drained fertile soil in sun or part shade. Dead-head to induce repeat-flowering.

PROPAGATION
Seed should be sown in mid-spring. Division can be done in early spring.

Coreopsis grandiflora
(Bigflower coreopsis)
Zone 7
Height: 3ft. (90cm) Spread: 18in. (45 cm)
Short-lived

Coreopsis grandiflora 'Calypso'

Zone 7
Height and spread: 18in. (45 cm)
Foliage variegated/Short-lived

Coreopsis grandiflora
'Early Sunrise'
Zone 7
Height and spread: 18in. (45 cm)
Short-lived

Coreopsis grandiflora 'Sunray'

Zone 7
Height: 30in. (75cm) Spread: 18in. (45 cm)
Short-lived

C

Coreopsis rosea 'American Dream'
(Rose tickseed)
Zone 4
Height: 2ft. (60cm) Spread: 1ft. (30cm)
Short-lived

Coreopsis 'Tequila Sunrise'
Zone 7
Height: 1ft. (30cm) Spread: 18in. (45 cm)
Foliage variegated/Short-lived

Coreopsis verticillata 'Grandiflora'
A.G.M. (Threadleaf coreopsis)
Zone 6
Height: 32in. (80 cm) Spread: 18in. (45 cm)

Coreopsis verticillata 'Moonbeam'
Zone 6
Height: 20in. (50cm) Spread: 18in. (45 cm)

Coreopsis verticillata 'Zagreb'
Zone 6
Height and spread: 1ft. (30cm)

CORIARIA *(Coriariaceae)*
Common names: None

A genus of eight species of trees, shrubs, subshrubs and rhizomatous, herbaceous perennials from high scrubland, woodland and grassland in warm climates in the temperate regions of the world. They are grown for their foliage and berries, the flowers being insignificant (see *C. terminalis*). The leaves are alternate, glossy, entire, and borne on arching stems. The berries may be black, red, purple or yellow, and they contain poisonous seeds.

✔ Handsome foliage	✘ Poisonous seeds
✔ Have berries after flowering	✘ Flowers insignificant
✔ Disease-free	
✔ Pest-free	

Coriaria terminalis
Zone 8
Height: 3ft. (90cm) Spread: 6ft. (2m)

CULTIVATION
Grow in well-drained, fertile, deep soil in a sheltered corner in sun.

PROPAGATION
Seed should be sown in a cold frame as soon as it is ripe. The rhizomes can be divided in spring. Greenwood cuttings can be taken in summer.

C

Coriaria terminalis var. *xanthocarpa*

Zone 8
Height: 3ft. (90cm) Spread: 5ft. (1.5m)

CORNUS *(Cornaceae)*

Common names: Cornel; dogwood

A genus of 45 species of trees and shrubs and a few perennials, from a wide variety of habitats such as grassland, swampland, woodland and scree, in the temperate northern hemisphere. The leaves are alternate, lance-shaped or ovate. The flowers are small stars, usually surrounded by bracts (as in *C. canadensis*), and are borne in terminal cymes in spring or summer. The flowers are followed by berries, which may be poisonous in some species, but not *C. canadensis*.

✔ Have berries after flowering
✔ Disease-free
✔ Pest-free

CULTIVATION
Grow in acid, moist soil in sun or part shade.

PROPAGATION
Seed should be sown in autumn Division can be carried out in spring.

Cornus canadensis A.G.M.

Zone 2
Height: 6in. (15cm) Spread: indefinite
Invasive

CORTADERIA *(Poaceae)*

Common names: Pampas grass

A genus of 25 species of evergreen perennial grasses from grassland in South America, New Zealand and New Guinea. They usually grow near water. They form large clumps of very stiff, linear, saw-edged leaves, and have plumes of white, silver or pale pink flower panicles. They may be hermaphroditic or dioecious.

✔ Evergreen   ✘ Highly allergenic
✔ Good for drying for winter   ✘ Leaves very sharp-edged
✔ Architectural plants
✔ Disease-free
✔ Pest-free

CULTIVATION
Grow in well-drained,fertile soil in sun.

PROPAGATION
Seed should be sown at 64°F (18°C) in spring; they can also be divided then.

Cortaderia selloana
'Pumila'

Zone 8
Height: 5ft. (1.5m) Spread: 4ft. (1.2m)

Cortaderia selloana
'Aureolineata' A.G.M.

Zone 8
Height: 7ft. (2.2m) Spread: 5ft. (1.5m)

Cortaderia selloana
'Rendatleri'

Zone 8
Height: 8ft. (2.5m) Spread: 6ft. (2m)

Cortaderia selloana
'Silver Fountain'

Zone 8
Height: 5ft. (1.5m) Spread: 4ft. (1.2m)

CORTUSA *(Primulaceae)*

Common names: None

A genus of eight species of herbaceous perennials that occur in high woodlands in Eurasia. The leaves are basal and round or heart-shaped. The flowers are funnel- or bell-shaped, and borne in one-sided umbels well above the rosette. They will not tolerate hot, dry conditions.

| ✔ Handsome foliage | ✘ Prone to slug damage |

CULTIVATION
Grow in moist, humus-rich, well-drained soil in a cool spot in part shade.

PROPAGATION
Seed should be sown in a cold frame as soon as it is ripe. They can be divided in spring.

Cortusa matthioli

Zone 7
Height: 1ft. (30cm) Spread: 6in. (15cm)

CORYDALIS *(Papaveraceae)*

Common names: None

A genus of 300 species of annuals, biennials and rhizomatous or tuberous perennials from rocky and woodland habitats in the temperate northern hemisphere. The majority are evergreen, but a few are herbaceous. The leaves are stem, opposite or alternate, three-ternate or three-pinnate, and finely-divided such as to look fern-like. The flowers are tubular, with two pairs of petals, the outer pair spurred and reflexed and the inner pair incurved. They are borne on terminal or axillary racemes.

✔ Good cut flowers	✘ Self-seeds
✔ Handsome foliage	✘ Prone to slug damage
✔ Low allergen	

CULTIVATION
Varies with the species. *Corydalis cheilanthifolia*; grow in well-drained fertile soil in sun or part shade. *CC. flexuosa*, *lutea*, *ochroleuca* and *ophiocarpa*; grow in moist, well-drained soil in sun or part shade. *Corydalis solida*; grow in sharply-drained soil in sun. Dead-head to prevent self-seeding.

PROPAGATION
Seed should be sown in an open frame as soon as it is ripe. Spring-flowering species should be divided in autumn, and autumn-flowering ones in spring.

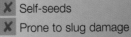

Corydalis cheilanthifolia

Zone 6
Height: 1ft. (30cm) Spread: 10in. (25 cm)
Long-flowering

Corydalis flexuosa

Zone 7
Height: 1ft. (30cm) Spread: 8in. (20cm)

Corydalis lutea (Yellow corydalis)

Zone 6
Height: 16in. (40cm) Spread: 1ft. (30cm)
Evergreen/Long-flowering

Corydalis ochroleuca

Zone 5
Height and spread: 1ft. (30cm)
Evergreen

Corydalis ophiocarpa

Zone 6
Height: 30in. (75cm) Spread: 1ft. (30cm)

Corydalis solida

Zone 6
Height: 1ft. (30cm) Spread: 6in. (15cm)

COSMOS *(Asteraceae)*
Common names: None

A genus of 25 species of annuals and tuberous perennials that are found in meadow and scrubland in southern U.S.A., and Central America. The leaves are pinnate and the lobes are ovate or diamond-shaped. The flowers are large, open, cup- or saucer-shaped, and solitary, on long stems over a long season in summer.

✔ Flowers perfumed   ✘ Prone to slug damage
✔ Good cut flowers
✔ Attracts bees
✔ Handsome foliage
✔ Long-flowering

Cosmos atrosanguineus
(Chocolate-scented cosmos)

Zone 8
Height: 30in. (75cm) Spread: 18in. (45 cm)

CULTIVATION
Grow in moist, fertile, well-drained soil in sun. Dead-head to prolong flowering. Protect against frost in winter, or lift tubers and dry off and store frost-free over winter.

PROPAGATION
Seed should be sown at 61°F (16°C) in mid spring.

CRAMBE *(Brassicaceae)*
Common names: Sea kale

A genus of 20 species of annuals and perennials from varied habitat such as coastal sand dunes, mountain slopes and open grassland in Eurasia, Turkey and tropical Africa. Their leaves are large, basal, pinnatisect or simple. The flowers are tiny, cross-shaped, and borne in very large panicles or racemes over a long period from summer to autumn. The stems are edible.

✔ Long-flowering	✔ Handsome foliage	✗ Resents disturbance
✔ Good cut flowers	✔ Architectural plants	✗ Prone to slug damage
✔ Attracts bees	✔ Culinary vegetables	

CULTIVATION
Grow in well-drained, deep, fertile soil in sun. May require staking.

PROPAGATION
Seed should be sown in a cold frame in spring or autumn. Division can be done in early spring, but is not tolerated well. Root cuttings can be taken in winter.

Crambe cordifolia
(Greater sea kale)

Zone 6
Height: 6ft. (2m) Spread: 5ft. (1.5m)

Crambe maritima
(Sea kale)

Zone 5
Height: 32in. (80 cm) Spread: 2ft. (60cm)

COTULA *(Asteraceae)*
Common names: Brass buttons

A genus of 55 species of annuals and perennials from moist habitats in Africa, South America, Mexico and Australia. They are prostrate, and have succulent stems and aromatic, linear lobed or toothed leaves. The flowers are button-like, and borne on thin stems in summer.

| ✔ Foliage aromatic |
| ✔ Disease-free |
| ✔ Pest-free |

CULTIVATION
Grow in a pond margin, bog garden or damp, humus-rich soil in sun. Dead-heading prolongs flowering.

PROPAGATION
Seed should be surface-sown in spring at 64°F (18°C).

Cotula coronopifolia

Zone 7
Height: 6in. (15cm) Spread: 1ft. (30cm)

C

COTYLEDON *(Crassulaceae)*

Common names: None

A genus of nine species of perennial succulents and evergreen subshrubs from deserts or shady regions of Southern Africa, Arabia and East Africa. Their leaves are stalked, fleshy, ovoid, and in opposite pairs. The flowers are bell-shaped or tubular, pendent, and borne in crowded terminal panicles in late summer and autumn.

✔ Evergreen

✔ Handsome foliage

✘ Prone to aphid attack

CULTIVATION

Under glass, grow in cactus compost in full light, with shade from sun. Water with moderation even in the growing season, avoiding the foliage, and keep completely dry in winter.

Out of doors, grow in sharply-draining, humus-rich soil in sun, with shade at mid-day.

PROPAGATION

Seed should be sown at 75°F (24°C) in spring. Root stem cuttings in spring or summer.

Cotyledon orbiculata

Zone 10
Height: 3ft. (90cm) Spread: 20in. (50cm)

Cotyledon orbiculata var. *oblonga*

Zone 10
Height: 3ft. (90cm) Spread: 20in. (50cm)

CRASPEDIA *(Asteraceae)*

Common names: Bachelor's buttons

A genus of eight species of annuals and perennials from the mountains of New Zealand, Tasmania and Australia. The leaves are in basal rosettes, and obovate or linear or spoon-shaped. The flowers are tiny, cup-shaped, surrounded by leafy bracts, and crowded in dense hemispherical heads on short stems in summer.

✔ Handsome foliage

✘ Prone to slug damage

CULTIVATION

Grow in sharply-draining, poor, humus-rich soil in sun. Protect against winter wet.

PROPAGATION

Seed should be sown at 64°F (18°C) in spring, when division can also be carried out.

Craspedia uniflora

Zone 8
Height: 18in. (45 cm) Spread: 14in. (35cm)

CRASSULA *(Crasulaceae)*
Common names: Jade plant

A genus of 150 species of annual or perennial succulents and evergreen subshrubs and shrubs, from moist or dry regions of South Africa in particular, but also Madagascar and Asia. They are grown for their foliage and flowers. The leaves are fleshy, opposite, and variously shaped. The flowers are tubular or funnel- or star-shaped, and borne in dense terminal cymes.

✔ Handsome foliage
✔ Evergreen
✔ Architectural plants

✘ Prone to aphid attack

CULTIVATION
Under glass, grow in cactus compost in full light. Water moderately in summer and sparingly in winter.

Out of doors, grow in sharply-draining, humus-rich, fertile soil in sun.

PROPAGATION
Seed should be sown at 64°F (18°C) in spring. Leaf or stem cuttings can be rooted in spring or summer.

Crassula arborescens
(Silver jade plant)

Zone 9
Height: 12ft. (4m) Spread: 6ft. (2m)

Crassula ovata
A.G.M. (Jade plant)

Zone 9
Height: 6ft. (2m) Spread: 3ft. (90cm)

Crassula ovata 'Variegata'

Zone 9
Height: 6ft. (2m) Spread: 3ft. (90cm)

Crassula perforata 'Variegata'

Zone 9
Height: 3ft. (90cm) Spread: 1ft. (30cm)

CREPIS *(Asteraceae)*
Common names: Hawk's beard

A genus of 200 species of annuals and perennials found in dry grassland and scree across the northern hemisphere. The leaves are inverse-lance-shaped, gray-green, pinnatifid, and resemble closely those of the dandelion. The flowers also resemble those of the dandelion, and are semi-double, and solitary or in many-flowered corymbs.

✔ Drought-tolerant
✔ Disease-free
✔ Pest-free

✘ Short-lived
✘ Self-seeds
✘ Resents disturbance

CULTIVATION
Grow in any soil that is not waterlogged, in sun. Dead-head to prevent self-seeding.

PROPAGATION
Seed should be sown in a frame as soon as it is ripe. Cuttings of lateral roots (but not tap roots) can be taken in winter.

Crepis incana A.G.M. (Pink dandelion)

Zone 8
Height and spread: 1ft. (30cm)

C

Crepis rubra

Zone 8
Height: 16in. (40cm) Spread: 6in. (15cm)

CRINUM *(Amaryllidaceae)*

Common names: Pyjama lily

A genus of 130 species of bulbous perennials found at water- and lake-sides across the tropics, and in South Africa. They may be evergreen or deciduous. The leaves are basal, strap-shaped. The flowers are large, funnel-shaped, sometimes perfumed, and borne from spring to autumn.

✔ Flowers perfumed	✘ All parts poisonous
✔ Good cut flowers	✘ Sap is skin-irritant
✔ Long-flowering	✘ Resents disturbance
✔ Disease-free	
✔ Pest-free	

CULTIVATION
The bulbs should be planted with the neck just above the surface in spring in moist, well-drained, humus-rich soil in sun.

PROPAGATION
Seed should be sown as soon as it is ripe. Remove offsets in spring.

Crinum macowanii

Zone 9
Height: 2ft. (60cm) Spread: 6in. (15cm)

Crinum x powellii A.G.M.

Zone 6
Height: 4ft. (1.2m) Spread: 1ft. (30cm)

Crinum x powellii 'Album' A.G.M.

Zone 6
Height: 4ft. (1.2m) Spread: 1ft. (30cm)

CROCOSMIA *(Iridaceae)*
Common names: Montbretia

A genus of seven species of cormous perennials from grassland in South Africa. The leaves are linear, erect, pleated or ribbed. The flowers are funnel-shaped, and borne in one-sided spikes from mid- to late summer. The species have been hybridized extensively and the original cross was given the unwieldy name of *C. x crocosmiiflora*. A large number of brightly-colored hybrids have been introduced since.

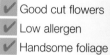

✔ Good cut flowers   ✖ Need to lift & divide often
✔ Low allergen
✔ Handsome foliage

CULTIVATION
Plant corms 4in. (10 cm) deep in spring in moist, humus-rich, well-drained soil in sun or pare shade. The corms must be dug up and separated before being replanted every few years in spring.

PROPAGATION
Divide in spring before growth starts.

Crocosmia x crocosmiiflora
'Carmin Brilliant' A.G.M.

Zone 7
Height: 32in. (80 cm) Spread: 4in. (10 cm)

Crocosmia x crocosmiiflora
'Citronella'

Zone 7
Height: 2ft. (60cm) Spread: 4in. (10 cm)

Crocosmia x crocosmiiflora
'Emily McKenzie'

Zone 7
Height: 2ft. (60cm) Spread: 4in. (10 cm)

Crocosmia x crocosmiiflora
'Jackanapes'

Zone 7
Height: 2ft. (60cm) Spread: 4in. (10 cm)

Crocosmia x crocosmiiflora
'Lady Hamilton'

Zone 7
Height: 32in. (80 cm) Spread: 4in. (10 cm)

Crocosmia x crocosmiiflora
'Solfatare' A.G.M.

Zone 7
Height: 32in. (80 cm) Spread: 4in. (10 cm)

Crocosmia
'Emberglow'

Zone 7
Height: 30in. (75cm) Spread: 4in. (10 cm)

C

Crocosmia
'Firebird'

Zone 7
Height: 32in. (80 cm) Spread: 4in. (10 cm)

Crocosmia 'Lucifer' A.G.M.

Zone 7
Height: 3ft. (90cm) Spread: 4in. (10 cm)

Crocosmia masoniorum
A.G.M.

Zone 7
Height: 4ft. (1.2m) Spread: 4in. (10 cm)

Crocosmia paniculata

Zone 7
Height: 4ft. (1.2m) Spread: 4in. (10 cm)

Crocosmia
'Severn Sunrise'

Zone 7
Height: 32in. (80 cm) Spread: 4in. (10 cm)

Crocosmia
'Solfatare' A.G.M.

Zone 8
Height: 32in. (80 cm) Spread: 4in. (10 cm)

Crocosmia
'Vulcan'

Zone 7
Height: 32in. (80 cm) Spread: 4in. (10 cm)

Crocosmia
'Walburton Yellow'

Zone 7
Height: 32in. (80 cm) Spread: 4in. (10 cm)

CROCUS *(Iridaceae)*
Common names: None

A genus of 80 species of cormous perennials found in Europe, North Africa, the Middle East, Central Asia and China. The leaves are erect or arching, linear, green with a pale central stripe of silver or cream; they appear with the flowers and elongate considerably after flowering. The flowers are formed by six tepals, in an inner and an outer ring of three; all six may be the same color, or each group of three may be of a different color. Some are perfumed. Some species require a dry summer dormancy, and so require alpine house treatment; only one (*C. kotschyanus*) is included here. The others are easy to cultivate.

✔ Attracts bees	✘ Need to lift & divide often
✔ Trouble-free	✘ Rodents love corms
✔ Pest-free	✘ Birds pluck flowers

CULTIVATION
Plant the corms in autumn, 4in. (10 cm) deep in sandy, well-drained fertile soil in sun. Corms get overcrowded, so they should be lifted and replanted every few years.

PROPAGATION
Seed should be sown instantly after ripening in a cold frame, and the seedlings left for two years before planting out. Cormlets can be separated during the dormant period.

Crocus chrysanthus
'Blue Pearl' A.G.M.
Zone 4
Height: 3in. (8 cm) Spread: 2in. (5cm)
Flowers perfumed

Crocus chrysanthus
'Cream Beauty' A.G.M.
Zone 4
Height: 3in. (8 cm) Spread: 2in. (5cm)
Flowers perfumed

Crocus kotschyanus A.G.M.
Zone 5
Height: 4in. (10 cm) Spread: 3in. (8 cm)

Crocus x luteus
'Golden Yellow' A.G.M.
Zone 4
Height: 4in. (10 cm) Spread: 2in. (5cm)

Crocus tomassinianus
'Ruby Giant'
Zone 5
Height: 4in. (10 cm) Spread: 1in. (2.5 cm)

Crocus chrysanthus
'Snow Bunting' A.G.M.
Zone 4
Height: 3in. (8 cm) Spread: 2in. (5cm)

CRYPTANTHUS *(Bromeliaceae)*

Common names: Starfish plant; Earth Star

A genus of 20 species of evergreen terrestrial perennials from dry forest areas in eastern Brazil at altitudes of up to 5,000 ft. (1,600m). Their strap-shaped, wavy-edged leaves are handsome, zoned, and borne in basal rosettes. The flowers are inconspicuous, and are borne in the depths of each rosette in summer.

C

 Evergreen

 Handsome foliage

✗ Flowers inconspicuous

CULTIVATION

Under glass, grow in terrestrial bromeliad compost in bright filtered light or full light, with some humidity. Water moderately during growth, and reduce in winter. Mist with tepid water in summer.

Out of doors, grow in acid to neutral, moist, fertile, well-drained soil in part shade.

PROPAGATION

Seed should be sown at 81°F (27°C) as soon as ripe. Separate offsets in early summer.

Cryptanthus bromelioides
'Tricolor' A.G.M.
Zone 9
Height: 16in. (40cm) Spread: indefinite
Invasive

Cryptanthus
'It'
Zone 9
Height: 1ft. (30cm) Spread: 18in. (45 cm)

Cryptanthus
'Pink Starlight'
Zone 9
Height: 8in. (20cm) Spread: 14in. (35cm)

Cryptanthus zonatus A.G.M.
Zone 9
Height: 5in. (12cm) Spread: 16in. (40cm)

Cryptanthus zonatus
'Zebrinus' (Zebra plant)
Zone 9
Height: 5in. (12cm) Spread: 16in. (40cm)

CTENANTHE *(Marantaceae)*

Common names: None

A genus of 15 species of rosette-forming, rhizomatous evergreen perennials from wet forest floor and thickets in Brazil and Costa Rica. Their leaves are ovate, or lance-shaped or inversely-lance-shaped, and handsomely marked. The flowers are tubular, and borne in terminal racemes or spikes throughout the year.

✔ Evergreen
✔ Long-flowering
✔ Handsome foliage

CULTIVATION

Under glass, grow in potting compost in bright indirect or filtered light in high humidity, and out of draughts, and in a constant temperature. Mist with soft, tepid water and water freely during growth. Water sparingly in winter. Repot annually in spring or early summer.

Out of doors, grow in moist, humus-rich, fertile soil in part shade.

PROPAGATION

Seed should be sown at 75°F (24°C) as soon as ripe, or in spring, when division can be carried out.

Ctenanthe burle-marxii

Zone 10
Height: 2ft. (60cm) Spread: 14in. (35cm)

Ctenanthe oppenheimiana
'Tricolor' A.G.M.

Zone 10
Height: 3ft. (90cm) Spread: 2ft. (60cm)

CUPHEA *(Lythraceae)*

Common names: Cigar flower

A genus of 250 species of annuals, perennials and shrubs from pastureland and clearings in woodland in south-eastern U.S.A., Mexico, and tropical and subtropical South and Central America. Their leaves are opposite, ovate or lance-shaped, toothed or entire, and sticky-hairy in *C. cyanea*. The flowers are tubular, and solitary or in panicles or racemes.

✔ Disease-free   ✗ Need to lift & divide often
                             ✗ Prone to aphid attack

CULTIVATION

Under glass, grow in loam-based potting compost in full light and shade from hot sun. Humidity should be moderate. Water freely during growth, but sparingly in winter. Prune in spring by cutting back to within 1in. (2.5 cm) of previous year's growth.

Out of doors, grow in well-drained fertile soil in sun or part shade.

PROPAGATION

Seed should be sown at 61°F (16°C) in early spring. Divide in late spring. Softwood cuttings can be rooted in late spring.

Cuphea cyanea

Zone 9
Height: 4ft. (1.2m) Spread: 3ft. (90cm)

C

Cuphea hyssopifolia
A.G.M. (False heather)

Zone 10
Height: 2ft. (60cm) Spread: 32in. (80 cm)

Cuphea ignea
A.G.M.

Zone 9
Height: 30in. (75cm) Spread: 3ft. (90cm)

CYCLAMEN *(Primulaceae)*
Common names: None

A genus of 19 species of tuberous perennials found in a wide range of habitat such as dry sand, alpine woodland and damp woodland from the Mediterranean to Somalia, to Iran. The leaves are heart-shaped or round, handsomely marbled in silver, and reddish-purple underneath. The flowers are nodding, with five twisted, reflexed petals of white, pink or red, and they may be perfumed. Cyclamen should be bought in active growth, and never as dry tubers as they do not grow away.

✔ Handsome foliage   ✗ All parts poisonous   ✗ Rodents gnaw tubers

CULTIVATION
Under glass, the tender CC. graecum and persicum should be planted with the upper surface of the tuber above the soil surface in a bulb frame or alpine house, in a mix of equal parts of sharp sand, loam and leaf mould, and kept totally dry and frost-free during dormancy.

Out of doors, all seven hardy species included should be grown in well-drained, humus-rich, fertile soil in part shade under trees to minimize summer wet.

PROPAGATION
Seed of hardy species should be soaked when it is ripe for 12 hours and, after rinsing, sown in darkness at 55°F (13°C) and at 59°F (15°C) for *CC. graecum* and *persicum*.

Cyclamen coum
A.G.M.

Zone 6
Height: 3in. (8 cm) Spread: 4in. (10 cm)

Cyclamen coum subsp. *coum*
forma. *albissimum*

Zone 6
Height: 3in. (8 cm) Spread: 4in. (10 cm)

Cyclamen graecum

Zone 9
Height: 4in. (10 cm) Spread: 6in. (15cm)

Cyclamen hederifolium A.G.M.

Zone 6
Height: 5in. (12cm) Spread: 6in. (15cm)
Self-seeds

C

Cyclamen parviflorum

Zone 7
Height: 2in. (5cm) Spread: 3in. (8 cm)

Cyclamen persicum

Zone 9
Height: 8in. (20cm) Spread: 6in. (15cm)
Flowers perfumed

Cyclamen repandum

Zone 7
Height: 6in. (15cm) Spread: 5in. (12cm)
Flowers perfumed

Cyclamen repandum subsp.
peloppenesiacum
Zone 7
Height: 6in. (15cm) Spread: 5in. (12cm)
Flowers perfumed

Cyclamen trochopteranthum

Zone 7
Height: 3in. (8 cm) Spread: 4in. (10 cm)
Flowers perfumed

CYMBOPOGON *(Poaceae)*
Common names: Lemon grass

A genus of 56 species of evergreen perennial grasses from savannah grassland in tropical, subtropical and warm temperate Asia and Africa. The foliage is aromatic, with leaves linear to lance-shaped and blue-green in color. The flowering spike is a panicle of spike-like racemes, enclosed in bracts, and borne in late summer and early autumn, but it does not flower freely under glass.

✔ Evergreen
✔ Handsome foliage
✔ Foliage aromatic
✔ Disease-free
✔ Pest-free

✘ Highly allergenic

Cymbopogon citratus

Zone 9
Height: 5ft. (1.5m) Spread: 3ft. (90cm)

CULTIVATION
Grow in moist, fertile, well-drained soil in sun.

PROPAGATION
Seed should be sown at 64°F (18°C) in spring. Division can be done in spring.

C

CYNARA *(Asteraceae)*
Common names: Cardoon; globe artichoke

A genus of 10 species of perennials from sunny well-drained slopes in the Canary Islands, north-west Africa and the Mediterranean region. They are clump-forming, and herbaceous. Some species are tall stately plants and make excellent specimen or architectural plants. The leaves are pinnatifid or bipinnatifid, glaucous-green or silver. The flowers are spherical, thistle-like, and solitary or in corymbs.

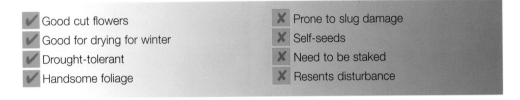

✔ Good cut flowers	✘ Prone to slug damage
✔ Good for drying for winter	✘ Self-seeds
✔ Drought-tolerant	✘ Need to be staked
✔ Handsome foliage	✘ Resents disturbance

CULTIVATION
Grow in well-drained, fertile soil in a sheltered corner in sun. Dead-head to prevent self-seeding.

PROPAGATION
Seed should be sown in a cold frame, and division can also be done then. Root cuttings can be taken in winter.

Cynara cardunculus (Cardoon)
Zone 6
Height: 5ft. (1.5m) Spread: 4ft. (1.2m)
Architectural plant

Cynara scolymus (Globe artichoke)
Zone 6
Height: 6ft. (2m) Spread: 4ft. (1.2m)
Architectural plant

CYNOGLOSSUM *(Boraginaceae)*
Common names: Chinese hound's tongue; Hound's tongue

A genus of 55 species of annuals, biennials and perennials from rocky slopes and grasslands at altitude in tropical and temperate regions. The perennials are short-lived. The leaves are alternate, rough, lance-shaped or ovate. The flowers are forget-me–not-like, blue, white or pink in color, tubular, borne in one-sided terminal cymes over a long period from spring to autumn.

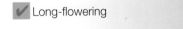

✔ Long-flowering	✘ Short-lived
	✘ Mildew prone

CULTIVATION
Grow in moist, well-drained, poor soil in sun or part shade. They become leafy and coarse if fed too rich a diet.

PROPAGATION
Seed should be sown in a cold frame in autumn or spring. Division can be carried out in spring.

Cynoglossum amabile A.G.M.
(Chinese forget-me-not)
Zone 7
Height: 2ft. (60cm) Spread: 1ft. (30cm)

C

Cynoglossum nervosum

Zone 5
Height: 32in. (80 cm) Spread: 2ft. (60cm)

Cynoglossum officinale

Zone 6
Height: 28in. (70 cm) Spread: 20in. (50cm)

CYPELLA *(Iridaceae)*
Common names: None

A genus of 15 species of bulbous perennials found in grassland and woodland in South and Central America. The leaves are lance-shaped or linear, and pleated. The unusual flowers have three large outer spreading tepals and three small inner incurved ones. They may be solitary or in terminal corymbs, and each lasts but one day but they are borne successively over a long period in summer or winter.

| ✔ Long-flowering | ✔ Pest-free |
| ✔ Disease-free | |

CULTIVATION
Under glass, grow in gritty, loam-based potting compost in bright filtered light, and with good ventilation. Water freely during the growing season, and dry off completely in winter. Keep frost-free.

Out of doors, grow in sharply-draining, humus-rich soil in sun. In cold regions, lift the bulbs in autumn and store in a dry, frost-free atmosphere over winter.

PROPAGATION
Seed should be sown as soon as it is ripe at 55°F (13°C).Offsets can be detached in late winter or spring., when dormant.

Cypella herbertii

Zone 9
Height: 2ft. (60cm) Spread: 4in. (10 cm)

CYPRIPEDIUM *(Orchidaceae)*
Common names: Lady's slipper orchid

A genus of 35 species of terrestrial, deciduous orchids that occur in dry woods and marshland in the temperate northern hemisphere, Mexico and South Asia. They are rhizomatous, and their leaves are ovate, elliptic or fan-shaped, folded, and in opposite pairs. The flowers are solitary, or in terminal racemes. Each has three spreading tepals of purple, red, pink or white, and a pouch that is slipper-shaped, which may be purple, red, pink, or yellow.

| ✔ Handsome foliage | ✘ Prone to slug damage |

CULTIVATION
Grow in moist, fertile, humus-rich, leafy, acid to neutral (except for *C. calceolus*, which prefers alkaline) soil in a sheltered corner. Mulch annually in winter with leaf mould.

PROPAGATION
Divide in spring, ensuring that some of the root ball soil is planted with each division, since it holds beneficial fungi, and replant at once.

Cypripedium acaule

Zone 5
Height and spread: 10in. (25 cm)

C

Cypripedium calceolus

Zone 5
Height and spread: 16in. (40cm)

Cypripedium parviflorum var.
pubescens
Zone 5
Height and spread: 10in. (25 cm)
Skin irritant

Cypripedium reginae

Zone 4
Height: 30in. (75cm) Spread: 1ft. (30cm)

CYRTANTHUS *(Amaryllidaceae)*

Common names: Fire lily

A genus of 50 species of bulbous perennials from grassland, forest, and scree in South Africa. They are herbaceous or semi-evergreen, and clump-forming. The leaves are basal, lance-shaped, and semi-erect. The flowers are tubular to funnel-shaped, and borne in umbels from spring to autumn.

✔ Long-flowering	✔ Disease-free
✔ Handsome foliage	✔ Pest-free

CULTIVATION

Under glass, plant bulbs in spring with their necks at soil level in sharply-draining loam-based potting compost, in full light or bright filtered light. Water freely during growth, keep just moist at 50°F (10°C) in winter.

Out of doors, plant the bulbs at twice their depth in spring in well-drained, humus-rich, fertile soil in sun.

PROPAGATION

Seed should be as soon as it is ripe at 64°F (18°C). Offsets can be detached in spring.

Cyrtanthus brachyscyphus

Zone 9
Height: 1ft. (30cm) Spread: 4in. (10 cm)

C

D

DACTYLIS
DACTYLORHIZA
DAHLIA
DARMERA
DAVALLIA
DELPHINIUM
DESCHAMPSIA
DESMODIUM
DIANELLA
DIANTHUS
DIASCIA
DICENTRA
DICKSONIA
DICTAMNUS
DIEFFENBACHIA
DIERAMA
DIETES
DIGITALIS
DIONAEA
DIPHYLLEIA
DIPLARRHENA
DISA
DISPORUM
DODECATHEON
DORONICUM
DRABA
DRACUNCULUS
DRYAS
DRYOPTERIS

DACTYLIS *(Poaceae)*
Common names: None

A genus of but two species of evergreen perennial grasses from Eurasia and North Africa. The leaves are linear. The flowering spike is a one-sided panicle of pale green, borne all summer.

- ✔ Handsome foliage
- ✔ Long-flowering
- ✘ Flowers insignificant

CULTIVATION
Grow in well-drained fertile soil in sun or part shade.

PROPAGATION
Divide in spring.

Dactylis glomerata
'Variegata'

Zone 5
Height: 18in. (45 cm) Spread: 10in. (25 cm)

DACTYLORHIZA *(Orchidaceae)*
Common names: Marsh orchid; spotted orchid

A genus of 30 species of tuberous, herbaceous terrestrial orchids from Eurasia, North Africa and North America. Their leaves are linear or lance-shaped, fleshy, and spotted in some species. The flowers are borne in dense, upright, terminal racemes, and may be red, purple, lilac, pink or white, with purple or green bracts; they appear in late spring or early summer.

- ✔ Handsome foliage
- ✔ Disease-free
- ✔ Pest-free

CULTIVATION
Grow in moist, humus-rich, well-drained soil in part shade.

PROPAGATION
Divide in early spring.

Dactylorhiza elata
A.G.M. (Robust marsh orchid)

Zone 6
Height: 2ft. (60cm) Spread: 6in. (15cm)

Dactylorhiza foliosa
A.G.M. (Madeiran orchid)

Zone 7
Height: 2ft. (60cm) Spread: 6in. (15cm)

Dactylorhiza fuchsii
(Common spotted orchid)

Zone 6
Height: 2ft. (60cm) Spread: 6in. (15cm)

Dactylorhiza praetermissa
(Southern marsh orchid)

Zone 6
Height: 2ft. (60cm) Spread: 6in. (15cm)

DAHLIA (Asteraceae)
Common names: None

A genus of 30 species (but over 20,000 cultivars) of tuberous perennials from Central America and Mexico. All are tender (Zone 10) except *D. merckii.* (Zone 9). The handsome foliage is pinnate, the lobes being toothed with rounded tips, or pinnatifid or pinnatisect. The flowers are borne from midsummer to autumn, and later in mild areas. Classification, based on flower size and shape, is beyond the scope of this book, and the interested reader is referred to the Royal Horticultural Society 'Plant Finder' for details.

D

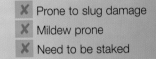

✔ Long-flowering	✘ Prone to slug damage
✔ Good cut flowers	✘ Mildew prone
✔ Attracts butterflies	✘ Need to be staked
✔ Handsome foliage	

CULTIVATION
Grow in humus-rich, fertile soil in sun. Dead-heading helps prolong flowering. Taller varieties may need to be staked. Lift and store the tubers, dust them with fungicide, dry off and store in a frost-free place over winter. Check them over regularly for any fungal infected bits, remove and dust the cut surface with fungicide.

PROPAGATION
Basal cuttings can be taken from tubers which have been brought on under glass and rooted in early spring in a propagator. Tubers started into growth later can be divided once new shoots are 1in. (2.5 cm) long, ensuring that each tuber division has a shoot. These can be planted out once all danger of frost has passed.

Dahlia
'Bishop of Llandaff' A.G.M.

Zone 10
Height: 4ft. (1.2m) Spread: 18in. (45 cm)

Dahlia
'David Howard' A.G.M.

Zone 10
Height: 4ft. (1.2m) Spread: 18in. (45 cm)

Dahlia
'Grenadier' A.G.M.

Zone 10
Height: 3ft. (90cm) Spread: 1ft. (30cm)

Dahlia imperialis

Zone 10
Height: 30ft. (10m) Spread: 6ft. (2m)
Architectural plant

Dahlia merckii

Zone 9
Height: 6ft. (2m) Spread: 3ft. (90cm)

Dahlia 'Moonfire' A.G.M.

Zone 10
Height: 3ft. (90cm) Spread: 30in. (75cm)

DARMERA *(Saxifragaceae)*
Common names: Umbrella plant

A monospecific genus of one rhizomatous plant from watersides in mountains in western U.S.A. Its leaves are large, peltate, round, toothed, and deeply-lobed, and appear after the flowers, which are small and pink and borne in cymes on tall stems in spring.

- ✔ Handsome foliage
- ✔ Architectural plant
- ✔ Disease-free
- ✔ Pest-free

CULTIVATION
Grow in a pond margin or wet or humus-rich soil in sun or part shade.

PROPAGATION
Seed should be sown in a cold frame in autumn or spring, or division can be carried out in spring.

Darmera peltata
A.G.M.

Zone 6
Height: 6ft. (2m) Spread: 5ft. (1.5m)

DAVALLIA *(Davalliaveae)*
Common names: Squirrel's foot fern

A genus of 34 species of rhizomatous ferns from watersides in China to Japan, Australasia, and the Mediterranean region. They are rhizomatous, epiphytic, deciduous and creeping. The fronds are three- or four-pinnate, finely-cut, and broad, and the segments are linear or triangular.

- ✔ Handsome foliage
- ✔ Disease-free
- ✔ Pest-free
- ✘ Invasive

CULTIVATION
Under glass, grow in a mix of equal parts sharp sand, leaf mould, bark, moss, pine needles and charcoal in bright indirect light with high humidity. Water with moderation over summer, but sparingly in winter.

Out of doors, grow in moist, leafy, humus-rich soil, or epiphytically, in part shade.

PROPAGATION
Sow spores at 70°F (21°C) as soon as they are ripe. Divide rhizomes in spring, ensuring that each division has roots.

Davallia mariesii
A.G.M.

Zone 9
Height: 6in. (15cm) Spread: indefinite

DELPHINIUM *(Ranunculaceae)*
Common names: None

A genus of 250 species of annuals, biennials and perennials from all parts of the world except the polar regions and Australia. They are mostly fibrous-rooted, but a few are tuberous. They are grown for their stately spires of flowers, and are indispensable members of the Cottage Garden or the herbaceous border, although some are small enough for the rock garden. The leaves are three-, five- or seven-lobed, and toothed. The flowers are shallow cups, spurred or hooded in some types, double or single, and borne in spikes or racemes or panicles. All parts are poisonous, and the sap is skin irritant. They are prone to slug damage and powdery mildew. They are classified, apart from the species, as:

Belladonna Group: Upright, to 4ft. (1.2m), branched plants with leaves palmately-lobed, and loose spikes of elfin-cap-like single flowers in early and again in late summer.

Elatum Group: The most popular type, with tall plants to 5.5ft. (1.7m) high, tapering flower spikes of single or double flowers with 5 large outer sepals and an inner eye of eight sepals, in early and midsummer, and again in autumn if cut back, and side shoots which flower in between.

Pacific Hybrids: These are short-lived, and so are grown usually as annuals or biennials. They are also tall, 5.5ft. (1.7m), and flower in spring and early summer.

✔ Repeat-flowering	✘ Mildew prone
✔ Good cut flowers	✘ Prone to slug damage
✔ Low allergen	✘ All parts poisonous
	✘ Foliage is skin-irritant

CULTIVATION
Grow in well-drained, fertile soil in a sheltered spot in sun. Stake as required. Dead-head, and cut back to lower side shoots to encourage repeat-flowering.

PROPAGATION
Seed of species should be sown in early spring at 55°F (13°C).

For cultivars, take pencil-slim basal cuttings with a heel from near the crown in early spring.

Delphinium beesianum 'Cliveden Beauty' (Belladonna Group)

Zone 3
Height: 4ft. (1.2m) Spread: 6in. (15cm)

Delphinium beesianum 'Peace' (Belladonna Group)

Zone 3
Height: 4ft. (1.2m) Spread: 18in. (45 cm)

Delphinium beesianum 'Volkerfrieden' (Belladonna Group)

Zone 3
Height: 4ft. (1.2m) Spread: 18in. (45 cm)

Delphinium belladonna Hybrid
(Belladonna Group)

Zone 3
Height: 4ft. (1.2m) Spread: 18in. (45 cm)

Delphinium Blue Jade Group
(Elatum Group)

Zone 3
Height: 5ft. (1.5m) Spread: 2ft. (60cm)

Delphinium cashmerianum
(Species)

Zone 5
Height: 16in. (40cm) Spread: 6in. (15cm)

Delphinium 'Conspicuous' A.G.M.
(Elatum Group)

Zone 3
Height: 4ft. (1.2m) Spread: 18in. (45 cm)

Delphinium
'Galahad' (Pacific hybrid)

Zone 3
Height: 5ft. (1.5m) Spread: 30in. (75cm)

Delphinium grandiflorum
'Blue Butterfly' (Species)

Zone 3
Height: 16in. (40cm) Spread: 8in. (20cm)

Delphinium Magic Fountain Series
(Elatum Group)

Zone 3
Height: 5ft. (1.5m) Spread: 2ft. (60cm)

Delphinium nudicaule
(Species)

Zone 8
Height: 2ft. (60cm) Spread: 8in. (20cm)

Delphinium speciosum
(Species)

Zone 6
Height: 30in. (75cm) Spread: 1ft. (30cm)

D

DESCHAMPSIA *(Poaceae)*

Common names: None

A genus of 50 species of perennial, evergreen grasses, which may be tuft-or tussock-forming. They are widespread in distribution in tropical mountains and in arctic and temperate marshland, moorland and woodland. The leaves are narrowly linear. The flowering spike is a panicle.

✔ Handsome seed-heads   ✘ Highly allergenic
✔ Evergreen
✔ Handsome foliage
✔ Disease-free
✔ Pest-free

CULTIVATION
Grow in acid to neutral, dry, or damp, humus-rich, soil in sun or part shade.

PROPAGATION
Seed should be sown in situ in spring or autumn. Division can be done in late spring to early summer.

Deschampsia caespitosa
'Northern Lights'
Zone 5
Height: 6ft. (2m) Spread: 5ft. (1.5m)
Architectural plant

Deschampsia flexuosa
'Tatra Gold'
Zone 5
Height: 20in. (50cm) Spread: 1ft. (30cm)

DESMODIUM *(Papilionaceae)*

Common names: Beggarweed

A genus of over 450 species of shrubs, sub shrubs and herbaceous perennials from subtropical and tropical regions of the world. Their leaves are pinnate to tripalmate, alternate. The flowers are pea-like, purple or white, and borne in axillary or terminal panicles or racemes in late summer or early autumn.

✔ Handsome foliage
✔ Trouble-free

CULTIVATION
Grow in any well-drained soil in sun.

PROPAGATION
Seed should be sown in a cold frame in autumn. Softwood cuttings can be taken in late spring.

Desmodium elegans

Zone 6
Height and spread: 5ft. (1.5m)

DIANELLA *(Phormiaceae)*

Common names: Flax lily

A genus of 30 species of rhizomatous or fibrous-rooted evergreen perennials from open woodland or heathland in the tropical or temperate parts of Asia, Australasia, East Africa and Madagascar. The flowers are tiny, pendent, star-shaped, blue, borne in loose panicles, and followed by blue berries.

✔ Evergreen

✔ Have berries after flowering

✔ Disease-free

✔ Pest-free

✘ Flowers insignificant

CULTIVATION

Under glass, grow in loam-based potting compost in full light with shade from hot sun. Water freely during growth, but keep just moist in winter.

Out of doors, grow in acid to neutral, humus-rich, well-drained soil in sun or part shade.

PROPAGATION

Seed should be sown at 61°F (16°C) in spring. Division can also be carried out then.

Dianella caerulea

Zone 9
Height: 2ft. (60cm) Spread: 1ft. (30cm)

Dianella nigra
(New Zealand Blackberry)

Zone 9
Height: 2ft. (60cm) Spread: 18in. (45 cm)

Dianella tasmanica
(Tasmanian Blueberry)

Zone 9
Height: 4ft. (1.2m) Spread: 18in. (45 cm)

Dianella tasmanica
'Variegata'

Zone 9
Height: 4ft. (1.2m) Spread: 18in. (45 cm)

DIANTHUS *(Caryophyllaceae)*

Common names: Carnation; Pink; Sweet William

A genus of 300 species from Eurasia, Africa and one from arctic U.S.A. They are evergreen, long-flowering, and drought-tolerant. They can be short-lived however, and are highly allergenic. The foliage is linear to lance-shaped, commonly gray-green or blue-gray, and beloved of rabbits and pigeons. The genus is classified as comprising three types of carnation (*Dianthus caryophyllus*, which will not be dealt with here) and three classes of pinks, (*Dianthus plumarius*).

Perpetual-flowering carnations: these are usually grown under glass, for exhibition and the cut-flower trade.

Malmaison carnations: these, too, are grown for the flower trade and exhibition.

Border carnations: summer-flowering, double plants in a range of colors and fancy- or picotee-edged.

Pinks: summer-flowering and grouped into alpine, old-fashioned or modern. They may be single or double, solitary or in cymes or umbels, and are sometimes clove-scented.

Dianthus barbatus (Sweet William)

Zone 4
Height: 28in. (70cm) Spread: 1ft. (30cm)
Short-lived

✔ Evergreen
✔ Handsome foliage
✔ Flowers perfumed
✔ Drought-tolerant
✔ Good cut flowers

✘ Prone to slug damage
✘ Short-lived
✘ Highly allergenic

CULTIVATION

Grow pinks in alkaline to neutral, well-drained soil in sun. Alpine species must have very sharp drainage. *DD. barbatus and chinensis* are almost invariably grown as biennials.

PROPAGATION

Seed of alpine species should be sown in a cold frame in early spring.

Cuttings of non-flowering shoots of perennial hybrid and species pinks can be taken in summer.

Dianthus
'Brilliance' (Modern Pink)

Zone 5
Height: 1ft. (30cm) Spread: 2ft. (60cm)

Dianthus callizonus

Zone 5
Height: 8in. (20cm) Spread: 18in. (45 cm)

Dianthus chinensis 'Carpet Series'

Zone 7
Height: 1ft. (30cm) Spread: 9in. (22cm)
Short-lived

Dianthus 'Cranmere Pool'
A.G.M. (Modern Pink)

Zone 3
Height: 18in. (45 cm) Spread: 1ft. (30cm)

Dianthus 'Dainty Dame'
(Modern pink)

Zone 3
Height: 6in. (15cm) Spread: 8in. (20cm)

Dianthus deltoids
A.G.M. (Maiden pink)

Zone 3
Height: 8in. (20cm) Spread: 1ft. (30cm)

Dianthus deltoides
'Leuchtfunk'

Zone 3
Height: 8in. (20cm) Spread: 1ft. (30cm)

Dianthus 'Devon Dove' A.G.M.
(PBR) (Modern Pink)

Zone 3
Height: 18in. (45 cm) Spread: 1ft. (30cm)

Dianthus
'Dewdrop' (Modern pink)

Zone 3
Height: 18in. (45 cm) Spread: 1ft. (30cm)

Dianthus
'Doris' A.G.M. (Modern Pink)

Zone 3
Height: 18in. (45 cm) Spread: 1ft. (30cm)

Dianthus 'Gran's Favourite'
A.G.M. (Modern Pink)

Zone 3
Height: 1ft. (30cm) Spread: 8in. (20cm)

Dianthus gratianopolitanus
A.G.M. (Cheddar pink)

Zone 3
Height: 6in. (15cm) Spread: 14in. (35cm)

Dianthus 'Haytor Rock'
A.G.M. (Modern pink)

Zone 3
Height: 18in. (45 cm) Spread: 1ft. (30cm)

Dianthus 'Houndspool Ruby'
A.G.M. (Modern pink)

Zone 3
Height: 18in. (45 cm) Spread: 1ft. (30cm)

Dianthus 'Inshriach Dazzler'
A.G.M. (Alpine pink)

Zone 3
Height: 4in. (10 cm) Spread: 6in. (15cm)

Dianthus knappii

Zone 3
Height: 16in. (40cm) Spread: 1ft. (30cm)

Dianthus 'Mrs Sinkins'
(Old-fashioned pink)

Zone 3
Height: 18in. (45 cm) Spread: 1ft. (30cm)

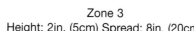

Dianthus myrtinervius
(Alpine pink)

Zone 3
Height: 2in. (5cm) Spread: 8in. (20cm)

Dianthus pavonius
A.G.M. (Alpine pink)

Zone 3
Height: 3in. (8 cm) Spread; 20 cm.(8in.)

Dianthus 'Prince Charming'
(Modern pink)

Zone 3
Height: 4in. (10 cm) Spread: 8in. (20cm)

Dianthus
'Queen of Henri' (Modern Pink)

Zone 3
Height: 18in. (45 cm) Spread: 8in. (20cm)

Dianthus 'Rose Joy'
A.G.M (Modern pink)

Zone 3
Height: 18in. (45 cm) Spread: 8in. (20cm)

Dianthus 'Royal Velvet'
(Modern pink)

Zone 3
Height: 18in. (45 cm) Spread: 8in. (20cm)

Dianthus superbus
(Alpine pink)

Zone 4
Height and spread: 8in. (20cm)

Dianthus 'Valda Wyatt'
A.G.M. (Modern pink)

Zone 3
Height and spread: 1ft. (30cm)

Dianthus 'Waithman Beauty'
(Modern pink)

Zone 3
Height: 1ft. (30cm) Spread: 8in. (20cm)

Dianthus 'Whatfield Joy'
(Modern pink)

Zone 3
Height: 8in. (20cm) Spread: 4in. (10 cm)

Dianthus 'Widecombe Fair'
(Modern pink)

Zone 3
Height: 1ft. (30cm) Spread: 8in. (20cm)

DIASCIA *(Scrophulariaceae)*

Common names: Twinspur

A genus of 50 annuals and perennials from the Drakensberg mountains of Southern Africa. They are long-flowering, mostly herbaceous, and generally short-lived. Some are suckering, and can be invasive. The leaves are ovate to linear, toothed. The flowers are borne in terminal racemes and are tubular, and five-lobed, with an upper spurred pair and three lower, larger ones; the upper lobes have a translucent window at the base. The flowering season is all summer provided they are dead-headed.

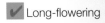 Long-flowering

✗ Prone to slug damage
✗ Short-lived

CULTIVATION
Grow in moist, well-drained soil in sun. Dead-head regularly. They dislike winter wet, summer drought and heavy soil. Shear over after flowering.

PROPAGATION
Seed should be sown at 64°F (18°C) in a cold frame as soon as ripe. Suckering species may be divided in spring. Softwood cuttings can be taken in spring, and semi-ripe cuttings in summer.

Diascia barberae 'Belmore Beauty'

Zone 8
Height: 10in. (25 cm) Spread: 20in. (50cm)
Variegated foliage

D

D

Diascia
'Coral Belle' A.G.M (PBR)

Zone 8
Height: 1ft. (30cm) Spread: 8in. (20cm)

Diascia
'Eclat'

Zone 8
Height: 1ft. (30cm) Spread: 10in. (25 cm)

Diascia
'Elizabeth'

Zone 8
Height: 1ft. (30cm) Spread: 14in. (35cm)

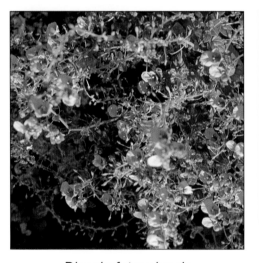

Diascia fetcaniensis

Zone 8
Height: 10in. (25 cm) Spread: 1ft. (30cm)

Diascia integerrima

Zone 8
Height: 1ft. (30cm) Spread: 30in. (75cm)
Invasive

Diascia
'Joyce's Choice' A.G.M.

Zone 8
Height: 1ft. (30cm) Spread: 8in. (20cm)

Diascia
'Lady Valerie' A.G.M.

Zone 8
Height: 1ft. (30cm) Spread: 8in. (20cm)

Diascia rigescens A.G.M.

Zone 8
Height and spread: 16in. (40cm)
Requires staking

Diascia
'Rose Queen'

Zone 8
Height: 18in. (45 cm) Spread: 1ft. (30cm)

Diascia
'Ruby Field' A.G.M.

Zone 8
Height: 10in. (25 cm) Spread: 18in. (45 cm)

Diascia vigilis
A.G.M.

Zone 8
Height: 1ft. (30cm) Spread: 45 cm.(18in.)

DICENTRA *(Papaveraceae)*
Common names: Bleeding heart; Dutchman's breeches

A genus of 20 annuals and perennials found in moist, woodland habitats in Asia and North America. They may be rhizomatous, fibrous-rooted or have fleshy tap roots, and some are highly invasive. The foliage is much-divided and fern-like. The pendent flowers are borne in arching panicles or racemes. Each flower has two pouched outer petals forming a heart-shaped outline, and two inner ones forming a hood over the anthers.

✔ Good cut flowers
✔ Low allergen
✔ Handsome foliage

✘ Prone to slug damage
✘ All parts poisonous
✘ Foliage skin-irritant

CULTIVATION
Grow in moist, humus-rich, fertile soil in part shade, except for *D. spectabilis*, which prefers full sun.

PROPAGATION
Seed should be sown in a cold frame as soon as it is rips, or in spring, at which time they can be divided. Root cuttings of *D.spectabilis* can be taken in winter.

Dicentra
'Adrian Bloom'

Zone 5
Height: 16in. (40cm) Spread: 18in. (45 cm)

Dicentra
'Bacchanal' A.G.M.

Zone 5
Height: 18in. (45 cm) Spread: 2ft. (60cm)

Dicentra
'King of Hearts'

Zone 5
Height: 1ft. (30cm) Spread: 18in. (45 cm)

Dicentra 'Pearl Drops'

Zone 5
Height: 1ft. (30cm) Spread: indefinite
Invasive

Dicentra scandens
(Climbing dicentra)

Zone 6
Height: 6ft. (2m) Spread: 18in. (45 cm)

Dicentra spectabilis
A.G.M.

Zone 6
Height: 3ft. (90cm) Spread: 18in. (45 cm)

Dicentra spectabilis
'Alba' A.G.M.

Zone 6
Height: 3ft. (90cm) Spread: 18in. (45 cm)

Dicentra spectabilis
'Gold Heart' (PBR)

Zone 6
Height: 3ft. (90cm) Spread: 18in. (45 cm)

Dicentra
'Spring Morning'

Zone 5
Height and spread: 18in. (45 cm)

DICKSONIA *(Dicksoniaceae)*

Common names: Tree fern

A genus of 25 species of semi-evergreen or evergreen ferns, which may be tree-like, with a trunk, or creeping, found in upland forest in Australasia, Asia and South America. They have trunk-like rhizomes (caudices) atop of which are pinnatifid or two- to four-pinnate, spreading fronds. Their sori are round, and run along the under margin of the frond segments.

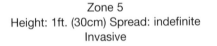

✔ Architectural plants
✔ Evergreen
✔ Handsome foliage
✔ Disease-free
✔ Pest-free

CULTIVATION
Grow in acid, humus-rich, soil in full or part shade. Hose over in hot dry spells.

PROPAGATION
Spores should be sown at 61°F (16°C) as soon as they are ripe.

Dicksonia antarctica A.G.M. (Soft tree fern; man fern; woolly tree fern)

Zone 8
Height: 15ft. (15m); Spread: 12ft. (4m)

Dicksonia squarrosa

A.G.M. Zone 9
Height: 18ft. (6 m) Spread: 12ft. (4m)

DICTAMNUS *(Rutaceae)*

Common names: Burning bush; dittany

A genus of but one species, *D. albus*, of perennial with several forms, from dry grassland in Eurasia, China and Japan. The leaves are pinnate, spiny and lemon scented. The flowers are asymmetrical, white or purple, and borne in long racemes, followed by fruits. The fruits and flowers produce a volatile, aromatic oil, which can be ignited on hot days.

✔ Flowers perfumed	✘ All parts poisonous
✔ Good cut flowers	✘ Foliage skin-irritant
✔ Good for drying for winter	✘ Highly allergenic
✔ Drought-tolerant	✘ Resent disturbance
✔ Foliage aromatic	

CULTIVATION
Grow in well-drained soil in sun or part shade.

PROPAGATION
Seed should be sown in a cold frame as soon as it is ripe. Division can be tried in spring or autumn, but is not tolerated well.

Dictamnus albus

Zone 3
Height: 3ft. (90cm) Spread: 2ft. (60cm)

Dictamnus albus
var. 'Purpureus'

Height: 3ft. (90cm) Spread: 2ft. (60cm)

DIEFFENBACHIA *(Araceae)*

Common names: Mother-in-law's tongue; Dumb cane

A genus of 30 species of evergreen perennials from tropical forest in the West Indies, North America and South America. They are grown for their foliage, as they seldom flower in cultivation. The leaves are large, paddle-shaped, fleshy, and usually handsomely-marked. The flowers take the form of cream spathes, and are borne from time to time throughout the year.

✔ Handsome foliage	✘ Prone to aphid attack	✘ Sap is skin irritant
	✘ All parts poisonous	✘ Rarely flowers in cultivation

CULTIVATION
Under glass, grow in loam-based potting compost in bright filtered light and high humidity. Water sparingly in winter, and allow full light. Repot in spring.

Out of doors, grow in moist, well-drained soil in part shade.

PROPAGATION
Tip cuttings can be taken in spring or summer. If stem sections containing a growth bud are laid flat on the soil surface, they will root.

Dieffenbachia picta

Zone 10
Height: 10ft. (3m) Spread: 2ft. (60cm)

Dieffenbachia picta
'Exotica'

Zone 10
Height: 3ft. (90cm) Spread: 16in. (40cm)

Dieffenbachia picta
'Super Tropic'

Zone 10
Height: 3ft. (90cm) Spread: 16in. (40cm)

DIERAMA *(Iridaceae)*

Common names: Angel's fishing rod; wandflower

A genus of 44 species of cormous perennials from mountainous regions of South Africa, tropical Africa and Ethiopia. The leaves are basal, semi-erect, narrowly linear and gray-green in some species. The flowers are bell- or funnel-shaped, purple, pink or white and borne in arching spikes.

✔ Good cut flowers	✔ Handsome foliage	✔ Pest-free
✔ Evergreen	✔ Handsome seed-heads	
✔ Low allergen	✔ Disease-free	

CULTIVATION
Plant corms 3in. (8 cm) deep in well-drained, humus-rich soil in spring. Do not allow to dry out in summer. Divide in spring, but divisions are slow to establish.

PROPAGATION
Seed should be sown in a cold frame as soon as it is ripe. Division can be done in spring, and divisions are slow to establish, but settle down in a season or two.

Dierama medium

Zone 9
Height and spread: 2ft. (60cm)

Dierama pendulum

Zone 7
Height: 6ft. (2m) Spread: 2ft. (60cm)
Architectural plant

Dierama pulcherrimum

Zone 7
Height: 5ft. (1.5m) Spread: 2ft. (60cm)
Architectural plant

DIETES *(Iridaceae)*
Common names: None

A genus of half a dozen species of rhizomatous, evergreen perennials found in tropical and South Africa, and Lord Howe Island, Australia. Their habitat varies from moist forest margins to dry bushland, to mountain cliffs. The leaves are basal, fleshy, erect, and linear or sword-shaped. The flowers are flat, short-lived, iris-like, and borne in succession from spring to summer.

✔ Evergreen
✔ Drought-tolerant
✔ Disease-free
✔ Pest-free

✘ Resent disturbance

CULTIVATION
Grow in moist, well-drained soil in sun or part shade.

PROPAGATION
Seed should be sown at 59°F (15°C) in spring or autumn. Division can be done in spring, but the divisions are very slow to establish.

Dietes bicolor

Zone 9
Height: 3ft. (90cm) Spread: 1ft. (30cm)

Dietes grandiflora

Zone 9
Height: 3ft. (90cm) Spread: 1ft. (30cm)

DIGITALIS (*Scrophulariaceae*)
Common names: Foxglove

A genus of 20 species of biennials and short-lived perennials from Eurasia and North Africa. They occur in grassy slopes, woodland and subalpine meadows. They are tall, architectural plants, but do not, however, require to be staked except in exposed sites. The British native foxglove, *D. purpurea* is a biennial, or at best a very short-lived perennial. The leaves are in basal rosettes, oblong or obovate, toothed or entire. The flowers are in one-sided upright racemes, tubular or bell-shaped, and often marked internally.

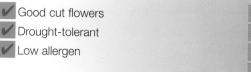

✔ Good cut flowers
✔ Drought-tolerant
✔ Low allergen

✘ All parts poisonous
✘ Foliage is skin-irritant
✘ Mildew prone
✘ Self-seeds

CULTIVATION
Grow in sun or part shade in any soil that is not waterlogged or tired. They self-seeds gently, so should be deadheaded as necessary.

PROPAGATION
Seed should be sown in a cold frame in spring.

Digitalis ferruginea
(Rusty foxglove)

Zone 7
Height: 4ft. (1.2m) Spread: 18in. (45 cm)

Digitalis
'Foxy Primrose'

Zone 5
Height: 3ft. (90cm) Spread: 1ft. (30cm)

Digitalis
'Glory of Roundway'

Zone 5
Height: 3ft. (90cm) Spread: 1ft. (30cm)

Digitalis grandiflora
A.G.M. (Yellow foxglove)

Zone 4
Height: 3ft. (90cm) Spread: 18in. (45 cm)

Digitalis
'John Innes Tetra'

(Zone 6)
Height: 3ft. (90cm) Spread: 1ft. (30cm)

Digitalis lanata
A.G.M. (Grecian foxglove)

Zone 7
Height: 2ft. (60cm) Spread: 1ft. (30cm)

Digitalis lutea
(Straw foxglove)

Zone 4
Height: 2ft. (60cm) Spread: 1ft. (30cm)

Digitalis x mertonensis
A.G.M.

Zone 5
Height: 3ft. (90cm) Spread: 2ft. (60cm)

Digitalis purpurea
(Biennial foxglove)

Zone 6
Height: 6ft. (2m) Spread: 2ft. (60cm)

DIONAEA *(Droseraceae)*

Common names: Venus' fly trap

A genus of but a single species of insectivorous perennial found in coastal bogs in the Carolinas, in eastern U.S.A. It is rosette-forming, and has yellow leaves, which have winged stalks and are spiny-edged. The flowers are white, cup-shaped, and borne in umbels on bare stems in early and midsummer.

✔ Handsome foliage	✘ Cultivation
✔ Disease-free	✘ Grow in acid, moist soil in sun.
✔ Pest-free	

PROPAGATION
Seed should be sown at 55°F (13°C) in a pot in a tray of water. Germination is erratic. Division can be done in spring, or leaf cuttings can be taken in early summer.

Dionaea muscipula

Zone 8
Height: 1ft. (30cm) Spread: 6in. (15cm)

DIPHYLLEIA *(Berberidaceae)*

Common names: Umbrella leaf

A genus of three species of rhizomatous perennials from Japan and North America, where they grow at watersides and in woodland. The leaves are large, toothed and peltate. The flowers are bowl-shaped, six-petalled, white, and borne in terminal cymes in late spring and early summer. They lose their petals very quickly, and are followed by blue berries.

✔ Good for drying for winter	✘ Prone to slug damage
✔ Handsome foliage	
✔ Have berries after flowering	

CULTIVATION
Grow in moist, humus-rich soil in full or part shade.

PROPAGATION
Seed should be sown in a cold frame as soon as it is ripe. The rhizomes can be divided in spring.

Diphylleia cymosa

Zone 7
Height: 3ft. (90cm) Spread: 1ft. (30cm)

DIPLARRHENA *(Iridaceae)*
Common names: None

A genus of just two species of evergreen perennials from Tasmania and south-east Australia where they grow in moist mountain slopes. The leaves are in basal clumps, and are long and linear. The flowers are perfumed, short-lived, white, iris-like, and enclosed by a pair of bracts; the inner tepals have yellow marks. They are solitary, and borne in late spring to early summer.

- ✔ Evergreen
- ✔ Good cut flowers
- ✔ Flowers perfumed
- ✔ Handsome seed-heads
- ✔ Disease-free
- ✔ Pest-free

CULTIVATION
Under glass, grow in loam-free potting compost in bright filtered light. Water freely during growth, but sparingly in winter.

Out of doors, grow in acid to neutral, moist, sharply-drained, humus-rich soil in sun or part shade in a warm corner.

PROPAGATION
Seed should be sown in a cold frame in spring or autumn. Divide the rhizomes in spring.

Diplarrhena moraea

Zone 7
Height: 2ft. (60cm) Spread: 10in. (25 cm)

DISA *(Orchidaceae)*
Common names: None

A genus of 100 species of terrestrial, cool-growing orchids found at high and low altitude in tropical Africa, South Africa and Madagascar, often near running water. They are rhizomatous, and mostly herbaceous, but some are evergreen. The leaves are lance-shaped or ovate. The flowers are red, veined in gold, with upper hooded and lower spreading perianth segments, and borne in terminal corymbs or racemes.

- ✔ Handsome foliage

CULTIVATION
This is not easy. Grow in peaty, mossy, sandy soil in part shade. Keep cool and humid in summer, and water freely, avoiding the foliage. Water very sparingly in winter, and also keep cool then too.

PROPAGATION
Divide in spring after growth starts.

Disa Kewensis

Zone 10
Height: 2ft. (60cm) Spread: 8in. (20cm)

Disa uniflora

Zone 10
Height: 2ft. (60cm) Spread: 8in. (20cm)

D

DISPORUM *(Convallariaceae)*

Common names: None

A genus of 20 species of perennials found in woodland in Asia, the Himalaya and temperate North America. The leaves are ovate or lance-shaped, scalloped, and alternate. The flowers are mostly pendent, narrow bells or tubules or cups, borne in few-flowered umbels in spring, and followed in autumn by berries, which may be orange, red or black.

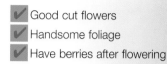

✔ Good cut flowers	✘ Prone to slug damage
✔ Handsome foliage	
✔ Have berries after flowering	

CULTIVATION
Grow in moist, well-drained humus-rich soil in half or full shade.

PROPAGATION
Seed should be sown in a cold frame in autumn. The rhizomes can be divided in spring as growth starts.

Disporum sessile
'Variegatum'

Zone 7
Height: 18in. (45 cm) Spread: 3ft. (90cm)

Disporum smithii

Zone 6
Height: 2ft. (60cm) Spread: 1ft. (30cm)

DODECATHEON *(Primulaceae)*

Common names: Shooting stars; American cowslip

A genus of 14 species of summer-dormant perennials from North America, where they grow in wet grassland, woodland or even alpine meadows. The basal leaves are ovate or spoon-shaped. The flowers are pendent, resembling cyclamen, with reflexed petals, and styles exposed, borne in umbels in spring.

✔ Good cut flowers	✘ Prone to slug damage

CULTIVATION
Grow in acid, well-drained, humus-rich soil in sun or part shade. Do not allow to dry out in the growing season. *D. pulchellum* requires moist shade.

PROPAGATION
Seed should be exposed to cold, and sown in a cold frame as soon as it is ripe. Division can be done in spring.

Dodecatheon meadia
A.G.M.

Zone 3
Height: 16in. (40cm) Spread: 10in. (25 cm)

D

Dodecatheon meadia
forma. *album*

Zone 3
Height: 16in. (40cm) Spread: 10in. (25 cm)

Dodecatheon pulchellum
A.G.M.

Zone 5
Height: 14in. (35cm) Spread: 6in. (15cm)

DORONICUM (*Asteraceae*)
Common names: Leopard's bane

A genus of 35 species of herbaceous perennials from scrubland, woodland, heathland and meadows across Eurasia, and in Siberia. They may be tuberous-rooted or rhizomatous. The leaves are basal and stem, ovate or elliptic. The flowers are daisy-like, yellow, solitary, or in corymbs, borne in spring or early summer.

✔ Good cut flowers

✘ Prone to slug damage
✘ Need to lift & divide often
✘ Mildew prone

CULTIVATION
Grow in sharply-drained but moist, humus-rich soil in part shade.

PROPAGATION
Seed should be sown in a cold frame in spring.

Doronicum
'Finesse'

Zone 6
Height: 20in. (50cm) Spread: 3ft. (90cm)

Doronicum
'Little Leo'

Zone 6
Height: 8in. (20cm) Spread: 1ft. (30cm)

Doronicum orientale
'Magnificum'

Zone 5
Height: 20in. (50cm) Spread: 3ft. (90cm)

Doronicum pardalianches

Zone 6
Height and spread: 3ft. (90cm)

Doronicum plantagineum

Zone 6
Height: 32in. (80cm) Spread: 18in. (45 cm)

DRABA *(Brassicaceae)*
Common names: None

A genus of 300 species of annuals and perennials from mountainous screes and rocky areas of Northern temperate and arctic regions, and temperate South America. The perennials are evergreen, and cushion-forming . The foliage is in rosettes of linear, oblong, ovate or spoon-shaped leaves.

✔ Evergreen

Draba longisiliqua
A.G.M.

Zone 6
Height: 4in. (10 cm) Spread: 8in. (20cm)

CULTIVATION
This is not too easy. Grow in sharply-drained, soil in full sun. Avoid wetting the foliage at all times, summer and winter alike—this means they need alpine house treatment in temperate climates.

PROPAGATION
Seed should be exposed to cold and then sown in a cold frame in autumn. Rosettes can be rooted in late spring.

DRACUNCULUS *(Araceae)*
Common names: Dragon arum

A genus of three species of tuberous perennials from the Mediterranean, the Canary Islands, and Madeira, where they grow on hillsides, waste ground and stony ground. The leaves are basal, pedate, and green flecked brown. The flowers have a large maroon spathe, a black spadix, are malodorous and borne in spring or summer.

✔ Good cut flowers
✔ Drought-tolerant
✔ Handsome foliage
✔ Architectural plant
✔ Disease-free
✔ Pest-free

✘ Need to lift & divide often
✘ Flowers malodorous

CULTIVATION
Plant tubers 6in. (15cm) deep in spring or autumn in well-drained, humus-rich soil in a warm corner in sun or part shade. Protect against frost in winter.

PROPAGATION
Offsets should be separated in spring or autumn.

Dracunculus vulgaris

Zone 9
Height: 5ft. (1.5m) Spread: 2ft. (60cm)

DRYAS *(Rosaceae)*
Common names: Mountain avens

A genus of three species of subshrubs found on rock ledges and cliffs in alpine and arctic regions of the world. Their leaves are leathery, oak-like, wrinkled and dark green. The flowers are single, white, solitary cup-or bell-shaped, appearing in late spring to early summer, and followed by fluffy seed-heads.

D

✔ Handsome foliage

✔ Handsome seed-heads

✔ Low allergen

✔ Disease-free

✔ Pest-free

CULTIVATION
Grow in humus-rich, well-drained soil in sun or part shade.

PROPAGATION
Seed should be sown in a cold frame as soon as it is ripe. Softwood cuttings can be taken in early summer. Rooted stems can be detached in spring.

Dryas octopetala
A.G.M.

Zone 2
Height: 4in. (10 cm) Spread: 3ft. (90cm)

DRYOPTERIS *(Dryopteridaceae)*
Common names: Buckler fern

A genus of 200 species of terrestrial ferns found in woodland, watersides, and amongst rocks in the mountains of the temperate northern hemisphere. They are mostly deciduous, but may be evergreen in warm climes or during mild winters in colder areas. The fronds are up to four-pinnate, or pinnatisect, and form shuttlecocks. Spores are produced in sori that are kidney-shaped.

✔ Handsome foliage

✔ Disease free

✔ Pest-free

CULTIVATION
Grow in moist, humus-rich soil in a sheltered corner in sun or part shade.

PROPAGATION
Spores should be sown at 59°F (15°C) as soon as they are ripe, but only *D. affinis* comes true from seed. Division can be carried out in spring or autumn.

Dryopteris affinis A.G.M.
(Golden male fern)
Zone 6
Height and spread: 3ft. (90cm)
Evergreen

Dryopteris affinis 'Crispa Gracilis'

Zone 6
Height and spread: 1ft. (30cm)
Evergreen

Dryopteris affinis 'Cristata'

Zone 6
Height and spread: 3ft. (90cm)
Evergreen

Dryopteris dilatata
'Crispa Whiteside' A.G.M.

Zone 5
Height: 3ft. (90cm) Spread: 4ft. (1.2m)

D

Dryopteris erythrosora
A.G.M.

Zone 8
Height: 2ft. (60cm) Spread: 15in. (38 cm)

Dryopteris filix-mas
'Linearis Polydactyla'

Zone 2
Height and spread: 3ft. (90cm)

E

ECCREMOCARPUS
ECHEVERIA
ECHINACEA
ECHINOPS
ECHIUM
EDRAIANTHUS
ELSCHOLTZIA
ELYMUS
EOMECON
EPIDENDRUM
EPIGAEA
EPILOBIUM
EPIPACTIS
EPIPREMNUM
EPISCIA
ERANTHIS
EREMURUS
ERIGERON
ERINUS
ERIOGONUM
ERIOPHYLLUM
ERODIUM
ERYSIMUM
ERYTHRONIUM
EUCHARIS
EUCOMIS
EUPATORIUM
EUPHORBIA
EURYOPS

ECCREMOCARPUS *(Bignoniaceae)*

Common names: Chilean gloryflower

A genus of five species of climbing perennials found in forest edges and scrubland in Peru and Chile. Their leaves are bipinnate, with a terminal tendril, and opposite, and they may be herbaceous or evergreen. The flowers are asymmetric tubules, borne in terminal racemes from late spring to autumn.

Long-flowering

Handsome foliage

Disease-free

CULTIVATION

Under glass, grow in gritty loam-based potting compost in full light. Water freely during growth, but sparingly in winter.

Out of doors, grow in well-drained soil in sun.

PROPAGATION

Seed should be sown at 61°F (16°C) in late winter/early spring. Tip cuttings can be rooted in spring or summer with bottom heat.

Eccremocarpus scaber
A.G.M.

Zone 9
Height: 15ft. (5m) Spread: 3ft. (90cm)

ECHEVERIA *(Crassulaceae)*

Common names: None

A genus of 150 species of succulents and subshrubs from dry desert lands in Texas, Mexico, and Central and South America. The fleshy leaves are usually in rosettes, and are alternate and spoon-shaped, triangular, linear or cylindrical. The flowers are borne in erect, tall racemes, cymes or panicles from the leaf axils. They have spreading petals, and keeled or angled tubes.

Evergreen

Handsome foliage

✗ Prone to aphid attack

CULTIVATION

Under glass, grow in cactus compost in full light. Water with moderation during growth, and keep just moist in winter.

Out of doors, grow in well-drained, poor soil in sun.

PROPAGATION

Seed should be sown at 66°F (19°C) as soon as is ripe. Offsets can be separated in spring, and leaf or stem cuttings can be rooted in spring.

Echeveria crenulata

Zone 8
Height: 1ft. (30cm) Spread: 20in. (50cm)

Echeveria peacockii

Zone 8
Height: 5in. (12cm) Spread: 10in. (25 cm)

Echeveria
'Perle d'azur'

Zone 8
Height: 1ft. (30cm) Spread: 8in. (20cm)

Echeveria pulvinata
A.G.M.

Zone 8
Height: 1ft. (30cm) Spread: 20in. (50cm)

ECHINACEA *(Asteraceae)*
Common names: None

A genus of nine species of perennials from dry prairie, woodland, and scree in eastern North America. They are rhizomatous, and have black fleshy roots. The leaves are linear or lance-shaped or ovate, toothed or pinnatifid, and bristly. The flowers are solitary, daisy-like, generally with reflexed petals and a prominent central yellow boss, and are borne in summer.

✔ Good cut flowers	✔ Pest-free	✘ Highly allergenic
✔ Repeat-flowering	✔ Attracts bees	✘ Resent disturbance
✔ Disease-free	✔ Attracts butterflies	

E

CULTIVATION
Grow in well-drained, humus-rich soil in sun, or light shade. They will repeat-flower if cut back as the blooms are fading.

PROPAGATION
Seed should be sown at 55°F (13°C) in spring. They can be divided in spring or autumn, but do not enjoy root disturbance, Root cuttings can be taken in late autumn or early winter.

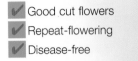

Echinacea pallida

Zone 5
Height: 4ft. (1.2m) Spread: 18in. (45 cm)

Echinacea purpurea

Zone 3
Height: 5ft. (1.5m) Spread: 18in. (45 cm)

Echinacea purpurea
'Elton Knight'

Zone 3
Height: 4ft. (1.2m) Spread: 18in. (45 cm)

Echinacea purpurea
'Kim's Knee High'

Zone 3
Height: 30in. (75cm) Spread: 18in. (45 cm)

Echinacea purpurea
'Magnus'

Zone 3
Height: 5ft. (1.5m) Spread: 45 cm.(18in.)

Echinacea purpurea
'Robert Bloom'

Zone 3
Height: 5ft. (1.5m) Spread: 18in. (45 cm)

E

Echinacea purpurea
'White Lustre'

Zone 3
Height: 5ft. (1.5m) Spread: 18in. (45 cm)

Echinacea purpurea
'White Swan'

Zone 3
Height: 4ft. (1.2m) Spread: 18in. (45 cm)

ECHINOPS *(Asteraceae)*
Common names: Globe thistle

A genus of 120 species of annuals, biennials and perennials from dry, grassland and hot scree slopes across Eurasia, India and mountains of tropical Africa. Their spiny leaves can be simple, or pinnatifid or pinnatisect, and are commonly glaucous or white-woolly. The flowers are spherical, terminal, solitary, and bristly with bracts.

- ✔ Good cut flowers
- ✔ Good for drying for winter
- ✔ Attracts bees
- ✔ Attracts butterflies
- ✔ Drought-tolerant

- ✘ Highly allergenic
- ✘ Self-seeds
- ✘ Prone to aphid attack

CULTIVATION
Grow in any well-drained, poor soil in sun or part shade. Dead-head to prevent self-seedsing.

PROPAGATION
Seed should be sown in mid-spring. Divide in spring or winter.

Echinops bannaticus

Zone 3
Height: 4ft. (1.2m) Spread: 2ft. (60cm)

Echinops ritro
A.G.M.

Zone 3
Height: 2ft. (60cm) Spread: 18in. (45 cm)

E

ECHIUM *(Boraginaceae)*

COMMON NAMES: BUGLOSS

A genus of 40 species of annuals, biennials, and short-lived, evergreen perennials and shrubs from stony rocky hillsides, open woodland, and grasslands in Eurasia, Africa, the Canary Islands, and the Mediterranean region. The leaves are both in basal rosettes and stem, and are hairy and bristly. The flowers are bell- or funnel-shaped, and are borne in spikes or panicles in summer.

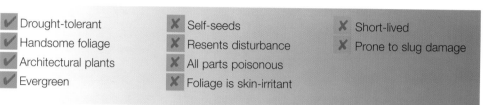

- ✔ Drought-tolerant
- ✔ Handsome foliage
- ✔ Architectural plants
- ✔ Evergreen
- ✘ Self-seeds
- ✘ Resents disturbance
- ✘ All parts poisonous
- ✘ Foliage is skin-irritant
- ✘ Short-lived
- ✘ Prone to slug damage

CULTIVATION

Under glass, grow in loam-based potting compost in full light. Water freely during growth but sparingly in winter.

CULTIVATION

Out of doors, grow in well-drained, fertile soil in sun. Protect against frost in winter.

PROPAGATION

Seed should be sown at 61°F (16°C) in summer.

Echium brevirame
Zone 9
Height: 8ft. (2.5m) Spread: 2ft. (60cm)

Echium decaisnei
Zone 9
Height: 6ft. (2m) Spread: 3ft. (90cm)

Echium pininiana
(Bugloss)
Zone 9
Height: 12ft. (4m) Spread: 3ft. (90cm)

Echium russicum
Zone 8
Height: 2ft. (60cm) Spread: 3ft. (90cm)

Echium webbii
Zone 9
Height: 18in. (45 cm) Spread: 8in. (20cm)

Echium wildpretii
Zone 9
Height: 6ft. (2m) Spread: 2ft. (60cm)

EDRAIANTHUS *(Campanulaceae)*
Common names: Grassy bells

A genus of two dozen species of short-lived perennials from sunny, well-drained regions of the Mediterranean across to the Caucasus mountains. They may be evergreen or herbaceous. The foliage is linear, grass-like. The flowers are bell-shaped, with leafy bracts, and solitary or in terminal heads, in summer.

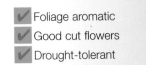

- ✔ Drought-tolerant
- ✘ Short-lived
- ✘ Prone to slug damage

Edraianthus pumilio
A.G.M.

Zone 6
Height: 1in. (2.5 cm) Spread: 6in. (15cm)

CULTIVATION
Grow in sharply-drained, humus-rich, limy soil in sun. Protect against winter wet.

PROPAGATION
Seed should be sown in an open frame in autumn. Softwood sideshoot cuttings can be taken in early summer.

ELSCHOLTZIA *(Lamiaceae)*
Common names: None

A genus of 35 species of annuals, perennials and subshrubs from dry hill- and road-sides in East and Central Asia. The leaves are aromatic, lance-shaped or ovate, and opposite. The flowers are two-lipped, tubular, in dense panicles in early summer.

- ✔ Foliage aromatic
- ✔ Good cut flowers
- ✔ Drought-tolerant
- ✔ Disease-free
- ✔ Pest-free

Elscholtzia stauntonii

Zone 4
Height: 4ft. (1.2m) Spread: 3ft. (90cm)

CULTIVATION
Grow in well-drained, fertile soil in sun.

PROPAGATION
Seed should be sown as soon as it is ripe at 55°F (13°C).Softwood cuttings can be taken in summer.

ELYMUS *(Poaceae)*
Common names: Wild rye

A genus of 150 species of grasses that are mostly perennial, from sandy areas in temperate regions in both hemispheres. They may be rhizomatous or tufted. The leaves are linear, flat, or rolled, and often blue or blue-green. The flowering spike consists of alternately-arranged, flattened spikelets. The genus includes the highly invasive couch grass, *E. repens,* but the species included here are non-invasive.

- ✔ Evergreen
- ✔ Handsome foliage
- ✘ Highly allergenic

CULTIVATION
Grow in moist, fertile, well-drained soil in sun. Shear back to ground level in autumn or late winter.

Elymus hispidus
(Blue wild rye)

Zone 5
Height: 30in. (75cm) Spread: 16in. (40cm)

Elymus magellanicus

Zone 5
Height: 6in. (15cm) Spread: 1ft. (30cm)

EOMECON *(Papaveraceae)*
Common names: None

A monospecific genus of *E. chionantha*, a highly invasive but beautiful rhizomatous perennial from watersides in East China. The leaves are heart-shaped, fleshy. The flowers are poppy-like, white, borne in loose panicles from late spring to midsummer.

✔ Handsome foliage

✘ Invasive
✘ Mildew prone
✘ Prone to slug damage

CULTIVATION
Grow in any well-drained moist, humus-rich, poor soil in sun or part shade. Feeding enhances its invasiveness.

PROPAGATION
Sow seed, divide or separate runners, all in spring.

Eomecon chionantha

Zone 7
Height: 16in. (40cm) Spread: indefinite

EPIDENDRUM *(Orchidaceae)*
Common names: None

A genus of 750 species of evergreen orchids from mountain forests up to 3250ft. (1000m) in all three Americas. They may be terrestrial or epiphytic, and vary widely from species to species, as do their leaves. Some have pseudobulbs. The flowers are borne in panicles or racemes.

✔ Evergreen

✘ Prone to aphid attack

CULTIVATION
Under glass, grow in terrestrial or epiphytic compost in high humidity and bright filtered light. Water freely during growth. Mist once or twice daily. Water sparingly in winter, and types with pseudobulbs should be kept dry then.

PROPAGATION
Divide when pot-bound, in spring.

Epidendrum 'Ballerina'

Zone 10
Height: 1ft. (30cm) Spread: 6in. (15cm)

E

EPIGAEA *(Ericaceae)*
Common names: Trailing arbutus; Mayflower

A genus of three species of evergreen subshrubs and shrubs from woodland in North America, Japan and Turkey. Their leaves are entire, tough, ovate or oblong, veined and dark green. The flowers are small, bell- or urn-shaped, or tubular, and borne n clusters or racemes in spring.

✔ Evergreen
✔ Handsome foliage

CULTIVATION
Under glass, grow in ericaceous compost in an alpine house in indirect light.

Out of doors, grow in acid, moist, humus-rich soil in part or deep shade.

PROPAGATION
Seed should be surface-sown at 55°F (13°C) as soon as ripe, and kept moist and warm until it germinates. Water with soft water.

Epigaea repens

Zone 2
Height: 3in. (8 cm) Spread: 1ft. (30cm)

EPILOBIUM *(Onagraceae)*
Common names: Willow herb

A genus of 200 species of annuals, biennials, perennials and subshrubs from wasteland, scree, and river gravel across the temperate parts of the world. The leaves are ovate or linear. The flowers are four-petalled, borne singly or in racemes, sometime over a long period from summer to autumn. Some species can be inveterate self-seedsers, and invasive, so should be allowed into the garden with caution.

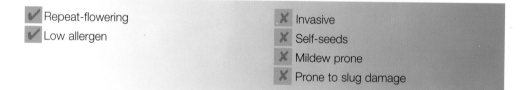
✔ Repeat-flowering
✔ Low allergen

✘ Invasive
✘ Self-seeds
✘ Mildew prone
✘ Prone to slug damage

CULTIVATION
Grow in moist, humus-rich, well-drained soil in sun or part shade. Dead-head to prevent self-seedsing and to encourage repeat-flowering.

PROPAGATION
Seed should be sown in a cold frame as soon as ripe. Division can be done in spring or autumn.

Epilobium angustifolium
'Album'

Zone 3
Height: 5ft. (1.5m) Spread:indefinite

Epilobium angustifolium (Rose bay willow herb; Fireweed)

Zone 3
Height: 5ft. (1.5m) Spread: indefinite

Epilobium dodonei
(Willow herb)

Zone 6
Height: 3ft. (90cm) Spread: indefinite

Epilobium glabellum

Zone 6
Height and spread: 8in. (20cm)
Short-lived

Epilobium glabellum
'White Wonder'
Zone 6
Height and spread: 8in. (20cm)
Short-lived

Epilobium hirsutum 'Variegatum'
(Codlins and cream)

Zone 8
Height: 6ft. (2m) Spread: indefinite

EPIMEDIUM *(Berberidaceae)*

Common names: Barrenwort; Bishop's mitre

A genus of 40 perennials from shady scrub or woodland from the Mediterranean across to temperate East Asia. They may be evergreen or herbaceous, and are rhizomatous. The leaves are mainly basal, two- or three-ternate, heart-shaped with pointed tips, and bronze-tinted in some species. The flowers are delicate, saucer- or cup-shaped, spurred, and borne in lax panicles or racemes.

✔ Low allergen
✔ Handsome foliage
✔ Good ground cover in shade

CULTIVATION
Grow in humus-rich, well-drained, fertile soil in part shade, although *E. x versicolor* will tolerate full sun. Shear over in late winter or early spring for best results.

PROPAGATION
Seed should be sown in a cold frame as soon as it is ripe. Divide in autumn.

Epimedium davidii

Zone 7
Height: 1ft. (30cm) Spread: 18in. (45 cm)

Epimedium grandiflorum
A.G.M.

Zone 5
Height and spread: 1ft. (30cm)

Epimedium x rubrum
A.G.M.

Zone 5
Height and spread: 1ft. (30cm)

Epimedium x versicolor

Zone 5
Height: 1ft. (30cm) Spread: 3ft. (90cm)
Evergreen

Epimedium x versicolor
'Sulphureum' A.G.M.
Zone 5
Height: 1ft. (30cm) Spread: 3ft. (90cm)
Evergreen

EPIPACTIS *(Orchidaceae)*

Common names: Helleborine

A genus of 24 species of terrestrial, rhizomatous orchids found in on dunes, in marshland, woodland or alpine meadows across the temperate northern hemisphere, plus a few from tropical Mexico, Africa and Thailand. Their leaves are ovate or lance-shaped, ribbed, and spirally arranged. The flowers have upper segments that curve in to form a helmet, with the lower lip forming a cup with a heart-shaped lobe below, and are borne in spikes. They make big colonies when happy.

✔ Handsome foliage	✘ Prone to slug damage

CULTIVATION
Grow in moist, well-drained humus-rich soil in part or full shade.

PROPAGATION
Division in spring, ensuring that each rhizome segment has a growing point.

Epipactis gigantea

Zone 6
Height: 16in. (40cm) Spread: 4ft. (1.2m)

EPIPREMNUM *(Araceae)*

Common names: None

A genus of eight species of evergreen climbers found in forest in the Western Pacific and South-East Asia. They are grown for their foliage, which may be entire or pinnate, even on the same plant, and is alternate.

✔ Evergreen	✘ All parts poisonous
✔ Handsome foliage	✘ Sap is skin-irritant
	✘ Requires support

CULTIVATION
Under glass, grow in loam-based potting compost in bright filtered or full light. Water freely during growth but with moderation in winter. Support must be provided. Tip-prune in spring to encourage branching.

Out of doors, grow in moist, well-drained soil in sun or part shade. Prune in spring for shape and size.

PROPAGATION
Layer in spring or summer. Leaf-bud or stem-tip cuttings may be rooted with bottom heat in summer.

Epipremnum aureum

Zone 10
Height: 40ft. (12 m) Spread: 6ft. (2m)

EPISCIA *(Gesneriaceae)*

Common names: Carpet plant; Flame flower

A genus of six species of stoloniferous terrestrial or epiphytic perennials from tropical forest and rocky regions in South America and Mexico. They have handsome, elliptic or oblong, hairy leaves in rosettes or whorls. The flowers are five-lobed salvers, and are solitary or borne in racemes from the leaf axils from spring to autumn.

Episcia cupreata

Zone 10
Height: 6in. (15cm) Spread: indefinite
Invasive

✔ Long-flowering   ✖ Prone to aphid attack
✔ Handsome foliage

CULTIVATION
Under glass, grow in loam-free, vermiculite-enriched potting compost, in bright filtered light and high humidity. Water with moderation during growth; keep just moist in winter.

Out of doors, grow in moist, sharply-draining, humus-rich soil in part shade.

PROPAGATION
Seed should be surface-sown at 77°F (25°C) as soon as ripe, or in spring. Separate plantlets, or divide in early to midsummer. Stem cutting may be rooted with bottom heat in early and midsummer.

ERANTHIS *(Ranunculaceae)*

Common names: Winter aconite

A genus of seven species of tuberous, perennials from wet woodland in Eurasia. The leaves are basal, pinnate or palmately lobed, and stem, forming a ruff below the flower. These are cup-shaped, and appear in early spring.

✔ Handsome foliage   ✖ Prone to slug damage
✔ Attracts bees   ✖ All parts poisonous
                             ✖ Sap is skin-irritant

CULTIVATION
Plant tubers 2in. (5cm) deep in autumn in fertile, humus-rich soil in sun or light shade; do not allow to dry out in summer.

PROPAGATION
Seed should be sown in a cold frame in spring. The tubers can be separated after flowering.

Eranthis hyemalis
A.G.M.

Zone 5
Height: 3in. (8 cm) Spread: 2in. (5cm)

EREMURUS *(Asphodelaceae)*

Common names: Foxtail lily; desert candle

A genus of 50 species of perennials found in semi-desert areas and dry grasslands of Central and West Asia. They have fleshy roots which radiate fan-wise just under the soil surface, and are easily damaged. The leaves are in basal rosettes, linear, folded. The flowers are star-shaped, have conspicuous stamens and are borne in tall dense racemes. They require winter cold to induce them to flower.

- ✔ Good cut flowers
- ✔ Drought-tolerant
- ✔ Low allergen
- ✔ Architectural plants
- ✘ Require staking
- ✘ Prone to slug damage

E

CULTIVATION
Grow in a sheltered corner in well-drained, gritty soil in full sun.

PROPAGATION
Seed should be sown in a cold frame in autumn. Division can be carried out after flowering.

Eremurus himalaicus
(Himalayan desert candle)

Zone 3
Height: 6ft. (2m) Spread: 2ft. (60cm)

Eremurus robustus
(Giant desert candle)

Zone 8
Height: 10ft. (3m) Spread: 3ft. (90cm)

Eremurus stenophyllus
(Bunge desert candle)

Zone 5
Height: 4ft. (1.2m) Spread: 2ft. (60cm)

ERIGERON *(Asteraceae)*

Common names: Fleabane

A genus of 200 species of annuals, biennials and perennials with world-wide distribution in dry grassland and mountains, but in North America in particular. The perennials may be bushy plants or low-growing alpines. The leaves are basal, large and oblong, or lance-shaped, smaller, narrower stem. The daisy-like flowers may be single or double, solitary or in corymbs, and are borne over a long season in summer. *E. karvinskianus* is the longest-flowering of all hardy perennials as it flowers for at least six months. They are good seaside plants.

- ✔ Repeat-flowering
- ✔ Good cut flowers
- ✔ Drought-tolerant
- ✔ Attracts bees
- ✔ Attracts butterflies
- ✘ Prone to slug damage
- ✘ Need to lift & divide often
- ✘ Highly allergenic

CULTIVATION
Grow in humus-rich, well-drained soil in sun. Do not allow to dry out in summer. Dead-head to encourage repeat-flowering.

PROPAGATION
Seed should be sown in a cold frame in spring. Divide in spring, when basal cuttings can also be taken.

Erigeron aurantiacus
(Daisy fleabane)

Zone 6
Height and spread: 1ft. (30cm)

Erigeron
'Charity'

Zone 5
Height: 2ft. (60cm) Spread: 18in. (45 cm)

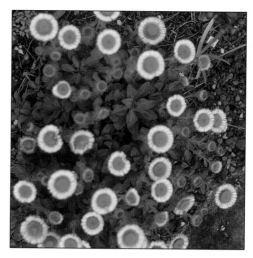

Erigeron compositus
(Fernleaf fleabane; Cutleaf daisy)

Zone 5
Height and spread: 4in. (10 cm)

Erigeron
'Dignity'

Zone 5
Height and spread: 20in. (50cm)

Erigeron
'Four Winds'

Zone 5
Height and spread: 20in. (50cm)

Erigeron glaucus
(Beach fleabane)

Zone 3
Height: 1ft. (30cm) Spread: 18in. (45 cm)

Erigeron karvinskianus
A.G.M. (Bonytip fleabane)

Zone 7
Height: 1ft. (30cm) Spread: 3ft. (90cm)

Erigeron philadelphicus

Zone 2
Height: 2ft. (60cm) Spread: 1ft. (30cm)

Erigeron
'Quakeress'

Zone 5
Height: 2ft. (60cm) Spread: 18in. (45 cm)

Erigeron 'Rotes Meer'

Zone 5
Height and spread: 2ft. (60cm)

Erigeron
'Schneewitschen'

Zone 5
Height and spread: 2ft. (60cm)

Erigeron
'Serenity'

Zone 5
Height: 30in. (75cm) Spread: 18in. (45 cm)

ERINUS *(Scrophulariaceae)*

Common names: Fairy foxglove

A genus of two species of perennials from rocky mountains in southern and Central Europe and North Africa. They are short-lived, and semi-evergreen. The leaves are in rosettes, and sticky, toothed, and inverse-lance-shaped. The flowers are two-lipped, and borne in terminal racemes in late spring to early summer.

Erinus alpinus
A.G.M.

Zone 6
Height and spread: 4in. (10 cm)

✔ Flowers perfumed
✔ Repeat-flowering
✔ Disease-free
✔ Pest-free
✖ Short-lived

CULTIVATION
Grow in well-drained,light soil in sun or part shade. Will repeat-flower if dead-headed.

PROPAGATION
Seed should be sown in an open frame in autumn, Rosettes can be rooted in spring.

ERIOGONUM *(Polygonaceae)*

Common names: St. Catherine's lace; Buckwheat;Umbrella plant

A genus of 150 species of annuals, subshrubs and perennials from the mountains and deserts of western U.S.A. The foliage of the smaller species is in rosettes, and may be white-wooly above or below. The leaves are ovate, rounded or linear. The flowers are small, cupped in bracts and borne in dense heads or umbels or cymes.

✔ Flowers long-lasting
✔ Disease-free
✔ Pest-free
✖ Resents disturbance

CULTIVATION
Grow in open, sharply-drained soil in sun. Dead-head after flowering.

PROPAGATION
Seed should be sown in an open frame in autumn. Rosettes can be rooted in spring or early summer.

Eriogonum latifoliium
subsp. *rubescens*

Zone 7
Height: 2ft. (60cm) Spread: 1ft. (30cm)

Eriogonum umbellatum
(Sulphur flower)

Zone 7
Height: 1ft. (30cm) Spread: 3ft. (90cm)

Eripgonum umbellatum
var. *torreyanum*

Zone 7
Height: 1ft. (30cm) Spread: 3ft. (90cm)

ERIOPHYLLUM *(Asteraceae)*
Common names: Golden yarrow; woolly sunflower

A genus of a dozen species annuals, perennials and subshrubs from mountainous scrubland in Australia. The leavers are alternate, pinnatifid or toothed, white-hairy. The flowers are daisy-like, single yellow with yellow discs, and borne in corymbs or cymes in summer.

✔ Long-flowering	✘ Invasive
✔ Drought-tolerant	✘ Prone to slug damage
✔ Handsome foliage	

CULTIVATION
Grow in sharply-draining, poor soil in sun. Shear over after flowering to maintain compactness.

PROPAGATION
Seed should be sown in an open frame in autumn. Divide in spring.

Eriophyllum lanatum
(Woolly eriophyllum)
Zone 5
Height and spread: 2ft. (60cm)
Birds use foliage for nests

Eriophyllum lanatum
'Pointe'
Zone 5
Height and spread: 1ft. (30cm)

ERODIUM *(Geraniaceae)*
Common names: Heron's bill; stork's bill

A genus of 60 species of annuals, perennials and subshrubs from rocky limestone habitats in Eurasia, North and South America, Australia and North Africa. The foliage is handsome, the leaves alternate, pinnate or pinnatisect. The flowers are geranium-like, solitary, or in terminal umbels, and are borne for long periods in late spring to late summer. They are excellent coastal plants.

✔ Long-flowering	✔ Disease-free	✘ Self-seeds
✔ Drought-tolerant	✔ Pest-free	
✔ Handsome foliage		

CULTIVATION
Grow in alkaline to neutral, sharply-draining, humus-rich soil in sun. Dead-heading prolongs flowering and prevents self-seedsing. Alpine species must be protected against winter wet.

PROPAGATION
Seed should be sown in an open frame as soon as it is ripe. Division can be done in spring, and basal stem cuttings can be rooted in late spring or early summer.

Erodium carvifolium

Zone 7
Height: 14in. (35cm) Spread: 8in. (20cm)

Erodium
'Fran's Choice'

Zone 7
Height and spread: 8in. (20cm)

Erodium x kolbianum

Zone 6
Height and spread: 8in. (20cm)

Erodium manescaui
(Pyrenees heronsbill)

Zone 6
Height: 18in. (45 cm) Spread: 8in. (20cm)

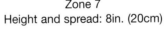

Erodium
'Merstham Pink'

Zone 6
Height: 9in. (22cm) Spread: 10in. (25 cm)

Erodium pelargoniiflorum
(Geranium heronsbill)

Zone 6
Height and spread: 1ft. (30cm)

Erodium
'Stephanie'

Zone 6
Height and spread: 1ft. (30cm)

Erodiun x variabile
'Purple Haze'

Zone 7
Height and spread: 1ft. (30cm)

ERYNGIUM *(Apiaceae)*
Common names: Sea holly

A genus of 230 species of annuals, biennials and tap-rooted evergreen or herbaceous perennials from dry coastal areas and rocky places in Eurasia, North Africa, China, Korea and Turkey, and fibrous-rooted, evergreen ones from marshland and wet grassland in Mexico, Brazil, Argentina and northern Central America. Their leaves are usually in basal rosettes, and are sword-shaped, and spiny, with prominent silver veins. The flowers are small and crowded into cylindrical or hemi-spherical, thistle-like umbels on branched stems.

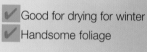

✔ Good cut flower	✔ Good for drying for winter	✘ Prone to slug damage
✔ Attracts bees	✔ Handsome foliage	✘ Resent disturbance
✔ Attracts butterflies		✘ Mildew prone

CULTIVATION
Depends on the habitat in nature:

Group 1: grow in dry, well-drained, poor soil in sun, and protected against winter wet.
Group 2: grow in moist, fertile soil in sun.

PROPAGATION
Seed should be sown in a cold frame as soon as it is ripe. They can be divided in spring, but do not enjoy the process. Root cuttings can be taken in winter.

Eryngium agavifolium
(Argentina, Group 2)
Zone 7
Height: 5ft. (1.5m) Spread: 2ft. (60cm)
Evergreen

Eryngium alpinum
(Europe, Group 1)
Zone 5
Height: 28in. (70cm) Spreads: 18in. (45 cm)

Eryngium alpinum 'Amethyst'
(Europe, Group 1)
Zone 5
Height: 28in. (70cm) Spread: 18in. (45 cm)

E

Eryngium alpinum 'Slieve Donard'
(Europe, Group 1)

Zone 5
Height: 28in. (70cm) Spread: 18in. (45 cm)

Eryngium bourgatii
(Europe, Group 1)

Zone 5
Height: 18in. (45 cm) Spread: 1ft. (30cm)

Erygium bourgatii 'Picos Blue'
(Europe, Group 1)

Zone 5
Height: 18in. (45 cm) Spread: 1ft. (30cm)

Eryngium eburneum
(South America, Group 2)
Zone 5
Height: 4ft. (1.2m) Spread: 1ft. (30cm)
Evergreen

Eryngium giganteum A.G.M.
(Europe, Group 1)
Zone 5
Height: 3ft. (90cm) Spread: 1ft. (30cm)
Short-lived

Eryngium horridum
(Americas, Group 2)
Zone 5
Height: 10ft. (3m) Spread: 3ft. (90cm)
Evergreen

Eryngium x oliverianum A.G.M.
(Europe, Group 1)

Zone 5
Height: 3ft. (90cm) Spread: 18in. (45 cm)

Eryngium pandanifolium
(Americas, Group 2)
Zone 8
Height: 12ft. (4m) Spread: 6ft. (2m)
Evergreen

Eryngium proteiflorum
(Mexico, Group 2)
Zone 8
Height: 3ft. (90cm) Spread: 2ft. (60cm)
Evergreen

Eryngium x tripartitium A.G.M.
(Europe, Group 1)

Zone 5
Height: 3ft. (90cm) Spread: 20in. (50cm)

Eryngium variifolium
(Morocco, Group 1)
Zone 7
Height: 16in. (40cm) Spread: 10in. (25 cm)
Evergreen

ERYSIMUM *(Brassicaceae)*
Common names: Wallflower

A genus of 80 species of annuals, biennials and perennials from limestone, well-draining soils in Eurasia, North Africa and North America. The perennials are mostly evergreen, but a few are herbaceous. The leaves are inversely-lance-shaped, toothed, hairy. The flowers have four petals, so are cross-shaped, and borne in corymb-like racemes over a long period from early spring to summer.

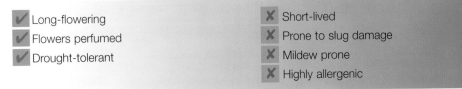

- ✔ Long-flowering
- ✔ Flowers perfumed
- ✔ Drought-tolerant
- ✘ Short-lived
- ✘ Prone to slug damage
- ✘ Mildew prone
- ✘ Highly allergenic

CULTIVATION
Grow in neutral to alkaline, well-drained, fertile soil in sun. Cut back gently after flowering to keep compact. *E. cheiri* is invariably grown as a biennial in cold countries.

PROPAGATION
Seed should be sown in a cold frame in spring. Heeled softwood or nodal cuttings can be taken from spring to summer.

Erysimum alpinum

Zone 6
Height and spread: 6in. (15cm)

Erysimum
'Apricot Delight'

Zone 7
Height: 2ft. (60cm) Spread: 28in. (70cm)

Erysimum 'Bowles' Mauve' A.G.M.

Zone 7
Height: 30in. (75cm) Spread: 2ft. (60cm)
Evergreen

Erysimum
'Bredon' A.G.M.

Zone 6
Height: 1ft. (30cm) Spread: 18in. (45 cm)

Erysimum cheiri
(Wallflower)

Zone 6
Height: 32in. (80cm) Spread: 16in. (40cm)

Erysimum
'Constant Cheer' A.G.M.

Zone 7
Height: 1ft. (30cm) Spread: 2ft. (60cm)

Erysimum helveticum

Zone 6
Height and spread: 4in. (10 cm)

Erysimum linifolium 'Variegatum'
(Alpine wallflower)
Zone 6
Height: 28in. (70cm) Spread: 10in. (25cm)
Evergreen

Erysimum 'Orange Flame'

Zone 7
Height: 4in. (10 cm) Spread: 1ft. (30cm)
Evergreen

Erysimum
'Sprite'

Zone 7
Height: 8in. (20cm) Spread: 18in. (45 cm)

Erysimum
'Walburton's Fragrant Sunshine'

Zone 7
Height: 1ft. (30cm) Spread: 6in. (15cm)

Erysimum
'Yellow Bird'

Zone 7
Height: 1ft. (30cm) Spread: 6in. (15cm)

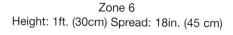

E

ERYTHRONIUM *(Liliaceae)*
Common names: Dog's tooth violet; Trout lily

A genus of 22 bulbous perennials from mountain meadows and deciduous woodland in Eurasia and North America. They have basal, broadly-elliptic, arching handsome leaves that may be marbled bronze in some species. The flowers are pendent, bell-shaped, and have six recurved tepals and prominent stamen. Up to 10 flowers are borne per stem, from spring to early summer.

✔ Handsome foliage   ✗ Prone to slug damage

CULTIVATION
The tooth-like bulbs should be planted 4in. (10 cm) deep in autumn in humus-rich, fertile, well-drained soil in part shade. Never buy dried-out bulbs, or allow bulbs to dry out, as they seldom recover.

PROPAGATION
Divide, and replant immediately, after flowering.

Erythronium californicum
'White Beauty' A.G.M.

Zone 5
Height: 14in. (35cm) Spread: 4in. (10 cm)

Erythronium dens-canis A.G.M.

Zone 3
Height: 6in. (15cm) Spread: 4in. (10 cm)

Erythronium grandiflorum

Zone 3
Height: 1ft. (30cm) Spread: 4in. (10 cm)

Erythronium helenae

Zone 5
Height: 14in. (35cm) Spread: 6in. (15cm)

Erythronium
'Pagoda' A.G.M.

Zone 5
Height: 14in. (35cm) Spread: 4in. (10 cm)

Erythronium tuolumnense A.G.M.

Zone 5
Height: 14in. (35cm) Spread: 3in. (8 cm)

EUCHARIS *(Amaryllidaceae)*

Common names: None

A genus of 17 species of bulbous perennials from moist forest in South and Central America. They are evergreen and summer-flowering. The basal leaves are glossy, lance-shaped or ovate or elliptic, wavy or folded. The flowers are daffodil-like, and composed of an inner and an outer row of three tepals each, and six fused stamens forming a cup.

✔ Handsome foliage
✔ Flowers perfumed
✔ Disease-free
✔ Pest-free

CULTIVATION
Grow in well-drained, humus-rich, fertile soil in light shade.

PROPAGATION
Remove offsets after flowering.

Eucharis amazonica

Zone 10
Height: 28in. (70cm) Spread: 6in. (15cm)

EUCOMIS *(Hyacinthaceae)*

Common names: None

A genus of 15 species of bulbous perennials from wet meadows and dry screes in tropical Southern Africa and South Africa. The leaves are in a basal rosette, glossy and strap-shaped. The flowers are small, star-shaped and surrounded by leafy bracts, and borne in a tight raceme over a long season in late summer and early autumn.

✔ Long-flowering   ✗ Prone to slug damage
✔ Good cut flowers
✔ Handsome foliage

CULTIVATION
Plant bulbs 6in. (15cm) deep in fertile, well-drained soil in sun. Do not allow to dry out in summer, and keep almost dry in winter.

PROPAGATION
Remove offsets in spring or sow seed at 61°F (16°C) in spring or autumn.

Eucomis autumnalis
A.G.M.

Zone 8
Height: 1ft. (30cm) Spread: 8in. (20cm)

Eucomis bicolor
A.G.M.

Zone 8
Height: 2ft. (60cm) Spread: 8in. (20cm)

Eucomis comosa
'Sparkling Burgundy'

Zone 8
Height: 20in. (50cm) Spread: 8in. (20cm)

Eucomis comosa
'Striata'

Zone 8
Height: 30in. (75cm) Spread: 8in. (20cm)

Eucomis pallidiflora
A.G.M.

Zone 8
Height: 28in. (70cm) Spread: 8in. (20cm)

Eucomis zambesiaca

Zone 8
Height: 10in. (25 cm) Spread: 6in. (15cm)

Eucomis
'Zeal Bronze'

Zone 8
Height: 28in. (70cm) Spread: 8in. (20cm)

EUPATORIUM *(Asteraceae)*

Common names: Hemp agrimony; Joe Pye weed; snakeroot

A genus of 40 species of annuals, perennials and shrubs from dry sandy and wet swampy, temperate and tropical, habitats in Eurasia, Africa and both Americas. The perennials are coarse, herbaceous, and best suited to the wild garden. Their leaves are alternate or opposite, entire or dissected, and toothed. The flowers are tubular, and solitary or borne in axillary or terminal panicles or corymbs.

✔ Attracts bees
✔ Attracts butterflies
✔ Good for drying for winter

✘ Prone to slug damage

CULTIVATION
Grow in moist soil in sun or part shade.

PROPAGATION
Seed should be sown in a cold frame in spring. Divide in spring.

Eupatorium album
(Hemp agrimony)

Zone 4
Height: 3ft. (90cm) Spread: 1ft. (30cm)

Eupatorium purpureum
(Joe Pye weed)
Zone 4
Height: 6ft. (2m) Spread: 3ft. (90cm)
Requires staking

Eupatorium rugosum 'Chocolate'
A.G.M. (White snakeroot)

Zone 6.
Height: 32in. (80cm) Spread: 28in. (70cm)

EUPHORBIA *(Euphorbiaceae)*
Common names: Spurge

A huge genus of 2,000 species of annuals, biennials, subshrubs, shrubs, trees, and succulents distributed, not surprisingly, over the continents and temperature zones. The perennials may be evergreen, semi-evergreen or herbaceous, and vary widely in their hardiness and cultural needs. Characteristic are their cyathia, cups of long-lasting bracts that surround nectarines and the insignificant flowers, which have much-reduced parts. The leaves are variable and often ephemeral. Gardeners tend to be 'euphoric' or 'euphobic' about them.

✔ Good cut flowers
✔ Handsome bracts

✘ All parts poisonous
✘ Sap is skin-irritant
✘ Flowers insignificant
✘ Resent disturbance
✘ Highly allergenic

Euphorbia amygdaloides
(Wood spurge) (Europe, Group 2)
Zone 7
Height: 80 cm.(32in.); Spread: 1ft. (30cm)
Evergreen

CULTIVATION
The categories of requirement are given for each entry:

Group 1: light, well-drained soil in sun.

Group 2: moist, humus-rich soil in dappled shade.

PROPAGATION
Seed of perennials should be sown in a cold frame as soon as it is ripe, or the next spring. Divide in spring. Basal cuttings can be taken in spring, and the cut surface must be dipped in lukewarm water to prevent 'bleeding'.

Euphorbia amygdaloides
'Purpurea' (Group 2)
Zone 7
Height: 32in. (80cm) Spread: 1ft. (30cm)
Handsome foliage/Evergreen

Euphorbia amygdaloides var.
robbiae A.G.M. (Group 2)
Zone 7
Height: 32in. (80cm) Spread: 1ft. (30cm)
Evergreen

Euphorbia characias
(Portugal, Group 1)
Zone 8
Height: 4ft. (1.2m) Spread: 3ft. (90cm)
Evergreen/Drought-tolerant

Euphorbia characias subsp.
characias (Group 1)
Zone 8
Height: 4ft. (1.2m) Spread: 1ft. (30cm)
Evergreen/Drought-tolerant

Euphorbia characuas subsp.
wulfenii A.G.M. (Group 1)
Zone 8
Height: 4ft. (1.2m) Spread: 1ft. (30cm)
Evergreen/Drought-tolerant

Euphorbia characias subsp.
wulfenii 'Variegata' (Group 1)
Zone 8
Height: 4ft. (1.2m) Spread: 1ft. (30cm)
Evergreen/Handsome foliage

Euphorbia cyparissias 'Fens Ruby'
(Cypress spurge) (Europe, Group 1)
Zone 4
Height: and spread: 16in. (40cm)
Drought-toleran

Euphorbia dulcis
'Chameleon' (Europe, Group 1)
Zone 5
Height and spread: 1ft. (30cm)
Drought-tolerant/Handsome foliage

Euphorbia griffithii
'Fireglow' (Asia, Group 2)

Zone 5
Height: 3ft. (90cm) Spread: 2ft. (60cm)

Euphorbia polychroma A.G.M.
(Europe, Group 1 or 2)
Zone 6
Height: 16in. (40cm) Spread: 2ft. (60cm)

Euphorbia polychroma
'Candy' (Group 1 or 2)
Zone 6
Height: 16in. (40cm) Spread: 2ft. (60cm)

Euphorbia rigida
(Mediterranean area, Group 1)
Zone 8
Height and spread: 2ft. (60cm)
Evergreen/Drought-tolerant

Euphorbia schillingii
A.G.M. (Group 2)

Zone 5
Height: 3ft. (90cm) Spread: 1ft. (30cm)

Euphorbia sikkimensis
(Group 2)

Zone 6
Height: 4ft. (1.2m) Spread: 18in. (45 cm)

EURYOPS *(Asteraceae)*

Common names: None

A genus of 100 species of annuals, perennials and shrubs found in rocky regions in southern Africa and one species in Yemen, Arabia. Their leaves are handsome, alternate, pinnatised or simple, linear or ovate, and gray-green. The daisy-like flowers have yellow ray and tallow disc petals, and are solitary or borne in groups of two or three, from late spring to early summer.

✔ Handsome foliage

✔ Disease-free

✔ Pest-free

Euryops acraeus
A.G.M.

Zone 7
Height and spread: 1ft. (30cm)

CULTIVATION

Under glass, grow in an alpine house in loam-based potting compost with extra sharp sand, in full light. Water freely during growth but very sparingly in winter.

Out of doors, grow in well-drained or sharply-draining fertile soil in sun. Trim over lightly after flowering to maintain compactness.

PROPAGATION

Seed should be sown at 55°F (13°C) in spring. Softwood cuttings can be taken in late spring, or semi-ripe ones in summer.

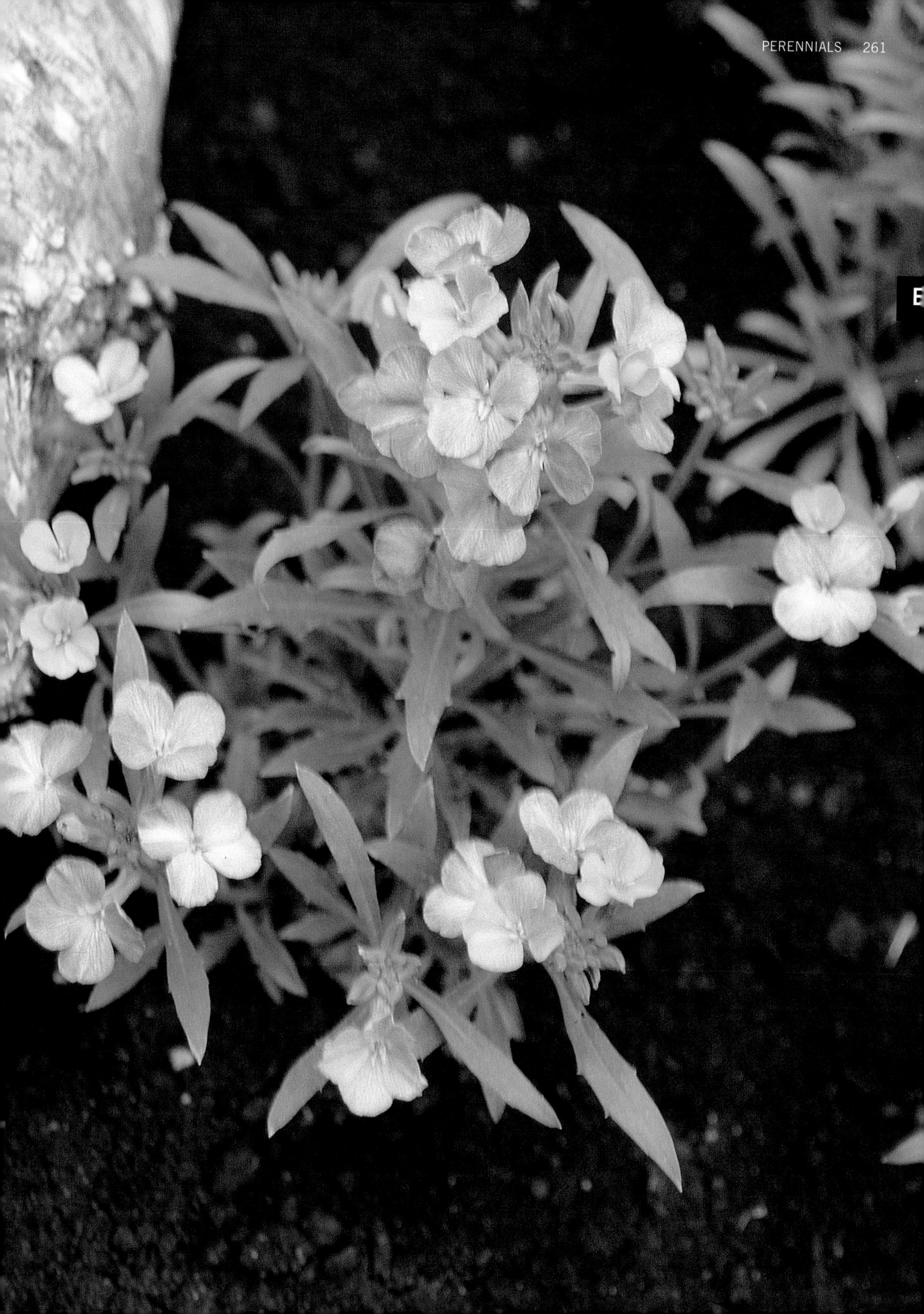

F

FARFUGIUM
FASCICULARIA
FELICIA
FERULA
FESTUCA
FILIPENDULA
FITTONIA
FOENICULUM
FRAGARIA
FRANCOA
FRITILLARIA
FUCHSIA

FARFUGIUM *(Asteraceae)*

Common names: None

A genus of 2 species of evergreen rhizomatous perennials from waterside and seaside in Japan. Their leaves are large, round, leathery and handsome. The flowers are tallow, small, and borne in loose corymbs in autumn and winter. They are excellent foliage plants for the border.

✔ Handsome foliage   ✘ Prone to slug damage

CULTIVATION
Grow in moist, fertile, well-drained soil in a sheltered corner in part shade.

PROPAGATION
Divide in spring.

Farfugium japonicum 'Argenteum'

Zone 8
Height and spread: 2ft. (60cm)

Farfugium japonicum 'Aureomaculatum' A.G.M.

Zone 8
Height and spread: 2ft. (60cm)

FASCICULARIA *(Bromeliaceae)*

Common names: None

A genus of five species of evergreen, rosette-forming, xerophytic, bromeliad perennials from coastal areas and mountains of Chile. They may be epiphytic or terrestrial (*F. bicolor* is the latter). The leaves are linear, arching, very spiny, tough, and green, but their inner sections turn red at flowering. The flowers are small, blue, surrounded by bracts and packed into a tight corymb in the center of the rosette, and followed by scaly, ovoid fruits.

✔ Evergreen   ✘ Prone to slug damage
✔ Handsome foliage   ✘ Resent disturbance

CULTIVATION
Grow in sharply-draining, poorish soil in sun. Protect against winter wet.

PROPAGATION
Seed should be sown at 81°F (27°C) in spring or winter. Division of offsets can be done in spring.

Fascicularia bicolor

Zone 8
Height: 18in. (45 cm) Spread: 2ft. (60cm)

FELICIA (Asteraceae)
Common names: Blue daisy

A genus of 80 species of annuals, subshrubs and perennials from sunny, open habitats in tropical and Southern Africa, and the Arabian peninsula. The leaves are linear or obovate or ovate, opposite, or alternate, and in a basal rosette in some. The flowers are single, blue, daisies with yellow discs borne over a long period in summer. All three species shown are evergreen subshrubs.

✔ Evergreen
✔ Drought-tolerant
✔ Long-flowering
✔ Disease-free
✔ Pest-free

CULTIVATION
Under glass, grow in loam-based potting compost in full light, with good ventilation and low humidity. Water moderately during summer, and sparingly in winter.

Out of doors, grow in well-drained, fertile soil in sun. Water sparingly in winter.

PROPAGATION
Stem-tip cuttings can be rooted in late summer.

Felicia amelloides 'Variegata'

Zone 9
Height and spread: 2ft. (60cm)
Variegated foliage

Felicia echinata

Zone 9
Height and spread: 2ft. (60cm)

Felicia petiolata

Zone 9
Height: and spread: 1ft. (30cm)

FERULA (Apiaceae)
Common names: Giant fennel

A genus of 170 species of tap-rooted, herbaceous perennials from dry grassy slopes and roadsides from the Mediterranean across to Central Asia. The leaves are basal, malodorous, and very finely-divided.. The flower are in flat, terminal racemes, on branching stems, and may not appear for a few years; moreover, they may be monocarpic. Not to be confused with edible fennel, *Foeniculum vulgare*, q.v.

✔ Architectural plants
✔ Evergreen
✔ Handsome foliage
✘ Resents disturbance
✘ Mildew prone
✘ Prone to slug damage

CULTIVATION
Grow in well-drained, fertile soil in sun. Dead-head if seed is not required, for best foliage effect.

PROPAGATION
Seed should be sown in a cold frame as soon as it is ripe, and in deep containers to allow room for tap roots.

Ferula communis
(Common giant fennel)

Zone 8
Height: 10ft. (3m) Spread: 2ft. (60cm)

FESTUCA *(Poaceae)*
Common names: Fescue

A genus of 400 species of evergreen, rhizomatous grasses found across the temperate regions of both hemispheres in the edge of streams and woodland, and in grassland. They are grown for their foliage, which is usually blue-green, and they need to be lifted and divided every few years to maintain the color. The leaves are rolled, folded or flat, lance-shaped, and veined. The flowers are brownish-green, and borne in dense panicles in early and midsummer.

- ✔ Evergreen
- ✔ Handsome foliage
- ✔ Disease-free
- ✔ Pest-free

- ✘ Highly allergenic

F

CULTIVATION
Grow in dry, fertile, well-drained soil in sun.

PROPAGATION
Sow seed, or divide, in spring.

Festuca amethystina
(Tufted fescue; large blue fescue)

Zone 5
Height: 18in. (45 cm) Spread: 10in. (25 cm)

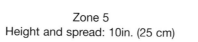

Festuca glauca
(Blue fescue; gray fescue)

Zone 5
Height and spread: 10in. (25 cm)

Festuca glauca
'Elijah Blue'

Zone 5
Height and spread: 10in. (25 cm)

Festuca ovina
'Tetra Gold'

Zone 5
Height and spread: 10in. (25 cm)

F

FILIPENDULA *(Rosaceae)*
Common names: Meadowsweet; queen of the meadow; dropwort

A genus of ten species of rhizomatous perennials which all are to be found in wet, habitats with the exception of *F. vulgaris*, which hails from chalky, dry grassland; all are found in the temperate northern hemisphere. The leaves are alternate, pinnate, with lobes five- to seven-lobed. The perfumed flowers are tiny, fluffy, and borne in dense corymbs, from late spring to late summer. They are best suited to the woodland garden.

 Flowers perfumed

✔ Handsome foliage

✘ Mildew prone

CULTIVATION
Grow all except *F. vulgaris* (which needs dry limy soil) in moist, well-drained, humus-rich soil in sun or part shade. *F. ulmaria* will grow in bog conditions.

PROPAGATION
Seed should be sown at 55°F (13°C) in a cold frame in spring or autumn. Division can be carried out in spring.

Filipendula purpurea A.G.M.
(Japanese meadowsweet)

Zone 6
Height: 4ft. (1.2m) Spread: 2ft. (60cm)

Filipendula ulmaria

Zone 6
Height: 3ft. (90cm) Spread: 2ft. (60cm)

Filipendula ulmaria
'Aurea'

Zone 6
Height: 4ft. (1.2m) Spread: 2ft. (60cm)

Filipendula ulmaria 'Variegata'
(Queen of the meadow)

Zone 6
Height: 4ft. (1.2m) Spread: 2ft. (60cm)

Filipendula vulgaris
(Dropwort)

Zone 3
Height: 2ft. (60cm) Spread: 18in. (45 cm)

FITTONIA *(Acanthaceae)*

Common names: Nerve plant; Painted net leaf

A genus of two species of evergreen perennials, from tropical rainforest in Peru in particular, and South America in general. They are grown for their foliage, as their flowers are insignificant, and borne very erratically. The leaves are oval to elliptic, opposite, and have prominent, colorful veins.

✔ Handsome foliage   ✘ Flowers insignificant

✔ Disease-free   ✘ Invasive

✔ Pest-free

CULTIVATION

Under glass, grow in loam-free potting compost, in indirect light and high humidity. Water carefully, keeping the compost just moist, to avert stem rot, at a constant temperature of 64°F (18°C).

Out of doors, grow in moist, humus-rich, well-drained leafy soil in part shade.

PROPAGATION

Take tip cuttings, or layer stems, in spring.

Fittonia verschaffeltii A.G.M.

Zone 10
Height: 6in. (15cm) Spread: indefinite
Invasive

Fittonia verschaffeltii var. *argyroneura* 'Nana' A.G.M.

Height: 4in. (10 cm) Spread: indefinite

FOENICULUM *(Apiaceae)*

Common names: Edible fennel

A genus of but a single species, *F. vulgare*, from sunny coastal habitats in the Mediterranean area. It is a tap-rooted aromatic perennial, but *F. vulgare* var. *azoricum* is biennial. The leaves are very finely-divided, ferny, and flavored of aniseed. The flowers are tiny, yellow, and borne in flat umbels, followed by aromatic seeds.

✔ Foliage aromatic   ✘ Prone to slug damage

✔ Good cut flower   ✘ Resents disturbance

✔ Handsome foliage   ✘ Highly allergenic

✔ Architectural plant   ✘ Self-seeds

✔ Culinary vegetable

CULTIVATION

Grow in moist, fertile, well-drained soil in sun. Dead-head to prevent self-seeding.

PROPAGATION

Seed should be sown *in situ* in spring.

Foeniculum vulgare 'Purpureum'

Zone 5
Height: 7ft. (2.2m) Spread: 2ft. (60cm)

FRAGARIA *(Rosaceae)*
Common names: Strawberry

A genus of a dozen species of evergreen or semi-evergreen, stoloniferous perennials from open woodland in Eurasia, North America and temperate Chile. Their leaves are radical, tripalmate and toothed. The flowers are single, five-petalled, and borne in cymes of up to 10 flowers; they are followed by edible fruit, except for *FF.* 'Lipstick' and 'Pink Panda', which are both sterile.

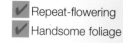

✔ Repeat-flowering ✘ Mildew prone
✔ Handsome foliage ✘ Invasive

CULTIVATION
Grow in moist, well-drained, fertile, alkaline soil in sun or part shade.

PROPAGATION
Seed should be sown at 64°F (18°C) in spring. Plantlets can be detached and planted out in autumn.

Fragaria x ananassa 'Variegata'
(Garden strawberry)
Zone 5
Height: 6in. (15cm) Spread: indefinite
Edible fruit

Fragaria
'Lipstick'

Zone 5
Height: 6in. (15cm) Spread: indefinite

Fragaria
'Pink Panda' (PBR)

Zone 5
Height: 6in. (15cm) Spread: indefinite

Fragaria vesca
(European wild strawberry)

Zone 5
Height: 6in. (15cm) Spread: indefinite

FRANCOA *(Saxifragaceae)*
Common names: Bridal wreath

A genus of either a single, but variable species, or five different species, of evergreen perennials from shaded rocky habitats in Chile. Their leaves are in rosettes, pinnatisect, hairy, wavy-edged, with several small lobes and one large terminal lobe. The flowers are small, four-petalled, pink or white, with handsome markings, are borne in terminal spike-like racemes.

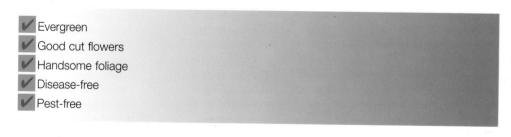

✔ Evergreen
✔ Good cut flowers
✔ Handsome foliage
✔ Disease-free
✔ Pest-free

CULTIVATION
Grow in moist, well-drained, humus-rich soil in sun or part shade. Protect against winter wet.

PROPAGATION
Seed should be sown at 75°F (24°C) in spring.

Francoa ramose

Zone 7
Height: 3ft. (90cm) Spread: 1ft. (30cm)

F

Francoa sonchifolia

Zone 7
Height: 3ft. (90cm) Spread: 18in. (45 cm)

Francoa sonchifolia
(Rodgerson's form)

Zone 7
Height: 3ft. (90cm) Spread: 18in. (45 cm)

FRITILLARIA *(Liliaceae)*
Common names: None

A genus of 100 species of bulbous perennials from a range of habitats such as scree, woodland and open meadows across the temperate Northern hemisphere from north-west America, the Mediterranean and south-west Asia. The leaves are lance-shaped, with one or two basal leaves and several opposite or alternate or whorled stem leaves. The bell- or saucer-shaped or tubular flowers are pendulous, solitary or in terminal racemes or umbels, and borne in spring or early summer. In some species there is an involucre of two or three rows of leaf-like bracts.

✔ Drought-tolerant

✘ Prone to slug damage
✘ Mice like bulbs

Fritillaria acmopetala
A.G.M. (Group 1)

Zone 7
Height: 16in. (40cm) Spread: 3in. (8 cm)

CULTIVATION
Plant the bulbs at four times their depth in:

Group 1: well-drained fertile soil in sun.

Group 2: sharply-draining, fertile soil and full sun.

Group 3: moisture-retentive, humus-rich soil with added leaf mould, in sun or light shade.

Group 4: well-drained, fertile soil in sun, and protection against rain when dormant, so require a frame or glasshouse in wet areas.

PROPAGATION
Seed should be sown in a cold frame in autumn, and keep cold till spring, when it will germinate. Divide offsets or separate bulbils in late summer.

Fritillaria hermonis
(Group 2 or 4)

Zone 8
Height: 1ft. (30cm) Spread: 3in. (8 cm)

Fritillaria imperialis
(Crown imperial) (Group 1)

Zone 4
Height: 4ft. (1.2m) Spread: 1ft. (30cm)

Fritillaria imperialis 'Maxima Lutea'
A.G.M. (Crown imperial) (Group 1)

Zone 4
Height: 4ft. (1.2m) Spread: 1ft. (30cm)

Fritillaria imperialis 'Rubra' (Crown
imperial) (Group 1)

Zone 4
Height: 4ft. (1.2m) Spread: 1ft. (30cm)

*Fritillaria meleagris (*Snake's head
fritillary) (Group 1 or 3)

Zone 4
Height: 1ft. (30cm) Spread: 4in. (10 cm)

Fritillaria michaelovski
A.G.M. (Group 2 or 4)

Zone 7
Height: 6in. (15cm) Spread: 2in. (5cm)

Fritillaria persica
(Group 1)

Zone 5
Height: 3ft. (90cm) Spread: 4in. (10 cm)

Fritillaria pudica
(Group 4)

Zone 6
Height: 6in. (15cm) Spread: 2in. (5cm)

Fritillaria raddeana
(Group 1 or 3)

Zone 4
Height: 2ft. (60cm) Spread: 8in. (20cm)

FUCHSIA *(Onagraceae)*
Common names: None

A genus of 100 species of shrubs, subshrubs, trees and some perennials from the mountains of Central and South America, and New Zealand. They may be deciduous or evergreen, and are evergreen especially in warm climates. They vary in their degree of hardiness from Zone 6 to Zone 10, so it is important to study this before buying if one intends to leave them out over winter. The leaves are elliptic to inversely-lance-shaped, toothed, and in pairs or whorls of three. The flowers are unique, and borne over a very long season from spring to autumn. Each flower is tubular or bell-shaped, with a tube which can be short or long, and widely-spreading sepals, below which is a skirt of four petals in single types, five–seven in semi-double types and over eight in double flowers. The sepals and petals can be of the same or different color. The flowers are borne in terminal clusters.

Fuchsia 'Bicentennial'

Zone 9
Height: 18in. (45 cm) Spread: 2ft. (60cm)

 Long-flowering

✔ Attracts bees

✔ Have berries after flowering

✖ Prone to aphid attack

CULTIVATION
Under glass, grow in loam-based or loam-free potting compost in bright filtered light with high to moderate humidity. Water freely during growth, and keep just moist in winter.

Out of doors, grow in moist, fertile, well-drained soil in sun or part shade, and out of cold drying winds. Cut back to base in spring.

PROPAGATION
Seed of species should be sown at 75°F (24°C) in spring. Cultivars should have softwood cuttings taken in spring, or semi-ripe cuttings in late summer, with bottom heat.

Fuchsia
'Chang' A.G.M.

Zone 9
Height: 2ft. (60cm) Spread: 18in. (45 cm)

Fuchsia
'Coralle' A.G.M.

Zone 9
Height: 3ft. (90cm) Spread: 2ft. (60cm)

Fuchsia
'Emile de Waldman'

Zone 9
Height: 32in. (80cm) Spread: 18in. (45 cm)

Fuchsia
'Firecracker' (PBR)

Zone 9
Height: 3ft. (90cm) Spread: 18in. (45 cm)

Fuchsia 'Genii' A.G.M.

Zone 9
Height and spread: 3ft. (90cm)
Golden foliage

F

Fuchsia
'Happy Wedding'

Zone 8
Height: 1ft. (30cm) Spread: 18in. (45 cm)

Fuchsia
'Heidi Ann' A.G.M.

Zone 9
Height and spread: 2ft. (60cm)

Fuchsia
'John Lockyer'

Zone 9
Height: 3ft. (90cm) Spread: 1ft. (30cm)

Fuchsia
'Love's Reward'

Zone 8
Height and spread: 18in. (45 cm)

Fuchsia
'Lye's Unique'

Zone 8
Height: 2ft. (60cm) Spread: 18in. (45 cm)

Fuchsia
'Madame Cornelissen' A.G.M.

Zone 6
Height: 3ft. (90cm) Spread: 1ft. (30cm)

Fuchsia magellanica
'Riccartonii' A.G.M.

Zone 6
Height: 10ft. (3m) Spread: 6ft. (2m)

Fuchsia magellanica
'Versicolor' A.G.M.

Zone 6
Height: 3ft. (90cm) Spread: 5ft. (1.5m)

Fuchsia
'Mrs Popple' A.G.M.

Zone 6
Height and spread: 4ft. (1.2m)

Fuchsia
'Phenomenal'

Zone 7
Height and spread: 1ft. (30cm)

Fuchsia
'Reading Show'

Zone 8
Height and spread: 1ft. (30cm)

Fuchsia
'Rose Fantasia'

Zone 9
Height: 32in. (80cm) Spread: 18in. (45cm)

Fuchsia
'Rufus'

Zone 7
Height: 30in. (75cm) Spread: 2ft. (60cm)

Fuchsia splendens
A.G.M.

Zone 9
Height: 6ft. (2m) Spread: 3ft. (90cm)

Fuchsia
'Thalia' A.G.M.

Zone 9
Height and spread: 3ft. (90cm)

Fuchsia
'The Doctor'

Zone 9
Height: 30in. (75cm) Spread: 18in. (45 cm)

Fuchsia
'Thornley's Hardy'

Zone 5
Height: 1ft. (30cm) Spread: 8in. (20cm)

F

Fuchsia
'Tom West'

Zone 9
Height and spread: 2ft. (60cm)

Fuchsia
'Turkish Delight'

Zone 9
Height: 2ft. (60cm) Spread: 18in. (45 cm)

G

GAILLARDIA
GALANTHUS
GALEGA
GALIUM
GALTONIA
GAURA
GAZANIA
GENTIANA
GERANIUM
GERBERA
GEUM
GILLENIA
GLADIOLUS
GLAUCIDIUM
GLAUCIUM
GLORIOSA
GLOTTIPHYLLUM
GLYCERIA
GLYCYRRHIZA
GONIOLIMON
GRAPTOPETALUM
GRINDELIA
GUNNERA
GUZMANIA
GYPSOPHILA

GAILLARDIA *(Asteraceae)*
Common names: Blanket flower

A genus of 30 species of annuals, biennials and short-lived perennials from open prairies and hillsides in North and South America. Their leaves are in basal rosettes, and stem, and entire, toothed, pinnatifid or lobed. The flowers are daisy-like, brightly-colored, single, solitary and borne over a long period in summer to autumn.

✔ Long-flowering	✘ Short-lived
✔ Good cut flowers	✘ Need staking
✔ Drought-tolerant	✘ Prone to slug damage
	✘ Mildew prone
	✘ Highly allergenic

G

CULTIVATION
Grow in well-drained fertile or poor soil in sun. Dead-head regularly to prolong flowering. Cut back stems to 6in. (15cm) after flowering, to encourage new growth before winter sets in.

PROPAGATION
Seed of species should be sown at 64°F (18°C) in early spring. Divide cultivars in spring, or take root cuttings in winter.

Gaillardia 'Burgunder'

Zone 4
Height: 2ft. (60cm) Spread: 18in. (45 cm)

Gaillardia grandiflora 'Red Plume' (PBR)

Zone 4
Height and spread: 18in. (45 cm)

Gaillardia 'Kobold'

Zone 4
Height: 1ft. (30cm) Spread: 18in. (45 cm)

GALANTHUS *(Amaryllidaceae)*
Common names: Snowdrop

A genus of 19 species of vigorous, bulbous perennials from rocky sites and upland woodland in Eurasia. The leaves are basal, strap-shaped, glaucous. Each bulb produces a single flower in late winter or early spring. The bulbs rapidly get overcrowded, and must be lifted and separated regularly to maintain vitality. The flowers are pendent, pear-shaped, and white with six tepals, three inner, marked green, and three outer.

✔ Flowers perfumed	✘ All parts poisonous
✔ Good cut flowers	✘ Bulbs skin-irritant
✔ Drought-tolerant	✘ Need to lift & divide often
✔ Attracts bees	

CULTIVATION
Plant the bulbs 6in. (15cm) deep in autumn in moist, well-drained, humus-rich soil in half shade.

PROPAGATION
Seed of the species should be sown as soon as it is ripe in an open frame. Lift and divide clumps of cultivars as soon as the leaves die down after flowering.

Galanthus
'Augustus'

Zone 4
Height: 6in. (15cm) Spread: 3in. (8 cm)

Galanthus
'Galatea'

Zone 4
Height: 3in. (8 cm) Spread: 2in. (5cm)

Galanthus nivalis

Zone 4
Height and spread: 4in. (10 cm)

GALEGA *(Papilionaceae)*

Common names: Goat's rue

A genus of six species of perennials from sunny, moist meadows and slopes in Eurasia and the mountains of East Africa. Their leaves are alternate, pinnate, blue-green. The flowers are pea-like, and in axillary racemes.

✔ Good cut flowers	✘ Need staking
✔ Attracts bees	✘ Self-seeds
	✘ Invasive

CULTIVATION
Grow in moist soil in sun or part shade. Dead-head to prevent self-seeding.

PROPAGATION
Soak seed of species for 12 hours and sow in a cold frame in spring. Divide cultivars between late autumn and spring.

Galega x hartlandii
'Alba' A.G.M.

Zone 4
Height: 5ft. (1.5m) Spread: 3ft. (90cm)

Galega
'Lady Wilson'

Zone 4
Height: 5ft. (1.5m) Spread: 3ft. (90cm)

Galega officinalis
(Common goat's rue)

Zone 4
Height: 5ft. (1.5m) Spread: 3ft. (90cm)

GALIUM *(Rubiaceae)*

Common names: Bedstraw

A genus of 400 species of annuals and rhizomatous perennials from wasteland, hedgerows, meadows and woodland in the temperate regions of the world. Their leaves are linear, and whorled. The tubular flowers are solitary or in terminal cymes or panicles.

- ✔ Flowers perfumed
- ✔ Attracts bees
- ✔ Disease-free
- ✔ Pest-free
- ✘ Invasive

CULTIVATION
Grow in any moist, humus-rich soil in sun or part shade.

PROPAGATION
Seed should be sown in shade in a cold frame as soon as it is ripe.

Divide in autumn or spring.

Galium odoratum
(Sweet woodruff)

Zone 5
Height: 18in. (45 cm) Spread: indefinite

GALTONIA *(Hyacinthaceae)*

Common names: Summer hyacinth

A genus of four species of bulbous perennials found in moist grassland in South Africa. Their leaves are basal, fleshy, semi-erect, and linear or lance-shaped. The flowers are pendent, white or green, and trumpet-shaped or tubular, are borne in late summer and are perfumed in some species.

- ✔ Attracts bees
- ✔ Low allergen
- ✔ Disease-free
- ✔ Pest free
- ✘ Self-seeds

CULTIVATION
Grow in moist, humus-rich, fertile, well-drained soil in sun. Do not allow to dry out in summer. Dead-head to prevent self-seeding.

PROPAGATION
Seed should be sown in a cold frame as soon as it is ripe. Remove offsets in spring.

Galtonia candicans
(Giant summer hyacinth)
Zone 5
Height: 4ft. (1.2m) Spread: 4in. (10 cm)
Flowers perfumed

Galtonia candicans 'Moonbeam'

Zone 5
Height: 4ft. (1.2m) Spread: 4in. (10 cm)
Flowers perfumed

Galtonia princeps

Zone 8
Height: 3ft. (90cm) Spread: 4in. (10 cm)

Galtonia viridiflora
A.G.M.

Zone 8
Height: 3ft. (90cm) Spread: 4in. (10 cm)

GAURA *(Onagraceae)*
Common names: None

A genus of 20 species of annuals, biennials and short-lived perennials from prairies and moist places in North America. The leaves are in rosettes, spoon- or lance-shaped or elliptic, and simple. The flowers are star-shaped, four-petalled, and borne in airy panicles or racemes. Each flower is short-lived, but they appear over a long season from summer to autumn.

✔ Repeat-flowering	✘ Short-lived
✔ Drought-tolerant	✘ Need staking
✔ Disease-free	
✔ Pest-free	

Gaura lindheimeri
A.G.M (White gaura)

Zone 4.
Height: 5ft. (1.5m) Spread: 3ft. (90cm)

CULTIVATION
Grow in moist, fertile, well-drained soil in sun or part shade. They are reasonably drought-tolerant.

PROPAGATION
Seed should be sown in a cold frame in spring. Divide in spring. Root softwood or basal cuttings in spring.

Gaura linheimeri
'Crimson Butterfly'

Zone 4
Height: 5ft. (1.5m) Spread: 3ft. (90cm)

Gaura lindheimeri
'Siskiyou Pink'

Zone 4
Height: 5ft. (1.5m) Spread: 3ft. (90cm)

GAZANIA *(Asteraceae)*
Common names: Treasure flower

A genus of 16 species of annuals and evergreen perennials from low-lying sands to high alpine meadows in southern Africa. The leaves are basal, gray-felted on one or both surfaces, entire or toothed, deeply-lobed to pinnatifid. The daisy-like flowers are solitary, dark-centered, brightly-colored, and borne over long periods in summer; they open only in sun.

✔ Long-flowering	✔ Good cut flowers	✘ Highly allergenic
✔ Evergreen	✔ Disease-free	
✔ Handsome foliage	✔ Pest-free	

CULTIVATION
Under glass, grow in a mix of loam-based potting compost and sharp sand, equal parts, in full light. Water freely during growth, and keep just moist in winter.

Out of doors, grow in well-drained sandy soil in sun. Dead-heading prolongs flowering. Protect against winter wet.

PROPAGATION
Seed should be sown at 68°F (20°C) in late winter or early spring. Basal cuttings can be taken in late summer or early autumn, and must be kept under glass over winter in cool or cold areas.

Gazania
'Aztec' A.G.M.

Zone 9
Height: 8in. (20cm) Spread: 1ft. (30cm)

Gazania
'Christopher Lloyd'

Zone 9
Height: 8in. (20cm) Spread: 1ft. (30cm)

Gazania Chansonette
Series A.G.M.

Zone 9
Height: 8in. (20cm) Spread: 1ft. (30cm)

G

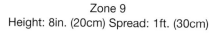

Gazania Daybreak
Series A.G.M.

Zone 9
Height: 8in. (20cm) Spread: 1ft. (30cm)

Gazania krebsiana

Zone 9
Height: 8in. (20cm) Spread: 1ft. (30cm)

Gazania rigens
'Variegata'

Zone 9
Height and spread: 8in. (20cm)

Gazania
'Sun Bathers'

Zone 9
Height: 10in. (25 cm) Spread: 1ft. (30cm)

Gazania Talent
Series A.G.M.

Zone 9
Height: 8in. (20cm) Spread: 30 cm.(1ft.)

Gazania Tiger Stripes
Series

Zone 9
Height: 8in. (20cm) Spread: 1ft. (30cm)

G

GENTIANA *(Gentianaceae)*
Common names: Gentian

A genus of 400 species of annuals, biennials and perennials from either alpine regions or woodland across the temperate regions of the world. The perennials may be herbaceous, semi-evergreen or evergreen. The leaves are in basal rosettes, and in opposite pairs on the stems. The flowers are large, trumpet- or bell-shaped, and flowering can be spring, summer or autumn.

✔ Good cut flowers
✔ Low allergen

✘ Prone to slug damage
✘ Resent disturbance

CULTIVATION
Grow gentians in moist, well-drained soil in sun, except in hot gardens, where they must be given shade. The soil requires to be acid in the case of the autumn-flowering species, *G. asclepiadea*.

PROPAGATION
Seed of species should be sown in an open frame as soon as it is ripe. Division can be carried out in spring, but is not well tolerated.

Gentiana angustifolia

Zone 7
Height: 4in. (10 cm) Spread: 1ft. (30cm)

G

Gentiana asclepiadea
A.G.M. (Willow gentian)

Zone 6
Height: 3ft. (90cm) Spread: 18in. (45 cm)

Gentiana asclepiadea var. *alba*
(White willow gentian)

Zone 6
Height: 3ft. (90cm) Spread: 18in. (45 cm)

Gentiana lutea
(Yellow gentian)

Zone 4
Height: 6ft. (2m) Spread: 2ft. (60cm)

Gentiana sceptrum

Zone 6
Height: 3ft. (90cm) Spread: 8in. (20cm)

Gentiana septemfida
A.G.M.

Zone 3
Height: 8in. (20cm) Spread: 1ft. (30cm)

Gentiana tibetica

Zone 6
Height: 2ft. (60cm) Spread: 1ft. (30cm)

GERANIUM *(Geraniaceae)*
Common names: Cranesbill

A genus of 400 species of annuals, biennials and herbaceous perennials from varied habitats, but not wet ones, in the temperate regions of both hemispheres. Their leaves are basal, which may persist over winter, and stem. They are palmately-lobed, usually five-pointed, toothed perhaps, and may be aromatic, or handsomely marked or textured. The flowers are generally saucer-shaped, and borne in umbels, panicles or cymes in summer, over long periods in some instances. Some types such as *G.* 'Ann Folkard' need plenty of elbow room. *G. pyrenaicum* 'Bill Wallis' comes true from seed. *G. tuberosum* is summer-dormant, and produces leaves in autumn and flowers in spring.

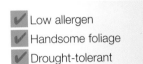

✔ Low allergen   ✖ Mildew prone

✔ Handsome foliage   ✖ Prone to slug damage

✔ Drought-tolerant

Cultivationgrow in fertile, well-drained soil in sun or part shade. Shear over after flowering to encourage new basal growth for the following season.

PROPAGATION
Seed of species should be sown as soon as it is ripe, or in spring. Cultivars and species can be divided in spring. Basal cuttings can be taken in spring, but require bottom heat.

Geranium 'Ann Folkard' A.G.M.

Zone 7
Height: 2ft. (60cm) Spread: 6ft. (2m)
Long-flowering

Geranium
'Brookside'

Zone 7
Height: 1ft. (30cm) Spread: 18in. (45 cm)

Geranium x cantabrigiense
Zone 5
Height: 1ft. (30cm) Spread: 2ft. (60cm)
Evergreen
Foliage aromatic

Geranium
'Chocolate Candy' (PBR)

Zone 7
Height: 6in. (15cm) Spread: 18in. (45 cm)

Geranium cinereum
'Ballerina' A.G.M.
Zone 5
Height: 6in. (15cm) Spread: 1ft. (30cm)
Long-flowering

Geranium cinereum
'Carol' (PBR)

Zone 5
Height: 6in. (15cm) Spread: 1ft. (30cm)

Geranium cinereum var.
subcaulescens A.G.M.

Zone 5
Height: 6in. (15cm) Spread: 1ft. (30cm)

Geranium harveyi

Zone 7
Height: 6in. (15cm) Spread: 8in. (20cm)

Geranium himalayense

Zone 4
Height: 18in. (45 cm) Spread: 2ft. (60cm)
Repeat-flowering

Geranium himalayense 'Plenum'

Zone 4
Height: 18in. (45 cm) Spread: 2ft. (60cm)
Repeat-flowering

G

Geranium ibericum
subsp. *jubatum*

Zone 6
Height: 20in. (50cm) Spread: 2ft. (60cm)

Geranium incanum

Zone 9
Height: 16in. (40cm) Spread: 2ft. (60cm)

Geranium 'Johnson's Blue' A.G.M.

Zone 4
Height: 18in. (45 cm) Spread: 30in. (75cm)
Long-flowering

Geranium macorrhizum
'Ingwersen's Variety' A.G.M.
Zone 4
Height: 1ft. (30cm) Spread: 2ft. (60cm)
Aromatic foliage

Geranium maculatum

Zone 4
Height: 2ft. (60cm) Spread: 45 cm.(18in.)
Long-flowering

Geranium maderense A.G.M.
Zone 9
Height and spread: 5ft. (1.5m)
Long-flowering
Evergreen

G

Geranium malviflorum

Zone 8
Height: 1ft. (30cm) Spread: 18in. (45 cm)

Geranium x oxonianum 'Rose Clair'

Zone 5
Height and spread: 2ft. (60cm)
Long-flowering

Geranium x oxonianum
'Spring Fling'
Zone 5
Height and spread: 1ft. (30cm)
Foliage variegated in spring Evergreen

Geranium palmatum
A.G.M.

Zone 9
Height and spread: 4ft. (1.2m)

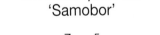

Geranium phaeum
'Samobor'

Zone 5
Height: 2ft. (60cm) Spread: 18in. (45 cm)

Geranium 'Philippe Vapelle'

Zone 7
Height: 16in. (40cm) Spread: 1ft. (30cm)
Long-flowering

Geranium
'Pink Spice' (PBR)

Zone 6
Height: 6in. (15cm) Spread: 1ft. (30cm)

Geranium pratense
(Meadow geranium)
Zone 5
Height: 3ft. (90cm) Spread: 2ft. (60cm)
Self-seeds

Geranium pratense
'Mr. Kendall Clarke' A.G.M.
Zone 5
Height: 3ft. (90cm) Spread: 2ft. (60cm)
Self-seeds

G

Geranium pratense
'Plenum Violaceum' A.G.M.
Zone 5
Height: 3ft. (90cm) Spread: 2ft. (60cm)
Need to lift & divide often

Geranium psilostemon A.G.M.

Zone 6
Height and spread: 4ft. (1.2m)
Long-flowering

Geranium pyrenaicum 'Bill Walls'
Zone 7
Height: 2ft. (60cm) Spread: 1ft. (30cm)
Long-flowering
Comes true from seed/Self-seeds

Geranium x riversleaianum
'Mavis Simpson'
Zone 7
Height: 1ft. (30cm) Spread: 4ft. (1.2m)
Long-flowering

Geranium x riversleaianum
'Russell Pritchard' A.G.M.
Zone 7
Height: 1ft. (30cm) Spread: 3ft. (90cm)
Long-flowering

Geranium sanguineum
'Ankum's Pride'
Zone 5
Height and spread: 1ft. (30cm)
Long-flowering

Geranium sanguineum 'Elsbeth'

Zone 5
Height: 8in. (20cm) Spread: 1ft. (30cm)
Long-flowering

Geranium sanguineum 'Shepherd's
Warning' A.G.M.
Zone 5
Height and spread: 6in. (15cm)
Long-flowering

Geranium sanguineum var. *striatum*
A.G.M.
Zone 5
Height: 4in. (10 cm) Spread: 6in. (15cm)
Long-flowering

G

Geranium sanguineum var.
striatum 'Splendens'

Zone 5
Height: 18in. (45 cm) Spread: 2ft. (60cm)

Geranium 'Stanhoe'

Zone 4
Height: 30in. (75cm) Spread: 2ft. (60cm)
Long-flowering

Geranium sylvaticum 'Album'
A.G.M. (Forest-loving cranesbill)
Zone 4
Height: 30in. (75cm) Spread: 2ft. (60cm)
Long-flowering

Geranium sylvaticum
'Amy Doncaster'
Zone 4
Height: 30in. (75cm) Spread: 2ft. (60cm)
Long-flowering

Geranium tuberosum

Zone 8
Height and spread: 10in. (25 cm)
Summer dormant

Geranium wallichianum
'Buxton's Variety'
Zone 7
Height: 1ft. (30cm) Spread: 3ft. (90cm)
Long-flowering

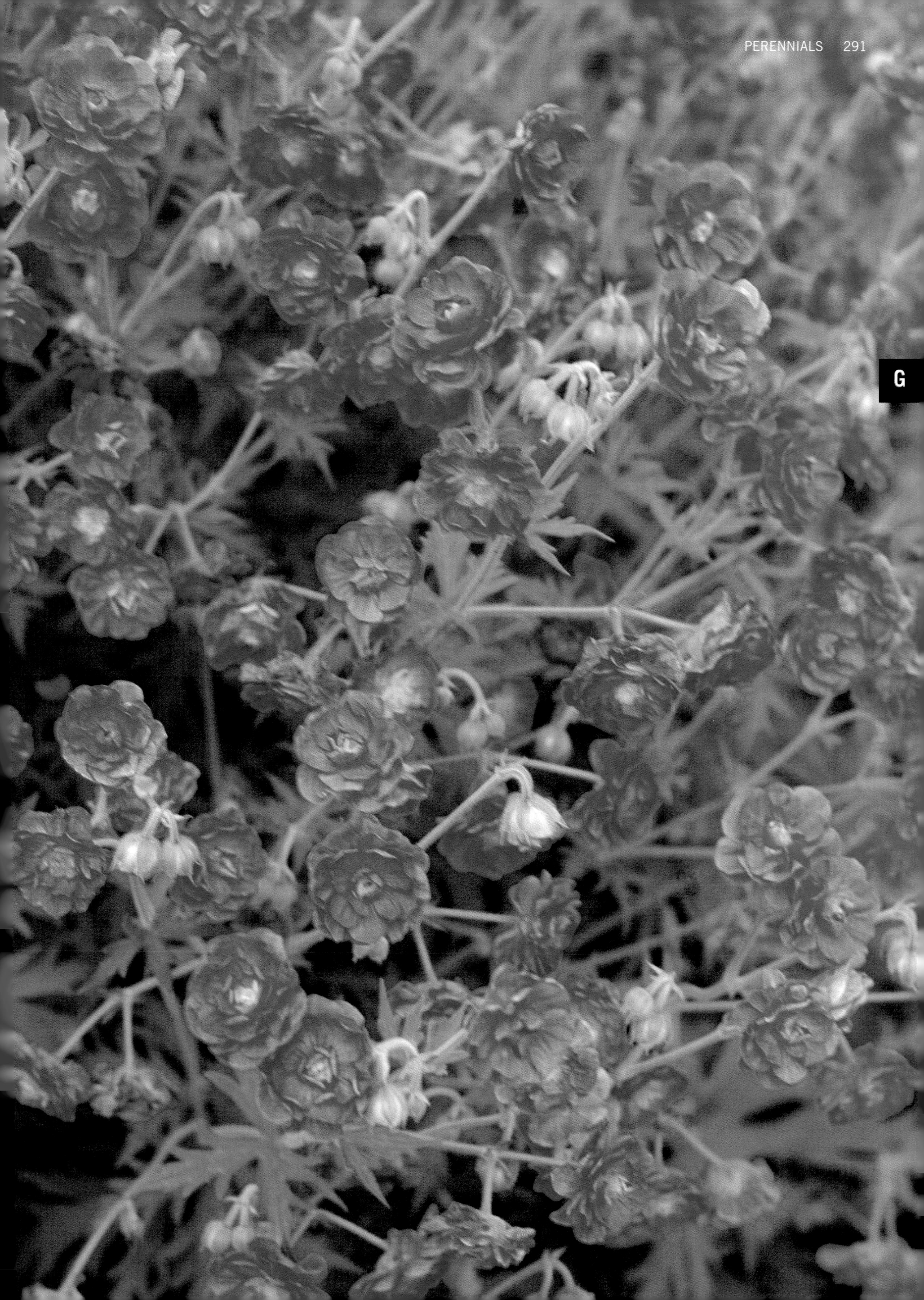

GERBERA *(Asteraceae)*

Common names: Transvaal daisy; Berberton daisy

A genus of 40 species of perennials from temperate grasslands in sub-Saharan Africa, Madagascar, Indonesia and Asia. Their leaves are in basal rosettes, may be entire or lobed, and toothed. The daisy-like flowers are large, solitary, long-lasting, and brightly -colored.

✔ Long-flowering   ✘ Prone to slug damage

✔ Good cut flowers   ✘ Resent disturbance

✔ Handsome foliage   ✘ Highly allergenic

CULTIVATION

Under glass, grow in loam-based potting compost in bright filtered light. Water freely during growth, but keep just moist in winter. Repot annually in spring

Out of doors, grow in well-drained, fertile soil in sun.

PROPAGATION

Seed should be sown at 64°F (18°C) in spring or autumn. Divide in spring, but they do not tolerate disturbance well.

Gerbera jamesonii

Zone 8
Height: 18in. (45 cm) Spread: 2ft. (60cm)

Gerbera jamesonii hybridus

Zone 8
Height: 18in. (45 cm) Spread: 2ft. (60cm)

Gerbera jamesonii
Pandora series

Zone 8
Height: 16in. (40cm) Spread: 18in. (45 cm)

GEUM *(Rosaceae)*

Common names: Avens

A genus of 30 species of rhizomatous or stoloniferous, evergreen perennials from arctic and temperate mountains, wet meadows or stream sides in Eurasia, Africa, New Zealand, and the Americas. Their leaves are wrinkled, pinnate or pinnatisect, scalloped or toothed, and in basal rosettes. The flowers are saucer-or bowl-shaped, five-petalled, pendent or upright, in cymes from late spring to summer. They can be shy-flowering unless lifted and divided very regularly; this should be done in spring.

✔ Evergreen   ✔ Attracts bees   ✘ Need to lift & divide often

✔ Good cut flowers   ✔ Low allergen   ✘ Shy-flowering

✔ Long-flowering   ✔ Handsome foliage

CULTIVATION

Grow in sun in well-drained fertile soil, except for *G. rivale*, which is a waterside or bog plant. All others resent waterlogged soil.

PROPAGATION

Seed should be sown in a cold frame in spring or autumn. Division can be done in spring or autumn, but spring is preferable.

G

Geum coccineum
(= *G. 'Borisii'*)

Zone 5
Height; 50 cm.(2 0in.); Spread: 1ft. (30cm)

Geum
'Dolly North'

Zone 5
Height and spread: 2ft. (60cm)

Geum elatum

Zone 5
Height and spread: 1ft. (30cm)

Geum
'Georgenberg'

Zone 5
Height and spread: 1ft. (30cm)

Geum
'Lady Stratheden' A.G.M.

Zone 6
Height and spread: 2ft. (60cm)

Geum
'Mrs J. Bradshaw' A.G.M.

Zone 6
Height and spread: 2ft. (60cm)

Geum
'Princess Juliana'

Zone 5
Height and spread: 2ft. (60cm)

Geum rivale
Water avens

Zone 3
Height: 2ft. (60cm) Spread: 18in. (45 cm)

Geum rivale
'Album'

Zone 3
Height: 2ft. (60cm) Spread: 1ft. (30cm)

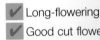

Geum rivale
'Coppertone'

Zone 3
Height: 2ft. (60cm) Spread: 18in. (45 cm)

Geum
'Tangerine'

Zone 3
Height and spread: 1ft. (30cm)

GILLENIA *(Rosaceae)*
Common names: Bowman's root

A genus of two species of rhizomatous perennials from North America, where they inhabit open woodland. Their leaves are palmate, with ovoid leaflets, toothed, and veined, and green-bronze in color. The flowers are star-shaped, white or pink, borne in airy, few-flowered panicles over a long period from spring to late summer.

✔ Long-flowering	✘ Prone to slug damage
✔ Good cut flower	✘ Need staking
✔ Handsome seed-heads	

CULTIVATION
Grow in acid to neutral, moist, fertile, well-drained soil in sun, with mid-day shade, or in part shade.

PROPAGATION
Seed should be sown in a cold frame in spring. Divide in spring or autumn.

Gillenia trifoliata

Zone 4
Height: 3ft. (90cm) Spread: 2ft. (60cm)

GLADIOLUS *(Iridaceae)*
Common names: None

A genus of 200 species of cormous, herbaceous perennials from marshy regions or dry grassland in South Africa in particular, but also in Madagascar, west Asia, east, west and north Africa, and Arabia. They have basal, erect, linear leaves. The flowers are borne in loose or dense spikes, and are open, funnel-shaped, with have six tepals, one upper, two side, and three small lower ones. Some are perfumed. *G. papilio* is very beautiful, but invasive.

✔ Good cut flowers	✘ Prone to slug damage
✔ Drought-tolerant	
✔ Low allergen	

CULTIVATION
Plant the corms in spring 6in. (15cm) deep in well-drained fertile soil in sun. In cold gardens, the corms of tender forms should be lifted in autumn, separated from the old ones, and stored dry and free of frost over winter.

PROPAGATION
Seed of hardy species should be sown in cold frame in spring. Cormlets should be separated in autumn.

Gladiolus callianthus
A.G.M. (Mozambique)
Zone 9
Height: 3ft. (90cm) Spread: 4in. (10 cm)
Flowers perfumed

Gladiolus cardinalis
(S. Africa)
Zone 9
Height: 3ft. (90cm) Spread: 4in. (10 cm)

Gladiolus communis subsp.
Byzantines A.G.M. (Spain, N. Africa)
Zone 6
Height: 3ft. (90cm) Spread: 4in. (10 cm)
Invasive/Need to lift & divide often

Gladiolus
'Green Woodpecker' A.G.M.
Zone 9
Height: 5ft. (1.5m) Spread: 5in. (12cm)

Gladiolus papilio (S. Africa)
Zone 8
Height: 3ft. (90cm) Spread: 3in. (8 cm)
Highly invasive

Gladiolus
'Robin Etta' A.G.M.

Zone 9
Height: 3ft. (90cm) Spread: 4in. (10 cm)

Gladiolus
'The Bride' A.G.M.

Zone 9
Height: 2ft. (60cm) Spread: 2in. (5cm)

Gladiolus tristis (S. Africa)

Zone 7
Height: 5ft. (1.5m) Spread: 2in. (5cm)
Flowers perfumed

G

GLAUCIDIUM *(Glaucidiaceae)*
Common names: None

A genus of a single species. *G. palmatum*, of rhizomatous perennial from mountain woodland in Japan. The leaves are handsome, toothed, veined, and palmately-lobed. The flowers are large, and poppy-like, and appear in late spring and early summer. It thrives best in cool gardens.

| ✔ Handsome foliage | ✘ Prone to slug damage. |
| | ✘ Resents disturbance |

CULTIVATION
Grow in moist, humus-rich, leafy, soil in a sheltered corner in part or deep shade.

PROPAGATION
Seed should be sown in an open frame in spring Divide with care in spring.

Glaucidium palmatum
A.G.M.

Zone 6
Height and spread: 18in. (45 cm)

GLAUCIUM *(Papaveraceae)*
Common names: Horned poppy

A genus of 25 species of annuals, biennials and perennials from waste or disturbed ground in Eurasia, the Middle East and North Africa. The perennials are short-lived, they dislike transplantation, and their roots are poisonous. The leaves are pinnatifid, ovate or round, and glaucous. The flowers are poppy-like, solitary, and terminal or axillary, borne in summer, and followed by long, curved seed-heads. These should be removed after flowering unless seed is required, since they self-seed freely. *G. grandiflorum* has scarlet or orange-red flowers, and silver foliage.

✔ Drought-tolerant	✔ Disease-free	✘ Short-lived
✔ Handsome seed-heads	✔ Pest-free	✘ Self-seeds
✔ Handsome foliage		✘ Resent disturbance

Glaucium flavum

Zone 7
Height: 3ft. (90cm) Spread: 18in. (45 cm)

CULTIVATION
Grow in well-drained soil in sun.

PROPAGATION
Seed should be sown *in situ* in spring or autumn.

Glaucium flavum
forma. *fulvum*

Zone 7
Height: 3ft. (90cm) Spread: 18in. (45 cm)

Glaucium grandiflorum

Zone 7
Height and spread: 20in. (50cm)

GLORIOSA *(Colchicaceae)*
Common names: None

A genus of but one species, *G. superba*, of tuberous, climbing perennial found in tropical India and Africa growing at riversides, and in forests and woodland. It is very variable.

✔ Long-flowering

✗ All parts poisonous
✗ Tubers skin-irritant
✗ Prone to aphid attack

CULTIVATION
Under glass, plant tubers 4in. (10 cm) deep in early spring in loam-based potting compost. Water freely during growth but keep dry in winter. Pot on in late winter.

Out of doors, grow in well-drained soil in sun. Protect against winter wet.

Gloriosa superba
A.G.M.

Zone 9
Height: 6ft. (2m) Spread: 1ft. (30cm)

GLOTTIPHYLLUM *(Aizoaceae)*
Common names: None

A genus of 60 species of succulent perennials found in semi-desert regions of South Africa. Their leaves are fleshy, glossy, strap-shaped and alternate or opposite. The flowers are daisy-like, solitary, and borne form the leaf axils from summer to late winter.

✔ Long-flowering
✔ Handsome foliage
✔ Disease-free
✔ Free of pests

CULTIVATION
Under glass, grow in cactus compost in full light. Water sparingly during growth, and keep just moist when dormant in spring.

Out of doors, grow in sharply-draining soil in sun. Protect against frost in winter.

PROPAGATION
Seed should be sown at 75°F (24°C) in late summer. Basal stem cuttings can be taken then too.

Glottiphyllum lagenicaulis

Zone 9
Height: 4in. (10 cm) Spread: 6in. (15cm)

GLYCERIA *(Poaceae)*

Common names: None

A genus of 16 species of marginal aquatic perennial grasses found in water up to 30in. (75cm) deep in temperate regions of New Zealand, Australia, South America, and the Northern hemisphere. They are dense, spreading plants.

- ✔ Handsome foliage
- ✔ Disease-free
- ✔ Pest-free
- ✘ Invasive
- ✘ Highly allergenic

CULTIVATION
Plant in a basket in water 6in. (15cm) deep, or in a bog or wet area in sun.

PROPAGATION
Divide in spring.

Glyceria maxima var. *variegata*

Zone 5
Height: 28in. (70cm) Spread: indefinite

GLYCYRRHIZA *(Papilionaceae)*

Common names: Liquorice

A genus of 20 species of perennials from both wet and dry habitats in North and South America, tropical Asia, and the Mediterranean region. They have pinnate, sticky leaves. The pea-like flowers are borne in spikes or racemes, but *G. glabra* is very shy flowering; liquorice is obtained from its roots, which can be harvested in autumn.

- ✔ Low allergen
- ✔ Handsome foliage
- ✔ Disease-free
- ✔ Pest-free
- ✘ Resent disturbance
- ✘ Shy-flowering

CULTIVATION
Grow in moist, deep soil in sun.

PROPAGATION
Seed should be sown outdoors in spring or autumn. Division, ensuring that at least one bud is on each division, can be done in spring.

Glycyrrhiza glabra
'Liquorice'

Zone 8
Height: 3ft. (90cm) Spread: 18in. (45 cm)

GONIOLIMON *(Plumaginaceae)*

Common names: Statice

A genus of 20 species of perennials from dry, hot habitats in north-west Africa, and Eurasia. Their leaves are in basal rosettes, leathery or fleshy, smooth and inverse-lance-shaped. The flowers are 'everlasting', tubular, with white sepals and red petals, and are borne in panicles in mid and late summer.

- ✔ Good cut flower
- ✔ Good for drying for winter
- ✔ Disease-free
- ✔ Pest-free

CULTIVATION
Grow in sharply-draining soil in sun.

PROPAGATION
Seed should be sown in a cold frame in spring. Root cuttings can be taken in winter.

Goniolimon tataricum

Zone 4
Height and spread: 1ft. (30cm)

G

GRAPTOPETALUM *(Crassulaceae)*
Common names: Mother-of-pearl plant

A genus of 17 species of evergreen perennials from stony grassland in Mexico and southern U.S.A. They are rosette-forming, and the leaves are fleshy, oval, pointed, and gray-green or purple-gray. The flowers are star- or bell-shaped, and borne in axillary cymes in spring or summer.

✔ Evergreen   ✘ Invasive

✔ Handsome foliage

✔ Disease-free

CULTIVATION
Under glass, grow in sharply-draining, loam-based potting compost in full light, at a temperature of 41°F (5°C) or above. Water freely in spring and summer, very sparingly in autumn and winter.

Out of doors, grow in sharply-draining fertile soil in sun or part shade.

PROPAGATION
Seed should be sown at 75°F (24°C), or take leaf or rosette cuttings in spring and summer.

Graptopetalum paraguayense

Zone 9
Height: 8in. (20cm) spread; indefinite

G

GRINDELIA *(Asteraceae)*
Common names: Rosinweed; Gum plant; Tarweed

A genus of 60 species of annuals, evergreen perennials, and subshrubs from dry, stony habitats in South, Central and North America. Their leaves are simple, toothed or entire, alternate and sticky, as are the stems. The daisy-like flowers are solitary, semi-double, yellow and borne on long stems in summer.

✔ Drought-tolerant   ✘ Need staking

✔ Evergreen

✔ Good cut flowers

✔ Disease-free

✔ Pest-free

CULTIVATION
Grow in well-drained soil in sun.

PROPAGATION
Seed should be sown in a cold frame in spring. Semi-ripe cuttings can be taken in summer.

Grindelia chiloensis

Zone 6
Height and spread: 3ft. (90cm)

GUNNERA *(Gunneraceae)*
Common names: None

A genus of 45 species of rhizomatous perennials from moist regions across the southern hemisphere. They may be evergreen or herbaceous, and come in a huge range of size from tiny to massive. They are grown primarily as foliage plants, since their very large leaves are handsome, round or heart-shaped, lobed and toothed. The flowers are tiny, yellow, and borne in dense spikes in summer.

✔ Handsome foliage   ✘ Require room

✔ Architectural plants   ✘ Flowers insignificant

                                      ✘ Prone to slug damage

CULTIVATION
Grow in soil that is permanently wet or moist, and humus-rich, in sun. They dislike cold, drying winds and hot summers.

PROPAGATION
Seed should be sown as soon as it is ripe; germination is slow. Leafy, basal bud cuttings can be taken in spring.

Gunnera manicata
A.G.M.

Zone 8
Height: 8ft. (2.5m) Spread: 12ft. (4m)

GUZMANIA *(Bromeliaceae)*

Common names: None

A genus of evergreen, epiphytic perennials from, in particular, the rainforests of the Andes at heights up to 11,000ft. (3,500m) but also from Florida, the West Indies and Central America. They have funnel-shaped rosettes of handsome, lance-shaped leaves, and tubular, short-stemmed, white or yellow flowers surrounded by brightly-colored bracts, in summer.

✔ Long-flowering   ✘ Epiphytic

✔ Handsome foliage

CULTIVATION
Under glass, grow in epiphytic bromeliad compost, or epiphytically, in indirect light or filtered light. Mist daily in summer with soft water, Water very sparingly in winter, and do not mist then.

Out of doors, grow on the branches of trees, in shade.

PROPAGATION
Seed should be sown at 81°F (27°C), or offsets removed, in spring.

Guzmania
'Sunstar'

Zone 10
Height and spread: 1ft. (30cm)

GYPSOPHILA *(Cartophyllaceae)*

Common names: Baby's breath

A genus of 100 species of annuals and perennials from limy, dry alpine screes or steppes all the way across from the Mediterranean to China. The perennials may be evergreen or herbaceous. Their leaves are linear to lance-shaped, glaucous, and in opposite pairs. The flowers are tiny, five-petalled, stars borne singly or in airy panicles, often over long periods in summer. Some species are dwarf alpines.

✔ Long-flowering   ✘ Highly allergenic

✔ Good cut flowers

✔ Attracts bees

✔ Drought-tolerant

CULTIVATION
Grow in alkaline to neutral, sharply-draining soil in sun, and protect against winter wet.

PROPAGATION
Seed should be sown in a cold frame in spring, or at 64°F (18°C) in autumn. Cultivars can be increased by grafting, and species by root cuttings, in late winter.

Gypsophila fastigiata
'Festival Pink'

Zone 5
Height and spread: 2ft. (60cm)

Gypsophila paniculata
(Baby's breath)
Zone 4
Height and spread: 4ft. (1.2m)
Long-flowering

Gypsohila repens A.G.M.
(Creeping gypsophila)
Zone 4
Height and spread: 1ft. (30cm)
Long-flowering

Gypsophila 'Rosenschleier' A.G.M.

Zone 4
Height and spread: 18in. (45 cm)
Long-flowering

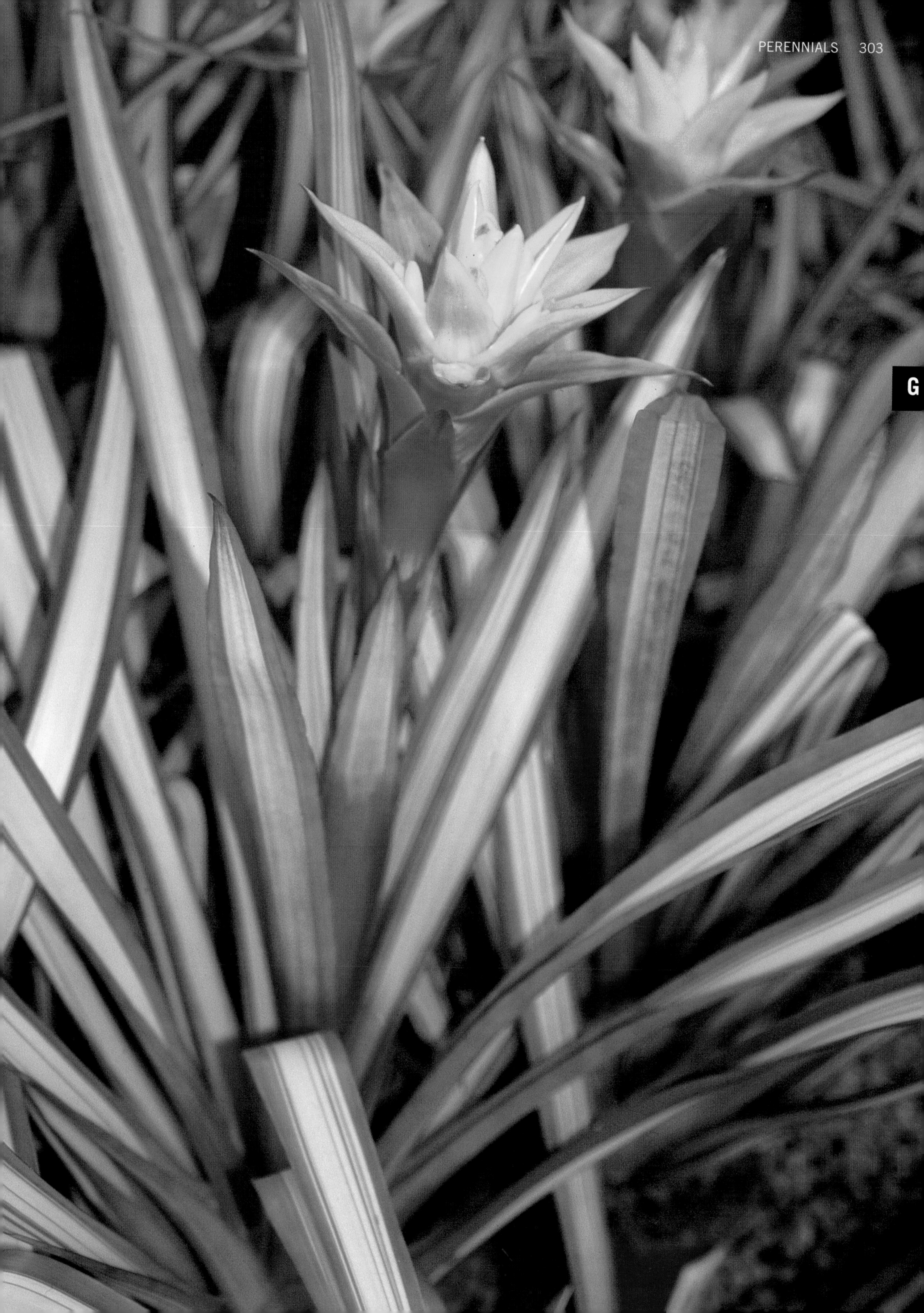
G

H

HABERLEA *(Gesneriaceae)*

Common names: None

A genus of just two species of evergreen perennials from shady, rocky regions of the Balkan peninsula. Their leaves are in basal rosettes, obovate, and scalloped. The flowers are two-lipped trumpets, borne in loose umbels from spring to early summer.

✔ Evergreen

✔ Handsome foliage

✔ Disease-free

✘ Prone to slug damage

✘ Resents disturbance

CULTIVATION

Under glass, grow in an alpine house in a mix of equal parts of loam-based potting compost and coarse grit, in bright indirect light. Water freely during growth, but sparingly in winter, avoiding the foliage.

Out of doors, grow in acid to neutral, moist, well-drained soil on its side in a wall or crevice, in a sheltered corner in part or full shade. Protect against winter wet.

PROPAGATION

Seed should be sown at 64°F (18°C) in spring. Leaf cuttings may be rooted in summer. Division can be tried in early summer, but is not tolerated well.

Haberlea rhodopensis
A.G.M.

Zone 6
Height: 6in. (15cm) Spread: 10in. (25 cm)

HACQUETIA *(Apiaceae)*

Common names: None

A genus of only a single species, *H. epipactis*, from woodlands in Europe. It is rhizomatous, and the small, yellow, long-lasting flowers, with their large green bracts, appear in late winter or early spring before the glossy, three-lobed leaves. The plant disappears completely by summer, so mark its position well.

✘ Prone to slug damage

✘ Resents disturbance

CULTIVATION

Grow in acid to neutral, moist, well-drained soil in part shade.

PROPAGATION

Seed should be sown in a cold frame as soon as it is ripe. Divide in spring but this is not tolerated well. Take root cuttings in winter.

Hacquetia epipactis
A.G.M.

Zone 7
Height: 2in. (5cm) Spread: 8in. (20cm)

HAKONECHLOA *(Poaceae)*

Common names: None

A genus of just one species of perennial grass, *H. macra*, from mountains and woodland in Japan. It is rhizomatous, and clump-forming. The leaves are linear, and arching, and the flowers are spikelets in panicles from late summer to mid-autumn. They are best appreciated if grown where they can tumble over a wall, or from a tall container.

✔ Handsome foliage

✔ Disease-free

✔ Pest-free

✘ Highly allergenic

CULTIVATION

Grow in moist, humus-rich, well-drained soil in sun or part shade, and in shade for variegated forms in particular.

PROPAGATION

Divide in spring.

Hakonechloa macra
'Alboaurea'

Zone 3
Height and spread: 18in. (45 cm)

Hakonechloa macra
'Aureola' A.G.M.

Zone 3
Height and spread: 18in. (45 cm)

Hakonechloa macra
'Mediovariegata'

Zone 3
Height and spread: 18in. (45 cm)

HAPLOPAPPUS *(Asteraceae)*
Common names: None

A genus of 160 species of annuals, perennials and shrubs found in open sunny places in both South and North America. Their leaves are entire or lobed, and opposite. The flowers are daisy-like, solitary, purple or yellow, and borne in summer.

- ✔ Good cut flowers
- ✔ Disease-free
- ✔ Pest-free

Haplopappus glutinosus

Zone 9
Height: 6in. (15cm) Spread: 1ft. (30cm)

CULTIVATION
Grow in alkaline to neutral, sharply-draining soil in sun. Protect against winter wet. Shear over after flowering to keep compact.

PROPAGATION
Seed should be sown in a cold frame as soon as it is ripe, or in spring. Softwood cuttings can be taken in spring.

HAWORTHIA *(Aloeaceae)*
Common names: Pearl plant

A genus of 150 species of perennial succulents from low and highland in southern Africa. They are rosette-forming, and the leaves are fleshy, triangular or ovate, and covered in tiny tubercles. He flowers are tubular or funnel-shaped, and are borne in loose racemes from spring to autumn.

- ✔ Evergreen
- ✔ Handsome foliage

CULTIVATION
Under glass, grow in cactus compost in bright filtered light, good ventilation and low humidity. Water with moderation in summer, very sparingly in winter.

Out of doors, grow in alkaline to neutral, sharply-draining soil in sun or part shade. Protect against winter wet.

PROPAGATION
Seed should be sown at 75°F (24°C) in spring. Divide, or separate offsets in spring.

Haworthia attenuata

Zone 9
Height and spread: 5in. (12cm)

Haworthia pumila

Zone 9
Height: 5in. (12cm) Spread: 18in. (45 cm)

H

HEDYCHIUM *(Zingiberaceae)*
Common names: Ginger lily; garland lily

A genus of 40 species of rhizomatous perennials from moist woodland in Asia. Their leaves are linear, shiny, and borne in two parallel rows. The two-lipped flowers are trumpet-shaped or tubular, perfumed in some species, and with large bracts, and borne in dense spikes.

- ✔ Good cut flowers
- ✔ Handsome foliage
- ✔ Architectural plants
- ✔ Handsome seed-heads
- ✔ Disease-free
- ✔ Pest-free

CULTIVATION
Under glass, grow in loam-based potting compost, with high humidity and good ventilation. Water freely in summer, and sparingly in winter.

Out of doors, grow in moist, humus-rich, well-drained soil in a warm corner in sun or part shade.

PROPAGATION
Seed should be sown at 75°F (24°C) as soon as it is ripe. Divide in spring. Bulbils of *H. greenei* should be sown when ripe.

Hedychium coronarium
'Garland flower'
Zone 9
Height: 10ft. (3m) Spread: 3ft. (90cm)
Flowers perfumed

Hedychium densiflorum

Zone 8
Height: 15ft. (5m) Spread: 6ft. (2m)
Flowers perfumed

Hedychium densiflorum 'Stephen'

Zone 8
Height: 15ft. (5m) Spread: 6ft. (2m)
Flowers perfumed

Hedychium forrestii

Zone 9
Height: 5ft. (1.5m) Spread: 2ft. (60cm)

H

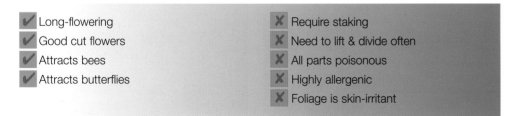

Hedychium greenei

Zone 10
Height: 6ft. (2m) Spread: 2ft. (60cm)

Hedychium yunnanense

Zone 9
Height: 3ft. (90cm) Spread: 2ft. (60cm)

H

HEDYSARUM *(Papilionaceae)*
Common names: French honeysuckle; Sulla sweet vetch

A genus of 100 species of perennials and subshrubs from prairies and mountains across the northern hemisphere. Their leaves are pinnate and alternate. The pea-like flowers are perfumed and borne in axillary racemes.

✔ Flowers perfumed
✔ Good cut flowers
✔ Attracts bees
✔ Disease-free
✔ Pest-free

✖ Resents disturbance
✖ Short-lived

CULTIVATION
Grow in gritty, sharply-draining, limy soil in sun.

PROPAGATION
Seeds should be sown in a cold frame as soon as it is ripe, or in spring. Divide in spring, but this is not tolerated well.

Hedysarum coronarium

Zone 3
Height: 3ft. (90cm) Spread: 2ft. (60cm)

HELENIUM *(Asteraceae)*
Common names: Helen's flower; Sneezeweed

A genus of 40 species of annuals, biennials and perennials from wet meadows and forest margins in Central and northern America. Their leaves are ovate or lance-shaped. The flowers are daisy-like, with yellow, orange or red ray florets and brown discs, borne on branching stems over a long period from late summer to mid-autumn.

✔ Long-flowering
✔ Good cut flowers
✔ Attracts bees
✔ Attracts butterflies

✖ Require staking
✖ Need to lift & divide often
✖ All parts poisonous
✖ Highly allergenic
✖ Foliage is skin-irritant

CULTIVATION
Grow in moist, fertile, well-drained soil in sun. Stake as necessary. Dead-heading prolongs flowering. Lift and divide every few years to maintain vigor.

PROPAGATION
Seed of species should be sown in a cold frame in spring. Divide species and cultivars in spring or autumn.

Helenium autumnale

Zone 3
Height: 5ft. (1.5m) Spread: 18in. (45 cm)

H

Helenium
'Bressingham Gold'

Zone 3
Height: 3ft. (90cm) Spread: 2ft. (60cm)

Helenium
'Crimson Beauty'

Zone 3
Height: 4ft. (1.2m) Spread: 2ft. (60cm)

Helenium
'Goldene Jugend'

Zone 5
Height: 32in. (80cm) Spread: 2ft. (60cm)

Helenium
'Madame Canivet'

Zone 3
Height: 3ft. (90cm) Spread: 2ft. (60cm)

Helenium
'Pumilum Magnificum'

Zone 5
Height: 3ft. (90cm) Spread: 2ft. (60cm)

Helenium puberulum

Zone 8
Height: 5ft. (1.5m) Spread: 2ft. (60cm)
Short-lived

Helenium
'Rubinzwerg' A.G.M.

Zone 5
Height: 3ft. (90cm) Spread: 2ft. (60cm)

Helenium
'Sahin's Early Flowerer' A.G.M.

Zone 5
Height: 3ft. (90cm) Spread: 2ft. (60cm)

Helenium
'Waldtraut' A.G.M.

Zone 3
Height: 3ft. (90cm) Spread: 2ft. (60cm)

HELIANTHEMUM *(Cistaceae)*
Common names: Rock rose; sun rose

A genus of 110 species of subshrubs found in open scrubland or alpine meadows around the Mediterranean, in Eurasia, and in South and North America. They may be evergreen or semi-evergreen. Their leaves are linear or oblong, and opposite, and silver or gray-green in some species. The flowers are saucer-shaped, brightly-colored, and borne in cymes over a long period from late spring to midsummer.

✔ Long-flowering	✔ Low allergen
✔ Evergreen	✔ Disease-free
✔ Drought-tolerant	✔ Pest-free

CULTIVATION
Grow in alkaline to neutral, well-drained soil in sun. Cut back after flowering to within 1in. (2.5 cm) of previous year's growth.

PROPAGATION
Seed of species should be sown in a cold frame in as soon as it is ripe, or in spring. Softwood cuttings of species and cultivars can be taken in late spring or early summer.

H

Helianthemum
'Ben Fhada'

Zone 6
Height and spread: 8in. (20cm)

Helianthemum
'Ben Hope'

Zone 6
Height and spread: 8in. (20cm)

Helianthemum
'Coppernob'

Zone 6
Height: 8in. (20cm) Spread: 1ft. (30cm)

Helianthemum
'Fireball'

Zone 6
Height: 8in. (20cm) Spread: 1ft. (30cm)

Helianthemum
'Lawrenson's Pink'

Zone 6
Height: 8in. (20cm) Spread: 1ft. (30cm)

Helianthemum nummularium

Zone 6
Height: 8in. (20cm) Spread: 1ft. (30cm)

H

Helianthemum
'Raspberry Ripple'

Zone 6
Height and spread: 8in. (20cm)

Helianthemum
'Windmill Gold'

Zone 6
Height and spread: 8in. (20cm)

H

HELIANTHUS *(Asteraceae)*
Common names: Sunflower

A genus of 80 species of annuals and perennials from both dry meadows and wet swamps in North, Central, and South America. Their leaves are simple, bristly, large, and opposite or alternate. The daisy-like flowers have yellow ray florets and yellow, brown or purple discs, and are solitary or borne in loose corymbs over a long period in summer. They do not flower well in cold gardens. Some are highly invasive.

✔ Long-flowering	✘ Require staking	✘ Prone to slug damage
✔ Good cut flowers	✘ Mildew prone	
✔ Attracts bees	✘ Highly allergenic	
✔ Pest-free	✘ Foliage is skin-irritant	

CULTIVATION
Grow in poor, alkaline to neutral, humus-rich moist soil (except *H. salicifolius*, which prefers dry soil) in sun.

PROPAGATION
Seed should be sown in a cold frame in spring. Divide in spring or autumn. Take basal cuttings in spring.

Helianthus
'Capenoch Star' A.G.M.

Zone 5
Height: 5ft. (1.5m) Spread: 30in. (75cm)

Helianthus decapetalus
(Thin-leaf sunflower)
Zone 5
Height: 4ft. (1.2m) Spread: indefinite
Invasive

Helianthus x doronicoides
Zone 5
Height: 5ft. (1.5m) Spread: 2ft. (60cm)
Invasive

Helianthus 'Lemon Queen'
Zone 5
Height: 6ft. (2m) Spread: indefinite
Invasive

H

Heliamthus
'Loddon Gold' A.G.M.

Zone 5
Height: 5ft. (1.5m) Spread: 3ft. (90cm)

Helianthus x multiflorus

Zone 5
Height: 6ft. (2m) Spread: 3ft. (90cm)

Helianthus salicifolius
(Willow-leaved sunflower)
Zone 4
Height: 8ft. (2.5m) Spread: 1ft. (30cm)
Handsome foliage/ Drought-tolerant

Helianthus
'Triomphe de Gand'

Zone 5
Height: 4ft. (1.2m) Spread: 3ft. (90cm)

HELICHRYSUM *(Asteraceae)*

Common names: Curry plant

A genus of 500 species of annuals, perennials and shrubs from dry sunny sites in South Africa and Australasia in particular, but also in Eurasia and other parts of Africa. The perennials may be herbaceous or evergreen. Their handsome leaves may be in basal rosettes or opposite, are linear, and may be white-woolly in some and aromatic in others. The flowers are shaving-brush- or daisy-like, solitary or in corymbs, and everlasting. Some species are very small, and require scree or alpine house conditions.

✔ Good cut flowers   ✘ Mildew prone
✔ Good for drying for winter
✔ Handsome foliage

Helichrysum chionophilum

Zone 8
Height: 8in. (20cm) Spread: 1ft. (30cm)

CULTIVATION
Grow in alkaline to neutral, well-drained soil in sun.

PROPAGATION
Seed should be sown at 61°F (16°C) in a cold frame as soon as it is ripe, or in spring. Divide in spring.

H

Helichrysum italicum A.G.M.

Zone 8.
Height: 2ft. (60cm) Spread: 3ft. (90cm)
Foliage aromatic

Helichrysum italicum subsp.
serotinum
Zone 8
Height: 16in. (40cm) Spread: 30in. (75cm)
Foliage aromatic

Helichrysum petiolare
A.G.M.

Zone 10
Height: 20in. (50cm) Spread: 2ft. (60cm)

Helichrysum petiolare
'Limelight' A.G.M.

Zone 10
Height: 1ft. (30cm) Spread: 2ft. (60cm)

Helichrysum petiolare
'Roundabout'

Zone 10
Height: 6in. (15cm) Spread: 1ft. (30cm)

Helichrysum
'Ruby Cluster'

Zone 8
Height: 1ft. (30cm) Spread: 8in. (20cm)

Helichrysum
'Schweffelicht'

Zone 6
Height: 16in. (40cm) Spread: 1ft. (30cm)

Helichrysum thianschianicum
'Goldkind'

Zone 6
Height and spread: 1ft. (30cm)

H

HELICTOTRICHON *(Poaceae)*

Common names: Blue oat grass

A genus of 50 species of perennial grasses found in wasteland, field margins and rocky slopes in temperate Eurasia and North America. They may be evergreen or deciduous, and are tussock-forming. The leaves are linear, flat or rolled, and blue-gray. The flowering spike is stiff, shiny, straw-colored, and in open panicles.

- ✔ Evergreen
- ✔ Handsome foliage
- ✔ Attractive seed-heads
- ✔ Handsome seed-heads
- ✔ Low allergen
- ✘ Highly allergenic
- ✘ Prone to rust

CULTIVATION
Grow in alkaline to neutral, well-drained, soil in sun.

PROPAGATION
Seed should be sown in a cold frame in spring, when division can also be carried out.

Helictotrichon sempervirens
A.G.M.

Zone 5
Height: 4ft. (1.2m) Spread: 2ft. (60cm)

HELIOPSIS *(Asteraceae)*

Common names: Ox eye

A genus of a dozen species of perennials from dry prairie and open woodland in North America. The leaves are lance-shaped or ovate, toothed, and opposite. The solitary, daisy-like flowers are yellow, with yellow discs.

- ✔ Good cut flowers
- ✔ Attracts bees
- ✘ Need staking
- ✘ Prone to slug damage
- ✘ Need to lift & divide often

CULTIVATION
Grow in moist, fertile, humus-rich, well-drained soil in sun. They may require to be staked. Lift and divide every few years to maintain vigor.

PROPAGATION
Seed should be sown in a cold frame in spring. Divide in autumn or spring. Take basal cuttings in spring.

Heliopsis helianthoides
'Bressingham Dubloon'

Height and spread: 3ft. (90cm)

Heliopsis helianthoides var. *scabra*
'Light of Loddon' A.G.M.

Zone 4
Height: 4ft. (1.2m) Spread: 2ft. (60cm)

Heliopsis helianthoides var. *scabra*
'Mars'

Zone 4
Height: 5ft. (1.5m) Spread: 2ft. (60cm)

Heliopsis 'Lorraine Sunshine' (PBR)

Zone 4
Height and spread: 1ft. (30cm)
Foliage variegated

HELLEBORUS *(Ranunculaceae)*
Common names: Hellebore

A genus of 15 species of rhizomatous perennials from a wide range of habitats across Eurasia; some grow in dry, sunny scrubland and rocky sites, whilst others prefer moist, woodland. Furthermore, most (including those dealt with here) like alkaline soil, but a few prefer it to be acid. Collectively they provide the gardener with excellent, weather-resistant flowers in winter. Their leaves are lobed or pedate, leathery and toothed, and they may be evergreen or herbaceous. The flowers may be open saucers or bells or tubules, outward-facing or pendent, and sometimes marked handsomely internally; they are perfumed in *H. odorus*. They appear from late winter to early spring.

Helleborus argutifolius
A.G.M.

Zone 7
Height: 4ft. (1.2m) Spread: 3ft. (90cm)

✔ Evergreen	✔ Winter-flowering	✘ All parts poisonous
✔ Good cut flowers		✘ Sap is skin-irritant
✔ Handsome foliage		✘ Prone to slug damage

CULTIVATION
They dislike very wet or very dry soil, and must have humus; grow in alkaline to neutral soil in sun or part shade.

PROPAGATION
Seed of species should be sown in a cold frame as soon as it is ripe. Divide species and cultivars after flowering.

Helleborus argutifolius
'Pacific Frost'

Zone 7
Height: 4ft. (1.2m) Spread: 3ft. (90cm)

Helleborus niger
(Christmas Rose)

Zone 3
Height: 1ft. (30cm) Spread: 18in. (45 cm)

Helleborus odorus

Zone 6
Height and spread: 20in. (50cm)
Flowers perfumed

Helleborus orientalis hybridus

Zone 6
Height: and spread: 20in. (50cm)

Helleborus x sternyii
Blackthorn Group A.G.M.
Zone 7
Height: 14in. (35cm) Spread: 1ft. (30cm)

Helleborus viridis
(Green hellebore)

Zone 6
Height and spread: 18in. (45 cm)

HEMEROCALLIS *(Hemerocallidaceae)*
Common names: Day lily

A genus of 15 species of perennials from meadowland, forest margins, and river valleys in Japan, China and Korea. They may be herbaceous, semi-evergreen or evergreen, and some are rhizomatous. Their leaves are strap-shaped, and arching. The flower shape varies from circular to triangular to star- or spider- shaped. They may be single or double, and are borne on erect, branching scapes over a long period in summer; each flower lasts but one day (or night in the case of nocturnal-flowering types) but is followed by others in succession.

✔ Repeat-flowering
✔ Low allergen
✔ Handsome foliage

✘ Prone to slug damage
✘ Need to lift & divide often

CULTIVATION
They dislike excessive shade and dry conditions; grow in moist, well-drained soil in sun, and do not let them dry out, especially before flowering time. Lift and divide every few years to maintain vigor.

PROPAGATION
Seed of species should be sown in a cold frame in spring or autumn. Cultivars and species can be divided in spring or autumn, but only in spring if evergreen.

Hemerocallis
'Amersham'

Zone 4
Height and spread: 28in. (70cm)

H

Hemerocallis
'Bette Davies' Eyes'

Zone 4
Height and spread: 26in. (65cm)

Hemerocallis
'Black Magic'

Zone 4
Height and spread: 2ft. (60cm)

Hemerocallis 'Cartwheels' A.G.M.

Zone 4
Height and spread: 30in. (75cm)
Evergreen

Hemerocallis
'Chemistry'

Zone 4
Height and spread: 28in. (70cm)

Hemerocallis
'Chicago Royal Robe'

Zone 4
Height: 2ft. (60cm) Spread: 6in. (15cm)

Hemerocallis
'Chicago Sunrise'

Zone 4
Height: 28in. (70cm) Spread: 6in. (15cm)

H

Hemerocallis 'Corky' A.G.M.

Zone 4
Height: 32in. (80cm) Spread: 1ft. (30cm)
Evergreen

Hemerocallis
'Frans Hals'

Zone 4
Height and spread: 2ft. (60cm)

Hemerocallis fulva
'Flore Pleno'

Zone 4
Height: 30in. (75cm) Spread: 3ft. (90cm)

Hemerocallis
'Golden Scroll'

Zone 4
Height: 30in. (75cm) Spread: 1ft. (30cm)

Hemerocallis 'Golden Zebra'

Zone 4
Height: 18in. (45 cm) Spread: 1ft. (30cm)
Foliage variegated

Hemerocallis
'Green Flutter' A.G.M.

Zone 4
Height: 20in. (50cm) Spread: 3ft. (90cm)

Hemerocallis
'King Haiglar'

Zone 4
Height: 28in. (70cm) Spread: 6in. (15cm)

Hemerocallis
'Lady Neva'

Zone 4
Height: 3ft. (90cm) Spread: 9in. (22cm)

Hemerocallis
'Little Grapette'

Zone 4
Height: 1ft. (30cm) Spread: 18in. (45 cm)

Hemerocallis
'Mighty Mogul'

Zone 4
Height: 1ft. (30cm) Spread: 18in. (45 cm)

Hemerocallis
'Silver Veil'

Zone 4
Height: 2ft. (60cm) Spread: 3ft. (90cm)

Hemerocallis
'Stafford'

Zone 4
Height: 28in. (70cm) Spread: 3ft. (90cm)

Hemerocallis
'Stella de Oro' A.G.M.

Zone 4
Height: 1ft. (30cm) Spread: 18in. (45 cm)

Hemerocallis
'Tutunkhamun'

Zone 4
Height: 2ft. (60cm) Spread: 3ft. (90cm)

HEPATICA *(Ranunculaceae)*

Common names: None

A genus of ten species of perennials from northern temperate woodlands. They have handsome leaves, which may be kidney-shaped or lobed, toothed or simple, and are often marbled in white or silver. The flowers are solitary, bowl- or star-shaped, and borne in early spring, often before the leaves.

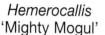 Handsome foliage

✗ Resents disturbance
✗ Prone to slug damage

CULTIVATION
Grow in moist, humus-rich, alkaline to neutral, soil in part shade.

PROPAGATION
Seed should be sown in an open frame as soon as it is ripe. Division can be tried in spring, but is not tolerated well.

Hepatica nobilis var. *japonica*

Zone 5
Height: 4in. (10 cm) Spread: 6in. (15cm)

HESPERIS *(Brasssicaceae)*

Common names: Sweet rocket; Dame's violet

A genus of 30 species of biennials and short-lived perennials from wasteland, stony ground and woodland across Eurasia. Their leaves are entire or pinnatifid, spoon-shaped or ovate. The flowers are single, cross-shaped, perfumed, and borne in loose panicles from spring to midsummer. Only the double forms are good for cutting.

✔ Flowers perfumed
✔ Attracts butterflies

✘ Mildew prone
✘ Prone to slug damage
✘ Resents disturbance
✘ Self-seeds
✘ Short-lived

CULTIVATION
Grow in moist, well-drained, alkaline to neutral, fertile soil in sun or part shade. Dead-head to prevent self-seeding.

PROPAGATION
Seed should be sown in situ in spring. Take basal cuttings in spring.

Hesperis matronalis

Zone 3
Height: 3ft. (90cm) Spread: 18in. (45 cm)

Hesperis matronalis var. *alba*

Zone 3
Height: 3ft. (90cm) Spread: 18in. (45 cm)

HETEROTHECA *(Asteraceae)*

Common names: Hairy golden aster

A genus of 20 species of annuals and perennials from open, dry, sunny sites in sandy soil in North America. The leaves are simple, alternate, ovate, toothed or entire, and silver-hairy in some species. The daisy-like flowers are yellow, and borne in corymbs from midsummer to early autumn.

✔ Handsome foliage
✔ Drought-tolerant
✔ Trouble-free

✘ Highly allergenic

Heterotheca villosa

Zone 5
Height: 32in. (80cm) Spread: 8in. (20cm)

CULTIVATION
Grow in sharply-draining soil in sun. Protect against winter wet.

PROPAGATION
Sow seed, or divide in spring.

HEUCHERA *(Saxifragaceae)*
Common names: Coral bells

A genus of 55 species of evergreen or semi-evergreen perennials from the Rocky Mountains of the U.S.A., and Mexico. They have clumps of heart-shaped or rounded, lobed, long-stalked, boldly-veined leaves, which are toothed in some species. They are first-class foliage plants, and make excellent ground-cove, even in shade. The flowers are small, tubular, with colorful calyces, and are borne in tall, narrow panicles or racemes in early summer.

✔ Handsome foliage

✔ Good cut flowers

✔ Attracts bees

✔ Low allergen

✘ Need to lift & divide often

CULTIVATION
Grow in moist, neutral, well-drained soil in sun or part shade, and even full shade provided the ground is moist. With time, they become woody, and lift above the surface, so need to be lifted and divided and replanted with the crown just at the soil surface.

PROPAGATION
Sow seed of species in a cold frame in spring; divide cultivars and species in autumn.

Heuchera
'Amber Waves'

Zone 7
Height and spread: 8in. (20cm)

Heuchera
'Beauty Colour'

Zone 5
Height and spread: 1ft. (30cm)

Heuchera
'Cancan' A.G.M.

Zone 5
Height: 6in. (15cm) Spread: 1ft. (30cm)

Heuchera
'Chocolate Ruffles' (PBR)

Zone 4
Height: 8in. (20cm) Spread: 1ft. (30cm)

Heuchera
'Fireworks' A.G.M.

Zone 4
Height and spread: 1ft. (30cm)

Heuchera
'Greenfinch'

Zone 4
Height: 3ft. (90cm) Spread: 2ft. (60cm)

Heuchera
'Helen Dillon'

Zone 5
Height and spread: 2ft. (60cm)

H

Heuchera
'Leuchtkafer' ('Firefly')

Zone 4
Height: 30in. (75cm) Spread: 1ft. (30cm)

Heuchera micrantha
'Palace Purple' A.G.M.

Zone 5
Height and spread: 2ft. (60cm)

Heuchera
'Mint Frost' (PBR)

Zone 5
Height and spread: 2ft. (60cm)

Heuchera
'Persian Carpet'

Zone 7
Height: 14in. (35cm) Spread: 2ft. (60cm)

Heuchera
'Pewter Moon'

Zone 7
Height: 16in. (40cm) Spread: 1ft. (30cm)

Heuchera
'Pluie de Feu'

Zone 5
Height: 18in. (45 cm) Spread: 1ft. (30cm)

Heuchera
'Plum Pudding'

Zone 5
Height and spread: 2ft. (60cm)

Heuchera
'Rachel'

Zone 7
Height and spread: 1ft. (30cm)

Heuchera
'Raspberry Regal' A.G.M.

Zone 4
Height and spread: 18in. (45 cm)

H

Heuchera
'Red Spangles'

Zone 4
Height: 20in. (50cm) Spread: 10in. (25 cm)

Heuchera
'Silver Indiana' (PBR)

Zone 5
Height: 2ft. (60cm) Spread: 18in. (45 cm)

Heuchera
'Strawberry Candy'

Zone 5
Height and spread: 18in. (45 cm)

Heuchera
'Van Gogh'

Zone 4
Height: 18in. (45 cm) Spread: 1ft. (30cm)

Heuchera
'Whirlwind'

Zone 7
Height: 1ft. (30cm) Spread: 8in. (20cm)

X HEUCHERELLA *(Saxifragaceae)*

Common names: None

An intergeneric hybrid genus between Heuchera and Tiarella of evergreen perennials. Their leaves are rounded or heart-shaped, boldly-veined, and often handsomely colored. They are excellent foliage plants. The flowers are tubular or bell-shaped, and borne in short panicles over a long period from spring to autumn.

✔ Evergreen
✔ Long-flowering
✔ Handsome foliage
✔ Low allergen

✔ Good cut flowers
✔ Disease-free
✔ Pest-free

CULTIVATION
Grow in acid to neutral, moist, well-drained soil in sun or part or full shade.

PROPAGATION
Division in spring or autumn.

x Heucherella alba
'Bridget Bloom'

Zone 5
Height: 16in. (40cm) Spread: 1ft. (30cm)

x Heucherella alba
'Rosalie'

Zone 5
Height: 16in. (40cm) Spread: 1ft. (30cm)

x Heucherella
'Burnished Bronze'

Zone 5
Height: 14in. (35cm) Spread: 1ft. (30cm)

x Heucherella
'Ink Spot'

Zone 5
Height: 14in. (35cm) Spread: 1ft. (30cm)

x Heucherella
'Quicksilver'

Zone 5
Height: 1ft. (30cm) Spread: 18in. (45 cm)

HIERACIUM *(Asteraceae)*

Common names: Hawkweed

A genus of 260 species of perennials from a wide diversity of habitats from meadow, grassland, dry slopes and farmed fields across the Northern hemisphere. Their leaves are in basal rosettes, entire or toothed, ovate. The dandelion-like flowers are in panicles or corymbs, in summer.

✔ Good cut flowers	✘ Self-seeds
✔ Drought-tolerant	✘ Prone to slug damage
✔ Handsome foliage	

CULTIVATION
Grow in well-drained poor soil in sun. Dead-head to prevent self-seeding.

PROPAGATION
Seed should be sown in a cold frame in spring, when division can also be carried out.

Hieracium lanatum

Zone 7
Height: 18in. (45 cm) Spread: 8in. (20cm)

Hieracium maculatum

Zone 6
Height: 32in. (80cm) Spread: 8in. (20cm)
Variegated foliage

Hieracium villosum

Zone 6
Height: 18in. (45 cm) Spread: 8in. (20cm)

HOLCUS *(Poaceae)*

Common names: None

A genus of eight species of annual and perennial grasses from grassland and woodland in Eurasia and North Africa. Their leaves are linear, folded or flat, green or blue-green. The inflorescence is a panicle of flattened, two-flowered spikelets in summer.

✔ Handsome foliage   ✘ Highly allergenic

✔ Disease-free   ✘ Self-seeds

CULTIVATION

Grow in moist, well-drained, fertile soil in sun or part shade. Dead-head after flowering to prevent self-seeding.

PROPAGATION

Divide in spring, as they do not come true from seed.

Holcus mollis
'Albovariegatus'

Zone 5
Height: 1ft. (30cm) Spread: 18in. (45 cm)

Holcus mollis
'White Fog'

Zone 5
Height: 1ft. (30cm) Spread: 18in. (45 cm)

HOMERIA *(Iridaceae)*
Common names: None

A genus of 31 species of perennials found in gritty slopes at low and high altitude in South Africa. Their leaves are basal and stem, strap-shaped or linear. The cup-shaped flowers are perfumed, and borne in succession on branched stems from spring to summer.

✔ Flowers perfumed
✔ Disease-free
✔ Pest-free

CULTIVATION
Under glass, plant corms 4in. (10 cm) deep in sharply-draining loam-based compost in full light and high humidity. Water freely during growth, and keep dry in winter.

Out of doors, grow in humus-rich, fertile, well-drained soil in sun.

PROPAGATION
Separate offsets in dormant period.

Homeria collina

Zone 9
Height: 16in. (40cm) Spread: 2in. (5cm)

Homeria flaccida

Zone 9
Height: 2ft. (60cm) Spread: 4in. (10 cm)

HORDEUM *(Poaceae)*
Common names: Barley; Squirrel-tail grass

A genus of 20 species of annual and perennial grasses which

grow on disturbed ground in temperate parts of both the north and south hemispheres. Their leaves are linear, rolled or flat, and green to blue-green. The flowering spike is arched, silky, broad, and dense, with bristly spikelets, and is borne in early and midsummer.

✔ Good for drying for winter   ✘ Highly allergenic
✔ Drought-tolerant
✔ Evergreen
✔ Handsome foliage
✔ Disease-free
✔ Pest-free

CULTIVATION
Grow in fertile, well-drained soil in sun.

PROPAGATION
Seed should be sown *in situ* in spring or autumn.

Hordeum jubatum

Zone 5
Height: 20in. (50 cm) Spread: 1ft. (30cm)

H

HORMINIUM (*Lamiaceae*)

Common names: Dragon's mouth; Pyrenean dead-nettle

A genus of one species, *H pyrenaicum*, from subalpine meadows and screes of the European Alps and the Pyrenees. Its ovate, toothed leaves are in basal rosettes. The flowers are bell-shaped or tubular, two-lipped, and borne in axillary whorls in summer.

✔ Handsome foliage   ✘ Prone to slug damage

CULTIVATION
Grow in well-drained, fertile soil in sun.

PROPAGATION
Divide in spring or sow seed in a cold frame in autumn.

Horminium pyrenaicum

Zone 7
Height: 8in. (20cm) Spread: 1ft. (30cm)

HOSTA (*Hostaceae*)

Common names: Plantain lily

A genus of 70 species of herbaceous perennials from sunny alpine meadows, rocky stream sides, woodland and volcanic cliffs in Japan, China, Korea and east Russia. They are grown for their foliage, which comes in dense mounds of heart-shaped or ovate or round leaves. Their flowers are pink or white, funnel- or bell-shaped, and borne in one-sided leafy or leafless scapes in summer, which are followed by handsome seed-heads; they can be perfumed in some instances.

✔ Handsome foliage   ✘ Very prone to slug damage
✔ Low allergen
✔ Good cut flowers

CULTIVATION
Grow in moist, fertile well-drained soil in a sheltered corner in full or part shade. Do not allow to dry out in summer. Flowering is less in deep shade. Take precautions against slugs and snails, as they damage the foliage even before it unfolds. Yellow-leaved forms color best in sun.

PROPAGATION
Since the majority of cultured forms are hybrids they can be propagated only by division; this should be done in early spring or late summer.

Hosta
'August Moon'

Zone 5
Height: 20in. (50cm) Spread: 30in. (75cm)

Hosta
'Brim Cup'

Zone 5
Height: 1ft. (30cm) Spread: 16in. (40cm)

Hosta crispula
A.G.M.

Zone 5
Height and spread: 3ft. (90cm)

Hosta
'Eric Smith'

Zone 5
Height: 4ft. (1.2m) Spread: 2ft. (60cm)

Hosta
'Fire and Ice'

Zone 5
Height: 2ft. (60cm) Spread: 18in. (45 cm)

Hosta fortunei var. *albopicta forma.*
'Aurea' A.G.M.

Zone 5
Height: 22in. (55cm) Spread: 3ft. (90cm)

Hosta
'Francee' A.G.M.

Zone 5
Height and spread: 32in. (80cm)

Hosta
'Frances Williams' A.G.M.

Zone 5
Height: 26in. (65cm) Spread: 3ft. (90cm)

Hosta
'Gold Standard'

Zone 5
Height: 26in. (65cm) Spread: 3ft. (90cm)

Hosta
'Ground Master'

Zone 5
Height: 20in. (50cm) Spread: 22in. (55cm)

Hosta 'Honeybells' A.G.M.

Zone 5
Height: 3ft. (90cm) Spread: 4ft. (1.2m)
Flowers perfumed

Hosta
'Lacy Belle'

Zone 5
Height: 18in. (45 cm) Spread: 2ft. (60cm)

Hosta
'Minuteman'

Zone 5
Height: 8in. (20cm) Spread: 1ft. (30cm)

H

Hosta montana
'Aureomarginata'

Zone 5
Height: 28in. (70cm) Spread: 3ft. (90cm)

Hosta
'Night before Christmas'

Zone 5
Height: 3ft. (90cm) Spread: 18in. (45 cm)

Hosta
'On Stage'

Zone 5
Height: 2ft. (60cm) Spread: 18in. (45 cm)

H

Hosta
'Patriot'

Zone 5
Height: 26in. (65cm) Spread: 18in. (45 cm)

Hosta plantaginea

Zone 5
Height: 30in. (75cm) Spread: 3ft. (90cm)
Flowers perfumed

Hosta rohdeifolia

Zone 5
Height: 3ft. (90cm) Spread: 45 cm.(18in.)

Hosta 'Royal Standard' A.G.M.

Zone 5
Height: 3ft. (90cm) Spread: 4ft. (1.2m)
Flowers perfumed

Hosta
'Samurai'

Zone 5
Height: 32in. (80cm) Spread: 3ft. (90cm)

Hosta
'Sea Gold Star'

Zone 5
Height: 32in. (80cm) Spread: 2ft. (60cm)

H

Hosta sieboldiana
(Siebold plantain lily)

Zone 5
Height: 3ft. (90cm) Spread: 4ft. (1.2m)

Hosta
'Snow Cap'

Zone 5
Height: 16in. (40cm) Spread: 2ft. (60cm)

Hosta 'So Sweet'

Zone 5
Height and spread: 2ft. (60cm)
Flowers perfumed

Hosta
'Sun Power'

Zone 5
Height: 3ft. (90cm) Spread: 3ft. (90cm)

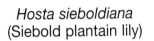

Hosta
'Super Nova'

Zone 5
Height: 32in. (80cm) Spread: 3ft. (90cm)

Hosta 'Sweet Susan'

Zone 5
Height: 18in. (45 cm) Spread: 28in. (70cm)
Flowers perfumed

Hosta
'Tall Boy'

Zone 5
Height and spread: 3ft. (90cm)

Hosta
'Tattoo'

Zone 5
Height and spread: 14in. (35cm)

Hosta undulata var. *undulata*
A.G.M.

Zone 5.
Height: 32in. (80cm) Spread: 18in. (45 cm)

Hosta
'Whirlwind'

Zone 5
Height: 16in. (40cm) Spread: 2ft. (60cm)

Hosta
'Wide Brim' A.G.M.

Zone 5
Height: 22in. (55cm) Spread: 3ft. (90cm)

HOUTTUYNIA *(Saururaceae)*
Common names: None

A genus of but a single rhizomatous perennial, *H. cordata*, found in wet or damp shady woodland and marshland in East Asia. It is highly invasive, and can be grown for ground cover. The leaves are simple, ovate, or heart-shaped, gray-green, and emit an orange smell when bruised. The flowers are tiny, greenish-yellow, and followed by white bracts, in spring.

✔ Aromatic foliage
✔ Low allergen
✔ Handsome foliage

✘ Invasive
✘ Prone to slug damage

CULTIVATION
Grow in a container in moist, humus-rich, fertile soil in sun or part shade, or in shallow water.

PROPAGATION
Seed should be sown in a cold frame as soon as it is ripe. Divide in spring.

Houttuynia cordata
'Chameleon'

Zone 5
Height: 1ft. (30cm) Spread: indefinite

Houttuynia cordata
'Flore Pleno'

Zone 5
Height: 1ft. (30cm) Spread: indefinite

Houttuynia cordata
'Variegata'

Zone 5
Height: 1ft. (30cm) Spread: indefinite

HOYA *(Asclepiadaceae)*

Common names: Wax plant

A genus of 200 species of evergreen climbing and shrubby perennials from rainforest, coastal bluffs, stream sides and escarpments in warm parts of Australia, Asia and the Pacific Islands. Their leaves are variously shaped, leathery, succulent, and in opposite pairs. The flowers have five spreading petals and a central corona of hooded stamens., and are borne in cymes from the upper leaf axils, and followed by handsome seed-heads.

✔ Evergreen

✔ Handsome foliage

✔ Disease-free

CULTIVATION
Under glass, grow in loam-based, sharply-draining potting compost, in indirect or shaded light, and moderate or high humidity. Water freely during growth, and keep just moist in winter.

Out of doors, grow in moist, well-drained soil in a sheltered corner, in sun, with shade at mid-day.

PROPAGATION
Seed should be sown at 75°F (24°C) in spring. Layer in spring or summer. Take semi-ripe cuttings, and root with bottom heat in late summer.

Hoya carnosa
'Tricolor'

Zone 10
Height: 20ft. (6 m) Spread: 6ft. (2m)

HYACINTHOIDES *(Hyacinthaceae)*

Common names: Bluebell

A genus of four bulbous perennials from wet meadows and deciduous woodland in North Africa and western Europe. They spread rapidly by self-seeding and bulb production. The basal leaves are glossy, linear, or strap-shaped. The perfumed flowers are bell-shaped or tubular, and borne in racemes in spring.

✔ Flowers perfumed
✔ Good cut flowers
✔ Handsome foliage
✔ Disease-free
✔ Pest-free

✘ All parts poisonous
✘ All parts skin-irritant
✘ Self-seeds
✘ Invasive

CULTIVATION
Plant bulbs 3in. (8 cm) deep in autumn in moist, humus-rich, well-drained soil in part shade. Dead-head to prevent self-seeding.

PROPAGATION
Separate bulbs in summer, or sow seed in a cold frame as soon as it is ripe.

Hyacinthoides non-scripta
(English bluebell)

Zone 5
Height: 16in. (40cm) Spread: 4in. (10cm)

Hyacinthoides non-scripta
var. *alba*

Zone 5
Height: 16in. (40cm) Spread: 4in. (10 cm)

Hyacinthoides non-scripta
var. *rosea*

Zone 5
Height: 16in. (40cm) Spread: 4in. (10 cm)

HYACINTHUS *(Hyacinthaceae)*
Common names: Hyacinth

A genus of three species of bulbous perennials from limestone cliffs and slopes at altitudes to 8,000ft. (2,600m) in Central and West Asia. Their leaves are basal, semi-erect, strap-shaped, channeled, and shiny green. The perfumed, bell-shaped flowers are borne in loose or dense racemes in early spring; they can be single or double.

- ✔ Flowers perfumed
- ✔ Drought-tolerant
- ✔ Attracts bees
- ✔ Disease-free
- ✔ Pest-free
- ✗ All parts poisonous
- ✗ Bulbs skin-irritant

CULTIVATION
Plant bulbs 4in. (10 cm) deep in autumn in fertile, well-drained soil in sun or part shade. Bulbs can be planted even deeper 16in. (40 cm.) provided drainage is good, and this permits overplanting with summer bedding.

PROPAGATION
Remove offsets in summer.

Hyacinthus orientalis
'Blue Jacket'

Zone 5
Height: 1ft. (30cm) Spread: 3in. (8 cm)

Hyacinthus orientalis
'City of Haarlam' A.G.M.

Zone 5
Height: 1ft. (30cm) Spread: 3in. (8 cm)

Hyacinthus orientalis
'Gipsy Queen' A.G.M.

Zone 5
Height: 1ft. (30cm) Spread: 3in. (8 cm)

Hyacinthus orientalis
'L' Innocence' A.G.M.

Zone 5
Height: 1ft. (30cm) Spread: 3in. (8 cm)

HYLOMECON *(Papaveraceae)*
Common names: None

A genus of but one species, *H. japonica*, of herbaceous rhizomatous perennial from east Asian woodlands. The leaves are basal, pinnate with ovate lobes and toothed. The flowers are single, solitary, yellow cups with four petals, borne from spring to summer.

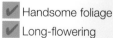

- ✔ Handsome foliage
- ✔ Long-flowering
- ✗ Prone to slug damage
- ✗ Invasive

CULTIVATION
Grow in acid to neutral, moist, humus-rich, well-drained soil in full or part shade.

PROPAGATION
Seed should be sown as soon as it is ripe, or divide in spring.

Hylomecon japonica

Zone 7
Height: 8in. (20cm) Spread: indefinite

H

HYMENOCALLIS *(Amaryllidaceae)*
Common names: None

A genus of bulbous perennials from rocky ground and grassland in southern U.S.A. down to South America. They may be evergreen or herbaceous. The leaves are basal, oblong, shiny green. The perfumed flowers have a resemblance to spidery daffodils in that they have a central cup, and long, twisted tepals.

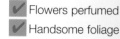 Flowers perfumed
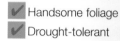 Handsome foliage

CULTIVATION
Grow in moist, fertile, well-drained soil in sun or part shade. Protect against winter wet.

PROPAGATION
Seed should be sown at 75°F (24°C) as soon as it is ripe. Remove offsets in spring.

Hymenocallis x festalis
A.G.M.

Zone 9
Height: 32in. (80cm) Spread: 1ft. (30cm)

H

HYPERICUM *(Clusiaceae)*
Common names: St. John's Wort

A genus of 400 species of shrubs, annuals, trees and herbaceous perennials from a wide range of habitats and climates across the world. Their leaves are variously shaped, and opposite or in whorls. The flowers are yellow, with pronounced stamens, and borne singly or in cymes—over a long period in many instances.

Handsome foliage   Prone to rust
Drought-tolerant

CULTIVATION
Grow in sharply-draining soil in sun or part shade.

PROPAGATION
Seed should be sown in a cold frame in autumn. Divide in spring or autumn.

Hypericum cerastioides

Zone 7
Height: 8in. (20cm) Spread: 18in. (45 cm)

Hypericum olympicum

Zone 6
Height and spread: 1ft. (30cm)

Hypericum olympicum
forma. *minus*

Zone 6
Height 4in. (10 cm) Spread: 8in. (20cm)

Hypericum perforatum

Zone 3
Height: 4ft. (1.2m) Spread: 2ft. (60cm)

HYSSOPUS *(Lamiaceae)*

Common names: Hyssop

A genus of five species of herbaceous perennials from dry, rocky and sandy sites from the Mediterranean to Central Asia. The aromatic foliage is linear, and blue-green or mid green. The tubular flowers are borne in whorls in narrow, terminal spikes.

- ✔ Foliage aromatic
- ✔ Attracts bees
- ✔ Attracts butterflies
- ✔ Low allergen
- ✔ Culinary vegetable
- ✔ Disease-free
- ✔ Pest-free

CULTIVATION

Grow in alkaline to neutral, fertile, well-drained soil in sun. Cut back to within 1in. (2.5 cm) of previous year's growth in mid-spring.

PROPAGATION

Seed should be sown in a cold frame in autumn. Softwood cuttings can be rooted in summer.

Height: 3ft. (90cm) Spread: 14in. (35cm)

H

Hyssopus officinalis
forma. *Albus*

Zone 3
Height: 2ft. (60cm) Spread: 3ft. (90cm)

IBERIS
IMPATIENS
IMPERATA
INCARVILLEA
INULA
IPHEION
IPOMOEA
IRESINE
IRIS
ISATIS
ISOPLEXIS
IXIA

I

IBERIS *(Brassicaceae)*
Common names: Candytuft

A genus of 40 species of annuals, evergreen subshrubs and perennials from porous, limy, sunny sites in Europe, the near East and North Africa. Their leaves are entire or pinnatisect, linear, and alternate. The flowers are cruciform, with two pairs of unevenly-sized petals, and borne in racemes or corymbs; they may be perfumed.

✔ Evergreen
✔ Low allergen
✔ Attracts bees
✔ Attracts butterflies

✘ Prone to slug damage

CULTIVATION
Grow in alkaline to neutral, moist, humus-rich, well-drained soil in sun. Trim over after flowering to maintain compactness.

PROPAGATION
Seed should be sown in a cold frame in autumn. Softwood cuttings can be taken in late spring and semi-ripe cuttings in summer.

Iberis semperflorens

Zone 7
Height: 1ft. (30cm) Spread: 2ft. (60cm)

Iberis sempervirens

Zone 4
Height: 8in. (20cm) Spread: 1ft. (30cm)

Iberis sempervirens
'Pinky Perpetual'

Zone 4
Height: 1ft. (30cm) Spread: 16in. (40cm)

Iberis sempervirens
'Weisse Zwerg'

Zone 4
Height: 4in. (10 cm) Spread: 8in. (20cm)

IMPATIENS *(Balsamaceae)*
Common names: Busy Lizzie

A genus of 850 species of annuals, subshrubs and evergreen perennials from a wide range of warm temperate and tropical habitats such as woodland, stream sides and lakesides across the northern hemisphere in particular. Their stems and foliage are succulent, brittle and fleshy. The leaves may be alternate, whorled or opposite. The flowers are asymmetric, five-petalled, spurred and sometimes hooded, and are borne singly or in clusters, over long periods in some instances. The seed-heads are explosive, and some species are rampant weeds for this reason.

✔ Long-flowering

✘ Prone to gray mould

CULTIVATION
Under glass, grow in any potting compost in full or bright filtered light, with moderate to high humidity. Water moderately in summer, and sparingly in winter.

Out of doors, grow in moist, humus-rich, well-drained soil in a warm spot in part shade.

PROPAGATION
Seed should be sown at 64°F (18°C) in early spring. Softwood cuttings of I. walleriana and I. New Guinea Group can be taken from spring to summer.

Impatiens
New Guinea Group

Zone 10
Height: 14in. (35cm) Spread: 1ft. (30cm)

Impatiens niamniamensis
'Congo Cockatoo'

Zone 10
Height: 3ft. (90cm) Spread: 14in. (35cm)

Impatiens omeina

Zone 8
Height: 6in. (15cm) Spread: 8in. (20cm)

Impatiens sodenii

Zone 10
Height: 8in. (20cm) Spread: 16in. (40cm)

I

Impatiens tinctoria

Zone 8
Height: 7ft. (2.2m) Spread: 3ft. (90cm)
Invasive

Impatiens walleriana
Accent series

Zone 10
Height and spread: 2ft. (60cm)

Impatiens walleriana
'Variegata'

Zone 10
Height and spread: 2ft. (60cm)

IMPERATA *(Poaceae)*
Common names: None

A genus of six species of rhizomatous perennial grasses from open grassland in tropical and warm-temperate Japan. The leaves are linear, flat, and pointed. They have erect spikelets in panicles in summer.

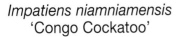

✔ Handsome foliage	✘ Self-seeds
✔ Disease-free	✘ Highly allergenic
✔ Pest-free	

CULTIVATION
Grow in moist, humus-rich, well-drained soil in sun or part shade.

PROPAGATION
Divide in spring or early summer.

Imperata cylindrica
'Rubra'

Zone 8
Height: 2ft. (60cm) Spread: 1ft. (30cm)

I

INCARVILLEA *(Bignoniaceae)*
Common names: None

A genus of 15 annuals and perennials from grassland and mountainous rocky regions in Asia. Their leaves are alternate, and pinnatisect or pinnate. The flowers are trumpet-shaped or tubular, and are held high on stiff stems, in panicles or racemes or singly, in early and midsummer. They are tap-rooted.

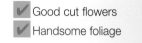

✔ Good cut flowers
✔ Handsome foliage
✘ Prone to slug damage
✘ Resents disturbance

CULTIVATION
Grow in moist, fertile well-drained soil in sun, but with some shade in midsummer. Do not transplant once established. Protect against excessive winter wet.

PROPAGATION
Seed should be sown in a cold frame in spring or autumn. Basal stem cuttings can be rooted in spring. Division can be tried in spring, but is not recommended.

Incarvillea compacta

Zone 6
Height: 1ft. (30cm) Spread: 16in. (40cm)

Incarvillea delavayi

Zone 6
Height: 2ft. (60cm) Spread: 1ft. (30cm)

Incarvillea delavayi forma. *alba*

Zone 6
Height: 2ft. (60cm) Spread: 1ft. (30cm)

Incarvillea delavayi 'Bees Pink'

Zone 6
Height: 2ft. (60cm) Spread: 1ft. (30cm)

Incarvillea mairei

Zone 4
Height: 20in. (50cm) Spread: 1ft. (30cm)

Incarvillea sinensis 'Alba'

Zone 4
Height: 34in. (85 cm) Spread: 1ft. (30cm)

Incarvillea
'Snowtop'

Zone 6
Height: 2ft. (60cm) Spread: 1ft. (30cm)

Incarvillea zhongdianensis

Zone 7
Height: 16in. (40cm) Spread: 8in. (20cm)

INULA *(Asteraceae)*

Common names: Sword-leaf Inula; elecampane

A genus of 100 species of annuals, biennials and perennials from temperate Europe and Africa, and subtropical Africa and Asia, where they grow in very diverse habitats such as dry mountainous and wet shady lowland. The majority, however, come from dry sunny sites. The leaves are basal and large, or smaller and stem, and ovate or linear or round. The flowers are daisy-like, flat, with yellow ray florets and discs; they are solitary or borne in panicles or corymbs in mid and late summer. Taller species may need to be staked, and rhizomatous ones may be invasive.

✔ Good cut flowers   ✘ Mildew prone
✔ Attracts bees

CULTIVATION
Grow in moist, fertile, deep soil in sun. *I. magnifica* tolerates boggy soils, and *II. helenium* and *hookeri* will tolerate some shade.

PROPAGATION
Seed should be sown in a cold frame in autumn or spring. Divide in spring or autumn.

Inula acaulis

Zone 6
Height: 4in. (10 cm) Spread: 1ft. (30cm)

Inula ensifolia

Zone 5
Height: 2ft. (60cm) Spread: 1ft. (30cm)

Inula helenium
(Elecampane)

Zone 5
Height: 5ft. (1.5m) Spread: 3ft. (90cm)

Inula hookeri

Zone 6
Height: 32in. (80cm) Spread: indefinite
Invasive

Inula magnifica

Zone 6
Height: 6ft. (2m) Spread: 3ft. (90cm)

Inula orientalis

Zone 6
Height: 3ft. (90cm) Spread: 2ft. (60cm)

Inula royleana
(Himalayan elecampane)

Zone 6
Height: 32in. (80cm) Spread: 18in. (45 cm)

IPHEION *(Alliaceae)*
Common names: None

A genus of ten species of bulbous perennials from rocky habitats and upland meadow in South America. Their leaves are basal, grass-like, narrow linear. The perfumed flowers are star-shaped, and borne singly or in pairs in late winter or spring. The leaves and bulbs smell of onions when crushed; the flowers smell of honey.

✔ Flowers perfumed
✔ Drought-tolerant

✘ Prone to slug damage

CULTIVATION
Plant bulbs 3in. (8 cm) deep in autumn in moist, humus-rich, well-drained soil in sun.

PROPAGATION
Seed should be sown in a cold frame as soon as it is ripe. Separate bulbs during summer dormancy.

Ipheion
'Alberto Castillo'

Zone 6
Height: 8in. (20cm) Spread: 2in. (5cm)

Ipheion uniflorum

Zone 6
Height: 8in. (20cm) Spread: 3in. (8 cm)

Ipheion uniflorum
'Wisley Blue' A.G.M.

Zone 6
Height: 8in. (20cm) Spread: 3in. (8 cm)

IPOMOEA (*Convolvulaceae*)

Common names: Morning glory; Sweet potato; Spanish flag

A genus of 500 species of annuals, and perennials, the majority of which are climbers, and some shrubs and trees. They occur in warm tropical and subtropical climates across the world, and in very diverse habitats such as dense woodland, open scrub, sand dunes and cliffs. Their leaves may be entire and simple, or dissected, lobed and toothed. The flowers are tubular or funnel-shaped, and solitary or in paniles, cymes or racemes.

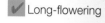 Long-flowering

✗ Mildew prone
✗ Seeds highly poisonous

CULTIVATION

Under glass, grow in loam-based potting compost in full light, with shade during the hottest part of the day. Water moderately in summer, sparingly in winter.

Out of doors, grow in well-drained fertile soil in sun, and out of cold winds. Trim for shape and size after flowering.

PROPAGATION

Seed should be sown, after being soaked for 24 hours, and chipped, at 64°F (18°C) in spring. Softwood, or semi-ripe cuttings can be taken in summer.

Ipomoea batatas
'Variegata'

Zone 9
Height: 6ft. (2m) Spread: 3ft. (90cm)

Ipomoea batatas
'Blackie'

Zone 9
Height: 6ft. (2m) Spread: 3ft. (90cm)

Ipomoea lobata

Zone 8
Height: 15ft. (5m) Spread: 3ft. (90cm)

IRESINE (*Amaranthaceae*)

Common names: None

A genus of 80 species of annuals, subshrubs and perennials from dry, open regions of Australia and South America. The perennials are short-lived, and grown for their colorful foliage. The leaves are entire, simple and opposite. The flowers are insignificant, green or white, and borne in spikes.

✔ Handsome foliage

✗ Short-lived
✗ Mildew prone

CULTIVATION

Under glass, grow in loam-based potting compost in sun with shade at midday. Water freely during growth, but sparingly in winter.

Out of doors, grow in moist, fertile, well-drained soil in sun. Cut back mature plants hard in spring.

PROPAGATION

Stem-tip cuttings can be taken at any time in warm regions, and in late summer in cold areas, and overwintered in heat. Pinch out seedlings to encourage compactness.

Iresine herbstii
'Aureoreticulata'

Zone 9
Height: 5ft. (1.5m) Spread: 3ft. (90cm)

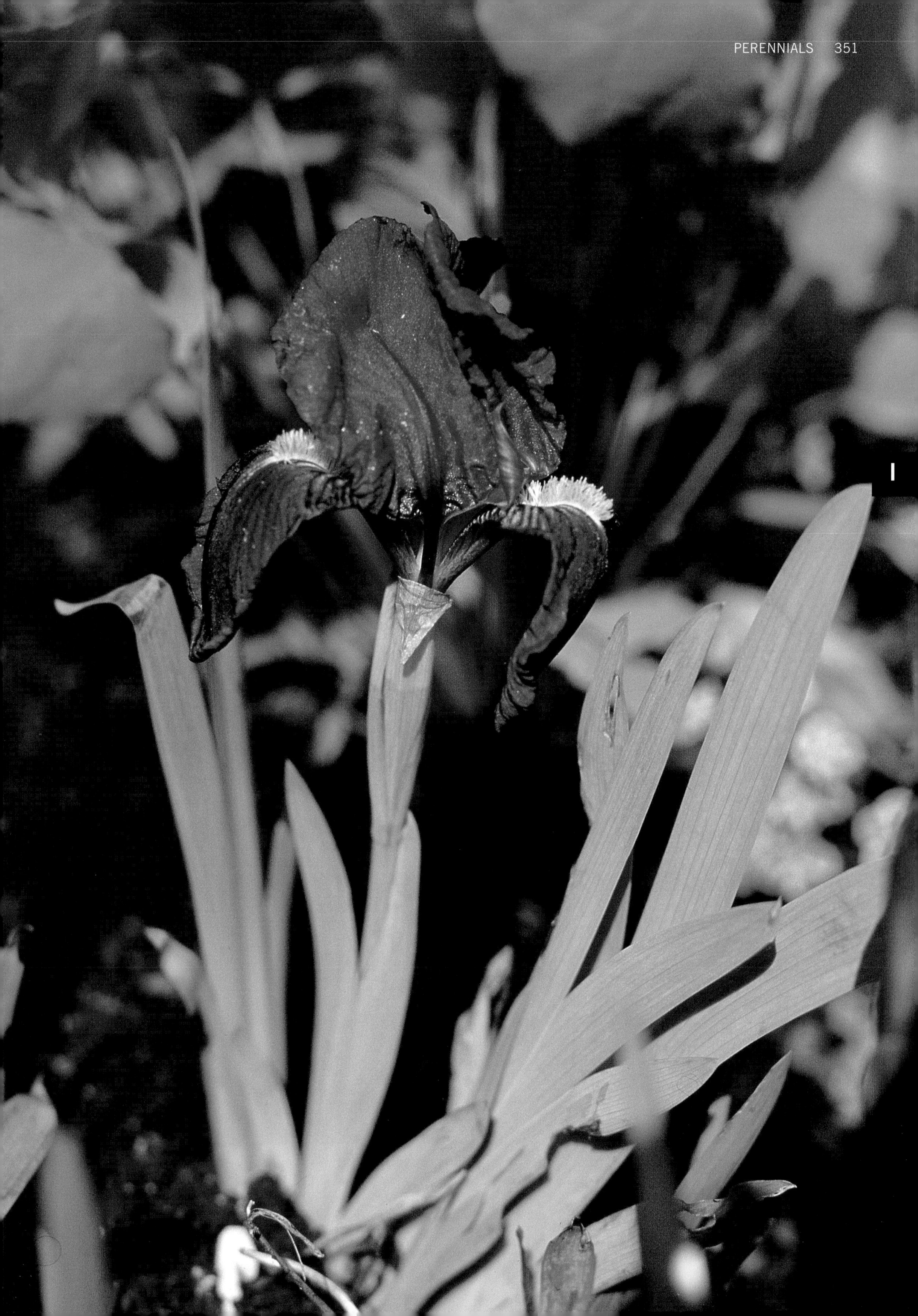

I

IRIS *(Iridaceae)*

Common names: Flag; Sword lily; Fleur de Lis

A genus of 300 species of perennials from very scattered and diverse habitats across the northern hemisphere. They may be bulbous, rhizomatous or fibrous-rooted, and evergreen or herbaceous. An iris flower has six tepals, deployed as three outer and three inner; the outer three are recurved, forming the 'falls', and are the most colorful part. In bearded irises each fall has a beard of hairs in the center, while Crested irises have a ridge or crest. The inner three tepals are usually upright, so are known as standards, although they may be horizontal or recurved—or even much-reduced as in *I danfordiae*. Finally, three modified styles known as stigma flaps reach out over the falls, and are an important element of the flower in some types. Irises are classified by the American Iris Society as follows; each entry has its classification indicated in brackets:

Bearded species and cultivars (B) This is a widely-cultivated group, and varies from dwarf to tall. They are rhizomarous, and like well-drained conditions.

Aril irises (A) This group of bearded irises includes *Onocyclus*, *regalia*, *Regeliocyclus* and *Aril* irises, which become dormant after summer-flowering and must be kept dry while dormant.

Beardless irises (Bl) include *Pacific Coast*, *Siberian*, *Spuria*, *Laevigate*, *Unguicularis* and *Louisiana* irises and are also rhizomatous. They generally have more flowers per stem than Bearded irises. They like well-drained conditions except for the *Laevigatae*, which prefer moist soil.

Crested irises (C) are rhizomatous, and spread freely. They like moist soil.

Bulbous irises (I) include *Juno*, *Reticulata*, and *Xiphium* irises, and are beardless and summer-dormant. They prefer well-drained soil.

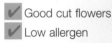

✔ Good cut flowers	✘ All parts poisonous
✔ Low allergen	✘ Prone to slug damage
	✘ Sap is skin-irritant

CULTIVATION

Bearded irises should be grown in acid to neutral well-drained soil in sun. Beardless irises should be grown in acid to neutral well-drained soil in sun or part shade, except that:

Unguiculares prefer sharply-draining, alkaline soil in sun.

Laevigate irises prefer wet or moist humus-rich acid soil.

Louisiana irises like damp humus-rich soil, but thrive only where summer temperatures are high.

Crested irises prefer moist, humus-rich soil in sun or part shade, and should be kept almost dry during dormancy.

Bulbous irises like alkaline to neutral, well-drained soil in sun, and should be kept just moist during dormancy.

Iris
'Brighteyes' (B)

Zone 6
Height: 16in. (40cm) Spread: indefinite

Iris chrysographes
(Bl Siberian)

Zone 5
Height: 20in. (50cm) Spread: indefinite

Iris confusa (C)

Zone 6
Height: 3ft. (90cm) Spread: indefinite
Evergreen

Iris cristata (C)

Zone 4
Height: 4in. (10 cm) Spread: indefinite

Iris danfordiae
(I Reticulata)

Zone 5
Height: 6in. (15cm) Spread: 3in. (8 cm)

Iris douglasiana
A.G.M. (BI Pacific Coast)
Zone 7
Height: 28in. (70cm) Spread: indefinite
Evergreen

Iris ensata
(BI Laevigate, Japan)
Zone 5
Height: 3ft. (90cm) Spread: indefinite

Iris ensata
'Freckled Geisha' (BI Laevigate)
Zone 5
Height: 3ft. (90cm) Spread: indefinite

Iris ensata
'Galatea Marx' (BI Laevigate)
Zone 5
Height: 3ft. (90cm) Spread: indefinite

Iris ensata
'Moonlight Waves' (BI Laevigate)
Zone 5
Height: 3ft. (90cm) Spread: indefinite

Iris graminea
A.G.M. (BI Spuria, Spain)
Zone 5
Height: 16in. (40cm) Spread: indefinite

Iris 'Holden Clough' A.G.M.
(BI Laevigate)
Zone 6
Height: 3ft. (90cm) Spread: indefinite
Evergreen

Iris innominata (BI Pacific Coast)
Zone 7
Height: 8in. (20cm) Spread: indefinite
Evergreen

Iris japonica (C) A.G.M.
Zone 7
Height: 18in. (45 cm) Spread: indefinite
Evergreen

I

I

Iris laevigata
A.G.M. (BI Laevigate)

Zone 4
Height: 2ft. (60cm) Spread: indefinite

Iris latifolia
A.G.M. (I Xiphium)

Zone 5
Height: 2ft. (60cm) Spread: 8in. (20cm)

Iris missouriensis
(BI)

Zone 9
Height: 20in. (50cm) Spread: indefinite

Iris pallida
'Argenteovariegata' (B)

Zone 6
Height: 4ft. (1.2m) Spread: indefinite

Iris pallida
'Variegata' A.G.M. (B)

Zone 6
Height: 4ft. (1.2m) Spread: indefinite

Iris 'Professor Blaauw'
(I Dutch Xiphium)

Zone 6
Height: 2ft. (60cm) Spread: 6in. (15cm)

Iris pseudacorus
(BI Laevigate)

Zone 6
Height: 4ft. (1.2m) Spread: indefinite

Iris pseudacorus
'Variegata' A.G.M.

Zone 6
Height: 4ft. (1.2m) Spread: indefinite

Iris pumila
(Dwarf B)

Zone 4
Height: 6in. (15cm) Spread: indefinite

Iris reticulata
A.G.M. (I Reticulata)

Zone 5
Height: 6in. (15cm) Spread: 5 cm.(3in.)

Iris sibirica
A.G.M. (BI)

Zone 4
Height: 3ft. (90cm) Spread: indefinite

Iris sibirica
'Limeheart'

Zone 4
Height: 3ft. (90cm) Spread: indefinite

I

Iris sibirica
'Wisley White' A.G.M.

Zone 4
Height: 3ft. (90cm) Spread: indefinite

Iris spuria
(BI)

Zone 4
Height: 3ft. (90cm) Spread: indefinite

Iris spuria
'Destination' (BI)

Zone 5
Height: 3ft. (90cm) Spread: indefinite

Iris tenax
(BI Pacific Coast)

Zone 7
Height: 14in. (35cm) Spread: indefinite

Iris
'Three Cherries' (B)

Zone 6
Height: 8in. (20cm) Spread: indefinite

Iris
'Tinkerbelle' (B)

Zone 6
Height: 8in. (20cm) Spread: indefinite

Iris tridentata
(B Pacific Coast)

Zone 5
Height: 28in. (70cm) Spread: indefinite

Iris uromovii
(Bl Spuria)

Zone 6
Height: 1ft. (30cm) Spread: indefinite

ISATIS *(Brassicaceae)*

Common names: Woad

A genus of 30 species of annuals, biennials and perennials from dry places such as waste ground and rocky sites in Eurasia. Their leaves are large ovate, entire or pinnate, basal or smaller, arrow-shaped stem. The flowers are four-petalled, cruciform, borne in loose racemes in early summer.

✔ Attracts bees	✘ Resents disturbance
✔ Disease-free	✘ Need to be staked
✔ Pest-free	✘ Short-lived
	✘ Self-seeds

Isatis tinctoria

Zone 7
Height: 4ft. (1.2m) Spread: 18in. (45 cm)

CULTIVATION
Grow in moist, fertile, well-drained soil in sun. Dead-head to prevent self-seeding.

PROPAGATION
Seed should be sown at 64°F (18°C) in a cold frame in autumn. Divide in spring, but this is not well tolerated.

ISOPLEXIS *(Scrophulariaceae)*

Common names: Canary Island foxglove

A genus of three species of evergreen subshrubs found in open parts of tree heather or laurel forest in the Canary Islands and Madeira. Their leaves are narrow, simple and toothed. The flowers are five-lobed, tubular, and borne in terminal racemes.

✔ Evergreen	✔ Disease-free
✔ Drought-tolerant	✔ Pest-free
✔ Architectural plants	

Isoplexis canariensis

Zone 9
Height: 5ft. (1.5m) Spread: 3ft. (90cm)

CULTIVATION
Under glass, grow in loam-based potting compost, in full or bright filtered light and moderate to high humidity. Water with moderation in summer, sparingly in winter.

Out of doors, grow in moist, fertile well-drained soil in sun or part shade, in a sheltered corner. Keep dry in winter, and water sparingly.

PROPAGATION
Seed should be sown at 75°F (24°C) in spring. Take softwood cuttings in spring or semi-ripe cuttings with bottom heat in summer.

Isoplexis isabellina

Zone 9
Height: 4ft. (1.2m) Spread: 3ft. (90cm)

Isoplexis sceptrum

Zone 9
Height: 6ft. (2m) Spread: 4ft. (1.2m)

IXIA *(Iridaceae)*
Common names: None

A genus of 50 species of cormous perennials found in dry and wet slopes in South Africa. Their leaves are basal and stem, and linear. The flowers are star-shaped saucers, often with dark centers, and are borne on long stems from early spring to summer.

✔ Drought-tolerant   ✔ Pest-free
✔ Disease-free

CULTIVATION
Under glass, plant corms 6in. (15cm) deep in autumn in gritty, loam-based potting compost in full light. Water freely at flowering time, but keep dry and frost-free in winter.

Out of doors, grow in well-drained soil in sun.

PROPAGATION
Seed should be sown in a cold frame when ripe. Separate offsets in autumn when dormant.

Ixia polystachya

Zone 9
Height: 3ft. (90cm) Spread: 4in. (10 cm)

JASIONE
JEFFERSONIA
JOVIBARBA
JUNCUS

J

JASIONE *(Campanulaceae)*
Common names: None

A genus of 20 species of annuals, biennials and perennials from open, dry grassland in the Mediterranean area, and temperate Europe. The leaves are in basal rosettes, simple and alternate. The flowers are scabious-like, solitary and terminal.

✔ Drought-tolerant   ✘ Prone to slug damage

CULTIVATION
Grow in sharply-draining, fertile soil in sun.

PROPAGATION
Seed should be sown in a cold frame as soon as it is ripe, or in spring. Divide in spring.

Jasione laevis

Zone 5
Height: 1ft. (30cm) Spread: 8in. (20cm)

JEFFERSONIA *(Berberidaceae)*
Common names: Twinleaf

A genus of two species of perennials from damp woodland and forest in North America and north-east Asia. Their leaves are kidney-shaped or bilobed or round. The white flowers are cup-shaped, and solitary on long stems well above the foliage in spring.

✔ Handsome foliage   ✘ Prone to slug damage

CULTIVATION
Grow in moist, humus-rich soil in part shade.

PROPAGATION
Seed should be sown in a cold frame as soon as it is ripe. Divide in spring.

Jeffersonia diphylla

Zone 5
Height: 8in. (20cm) Spread: 6in. (15cm)

JOVIBARBA *(Crassukaceae)*
Common names: None

A genus of six species of evergreen, rosette-forming perennials from the European mountains; it resembles Sempervivum closely. The rosettes are symmetrical, and the leaves hairy and fleshy. The flowers are small, bell-shaped, have six petals, and are borne on leafy stems in summer.

✔ Handsome foliage   ✔ Disease-free
✔ Evergreen   ✔ Pest-free
✔ Drought-tolerant

CULTIVATION
Grow in sharply-draining soil in sun.

PROPAGATION
Separate and root offsets in late spring or early summer.

Jovibarba heuffelii

Zone 6
Height: 8in. (20cm) Spread: 1ft. (30cm)

J

Jovibarba hirta subsp. *allionii*

Zone 7
Height: 6in. (15cm) Spread: 1ft. (30cm)

JUNCUS *(Juncaceae)*
Common names: Rush

A genus of 300 species of grass-like rhizomatous perennials from acid, wet soil in cool regions across the world. The leaves are narrow, small, and often reduced to basal sheaths. The flower stems may be twisted or variegated. The flowers have six tepals, and are small, green or brown, and borne in cymes in midsummer.

✔ Long-flowering
✔ Handsome foliage
✔ Disease-free
✔ Pest-free

✗ Invasive
✗ Self-seeds
✗ Highly allergenic

CULTIVATION
Grow in wet or very moist, acid soil in sun or part shade.

PROPAGATION
Seed should be sown at 54°F (12°C) in spring. Divide in spring or summer.

Juncus effusus
'Spiralis'

Zone 4
Height: 1ft. (30cm) Spread: indefinite

KALANCHOE
KIRENGESHOMA
KNAUTIA
KNIPHOFIA
KOHLERIA

K

KALANCHOE (Crassulaceae)

Common names: None

A genus of 130 species of annual, biennial and perennial succulents, shrubs and small trees from shady parts of the Yemen, Saudi Arabia, Central Africa, South Africa, Madagascar, Australia, Asia and tropical Americas. Their leaves are fleshy, simple to pinnatisect, toothed or scalloped, and alternate, opposite or whorled. The flowers are four-lobed, bell- or urn-shaped or tubular, and borne in terminal panicles.

✔ Handsome foliage
✔ Long-flowering

CULTIVATION
Under glass, grow in loam-based potting compost, with added grit, in bright filtered light. Water moderately during growth, and keep just moist in winter

Out of doors, grow in humus-rich, fertile, well-drained soil in part shade.

PROPAGATION
Seed should be sown at 70°F (21°C) in early spring. Separate offsets or plantlets, or take stem cuttings in spring or summer.

Kalanchoe blossfeldiana

Zone 10
Height and spread: 16in. (40cm)

Kalanchoe thyrsiflora

Zone 10
Height: 2ft. (60cm) Spread: 1ft. (30cm)

KIRENGESHOMA (Hydranbeaceae)

Common names: None

A genus of two species of rhizomatous perennials from Japanese and Korean woodland. Their leaves are large, gray-green, broad, ovate and paired. The flowers are yellow, tubular, waxy, and in pendent, nodding cymes of three from summer to early autumn.

✔ Good cut flowers   ✘ Prone to slug damage
✔ Low allergen
✔ Handsome foliage

CULTIVATION
Grow in acid to neutral, leafy, moist soil in a sheltered corner in part shade.

PROPAGATION
Seed should be sown in a cold frame as soon as it is ripe, or in spring. Germination is erratic. Divide in spring as growth is beginning.

Kirengeshoma palmata
A.G.M.

Zone 5
Height: 4ft. (1.2m) Spread: 6ft. (2m)

KNAUTIA *(Dipsacaceae)*
Common names: Macedonian scabious; Field scabious

A genus of 40 species of annuals and perennials from limestone woodland, grassland and scrub in Eurasia and North Africa. Their leaves are basal in rosettes, simple or pinnatifid, and stem, opposite. The flowers are scabious-like, with a pincushion of stamens and are surrounded by cup-shaped involucres of hairy or toothed bracts, on tall stems in early or mid summer.

✔ Good cut flowers   ✘ Require staking
✔ Drought-tolerant
✔ Attracts bees

CULTIVATION
Grow in alkaline to neutral, fertile, well-drained soil in sun.

PROPAGATION
Seed should be sown, or basal cuttings taken, in spring.

Knautia arvensis

Zone 6
Height: 5ft. (1.5m) Spread: 18in. (45cm)

Knautia macedonica

Zone 6
Height: 32in. (80cm) Spread: 18in. (45cm)

KNIPHOFIA *(Asphodelaceae)*
Common names: Red hot poker; torch lily

A genus of 70 species of herbaceous or evergreen perennials from tropical and Southern Africa, where they grow on stream sides and other moist sites such as grasslands and mountainsides. Their leaves are arching, linear or strap-shaped. The flowers are cylindrical or tubular, pendent, and borne on erect, dense, spike-like racemes in early, mid or late summer.

✔ Attracts bees   ✘ Need to be staked
✔ Good cut flowers
✔ Low allergen

CULTIVATION
Grow in any moist, humus-rich, deep, well-drained soil in sun or part shade.

PROPAGATION
Seed of species should be sown in a cold frame in spring. Cultivars should be divided in late spring, when basal cuttings can also be taken.

Kniphofia 'Atlanta'

Zone 7
Height: 4ft. (1.2m) Spread: 32in. (80cm)
Evergreen

Kniphofia
'Bees Sunset'

Zone 7
Height: 3ft. (90cm) Spread: 2ft. (60cm)

Kniphofia caulescens A.G.M.

Zone 7
Height: 4ft. (1.2m) Spread: 2ft. (60cm)
Evergreen

Kniphofia
'Fiery Fred'

Zone 7
Height: 4ft. (1.2m) Spread: 2ft. (60cm)

Kniphofia 'Green Jade'

Zone 7
Height: 5ft. (1.5m) Spread: 30in. (75cm)
Evergreen

Kniphofia
'Little Maid' A.G.M.

Zone 7
Height: 2ft. (60cm) Spread: 18in. (45cm)

Kniphofia natalensis

Zone 8
Height: 32in. (80cm) Spread: 1ft. (30cm)

Kniphofia pauciflora

Zone 8
Height and spread: 1ft. (30cm)

Kniphofia
'Spanish Gold'

Zone 7
Height: 4ft. (1.2m) Spread: 2ft. (60cm)

Kniphofia
'Shining Sceptre'

Zone 7
Height: 4ft. (1.2m) Spread: 2ft. (60cm)

Kniphofia
'Sunningdale Yellow' A.G.M.

Zone 7
Height: 4ft. (1.2m) Spread: 2ft. (60cm)

Kniphofia thompsonii var.
snowdenii

Zone 8
Height: 3ft. (90cm) Spread: 18in. (45cm)

Kniphofia triangularis
(=galpinii) A.G.M.

Zone 8
Height: 3ft. (90cm) Spread: 18in. (45cm)

KOHLERIA *(Gesneriaceae)*
Common names: None

A genus of 50 species of rhizomatous perennials and subshrubs from tropical rainforest in North, Central, and South America. Their foliage is linear or lance-shaped, hairy, toothed or scalloped, and opposite or in whorls. The flower stems and flowers are also hairy. The flowers are bell- or tubular-shaped, formed in the leaf axils in pairs or singly, and in racemes in summer and autumn.

✔ Handsome foliage
✔ Self-seeds

K

CULTIVATION
Grow in moist, humus-rich, well-drained soil in part shade.

PROPAGATION
Divide in spring.

Kohleria glauca

Zone 10
Height: 5ft. (1.5m) Spread: 1ft. (30cm)

K

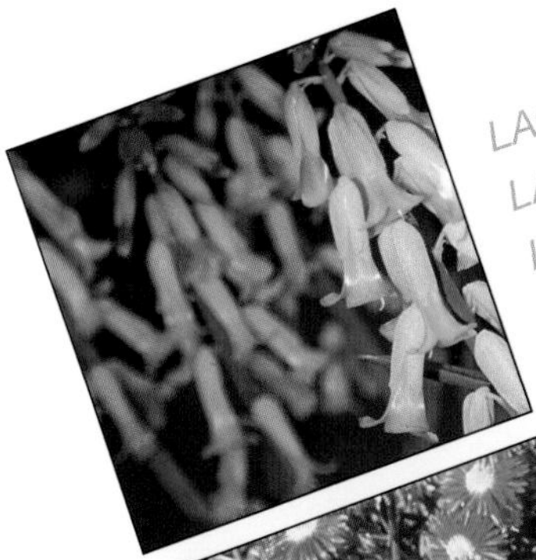

LACHENALIA
LAMIUM
LAMPRANTHUS
LATHYRUS
LAVANDULA
LAVATERA
LEDEBOURIA
LEONOTIS
LEONTODON
LEONTOPODIUM
LEPTINELLA
LEUCANTHEMELLA
LEUCANTHEMOPSIS
LEUCANTHEMUM
LEUCOJUM
LEVISTICUM
LEWISIA
LEYCESTERIA
LEYMUS
LIATRIS
LIBERTIA
LIGULARIA
LILIUM

LIMONIUM
LINARIA
LINUM
LIRIOPE
LITHODORA
LOBELIA
LOBULARIA
LOPHOSPEMUM
LOTUS
LUDISIA
LUNARIA
LUPINUS
LUZULA
LYCHNIS
LYSICHITON
LYSIMACHIA
LYTHRUM

L

LACHENALIA *(Hyacinthaceae)*
Common names: None

A genus of 90 species of bulbous perennials from dry and wet grassland in South Africa. Their leaves are basal, variously shaped, and sometimes handsomely spotted. The colorful flowers are cylindrical, bell-shaped or tubular, borne in spikes or racemes from autumn to spring.

- ✔ Long-flowering
- ✔ Handsome foliage
- ✔ Disease-free
- ✔ Winter-flowering

CULTIVATION
Under glass, plant bulbs 4in. (10 cm) deep in spring in loam-based potting compost. Water freely during growth, but dry off over summer.

Out of doors, grow in sharply-draining, humus-rich soil in sun.

PROPAGATION
Seed should be sown at 64°F (18°C) as soon as it is ripe. Separate bulbils in autumn.

Lachenalia aloides lutea

Zone 9
Height: 1ft. (30cm) Spread: 3in. (8 cm)

Lachenalia 'Namaqualand'

Zone 9
Height: 1ft. (30cm) Spread: 4in. (10 cm)

LAMIUM *(Lamiaceae)*
Common names: Dead nettle

A genus of 50 species of annuals and rhizomatous perennials from wet woodland and dry scrubland in the circum-Mediterranean area. Their foliage is ovate, opposite, wrinkled and toothed. The two-lipped, solitary flowers are borne in whorls on spikes from late spring to summer. Some forms are very invasive.

- ✔ Low allergen
- ✔ Handsome foliage
- ✔ Good ground cover
- ✘ Prone to slug damage
- ✘ Mildew prone
- ✘ Self-seeds

CULTIVATION
Grow in moist, poor, well-drained soil in part or full shade.

PROPAGATION
Sow seed in a cold frame, or divide, in spring or autumn.

Lamium galeobdolon

Zone 6
Height: 2ft. (60cm) Spread: indefinite
Invasive

Lamium galeobdolon
'Herrmann's Pride'
Zone 6
Height: 2ft. (60cm) Spread: indefinite
Invasive

Lamium maculatum
Zone 4
Height: 8in. (20cm) Spread: 4ft. (1.2m)

Lamium maculatum
'Aureum'
Zone 4
Height: 8in. (20cm) Spread: 4ft. (1.2m)

Lamium maculatum
'Beacon Silver'
Zone 4
Height: 8in. (20cm) Spread: 4ft. (1.2m)

Lamium maculatum forma. *album*
Zone 4
Height: 8in. (20cm) Spread: 4ft. (1.2m)

Lamium maculatum
'Golden Anniversary'
Zone 4
Height: 8in. (20cm) Spread: 4ft. (1.2m)

Lamium maculatum
'Ickwell Beauty'
Zone 4
Height: 8in. (20cm) Spread: 4ft. (1.2m)

Lamium maculatum
'White Nancy'
Zone 4
Height: 8in. (20cm) Spread: 4ft. (1.2m)

Lamium orvala
Zone 6
Height: 8in. (20cm) Spread: 1ft. (30cm)

L

LAMPRANTHUS *(Aizoaceae)*

Common names: None

A genus of 180 species of succulent perennials found in coastal semi-desert regions of South Africa. Their three-angled leaves are cylindrical and opposite. The daisy-like, solitary flowers are borne from summer to early autumn.

- ✔ Evergreen
- ✔ Long-flowering
- ✖ Prone to aphid attack

CULTIVATION
Under glass, grow in cactus compost in full light. Water with moderation during growth, but sparingly at all other times.

Out of doors, grow in very sharply-draining soil in sun. Protect against frost in winter.

PROPAGATION
Seed should be sown 75°F (24°C) in spring. Stem cuttings can be taken in summer.

Lampranthus spectabilis

Zone 9
Height: 1ft. (30cm) Spread: indefinite

LATHYRUS *(Papilionaceae)*

Common names: Everlasting sweet pea; Perennial pea vine; Spring vetchling

A genus of 150 species of annuals and perennials from temperate regions of South America, North Africa, and across the temperate northern hemisphere, where they inhabit sunny, slopes, banks, woodland and wastelands. Their foliage is pinnate, and alternate on winged stems. The pea-like flowers are often perfumed, and borne singly or in racemes from the leaf axils in late spring and summer. Some are evergreen, others herbaceous. Some are climbers, others are clump-forming.

- ✔ Drought-tolerant
- ✔ Handsome foliage
- ✔ Attractive seed-pods
- ✖ Seeds poisonous
- ✖ Prone to slug damage
- ✖ Resents disturbance

CULTIVATION
Grow in well-drained, fertile, humus-rich soil in sun or light shade.

PROPAGATION
Seed should be soaked, and sown in a cold frame in early spring. Division can be done then also, but may not be tolerated well.

Lathyrus aureus
(Clump-forming)

Zone 6
Height: 2ft. (60cm) Spread: 1ft. (30cm)

Lathyrus grandiflorus
(Climber)

Zone 6
Height: 5ft. (1.5m) Spread: 1ft. (30cm)

Lathyrus latifolius
A.G.M. (Climber)

Zone 5
Height: 6ft. (2m) Spread: 1ft. (30cm)

Lathrus vernus
A.G.M. (Clump-forming)

Zone 4
Height and spread: 18in. (45cm)

Lathyrus vernus var. *albororeus*
A.G.M.

Zone 4
Height and spread: 18in. (45cm)

LAVANDULA *(Lamiaceae)*
Common names: Lavender

A genus of 25 species of evergreen, aromatic subshrubs and shrubs from dry, sunny rocky regions of Madeira, the Canary Islands, the circum-Mediterranean area, Asia and India. Their leaves may be entire and simple or pinnatifid, pinnate or bipinnate. The perfumed flowers are two-lipped, and tubular, and especially attractive to bees.

✔ Flowers perfumed	✔ Drought-tolerant	✘ Highly allergenic
✔ Foliage aromatic	✔ Good for drying for winter	
✔ Attracts bees	✔ Evergreen	

CULTIVATION
Grow in well-drained fertile soil in sun. Cut back after flowering to within 1in. (2.5 cm) of previous year's growth.

PROPAGATION
Seed should be sown in a cold frame in spring. Take semi-ripe cuttings in summer.

Lavandula canariensis

Zone 9
Height: 5ft. (1.5m) Spread: 18in. (45cm)

Lavandula x intermedia
A.G.M. (English lavender)

Zone 5
Height and spread: 20in. (50cm)

Lavandula stoechas
A.G.M. (French Lavender)

Zone 8
Height and spread: 2ft. (60cm)

L

LAVATERA *(Malvaceae)*
Common names: Mallow

A genus of 25 species of annuals, biennials, perennials, subshrubs and shrubs from dry, stony and coastal rocky places in Eurasia, Australia, the Canary Islands, Australia and California. The perennials are short-lived, and can be evergreen or herbaceous. The leaves are palmately-lobed, alternate and long-stalked. The flowers are five-petalled, saucer- or funnel-shaped, borne in racemes or singly in summer, over a long period in most instances.

✔ Long-flowering
✔ Good cut flowers
✔ Drought-tolerant
✔ Low allergen

✘ Short-lived

CULTIVATION
Grow in sandy, light, well-drained soil in a sheltered corner in sun.

PROPAGATION
Take softwood or greenwood cuttings in spring.

Lavatera arborea 'Variegata'

Zone 8
Height: 10ft. (3m) Spread: 5ft. (1.5m)
Evergreen

Lavatera 'Barnsley' A.G.M.

Zone 7
Height: 6ft. (2m) Spread: 4ft. (1.2m)
Semi-evergreen

Lavatera 'Bredon Springs'

Zone 8
Height: 6ft. (2m) Spread: 4ft. (1.2m)
Semi-evergreen

Lavatera 'Burgundy Wine'

Zone 7
Height: 4ft. (1.2m) Spread: 3ft. (90cm)
Semi-evergreen

Lavatera 'Candy Floss'

Zone 8
Height: 6ft. (2m) Spread: 4ft. (1.2m)
Semi-evergreen

Lavatera thuringiaca 'Ice Cool'

Zone 8
Height and spread: 5ft. (1.5m)

L

LEDEBOURIA *(Hyacinthaceae)*
Common names: None

A genus of 16 species of evergreen bulbous perennials from dry, open, sunny or seasonally dry parts of South Africa. Their foliage is handsomely-marked, and the lily-of-the-valley-like flowers are small, bell- or urn-shaped, and borne in racemes in spring and summer.

- ✔ Handsome foliage
- ✔ Evergreen
- ✔ Trouble-free

CULTIVATION
Under glass, plant bulbs with their necks just above soil level in loam-based potting compost in full light.Water freely during growth and keep just moist in winter.

Out of doors, grow in well-drained soil in sun.

PROPAGATION
Sow seed under glass in spring or autumn, or remove offsets in spring.

Ledebouria socialis

Zone 9
Height: 4in. (10 cm) Spread: 2in. (5cm)

LEONOTIS *(Lamiaceae)*
Common names: Lion's ear

A genus of 30 species of annuals, perennials, subshrubs and shrubs from rocky regions and high grassland in South Africa in particular, but *L. nepetifoilia* is found across the tropics. Their foliage is ovate or lance-shaped, and opposite, on square stems. The two-lipped flowers are borne in whorls on leafy racemes.

- ✔ Drought-tolerant
- ✔ Handsome foliage
- ✔ Architectural plants

- ✘ Invasive

CULTIVATION
Grow in well-drained, fertile soil in sun.

PROPAGATION
Seed should be sown at 64°F (18°C) in spring. Take greenwood cuttings in late spring-summer.

Leonotis dysophylla

Zone 9
Height: 10ft. (3m) Spread: indefinite

Leonotis leonurus

Zone 9
Height: 8ft. (2.5m) Spread: indefinite

Leonotis ocymifolia

Zone 9
Height: 10ft. (3m) Spread: indefinite

LEONTODON *(Asteraceae)*
Common names: Hawkbit

A genus of 40 annuals and rosette-forming perennials from temperate Eurasia and from the Mediterranean across to Iran. The leaves are entire or pinnatifid, hairy, rough. The flowers are like daisies, and borne in flat-topped racemes in early summer, and again later if deadheaded.

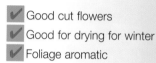

✔ Repeat-flowering   ✘ Self-seeds
✔ Good cut flowers   ✘ Highly allergenic

CULTIVATION
Grow in moist, humus-rich, well-drained soil in sun. Dead-head to prevent self-seeding and to encourage repeat-flowering.

PROPAGATION
Seed should be sown in a cold frame as soon as is ripe, or in spring, when division can also be carried out.

Leontodon rigens
(formerly *Microseris rigens*)

Zone 8
Height: 2ft. (60cm) Spread: 1ft. (30cm)

LEONTOPODIUM *(Asteraceae)*
Common names: Edelweiss

A genus of 35 species of perennials from grassland and stony areas in the mountains of Eurasia. Their leaves are basal, simple, hairy and entire. The flowers are composed of cream disc florets surrounded by leafy, felted white bracts in terminal cymes.

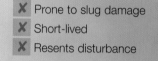

✔ Good cut flowers   ✘ Prone to slug damage
✔ Good for drying for winter   ✘ Short-lived
✔ Foliage aromatic   ✘ Resents disturbance

CULTIVATION
Grow in alkaline to neutral, well-drained soil in sun. Protect against winter wet.

PROPAGATION
Seed should be sown in a cold frame as soon as it is ripe. Division can be done in early spring, but is not tolerated well.

Leontopodium alpinum

Zone 4
Height and spread: 6in. (15cm)

LEPTINELLA *(Asteraceae)*
Common names: None

A genus of 30 species of annuals and perennials from subalpine grassland and rocky sites in South America and Australasia. They form dense cushions of pinnate, pinnatifid or pinnatisect, aromatic, leaves. The solitary button-like flowers are borne on short stems in late spring or early summer.

✔ Foliage aromatic
✔ Drought tolerant
✔ Trouble-free

CULTIVATION
Grow in sharply-draining soil in sun.

PROPAGATION
Seed should be sown in a cold frame as soon as ripe. Divide in spring.

Leptinella dendyi

Zone 8
Height: 16in. (40cm) Spread: 4in. (10 cm)

L

Leptinella squalida
'Platt's Black'

Zone 5
Height: 6in. (15cm) Spread: indefinite

LEUCANTHEMELLA *(Asteraceae)*
Common names: None

A genus of two species of perennials from marshland and wet places, one from East Asia, and the one included here, from south-east Europe. The foliage is alternate, lance-shaped, entire or toothed. The daisy-like flowers are single, and solitary or in corymbs of up to eight, in autumn.

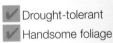

- ✘ Highly allergenic
- ✘ Prone to slug damage
- ✘ Needs staking

CULTIVATION
Grow in moist soil in sun or part shade.

PROPAGATION
Take basal cuttings, or divide in spring.

Leucanthemella serotina
A.G.M.

Zone 7
Height: 5ft. (1.5m) Spread: 3ft. (90cm)

LEUCANTHEMOPSIS *(Asteraceae)*
Common names: None

A genus of six species of perennials from the mountains of southern Europe and North Africa. They are cushion- or mat-forming, short-lived, and their spoon-shaped leaves are pinnatifid, pinnatisect or lobed palmately. The flowers are daisy-like, single, solitary, and borne in summer.

- ✔ Drought-tolerant
- ✔ Handsome foliage
- ✘ Short-lived

CULTIVATION
Grow in sharply-draining soil in sun.

PROPAGATION
Seed should be sown in a cold frame as soon as ripe. Take basal cuttings, or divide, in spring.

Leucanthemopsis alpina

Zone 6
Height: 4in. (10 cm) Spread: 6in. (15cm)

LEUCANTHEMUM *(Asteraceae)*
Common names: Shasta daisy

A genus of annuals and perennials from moist meadows and grassland and dry rocky slopes in the mountains of temperate Eurasia. Their leaves are entire or deeply pinnatifid, lobed, toothed or scalloped. The daisy-like solitary flowers usually have white ray florets and yellow disc florets, and are borne over a long period in summer. The herbaceous forms require staking.

Leucanthemum graminifolium

Zone 7
Height and spread: 1ft. (30cm)

✔ Good cut flowers
✔ Long-flowering
✔ Handsome foliage

✘ Prone to slug damage
✘ Require staking
✘ Highly allergenic

CULTIVATION
Grow in moist, well-drained soil in sun or part shade.

PROPAGATION
Seed of species should be sown in a cold frame in autumn or spring. Divide cultivars in early spring or late summer.

Leucanthemum x superbum
'Aglaia' A.G.M.

Zone 5
Height and spread: 2ft. (60cm)

Leucanthemum x superbum
'Barbara Bush'

Zone 5
Height and spread: 2ft. (60cm)

Leucanthemum x superbum
'Beaute Nivelloise'

Zone 5
Height: 34in. (85 cm) Spread: 2ft. (60cm)

Leucanthemum x superbum
'Droitwich Beauty'

Zone 5
Height: 3ft. (90cm) Spread: 2ft. (60cm)

Leucanthemum x superbum
'Phyllis Smith'

Zone 5
Height: 3ft. (90cm) Spread: 2ft. (60cm)

Leucanthemum x superbum
'Snowcap'

Zone 5
Height and spread: 18in. (45cm)

Leucanthemum x superbum
'Sonnenschein'

Zone 5
Height: 3ft. (90cm) Spread: 2ft. (60cm)

Leucanthemum x superbum
'White Iceberg'

Zone 5
Height: 3ft. (90cm) Spread: 2ft. (60cm)

Leucanthenum x superbum
'Wirral Supreme'

Zone 5
Height: 32in. (80cm) Spread: 2ft. (60cm)

LEUCOJUM *(Amaryllidaceae)*

Common names: Snowflake

A genus of ten species of bulbous perennials from a wide diversity of habitat from damp or wet woodland (as for the two species included here) to dry, sandy dunes or scrubland from west Europe to the Middle East and North Africa. The leaves are basal, strap-shaped, or linear. The snowdrop-like flowers are pendent, or nodding, bell-shaped, white mostly, but may be pink, and borne up to eight per stem in spring or autumn. Some types are perfumed.

✔ Good cut flowers   ✘ Prone to slug damage

CULTIVATION
Plant bulbs 4in. (10 cm) deep in autumn in moist or even wet, humus-rich soil in sun.

PROPAGATION
Seed should be sown in a cold frame in autumn, or separate offsets as soon as the foliage dies down.

L

Leucojum aestivum
(Summer snowflake)
Zone 4
Height: 2ft. (60cm) Spread: 4in. (10 cm)
Flowers perfumed

Leucojum vernum
A.G.M. (Spring snowflake)
Zone 5
Height: 1ft. (30cm) Spread: 3in. (8 cm)

L

LEVISTICUM *(Apiaceae)*
Common names: Lovage

A genus of one species of perennial, *L. officinale*, from the mountains of Eastern Europe. Its leaves are two- or three-pinnate, and diamond-shaped or triangular, and contact with it may cause photodermatitis. The roots and stems are celery-scented, and are used in salads. The seeds are used for flavoring. The flowers are star-shaped, borne in umbels, greenish-yellow, and appear in midsummer.

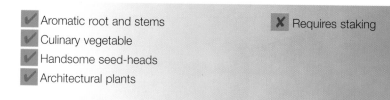

✔ Aromatic root and stems
✔ Culinary vegetable
✔ Handsome seed-heads
✔ Architectural plants

✖ Requires staking

CULTIVATION
Grow in moist, fertile, well-drained soil in sun.

PROPAGATION
Divide in spring, or sow seed as soon as ripe.

Levisticum officinale

Zone 4
Height: 6ft. (2m) Spread: 3ft. (90cm)

LEWISIA *(Portulacaceae)*
Common names: None

A genus of 20 species of perennials from western North America. They may be evergreen or herbaceous. The evergreen species (such as the one featured here) are found in shady spots among rocks or in crevices, whilst the deciduous species are found in open grassland or meadows. They have fleshy rootstocks, and tufts of variously-shaped, fleshy leaves. The flowers are saucer- or funnel-shaped, and are borne singly, or in panicles or cymes over a long period in spring and summer.

✔ Long-flowering
✔ Handsome foliage

✔ Drought-tolerant

✖ Prone to slug damage

CULTIVATION
Grow in acid to neutral, sharply-draining, humus-rich soil in full sun if herbaceous and in part shade if evergreen. They are excellent wall plants. Protect both forms against winter wet, and herbaceous ones against summer wet when dormant.

PROPAGATION
Remove offsets from evergreen species in early summer. Seed should be sown in a cold frame in autumn, but *L cotyledon* hybrid seed does not come true.

Lewisia cotyledon hybrid

Zone 6
Height: 1ft. (30cm) Spread: 16in. (40cm)
Evergreen

L

LEYCESTERIA *(Caprifoliaceae)*
Common names: None

A genus of six species of subshrubs and shrubs from mountain woodland and cliffs in Burma, India, China and the Himalayas. Their leaves are long-pointed, ovate, entire or toothed, and opposite. The flowers are tubular, and borne in whorls on spikes or axillary racemes in summer and early autumn.

✔ Architectural plants
✔ Disease-free
✔ Pest-free

CULTIVATION
Grow in well-drained soil in sun or part shade.

PROPAGATION
Seed should be sown in a cold frame in autumn. Softwood cuttings may be taken in summer.

Leycesteria formosa

Zone 7
Height and spread: 6ft. (2m)
Handsome foliage

LEYMUS *(Poaceae)*

Common names: None

A genus of 40 species of rhizomatous, perennial grasses from temperate grassland in the northern hemisphere, and one species from Argentina. The glaucous leaves are linear, stiff, and flat or rolled. They have narrow, linear racemes of paired spikes all summer.

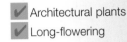

- ✔ Architectural plants
- ✔ Long-flowering
- ✘ Invasive
- ✘ Highly allergenic

CULTIVATION
Grow in well-drained, light soil in sun.

PROPAGATION
Divide between spring and autumn.

Leymus arenarius

Zone 6
Height: 5ft. (1.5m) Spread: indefinite

LIATRIS *(Asteraceae)*

Common names: Blazing star; Gayfeather

A genus of 20 species of perennials found for the greater part in dry, stony ground or open woodland (except for *L. spicata*, which is the only one in widespread cultivation, which prefers moist sites) in central and east North America. The rootstock is tuber- or corm-like, and is liked by mice. Their leaves are linear, lance-shaped or ovate, and alternate. The flowers are button-shaped, tubular, and composed of disc florets in white, red, or pink, in late summer and early autumn. They are borne on stiff spikes that open, unusually, from above downwards.

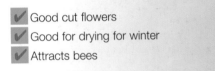

- ✔ Good cut flowers
- ✔ Good for drying for winter
- ✔ Attracts bees
- ✘ Need to lift & divide often
- ✘ Prone to slug damage
- ✘ Mice eat corms

CULTIVATION
Grow in moist, well-drained fertile soil in sun. Does not survive the winter in wet soils.

PROPAGATION
Seed should be sown in a cold frame in autumn. Divide in spring.

Liatris spicata

Zone 3
Height: 4ft. (1.2m) Spread: 18in. (45cm)

Liatris spicata
'Alba'

Zone 3
Height: 4ft. (1.2m) Spread: 18in. (45cm)

Liatris spicata
'Kobold'

Zone 3
Height: 20in. (50cm) Spread: 18in. (45cm)

LIBERTIA *(Iridaceae)*
Common names: None

A genus of 20 species of rhizomatous perennials from moist, grassy or dry scrub areas in New Zealand, New Caledonia and temperate South and North America. They are evergreen and clump-forming. Their leaves are leathery, linear, and mainly basal, but with a few stem. The flowers are saucer-shaped, six-tepalled, arranged in three small outer and three broad inner rows, and surrounded by bracts. They are borne in panicles in from late spring to early summer, and are followed by glossy seed-heads.

✔ Good cut flowers
✔ Handsome seed-heads
✔ Trouble-free

CULTIVATION
Grow in moist, well-drained, humus-rich soil in sun.

PROPAGATION
Seed should be sown as soon as ripe. Divide in spring.

Libertia formosa

Zone 8
Height: 3ft. (90cm) Spread: 2ft. (60cm)
Long-flowering

Libertia grandiflora

Zone 8
Height: 3ft. (90cm) Spread: 2ft. (60cm)

Libertia ixiodes

Zone 8
Height and spread: 2ft. (60cm)

Libertia peregrinans 'Gold Leaf'

Zone 8
Height: 3ft. (90cm) Spread: 2ft. (60cm)
Invasive

Libertia sessiliflora

Zone 8
Height: 3ft. (90cm) Spread: 2ft. (60cm)

L

LIGULARIA *(Asteraceae)*

Common names: None

A genus of 150 species of large perennials from wet scrub, grassland or woodland, stream sides and ditches in east and central Asia. They have large, basal, round, heart-shaped or ovate leaves, and small, alternate stem leaves. The daisy-like flowers have yellow or orange ray florets and yellow or brown disc florets, and are borne in racemes or corymbs on erect stems. Taller varieties need to be staked.

✔ Architectural plants
✔ Handsome foliage
✔ Attracts bees

✘ Highly allergenic
✘ Prone to slug damage

CULTIVATION

Grow in moist, deep, fertile soil in sun but with shade at mid-day, or in half shade.

PROPAGATION

Sow seed, or divide, in spring or autumn.

Ligularia dentata

Zone 4
Height: 5ft. (1.5m) Spread: 3ft. (90cm)

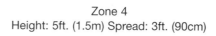

Ligularia dentata 'Britt Marie Crawford'

Zone 4
Height: 5ft. (1.5m) Spread: 3ft. (90cm)

Ligularia dentata 'Desdemona' A.G.M.

Zone 4
Height and spread: 3ft. (90cm)

Ligularia dentata 'Othello'

Zone 4
Height: 3ft. (90cm) Spread: 2ft. (60cm)

Ligularia x hessei

Zone 5
Height: 6ft. (2m) Spread: 3ft. (90cm)

Ligularia hodgsonii

Zone 5
Height: 3ft. (90cm) Spread: 2ft. (60cm)

L

Ligularia japonica

Zone 5
Height: 6ft. (2m) Spread: 3ft. (90cm)

Ligularia x palmatiloba

Zone 5
Height: 3ft. (90cm) Spread: 2ft. (60cm)

Ligularia przewalski

Zone 5
Height: 6ft. (2m) Spread: 3ft. (90cm)

Ligularia
'The Rocket' A.G.M.

Zone 4
Height: 6ft. (2m) Spread: 3ft. (90cm)

Ligularia
'Wiehenstephan'

Zone 5
Height: 6ft. (2m) Spread: 3ft. (90cm)

LILIUM *(Liliaceae)*
Common names: lily

A genus of 400 species of mainly bulbous, with a few rhizomatous, perennials from woodland
and scrub in Eurasia, the Philippines, and North America. Their leaves are glossy, linear to lance-
shaped, and in whorls or alternate on the stems. The flowers have six tepals and six stamens,
and may be bell-, trumpet-, star-, bowl-, or funnel-shaped, or of Turk's-cap form, and may be
perfumed. They may face up, sideways or down. The tepals may be spotted or lined. Taller
varieties need to be staked. Since, with rare exceptions, lilies do not spread, no quantification is
given here. Lilies are classified according to the National Lily Register of 1982, with amendments
by the Royal Horticultural Society, 1992, as follows:

Division 1: Asiatic hybrids

Division 2: Martagon hybrids.

Division 3: Candidum hybrids

Division 4: American hybrids.

Division 5: Longiflorum hybrids

Division 6: Trumpet and Aurelian hybrids

Lilium
'African Queen' (Div. 6, Acid soil)
Zone 8
Height: 6ft. (2m)
Flowers perfumed

Division 7: Oriental hybrids

Division 8: Other hybrids

Division 9: True species

The interested reader is referred to specialist groups for further details.

 Good cut flowers   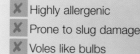 Highly allergenic   ✗ Rabbits like plants

✔ Attracts bees   ✗ Prone to slug damage

✗ Voles like bulbs

CULTIVATION

Plant the bulbs in autumn at a depth equivalent to three times the height of the bulb, in sharply-draining, fertile, humus-rich, soil in sun or light shade. The majority prefer acid soil, but others like limy soil, so details are given for each entry. Bulbs of Lilium candidum must be planted close to the soil surface.

PROPAGATION

Sow seed of species as soon as it is ripe. Remove offsets or scales or bulbils from bulbs, or bulbils from stems (where this occurs) as soon as the foliage dies down in late summer.

Lilium bulbiferum
(Orange lily) (Div. 9, Any soil)

Zone 7
Height: 5ft. (1.5m) Spread: indefinite

Lilium candidum (Madonna lily)
(Div. 9, Alkaline soil)
Zone 6
Height: 6ft. (2m)
Flowers perfumed

Lilium formosanum
(Formosa lily) (Div. 9, Acid soil)
Zone 5
Height: 5ft. (1.5m)
Flowers perfumed

Lilium formosanum var. *pricei*
A.G.M. (Div. 9, Acid soil)
Zone 5
Height: 1ft. (30cm)
Flowers perfumed

Lilium grayi (Div. 9, Acid soil)

Zone 5
Height: 5ft. (1.5m)
Flowers perfumed

Lilium henryi
A.G.M. (Div. 9, Alkaline soil)
Zone 5
Height: 10ft. (3m)
Flowers perfumed

Lilium lancifolium
(Div. 9, Acid soil)

Zone 4
Height: 5ft. (1.5m)

L

Lilium longiflorum
'Elegant Lady' (Div 5, Any soil)

Zone 4
Height: 4ft. (1.2m)

Lilium martagon
(Turk's cap lily) (Div. 9, Any soil)

Zone 4
Height: 6ft. (2m)

Lilium martagon var. *album* A.G.M
(Div. 9, Any soil)

Zone 4
Height: 6ft. (2m)

Lilium monadelphum (Caucasian
lily) (Div. 9, Alkaline soil)
Zone 5
Height: 5ft. (1.5m)
Flowers perfumed

Lilium 'Pink Perfection Group'
A.G.M. (Div. 6, Any soil)
Zone 7
Height: 6ft. (2m)
Flowers perfumed

Lilium pumilum
(Coral lily) (Div. 9, Acid soil)
Zone 5
Height: 18in. (45cm)
Flowers perfumed

Lilium pyrenaicum
A.G.M. (Div. 9, Alkaline soil)
Zone 3
Height: 3ft. (90cm)
Flowers malodorous

Lilium regale
(Regal lily) (Div. 9, Any soil)
Zone 5
Height: 6ft. (2m)
Flowers perfumed

Lilium speciosum var. *album*
(Div. 9)
Zone 8
Height: 5ft. (1.5m) Acid soil
Flowers perfumed

LIMONIUM *(Plumbaginaceae)*

Common names: Statice; Sea lavender

A genus of 150 species of annuals, biennials, evergreen and herbaceous perennials and subshrubs from deserts, coasts and salt marshes across the world. Their leaves are in basal rosettes, simple, entire or pinnatifid, tapered. The flowers are small, and papery, with similar bracts, and borne in one-sided panicles over a long period in summer and autumn.

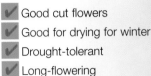

✔ Good cut flowers   ✘ Mildew prone

✔ Good for drying for winter   ✘ Resents disturbance

✔ Drought-tolerant

✔ Long-flowering

CULTIVATION
Grow in sharply-draining soil in sun.

PROPAGATION
Sow seed or divide, in spring.

Limonium bourgaei

Zone 7
Height: 16in. (40cm) Spread: 1ft. (30cm)

Limonium latifolium

Zone 5
Height: 3ft. (90cm) Spread: 18in. (45cm)
Evergreen

Limonium preauxii

Zone 9
Height: 28in. (70cm) Spread: 1ft. (30cm)

Limonium sinuatum

Zone 9
Height: 16in. (40cm) Spread: 4in. (10 cm)

LINARIA *(Scrophulariaceae)*

Common names: Toadflax

A genus of 100 species of annuals, biennials and herbaceous perennials from sunny, dry regions such as scree in the Mediterranean area, and temperate parts of the northern hemisphere. Their leaves are ovate, linear or lance-shaped, gray-green, and whorled lower down and alternate higher up the stem. The flowers are spurred, two-lipped, snapdragon-like, and borne in terminal racemes from spring to autumn.

✔ Long-flowering   ✘ Self-seeds

✔ Good cut flowers   ✘ Mildew prone

✔ Drought-tolerant

CULTIVATION
Grow in sharply-draining soil in sun.

PROPAGATION
Seed should be sown in a cold frame in early spring. Divide, or take softwood cuttings, in spring.

Linaria purpurea
(Purple toadflax)

Zone 6
Height: 3ft. (90cm) Spread: 1ft. (30cm)

Linaria purpurea
'Canon Went'

Zone 6
Height: 2ft. (60cm) Spread: 1ft. (30cm)

Linaria purpurea
'Springwood White'

Zone 6
Height: 3ft. (90cm) Spread: 1ft. (30cm)

Linaria purpurea
'Winifred's Delight'

Zone 6
Height and spread: 1ft. (30cm)

Linaria trionithophora
(Three birds flying)
Zone 7
Height: 4ft. (1.2m) Spread: indefinite
Invasive

LINUM *(Linaceae)*
Common names: Flax

A genus of 200 species of annuals, biennials, perennials, subshrubs and shrubs from dry grassland and scrubland in the temperate northern hemisphere. The perennials may be evergreen, semi-evergreen or herbaceous. Their leaves are simple, lance-shaped, gray-green and either alternate or opposite. The flowers are five-petalled and saucer-shaped, and are borne in racemes, cymes, panicles or corymbs over a long period in summer.

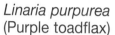

✓ Drought-tolerant
✓ Long-flowering
✓ Handsome foliage
✓ Attracts bees

✗ Short-lived
✗ Prone to slug damage
✗ Resents disturbance

Linum flavum
'Compactum'

Zone 5
Height: 6in. (15cm) Spread: 8in. (20cm)

CULTIVATION
Grow in sharply-draining, humus-rich soil in sun. Protect against winter wet.

PROPAGATION
Seed should be sown in a cold frame in spring or autumn. Stem-tip cuttings can be taken in early summer.

Linum
'Gemmell's Hybrid' A.G.M.

Zone 6
Height: 6in. (15cm) Spread: 8in. (20cm)

Linum monogynum

Zone 8
Height: 2ft. (60cm) Spread: 1ft. (30cm)

Linum narbonense
(Narbonne flax)

Zone 5
Height: 2ft. (60cm) Spread: 18in. (45cm)

Linum perenne

Zone 5
Height: 2ft. (60cm) Spread: 1ft. (30cm)

LIRIOPE *(Convallariaceae)*

Common names: Lily-turf

A genus of half a dozen species of perennials from acid woodland in Japan, China, Taiwan and Vietnam They may be rhizomatous or tuberous, evergreen or semi-evergreen. Their leaves are in clumps, arching, linear, and radical. The flowers are small, open only slightly, and are borne in dense spikes in early to late autumn, and followed by black berries.

✔ Evergreen
✔ Drought-tolerant
✔ Good cut flowers
✔ Low allergen
✔ Have berries after flowering

✘ Prone to slug damage

CULTIVATION
Grow in acid, light, moist, well-drained soil in a sheltered corner in sun or part shade.

PROPAGATION
Sow seed, or divide, in spring.

Liriope muscari
A.G.M (Big blue lily-turf)

Zone 6
Height: 1ft. (30cm) Spread: 18in. (45cm)

Liriope muscari
'John Burch'

Zone 6
Height: 1ft. (30cm) Spread: 18in. (45cm)

LITHODORA *(Boraginaceae)*

Common names: None

A genus of seven species of subshrubs and shrubs from scrub, woodland, and thickets across south Europe and into turkey and Algeria. Their leaves are linear, elliptic or lance-shaped, and hairy. The flowers are five-lobed funnels, produced on leafy terminal cymes over long periods in late spring and summer.

✔ Long-flowering
✔ Evergreen
✔ Trouble-free

CULTIVATION
Grow in alkaline to neutral, well-drained soil in sun.

PROPAGATION
Take semi-ripe cuttings in summer.

Lithodora diffusa
'Alba'

Zone 7
Height: 6in. (15cm) Spread: 32in. (80cm)

Lithodora diffusa
'Heavenly Blue' A.G.M.

Zone 7
Height: 6in. (15cm) Spread: 32in. (80cm)

L

L

LOBELIA *(Campanulaceae)*
Common names: None

A genus of 370 species of annuals, aquatics, perennials and shrubs from both temperate and tropical regions across the world, but from the Americas in particular. The habitat range is wide, varying from desert to dry mountain slopes to wet meadows, river banks and marshland. Their leaves are simple and alternate. The flowers are two-lipped, five-lobed, tubular, and solitary or borne in terminal racemes in summer. Tender forms such as *L. erinus* are grown as annuals in cold climates.

✔ Good cut flowers

✘ Short-lived
✘ Skin irritant
✘ Prone to slug damage

CULTIVATION
Grow in moist, or wet deep, fertile soil in sun.

PROPAGATION
Seed should be sown at 64°F (18°C) as soon as it is ripe, or divide in spring.

Lobelia
'Bees Flame'

Zone 7
Height: 3ft. (90cm) Spread: 1ft. (30cm)

Lobelia
'Butterfly Rose'

Zone7
Height: 3ft. (90cm) Spread: 1ft. (30cm)

Lobelia cardinalis A.G.M.

Zone 3
Height: 3ft. (90cm) Spread: 1ft. (30cm)

Lobelia erinus

Zone 9
Height: 8in. (20cm) Spread: 6in. (15cm)

Lobelia
'Eulalia Burridge'

Zone 8
Height: 30in. (75cm) Spread: 1ft. (30cm)

Lobelia
'Fan Tiefrot'

Zone 3
Height: 2ft. (60cm) Spread: 10in. (25cm)

Lobelia
'Fan Zinnoberrosa' A.G.M.

Zone 3
Height: 2ft. (60cm) Spread: 10in. (25cm)

L

Lobelia x gerardii
'Vedrariensis'

Zone 7
Height: 4ft. (1.2m) Spread: 1ft. (30cm)

Lobelia
'Kompliment Scharlach' A.G.M.

Zone 7
Height: 3ft. (90cm) Spread: 1ft. (30cm)

Lobelia 'Queen Victoria' A.G.M.

Zone 3
Height: 3ft. (90cm) Spread: 1ft. (30cm)
Flowers scarlet

Lobelia siphilitica

Zone 5
Height: 4ft. (1.2m) Spread: 1ft. (30cm)

Lobelia siphilitica
'Alba'

Zone 5
Height: 4ft. (1.2m) Spread: 1ft. (30cm)

Lobelia tupa

Zone 8
Height: 3ft. (90cm) Spread: 1ft. (30cm)

Lobelia
'Will Scarlet'

Zone 7
Height: 3ft. (90cm) Spread: 1ft. (30cm)

LOBULARIA *(Brassicaceae)*

Common names: None

A genus of five species of annuals and short-lived perennials from stony ground, seashore, and disturbed ground in the Mediterranean area and the Canary Islands. Their leaves are narrowly linear. The flowers are perfumed, four-petalled and cruciform, and are borne in terminal racemes in summer and early autumn.

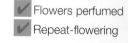

| ✔ Flowers perfumed | ✘ Short-lived |
| ✔ Repeat-flowering | ✘ Prone to slug damage |

CUTLIVATION
Grow in well-drained, light soil in sun.

PROPAGATION
Seed should be sown *in situ* in late spring.

Lobularia maritima

Zone 8
Height and spread: 1ft. (30cm)

LOPHOSPEMUM *(Scrophulariaceae)*

Common names: Creeping gloxinia

A genus of eight species of perennial climbing plants and shrubs from rocky slopes in Central and North America. Their leaves are entire or toothed, round or triangular. The funnel-shaped or tubular flowers are solitary or axillary, and borne over a long period in summer and autumn.

✔ Handsome foliage
✔ Long-flowering
✔ Trouble-free

CULTIVATION
Grow in moist, fertile, sharply-draining soil in sun.

PROPAGATION
Seed should be sown at 75°F (24°C) in spring. Semi-ripe cuttings can be rooted in late summer.

Lophospermum erubescens
A.G.M.
Zone 9
Height: 10ft. (3m) Spread: 3ft. (90cm)
Evergreen climber

L

LOTUS *(Papilionaceae)*

Common names: Parrot's beak; Pelican's beak; Bird's foot trefoil

A genus of 150 species of annuals, perennials and subshrubs found in dry stony areas or in pastureland across the world. Their leaves are simple, pinnate or palmate, and alternate. The pea-like flowers are solitary or in axillary or terminal clusters.

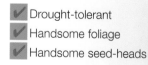

✔ Drought-tolerant	✘ Short-lived
✔ Handsome foliage	✘ Self-seeds
✔ Handsome seed-heads	

CULTIVATION
Grow in well-drained soil in sun.

PROPAGATION
Seed should be sown in spring, and for tender species, at 75°F (24°C).

Lotus berthelotii
A.G.M.

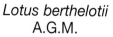

Zone 10
Height: 8in. (20cm) Spread: indefinite

Lotus corniculatus

Zone 5
Height: 1ft. (30cm) Spread: 18in. (45cm)

Lotus creticus

Zone 8
Height: 2ft. (60cm) Spread:45 cm.(18in.)

Lotus maculatus A.G.M.

Zone 10
Height: 8in. (20cm) Spread: indefinite

LUDISIA *(Orchidaceae)*

Common names: None

A genus of but a single species, *L. discolor*, of terrestrial perennial orchid from China and Indonesia. The leaves are subcordate to elliptic, velvety, papillose, red-bronze, with prominent veins, and banding. The small, white flowers are borne in terminal racemes in winter.

✔ Handsome foliage

CULTIVATION
Under glass, grow in loam-based compost in full light. Water moderately in summer, sparingly in winter.

Out of doors, grow in well-drained, humus-rich, fertile soil in part shade. Protect against frost in winter.

PROPAGATION
Division in spring.

Ludisia discolor

Zone 9
Height: 6in. (15cm) Spread: 1ft. (30cm)

LUNARIA *(Cruciferae)*

Common names: Honesty; Satin flower

A genus of three species, annual or perennial, found in uncultivated fields and disturbed ground in Eurasia. Their leaves are ovate or triangular, and toothed. The flowers are four-petalled, cruciform, and borne in tall, terminal racemes in late spring and summer.

✔ Flowers perfumed
✔ Good cut flowers
✔ Attracts butterflies
✔ Handsome seed-heads
✔ Good for winter drying

✘ Self-seeds

CULTIVATION
Grow in moist, well-drained soil in sun or part shade. Dead-head to prevent self-seeding if seed-heads are not required.

PROPAGATION
Sow seed in spring.

Lunaria rediviva (Perennial honesty)

Zone 8
Height: 3ft. (90cm) Spread: 1ft. (30cm)

L

L

LUPINUS *(Papilionaceae)*

Common names: Lupin

A genus of 200 species of annuals, perennials and subshrubs from dry, high grassland or cliffs or coastal sands or riversides in the circum-Mediterranean area and the Americas. Their leaves are basal, palmate with lance-shaped leaflets, which are softly hairy. The pea-like flowers are borne on tall terminal spikes in summer; they will repeat-flower if deadheaded at once.

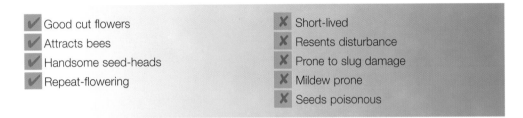

- ✔ Good cut flowers
- ✔ Attracts bees
- ✔ Handsome seed-heads
- ✔ Repeat-flowering
- ✘ Short-lived
- ✘ Resents disturbance
- ✘ Prone to slug damage
- ✘ Mildew prone
- ✘ Seeds poisonous

CULTIVATION
Grow in soil that is just on the acid side, well-drained, light and fertile, in sun or part shade. Dead-head to encourage repeat-flowering.

PROPAGATION
Seed should be nicked, or soaked for 24 hours and sown in spring or autumn.

Lupinus arboreus
A.G.M. (Tree lupin)

Zone 8
Height and spread: 6ft. (2m)

Lupinus
'Band of Nobles' series A.G.M.

Zone 5
Height: 5ft. (1.5m) Spread: 30in. (75cm)

Lupinus
'Chandelier'

Zone 5
Height: 3ft. (90cm) Spread: 30in. (75cm)

Lupinus
'Imperial Rose'

Zone 5
Height: 4ft. (1.2m) Spread: 30in. (75cm)

Lupinus
'Lulu'

Zone 5
Height: 3ft. (90cm) Spread: 30in. (75cm)

Lupinus
'My Castle'

Zone 5
Height: 3ft. (90cm) Spread: 30in. (75cm)

Lupinus
'Noble Maiden'

Zone 5
Height: 3ft. (90cm) Spread: 30in. (75cm)

Lupinus
'Ruby Lantern'

Zone 5
Height: 4ft. (1.2m) Spread: 30in. (75cm)

Lupinus
'The Chatelaine'

Zone 5
Height: 3ft. (90cm) Spread: 30in. (75cm)

Lupinus
'The Governor'

Zone 5
Height: 3ft. (90cm) Spread: 30in. (75cm)

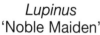

Lupinus
'The Page'

Zone 5
Height: 3ft. (90cm) Spread: 30in. (75cm)

LUZULA *(Juncaceae)*

Common names: Woodrush

A genus of 80 species of perennials from bog, fen, moor, heath, scrub, woodland and grassland across the temperate regions of the world. They are tuft-forming, grass-like, and evergreen for the most part, and some are rhizomatous or stoloniferous. Their leaves are broadly linear, stem and basal, flat or grooved, and fringed by white hairs. The flowers are in terminal clusters in spring and summer.

✔ Evergreen
✔ Handsome foliage
✔ Trouble-free

✘ Highly allergenic

Luzula sylvatica
'Aurea'

Zone 6
Height: 32in. (80cm) Spread: 18in. (45cm)

CULTIVATION
Grow in moist, humus-rich, fertile, well-drained soil in sun or part shade.

PROPAGATION
Seed should be sown in spring or autumn. Divide in late spring-early summer.

LYCHNIS *(Caryophyllaceae)*
Common names: Campion; Catchfly; Flower of Love; Ragged robin

A genus of 20 species of biennial and perennials from alpine and woodland and wet meadows in arctic and northern temperate regions. Their foliage is simple, hairy, lance-shaped. The flowers are five-petalled, tubular or star-shaped or salverform, and are borne in terminal panicles or cymes.

✔ Good cut flowers	✘ Short-lived
✔ Drought-tolerant	✘ Prone to slug damage
✔ Repeat-flowering	✘ Self-seeds

CULTIVATION
Grow in well-drained fertile in sun or part shade. *L chalcedonica* prefers moist soil. Dead-head to prevent self-seeding and to prolong flowering.

PROPAGATION
Seed should be sown in a cold frame as soon as it is ripe, or in spring.

Lychnis alpina

Zone 5
Height and spread: 6in. (15cm)

Lychnis x arkwrightii
'Vesuvius'

Zone 5
Height: 18in. (45cm) Spread: 1ft. (30cm)

Lychnis chalcedonica
(Maltese cross)

Zone 4
Height: 4ft. (1.2m) Spread: 1ft. (30cm)

Lychnis chalcedonica
'Rosea'

Zone 4
Height: 4ft. (1.2m) Spread: 1ft. (30cm)

Lychnis coronaria
(Rose campion)

Zone 4
Height: 32in. (80cm) Spread: 18in. (45cm)

Lychnis coronaria
'Alba' A.G.M.

Zone 4
Height: 32in. (80cm) Spread: 18in. (45cm)

Lychnis coronaria
Oculata Group

Zone 4
Height: 32in. (80cm) Spread: 1ft. (30cm)

Lychnis coronaria
(Pink form)

Zone 4
Height: 32in. (80cm) Spread: 1ft. (30cm)

Lychnis flos-cuculi albiflora
(White ragged robin)

Zone 5
Height: 32in. (80cm) Spread: 3ft. (90cm)

Lychnis flos-jovis
(Flower of Love; Flower of Jupiter)

Zone 5
Height: 2ft. (60cm) Spread: 18in. (45cm)

Lychnis flos-jovis
'Hort's Variety'

Zone 5
Height: 1ft. (30cm) Spread: 18in. (45cm)

Lychnis miqueliana

Zone 6
Height: 2ft. (60cm) Spread: 1ft. (30cm)

Lychnis viscaria
'Splendens Plena' A.G.M.

Zone 4
Height and spread: 18in. (45cm)

L

LYSICHITON *(Araceae)*

Common names: Skunk cabbage

A genus of two species of rhizomatous, aquatic perennials, one (*L. americanus*) from west North America and one (*L. camtschatcensis*) from north-east Asia. Their leaves are large, ovate or oblong, glossy, and in basal clusters. The flowers are white or yellow spathes that have small green flowers, with a musky smell.

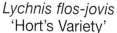
☑ Handsome foliage
☑ Trouble-free
✗ Flowers malodorous

CULTIVATION
Grow in moist or wet soil, or in shallow water in humus-rich fertile soil in sun or part shade.

PROPAGATION
Seed should be sown as soon as ripe in wet soil. Remove offsets in spring or summer.

Lysichiton americanus A.G.M.
(Yellow skunk cabbage)

Zone 6
Height: 3ft. (90cm) Spread: 4ft. (1.2m)

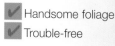

Lysichiton camtschatcensis
A.G.M. (White skunk cabbage)

Zone 6
Height and spread: 30in. (75cm)

LYSIMACHIA *(Primulaceae)*

Common names: Loosestrife; Creeping Jenny

A genus of 150 species of perennials from wet grassland or damp woodland or at watersides of northern temperate regions and South American subtropical areas. Their foliage is entire, simple, scalloped or toothed, and sometimes hairy. The flowers are five-petalled, cup- or star-shaped, and solitary or in terminal panicles or racemes. Some species are invasive, and taller ones require to be staked.

✔ Good cut flowers
✔ Handsome foliage
✔ Low allergen

✘ Prone to slug damage

CULTIVATION
Grow in moist, humus-rich, well-drained soil in sun or part shade. Do not allow to dry out in summer.

PROPAGATION
Seed should be sown outdoors in spring. Divide in spring or autumn.

Lysimachia ciliata
(Fringed loosestrife)

Zone 4
Height: 4ft. (1.2m) Spread: 2ft. (60cm)

Lysimachia ciliata
'Firecracker' A.G.M.

Zone 4
Height: 4ft. (1.2m) Spread: 2ft. (60cm)

Lysimachia clethroides A.G.M.
(Gooseneck loosestrife)

Zone 4
Height: 3ft. (90cm) Spread: indefinite

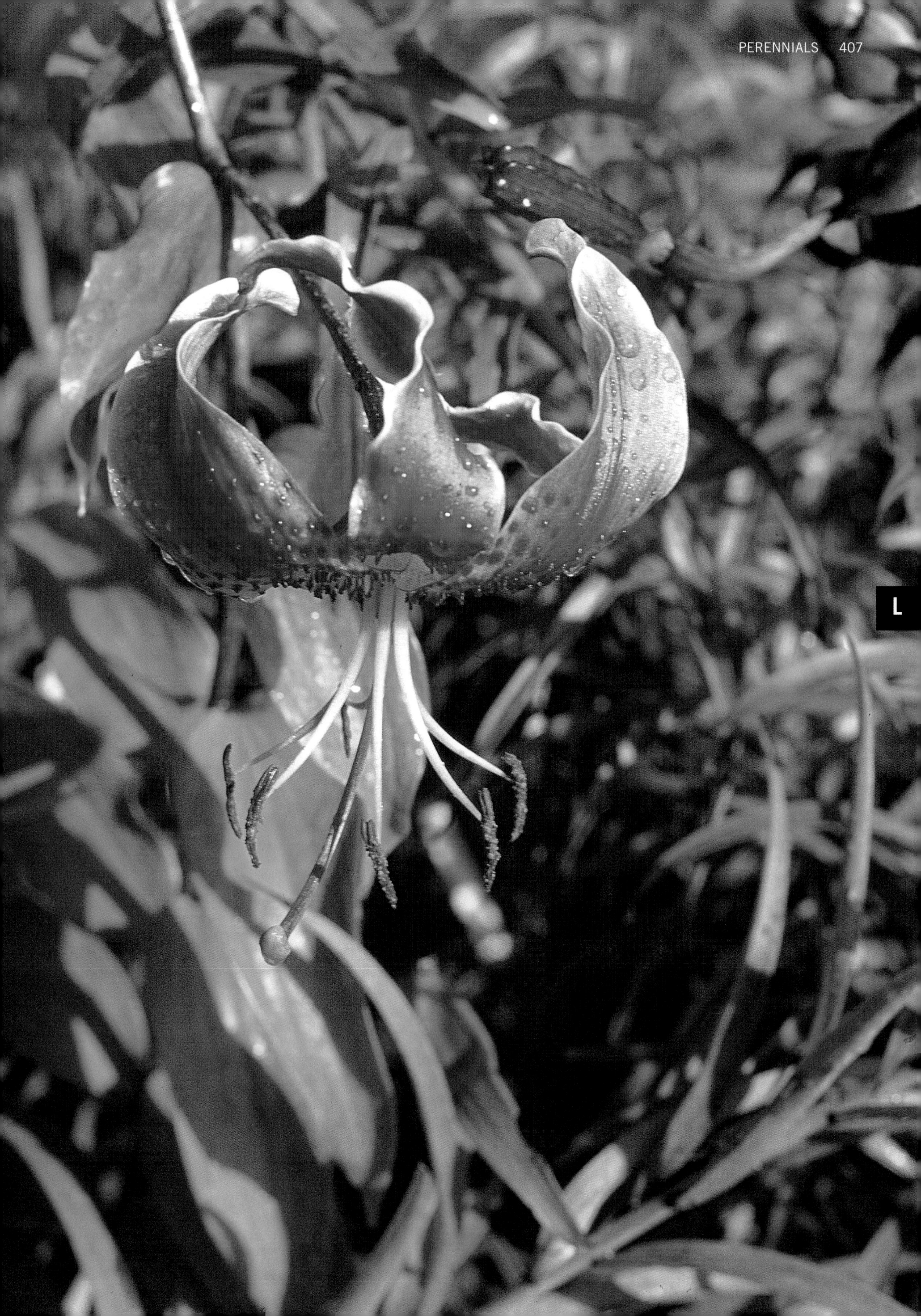

Lysimachia congestiflora
'Outback Sunset' (PBR)
Zone 9
Height: 8in. (20cm) Spread: 20in. (50cm)
Long-flowering

Lysimachia ephemerum

Zone 7
Height: 3ft. (90cm) Spread: 1ft. (30cm)

Lysimachia nummularia 'Aurea' A.G.M.
(Creeping Jenny; Creeping Charlie)

Zone 5
Height: 2in. (5cm) Spread: indefinite

Lysimachia punctata
(Yellow loosestrife)

Zone 5
Height: 3ft. (90cm) Spread: indefinite

Lysimachia punctata
'Alexander'

Zone 5
Height: 3ft. (90cm) Spread: indefinite

LYTHRUM *(Lythraceae)*

Common names: Loosestrife

A genus of 38 species of annuals and perennials found in ditches, riversides, wet meadows and scrubland across the temperate northern hemisphere. Their leaves are ovate or linear or lance-shaped, stalkless and opposite. The flowers are small, star-shaped funnels, and are formed singly or in groups in the leaf axils over a long period from midsummer to autumn. Some are invasive weeds.

✔ Long-flowering
✔ Good cut flowers
✔ Attracts bees
✔ Low allergen

✘ Prone to slug damage
✘ Self-seeds

CULTIVATION
Grow in moist, fertile, soil in sun. Dead-head to prevent self-seeding.

PROPAGATION
Seed should be sown at 64°F (18°C) in spring. Divide or take basal cuttings in spring.

Lythrum salicaria
(Purple loosestrife)

Zone 3
Height: 4ft. (1.2m) Spread: 18in. (45cm)

Lythrum salicaria
'Blush'

Zone 3
Height: 4ft. (1.2m) Spread: 18in. (45cm)

Lythrum salicaria
'Feuerkerze' (Firecandle) A.G.M.

Zone 3
Height: 5ft. (1.5m) Spread: 18in. (45cm)

Lythrum salicaria
'Robert'

Zone 3
Height: 4ft. (1.2m) Spread: 18in. (45cm)

Lythrum virgatum
'The Rocket'

Zone 4
Height: 3ft. (90cm) Spread: 18in. (45cm)

L

M

MACLEAYA
MAIANTHEMUM
MALVA
MALVASTRUM
MANDEVILLA
MARRUBIUM
MATTEUCCIA
MATTHIOLA
MAZUS
MECONOPSIS
MEGACARPAEA
MELIANTHUS
MELICA
MELISSA
MELLITIS
MENTHA
MERTENSIA
MILIUM
MIMULUS
MIRABILIS

MISCANTHUS
MITCHELLA
MOLINIA
MONARDA
MONSTERA
MORAEA
MORINA
MORISIA

MUKDENIA
MUSCARI
MYOSOTIDIUM
MYOSOTIS
MYRIOPHYLLUM
MYRRHIS

MACLEAYA *(Papaveraceae)*

Common names: None

A genus of three species of rhizomatous perennials from woodland, meadow and scrubland in Japan and China. Their handsome leaves are gray-green, heart-shaped, palmately-lobed, with round, toothed lobes and conspicuous veins. The flowers are tubular, lack petals, but have up to four sepals, and a clump of stamens, and are borne in airy panicles. All can be invasive.

✔ Good cut flowers	✘ Invasive
✔ Handsome foliage	✘ Prone to slug damage
✔ Low allergen	
✔ Architectural plants	

CULTIVATION
Grow in any soil, but preferably moist, in sun or part shade. They dislike cold drying winds.

PROPAGATION
Seed should be sown in a cold frame in spring. Separate rooted parts of rhizomes during dormancy. Root cuttings can be taken in winter.

Macleaya cordata A.G.M.

Zone 3
Height: 8ft. (2.5m) Spread: indefinite

Macleaya microcarpa

Zone 5
Height: 7ft. (2.2m) Spread: indefinite

MAIANTHEMUM *(Convallariaceae)*

Common names: May lily

A genus of three species of rhizomatous, creeping, invasive perennials from temperate northern hemisphere woodland. The leaves are heart-shaped, alternate. The flowers are tiny, fluffy, four-tepalled, stars borne in terminal racemes in early summer, and followed by red berries.

✔ Have berries after flowering	✘ Prone to slug damage
✔ Good ground cover in shade	✘ Invasive

CULTIVATION
Grow in acid to neutral, moist, well-drained soil in part or deep shade.

PROPAGATION
Seed should be sown in a cold frame as soon as ripe. Separate rooted runners in spring.

Maianthemum bifolium
(Wild lily-of-the-valley)

Zone 3
Height: 6in. (15cm) Spread: indefinite.

M

MALVA *(Malvaceae)*
Common names: Mallow

A genus of 30 species of annuals, biennials and perennials from open dry habitats such as waste ground, and roadsides in North Africa, temperate Asia, and Europe. Their leaves are alternate, round, kidney- or heart-shaped, entire or toothed, or shallowly lobed, or pinnatisect. The five-petalled flowers are saucer- or funnel-shaped, and surrounded by up to three bracts, and are solitary or borne in clusters in the leaf axils or in terminal racemes, in spring, summer or autumn.

✔ Long-flowering   ✘ Self-seeds

✔ Attracts bees   ✘ Short-lived

CULTIVATION
Grow in moist, fertile, well-drained soil in sun. Taller forms require to be staked. Dead-head to prevent self-seeding.

PROPAGATION
Seed should be sown *in situ* or in seed trays in spring or early summer. Basal cuttings can be taken in spring.

Malva moschata
(Musk mallow)

Zone 3
Height: 3ft. (90cm) Spread: 2ft. (60cm)

Malva moschata forma.
'Alba' A.G.M.

Zone 3
Height: 3ft. (90cm) Spread: 2ft. (60cm)

Malva sylvestris

Zone 5
Height: 4ft. (1.2m) Spread: 2ft. (60cm)

Malva sylvestris
'Primley Blue'

Zone 5
Height: 8in. (20cm) Spread: 2ft. (60cm)

Malva sylvestris
'Zebrina'

Zone 5
Height: 5ft. (1.5m) Spread: 2ft. (60cm)

M

M

MALVASTRUM *(Malvaceae)*

Common names: None

A genus of 30 species of evergreen perennials and shrubs from dry, rocky prairies or outcrops or alluvial soils in both South and North America. Their leaves are lance-shaped, rounded, entire or lobed, and often toothed. The flowers are cup- or funnel-shaped, solitary or axillary, or borne in spikes or racemes, in summer.

✔ Long-flowering   ✖ Invasive
✔ Drought-tolerant
✔ Trouble-free

CULTIVATION
Grow in well-drained soil in sun.

PROPAGATION
Sow seed in spring, or separate rooted runners in summer.

Malvastrum lateritium

Zone 8
Height: 6in. (15cm) Spread: indefinite
Invasive

MANDEVILLA *(Apocynaceae)*

Common names: None

A genus of 120 species of tuberous-rooted climbers and perennials from tropical woodland in South and Central America. Their leaves are simple, and opposite, with pointed tips and heart-shaped bases, and the stems have a milky sap that is skin-irritant. The flowers are tubular to salverform, five-lobed, and borne in axillary racemes in summer.

✔ Handsome foliage   ✖ Sap is skin-irritant
✔ Trouble-free   ✖ All parts poisonous

CULTIVATION
Grow in moist, fertile, well-drained soil in sun, but with shade at mid-day. Prune in late winter/early spring by cutting sideshoots back to within 3 or four buds of the permanent framework.

PROPAGATION
Seed should be sown at 73°F (23°C) in spring. Softwood cuttings can be taken in spring, and semi-ripe cuttings in summer, and rooted with bottom heat.

Mandevilla splendens

Zone 10
Height: 20ft. (6m) Spread: 3ft. (90cm)

MARRUBIUM *(Lamiaceae)*

Common names: Horehound

A genus of 40 species of perennials from dry, stony, sunny habitats in temperate Asia and the Mediterranean area of Europe. Their leaves are ovate, malodorous, and in opposite alternate pairs. The flowers are tubular, two-lipped, and borne in axillary whorls.

✔ Drought-tolerant   ✖ Self-seeds
✔ Handsome foliage
✔ Trouble-free

CULTIVATION
Grow in well-drained soil in a sheltered corner in sun. Protect against winter wet.

PROPAGATION
Seed should be sown in a cold frame in spring; germination is likely to be erratic. Softwood cuttings can be rooted in spring.

Marrubium peregrinum

Zone 8
Height: 2ft. (60cm) Spread: 1ft. (30cm)

MATTEUCCIA *(Woodsiaceae)*

Common names: Shuttlecock fern; ostrich fern

A genus of four species of terrestrial, rhizomatous, deciduous ferns from deciduous woodland in Eurasia and North America. The fronds that appear in spring are shuttlecock-like, lance-shaped, pinnate to two-pinnatifid, sterile. Later, in summer, fertile, small, dark, erect, fronds appear, and persist over winter.

- ✔ Handsome foliage
- ✔ Evergreen
- ✔ Trouble-free

CULTIVATION
Grow in acid to neutral, moist, well-drained soil in part shade.

PROPAGATION
Spores should be sown at 59°F (15°C) as soon as ripe. Divide in early spring.

Matteuccia struthiopteris
A.G.M.

Zone 2
Height: 5ft. (1.5m) Spread: 3ft. (90cm)

MATTHIOLA *(Brassicaceae)*

Common names: None

A genus of 55 species of annuals, perennials and subshrubs from hilly regions and scrubland across Eurasia and in South Africa. Their leaves are simple or lobed or pinnatifid, lance-shaped, and gray-green. The flowers are cruciform, perfumed, and borne in terminal spikes over a long period in summer. *M. incana* is grown usually as an annual.

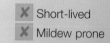
- ✔ Long-flowering
- ✔ Flowers perfumed
- ✔ Handsome foliage
- ✘ Short-lived
- ✘ Mildew prone

CULTIVATION
Grow in alkaline to neutral, moist, well-drained soil in a sheltered corner in sun.

PROPAGATION
Seed should be sown in a cold frame in spring or summer, and the seedlings overwintered under glass.

M

Matthiola incana
Ten Week Series

Zone 6
Height: 1ft. (30cm) Spread: 10in. (25cm)

Matthiola
(Pink perennial)

Zone 7
Height: 18in. (45cm) Spread: 1ft. (30cm)

Matthiola
(White perennial)

Zone 7
Height: 18in. (45cm) Spread: 1ft. (30cm)

MAZUS *(Scrophulariaceae)*

Common names: None

A genus of 30 species of annuals and mat-forming, creeping perennials from wet lowland and highland habitats in the Himalayas, Pakistan, India, China, Japan, south-east Asia and Australasia. The leaves are obovate, spoon-shaped or linear, toothed, and opposite. The flowers are tubular, with upright upper and spreading lower lips, produced from the leaf axils in few-flowered racemes in late spring to early summer.

✔ Good ground cover	✘ Prone to slug damage

CULTIVATION
Grow in moist, well-drained soil in a sheltered corner in sun.

PROPAGATION
Seed should be sown in a cold frame in autumn or spring, when division can also be carried out.

Mazus reptans

Zone 3
Height: 2in. (5cm) Spread: 18in. (45cm)

MECONOPSIS *(Papaveraceae)*

Common names: Poppy

A genus of 45 species of annuals, biennials and perennials from shaded, moist, mountainous areas such as woodland, scree, scrub or rocky slopes in the Himalayas, Burma, China and one (*M. cambrica*) from western Europe. The leaves are in basal rosettes, simple or pinnate, lobed, toothed or pinnatisect, and hairy or bristly. A single flowering stem is produced per rosette, and this may be unbranched with a solitary flower or branched high up, and carrying solitary flowers or several in short racemes, the upper ones opening first. The individual flowers have up to nine petals, are saucer- or cup-shaped, and pendent sometimes, and followed by handsome furry seed-pods. They may be monocarpic or short-lived.

✔ Handsome foliage	✘ Short-lived
	✘ Prone to slug damage
	✘ Required to be staked

CULTIVATION
Meconopsis perform best in gardens with cool, wet summers, and will not tolerate hot, dry sites. The soil should be acid to neutral, moist, humus-rich and sharply-draining. Part shade is ideal. Do not allow to dry out in summer. Allow short-lived species to build up several crowns by deadheading to prevent flowering, in order to prolong length of life.

PROPAGATION
Seed should be sown in a cold frame, preferably as soon as ripe, or in spring. Overwinter seedlings under glass. Divide after flowering.

Meconopsis betonicifoliia
A.G.M. (Himalayan blue poppy)

Zone 7
Height: 4ft. (1.2m) Spread: 18in. (45cm)

Meconopsis betonicifolia var. *alba*

Zone 7
Height: 4ft. (1.2m) Spread: 18in. (45cm)

Meconopsis cambrica
(Welsh poppy)
Zone 6
Height: 18in. (45cm) Spread: 1ft. (30cm)
Long-flowering

Meconopsis cambrica var. *aurantiaca*
'Plena' (Double orange Welsh poppy)
Zone 6
Height: 18in. (45cm) Spread: 1ft. (30cm)
Long-flowering

Meconopsis cambrica 'Flore Pleno'
Zone 6
Height: 18in. (45cm) Spread: 1ft. (30cm)
Long-flowering

Meconopsis chelidoniifolia

Zone 8
Height: 3ft. (90cm) Spread: 2ft. (60cm)

Meconopsis dhwojii
Zone 8
Height: 3ft. (90cm) Spread: 1ft. (30cm)
Evergreen
Monocarpic

Meconopsis grandis
A.G.M.

Zone 5
Height: 4ft. (1.2m) Spread: 2ft. (60cm)

M

Meconopsis latifolia

Zone7
Height: 4ft. (1.2m) Spread: 2ft. (60cm)

Meconopsis napaulensis

Zone 8
Height: 8ft. (2.5m) Spread: 3ft. (90cm)

Meconopsis paniculata

Zone 8
Height: 6ft. (2m) Spread: 2ft. (60cm)

Meconopsis punicea

Zone 7
Height: 30in. (75cm) Spread: 1ft. (30cm)

Meconopsis quintuplinervia
A.G.M.

Zone 8
Height: 18in. (45cm) Spread: 1ft. (30cm)

Meconopsis regia

Zone 8
Height: 6ft. (2m) Spread: 3ft. (90cm)

Meconopsis x sheldonii

Zone 6
Height: 5ft. (1.5m) Spread: 2ft. (60cm)

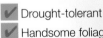

Meconopsis x sheldonii
'Slieve Donard' A.G.M.

Zone 6
Height: 5ft. (1.5m) Spread: 2ft. (60cm)

MEGACARPAEA *(Cruciferae)*

Common names: None

A genus of seven tap-rooted perennials from dry, open, sunny sites in Eurasia and China. The leaves are toothed, and pinnate, with ovate lobes. The small flowers are in dense panicles, or racemes, in spring and early summer.

✔ Drought-tolerant	✘ Resents disturbance
✔ Handsome foliage	✘ Short-lived

CULTIVATION
Grow in well-drained fertile soil in sun.

PROPAGATION
Seed should be sown in a cold frame when ripe.

Megacarpaea polyandra

Zone 7
Height: 6ft. (2m) Spread: 2ft. (60cm)

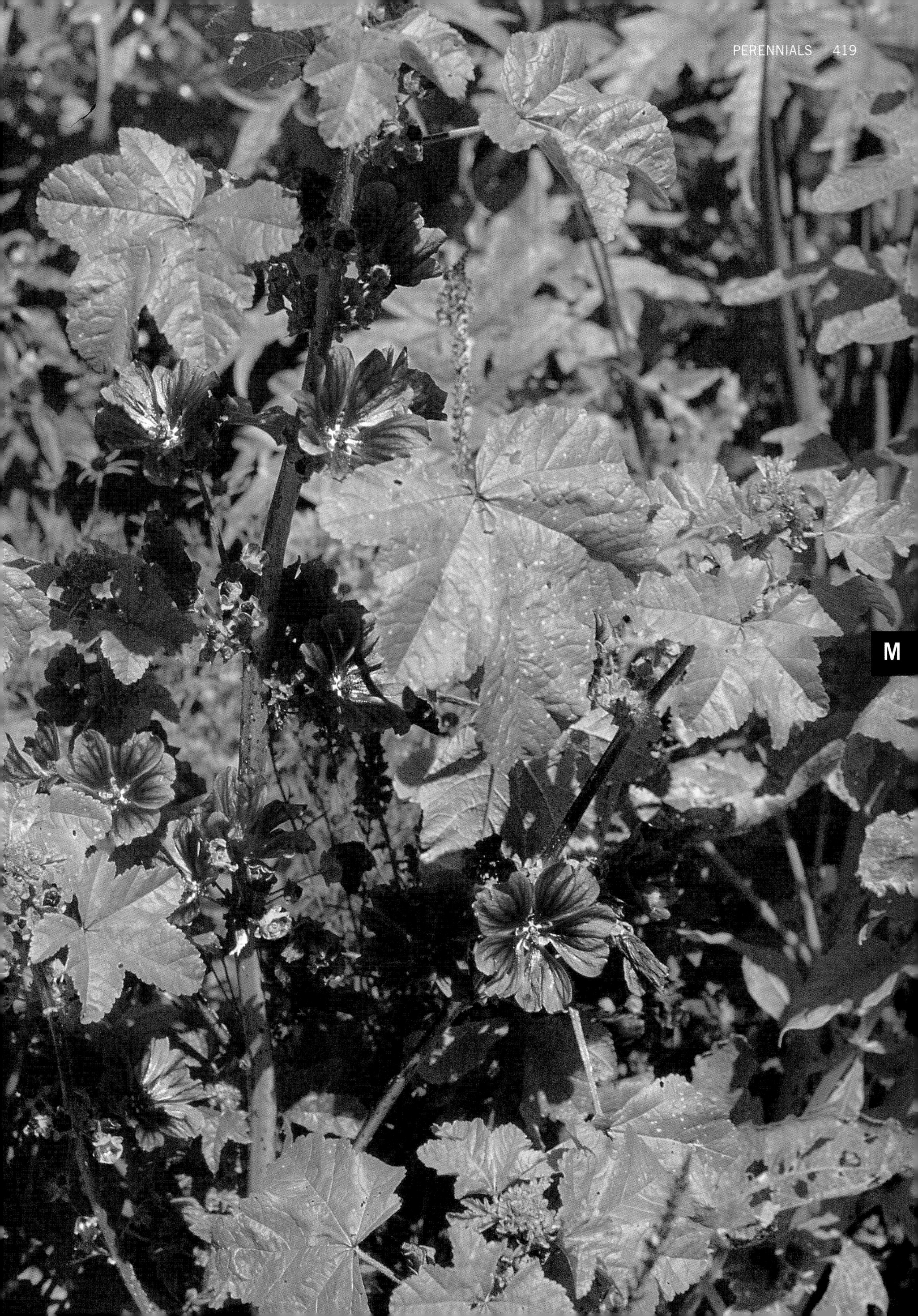

MELIANTHUS *(Melianthaceae)*

Common names: Honey bush

A genus of six species of evergreen subshrubs from high grassland in southern Africa. The handsome leaves are pinnate, alternate, and blue-green or gray-green. The flowers are small, brick red or crimson-brown, with five irregular sepals and petals forming a hood and spurs, and are borne in erect, spiky racemes from late spring to early summer.

- ✔ Evergreen
- ✔ Drought-tolerant
- ✔ Handsome foliage
- ✔ Trouble-free
- ✔ Architectural plants

CULTIVATION
Grow in moist, well-drained soil in a sheltered corner in sun. Protect against cold drying winds and winter wet, and against frost in cold areas, where they are herbaceous and recover in spring.

PROPAGATION
Seed should be sown at 64°F (18°C) in spring. Basal or softwood cuttings can be taken in spring, and rooted suckers can also be detached then.

Melianthus major

Zone 9
Height and spread: 10ft. (3m)

MELICA *(Poaceae)*

Common names: Melick

A genus of 75 species of rhizomatous, clump-forming, herbaceous perennial grasses from grassland in the temperate world, with the exception of Australia. The foliage is arching, linear and in-rolled. The inflorescence is of panicles of laterally compressed spikelets.

- ✔ Disease-free
- ✔ Pest-free
- ✔ Handsome foliage
- ✘ Highly allergenic

CULTIVATION
Grow in moist, well-drained soil in light shade.

PROPAGATION
Seed should be sown *in situ* as soon as ripe. Divide in spring as is starting into growth.

Melica nutans
(Wood melick; Mountain melick)

Zone 6
Height: 18in. (45cm) Spread: 1ft. (30cm)

MELISSA *(Lamiaceae)*

Common names: Balm

A genus of three species of herbaceous perennials from damp wasteland, from sea level to hills in Eurasia. The leaves are aromatic, smelling strongly of lemon when crushed, ovate, and opposite. The flowers are two-lipped, tubular, and borne in leafy spikes in summer.

- ✔ Long-flowering
- ✔ Attracts bees
- ✔ Foliage aromatic
- ✘ Self-seeds
- ✘ Mildew prone
- ✘ Require staking

CULTIVATION
Grow in well-drained, poor soil in sun. Protect against winter wet. Cut back hard in spring.

PROPAGATION
Seed should be sown in a cold frame in spring. Divide in spring or autumn.

Melissa officinalis
'Aurea' (Lemon balm)

Zone 4
Height: 4ft. (1.2m) Spread: 2ft. (60cm)

MELLITIS *(Lamiaceae)*

Common names: None

A genus of a single species, *M. melissophyllum*, from light woodland across Europe and west Asia. The leaves are oval, honey-scented, opposite in pairs. The two-lipped flowers are borne in whorls from the upper leaf axils in spring and early summer.

- ✔ Foliage aromatic
- ✔ Handsome foliage
- ✔ Attracts bees
- ✔ Trouble-free

CULTIVATION
Grow in moist, well-drained, fertile soil in part shade. Do not allow to dry out in summer.

PROPAGATION
Seed should be sown in a cold frame as soon as it is ripe, or in spring. Divide in early spring.

Mellitis melissophyllum

Zone 6
Height: 28in. (70cm) Spread: 20in. (50cm)

MENTHA *(Lamiaceae)*

Common names: Mint

A genus of 25 species of annuals and rhizomatous perennials from wet or moist or aquatic habitats in Eurasia and Africa. Their aromatic leaves are round or lance-shaped. The two-lipped flowers are bell-shaped or tubular, are surrounded by leafy bracts, and appear in clusters in spikes in summer. They can be invasive.

- ✔ Foliage aromatic
- ✔ Attracts bees
- ✔ Handsome foliage
- ✔ Low allergen
- ✔ Good for drying for winter
- ✘ Mildew prone
- ✘ Flowers insignificant

CULTIVATION
Grow in moist, poor soil in sun.

PROPAGATION
Sow seed in a cold frame, or divide in spring. Tip cuttings can be taken in spring or summer.

M

Mentha x gracilis
'Variegata' (Gingermint)

Zone 7
Height: 18in. (45cm) Spread: indefinite

Mentha x suaveolens
'Variegata' (Applemint)

Zone 6
Height: 3ft. (90cm) Spread: indefinite

M

MERTENSIA *(Boraginaceae)*
Common names: None

A genus of 50 species of perennials, sometimes prostrate, from wet meadows coasts and woodlands of Greenland, Eurasia and North America. Their leaves are lance-shaped or round, alternate, blue-green or gray-green. The flowers are bell-shaped or tubular, pendent, five-lobed, blue, and borne in cymes over a long period.

✔ Good cut flowers   ✘ Self-seeds
✔ Handsome foliage   ✘ Prone to slug damage
✔ Low allergen   ✘ Resents disturbance
✔ Long-flowering

CULTIVATION
Grow in moist, humus-rich, well-drained soil, or sharply-drained in the case of *M. simplicissima*, in part shade.

PROPAGATION
Seed should be sown in a cold frame in autumn; ensure that the seedlings do not dry out over winter.

Mertensia pulmonariodes
A.G.M.

Zone 3
Height: 18in. (45cm) Spread: 10in. (25cm)

Mertensia simplicissima

Zone 6
Height: 3ft. (90cm) Spread: 1ft. (30cm)

MILIUM *(Poaceae)*
Common names: None

A genus of six species of perennial grasses from temperate woodland in North America and Eurasia. Their leaves are linear, flat, pale green or yellow-green, and the flowers are panicles of spreading spikelets borne from late spring to midsummer.

✔ Handsome foliage   ✘ Self-seeds
✔ Trouble-free   ✘ Highly allergenic

CULTIVATION
Grow in reliably moist, well-drained soil in sun or part shade.

PROPAGATION
Seed should be sown *in situ* in spring. Divide in spring.

Milium effusum aureum
'Bowles' Golden Grass'
Zone 6
Height: 2ft. (60cm) Spread: 1ft. (30cm)
Comes true from seed

M

MIMULUS *(Scrophulariaceae)*
Common names: Monkey flower; Musk

A genus of 150 species of annuals, perennials and shrubs, mostly from damp ground but occasionally from desert, in the Americas, Asia, Australia and Southern Africa. Their leaves are linear, entire or toothed, and opposite. The flowers are snapdragon-like, two-lipped, two-lobed, trumpet- or funnel-shaped or tubular, and are borne in the leaf axils or in racemes from spring to autumn.

- ✔ Long-flowering
- ✔ Low allergen
- ✘ Mildew prone
- ✘ Prone to slug damage
- ✘ Self-seeds
- ✘ Short-lived

CULTIVATION
Grow in wet or moist humus-rich soil, except *M. aurantiacus*, which requires sharply-draining soil, in sun or light shade. *M. luteus* can be grown in shallow water.

PROPAGATION
Seed of hardy perennials should be sown in a cold frame in autumn or spring. Seed of tender species should be sown at 54°F (12°C) in spring. Divide both in spring.

Mimulus
'Andean Nymph' A.G.M.

Zone 6
Height: 8in. (20cm) Spread: 1ft. (30cm)

Mimulus aurantiacus
A.G.M.

Zone 8
Height and spread: 3ft. (90cm)

Mimulus cardinalis
A.G.M. (Scarlet monkey flower)

Zone 7
Height: 3ft. (90cm) Spread: 2ft. (60cm)

Mimulus
'Highland Orange'

Zone 6
Height: 8in. (20cm) Spread: 1ft. (30cm)

Mimulus lewisii
A.G.M.

Zone 5
Height: 2ft. (60cm) Spread: 18in. (45cm)

Mimulus luteus
(Yellow monkey flower)

Zone 7
Height: 1ft. (30cm) Spread: 2ft. (60cm)

Mimulus luteus
'Variegatus'

Zone 7
Height: 1ft. (30cm) Spread: 2ft. (60cm)

M

Mimulus
'Malibu Red'

Zone 6
Height: 8in. (20cm) Spread: 1ft. (30cm)

Mimulus moschatus

Zone 7
Height and spread: 1ft. (30cm)

Mimulus puniceus

Zone 9
Height and spread: 5ft. (1.5m)

MIRABILIS *(Nyctaginaceae)*

Common names: Four o'clock flower

A genus of 50 species of annuals and perennials from open, sunny, dry habitats in the Americas. The perennials are tuberous, and have ovate, opposite leaves. The flowers are large, trumpet-shaped, perfumed, and are borne in axillary corymbs or panicles over a long period in summer.

✔ Long-flowering
✔ Flowers perfumed

✘ Prone to slug damage

CULTIVATION
Grow in well-drained, fertile soil in sun. Lift tubers as for Dahlias, and store frost-free over winter in cold areas.

PROPAGATION
Seed should be sown at 64°F (18°C) in spring. Divide tubers after flowering.

Mirabilis jalapa

Zone 8
Height and spread: 2ft. (60cm)

M

MISCANTHUS *(Poaceae)*

Common names: Zebra grass

A genus of 20 species of perennial grasses found in moist marshland or meadows in Africa and East Asia. They may be evergreen or herbaceous, rhizomatous or tufted. The leaves are lance-shaped or linear, arching, folded, and gray- or blue-green. The flowers are in dense, terminal arching panicles of hairy, silvery, spikes in late summer or autumn. They make excellent specimen plants.

✔ Handsome foliage
✔ Architectural plants
✔ Trouble-free

✘ Resents disturbance
✘ Highly allergenic

CULTIVATION
Grow in any soil that is moist, fertile, well-drained, in sun. Protect against winter wet.

PROPAGATION
Seed should be sown in a cold frame in spring. Divide in spring as new growth is appearing, but divisions are slow to establish.

Miscanthus sinensis
'Zebrinus'

Zone 4
Height: 12ft. (4m) Spread: 4ft. (1.2m)

MITCHELLA *(Rubiaceae)*

Common names: Partridge berry; Creeping box

A genus of two species of evergreen, trailing perennials from woodland in Japan and North America. The stems root at the nodes, and so spread is considerable. The leaves are lance-shaped or ovate. The fragrant flowers are small, white funnels, in summer, and are followed by red berries.

 Flowers perfumed   Have berries after flowering
 Evergreen   Trouble-free

CULTIVATION
Grow in acid to neutral, moist, well-drained soil in part shade.

PROPAGATION
Sow seed, or separate rooted runners, in spring.

Mitchella repens
(U.S.A.) (Creeping box)

Zone 3
Height: 2in. (5cm) Spread: 1ft. (30cm)

MOLINIA *(Poaceae)*

Common names: Purple moor grass

A genus of two species of perennial grasses from damp moorland in Eurasia. The leaves are in dense clumps, linear, and the flowers are in compressed, purple, spikelets in open, graceful panicles well above the foliage from spring to autumn.

Long-flowering   ✗ Highly allergenic
Handsome seed-heads
Architectural plants

CULTIVATION
Grow in acid to neutral, moist, well-drained soil in sun or part shade.

PROPAGATION
Seed of species should be sown in a cold frame in spring. Divide all forms in spring.

Molinia caerulea
'Variegata'

Zone 5
Height: 2ft. (60cm) Spread: 16in. (40cm)

MONARDA *(Lamiaceae)*

Common names: Bergamot

A genus of 15 species of annuals and rhizomatous perennials from prairie, and dry scrubland and woodland in North America. Their leaves are oval or lance-shaped, toothed and aromatic, with conspicuous veins, and opposite and alternate. The sage-like flowers are tubular, two-lipped, with the upper being hooded and erect and the lower three-lobed, usually with colored bracts, and borne in terminal whorls from midsummer to early autumn.

Long-flowering   ✗ Require to be staked
Foliage aromatic   ✗ Prone to slug damage
Good cut flowers   ✗ Mildew prone
Low allergen
Attracts bees

CULTIVATION
Grow in moist, humus-rich, well-drained soil in sun or part shade. Do not allow to dry out in summer, and protect against winter wet.

PROPAGATION
Sow seed, or divide, or take basal cuttings in spring.

Monarda
'Aquarius'

Zone 4
Height: 3ft. (90cm) Spread: 18in. (45cm)

Monarda
'Balance'

Zone 4
Height: 3ft. (90cm) Spread: 18in. (45cm)

Monarda
'Cambridge Scarlet' A.G.M.

Zone 4
Height: 3ft. (90cm) Spread: 18in. (45cm)

Monarda
'Croftway Pink' A.G.M.

Zone 4
Height: 3ft. (90cm) Spread: 18in. (45cm)

Monarda didyma
(Bee balm)

Zone 4
Height: 3ft. (90cm) Spread: 18in. (45cm)

Monarda fistulosa

Zone 4
Height: 4ft. (1.2m) Spread: 18in. (45cm)

Monarda
'Gardenview Scarlet'

Zone 4
Height: 3ft. (90cm) Spread: 18in. (45cm)

Monarda
'Isla'

Zone 4
Height: 3ft. (90cm) Spread: 18in. (45cm)

Monarda
'Loddon Crown' A.G.M.

Zone 4
Height: 3ft. (90cm) Spread: 18in. (45cm)

Monarda
'Prairienacht'

Zone 4
Height: 3ft. (90cm) Spread: 18in. (45cm)

M

M

Monarda punctata

Zone 4
Height: 3ft. (90cm) Spread: 18in. (45cm)

Monarda
'Ruby Glow'

Zone 4
Height: 3ft. (90cm) Spread: 18in. (45cm)

Monarda
'Scorpion'

Zone 4
Height: 3ft. (90cm) Spread: 18in. (45cm)

Monarda
'Squaw'

Zone 4
Height: 3ft. (90cm) Spread: 18in. (45cm)

Monarda
'Twins'

Zone 4
Height: 3ft. (90cm) Spread: 18in. (45cm)

MONSTERA *(Araceae)*

Common names: Swiss cheese plant

A genus of 22 species of evergreen climbers found in tropical rainforest in all three Americas. Their leaves vary with the age of the plant, and can be entire or lobed or deeply pinnatifid. The flowers are tiny, borne singly in the leaf axils in spathes, and are followed by edible fruits.

✔ Handsome foliage	✘ Flowers insignificant
✔ Fruits edible	✘ All parts except fruit poisonous
✔ Evergreen	✘ Fruit is skin-irritant

CULTIVATION
Under glass, grow in loam-based potting compost in bright indirect light and moderate to high humidity. Water freely in summer, sparingly in winter.

Out of doors, grow in moist, well-drained humus-rich soil in part shade. Prune in spring for size and shape.

PROPAGATION
Seed should be sown at 75°F (24°C) as soon as ripe. Layering can be done in autumn. Leaf or tip cuttings can be taken in summer, and rooted with bottom heat.

Monstera deliciosa
'Variegata' A.G.M.

Zone 10
Height: 70ft. (20m); Spread: 6ft. (2m)

M

MORAEA *(Iridaceae)*
Common names: None

A genus of 120 species of cormous perennials from moist grassland across Africa. They are herbaceous, or at best, semi-evergreen in cold gardens, but may be evergreen in warm sites. Their leaves are both basal and stem, linear, or lance-shaped, rolled or flat, and channeled. The iris-like flowers are produced in clusters within paired bracts, are short-lived but borne in succession from spring to summer.

✔ Repeat-flowering   ✔ Trouble-free

✔ Good cut flowers

CULTIVATION
Plant corms 3in. (8 cm) deep in spring or autumn in well-drained, humus-rich, fertile soil in sun, with shade at mid-day. Water freely during growth, and dry off during their midsummer to autumn dormancy.

PROPAGATION
Sow seed of tender species in a cold frame in spring, and of hardy species under glass in autumn. Separate offsets during dormancy.

Moraea spathulata

Zone 8
Height: 3ft. (90cm) Spread: 3in. (8 cm)

MORINA *(Morinaceae)*
Common names: None

A genus of five species of evergreen perennials found in open grassy and rocky slopes, and open woodland from eastern Europe, Turkey, across to Central Asia, the Himalayas and China. Their handsome leaves are in basal rosettes, glossy, lance-shaped, scalloped and spiny-toothed, and stem, where they get progressively smaller as they ascend. The flowers have long perianth tubes, are two-lipped and borne in spikes, in clusters above whorled, spiny bracts, in summer.

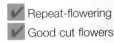

✔ Evergreen   ✘ Prone to slug damage

✔ Good cut flowers

✔ Good for drying for winter

✔ Handsome seed-heads

✔ Handsome foliage

CULTIVATION
Grow in sharply-draining, poor, soil in sun. Protect against winter wet.

PROPAGATION
Seed should be sown in a cold frame, one seed per compartment, in gritty compost, as soon as ripe.

Morina longifolia

Zone 6
Height: 3ft. (90cm) Spread: 2ft. (60cm)

Morina nepalensis

Zone 6
Height: 18in. (45cm) Spread: 1ft. (30cm)

MORISIA *(Brassicaceae)*
Common names: None

A genus of but one species of perennial, *M. monanthos*, found in sandy soils in Corsica and Sardinia. It is tap-rooted, and rosette-forming. The leaves are pinnatifid. The relatively large, saucer-shaped, four-petalled, yellow flowers are almost sessile, and appear in late spring and early summer.

 Handsome foliage

CULTIVATION
Under glass, grow in equal parts of grit and loam-based potting compost in full light.

Out of doors, grow in sharply-draining, fertile soil in sun.

PROPAGATION
Seed should be sown in a cold frame in spring. Root cuttings can be taken in winter, under glass.

Morisia monanthos
'Fred Hemingway'

Zone 7
Height: 2in. (5cm) Spread: 4in. (10 cm)

MUKDENIA *(Saxifragaceae)*
Common names: None

A genus of two species of rhizomatous, herbaceous perennials from woodland in China and Korea. Their handsome leaves are palmate, with between five and nine lobes, and toothed. The flowers are small, bell-shaped, five- or six-petalled, white, and borne above the leaves in panicles or racemes in spring. They dislike hot dry gardens.

 Handsome foliage   ✘ Prone to slug damage

CULTIVATION
Grow in moist, leafy, well-drained soil in part shade.

PROPAGATION
Seed should be sown in a cold frame in autumn. Divide in spring as growth commences.

M

Mukdenia rossii

Zone 6
Height: 14in. (35cm) Spread: 16in. (40cm)

MUSCARI *(Hyacinthaceae)*
Common names: Grape hyacinth

A genus of 30 species of bulbous perennials from high screes, steppes and low woodland in the Mediterranean area and south-west Asia. The leaves are in basal clusters, inversely lance-shaped or linear, and channeled. The tiny flowers are bell-shaped, spherical or tubular, and are borne in terminal racemes on leafless stems in spring or autumn. The lower flowers alone are fertile, and the upper sterile flowers are usually of paler color. The clumps get overcrowded and must be lifted and divided and replanted in summer when dormant. Some species are invasive.

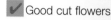 Good cut flowers   ✘ Need to lift & divide often
                                       ✘ Self-seeds

CULTIVATION
Plant bulbs 4in. (10 cm) deep in autumn in moist, fertile, well-drained soil in sun.

PROPAGATION
Sow seed in a cold frame in autumn or separate offsets in summer.

Muscari armeniacum A.G.M.

Zone 4
Height: 8in. (20cm) Spread: 2in. (5cm)
Invasive

Muscari azureum
A.G.M.

Zone 8
Height: 4in. (10 cm) Spread: 2in. (5cm)

Muscari comosum
'Plumosum'

Zone 4
Height: 2ft. (60cm) Spread: 2in. (5cm)

Muscari latifolium

Zone 4
Height: 8in. (20cm) Spread: 2in. (5cm)

MYOSOTIDIUM *(Boraginaceae)*

Common names: Chatham Islands forget-me-not

A genus of one species of evergreen perennial, *M. hortensia*, from a single location—the sandy or rocky coasts on Chatham Island, New Zealand. The handsome leaves are large, glossy and simple. The forget-me-not like flowers are blue, white-edged, and are borne in cymes in early summer.

✔ Evergreen	✘ Prone to slug damage
✔ Good cut flowers	
✔ Handsome foliage	

CULTIVATION
Does not flourish except in cool, damp gardens, preferably by the sea. Grow in moist, gritty, humus-rich, soil in a sheltered corner, in light shade.

PROPAGATION
Seed should be sown as soon as ripe, or in autumn. Divide in spring.

Myosotidium hortensia

Zone 8
Height: 2ft. (60cm) Spread: 3ft. (90cm)

MYOSOTIS *(Boraginaceae)*

Common names: Forget-me-not

A genus of 50 species of annuals, biennials and perennials from woodland, meadow, swampland or pond sides in Eurasia, North and South America, and Australasia. Their leaves are of various shapes, hairy and opposite. The flowers are salverform, five-lobed, white or blue with yellow or white eyes, and borne in cymes in early summer. They are short-lived, but self-seed freely.

✔ Good cut flowers	✘ Short-lived
	✘ Self-seeds
	✘ Mildew prone
	✘ Prone to slug damage

CULTIVATION
Grow in moist, fertile, well-drained soil in sun, with shade at mid-day, or in part shade. *M. scorpiodes* is a marginal aquatic plant, but can be grown in reliably moist soil.

PROPAGATION
Seed should be sown in a cold frame in early summer. Seed of *M. scorpiodes* must be sown in moist compost, and it can be divided in spring.

Myosotis scorpiodes
(Water forget-me-not)

Zone 5
Height and spread: 1ft. (30cm)

M

M

MYRIOPHYLLUM *(Haloragaceae)*

Common names: Milfoil: Parrot feather

A genus of 45 species of marginal or submerged aquatic annuals and perennials from streams and ponds all over the world, but in the southern hemisphere predominantly. Their foliage is very handsome, the underwater leaves being oblong or round or linear, pinnatifid, and with fine hair-like segments, and the above-surface leaves lance-shaped and entire or toothed.

✔ Handsome foliage   ✘ Invasive

CULTIVATION
Grow in baskets of loamy soil at a depth of 3ft. (90cm) in sun.

PROPAGATION
Root segment or tip cuttings in the pool bottom.

Myriophyllum aquaticum
(Parrot Feather; diamond milfoil)

Zone 10
Height: 2in. (5cm) Spread: indefinite

MYRRHIS *(Apiaceae)*

Common names: Myrrh; Sweet Cicely

A genus of one species of aromatic perennial, *M. odorata*, from the mountains of southern Europe, but naturalized widely in damp sites across Eurasia. Its bright green, ferny leaves are two- or three-pinnate, with a deeply-toothed, oblong pinnate. The white flowers are small, and borne in compound umbels in early summer, and followed by shiny brown fruits.

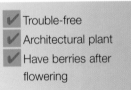

✔ Handsome foliage   ✔ Trouble-free   ✘ Self-seeds
✔ Good cut flowers   ✔ Architectural plant   ✘ Resents disturbance
✔ Aromatic foliage   ✔ Have berries after
✔ Culinary vegetable   flowering

CULTIVATION
Grow in moist, fertile well-drained soil in part shade. Remove flower–heads to improve quality of leaf flavor. Leaves can be harvested all summer.

PROPAGATION
Seed should be sown in a cold frame as soon as it is ripe or in spring. Divide in spring or autumn.

Myrrhis odorata

Zone 5
Height: 6ft. (2m) Spread: 5ft. (1.5m)

NARCISSUS
NECTAROSCORDUM
NEMESIA
NEOREGELIA
NEPETA
NEPHROLEPIS
NERINE
NICOTIANA
NIEREMBERGIA
NOLANA
NOMOCHARIS
NYMPHAEA
NYMPHOIDES

N

NARCISSUS *(Amaryllidaceae)*
Common names: Daffodil; jonquil

A genus of 50 species of bulbous perennials from a widely diverse range of habitat and height such as sea-level meadows and river silts to subalpine rock crevices, in North Africa and Europe. Their foliage is basal and strap-shaped. The flowers have six spreading petals (perianth segments) surrounding a narrow corona in the form of a cup or trumpet. The petals and corona can be of the same, or differing colors. Daffodils are classified by the Royal Horticultural Society into thirteen divisions as follows:

Division 1: Trumpet

Division 2: Large-cupped

Division 3: Small-cupped

Division 4: Double

Division 5: Triandrus

Division 6: Cyclamineus

Division 7: Jonquilla

Division 8: Tazetta

Division 9: Poeticus

Division 10: Bulbocodium

Division 11: Split-corona

Division 12: Miscellaneous

Division 13: Species

The interested reader is referred to specialist books and societies.

✓ Good cut flowers
✓ Flowers perfumed

✗ Need to lift & divide often
✗ Prone to slug damage
✗ Sap is skin-irritant

CULTIVATION
Plant bulbs one and a half times their depth in autumn in fertile, well-drained soil that is reliably moist during the growing season, in sun or light shade (The figure for 'spread' with each entry also serves as a guide to 'planting distance'). For the following species, the soil must be acid to neutral: *NN. asturensis, bulbocodium, cyclamineus* and *triandrus* and their hybrids. *NN. jonquilla* and *tazetta* prefer alkaline soil.

PROPAGATION
Seed of species should be sown in a cold frame as soon as ripe. Separate offsets of cultivars in early summer as growth has died down, or in autumn before growth starts.

N

Narcissus
'Actaea' A.G.M. (Div. 9)

Zone 4
Height: 18in. (45cm) Spread: 6in. (15cm)

Narcissus
'Baby Moon' (Div. 7)

Zone 4
Height: 10in. (25cm) Spread: 3in. (8 cm)

Narcissus
'Bantam' A.G.M. (Div. 2)

Zone 4
Height: 10in. (25cm) Spread: 6in. (15cm)

Narcissus
'Bravoure' A.G.M. (Div. 1)

Zone 4
Height: 18in. (45cm) Spread: 6in. (15cm)

Narcissus bulbocodium A.G.M.
(Div. 10)

Zone 6
Height: 6in. (15cm) Spread: 3in. (8 cm)

Narcissus bulbocodium var.
praecox

Zone 6
Height: 6in. (15cm) Spread: 3in. (8 cm)

Narcissus
'Canaliculatus' (Div. 8)

Zone 8
Height: 5in. (12cm) Spread: 6in. (15cm)

Narcissus cyclamineus
A.G.M. (Div. 10)

Zone 5
Height: 8in. (20cm) Spread: 3in. (8 cm)

Narcissus
'February Gold' A.G.M. (Div. 6)

Zone 6
Height: 1ft. (30cm) Spread: 3in. (8 cm)

Narcissus
'Hawera' A.G.M. (Div. 5)

Zone 4
Height: 7in. (18cm) Spread: 3in. (8 cm)

Narcissus
'Ice Follies' A.G.M. (Div. 2)

Zone 6
Height: 16in. (40cm) Spread: 6in. (15cm)

Narcissus
'Jack Snipe' A.G.M. (Div. 6)

Zone 6
Height: 8in. (20cm) Spread: 3in. (8 cm)

Narcissus
'Jetfire' A.G.M. (Div. 6.)

Zone 6
Height: 8in. (20cm) Spread: 6in. (15cm)

Narcissus jonquilla
A.G.M. (Div. 10)

Zone 4
Height: 1ft. (30cm) Spread: 3in. (8 cm)

N

Narcissus
'Jumblie' A.G.M. (Div. 12)

Zone 4
Height: 1ft. (30cm) Spread: 3in. (8 cm)

Narcissus
'Lemon Beauty' (Div. 11)

Zone 4
Height: 18in. (45cm) Spread: 4in. (10 cm)

Narcissus
'Minnow' A.G.M. (Div. 8)

Zone 8
Height: 7in. (18cm) Spread: 3in. (8 cm)

Narcissus obvallaris
A.G.M. (Div. 10)

Zone 4
Height: 1ft. (30cm) Spread: 6in. (15cm)

Narcissus
'Pipit' (Div. 7)

Zone 4
Height: 10in. (25cm) Spread: 3in. (8 cm)

Narcissus
'Rippling Waters' (Div. 5)

Zone 4
Height: 8in. (20cm) Spread: 3in. (8 cm)

Narcissus
'Rip van Winkle' (Div. 4)

Zone 4
Height and spread: 6in. (15cm)

Narcissus romieuxii
A.G.M (Div. 13)

Zone 4
Height: 4in. (10 cm) Spread: 6in. (15cm)

Narcissus
'Salome' (Div. 2)

Zone 4
Height: 18in. (45cm) Spread: 6in. (15cm)

Narcissus
'Silver Chimes' (Div. 8)

Zone 4
Height: 1ft. (30cm) Spread: 6in. (15cm)

Narcissus 'Sir Winston Churchill'
A.G.M. (Div.4)

Zone 4
Height: 14in. (35cm) Spread: 6in. (15cm)

Narcissus
'Sundial' (Div. 7)

Zone 4
Height: 8in. (20cm) Spread: 3in. (8 cm)

Narcissus tazetta (Div 13)

Zone 4
Height: 20in. (50cm) Spread: 4in. (10 cm)

Narcissus
'Tete-a-tete' A.G.M. (Div. 12)

Zone 4
Height and spread: 6in. (15cm)

Narcissus
'Thalia' (Div. 5)

Zone 4
Height: 14in. (35cm) Spread: 3in. (8 cm)

N

NECTAROSCORDUM *(Alliaceae)*

Common names: None

A genus of three species of bulbous perennials from wet, shady woodland or dry mountains or rocky places in Eurasia. Their leaves are linear, channeled or keeled, and smell of garlic. The flowers are bell-shaped, and borne in loose umbels of 20-30 flowers in summer.

- ✔ Foliage aromatic
- ✔ Good cut flowers
- ✔ Disease-free
- ✔ Pest-free
- ✘ Invasive
- ✘ Self-seeds

Nectaroscordum siculum

Zone 6
Height: 5ft. (1.5m) Spread: 6in. (15cm)

CULTIVATION
Grow in well-drained, fertile soil in sun or part shade. Dead-head to prevent self-seeding.

PROPAGATION
Seed should be sown in a cold frame in autumn or spring. Separate offsets in summer.

NEMESIA *(Scrophulariaceae)*

Common names: None

A genus of 50 annuals, perennials and subshrubs from coastal sands or inland scrubland or disturbed soil in South Africa. Their leaves are lance-shaped or linear, toothed, and opposite. The trumpet-shaped flowers are two-lipped, and have six lobes, four upper and two lower, and are borne singly in the leaf axils, or in racemes, from spring to autumn.

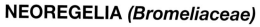

✔ Long-flowering
✔ Good cut flowers

CULTIVATION
Grow in acid to neutral, moist, fertile, well-drained soil in sun.

PROPAGATION
Seed should be sown at 59°F (15°C) in spring. Tip cuttings can be taken in late summer, and must be overwintered in a frost-free environment.

Nemesia denticulata
A.G.M.

Zone 8
Height: 16in. (40cm) Spread: 8in. (20cm)

NEOREGELIA *(Bromeliaceae)*

Common names: None

A genus of 70 species of evergreen perennials from coastal scrubland, rainforest and woodland in South America. They may be terrestrial or epiphytic, stoloniferous or rhizomatous. Their leaves are spiny-edged, borne in rosettes, and variable, and have brightly-colored central parts at flowering time. The tubular, long-lasting flower nestles in the heart of the rosette, in summer.

✔ Evergreen
✔ Flowers long-lasting

CULTIVATION
Under glass, grow in bromeliad compost in bright, filtered light. Water freely into the rosette in spring and summer, but sparingly in winter.

Out of doors, grow in sharply-draining soil in light shade.

PROPAGATION
Offsets can be detached in spring or summer. Seed should be sown at 81°F (27°C) as soon as it is ripe.

Neoregelia carolinae

Zone 10
Height: 1ft. (30cm) Spread: 28in. (70cm)

N

Neoregelia carolinae
'Flandria'

Zone 10
Height: 1ft. (30cm) Spread: 28in. (70cm)

Neoregelia carolinae
'Tricolor' A.G.M.

Zone 10
Height: 1ft. (30cm) Spread: 28in. (70cm)

Neoregelia
'Madame van Durne'

Zone 10
Height: 1ft. (30cm) Spread: 28in. (70cm)

NEPETA *(Lamiaceae)*
Common names: Catmint

A genus of 250 species of annuals and perennials from a wide variety of habitats in the temperate northern hemisphere. They grow in cool moist and hot dry sites, in lowland or mountainous regions. Their leaves are ovate or lance-shaped, toothed or scalloped, hairy, gray-green, and in opposite pairs. Some species have aromatic leaves. The two-lipped flowers are tubular, and borne in interrupted axillary whorls, in summer, and over a long period in most species. Some species self-seed freely.

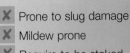

✔ Long-flowering
✔ Foliage aromatic
✔ Drought-tolerant
✔ Attracts bees
✔ Attracts butterflies

✘ Prone to slug damage
✘ Mildew prone
✘ Require to be staked
✘ Attracts cats

CULTIVATION
Grow in any soil that is well-drained, in sun. *NN. subsessilis* and *govaniana* prefer moist soil and a cool spot.

PROPAGATION
Seed should be sown in a cold frame in autumn. Divide in spring or autumn. Softwood cuttings can be taken in summer.

Nepeta govaniana

Zone 5
Height: 3ft. (90cm) Spread: 2ft. (60cm)

Nepeta longipes

Zone 5
Height: 2ft. (60cm) Spread: 18in. (45cm)

Nepeta sibirica

Zone 3
Height: 3ft. (90cm) Spread: 18in. (45cm)

Nepeta 'Six Hills Giant'

Zone 3
Height: 3ft. (90cm) Spread: 18in. (45cm)

Nepeta subsessilis

Zone 7
Height: 3ft. (90cm) Spread: 1ft. (30cm)

Nepeta subsessilis 'Sweet Dreams'

Zone 7
Height: 3ft. (90cm) Spread: 1ft. (30cm)

Nepeta tuberosa

Zone 8
Height: 3ft. (90cm) Spread: 1ft. (30cm)

N

NEPHROLEPIS *(Oleandraceae)*

Common names: Sword fern

A genus of 30 species of rhizomatous ferns from rainforest or open habitats in the tropics and subtropical regions worldwide. They may be epiphytic or terrestrial, evergreen or semi-evergreen. The fronds are in dense clusters, and may be upright or pendent. The pinnae are linear, and may be simple, forked or divided.

✔ Evergreen   ✘ Invasive
✔ Handsome foliage

CULTIVATION
Under glass, grow in loamy, sharply-draining compost in bright filtered light, with good ventilation and high humidity. Water moderately with soft water during growth, and sparingly in winter.

Out of doors, grow in moist, sharply-draining, humus-rich, fertile soil in part shade.

PROPAGATION
Spores should be sown at 70°F (21°C) as soon as ripe. Rooted runners can be separated in early spring.

Nephrolepis exaltata
A.G.M.

Zone 10
Height: 6ft. (2m) Spread: indefinite

NERINE *(Amaryllidaceae)*

Common names: None

A genus of 30 species of summer-dormant bulbous perennials from invariably dry and well-drained habitats in South Africa. Their leaves are strap-shaped, and appear after the flowers. The flowers are lily-like, have recurved tepals and are borne in spherical umbels in autumn.

✔ Good cut flowers   ✔ Drought-tolerant   ✘ All parts poisonous
✔ Flowers weather-resistant ✔ Flowers perfumed   ✘ Prone to slug damage
✔ Long-flowering

CULTIVATION
Under glass, plant the bulbs in spring or autumn with their tips level with the soil surface in loam-based potting compost in full light. Water freely when in active growth. Keep dry during summer dormancy.

Out of doors, plant in early spring in well-drained soil in sun. They flower best when pot-bound, or bulbs are congested.

PROPAGATION
Seed should be sown at 55°F (13°C) as soon as ripe. Division can be carried out after flowering.

Nerine bowdenii
A.G.M.

Zone 8
Height: 18in. (45cm) Spread: 4in. (10 cm)

N

Nerine bowdenii
'Variegata'

Zone 8
Height: 18in. (45cm) Spread: 4in. (10 cm)

Nerine bowdenii
'Wellsii'

Zone 8
Height: 18in. (45cm) Spread: 4in. (10 cm)

NICOTIANA *(Solanaceae)*
Common names: Tobacco plant

A genus of 67 species of annuals, biennials, perennials and shrubs from usually moist sites on mountain slopes and valley floors in North America, Australia, and tropical South America. Their leaves are ovate to linear, alternate, and hairy-glandular. The tubular or trumpet-shaped flowers are borne in panicles or racemes over long periods in summer and autumn. They may be scented, and open usually at night or during the evening, and during the day only if grown in part shade—except for *NN. alata* and *x sanderae*, which open in sun.

✔ Long-flowering

✘ Foliage is skin-irritant
✘ Prone to aphid attack
✘ Require staking
✘ Short-lived

CULTIVATION
Grow in moist, fertile, well-drained soil in sun or part shade.

PROPAGATION
Seed should be surface-sown at 64°F (18°C) in spring.

Nicotiana glauca

Zone 8
Height and spread: 10ft. (3m)
Handsome foliage

Nicotiana
'Havana Apple Blossom'

Zone 7
Height: 14in. (35cm) Spread: 1ft. (30cm)

Nicotiana
'Lime Green' A.G.M.

Zone 7
Height: 18in. (45cm) Spread: 1ft. (30cm)

N

Nicotiana Roulette Series

Zone 8
Height and spread: 10in. (25cm)

Nicotiana sylvestris A.G.M.

Zone 8
Height: 5ft. (1.5m) Spread: 2ft. (60cm)
Flowers perfumed

NIEREMBERGIA *(Solanaceae)*

Common names: Cup flower

A genus of 20 species of annuals, perennials and shrubs from sunny, wet habitats in temperate South America. Their leaves are entire, and alternate. The flowers are open, bell- or cup-shaped, and borne in summer.

✔ Long-flowering

✘ Prone to slug damage
✘ Prone to aphid attack

CULTIVATION
Grow in a sheltered corner in moist, well-drained soil in sun.

PROPAGATION
Seed should be sown at 59°F (15°C) in spring or autumn. Division can be carried out in spring.

Nierembergia scoparia
'Mont Blanc'

Zone 8
Height and spread: 8in. (20cm)

Nierembergia repens
(White cupflower)

Zone 8
Height: 2in. (5cm) Spread: indefinite

NOLANA *(Solanaceae)*

Common names: None

A genus of 18 species of annuals, perennials and subshrubs found in semi-deserts regions of Chile and Peru. Their leaves are simple, whorled or alternate, and may be succulent. The flowers are five-petalled broad trumpets, and are solitary or borne in clumps in the leaf axils in summer.

✘ Prone to aphid attack

CULTIVATION
Under glass, grow in loam-based potting compost in full light. Water moderately during growth, but sparingly in winter.

Out of doors, grow in any soil that is fertile, in sun.

PROPAGATION
Seed should be sown at 59°F (15°C) in spring, or *in situ* in late spring, or in autumn.

Nolana paradoxa
'Blue Bird'

Zone 9
Height: 10in. (25cm) Spread: 2ft. (60cm)

NOMOCHARIS *(Liliaceae)*
Common names: None

A genus of seven species of bulbous perennials from moist meadows and woodland in the mountains of China, Tibet, Burma and Northern India. Their leaves are linear to ovate, borne along the stems in whorls or pairs or groups of three. The handsome flowers are flat or saucer-shaped, and six-tepalled. They are often spotted. They dislike hot, dry gardens.

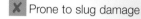
✗ Prone to slug damage

CULTIVATION
Plant bulbs 6in. (15cm) deep in winter or spring in acid, reliably moist, humus-rich soil in part shade in hot gardens and in sun in cool gardens.

PROPAGATION
Seed should be sown at 50°F (10°C) in spring or autumn.

Nomocharis aperta

Zone 7
Height: 32in. (80cm) Spread: 4in. (10 cm)

Nomocharis pardanthina

Zone 7
Height: 3ft. (90cm) Spread: 4in. (10 cm)

NYMPHAEA *(Nymphaeaceae)*
Common names: Water lily

A genus of 50 species of rhizomatous or tuberous, herbaceous submerged-aquatic perennials found worldwide. Their floating leaves are bilobed, large and sometimes marked handsomely. The flowers have many petals and four sepals, and are held just above the water surface, in summer. The majority of those in cultivation are hybrids.

✔ Handsome foliage
✔ Shade from leaves reduces growth of algae

CULTIVATION
Plant in summer in baskets of aquatic compost, propped on bricks, such that 10in. (25cm) of water is above the crown, in still water. When the plants are established, the planting depth can be doubled to 20in. (50cm) above the crown.

PROPAGATION
Divide rhizomes or separate offsets in summer.

Nymphaea alba

Zone 5
Height: 2in. (5cm) Spread: 5ft. (1.5m)

Nymphaea
'Chromatella' A.G.M.

Zone 4
Height: 2in. (5cm) Spread: 5ft. (1.5m)

Nymphaea
'Escarboucle' A.G.M.

Zone 4
Height: 2in. (5cm) Spread: 5ft. (1.5m)

Nymphaea
'James Brydon' A.G.M.

Zone 4
Height: 2in. (5cm) Spread: 4ft. (1.2m)

NYMPHOIDES *(Menyanthaceae)*

Common names: Floating heart

A genus of 20 species of vigorous, rhizomatous, submerged-aquatic, herbaceous perennials from across the world. Their leaves are heart- or kidney-shaped, and lie on the surface. The flowers are held above the surface on short stems, and are yellow or white cups, borne in summer.

✔ Handsome foliage

✔ Disease-free

✔ Pest-free

✔ Shade from leaves restricts growth of algae

N

CULTIVATION

Grow in a planting basket in aquatic compost, in still water of under 2ft. (60cm) in depth, or at the pond margin.

PROPAGATION

Separate runners during summer.

Nymphoides peltata

Zone 6
Height: 4in. (10 cm) Spread: indefinite

OENANTHE
OENOTHERA
OLSYNIUM
OMPHALODES
ONOCLEA
ONOSMA
OPHIOPOGON
OPHRYS
ORCHIS
ORIGANUM
ORNITHOGALUM
OROSTACHYS
ORTHROSANTHUS
OSMUNDA
OSTEOSPERMUM
OSTROWSKIA
OTHONNA
OURISIA
OXALIS

O

OENANTHE *(Apiaceae)*
Common names: None

A genus of 30 species of perennials from wet meadows, marshland and bogs in South Africa, Australia and the northern hemisphere. Their leaves are pinnate and alternate. The flowers are five-petalled, small, star-shaped and borne in compound umbels in late summer. All parts poisonous, even deadly in some species, except *O. javanica*, which is edible.

- ☒ Flowers insignificant
- ☒ Prone to slug damage
- ☒ Prone to aphid attack

CULTIVATION
Grow in wet or reliably moist soil in a sheltered corner in sun or part shade.

PROPAGATION
Divide in late spring or take stem-tip cuttings in spring.

Oenanthe javanica 'Flamingo'

Zone 10
Height: 16in. (40cm) Spread: 3ft. (90cm)
Culinary vegetable/Variegated foliage

OENOTHERA *(Onagraceae)*
Common names: Evening primrose; Sundrops

A genus of 125 species of annuals, biennials and short-lived perennials from North America in particular, but a few from South America. They are found in sunny, well-drained sites, or in deserts. They may be tap-rooted, rhizomatous or fibrous-rooted; the first category does not transplant well. Their leaves may be in basal rosettes, or stem or both, and are simple or pinnatifid, entire or toothed, and lance-shaped. The flowers may be trumpet- or saucer- or cup-shaped, white, yellow or pink, and solitary or borne in racemes over a long period in summer. Some are perfumed. The flowers open at dawn or dusk, and last only a short time.

- ☑ Long-flowering
- ☑ Drought-tolerant
- ☑ Attracts bees
- ☒ Short-lived
- ☒ Self-seeds
- ☒ Prone to slug damage

CULTIVATION
Grow in sharply-draining, fertile soil in sun. *O. speciosa* dislikes winter wet.

PROPAGATION
Seed should be sown in a cold frame in early spring; tap-rooted forms should be grown individually in pots, and planted out directly. Divide in early spring, but tap-rooted forms do not take kindly to it (see individual entries). Softwood cuttings of unflowered shoots can be taken from late spring to midsummer.

Oenothera
'Crown Imperial'

Zone 5
Height: 32in. (80cm) Spread: 1ft. (30cm)

Oenothera deltoides

Zone 9
Height: 1ft. (30cm) Spread: 8in. (20cm)
Resents disturbance

Oenothera fruticosa
(Common sundrops)
Zone 4
Height: 3ft. (90cm) Spread: 1ft. (30cm)
Resents disturbance

Oenothera fruticosa subsp. *glauca*
'Erica Robin'
Zone 4
Height and spread: 1ft. (30cm)
Foliage variegated/Resents disturbance

Oenothera fruticosa
'Fyrverkeri' A.G.M.
Zone 4
Height: 3ft. (90cm) Spread: 1ft. (30cm)
Resents disturbance

Oenothera fruticosa 'Youngii'
Zone 4
Height: 3ft. (90cm) Spread: 1ft. (30cm)
Resents disturbance

Oenothera glazioviana
Zone 3
Height: 5ft. (1.5m) Spread: 2ft. (60cm)
Prolific self-seeder/Requires staking

Oenothera macrocarpa A.G.M.
Zone 5
Height: 6in. (15cm) Spread: 18in. (45cm)
Resents disturbance

Oenothera nuttallii
Zone 5
Height: 6in. (15cm) Spread: 18in. (45cm)
Resents disturbance

Oenothera rosea
Zone 6
Height: 2ft. (60cm) Spread: 1ft. (30cm)

Oenothera speciosa
(Showy evening primrose)
Zone 5
Height and spread: 1ft. (30cm)
Resents disturbance

Oenothera speciosa
'Rosea' (Showy evening primrose)
Zone 5
Height and spread: 1ft. (30cm)
Resents disturbance

O

Oenothera speciosa 'Siskiyou'
(Showy evening primrose)
Zone 5
Height and spread: 1ft. (30cm)
Resents disturbance

Oenothera stubbei

Zone 8
Height: 4ft. (1.2m) Spread: 1ft. (30cm)
Resents disturbance/Requires staking

OLSYNIUM *(Iridaceae)*

Common names: None

A genus of a dozen species of perennials from moist grassland at sea level and altitude in South and North America. They are clump-forming, and fibrous-rooted. Their leaves are basal, linear or lance-shaped. The flowers are pendent, bell- or trumpet-shaped, and borne in spring.

✔ Disease-free
✔ Pest-free

CULTIVATION
Grow in moist, humus-rich, soil in part shade.

PROPAGATION
Seed should be sown in a cold frame in autumn. The seedlings reach flowering size only after two or three years.

Olsynium douglasii
A.G.M.

Zone 9
Height: 1ft. (30cm) Spread: 4in. (10 cm)

OMPHALODES *(Boraginaceae)*

Common names: Navelwort

A genus of 28 species of annuals, biennials and perennials from a variety of habitats in Eurasia and North Africa. They may be herbaceous, semi-evergreen or evergreen. Their leaves are in basal clusters, ovate, pointed, and veined. The flowers are forget-me-not-like, blue or white, and are borne singly or in terminal cymes in spring and summer. They will repeat-flower if dead-headed.

✔ Repeat-flowering   ✘ Prone to slug damage
✔ Low allergen

CULTIVATION
Grow in moist, humus-rich soil in part shade.

PROPAGATION
Seed should be sown in a cold frame in spring, when division can also be carried out.

Omphalodes cappadocica
'Cherry Ingram' A.G.M.

Zone 6
Height and spread: 1ft. (30cm)

Omphalodes cappadocica
'Starry Eyes'

Zone 6
Height: 1ft. (30cm) Spread: 18in. (45cm)

ONOCLEA *(Woodsiaceae)*

Common names: Sensitive fern

A genus of one species of terrestrial deciduous fern, *O. senibilis*, from damp ground in eastern North America and East Asia. Sterile, long-stemmed, pinnate or pinnatisect fronds arise singly from spreading rhizomes in spring. In late summer fertile two-pinnate fronds appear.

Onoclea sensibilis
A.G.M.

Zone 4
Height: 2ft. (60cm) Spread: indefinite

✔ Handsome foliage	✘ Invasive
✔ Disease-free	
✔ Pest-free	

CULTIVATION
Grow in acid to neutral, moist, humus-rich, fertile soil in a sheltered corner in light shade.

PROPAGATION
Spores should be sown at 61°F (16°C) as soon as they are ripe, or division can be done in spring.

ONOSMA *(Boraginaceae)*

Common names: None

A genus of 150 species of biennials and perennials from sunny, rocky habitats from the Mediterranean across to Turkey. Their leaves are simple, alternate, and finely hairy. The flowers are tubular, pendent, and borne in cymes in summer.

✔ Drought-tolerant	✘ Prone to slug damage
	✘ Foliage is skin-irritant
	✘ Prone to aphid attack

CULTIVATION
Grow in a wall or in very sharply-draining soil in sun. Protect against excessive wet, especially in winter.

PROPAGATION
Seed should be sown in a open frame in autumn.

Onosma alborosea

Zone 7
Height and spread: 10in. (25cm)
Evergreen

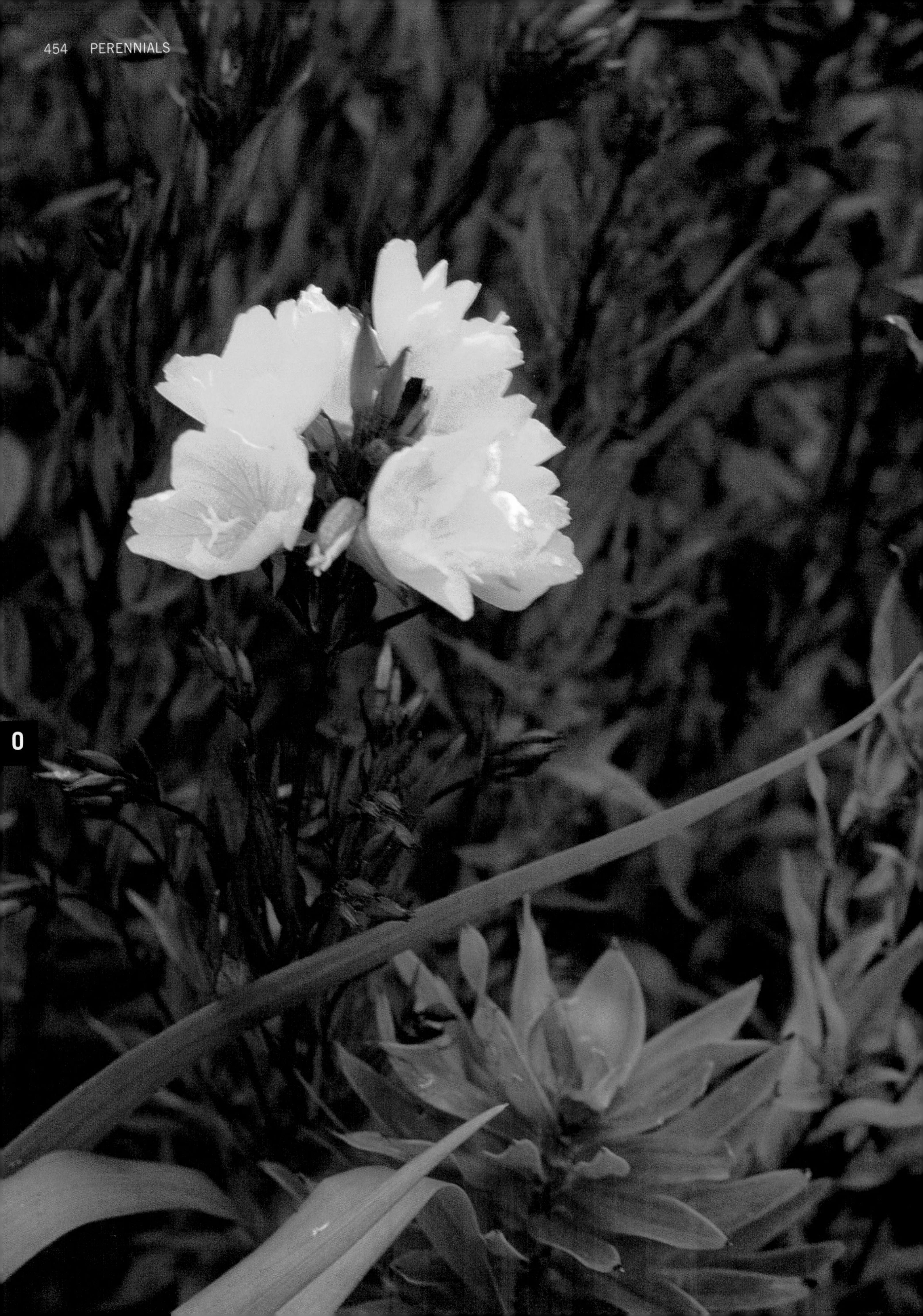

OPHIOPOGON *(Convallariaceae)*

Common names: Lilyturf

A genus of 50 species of evergreen perennials from shady woodland or scrubland in China and Japan. They may be rhizomatous or stoloniferous. Their grassy leaves are in dense tufts. The small, bell-shaped flowers are borne in racemes in summer, followed by glossy black or blue fruits.

 Evergreen

✔ Have berries after flowering

✔ Disease-free

✖ Prone to slug damage

CULTIVATION
Grow in acid to neutral, moist, well-drained soil in sun or part shade.

PROPAGATION
Seed should be sown in a cold frame as soon as it is ripe. Divide in spring.

Ophiopogon jaburan
'Vittatus'

Zone 7
Height: 2ft. (60cm) Spread: 1ft. (30cm)

Ophiopogon planiscapus
'Nigrescens' A.G.M.

Zone 6
Height: 8in. (20cm) Spread: 1ft. (30cm)

OPHRYS *(Orchidaceae)*

Common names: None

A genus of 30 species of herbaceous, terrestrial orchids found in grassland, mountainsides, woodland and marshland in Asia, Europe, the Mediterranean islands and North Africa. Their leaves are in basal rosettes, and ovate or oblong or lance-shaped. The flower stems have small, bract-like leaves, and three-sepalled, twin-petalled flowers that resemble the abdomen of an insect or bee, are borne in racemes in spring and early summer.

✔ Disease-free

✖ Prone to slug damage

CULTIVATION
Under glass, plant dormant tubers in autumn in an alpine house in terrestrial orchid compost in bright filtered light. Water moderately during growth, keep dry and frost-free at all other times.

Out of doors, grow in sharply-draining, humus-rich, leafy soil in part shade.

PROPAGATION
Offsets should be separated in autumn.

Ophrys cretensis

Zone 8
Height: 1ft. (30cm) Spread: 6in. (15 cm)

ORCHIS *(Orchidaceae)*
Common names: Orchid

A genus of 35 species of tuberous, terrestrial, herbaceous, perennial orchids from Eurasia, where they grow in open grassland, often dry and poor. Their leaves are in rosettes, linear to ovate, and spotted in some species. The flowers are in dense, upright racemes, from spring to summer. Flowers in some species are malodorous. They are usually grown in an Alpine house, but can be grown in the open garden with some difficulty.

✔ Handsome foliage ✘ Prone to slug damage

CULTIVATION
Under glass, grow in terrestrial orchid compost in bright filtered light. Water moderately during growth, keep dry and frost-free in winter.

Out of doors, grow in acid to neutral, sharply-draining soil in part shade.

PROPAGATION
Offsets should be separated in spring.

Orchis italica

Zone 5
Height: 18in. (45cm) Spread: 6in. (15cm)

Orchis mascula
(Early purple orchid)

Zone 5
Height: 1ft. (30cm) Spread: 6in. (15cm)

ORIGANUM *(Lamiaceae)*
Common names: Marjoram; Oregano

A genus of 20 species of herbaceous perennials and evergreen subshrubs from mountainous, open habitats in the Mediterranean area and south-west Asia. Their aromatic leaves are simple, ovate, and in opposite pairs. The flowers are funnel-shaped or tubular, two-lipped, and surrounded by brightly-colored bracts. They are borne in spiked whorls, over long periods in summer and autumn. Some are culinary herbs.

✔ Long-flowering ✘ Prone to aphid attack
✔ Foliage aromatic
✔ Attracts bees
✔ Disease-free

CULTIVATION
Grow in limy, sharply-drained, soil in sun.

PROPAGATION
Seed should be sown at 55°F (13°C) in spring, or in autumn. Divide in spring or take basal cuttings in late spring.

Origanum amanum A.G.M.

Zone 8
Height: 8in. (20cm) Spread: 1ft. (30cm)

Origanum
'Buckland'

Zone 7
Height: 8in. (20cm) Spread: 6in. (15cm)

Origanum laevigatum
A.G.M.

Zone 8
Height: 2ft. (60cm) Spread: 18in. (45cm)

Origanum laevigatum
'Herrenhausen' A.G.M.

Zone 8
Height and spread: 18in. (45cm)

Origanum vulgare
'Aureum' A.G.M.

Zone 5
Height: 2ft. (60cm) Spread: 1ft. (30cm)

Origanum vulgare
'County Cream'

Zone 5
Height and spread: 1ft. (30cm)

Origanum vulgare
'Gold Tip'

Zone 5
Height: 16in. (40cm) Spread: 1ft. (30cm)

Origanum vulgare
'Thumble's Variety'

Zone 5
Height and spread: 1ft. (30cm)

ORNITHOGALUM *(Hyacinthaceae)*
Common names: Star of Bethlehem

A genus of 80 species of bulbous perennials from a range of habitats such as meadows, woodland and dry hillsides in Europe, the Mediterranean, Asia, Russia, South Africa and tropical Africa. Their leaves are basal, and obovate or linear. The flowers are funnel- or star- or cup-shaped, and are borne in racemes on leafless stems in spring or summer. Some are perfumed. *OO. nutans* and *umbellatum* are invasive.

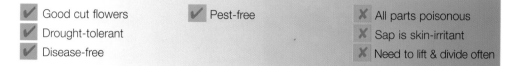

✔ Good cut flowers	✔ Pest-free	✘ All parts poisonous
✔ Drought-tolerant		✘ Sap is skin-irritant
✔ Disease-free		✘ Need to lift & divide often

CULTIVATION
Under glass, tender forms should be grown in loam-based potting compost in full light, but shaded from the mid-day sun. Water freely in summer, and keep dry in winter. Repot annually in spring.

Out of doors, plant bulbs of hardy species 4in. (10 cm) deep in autumn in well-drained, fertile soil in sun.

PROPAGATION
Separate offsets when dormant. Sow seed in a cold frame in autumn or spring.

Ornithogalum arabicum

Zone 9
Height: 32in. (80cm) Spread: 6in. (15cm)

Ornithogalum dubium

Zone 9
Height: 1ft. (30cm) Spread: 6in. (15cm)

Ornithogalum longibracteatum

Zone 9
Height: 5ft. (1.5m) Spread: 6in. (15cm)

Ornithogalum magnum

Zone 7
Height: 32in. (80cm) Spread: 1ft. (30cm)

Ornithogalum nutans A.G.M.

Zone 6
Height: 2ft. (60cm) Spread: 4in. (10 cm)
Invasive

O

Ornithogalum thyrsoides
'Chincherinchee'
Zone 9
Height: 32in. (80cm) Spread: 4in. (10 cm)
Requires staking

Ornithogalum umbellatum
Zone 5
Height: 1ft. (30cm) Spread: 4in. (10 cm)
Invasive

OROSTACHYS *(Crassulaceae)*

Common names: None

A genus of ten species of monocarpic, rosette-forming perennials from rocky lowland and mountains of Russia, China, Japan and both Koreas. The leaves are fleshy, and the rosettes dense, and spherical. The flowers are star-shaped, and borne in terminal racemes in summer and autumn. The flowering rosette dies, but new rosettes are produced freely.

✔ Evergreen   ✘ Monocarpic
✔ Long-flowering
✔ Disease-free

CULTIVATION
Under glass, grow in cactus compost in full light. Water freely in summer, keep dry in winter.

Out of doors, grow in poor, sharply-drained soil in sun.

PROPAGATION
Seed should be sown at 64°F (18°C) in spring. Separate offsets in spring.

Orostachys furusei

Zone 7
Height: 4in. (10 cm) Spread: 10in. (25cm)

Orostachys spinosa

Zone 4
Height: 14in. (35cm) Spread: 1ft. (30cm)

ORTHROSANTHUS *(Iridaceae)*
Common names: None

A genus of seven species of rhizomatous, evergreen perennials from sandy soils in tropical America and Australia. Their leaves are linear or strap-shaped, arching or upright. The flowers are saucer- or bell-shaped, and borne in loose terminal panicles in late spring and summer. Whilst individual flowers are short-lived, they are borne in succession over a few weeks.

✔ Evergreen   ✘ Short-lived
✔ Repeat-flowering
✔ Drought-tolerant

CULTIVATION
Under glass, grow in sharply-draining, loam-based, potting compost in full light. Water with moderation during summer, keep dry in winter.

Out of doors, grow in sharply-draining fertile soil in sun.

PROPAGATION
Seed should be sown at 64°F (18°C) in spring, when division can also be done.

Orthrosanthus chimboracensis

Zone 9
Height: 2ft. (60cm) Spread: 4in. (10 cm)

Orthrosanthus laxus

Zone 9
Height: 18in. (45cm) Spread: 3in. (8 cm)

OSMUNDA *(Osmundaceae)*
Common names: None

A genus of a dozen species of deciduous, rhizomatous, terrestrial ferns from wet areas and stream sides across the world, except Australia. The sterile fronds vary widely in shape, and have nice autumn coloring. The fertile fronds have reduced pinnae, and greenish sporangia, and they too change color in autumn.

✔ Handsome foliage
✔ Disease-free
✔ Pest-free

CULTIVATION
Grow in acid to neutral, moist, humus-rich, fertile soil in light shade.

PROPAGATION
Spores should be sown at 61°F (16°C) within a few days of ripening in summer, as they lose viability very quickly. Divide in spring or autumn.

Osmunda cinnamomea

Zone 3
Height: 3ft. (90cm) Spread: 2ft. (60cm)

OSTEOSPERMUM *(Asteraceae)*
Common names: None

A genus of 70 species of annuals, subshrubs and evergreen perennials from grassland, rocky slopes, and forest edges in Southern Africa and the Arabian peninsula. Their leaves are linear to ovate, alternate and entire or lobed or toothed. The daisy-like flowers are solitary, or borne in open panicles over a long period from spring to autumn, especially if dead-headed. The ray and disc florets may be of similar or different color.

✔ Long-flowering
✔ Evergreen
✔ Good cut flowers
✔ Disease-free

✘ Highly allergenic
✘ Prone to aphid attack

CULTIVATION
Grow in well-drained fertile soil in sun. Dead-head to prolong flowering.

PROPAGATION
Seed should be sown at 64°F (18°C) in spring. Semi-ripe cuttings can be taken in late summer, and softwood cuttings in late spring.

Osteospermum
'Buttermilk' A.G.M.

Zone 9
Height and spread: 2ft. (60cm)

Osteospermum caulescens
'White Pim' A.G.M.

Zone 8
Height: 4in. (10 cm) Spread: 2ft. (60cm)

Osteospermum
'Gold Sparkler'

Zone 8
Height and spread: 2ft. (60cm)

Osteospermum jucundum
A.G.M.

Zone 7
Height: 20in. (50cm) Spread: 3ft. (90cm)

Osteospermum jucundum var.
compactum

Zone 7
Height: 8in. (20cm) Spread: 18in. (45cm)

Osteospermum
'Nairobi Purple'

Zone 9
Height: 6in. (15cm) Spread: 3ft. (90cm)

Osteospermum
'Silver Sparkler' A.G.M.

Zone 8
Height: 18in. (45cm) Spread: 3ft. (90cm)

O

Osteospermum
'Sirius'

Zone 8
Height and spread: 1ft. (30cm)

Osteospermum
'Sunny Alex'

Zone 8
Height and spread: 1ft. (30cm)

Osteospermum
'Whirligig' A.G.M.

Zone 8
Height and spread: 2ft. (60cm)

Osteospermum
'Zaire'

Zone 8
Height: 1ft. (30cm) Spread: 18in. (45cm)

Osteospermum
'Zimbar'
Zone 9
Height and spread: 18in. (45cm)

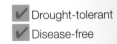

OSTROWSKIA *(Campanulaceae)*

Common names: None

A genus of but a single species of tap-rooted perennial, *O. magnifica*, from dry, stony hillsides in Tajilistan and Uzbekistan. Its leaves are toothed, glaucous, ovate, and in whorls. It has few-flowered racemes of outward-facing, bell-shaped, pale or dark blue flowers in early and midsummer.

✔ Drought-tolerant		✘ Prone to slug damage	
✔ Disease-free		✘ Resents disturbance	

CULTIVATION
Grow in moist, deep, well-drained soil in sun. Keep dry in winter.

PROPAGATION
Seed should be sown singly in a cold frame as soon as ripe. It takes at least three years to reach flowering size, and seedlings should be moved on with great care.

Ostrowskia magnifica

Zone 7
Height: 5ft. (1.5m) Spread: 18in. (45cm)

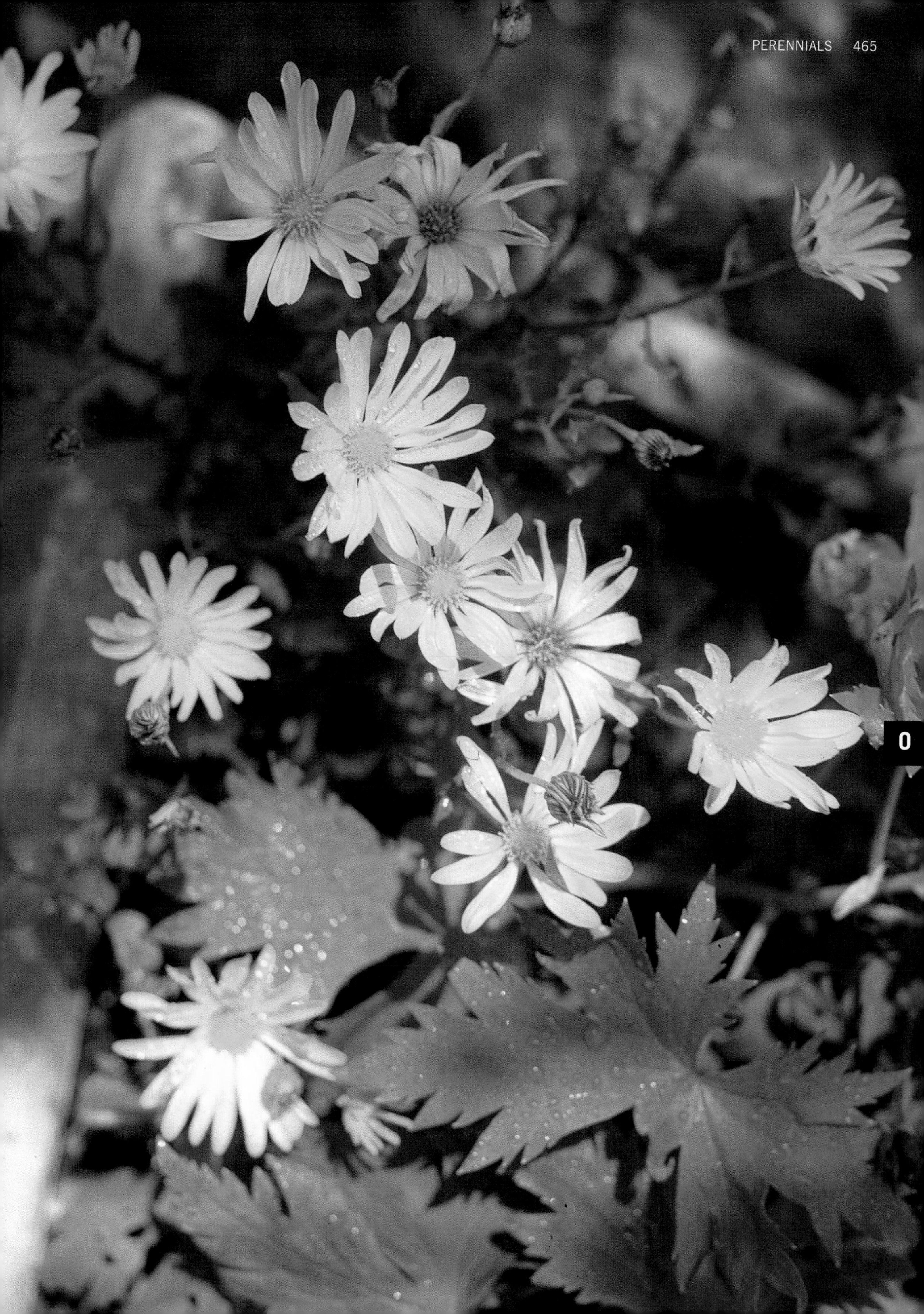

OTHONNA *(Asteraceae)*

Common names: None

A genus of 150 species of shrubby or succulent perennials and shrubs from dry hilly regions of North Africa and South Africa. Their leaves are fleshy, dissected or entire, toothed or lobed, and spoon-shaped. The daisy-like flowers are solitary or borne in corymbs in late summer to winter.

✔ Drought-tolerant   ✘ Prone to aphid attack
✔ Handsome foliage
✔ Disease-free

CULTIVATION
Under glass, grow in cactus compost in full light. Water with moderation in summer, keep fairly dry in winter.

Out of doors, grow in sharply-draining soil in sun.

Othonna cheirifolia

Zone 8
Height: 1ft. (30cm) Spread: 2ft. (60cm)

OURISIA *(Scrophulariaceae)*

Common names: None

A genus of 25 species of mostly rhizomatous perennials from alpine parts of Antarctica, Tasmania, New Zealand and South Africa. They may be evergreen or semi-evergreen. Their leaves are radical, with conspicuous veins. The flowers are short-tubed, with five lobes, of which the upper two are smaller than the lower three. They are solitary, or in racemes or whorls, from leafless stems.

✔ Long-flowering   ✘ Prone to slug damage
✔ Evergreen
✔ Disease-free

CULTIVATION
Under glass, grow in an alpine house in loamy, gritty compost, and do not allow to dry out in winter.

Out of doors, grow in moist, fertile, humus-rich soil in part shade. They dislike hot dry gardens. Rhizomatous species must be lifted and divided regularly, or they lose vigor.

PROPAGATION
Seed should be sown in a cold frame as soon as ripe, or in spring. Rhizomatous forms can be divided in spring. Separate rooted runners of mat-forming species (such as *O. coccinea*) in spring.

Ourisia coccinea

Zone 7
Height: 8in. (20cm) Spread: indefinite
Invasive

OXALIS *(Oxalidaceae)*

Common names: Shamrock; Sorrel

A genus of 500 species of bulbous, tuberous, rhizomatous or fibrous-rooted annuals and perennials; some of the latter, such as *OO. acetosella* and *pes-caprae*, are very invasive weeds, and others, such as *O. obtusa*, are tricky in cultivation and need to be grown in troughs, or given alpine house treatment. They occur in dry, open or woodland sites across the world, but in South America and South Africa in particular. Their leaves are clover-like, i.e. *palmate*, and may fold up at night. The flowers are cup- or funnel- or bowl-shaped, and solitary or in cymes; they open only in sunlight. Woodland species can be naturalized in shade.

✔ Drought-tolerant   ✔ Handsome foliage   ✘ Prone to slug damage

CULTIVATION
Under glass, grow in gritty, loam-based potting compost, low humidity and filtered light. Water with moderation during growth, and keep almost dry in winter.

Out of doors, grow woodlanders such as *O. acetosella*, in moist, fertile, humus-rich soil in part shade, and all others listed in well-drained soil in sun.

PROPAGATION
Seed should be sown at 64°F (18°C) in late winter or early spring. Divide in spring.

Oxalis acetosella

Zone 3
Height: 2in. (5cm) Spread: indefinite
Drought-tolerant

Oxalis adenophylla A.G.M.

Zone 5
Height: 4in. (10 cm) Spread: 6in. (15cm)
Drought-tolerant

Oxalis enneaphylla A.G.M.

Zone 6
Height: 3in. (8 cm) Spread: 6in. (15cm)
Drought-tolerant

Oxalis lobata

Zone 8
Height and spread: 4in. (10 cm)
Drought-tolerant

Oxalis pes-caprae

Zone 9
Height: 5in. (12cm) Spread: indefinite
Drought-tolerant/Self-seeds

Oxalis purpurea

Zone 8
Height: 4in. (10 cm) Spread: 6in. (15cm)

Oxalis tetraphylla

Zone 8
Height and spread: 6in. (15cm)
Drought-tolerant

Oxalis tetraphylla 'Iron Cross'

Zone 8
Height and spread: 6in. (15cm)
Drought-tolerant

Oxalis triangularis

Zone 9
Height and spread: 6in. (15cm)
Drought-tolerant

Oxalis tuberosa

Zone 7
Height: 10in. (25cm) Spread: 6in. (15cm)

O

PACHYPHRAGMA
PAEONIA
PALLENIS
PANDOREA
PAPAVER
PARADISEA
PARAHEBE
PARAQUILEGIA
PARIS
PARNASSIA
PARTHENOCISSUS
PASSIFLORA
PATRINIA
PELARGONIUM
PELTOBOYKINIA
PENSTEMON
PENTAGLOTTIS
PENTAS
PEPEROMIA
PERICALLIS
PEROVSKIA
PERSICARIA
PETASITES
PETREA
PETRORHAGIA
PETUNIA
PEUCEDANUM
PHALARIS
PHLOMIS
PHLOX
PHORMIUM
PHUOPSIS
PHYGELIUS
PHYSALIS
PHYSOPLEXIS
PHYSOSTEGIA
PHYTEUMA
PHYTOLACCA
PILEA
PILOSELLA
PIMPINELLA
PINGUICULA
PLANTAGO
PLATYCERIUM
PLATYCODON
PLECTRANTHUS

PLEIOBLASTUS
PLEIONE
PODOPHYLLUM
PODRANEA
POLEMONIUM
POLYGALA
POLYGONATUM
POLYPODIUM
POLYSTICHIUM
PONTEDERIA
PORTULACARIA
POTENTILLA
PRATIA
PRIMULA
PROTEA
PRUNELLA
PTERIS
PTEROCEPHALUS
PTEROCEPHALUS
PULMONARIA
PULSATILLA
PUSCHKINIA

P

PACHYPHRAGMA *(Brassicaceae)*

Common names: None

A genus of but a single species, *P. macrophyllum*, of semi-evergreen, rhizomatous perennial found in moist beech woodland in Turkey and the Caucasus. Its large leaves are basal, shiny, and long-stalked. The flowers are four-petalled, white, borne in flat corymbs in spring, and are foul-smelling. They are followed by fruits of inverse-heart-shape.

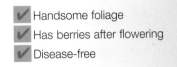

✔ Handsome foliage	✘ Prone to slug damage
✔ Has berries after flowering	✘ Flowers malodorous
✔ Disease-free	

CULTIVATION
Grow in moist, humus-rich soil in part shade.

PROPAGATION
Seed should be sown in a cold frame in autumn. Divide in spring or take basal stem cuttings in late spring.

Pachyphragma macrophyllum

Zone 7
Height: 6in. (15cm) Spread: 3ft. (90cm)

PAEONIA *(Paeoniaceae)*

Common names: Peony rose

A genus of 30 species of herbaceous perennials, subshrubs and shrubs from rocky scrubland and meadowland across Eurasia and western North America. Their leaves are pinnate or two-ternate, with oval or obovate lobes and entire or lobed leaflets. The flowers may be single, semi-double, anemoniform or double, and saucer- cup- or bowl-shaped, with five to ten petals and five sepals. They are solitary, but several can occur to a stem. They are classified as 'Very large' (over 8in. (20cm)), 'Large' (over 6in. (15cm)), 'Medium-sized' (over 4in. (10cm)), or 'Small' (under 4in. (10cm)). Some have attractive seed-heads.

✔ Long-lived	✘ Resent disturbance
✔ Good cut flowers	✘ All parts poisonous
✔ Handsome foliage	

CULTIVATION
Grow in moist, deep, fertile, well-drained soil in sun or part shade. They may need to be staked. Tree peonies need a sheltered corner.

PROPAGATION
Seed of herbaceous peonies should be sown outdoors in Autumn or early winter, but may take a year or two, even three, to germinate. Divide in spring or autumn, but this is not well tolerated. Take root cuttings in winter. Tree peonies should have semi-ripe cuttings taken in summer.

Paeonia
'Black Pirate'

Zone 6
Height and spread: 3ft. (90cm)

Paeonia broteroi

Zone 7
Height and spread: 20in. (50cm)

Paeonia delavayi
A.G.M. (Tree peony)

Zone 6
Height: 6ft. (2m) Spread: 4ft. (1.2m)

P

Paeonia lactiflora
'Bowl of Beauty' A.G.M.

Zone 6
Height: 4ft. (1.2m) Spread: 1ft. (30cm)

Paeonia lactiflora
'Lady Alexandra Duff' A.G.M.

Zone 6
Height and spread: 28in. (70cm)

Paeonia mascula subsp. *aretina*

Zone 8
Height and spread: 3ft. (90cm)

Paeonia mascula subsp. *russii*

Zone 8
Height and spread: 18in. (45cm)

Paeonia mascula subsp. *triternata*

Zone 8
Height and spread: 18in. (45cm)

Paeonia mlokosewitschii
A.G.M.

Zone 6
Height and spread: 3ft. (90cm)

P

Paeonia obovata var. *alba*
A.G.M.

Zone 7
Height and spread: 28in. (70cm)

Paeonia officinalis

Zone 8
Height and spread: 28in. (70cm)

Paeonia
'Oriental Gold'

Zone 7
Height and spread: 3ft. (90cm)

Paeonia
'Renown'

Zone 7
Height and spread: 4ft. (1.2m)

Paeonia
'Sarah Bernhardt' A.G.M.

Zone 7
Height and spread: 3ft. (90cm)

Paeonia tenuifolia

Zone 8
Height and spread: 28in. (70cm)

Paeonia veitchii

Zone 8
Height and spread: 2ft. (60cm)

Paeonia
'White Wings'

Zone 8
Height and spread: 34in. (85cm)

PALLENIS *(formerly Asteriscus)(Asteraceae)*

Common names: None

A genus of four species of perennials from dry, sunny habitats in he Canary Islands, the Cape Verde Islands and the Mediterranean region. Their leaves are hairy, and oblong or spoon-shaped. The flowers are solitary, single, orange-yellow daisies, borne over a long period in autumn. They are good seaside plants.

✔ Long-flowering
✔ Drought-tolerant
✔ Disease-free
✔ Pest-free

CULTIVATION
Grow in sharply-draining soil in sun.

PROPAGATION
Seed should be sown at 70°F (21°C) in a cold frame in spring.

Pallenis maritimus

Zone 8
Height: 10in. (25cm) Spread: 8in. (20cm)

PANDOREA *(Bignoniaceae)*
Common names: None

A genus of six species of evergreen, twining, climbers from rainforest at sea-level and up to 10,000ft. (3,000m) in Australasia and Malaysia. Their leaves are pinnate, whorled or opposite, with seven pairs of leaflets. The flowers are fragrant, tubular, five-petalled, and borne in panicles or racemes from spring to summer.

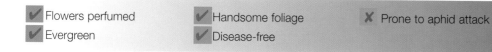

✔ Flowers perfumed	✔ Handsome foliage	✘ Prone to aphid attack
✔ Evergreen	✔ Disease-free	

CULTIVATION
Under glass, grow in loam-based potting compost in full light. Water moderately in summer, sparingly in winter.

Out of doors, grow in moist, fertile, well-drained soil in sun. Provide support.

PROPAGATION
Seed should be sown at 64°F (18°C) in spring. Layer in spring. Take greenwood cuttings with bottom heat in summer.

Pandorea jasminoides
'Rosea'

Zone 9
Height: 15ft. (5m) Spread: 2ft. (60cm)

PAPAVER *(Papaveraceae)*
Common names: Poppy

A genus of 70 species of annuals, biennials and tap-rooted perennials from a range of sunny habitats from low to high altitude and subarctic to temperate regions of Eurasia, South Africa, Australia and western North America. Their leaves vary from simple to pinnate to pinnatisect, smooth to bristly, toothed and gray-green or green. The flowers are short-lived, cup- or bowl- or saucer-shaped, four-petalled, brightly-colored, and with basal marking or spotting. They may be solitary or in racemes or panicles, and are followed by large seed-heads.

✔ Good cut flowers	✘ Prone to aphid attack
✔ Drought-tolerant	✘ Self-seeds
✔ Low allergen	✘ Resent disturbance

CULTIVATION
Grow infertile, well-drained deep soil in sun, but P. alpinum requires sharply-draining soil. Dead-head to prevent self-seeding, unless seed is required.

PROPAGATION
Seed should be sown in a cold frame in spring. Divide in spring but they do not respond well. Root cuttings can be taken in late autumn or early winter.

Papaver anomalum album

Zone 7
Height: 16in. (40cm) Spread: 6in. (15cm)

Papaver atlanticum

Zone 6
Height: 1ft. (30cm) Spread: 6in. (15cm)

Papaver fauriei

Zone 2
Height and spread: 4in. (10 cm)

P

P

Papaver 'Fireball'

Zone 7
Height: 1ft. (30cm) Spread: indefinite
Invasive

Papaver glaucum

Zone 8
Height: 20in. (50cm) Spread: 6in. (15cm)

Papaver miyabeanum

Zone 2
Height: 4in. (10 cm) Spread: 2in. (5cm)

Papaver orientale
'Allegro'

Zone 3
Height: 3ft. (90cm) Spread: 30in. (75cm)

Papaver orientale
'Beauty of Livermere' A.G.M.

Zone 3
Height: 4ft. (1.2m) Spread: 3ft. (90cm)

Papaver orientale
'Black and White' A.G.M.

Zone 3
Height and spread: 3ft. (90cm)

Papaver orientale
'Charming'

Zone 3
Height and spread: 3ft. (90cm)

P

Papaver orientale
'Harvest Moon'

Zone 3
Height and spread: 3ft. (90cm)

Papaver orientale
'Lady Roscoe'

Zone 3
Height and spread: 3ft. (90cm)

Papaver orientale
'Patty's Plum'

Zone 3
Height and spread: 3ft. (90cm)

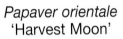

Papaver orientale
'Pizzicato'

Zone 3
Height and spread: 3ft. (90cm)

Papaver rupifragum

Zone 7
Height: 18in. (45cm) Spread: 8in. (20cm)

Papaver rupifragum
'Flore Pleno'

Zone 7
Height: 18in. (45cm) Spread: 8in. (20cm)

Papaver spicatum

Zone 8
Height: 2ft. (60cm) Spread: 6in. (15cm)

PARADISEA *(Asphodelaceae)*
Common names: St Bruno's lily; Paradise lily

A genus of two species of rhizomatous perennials found in damp woodland and meadows, and subalpine regions of southern Europe. Their leaves are basal, linear and gray-green. The flowers are perfumed, six-tepalled, trumpets borne on loose racemes, in late spring or early summer.

✔ Good cut flowers   ✘ Prone to slug damage
✔ Flowers perfumed

CULTIVATION
Grow in moist, fertile, well-drained soil in sun or part shade.

PROPAGATION
Seed should be sown in a cold frame as soon as ripe, or in spring. Divide after flowering, or in spring.

Paradisea liliastrum
A.G.M.

Zone 7
Height: 2ft. (60cm) Spread: 1ft. (30cm)

Paradisea lusitanicum

Zone 8
Height: 4ft. (1.2m) Spread: 16in. (40cm)

PARAHEBE *(Scrophulariaceae)*
Common names: None

A genus of 30 species of shrubs and perennials from Australasia. Their leaves are ovate, toothed and opposite. The flowers are small, saucer-shaped, and have four or five petals of uneven size, borne in erect, axillary racemes in late summer.

✔ Evergreen   ✘ Prone to slug damage
✔ Handsome foliage   ✘ Self-seeds

CULTIVATION
Grow in well-drained soil in sun, and in a warm corner in cold gardens.

PROPAGATION
Seed should be sown in a cold frame as soon as ripe, or in spring. Divide in early spring, or after flowering.

Parahebe perfoliata
A.G.M.

Zone 9
Height: 32in. (80cm) Spread: 18in. (45cm)

PARAQUILEGIA *(Ranunculaceae)*

Common names: None

A genus of six species of perennials found in rock crevices and scree in the Himalayas and the mountains of China and Central Asia. Their foliage is ferny, ternate to triternate, alternate, and gray- or blue-green. The flowers are columbine-like, solitary and cup-shaped, and appear in spring.

✔ Handsome foliage

✔ Drought-tolerant

✖ Prone to slug damage

CULTIVATION
Grow in an alpine house in sharply-draining compost, or outdoors in limy, well-drained soil in sun. Protect against winter wet.

PROPAGATION
Sow seed in an open frame as soon as ripe.

Paraquilegia anemonoides

Zone 5
Height and spread: 4in. (10 cm)

PARIS *(Trilliaceae)*

Common names: None

A genus of 20 species of rhizomatous perennials from woodland in Eurasia. Their leaves are variable, ovate to lance-shaped and lie just below the star- or spider-shaped, green flowers, which are followed by handsome seed-heads.

✔ Handsome foliage

✔ Handsome seed-heads

✖ Seeds poisonous

✖ Prone to slug damage

CULTIVATION
Grow in moist, fertile, loamy soil in part shade.

PROPAGATION
Seed should be sown in a cold frame in autumn. Divide after foliage dies down.

Paris japonica

Zone 8
Height: 1ft. (30cm) Spread: 10in. (25cm)

Paris polyphylla

Zone 7
Height: 3ft. (90cm) Spread: 1ft. (30cm)

P

PARNASSIA *(Parnassiaceae)*

Common names: Grass of Parnassus; Bog star

A genus of 15 species of herbaceous perennials from bogland in the temperate northern hemisphere. Their leaves are in basal rosettes, and vary from ovate to heart- or kidney-shaped. The flowers are large, solitary, saucer- or bell-shaped, borne in spring or summer.

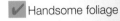 Handsome foliage   ✗ Prone to slug damage

CULTIVATION
Grow in wet, but non-stagnant, humus-rich soil in sun.

PROPAGATION
Seed should be sown in reliably moist compost in a cold frame in autumn. Divide in spring or autumn.

Parnassia nubicola

Zone 4
Height: 1ft. (30cm) Spread: 6in. (15cm)

PARTHENOCISSUS *(Vitaceae)*

Common names: Virginia creeper

A genus of ten species of herbaceous climbers from forest in the Himalayas, North America and East Asia. They may twine, but usually adhere by disc-shaped suckers on the tendrils. Their leaves are palmate or lobed or fully-divided leaves, and color well in autumn. The flowers are inconspicuous, and have four or five petals, and appear in summer, followed sometimes by black or blue berries.

✔ Handsome foliage   ✗ Flowers insignificant
✔ Disease-free   ✗ Berries poisonous
✔ Pest-free
✔ Harbor bird life

CULTIVATION
Grow in fertile well-drained soil in sun or part shade. Prune for size and shape in early winter and summer too if needed.

PROPAGATION
Seed should be sown in a cold frame in autumn. Take cuttings as follows: softwood in early summer; greenwood in midsummer; hardwood in winter.

Parthenocissus henryana A.G.M.
(Chinese Virginia creeper)

Zone 7
Height: 30ft. (10m) Spread: 9ft. (3m)

Parthenocissus tricuspidata
A.G.M (Boston ivy)

Zone 4
Height: 70ft. (20m) Spread: 15ft. (5m)

PASSIFLORA *(Passifloraceae)*

Common names: Passion flower; Granadilla

A genus of over 400 species of annuals, perennials, shrubs, trees and vigorous tendril climbers, from grassland and tropical woodland in the Americas, tropical Asia and Australasia. Their leaves are simple or up to nine-lobed, round or elliptic or ovate, and alternate. The flowers are solitary or borne in racemes from the leaf axils, and are followed by fleshy, edible fruits. The flowers have a central stalk bearing the ovary and stamens, and a corna of several fleshy layers.

✔ Evergreen
✔ Low allergen

✘ Invasive

CULTIVATION

Under glass, grow in loam-based potting compost, in full light, with midday shade. Water freely during growth, but sparingly in winter.

Out of doors, grow in moist, well-drained soil in a sheltered corner, in sun., or part shade.

PROPAGATION

Seed should be sown at 64°F (18°C) in spring. Layer in spring or summer. Semi-ripe cuttings may be taken in summer.

Passiflora caerulea
A.G.M.

Zone 7
Height: 30ft. (10m) Spread: 3ft. (90cm)

Passiflora quadrangularis
A.G.M.

Zone 10
Height: 50ft. (15m) Spread: 6ft. (2m)

PATRINIA *(Valerianaceae)*

Common names: None

A genus of 15 species of herbaceous perennials grassy mountain meadows in Siberia and Japan. Their leaves are basal and vary from round to ovate to palmate to pinnate. The small flowers are cup-shaped and borne in panicles in summer.

✔ Handsome foliage
✔ Good ground cover in shade

✘ Prone to slug damage

CULTIVATION

Grow in moist, humus-rich soil in part or full shade.

PROPAGATION

Seed should be sown in a cold frame as soon as it is ripe. Divide in spring.

Patrinia triloba

Zone 5
Height: 20in. (50cm) Spread: 1ft. (30cm)

P

PELARGONIUM *(Geraniaceae)*

Common names: None

A genus of 230 species of perennials, subshrubs and shrubs from deserts and mountains of South Africa, They are referred to generally, but erroneously, as Geraniums. Most pelargoniums in cultivation are cultivars, and few species are grown. Their leaves vary but are mostly pinnate or palmate, on long stalks; some are aromatic. The five-petalled flowers are funnel- or saucer- or star- or trumpet-shaped, borne on long stems, in clusters known as pseudoumbels, appearing from spring to summer in temperate zones, but all year in tropical regions. Six horticultural classes are recognized, but there are four main groups, and each entry has its classification indicated in brackets:

Zonal (Z) the largest group by far. They are bushy, evergreen, perennials with succulent stems. The leaves are round, green or pale green, or bicolored or tricolored, in concentric zones, or in a butterfly-shaped central zone. The flowers may be single, semi-double or double, in a wide range of colors. The double forms do not withstand bad weather. Further subdivisions of zonal pelargoniums are further subdivided as follows:

Cactus-flowered (ZCF) flowers resemble those of cactus dahlias, with quilled petals

Fancy-leaved (ZFL) grown for foliage value, flowers small

Rosebud (ZR) double-flowered with rosebud centers

Single-flowered (ZS) have no more than five petals

Double-flowered (ZD) have more than five petals.

Stellar-flowered (ZSF) flowers star-shaped

Regal (R) these are busy, evergreen perennials with rounded leaves that may be toothed or lobed. The flowers come in several colors, and are usually single, occasionally double, in clusters.

Ivy-leaved (I) these are trailing, evergreen perennials with fleshy, stiff, lobed green leaves. The flowers are produced in clusters in a wide range of colors. They are excellent for hanging baskets.

Scented-leaved (S) these shrubby evergreen perennials have variably-shaped leaves which release a scent when touched. The leaves may be plain green or variegated or silver or gold. The flowers are small, single, and in several colors, and borne in clusters.

The two other classes are Angel and Unique, but are for specialist growers and are not covered here.

✔ Evergreen
✔ Long-flowering
✔ Handsome foliage

✖ Foliage is skin-irritant
✖ Prone to aphid attack

CULTIVATION

Under glass, grow in loam-based or loam-free potting compost in full light, with good ventilation and shade from hot sun. Dead-head regularly. Water moderately during growth, and sparingly in winter. Cut back by two-thirds if to be kept cool, and keep almost dry. Repot in late winter as growth commences.

Out of doors, grow in alkaline to neutral, well-drained soil in sun, except for Regals, which prefer light shade. Dead-head to keep flowering. Lift in autumn, cut back by one-third, and store in dry, frost-free conditions.

PROPAGATION

Seed of species should be sown at 64°F (18°C) in late winter and early spring. Softwood cuttings can be taken in spring, late summer or early autumn.

Pelargonium 'Bristol' (ZFL)

Zone 10
Height and spread: 1ft. (30cm)
Variegated leaves

Pelargonium capitatum

Zone 10
Height: 3ft. (90cm) Spread: 10in. (25cm)
Foliage aromaticPelargonium capitatum

Pelargonium
'Caroline Schmidt' (ZD)

Zone 10
Height: 8in. (20cm) Spread: 1ft. (30cm)

Pelargonium
'Cathay' (ZSF)

Zone 10
Height: 8in. (20cm) Spread: 1ft. (30cm)

Pelargonium
'Chocolate Peppermint' A.G.M. (S)

Height: 1ft. (30cm) Spread: 18in. (45cm)

Pelargonium 'Contrast' (ZFL)

Zone 10
Height: 1ft. (30cm) Spread: 8in. (20cm)
Variegated leaves

Pelargonium crispum
'Variegatum' A.G.M.
Zone 10
Height: 18in. (45cm) Spread: 6in. (15cm)
Foliage aromatic

Pelargonium
'Crystal Palace Gem' (ZFL)
Zone 10
Height: 1ft. (30cm) Spread: 8in. (20cm)
Variegated leaves

Pelargonium 'Elbe Silver' (PBR) (I)

Zone 10
Height: 8in. (20cm) Spread: 1ft. (30cm)
Variegated leaves

P

Pelargonium endlicherianum

Zone 7
Height: 10in. (25cm) Spread: 6in. (15cm)
Hardy pelargonium

Pelargonium 'Evka' (PBR) (I)

Zone 10
Height: 8in. (20cm) Spread: 1ft. (30cm)
Variegated

Pelargonium exstipulatum

Zone 10
Height: 18in. (45cm) Spread: 8in. (20cm)

P

Pelargonium
'Fragrans Variegatum' (S)
Zone 10
Height: 10in. (25cm) Spread: 8in. (20cm)
Foliage aromatic/Variegated leaves

Pelargonium
'Francis Parmenter' (I)

Zone 10
Height: 6in. (15cm) Spread: 8in. (20cm)

Pelargonium
'Frank Headley' A.G.M. (ZFL)
Zone 10
Height: 8in. (20cm) Spread: 1ft. (30cm)
Variegated leaves

Pelargonium grandiflorum hybrid

Zone 10
Height: 45 cm.)18 9n.); Spread: 1ft. (30cm)

Pelargonium
'Grey Lady Plymouth' (S)

Zone 10
Height: 16in. (40cm) Spread: 8in. (20cm)

Pelargonium
'Happy Thought' A.G.M. (ZFL)

Zone 10
Height: 18in. (45cm) Spread: 10in. (25cm)

P

Pelargonium
'Lady Plymouth' A.G.M. (S)

Height: 16in. (40cm) Spread: 8in. (20cm)
Variegated leaves

Pelargonium 'Lass O'Gowrie' (ZFL)

Zone 10
Height: 16in. (40cm) Spread: 1ft. (30cm)
Variegated leaves

Pelargonium 'L'Elegante' A.G.M. (I)

Zone 10
Height: 10in. (25cm) Spread: 8in. (20cm)
Variegated leaves

Pelargonium 'Masterpiece' (ZD)

Zone 10
Height: 14in. (35cm) Spread: 1ft. (30cm)

Pelargonium 'Michaela' (I)

Zone 10
Height: 8in. (20cm) Spread: 1ft. (30cm)
Variegated leaves

Pelargonium
'Mr. Henry Cox' A.G.M. (ZFL)
Zone 10
Height: 1ft. (30cm) Spread: 5in. (12cm)
Variegated leaves

Pelargonium 'Mrs. Parker' (ZFL)

Zone 10
Height: 1ft. (30cm) Spread: 8in. (20cm)
Variegated leaves

Pelargonium 'Mrs. Pollock' (ZFL)

Zone 10
Height: 1ft. (30cm) Spread: 6in. (15cm)
Variegated leaves

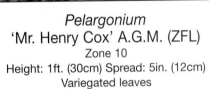

Pelargonium
'Mrs. Salter Bevis' (ZCF)

Zone 10
Height: 10in. (25cm) Spread: 8in. (20cm)

Pelargonium 'Occold Shield' (ZFL)

Zone 10
Height: 1ft. (30cm) Spread: 10in. (25cm)
Variegated leaves

Pelargonium 'Pelgardini' (ZFL)

Zone 10
Height: 10in. (25cm) Spread: 8in. (20cm)
Variegated leaves

P

Pelargonium peltatum (I)

Zone 10
Height: 4in. (10 cm) Spread: 18in. (45cm)

Pelargonium regale hybrid (R)

Zone 10
Height and spread: 18in. (45cm)

Pelargonium 'Robert Fish' (ZFL)

Zone 10
Height and spread: 1ft. (30cm)
Variegated leaves

Pelargonium
'Rouletta Mexicana' (I)
Zone 10
Height: 18in. (45cm) Spread: 8in. (20cm)
Double flowers/Variegated leaves

Pelargonium
'Splendide'

Zone 10
Height: 1ft. (30cm) Spread: 8in. (20cm)

Pelargonium 'Tomcat' (PBR) (I)

Zone 10
Height: 8in. (20cm) Spread: 1ft. (30cm)
Double flowers

P

Pelargonium 'Vancouver
Centennial' A.G.M. (ZSF)

Height: 1ft. (30cm) Spread: 8in. (20cm)

Pelargonium 'Wantirna' (ZFL)

Zone 10
Height and spread: 8in. (20cm)
Variegated leaves

P

PELTOBOYKINIA *(Saxifragaceae)*
Common names: None

A genus of two species of rhizomatous perennials from high woodland in Southern Japan. Their leaves are large, peltate or pinnate, toothed, shiny, and mid- or olive-green. The smallish, short-lived flowers are open bells of pale green, and are borne in terminal cymes in summer.

✔ Handsome foliage ✘ Flowers short-lived
✔ Disease-free
✔ Pest-free
✔ Good ground cover in shade

CULTIVATION
Grow in moist, fertile soil in part shade.

PROPAGATION
Seed should be sown in a cold frame in spring. Divide in spring or autumn.

Peltoboykinia tellimoides

Zone 7
Height: 3ft. (90cm) Spread: 30in. (75cm)

PENSTEMON *(Scrophulariaceae)*
Common names: None

A genus of 250 species of perennials and subshrubs from a variety of habitats such as alpine and subalpine regions and open plains in Central and North America. Their leaves are lance-shaped or linear, and opposite or alternate on the stems. The flowers are tubular or funnel-shaped, two-lipped; the upper lip is two-lobed, the lower three-lobed. They are borne in panicles or racemes over a long period in summer.

✔ Long-flowering ✘ Prone to slug damage
✔ Low allergen ✘ Mildew prone

CULTIVATION
Grow in well-drained fertile soil in sun or part shade. Dead-head to preserve vitality.

PROPAGATION
Seed of the species should be sown at 64°F (18°C) in a cold frame in late winter or spring. Divide cultivars in spring, or take softwood cuttings in early summer, or semi-ripe cuttings in midsummer.

P

Penstemon 'Andenken an Friedrich Hahn' A.G.M.

Zone 7
Height: 30in. (75cm) Spread: 2ft. (60cm)

Penstemon barbatus

Zone 3
Height: 5ft. (1.5m) Spread: 20in. (50cm)

Penstemon cardwellii forma. *albus*

Zone 8
Height: 8in. (20cm) Spread: 1ft. (30cm)

Penstemon 'Charles Rudd'

Zone 7
Height: 2ft. (60cm) Spread: 18in. (45cm)

Penstemon
'Cherry Ripe' A.G.M.

Zone 7
Height: 3ft. (90cm) Spread: 18in. (45cm)

Penstemon
'Chester Scarlet' A.G.M.

Zone 7
Height: 2ft. (60cm) Spread: 18in. (45cm)

Penstemon crandallii subsp.
glabrescens

Zone 3
Height: 4ft. (1.2m) Spread: 18in. (45cm)

Penstemon digitalis

Zone 3
Height: 3ft. (90cm) Spread: 18in. (45cm)

Penstemon digitalis 'Husker Red'

Zone 3
Height: 3ft. (90cm) Spread: 18in. (45cm)
Foliage red

P

Penstemon 'Drinkstone'

Zone 7
Height: 32in. (80cm) Spread: 18in. (45cm)

Penstemon
'Flamingo'

Zone 7
Height: 3ft. (90cm) Spread: 1ft. (30cm)

Penstemon heterophyllus
'Blue Springs'

Zone 8
Height and spread: 20in. (50cm)

Penstemon
'Hidcote Pink' A.G.M.

Zone 7
Height: 30in. (75cm) Spread: 18in. (45cm)

Penstemon
'Hopley's Variegated'

Zone 7
Height: 2ft. (60cm) Spread: 18in. (45cm)

Penstemon isophyllus

Zone 9
Height: 28in. (70cm) Spread: 1ft. (30cm)

Penstemon
'Modesty'

Zone 7
Height: 32in. (80cm) Spread: 18in. (45cm)

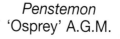

Penstemon
'Osprey' A.G.M.

Zone 7
Height: 3ft. (90cm) Spread: 18in. (45cm)

P

Penstemon
'Peace'

Zone 7
Height: 2ft. (60cm) Spread: 18in. (45cm)

Penstemon
'Pennington Gem' A.G.M.

Zone 7
Height: 30in. (75cm) Spread: 18in. (45cm)

Penstemon pinifolius
A.G.M.

Zone 8
Height: 16in. (40cm) Spread: 10in. (25cm)

Penstemon pinifolius
'Mersea Yellow'

Zone 8
Height: 16in. (40cm) Spread: 10in. (25cm)

Penstemon
'Pershore Pink Necklace'

Zone 7
Height: 3ft. (90cm) Spread: 18in. (45cm)

Penstemon
'Port Wine' A.G.M.

Zone 7
Height: 3ft. (90cm) Spread: 18in. (45cm)

Penstemon procerus
var. *tolmei*

Zone 3
Height: 16in. (40cm) Spread: 10in. (25cm)

Penstemon
'Red Emperor'

Zone 7
Height: 3ft. (90cm) Spread: 18in. (45cm)

Penstemon
'Rubicundus' A.G.M.

Zone 7
Height: 4ft. (1.2m) Spread: 18in. (45cm)

P

Penstemon rupicola
'Diamond Lake'

Zone 8
Height: 8in. (20cm) Spread: 18in. (45cm)

Penstemon
'Sour Grapes'

Zone 7
Height: 2ft. (60cm) Spread: 18in. (45cm)

Penstemon
'Stapleford Gem' A.G.M.

Zone 7
Height: 2ft. (60cm) Spread: 18in. (45cm)

Penstemon
'Volcano Kilimanjaro'

Zone 7
Height: 3ft. (90cm) Spread: 18in. (45cm)

Penstemon
'Volcano Stromboli'

Zone 7
Height: 3ft. (90cm) Spread: 18in. (45cm)

Penstemon
'White Bedder' A.G.M.

Zone 7
Height: 28in. (70cm) Spread: 1ft. (30cm)

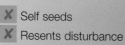
Penstemon
'Whitethroat'

Zone 7
Height: 3ft. (90cm) Spread: 18in. (45cm)

PENTAGLOTTIS *(Boraginaceae)*
Common names: Green alkanet

A genus of a single tap-rooted perennial, *P. sempervirens*, from shaded, damp areas, woodland edges and hedgerows in south-west Europe. Its leaves are in basal rosettes, rough, veined, ovate. The stem leaves are smaller. The flower is forget-me–not-like, borne in leafy cymes in spring and early summer. It is naturalized in Britain and Belgium.

✔ Disease-free
✔ Pest-free
✔ Good ground cover in shade

✘ Self seeds
✘ Resents disturbance

CULTIVATION
Grow in moist, humus-rich soil in part or deep shade. Dead-head to prevent self-seeding.

PROPAGATION
Seed should be sown in a cold frame when ripe, or in spring. Divide in spring; if broken root portions are left behind, each will sprout.

Pentaglottis sempervirens

Zone 7
Height and spread: 3ft. (90cm)

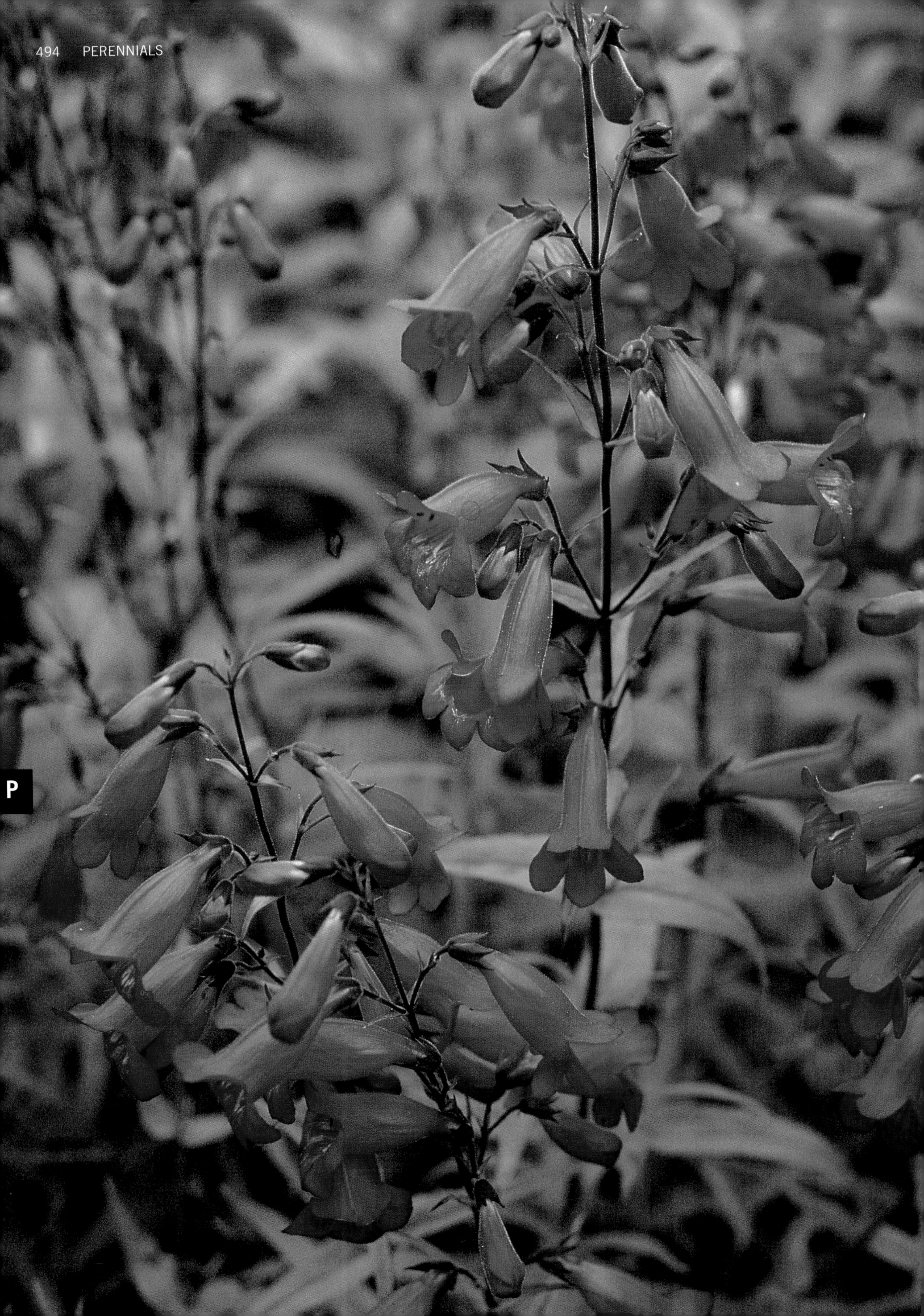

P

PENTAS *(Rubiaceae)*

Common names: None

A genus of 40 species of biennials, perennials and shrubs from scrubland and forest edges in Arabia, Madagascar and tropical Africa. Their leaves are ovate or elliptic or lance-shaped, and whorled or opposite. The flowers are salverform, five-petalled, and borne in domed or flat corymbs from spring to autumn.

✔ Drought-tolerant
✔ Evergreen
✔ Long-flowering

✘ Prone to aphid attack

CULTIVATION
Under glass, grow in sharply-draining, loam-based potting compost, in bright filtered light. Water freely during growth, sparingly in winter.

Out of doors, grow in well-drained fertile soil in sun.

PROPAGATION
Seed should be sown at 64°F (18°C) in spring. Softwood cuttings may be taken at any time.

Pentas lanceolata
(Egyptian star cluster)

Zone 10
Height: 6ft. (2m) Spread: 3ft. (90cm)

PEPEROMIA *(Piperaceae)*

Common names: None

A genus of over 1,000 species of evergreen perennials from habitats ranging from high-altitude cloud forest to near-desert in tropical and subtropical regions of the world. They have root systems that are short-lived, but the plants can absorb water from the atmosphere, and store it. They may be succulent or rosette-forming. Their leaves are fleshy, elliptic or heart-shaped or ovate, and in whorls or alternate. The flowers are small, greenish-white, and borne in spikes in late summer, but flowering is unreliable.

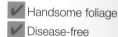

✔ Handsome foliage
✔ Disease-free

✔ Pest-free

✘ Flowers insignificant

CULTIVATION
Under glass, grow in any potting compost in bright indirect light during growth, and in full light in winter. High humidity is required during spring and summer, and they must be misted daily. Water moderately in summer, sparingly in winter, with soft, tepid water.

Out of doors, grow in moist, humus-rich, well-drained soil in part shade.

PROPAGATION
Seed should be sown at 75°F (24°C) when ripe. Softwood, leaf or leaf-bud cuttings may be taken during growth and offsets can be removed from rosette-forming types.

P

Peperomia argyreia
A.G.M.

Zone 10
Height: 8in. (20cm) Spread: 6in. (15cm)

Peperomia caperata
'Little Fantasy' A.G.M.

Zone 10
Height and spread: 3in. (8cm)

Peperomia clusiifolia
'Variegata'

Zone 10
Height: 10in. (25cm) Spread: 6in. (15cm)

Peperomia obtusifolia
A.G.M.

Zone 10
Height and spread: 10in. (25cm)

Peperomia obtusifolia
'Variegata'

Zone 10
Height and spread: 10in. (25cm)

PERICALLIS (Asteraceae)

Common names: None

A genus of 15 species of subshrubs and perennials from rocky outcrops and slopes in the Canary Islands. Their leaves are arrow-shaped or round or lance-shaped, and in basal rosettes or alternate. The daisy-like flowers are solitary or borne in corymbs from winter to late autumn.

✔ Long-flowering   ✘ Winter-flowering

CULTIVATION
Under glass, grow in loam-based potting compost in full light, with midday shade. Water with moderation during growth, but sparingly in winter.

Out of doors, grow in well-drained soil in sun, with shade at midday, or in part shade. Dead-head to prolong flowering.

PROPAGATION
Seed should be sown at 64°F (18°C) in spring or up to midsummer. Semi-ripe cuttings may be rooted in summer.

Pericallis lanata
Kew form

Zone 9
Height: 3ft. (90cm) Spread: 1ft. (30cm)

P

PEROVSKIA (Lamiaceae)

Common names: None

A genus of seven species of herbaceous subshrubs found in rocky sites from Central Asia across to the Himalayas. Their leaves are aromatic, ovate, oblong or lance-shaped, deeply-divided, opposite and gray-green. The flowers are small, tubular, two-lipped, and borne in terminal panicles in late summer and early autumn.

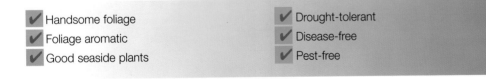

✔ Handsome foliage   ✔ Drought-tolerant
✔ Foliage aromatic   ✔ Disease-free
✔ Good seaside plants   ✔ Pest-free

CULTIVATION
Grow in well-drained soil in sun. Prune in early spring by cutting back to low permanent framework.

PROPAGATION
Softwood cuttings can be taken in late spring, and semi-ripe cuttings in summer.

Perovskia atriplicifolia

Zone 6
Height: 4ft. (1.2m) Spread: 3ft. (90cm)

Perovskia
'Blue Spire' A.G.M.

Zone 6
Height: 4ft. (1.2m) Spread: 3ft. (90cm)

PERSICARIA *(Polygonaceae)*
Common names: Snakeweed; Mountain fleece

A genus of 80 species of annuals, perennials and a few subshrubs from a range of habitats across the world. They may be evergreen or semi-evergreen or herbaceous, rhizomatous or stoloniferous. Their leaves are simple, entire, of various shapes, with larger basal and smaller stem. The small flowers are cup- or bell- or funnel-shaped, long-lasting, and borne in spikes or racemes in summer. They are followed by brownish berries.

✔ Long-flowering	✘ Sap poisonous
✔ Good cut flowers	✘ Sap skin-irritant

CULTIVATION
Grow in any moist soil in sun or part shade.

PROPAGATION
Seed should be sown in a cold frame in spring. Divide in spring or autumn.

Persicaria affinis 'Superba' A.G.M.

Zone 3
Height: 10in. (25cm) Spread: indefinite.
Invasive

P

Persicaria amplexicaulis

Zone 5
Height and spread: 4ft. (1.2m)

Persicaria amplexicaulis
'Firetail' A.G.M.

Zone 5
Height and spread: 4ft. (1.2m)

Persicaria amplexicaulis
var. *pendula*

Zone 5
Height: 2ft. (60cm) Spread: 4ft. (1.2m)

Persicaria bistorta
subsp. *carnea*

Zone 4
Height: 28in. (70cm) Spread: 18in. (45cm)

Persicaria bistorta
'Superba'

Zone 4
Height: 3ft. (90cm) Spread: 4ft. (1.2m)

Persicaria campanulata

Zone 8
Height and spread: 3ft. (90cm)

Persicaria campanulata
'Rosenrot'

Zone 8
Height and spread: 3ft. (90cm)

Persicaria capitata

Zone 8
Height: 3in. (8cm) Spread: indefinite
Invasive

Persicaria capitata 'Pink Bubbles'

Zone 8
Height: 3in. (8cm) Spread: indefinite
Invasive

Persicaria microcephala
'Red Dragon'

Zone 5
Height and spread: 18in. (45cm)

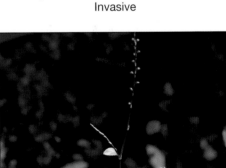

Persicaria polymorpha

Zone 8
Height: 2ft. (60cm) Spread: 18in. (45cm)

Persicaria virginiana
'Painter's Palette'
Zone 5
Height and spread: 4ft. (1.2m)
Variegated foliage/Flowers inconspicuous

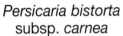

PETASITES *(Asteraceae)*

Common names: Butterbur; Sweet coltsfoot

A genus of 15 species of rhizomatous perennials from both lowland wet swamps and stream sides, and highland meadows in Eurasia and North America. Their leaves are large basal, kidney- or heart-shaped, or small stem, and scaly. The male and female flowers are on separate plants, and have ray and disc florets of white, yellow or purple; they are solitary or borne in dense panicles, corymbs or racemes in late winter to early spring.

✔ Attracts bees

✔ Handsome foliage

✔ Disease-free

✔ Pest-free

✔ Good ground cover in shade

✔ Winter-flowering

✘ Invasive

CULTIVATION
Grow in moist, but not stagnant, fertile humus-rich soil in part or full shade.

PROPAGATION
Divide in spring or autumn.

Petasites japonicus var. *giganteus*
'Nishiki-buki'

Zone 5
Height: 4ft. (1.2m) Spread: 5ft. (1.5m)

Petasites japonicus var. *giganteus*
'Variegatus'

Zone 5
Height: 4ft. (1.2m) Spread: 5ft. (1.5m)

PETREA *(Verbenaceae)*

Common names: Purple wreath; Queen's wreath

A genus of 30 species of climbers, shrubs, and trees found in woodland from Mexico and tropical South America. Their leaves are simple, elliptic, veined, and in opposite pairs or whorled. The flowers are five-petalled salvers, and are borne in racemes or panicles from the upper leaf axils.

✔ Winter-flowering

✘ Requires support

CULTIVATION
Under glass, grow in loam-based potting compost in full light. Water with moderation during growth, but sparingly in winter.

Out of doors, grow in moist, well-drained soil in sun. Prune in late winter or early spring for size and height, by cutting back sideshoots to within three or four buds of permanent growth.

PROPAGATION
Semi-ripe cuttings can be rooted with bottom heat in summer. Layer in late winter.

Petrea volubilis

Zone 10
Height: 40ft. (12m) Spread: 5ft. (1.5m)

P

PETRORHAGIA *(Caryophyllaceae)*
Common names: None

A genus of 30 species of annuals and perennials, from sandy, rocky habitats in central and southern Europe. Their leaves are lance-shaped, linear or oblong, and keeled in some species. The flowers are five-petalled salvers, and are borne in cymes or panicles over long periods in summer.

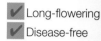 Long-flowering
✔ Disease-free

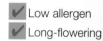 Prone to slug damage

CULTIVATION
Grow in any well-drained soil in sun.

PROPAGATION
Seed should be sown in a cold frame in autumn. Stem-tip cuttings may be taken in early summer.

Petrorhagia saxifraga

Zone 6
Height: 4in. (10 cm) Spread: 8in. (20cm)

PETUNIA *(Solanaceae)*
Common names: None

A genus of 40 species of annuals and perennials from disturbed ground, stony slopes and steppes of South America. Their leaves are lance-shaped and opposite or alternate. The flowers are solitary, five-lobed, trumpets or saucers, borne in the upper leaf axils from late spring to autumn. In cold climates, petunias are grown invariably as annuals.

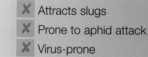 Low allergen
✔ Long-flowering

 Attracts slugs
✘ Prone to aphid attack
✘ Virus-prone

CULTIVATION
Under glass, grow in loam-based potting compost in full light. Water freely during growth, but with moderation in winter.

Out of doors, grow in well-drained soil in a sheltered corner in sun. Dead-head to prolong flowering.

PROPAGATION
Seed should be sown at 64°F (18°C) in autumn or spring. Softwood cuttings may be taken in summer.

Petunia
'Prism Sunshine'

Zone 7
Height: 10in. (25cm) Spread: 16in. (40cm)

P

Petunia
'Summer Morn'

Zone 7
Height: 1ft. (30cm) Spread: 18in. (45cm)

Petunia Surfinia
series

Zone 7
Height: 16in. (40cm) Spread: 3ft. (90cm)

Petunia Ultra
series

Zone 7
Height: 1ft. (30cm) Spread: 3ft. (90cm)

PEUCEDANUM *(Umbelliferae)*

Common names: None

A genus of 170 species of perennials and shrubs from Eurasia and tropical and southern Africa. The leaves are pinnate or ternate, gray-green. The flowers are white, small and borne in compound umbels in summer.

✔ Handsome foliage

CULTIVATION
Grow in fertile, well-drained soil in part shade.

PROPAGATION
Seed should be sown in a cold frame in spring, or divide then.

Peucedanum ostruthium
'Daphnis'

Zone 5
Height: 28in. (70cm) Spread: indefinite

PHALARIS *(Poaceae)*

Common names: Ribbon grass; Reed canary grass

A genus of 15 species of annual and perennial grasses from very varied habitats such as moist lakeside and dry slopes in temperate regions of the world. The perennials are rhizomatous, and evergreen. The leaves are linear, flat, pointed. The flowers are in ovoid spikelets in compact panicles. They are very invasive.

✔ Evergreen

✔ Handsome foliage

✔ Disease-free

✔ Pest-free

✔ Good ground cover

✘ Invasive

✘ Highly allergenic

CULTIVATION
Grow in any soil in sun or part shade. Variegated cultivars are liable to revert, so cut back hard in late spring or early summer to encourage new variegated leaves to form.

PROPAGATION
Divide in spring or early summer.

Phalaris arundinacea

Zone 4
Height: 5ft. (1.5m) Spread: indefinite

Phalaris arundinacea
var. *picta* 'Feesey'
Zone 4
Height: 5ft. (1.5m) Spread: indefinite
Foliage variegated

PHLOMIS *(Lamiaceae)*

Common names: None

A genus of 100 species of herbaceous perennials and evergreen subshrubs from rocky regions of Eurasia and North Africa. Their leaves are ovate or lance-shaped, opposite, light green or gray-green, and hairy in some. The deadnettle-like flowers are tubular, hooded, and borne in dense axillary whorls in early and mid-summer.

✔ Good cut flowers
✔ Disease-free
✔ Good for drying for winter
✔ Drought-tolerant
✔ Handsome foliage

CULTIVATION
Grow in any well-drained fertile soil in sun. Prune subshrubs after flowering for shape and size.

PROPAGATION
Seed should be sown at 64°F (18°C) in spring Divide perennials in spring.

Phlomis bovei

Zone 9
Height and spread: 3ft. (90cm)

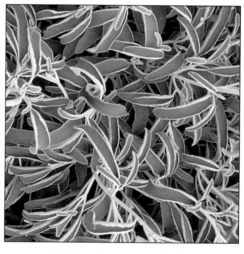

Phlomis chrysophylla
A.G.M.

Zone 9
Height: 3ft. (90cm) Spread: 4ft. (1.2m)

Phlomis fruticosa A.G.M.

Zone 7
Height: 3ft. (90cm) Spread: 5ft. (1.5m)
Evergreen

Phlomis italica

Zone 8
Height: 3ft. (90cm) Spread: 2ft. (60cm)
Evergreen

Phlomis tuberosa 'Amazone'

Zone 6
Height: 5ft. (1.5m) Spread: 4ft. (1.2m)
Evergreen

P

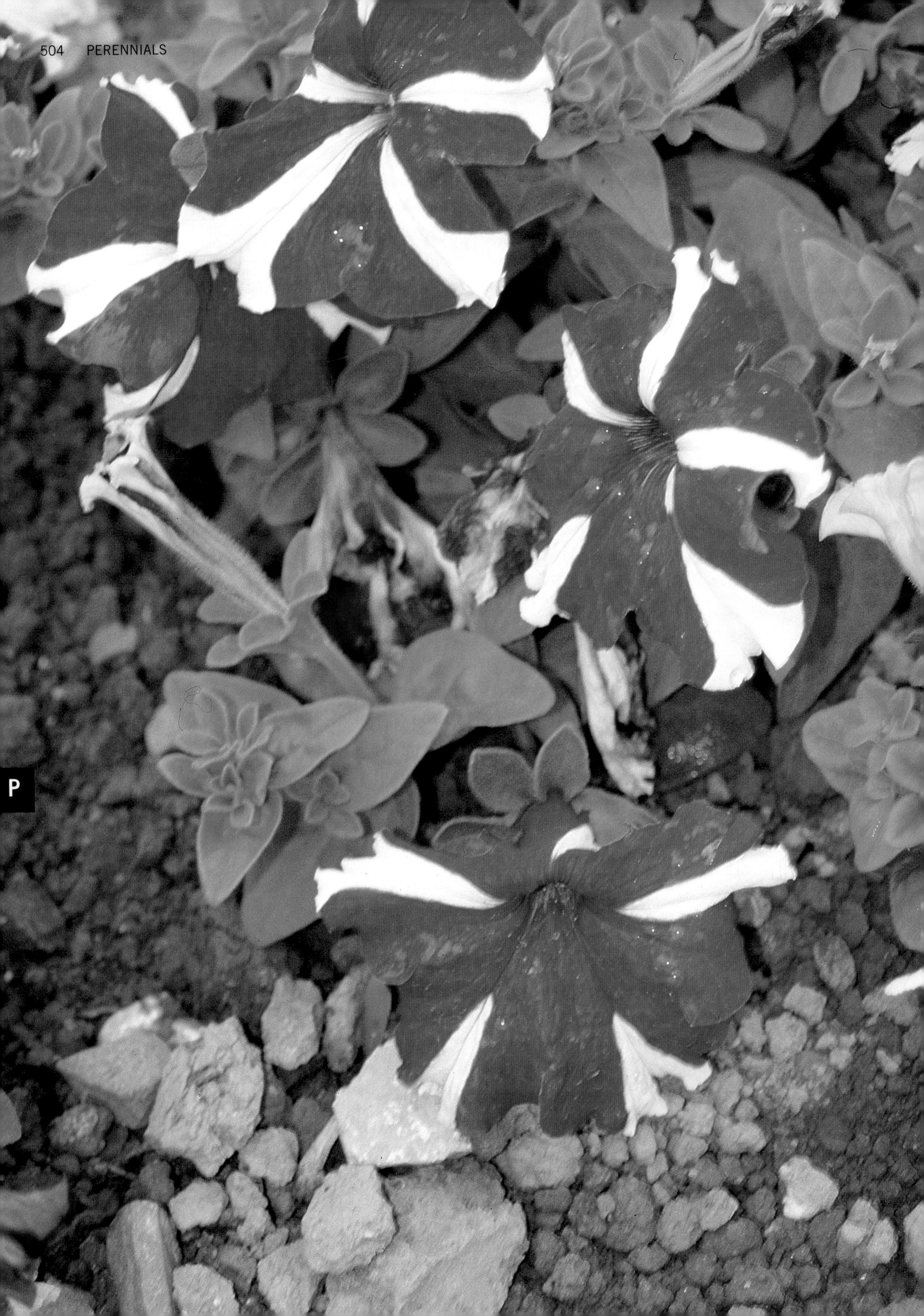

PHLOX *(Polemoniaceae)*
Common names: None

A genus of 67 species of annuals, perennials and shrubs found almost exclusively in North America, with one from Russia. The perennials may be evergreen or herbaceous. Their leaves are simple, entire, ovate or linear, and usually opposite, although the upper ones may be alternate. The flowers are salverform, with a narrow basal tubular part, and five petals. Species from dry stony habitats are cushion-forming, and flower in spring. Woodland species are trailing, like shady sites, and flower in early summer. The taller herbaceous border phloxes are from riversides, and have corymbs of flowers in midsummer, and are excellent for cutting.

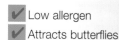

✔ Low allergen ✘ Prone to slug damage
✔ Attracts butterflies ✘ Mildew prone

Phlox adsurgens
'Wagon Wheel' (Group 2)

Zone 6
Height and spread: 1ft. (30cm)

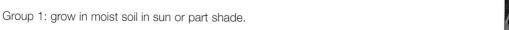

Cultivation varies with the type, and the three distinct types of need are as follows:

Group 1: grow in moist soil in sun or part shade.

Group 2: grow in moist, well-drained soil in part shade (woodlanders)

Group 3: grow in moist, humus-rich, well-drained soil in part shade.

PROPAGATION
Seed of species perennials should be sown in a cold frame when ripe, or in spring. Cultivars can be divided in spring or autumn. Softwood cuttings of non-flowering shoots can be taken from cushion-forming species in spring. Rooted runners of trailing varieties can be detached in spring or autumn.

Phlox carolina
'Bill Baker' A.G.M. (Group 1)

Zone 5
Height: 18in. (45cm) Spread: 1ft. (30cm)

P

Phlox carolina
'Magnificence' (Group 1)

Zone 5
Height and spread: 3ft. (90cm)

Phlox
'Chattahoochee' A.G.M. (Group 2)

Zone 4
Height: 6in. (15cm) Spread: 1ft. (30cm)

Phlox divaricata
'Blue Dreams' (Group 2)

Zone 4
Height: 14in. (35cm) Spread: 20in. (50cm)

Phlox douglasii
'Eva'

Zone 5
Height: 8in. (20cm) Spread: 1ft. (30cm)

Phlox maculata
(Group 1)

Zone 5
Height: 3ft. (90cm) Spread: 18in. (45cm)

Phlox maculata
'Natascha' (Group 1)

Zone 5
Height: 3ft. (90cm) Spread: 18in. (45cm)

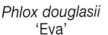

Phlox paniculata
'Becky Towe' (Group 1)
Zone 4
Height and spread: 3ft. (90cm)
Variegated foliage/Good cut flower

Phlox paniculata
'Blue Paradise' (Group 1)
Zone 4
Height and spread: 3ft. (90cm)
Good cut flower/Variegated foliage

Phlox paniculata
'Fujiyama' A.G.M. (Group 1)
Zone 4
Height: 30in. (75cm) Spread: 3ft. (90cm)
Good cut flower

Phlox paniculata
'Harlequin' (Group 1)
Zone 4
Height and spread: 3ft. (90cm)
Good cut flower/Variegated foliage

Phlox panicukata
'Jules Sandeau' (Group 1)
Zone 4
Height and spread: 3ft. (90cm)
Good cut flower

Phlox paniculata
'Norah Leigh' (Group 1)
Zone 4
Height and spread: 3ft. (90cm)
Good cut flower/Variegated foliage

Phlox paniculata
'Otley Choice' (Group 1)
Zone 4
Height and spread: 3ft. (90cm)
Good cut flower

Phlox paniculata
'Pink Posie' (PBR) (Group 1)
Zone 4
Height and spread: 3ft. (90cm)
Good cut flower/Variegated foliage

Phlox paniculata
'Rijnstroom'

Zone 4
Height and spread: 3ft. (90cm)

Phlox paniculata
'Starfire' (Group 1)
Zone 4
Height: 4ft. (1.2m) Spread: 3ft. (90cm)
Good cut flower

Phlox x procumbens 'Variegata'
(Group 2 or 3)

Zone 4
Height: 4in. (10 cm) Spread: 1ft. (30cm)

Phlox subulata
'Nettleton Variation' (Group 3)

Zone 3
Height: 6in. (15cm) Spread: 20in. (50cm)

P

PHORMIUM *(Phormiaceae)*

Common names: Mountain flax; New Zealand flax

A genus of two species, *PP cookianum* and *tenax*, of evergreen perennials found in various habitats such as scrubland, swampland, riversides and hillsides from sea level to mountain in New Zealand. The leaves are large, long linear, keeled, folded into a 'v' at the base, and handsomely marked in many cultivars. The flowers are small, nondescript, six-tepalled, abundant and borne in upright panicles on leafless stems in summer. They make excellent specimen or architectural plants.

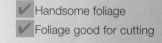

✔ Evergreen
✔ Low allergen
✔ Disease-free
✔ Handsome foliage
✔ Foliage good for cutting

CULTIVATION
Grow in moist, well-drained fertile soil in sun.

PROPAGATION
Seed should be sown at 64°F (18°C) in spring. Divide in spring.

Phormium
'Bronze Baby'

Zone 8
Height: and spread: 32in. (80cm)

Phormium cookianum
'Jester'

Zone 8
Height: 6ft. (2m) Spread: 10ft. (3m)

Phormium cookianum subsp.
hookeri 'Cream Delight' A.G.M.

Zone 8
Height: 6ft. (2m) Spread: 10ft. (3m)

Phormium cookianum
'Tricolor' A.G.M.

Zone 8
Height: 6ft. (2m) Spread: 10ft. (3m)

Phormium
'Daydream'

Zone 8
Height and spread: 6ft. (2m)

Phormium 'Dazzler'

Zone 8
Height: 3ft. (90cm) Spread: 4ft. (1.2m)

Phormium
'Duet' A.G.M.

Zone 8
Height and spread: 4ft. (1.2m)

Phormium
'Flamingo'

Zone 8
Height and spread: 6ft. (2m)

Phormium
'Jester'

Zone 8
Height and spread: 4ft. (1.2m)

Phormium
'Maori Maiden'

Zone 8
Height and spread: 4ft. (1.2m)

P

Phormium
'Maori Queen'

Zone 8
Height and spread: 4ft. (1.2m)

Phormium
'Maori Sunrise'

Zone 8
Height and spread: 4ft. (1.2m)

Phormium
'Pink Stripe'

Zone 8
Height and spread: 5ft. (1.5m)

Phormium
'Sundowner' A.G.M.

Zone 8
Height: 6ft. (2m) Spread: 10ft. (3m)

Phormium tenax
A.G.M.

Zone 8
Height: 12ft. (4m) Spread: 6ft. (2m)

Phormium tenax
'Variegatum' A.G.M.

Zone 8
Height: 12ft. (4m) Spread: 6ft. (2m)

P

Phormium tenax veitchii

Zone 8
Height and spread: 6ft. (2m)

Phormium tenax
'Yellow Wave' A.G.M.

Zone 8
Height and spread: 6ft. (2m)

P

PHUOPSIS *(Rubiaceae)*

Common names: None

A genus of a single species of perennial, *P. stylosa*, found in open hilly sites in the Caucasus and north-east Iran. It is mat-forming, and stem-rooting. Its leaves are elliptic, and in whorls. The flowers are small, with five spreading petals, perfumed, and borne in tight clusters at the ends of the stems over a long period in summer.

✔ Flowers perfumed   ✘ Self-seeds
✔ Long flowering
✔ Disease-free
✔ Pest-free

CULTIVATION
Grow in moist, sharply-drained fertile soil in sun or part shade. Shear over after flowering to maintain compactness.

PROPAGATION
Seed should be sown in a cold frame in autumn. Divide in spring. Stem-tip cuttings can be taken from spring to early summer.

Phuopsis stylosa

Zone 7
Height: 6in. (15cm) Spread: 30in. (75cm)

PHYGELIUS *(Scrophulariaceae)*

Common names: None

A genus of two species of suckering, evergreen subshrubs or shrubs from wet slopes and stream sides in South Africa. Their leaves are lance-shaped or ovate, and opposite. The flowers are tubular, pendent, and borne in panicles over a long period in summer and early autumn.

✔ Long-flowering   ✘ Invasive
✔ Evergreen
✔ Good cut flowers
✔ Disease-free

CULTIVATION
Grow in moist, fertile, well-drained soil in sun. Dead-head to prolong flowering time. Prune in spring for shape and size; they can be cut back to the base.

PROPAGATION
Seed should be sown in a cold frame in spring. Separate rooted suckers in spring. Softwood cuttings may be taken in late spring.

Phygelius aequalis

Zone 8
Height and spread: 4ft. (1.2m)

P

Phygelius aequalis
'Sensation' (PBR)

Zone 8
Height: 4ft. (1.2m) Spread: 3ft. (90cm)

Phygelius aequalis
'Yellow Trumpet' A.G.M.

Zone 8
Height and spread: 4ft. (1.2m)

Phygelius x rectus
'Moonraker'

Zone 8
Height and spread: 5ft. (1.5m)

Phygelius x rectus
'Salmon Leap' A.G.M.

Zone 8
Height: 4ft. (1.2m) Spread: 5ft. (1.5m)

Phygelius x rectus
'Sunshine'

Zone 8
Height and spread: 4ft. (1.2m)

Phygelius x rectus
'Winchester Fanfare'

Zone 8
Height and spread: 5ft. (1.5m)

PHYSALIS *(Solanaceae)*

Common names: Ground cherry

A genus of 80 species of annuals and perennials found in well-drained sunny or lightly-shaded habitats across the world, but in the Americas in particular. Their leaves are pinnatifid or entire, alternate or whorled. The flowers are insignificant, bell-shaped, and borne singly or in clusters in the leaf axils in summer. They are followed by berries enclosed in transparent, papery red or orange calyces, which persist throughout the winter, and are useful for drying for winter decoration.

✔ Good for drying for winter	✘ All parts except berries poisonous
✔ Drought-tolerant	✘ Foliage is skin-irritant
✔ Handsome seed-heads	✘ Invasive

CULTIVATION
Grow in any well-drained soil in sun or part shade.

PROPAGATION
Seed should be sown in a cold frame in spring. Divide in spring.

Physalis alkekengi var. *franchettii*

Zone 6
Height: 30in. (75cm) Spread: indefinite

PHYSOPLEXIS *(Campanulaceae)*

Common names: Devil's claw

A genus of a single species of hardy herbaceous perennial, *P. comosa*, from rock crevices in the European Alps. The leaves are heart-shaped, deeply-toothed and in basal tufts. The unusual pink flowers are bottle-shaped, and in basal clusters.

✔ Disease-free	✘ Prone to slug damage

CULTIVATION
Under glass, grow in an alpine house in a mix of equal parts loam, leaf mould and grit.

Out of doors, not easy. Grow in poor, alkaline to neutral, sharply-drained soil in sun, with shade at midday.

PROPAGATION
Seed should be sown in an open frame in autumn.

Physoplexis comosa

Zone 6
Height: 4in. (10 cm) Spread: 6in. (15cm)

P

PHYSOSTEGIA *(Lamiaceae)*
Common names: Obedient plant

A genus of a dozen species of rhizomatous, herbaceous perennials found in sunny but moist sites in eastern North America. Their leaves are variable, perhaps toothed, and in alternate pairs. The flowers are two-lipped, tubular, and are borne in racemes in summer. If any given flower is moved, it remains in the new position.

✔ Good cut flowers   ✘ Prone to slug damage
✔ Low allergen   ✘ Invasive

CULTIVATION
Grow in moist fertile soil in sun or part shade.

PROPAGATION
Seed should be sown in a cold frame in autumn. Divide in late winter or early spring.

Physostigia virginiana

Zone 4
Height: 4ft. (1.2m) Spread: indefinite

Physostigia virginiana
'Alba'

Zone 4
Height: 4ft. (1.2m) Spread: indefinite

Physostigia virginiana subsp.
speciosa 'Bouquet Rose'

Zone 4
Height: 4ft. (1.2m) Spread: indefinite

Physostigia virginiana
'Summer Snow' A.G.M.

Zone 4
Height: 4ft. (1.2m) Spread: indefinite

Physostigia virginiana subsp.
speciosa 'Variegata'

Zone 4
Height: 4ft. (1.2m) Spread: indefinite

P

PHYTEUMA *(Campanulaceae)*

Common names: Horned rampion

A genus of 40 species of perennials from open mountain regions, woodland, and meadows in Eurasia. Their leaves are large basal, simple, toothed perhaps, and smaller stem. The flowers are tubular, five-lobed, and borne in rounded clusters or terminal spikes, each flowerhead encased in leafy bracts.

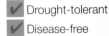

✔ Drought-tolerant

✔ Disease-free

✘ Prone to slug damage

CULTIVATION
Grow in well-drained, fertile soil in sun.

PROPAGATION
Seed should be sown in a cold frame in autumn.

Phyteuma orbiculare
(Roundheaded rampion)

Zone 6
Height: 20in. (50cm) Spread: 18in. (45cm)

Phyteuma spicatum
(Spiked rampion)

Zone 6
Height: 32in. (80cm) Spread 18in. (45cm)

PHYTOLACCA *(Phytolaccaceae)*

Common names: Pokeweed

A genus of 25 species of perennials, shrubs and trees from open fields and woodland in subtropical and tropical Asia, Africa and the Americas. Their leaves are ovate to elliptic, entire, and alternate. The flowers are small, petal-less, shallow cups borne in panicles or racemes on colored stems in late summer, and followed by round, dark red or black berries.

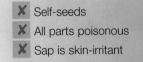

✔ Has berries after flowering

✘ Self-seeds

✘ All parts poisonous

✘ Sap is skin-irritant

CULTIVATION
Grow in moist, fertile soil in sun or part shade.

PROPAGATION
Seed should be sown at 64°F (18°C) in early spring.

Phytolacca americana

Zone 4
Height: 12ft. (4m) Spread: 3ft. (90cm)
All parts lethal

Phytolacca polyandra

Zone 6
Height: 6ft. (2m) Spread: 2ft. (60cm)

PILEA *(Urticaceae)*

Common names: Aluminum plant; Friendship plant; Artillery plant

A genus of 600 annuals and evergreen perennials from rainforest in tropical regions worldwide, with the exception of Australia. Their leaves are textured, handsomely marked, opposite, and vary in color and shape. The flowers are insignificant, and borne in the leaf axils singly or in panicles.

✔ Handsome foliage

✘ Flowers insignificant
✘ Mildew prone

CULTIVATION
Under glass, grow in pans of loam-free potting compost, in high humidity and bright filtered light. Water with moderation during growth, sparingly in winter.

Outside of doors, grow in moist soil in part or full shade.

PROPAGATION
Seed should be sown at 75°F (24°C) in spring. Stem-tip cuttings can be rooted in spring with bottom heat. Detach or divide rosettes in spring.

Pilea cadierei
A.G.M. (Aluminum plant)

Zone 10
Height: 1ft. (30cm) Spread: 8in. (20cm)

Pilea involucrata
(Friendship plant)

Zone 10
Height: 4in. (10 cm) Spread: 1ft. (30cm)

Pilea microphylla
(Artillery plant)

Zone 10
Height and spread: 1ft. (30cm)

Pilea numulariifolia
'Bronze'

Zone 10
Height: 6in. (15cm) Spread: 2ft. (60cm)

PILOSELLA *(Asteraceae)*
Common names: None

A genus of 20 species of rhizomatous perennials from a range of habitats such as dunes, grassland, open woodland and dry slopes in North Africa and Eurasia. Their leaves are mostly in basal rosettes, and are ovate, spoon-shaped or lance-shaped, toothed or entire, with a few stem leaves. The dandelion-like flowers are solitary or borne in terminal clusters in summer.

✔ Drought-tolerant
✔ Disease-free
✔ Pest-free

✘ Self-seeds
✘ Highly allergenic

CULTIVATION
Grow in dry or well-drained poor soil in sun or part shade. Dead-head to prevent self-seeding.

PROPAGATION
Seed should be sown out of doors in spring, or divide then.

Pilosella aurantiaca

Zone 5
Height: 1ft. (30cm) Spread: 30in. (75cm)

PIMPINELLA *(Apiaceae)*
Common names: None

A genus of 150 species of annuals, biennials and tap-rooted perennials from woodland, grassland and hedgerows in Eurasia, North Africa and South America. Their leaves are pinnate, or simple. The flowers are tiny, star-shaped, and borne in crowded, compound umbels in spring, followed by round fruits.

✘ Self-seeds
✘ Mildew prone
✘ Prone to slug damage

✘ Resent disturbance.
✘ Prone to aphid attack

CULTIVATION
Grow in moist, fertile soil in sun or part shade.

PROPAGATION
Sow seed in a cold frame as soon as it is ripe. Prick seedlings out into deep containers in order to reduce root damage when planting out later.

Pimpinella major
'Rosea'

Zone 5
Height: 3ft. (90cm) Spread: 2ft. (60cm)

P

PINGUICULA *(Lentibulariaceae)*
Common names: Butterwort

A genus of 45 species of insectivorous perennials from bogland across the northern hemisphere and in South America. Their leaves are in rosettes, lance-shaped, or round, and secrete mucilage. The flowers are solitary, two-lipped, spurred trumpets, the upper lip being two-lobed and the lower three-lobed, borne in summer.

✔ Help to control aphids
✔ Disease-free

✘ Prone to slug damage

CULTIVATION
Under glass, grow in an alpine house in a mixture of equal parts sphagnum moss and peat, in bright filtered light. Water freely during growth, sparingly in winter.

Out of doors, grow in wet peaty, poor soil in sun or part shade.

PROPAGATION
Seed should be surface-sown at 64°F (18°C) on damp sphagnum moss as soon as it is ripe. Divide in late winter.

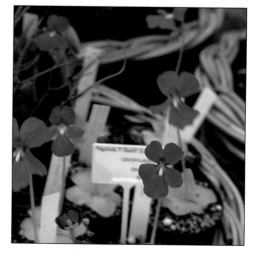

Pinguicula alpina

Zone 3
Height: 6in. (15cm) Spread: 4in. (10cm)

Pinguicula
'Hans'

Zone 10
Height: 6in. (15cm) Spread: 4in. (10cm)

Pinguicula lutea

Zone 8
Height: 20in. (50cm) Spread: 4in. (10cm)

PLANTAGO *(Plantaginaceae)*

Common names: Plantain

A genus of 200 species of annuals, biennials, evergreen perennials and shrubs from varied habitats worldwide. Some are very invasive. Their leaves are in basal rosettes, round or linear. The flowers are tiny, tubular, four-petalled, and borne in spikes in summer.

✔ Drought-tolerant
✔ Evergreen

✗ Highly allergenic
✗ Prone to aphid attack
✗ Self-seeds

CULTIVATION
Grow in acid to neutral, sharply-drained soil in sun. Protect against winter wet.

PROPAGATION
Seed should be sown in a cold frame in autumn. Divide in spring.

P

Plantago lanceolata
'Streaker'

Zone 6
Height: 16in. (40cm) Spread: 1ft. (30cm)

Plantago major
'Rosularis'

Zone 5
Height and spread: 1ft. (30cm)

Plantago major
'Rubrifolia'

Zone 5
Height and spread: 1ft. (30cm)

PLATYCERIUM *(Polypodiaceae)*
Common names: Staghorn fern

A genus of 15 species of evergreen rhizomatous, epiphytic ferns found in tropical and temperate rainforest in Asia, Africa, Australia and South America. They have sterile and fertile fronds, covered on both sides by small star-shaped hairs. The fertile fronds are wedge-shaped, leathery, gray-green, and forked, and are shed when old. The sterile fronds are oblong or round, lobed irregularly, and become brown as they age, forming a basket at the base of the plant. Spores form in patches underneath the fertile fronds. Some species form plantlets from runners from the nest.

✔ Evergreen ✔ Disease-free
✔ Handsome foliage

CULTIVATION
Under glass, grow epiphytically in a mix of equal parts of sphagnum moss, peat or leaf mould, and charcoal, in bright filtered light. Water freely during growth, and sparingly in winter. Mist daily during growth.

Out of doors, grow epiphytically on a tree in part shade.

PROPAGATION
Spores should be sown at 70°F (21°C) when ripe. Detach plantlets from runners.

Platycerium bifurcatum
A.G.M.

Zone 10
Height: 3ft. (90cm) Spread: 32in. (80cm)

Platycerium superbum

Zone 10
Height: 6ft. (2m) Spread: 5ft. (1.5m)

PLATYCODON *(Campanulaceae)*
Common names: Balloon flower

A genus of just one species of herbaceous perennial, *P. grandiflorus*, from mountain meadows and grassy slopes in East Asia. The leaves are ovate or lance-shaped, toothed, and bluish-green. The flowers are large, five-petalled open bells, borne in clusters in late summer. It dies down soon afterwards, and is very late to reappear, so mark its position carefully.

Platycodon grandiflorus
A.G.M.

Zone 4
Height: 2ft. (60cm) Spread: 1ft. (30cm)

✔ Good cut flowers ✘ Prone to slug damage
✔ Low allergen ✘ Needs to be staked
 ✘ Resent disturbance

CULTIVATION
Grow in reliably moist, deep, loamy, fertile well-drained soil in sun or part shade.

PROPAGATION
Seed should be sown in situ or in pots in a cold frame in spring. Detach rooted basal shoots or divide, in summer.

P

Platycodon grandiflorus
forma. *albus*

Zone 4
Height: 2ft. (60cm) Spread: 1ft. (30cm)

Platycocdon grandiflorus
'Fuji Pink'

Zone 4
Height: 2ft. (60cm) Spread: 1ft. (30cm)

PLECTRANTHUS *(Lamiaceae)*

Common names: None

A genus of 350 species of annuals, evergreen perennials and succulents and shrubs from Asia, Africa, Madagascar and Australasia. They are grown for their foliage and flowers. Their leaves are ovate or heart-shaped, scalloped, toothed or wavy-edged, aromatic, soft and furry in some species. The flowers are tubular, small, two-lipped, whorled, and are borne in terminal spikes, or panicles or racemes.

✔ Evergreen ✔ Pest-free
✔ Disease-free ✔ Handsome foliage

CULTIVATION
Under glass, grow in loam-based potting compost, in full light, but shaded from hot sun. Water freely during growth, moderately in winter.

CULTIVATION
Out of doors, grow in well-drained fertile soil in light shade.

PROPAGATION
Seed should be sown at 75°F (24°C) when ripe. Divide in spring. Stem-tip cuttings can be taken at any time.

Plectranthus argentatus

Zone 10
Height and spread: 3ft. (90cm)

Plectranthus ciliatus

Zone 10
Height: 18in. (45cm) Spread: indefinite
Invasive

Plectranthus ciliatus
'Sasha'

Zone 10
Height: 18in. (45cm) Spread: indefinite

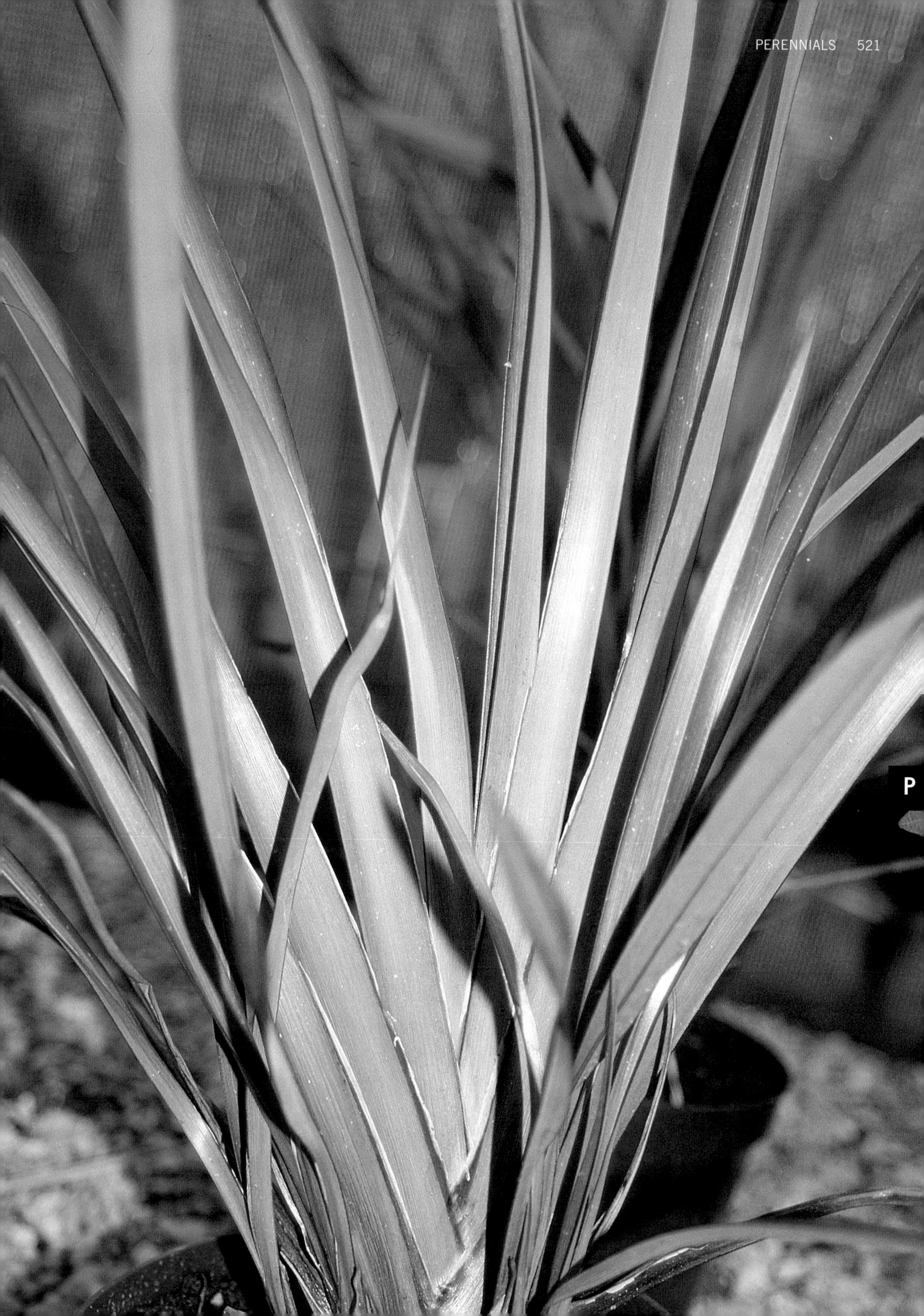

Plectranthus forsteri
(= coleiodes) 'Marginatus'

Zone 10
Height: 10in. (25cm) Spread: 3ft. (90cm)

Plectranthus fruticosus

Zone 10
Height: 6ft. (2m) Spread: 18in. (45cm)

Plectranthus fruticosus
'James'

Zone 10
Height: 6ft. (2m) Spread: 1ft. (30cm)

Plectranthus madagascarensis
(Mintleaf)
Zone 10
Height: 1ft. (30cm) Spread: indefinite
Invasive

Plectranthus oertendahlii
A.G.M.

Zone 10
Height: 8in. (20cm) Spread: 3ft. (90cm)

PLEIOBLASTUS *(Poaceae)*

Common names: None

A genus of 20 rhizomatous, evergreen bamboos from woodland and wood margins in Japan and China. Their leaves are lance-shaped or linear, with bristly white edges, and often tessellated and variegated. They are upright-growing, and the canes are woody. The flowers are insignificant, but seldom appear. Some types are highly invasive. The terminology of the genus is very confused.

✔ Evergreen

✔ Disease-free

✔ Pest-free

✘ Flowers insignificant

CULTIVATION
Grow in moist, fertile, well-drained soil in a sheltered corner in sun or part shade.

PROPAGATION
Separate rhizomes in spring, but do not allow to dry out until established.

Pleioblastus auricomus
'Variegatus'

Zone 7
Height and spread: 5ft. (1.5m)

Pleioblastus kongosanensis
'Aureostriatus'
Zone 7
Height: 6ft. (2m) Spread: indefinite
Invasive

Pleioblastus pygmaeus

Zone 7
Height: 16in. (40cm) Spread: 3ft. (90cm)

Pleioblastus vareigatus
A.G.M.

Zone 7
Height: 30in. (75cm) Spread: 4ft. (1.2m)

PLEIONE *(Orchidaceae)*
Common names: None

A genus of 20 species of epiphytic or terrestrial, herbaceous orchids from Northern India, South China and Taiwan. They have pseudo-bulbs that produce one or two folded elliptic or lance-shaped leaves. The flowers are generally solitary, and are borne mostly in spring, but can appear at any time.

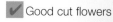 Good cut flowers

X Prone to slug damage
X Prone to aphid attack

CULTIVATION
Under glass, they like cool conditions, so grow in epiphytic or terrestrial orchid compost in shallow pans in an alpine house, cool greenhouse or on a windowsill in bright filtered light, with moderate humidity. Water freely in spring and summer, and dry off in winter, Repot annually before flowering time.

Out of doors, grow *P. formosana* in sharply-draining, leafy, humus-rich soil in a sheltered corner in part shade.

PROPAGATION
Divide annually when repotting, and discard old pseudobulbs.

Pleione
'Avalanche'

Zone 8
Height: 4in. (10cm) Spread: 10in. (25cm)

Pleione formosana
A.G.M.

Zone 8
Height: 6in. (15cm) Spread: 1ft. (30cm)

Pleione pleionoides
(= speciosa)

Zone 8
Height: 3in. (8cm) Spread: 4in. (10cm)

Pleione Shantung group

Zone 8
Height: 3in. (8cm) Spread: 4in. (10cm)

PODOPHYLLUM *(Berberidaceae)*

Common names: None

A genus of nine species of rhizomatous perennials from forest and scrubland in North America, and from the Himalayas to China and Taiwan. They are grown for their foliage and flowers. Each plant has one or two peltate, palmately-lobed leaves, veined conspicuously and often handsomely marked in brown or purple. The flowers are cup-shaped, terminal, solitary or in umbels, and are followed by large yellow or red fruits.

✔ Handsome foliage	✘ All parts poisonous
✔ Handsome fruits after flowering	✘ Prone to slug damage

CULTIVATION
Grow in moist, humus-rich leafy soil in part or full shade.

PROPAGATION
Seed should be sown in a cold frame as soon as ripe. Divide in spring or late summer.

Podophyllum hexandrum

Zone 6
Height: 18in. (45cm) Spread: 1ft. (30cm)

PODRANEA *(Bignoniaceae)*

Common names: Trumpet vine

A genus of just two species of evergreen climbers, one found in South Africa and one (*P. ricasoliana*) in Zimbabwe, in open woodland. Their leaves are in opposite pairs, and pinnate. The foxglove-like, trumpet-shaped flowers are borne in panicles from winter to summer, but they do not flower well in cold areas.

✔ Evergreen

CULTIVATION
Under glass, grow in loam-based potting compost in bright filtered light. Water with moderation during growth, and sparingly in winter.

Out of doors, grow in moist, fertile soil in part or deep shade. Prune after flowering by cutting back sideshoots to within 3 or 4 buds of permanent framework.

PROPAGATION
Seed should be sown at 64°F (18°C) in spring. Layer in spring. Semi-ripe cuttings may be taken in summer.

Podranea ricasoliana
(Pink Trumpet vine)

Zone 9
Height: 15ft. (5m) Spread: 3ft. (90cm)

P

POLEMONIUM *(Polemoniaceae)*
Common names: Jacob's ladder

A genus of 25 species of annuals and mainly rhizomatous perennials from varied habitats such as stony alpine, or even arctic, soils and damp meadows, woodland and stream sides in Eurasia and North and Central America. Their leaves are in basal clumps, asymmetrically pinnate, with many leaflets and smaller stem leaves. The flowers are tubular, or bell-, funnel- or saucer-shaped, with spreading mouths. They are solitary or borne in terminal or axillary cymes in late spring. Some are short-lived, and some need to be staked.

✔ Good cut flowers   ✘ Self-seeds
✔ Low allergen   ✘ Mildew prone
✔ Attracts bees

CULTIVATION
Grow in moist, well-drained soil (or sharply-drained in the case of alpine species) in sun or part shade. Dead-head to prevent self-seeding.

PROPAGATION
Seed should be sown in a cold frame in spring or autumn. Divide in spring.

Polemonium caeruleum

Zone 2
Height: 3ft. (90cm) Spread: 1ft. (30cm)
Requires to be staked

Polemonium caeruleum subsp.
caruleum var. *album*

Zone 2
Height: 3ft. (90cm) Spread: 1ft. (30cm)

Polemonium caeruleum
'Brise D'Anjou'
Zone 2
Height: 30in. (75cm) Spread: 1ft. (30cm)
Variegated foliage

Polemoniun carneum

Zone 6
Height: 18in. (45cm) Spread: 8in. (20cm)

Polemonium carneum
'Apricot Delight'

Zone 6
Height: 18in. (45cm) Spread: 20 cm.(8in.)

Polemonium
'Lambrook Mauve' A.G.M.

Zone 6
Height and spread: 18in. (45cm)

Polemonium 'Pam'

Zone 2
Height: 2ft. (60cm) Spread: 1ft. (30cm)
Variegated foliage

Polemonium pauciflorum

Zone 7
Height and spread: 20in. (50cm)
Short-lived

Polemonium reptans
'Blue Pearl'

Zone 4
Height: 28in. (70cm) Spread: 18in. (45cm)

POLYGALA *(Polygalaceae)*
Common names: Milkwort; Snakeroot; Seneca

A genus of 500 species of annuals, evergreen perennials, subshrubs and shrubs from a wide variety of habitats across the world, with the exception of the Arctic, New Zealand, and Polynesia. Their leaves are linear or rounded, whorled, or opposite, or alternate, and leathery. The pea-like flowers are borne in axillary or terminal racemes in summer or autumn.

✔ Evergreen   ✘ Prone to aphid attack under glass

CULTIVATION
Under glass, grow in loam-free potting compost in full light, with shade from hot sun, with good ventilation. Water freely during growth, sparingly in winter.

Out of doors, grow in sharply-draining, humus-rich, fertile soil in sun or part shade.

PROPAGATION
Seed of tender species should be sown at 59°F (15°C) in spring, and of hardy species in an open frame in autumn. Softwood cuttings may be taken in early summer and semi-ripe cuttings in mid to late summer.

P

Polygala chamaebuxus

Zone 6
Height: 6in. (15cm) Spread: 1ft. (30cm)

Polygala myrtifolia

Zone 9
Height: 8ft. (2.5m) Spread: 6ft. (2m)
Long-flowering

POLYGONATUM *(Convallariaceae)*
Common names: Solomon's seal

A genus of 50 species of rhizomatous perennials from woodland in temperate parts of North America and Eurasia. Their leaves are ovate or linear or elliptic, and in whorls, or opposite or alternate. The flowers are tubular or bell-shaped, pendent or upright, and solitary or in clusters along the lower side of the stem, and are followed by black or red fruits.

✔ Good cut flowers
✔ Have berries after flowering

✘ Prone to slug damage.
✘ All parts poisonous
✘ Self-seeds

CULTIVATION
Grow in moist, fertile, well-drained soil in sun or part shade.

PROPAGATION
Seed should be sown in a cold frame in autumn. Divide with care in spring, as the new shoots are very brittle.

Polygonatum x hybridum
A.G.M.

Zone 6
Height: 5ft. (1.5m) Spread: 1ft. (30cm)

Polygonatum multiflorum
'Striatum'

Zone 6
Height: 3ft. (90cm) Spread: 1ft. (30cm)

Polygonatum stewartianum

Zone 6
Height: 3ft. (90cm) Spread: 10in. (25cm)

POLYPODIUM *(Polypodiaceae)*
Common names: Polypody

A genus of 75 species of epiphytic or terrestrial ferns from sand dunes, walls, banks and rocks in the tropical and temperate regions of all three Americas, and elsewhere. Tropical forms tend to be epiphytic, whilst temperate types are generally terrestrial. Their fronds are lance-shaped, simple or pinnate or pinnatifid, and borne at random in two rows along the rhizomes. The sori are arranged in two rows either side of the midrib of the frond or pinna. Some species are invasive.

✔ Handsome foliage
✔ Disease-free

✔ Pest-free

Polypodium cambricum
'Omnilacerum Oxford'
Zone 6
Height: 2ft. (60cm) Spread: indefinite
Invasive

CULTIVATION
Under glass, grow in equal parts of charcoal, perlite and fine bark, or epiphytically, by wrapping the rhizomes in moss, and attaching to osmunda fiber or any other suitable medium, in bright filtered light. Water moderately during growth, sparingly in winter.

Out of doors, grow in a sheltered corner in sharply-drained humus-rich soil (alkaline in the case of *P.cambricum*) in sun or light shade.

PROPAGATION
Spores should be sown at 61°F (16°C) when ripe. Division can be done from spring to early summer.

P

Polypodium cambricum
'Semilacerum Robustum'
Zone 6
Height: 2ft. (60cm) Spread: indefinite
Invasive

Polypodium interjectum
'Cornubiense' A.G.M.

Zone 5
Height: 2ft. (60cm) Spread: 18in. (45cm)

Polypodium vulgare
'Cornubiense Grandiceps'
Zone 3
Height: 16in. (40cm) Spread: indefinite
Invasive.

POLYSTICHIUM *(Dryopteridaceae)*
Common names: Holly fern; Shield fern

A genus of 200 species of rhizomatous, terrestrial ferns found in varied habitats such as tropical forest and alpine cliffs across the world. They are mostly evergreen, and their fronds are lance-shaped, or pinnate to tripinnate, and spring from the rhizomes in shuttlecock-shaped crowns. The pinnae are lobed, and end in a bristle. The sori are on the underside, and are protected by an indusium. The terminology is very complex.

- ✔ Evergreen
- ✔ Drought-tolerant
- ✔ Handsome foliage

CULTIVATION
Grow in sharply-drained, humus-rich soil in part or full shade. Protect against severe winter wet. Remove dead fronds regularly.

PROPAGATION
Spores should be sown at 61°F (16°C) when ripe. Divide in spring. Fronds with bulbils can be detached in autumn.

Polystichium setiferum
A.G.M.

Zone 7
Height: 4ft. (1.2m) Spread: 3ft. (90cm)

P

Polystichium setiferum
'Congestum'

Zone 7
Height: 20in. (50cm) Spread: 2ft. (60cm)

Polystichium setiferum
Divisilobum Group

Zone 7
Height: 28in. (70cm) Spread: 3ft. (90cm)

Polystichium setiferum
'Divisilobum Densum' A.G.M.

Zone 7
Height: 28in. (70cm) Spread: 3ft. (90cm)

P

Polystichium setiferum
'Divisilobum Herrenhausen'

Zone 7
Height: 28in. (70cm) Spread: 3ft. (90cm)

Polystichium setiferum
'Pulcherrimum Bevis' A.G.M.

Zone 7
Height: 18in. (45cm) Spread: 3ft. (90cm)

Polystichium setiferum
'Wollaston'

Zone 7
Height: 2ft. (60cm) Spread: 3ft. (90cm)

PONTEDERIA *(Pontederiaceae)*

Common names: Pickerel weed

A genus of five species of marginal aquatic perennials from ditches and freshwater marshland in all three Americas. Their leaves are linear or lance-shaped, glossy, and submerged and floating. The flowers are tubular, two-lipped, and borne in terminal spikes in late summer; they do not open fully except in sun.

✔ Good cut flowers	✘ Resents disturbance
✔ Long-flowering	✘ Mildew prone
✔ Drought-tolerant	✘ Prone to slug damage
✔ Handsome foliage	
✔ Handsome seed-heads	
✔ Low allergen	

CULTIVATION
Grow in baskets of aquatic compost in water no deeper than 5in. (12cm) in sun.

PROPAGATION
Seed should be sown in moist compost outdoors as soon as it is ripe. Divide in late spring.

Pontederia cordata
A.G.M.

Zone 3
Height: 4ft. (1.2m) Spread: 32in. (80cm)

PORTULACARIA *(Portulacaceae)*

Common names: Elephant bush

A genus of either a single species with three variants, or of three species of perennial succulents from semi-arid regions of Central and South Africa, and Mozambique. The leaves and stems are fleshy. The flowers are inconspicuous, cup-shaped, and in racemes or cymes.

✔ Evergreen	✘ Flowers inconspicuous
✔ Disease-free	
✔ Handsome foliage	

CULTIVATION
Under glass, grow in grit-enhanced, loam-based potting compost in full light. Water freely during growth, keep almost dry in winter.

Out of doors, grow in very sharply-draining soil in sun or part shade.

PROPAGATION
Stem sections may be rooted with bottom heat in spring.

Portulacaria afra
'Foliisvariegatus'

Zone 9
Height: 10ft. (3m) Spread: 5ft. (1.5m)

POTENTILLA *(Rosaceae)*
Common names: Cinquefoil

A genus of 500 species of annuals, biennials, herbaceous perennials, subshrubs and shrubs found in habitats such as mountain screes and lowland meadows in the northern hemisphere. Their leaves are pinnate or three- to seven-palmate, veined, and wrinkled. The flowers are cup- or star- or saucer-shaped, five-petalled, borne singly or in cymes or panicles over a long period from spring to autumn.

✔ Long-flowering
✔ Attracts bees
✔ Disease-free
✔ Low allergen
✔ Pest-free

CULTIVATION
Grow well-drained soil, or sharply-draining in the case of alpine species, in sun.

PROPAGATION
Seed should be sown in a cold frame, or division carried out, in spring or autumn.

Potentilla argentea
Zone 4
Height: 20in. (50cm) Spread: 1ft. (30cm)

Potentilla atrosanguinea
Zone 5
Height: 3ft. (90cm) Spread: 2ft. (60cm)

Potentilla aurea
Zone 5
Height: 4in. (10cm) Spread: 8in. (20cm)

Potentilla 'Blazeaway'
Zone 5
Height: 18in. (45cm) Spread: 2ft. (60cm)

Potentilla 'Flamenco'
Zone 5
Height: 18in. (45cm) Spread: 2ft. (60cm)

Potentilla fruticosa
Zone 2
Height: 3ft. (90cm) Spread: 5ft. (1.5m)

P

Potentilla fruticosa
'Abbotswood Silver'

Zone 2
Height: 3ft. (90cm) Spread: 5ft. (1.5m)

Potentilla fruticosa 'Vilmoriniana'

Zone 2
Height: 3ft. (90cm) Spread: 5ft. (1.5m)
Handsome foliage

Potentilla
'Gloire de Nancy'

Zone 5
Height: 18in. (45cm) Spread: 2ft. (60cm)

Potentilla x hopwoodiana

Zone 5
Height: 30in. (75cm) Spread: 2ft. (60cm)

Potentilla megalantha
A.G.M.

Zone 5
Height: 1ft. (30cm) Spread: 6in. (15cm)

Potentilla nepalensis
(Nepalese cinqufoil)

Zone 5
Height: 3ft. (90cm) Spread: 2ft. (60cm)

P

Potentilla nepalensis
'Miss Willmott' A.G.M.

Zone 5
Height: 18in. (45cm) Spread: 2ft. (60cm)

Potentilla neumanniana
'Nana'

Zone 5
Height: 4in. (10cm) Spread: 1ft. (30cm)

Potentilla recta
'Warrenii'

Zone 4
Height: 2ft. (60cm) Spread: 18in. (45cm)

Potentilla rupestris

Zone 5
Height: 18in. (45cm) Spread: 1ft. (30cm)

Potentilla x tonguei

Zone 5
Height: 4in. (10cm) Spread: 1ft. (30cm)

Potentilla
'William Rollison' A.G.M.

Zone 5
Height: 18in. (45cm) Spread: 2ft. (60cm)

PRATIA *(Campanulaceae)*

Common names: None

A genus of 20 species of evergreen perennials from Asia, Africa, Australia, South America and New Zealand. They are prostrate and spread, making good ground cover. Their leaves are ovate to round, toothed, and alternate. The sessile flowers are small, but massed, solitary, two-lipped, white or blue stars, borne over a long period in summer.

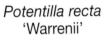

✔ Long-flowering
✔ Evergreen
✔ Good ground cover in shade

✖ Invasive
✖ Prone to slug damage

CULTIVATION
Grow in moist soil in part or deep shade.

PROPAGATION
Divide at any time, but do not allow divisions to dry out until established.

Pratia pedunculata
'County Park'

Zone 7
Height: 1in. (2.5cm) Spread: indefinite

PRIMULA *(Primulalaceae)*
Common names: None

A genus of 400 species of perennials from a variety of habitats such as marshland and bog to alpine regions, mainly in the northern hemisphere, although a few are found below the Equator. They are mostly herbaceous, but a few are evergreen. Their leaves are in basal rosettes, and are ovate or linear. The flowers are bell- or funnel-shaped, or tubular or salverform, and solitary or in racemes, umbels or whorls, and may be clustered among the leaves or held aloft on stiff stems. Some species have leaves, stems and calyces covered in a waxy, white farina. The classification of primulas is very complex, but for general purposes, they can be placed into four main groups:

Alpine primulas (A) are evergreen hybrid auriculas, which may be subdivided further into alpine, show, and border subgroups, and the first two are for addicts only and are not covered here. Border auriculas are robust garden plants, white with farina often and perfumed sometimes.

Candelabra primulas (C) are herbaceous perennials with flowers in tiers along the stem. They are best when naturalized in a bog or beside a stream.

Primrose-Polyanthus primulas (P) are also diverse, evergreen or herbaceous, perennial winter- to spring-flowering hybrids from complex crosses involving many species. Their flowers are borne in bunched clusters called fascicles, and umbels, or both on one plant. The distinction between the two groups has become fuzzy by virtue of interbreeding between the two, but the polyanthus group has umbels of flowers on tall stems, whereas the primrose group has solitary flowers in the basal rosette. Both are grown as biennial bedding plants.

Species primulas (S) these are grouped into 30 classes, the details of which need not concern us here.

✘ Prone to slug damage
✘ Prone to aphid attack
✘ Highly allergenic
✘ Foliage skin-irritant

CULTIVATION
Several categories of requirement are recognized:

Group 1: grow in moist, well-drained, humus-rich soil in sun or part shade.

Group 2: grow in moist, acid to neutral, humus-rich soil in part shade.

Group 3: grow in sharply-draining, moist, acid soil in part shade. Protect against winter wet.

Group 4: grow in an alpine house in gritty, loam-based, leafy, compost. Do not wet the foliage if mealy.

Group 5: grow in moist, sharply-draining, alkaline, humus-rich soil in sun with shade at mid-day.

Group 6: grow under glass in the house or a temperate glasshouse in a mix of four parts loam-based potting compost, 1 part grit and one part leaf mould, in bright filtered light. Water moderately during growth, keep just moist in winter.

PROPAGATION
Seed of tender species should be surface-sown in early spring, and of hardy species in an open frame as soon as ripe, or in early spring. Division can be carried out between autumn and early spring. Basal cuttings or offsets can be taken in autumn or early spring. Root cuttings may be taken during winter dormancy.

Primula auricula
hort. A.G.M. (A) (Group 1,4 or 5)

Zone 3
Height and spread: 8in. (20cm)

Primula bulleyana
A.G.M. (C) (Group 2)

Zone 6
Height and spread: 2ft. (60cm)

Primula capitata
(S) (Group 2)

Zone 5
Height: 16in. (40cm) Spread: 8in. (20cm)

Priimula chungensis
(C) (Group 2)

Zone 6
Height: 32in. (80cm) Spread: 2ft. (60cm)

Primula
'Cowichan Amethyst' (P) (Group 1)

Zone 5
Height: 10in. (25cm) Spread: 18in. (45cm)

Primula denticulata
A.G.M. (S) (Group 1 or 2)

Zone 5
Height and spread: 18in. (45cm)

Primula denticulata
var. *alba* (S) (Group 1 or 2)

Zone 5
Height and spread: 18in. (45cm)

Primula
'Inverewe' A.G.M. (C) (Group 2)

Zone 6
Height: 30in. (75cm) Spread: 2ft. (60cm)

Primula japonica
A.G.M. (C) (Group 2)

Zone 5
Height and spread: 18in. (45cm)

P

Primula japonica
'Alba' (C) (Group 2)

Zone 5
Height and spread: 18in. (45cm)

Primula japonica
'Miller's Crimson' (C) (Group 2)

Zone 5
Height: and spread: 18in. (45cm)

Primula juliae
(S) (Group 1,2 or 4)

Zone 5
Height: 4in. (10cm) Spread: 10in. (25cm)

Primula marginata
A.G.M. (A) (Group 4 or 5)

Zone 7
Height: 6in. (15cm) Spread: 1ft. (30cm)

Primula marginata 'Boothman's
Variety' (A) (Group 4 or 5)

Zone 7
Height and spread: 10in. (25cm)

Primula obconica
(Group 6)

Zone 8
Height: 16in. (40cm) Spread: 10in. (25cm)

Primula prolifera
A.G.M. (C) (Group 2)

Zone 6
Height and spread: 2ft. (60cm)

Primula pulverulenta
A.G.M. (C) (Group 2)

Zone 6
Height: 3ft. (90cm) Spread: 2ft. (60cm)

Primula rosea
A.G.M.(S) (Group 2)

Zone 6
Height and spread: 8in. (20cm)

Primula sikkimensis
(S) (Group 2)

Zone 6
Height: 3ft. (90cm) Spread: 2ft. (60cm)

Primula veris
A.G.M. Cowslip (S) (Group 1 or 2)

Zone 5
Height and spread: 10in. (25cm)

P

Primula vialii
A.G.M. (S)(Group 2)

Zone 7
Height: 2ft. (60cm) Spread: 1ft. (30cm)

Primula vulgaris
Primrose (S) (Group 2)

Zone 6
Height: 8in. (20cm) Spread: 1ft. (30cm)

PROTEA *(Proteaceae)*

Common names: None

A genus of 115 species of evergreen subshrubs or trees found in dry scrubland and rocky hills in tropical Africa and South Africa. Their leaves are leathery, simple, entire and alternate or spiraled. The flowers are solitary, terminal, and borne in cone-shaped clusters surrounded by petal-like bracts. Each floret is tubular, and splits into four terminal sepals to reveal the style.

✔ Evergreen
✔ Disease-free

✔ Pest-free

CULTIVATION

Under glass, grow in a mix of equal parts loam, charcoal, grit, and peat in full light. Water with moderation during spring and summer, and sparingly in winter.

Out of doors, grow in acid to neutral, poor, well-drained soil in sun. Prune for form and size in late winter or early spring.

PROPAGATION

Seed should be sown at 64°F (18°C) as soon as it is ripe or in spring. Semi-ripe cuttings can be taken in summer.

Protea cynaroides
(King protea)

Zone 9
Height and spread: 4ft. (1.2m)

P

PRUNELLA *(Lamiaceae)*

Common names: Self-heal

A genus of seven species of perennials from open woodland, sunny banks and dry grassland in Eurasia, North Africa and North America. They are semi-evergreen, prostrate and root as they go. Their leaves are basal or in tufts on the stems, ovate or linear, simple or lobed. The flowers are tubular, two-lipped, and borne in dense upright spikes in summer.

✔ Attracts bees
✔ Low allergen
✔ Disease-free
✔ Drought-tolerant

✗ Invasive
✗ Prone to slug damage
✗ Self-seeds

CULTIVATION

Grow in any soil in sun or part shade. Dead-head to prevent self-seeding.

PROPAGATION

Sow seed at 54°F (12°C) in spring. Divide in spring or autumn.

Prunella grandiflora

Zone 5
Height: 6in. (15cm) Spread: indefinite

Prunella grandiflora
'Pink Loveliness'

Zone 5
Height: 6in. (15cm) Spread: indefinite

PTERIS *(Pteridaceae)*
Common names: Brake; Dish fern; Table fern

A genus of 280 species of terrestrial, rhizomatous ferns found in subtropical and tropical regions across the world. They may be deciduous, semi-evergreen or evergreen. Their fronds are closely spaced, pinnatisect or pinnate to four-pinnate. Spores form along the frond edges, which bend over to protect them.

✔ Handsome foliage

CULTIVATION
Under glass, grow in a mix of equal parts sharp sand, charcoal, leaf mould and loam-based potting compost (and limestone chips in the case of *P. cretica*), in bright filtered light and high humidity. Water freely during growth, sparingly in winter.

Out of doors, grow in moist, well-drained, humus-rich soil in part or full shade.

PROPAGATION
Spores should be sown at 70°F (21°C) when ripe.

Pteris cretica
'Albolineata' A.G.M.

Zone 10
Height: 30in. (75cm) Spread: 2ft. (60cm)

Pteris ensiformis
'Evergemiensis'

Zone 10
Height and spread: 1ft. (30cm)

PTEROCEPHALUS *(Dipsacaceae)*

Common names: None

A genus of 25 species of annuals, perennials and evergreen shrubs from waste ground, rocky slopes and roadsides in tropical Africa to Central Asia, the Mediterranean region, the Himalayas and Western China. Their leaves are simple, entire or pinnatifid, and sometimes scalloped. The scabious-like flowers are tubular, solitary, and in dense flattened heads in summer, and are followed by papery seed-heads.

✔ Evergreen
✔ Disease-free
✔ Handsome seed-heads
✔ Pest-free

Pterocephalus perennis

Zone 6
Height: 3in. (8cm) Spread: 8in. (20cm)

CULTIVATION
Grow in any well-drained soil in sun.

PROPAGATION
Seed should be sown in a cold frame in autumn. Stem-tip cuttings can be taken in summer.

PULMONARIA *(Boraginaceae)*

Common names: Lungwort

A genus of 14 species of rhizomatous perennials from both alkaline and acid soils in stream sides, woodland and mountainous regions of Eurasia Their leaves are basal and stem, simple, ovate or oblong, hairy and often handsomely marked in silver or white. New leaves appear after flowering, and they are the most handsomely marked. The flowers are funnel-shaped, five-lobed, and borne in cymes in late winter or early spring.

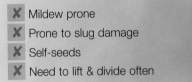

✔ Winter-flowering   ✘ Mildew prone
✔ Attracts bees   ✘ Prone to slug damage
✔ Low allergen   ✘ Self-seeds
                         ✘ Need to lift & divide often

CULTIVATION
Grow in moist, well-drained humus-rich soil in part or full shade,but *P. officinalis* tolerates full sun. Remove dead leaves regularly.

PROPAGATION
Seed of species should be sown in pans out of doors as soon as it is ripe. Divide cultivars after flowering or in autumn. Root cuttings can be taken in midwinter.

Pulmonaria angustifolia
A.G.M. (Cowslip lungwort)

Zone 3
Height: 1ft. (30cm) Spread: 18in. (45cm)

Pulmonaria
'Diana Clare'

Zone 3
Height: 1ft. (30cm) Spread: 18in. (45cm)

Pulmonaria longifolia
'Majeste'

Zone 6
Height: 1ft. (30cm) Spread: 18in. (45cm)

Pulmonaria officinalis
(Soldiers and sailors)

Zone 6
Height: 10in. (25cm) Spread: 2ft. (60cm)

Pulmonaria
'Opal' (PBR)

Zone 6
Height: 1ft. (30cm) Spread: 18in. (45cm)

Pulmonaria rubra
'Bowles' Red'

Zone 5
Height: 16in. (40cm) Spread: 3ft. (90cm)

Pulmonaria rubra
'David Ward'

Zone 5
Height: 16in. (40cm) Spread: 3ft. (90cm)

Pulmonaria saccharata
(Bethlehem sage)

Zone 3
Height: 1ft. (30cm) Spread: 2ft. (60cm)

PULSATILLA *(Ranunculaceae)*

Common names: None

A genus of 30 species of herbaceous perennials from alpine meadows in North America and Europe. Their leaves are fern-like, finely-dissected, and the flowers are cup- or bell-shaped, solitary, and borne in spring and early summer. The spherical seed-heads are silky-silver.

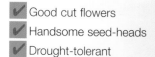

✔ Good cut flowers	✘ All parts poisonous
✔ Handsome seed-heads	✘ Sap is skin irritant
✔ Drought-tolerant	✘ Resent disturbance

CULTIVATION
Grow in very well drained soil in sun. Protect against winter wet.

PROPAGATION
Seed should be sown in a cold frame as soon as ripe. Root cuttings may be taken in winter.

Pulsatilla alpina
subsp. *apiifolia*

Zone 5
Height: 1ft. (30cm) Spread: 8in. (20cm)

P

Pulsatilla vulgaris
A.G.M.

Zone 5
Height and spread: 8in. (20cm)

Pulsatilla vulgaris
'Alba' A.G.M.

Zone 5
Height and spread: 20 cm.(8in.)

Pulsatilla vulgaris rosea

Zone 5
Height and spread: 8in. (20cm)

Pulsatilla vulgaris
var. *rubra*

Zone 5
Height and spread: 8in. (20cm)

PUSCHKINIA *(Hyacinthaceae)*
Common names: Striped squill

A genus of but a single species of bulbous perennial, *P. scilloides*, from damp grassland where snow has recently melted, in the Middle East. The leaves are basal, paired, semi-erect, and linear. The flowers are small, bell-shaped, pale blue with darker blue stripes, and borne in densely-packed racemes in spring.

✔ Drought-tolerant

CULTIVATION
Grow in any soil in sun or part shade.

PROPAGATION
Seed should be sown in a cold frame in summer or autumn. Separate offsets in summer as the foliage is dying down.

Puschkinia scilloides
var. *libanotica*

Zone 5
Height: 8in. (20cm) Spread: 2in. (5cm)

R

RAMONDA
RANUNCULUS
RAOULIA
RATIBIDA
REHMANNIA
REINECKEA
RHEUM
RHIPSALIDOPSIS
RHODANTHEMUM
RHODIOLA
RHODOCHITON
RHODOHYPOXIS
RICINUS
RODGERSIA
ROHDEA
ROMNEYA
ROMULEA
ROSCOEA
ROSULARIA
RUDBECKIA
RUELLIA
RUMEX
RUSSELIA
RUTA

RAMONDA *(Gesneriaceae)*
Common names: Rosette mullein

A genus of three species of evergreen perennials from cliff faces and rocky crevices in north-east Spain. The leaves are in basal rosettes, crinkled, hairy, and variously shaped. The flowers have between four and six petals, and are solitary, or borne in panicles in spring and early summer.

✓ Evergreen
✓ Handsome foliage

✗ Very prone to slug damage

CULTIVATION
Under glass, grow in an alpine house in a mix of equal parts loam, grit, and leaf mould in bright filtered light, with shade from hot sun.

Out of doors, grow in a wall on their side or in moist, sharply-drained soil in part shade. Do not allow to dry out, and protect against excessive winter wet.

PROPAGATION
Seed should be sown in a cold frame as soon as it is ripe, and do not prick out until several pairs of leaves have developed. Leaf cuttings can be rooted in early autumn.

Ramonda myconi

Zone 6
Height: 4in. (10cm) Spread: 6in. (15cm)

RANUNCULUS *(Ranunculaceae)*
Common names: Buttercup; Crowfoot

A genus of 400 species of annuals, biennials and perennials found in a range of habitats such as grassland, damp woodland, bogs, mountain screes, summer-dry sites and even in shallow water, in temperate regions of both hemispheres. They may be tuberous, rhizomatous or fibrous-rooted, and some spread by runners. The perennials are mostly herbaceous, but a few are evergreen. Their cultural needs vary. Their leaves may be in basal rosettes or stem-clasping, and vary considerably in shape from simple and entire to toothed, to palmate to pinnatisect. The flowers are cup- or bowl- or saucer-shaped, five-petalled, and borne singly or in panicles in spring.

✗ Sap is skin-irritant
✗ Mildew prone
✗ Prone to slug damage
✗ Highly allergenic

CULTIVATION REQUIREMENTS FALL INTO GROUPS AS FOLLOWS:
Group 1: grow woodland types in moist, humus-rich soil in part or full shade.

Group 2: grow in moist, fertile well-drained soil in sun or part shade

Group 3: grow high alpine types in an alpine house in a mix of equal parts grit, loam and leaf mould or out of doors in very sharply-drained soil in sun.

Group 4: grow aquatic types in the pool margin, or in baskets of aquatic compost in still water, no deeper than 9in. (22cm). *R. aquatilis* will grow in moving water, however, and can be planted up to 2ft. (60cm) deep.

Group 5: grow tuberous forms, which need a dry summer dormancy, in an alpine house or frame in the soil mix as detailed for Group 3.

PROPAGATION
Seed of alpines should be sown in an open frame while still green; germination may not occur for a year or two. Seed of perennials of all other types should be sown in a cold frame as soon as it is ripe, or they can be divided in spring. Tuberous species should be divided, and bulbils detached in those types where they form, in spring or autumn.

R

Ranunculus acris
'Flore Pleno' (Group 1 or 2)
Zone 5
Height: 3ft. (90cm) Spread: 10in. (25cm)
Good cut flower

Ranunculus aquatilis (Group 4)

Zone 5
Height: 1in. (2.5cm) Spread: indefinite
Evergreen

Ranunculus bulbosus
'F.M. Burton' (Group 2)
Zone 7
Height: 30in. (75cm) Spread: 1ft. (30cm)
Good cut flower

Ranunculus constantinopolitanus
(Group 1 or 2)

Zone 7
Height: 28in. (70cm) Spread: 1ft. (30cm)

Ranunculus cortusifolius (Group 2)

Zone 9
Height: 4ft. (1.2m) Spread: 2ft. (60cm)
Good cut flower/Flowers perfumed

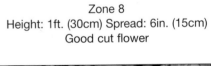

Ranuncukus creticus (Group 2)

Zone 8
Height: 1ft. (30cm) Spread: 6in. (15cm)
Good cut flower

Ranunculus ficaria
(Lesser celandine) (Group 1)
Zone 5
Height: 2in. (5cm) Spread: 18in. (45cm)
Highly invasive

Ranunculus ficaria
'Brazen Hussy' (Group 1)
Zone 5
Height: 2in. (5cm) Spread: 18in. (45cm)
Highly invasive

Ranunculus gramineus
A.G.M. (Group 2)
Zone 7
Height: 1ft. (30cm) Spread: 8in. (20cm)
Good cut flower

R

Ranunculus lingua (Group 4)

Zone 4
Height: 4ft. (1.2m) Spread: 6ft. (2m)
Good cut flower;

Ranunculus lyalii (Group 1 or 2)

Zone 6
Height: 3ft. (90cm) Spread: 14in. (35cm)
Evergreen

Ranunculus psilostachys
(Group 5)

Zone 6
Height: 1ft. (30cm) Spread: 8in. (20cm)

RAOULIA *(Asteraceae)*
Common names: None

A genus of 20 species of evergreen perennials from high screes and lowland rocky places in New Zealand. The spoon- or diamond-shaped or linear silvery leaves form dense cushions, or mats. The flowers are small, disc-shaped, solitary or in terminal clusters, borne in late spring or early summer. They like mild winters and cool summers.

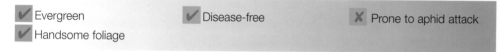

✔ Evergreen   ✔ Disease-free   ✘ Prone to aphid attack
✔ Handsome foliage

CULTIVATION
Under glass, grow in an alpine house in bright filtered light in a mix of equal parts loam, sharp sand and leaf mould, with a generous top dressing of grit. Water freely, but not over the foliage, during growth, but sparingly in winter.

Out of doors, grow in sharply-draining, humus-rich moist soil in full sun, but in part shade in warm dry gardens.

PROPAGATION
Mat-forming species should have rooted stems separated in spring. Cushion-forming species should have rosettes rooted in shade in early summer.

Raoulia hookeri

Zone 7
Height: 1in. (2.5cm) Spread: 8in. (20cm)

RATIBIDA *(Asteraceae)*
Common names: Mexican hat; Prairie cone flower

A genus of half a dozen species of biennials and perennials from North American and Mexican prairies. Their leaves are alternate, pinnatifid or pinnate. The daisy-like flowers have yellow ray florets and brown disc florets heaped into a central cone or boss, and are solitary and borne over long periods in summer.

✔ Long-flowering   ✘ Highly allergenic
✔ Good cut flowers
✔ Disease-free
✔ Pest-free
✔ Drought-tolerant

CULTIVATION
Grow in alkaline to neutral, dry well-drained soil in sun.

PROPAGATION
Seed should be sown in a cold frame in early spring. Young plants may be divided in spring, but old plants are too woody.

Ratibida columnaris

Zone 3
Height: 3ft. (90cm) Spread: 1ft. (30cm)

R

R

Ratibida pinnata

Zone 3
Height: 4ft. (1.2m) Spread: 18in. (45cm)

REHMANNIA *(Scrophulariaceae)*

Common names: Beverly-bells

A genus of nine species of perennials from stony sites and woodland in China. Their large leaves are in basal rosettes, oblong or obovate, toothed or lobed, hairy and veined. The foxglove-like flowers are two-lipped, and borne in terminal racemes over a long period in summer and autumn.

✔ Long-flowering	✘ Short-lived
✔ Drought-tolerant	✘ Prone to slug damage

CULTIVATION
Under glass, grow in loam-based potting compost in bright filtered light. Water freely during growth, keep just moist in winter.

Out of doors, grow in a sheltered corner in well-drained, humus-rich soil in sun.

PROPAGATION
Seed should be sown at 61°F (16°C) in late winter. Runners can be separated in spring. Root cuttings may be taken in late autumn or softwood cuttings of basal shoots in late spring.

R

Rehmannia elata
(Beverly-bells Rehmannia)

Zone 9
Height: 4ft. (1.2m) Spread: 20in. (50cm)

Rehmannia glutinosa
A.G.M.

Zone 9
Height and spread: 1ft. (30cm)

REINECKEA *(Convallariaceae)*
Common names: None

A genus of just a single species of rhizomatous, evergreen perennial, *R. carnea*, from sandy open areas or deciduous woodland in Japan and China. The leaves are linear or lance-shaped, arching, and borne in two ranks from the rhizomes. The flowers are shallow cups, with six reflexed segments, and are borne in dense terminal spikes in summer. They followed by red berries if summer is warm. It is shy-flowering where summers are cool.

✔ Evergreen	✖ Shy-flowering
✔ Has berries after flowering	✖ Prone to slug damage
✔ Flowers perfumed	

CULTIVATION
Grow in acid to neutral, moist, well-drained soil in part shade.

PROPAGATION
Seed should be sown in a cold frame as soon as it is ripe. Take rhizomes from the edges of clumps in spring.

Reineckea carnea

Zone 7
Height: 8in. (20cm) Spread: 2ft. (60cm)

RHEUM *(Polygonaceae)*
Common names: Rhubarb

A genus of 50 species of rhizomatous perennials from a variety of habitats such as scrubland, rocky slopes, marshy meadows and watersides in Eurasia, the Himalayas, and China. They are cultivated for their large handsome leaves and imposing flower spikes. Their leaf buds are often bright red, and the leaves are round, palmately-lobed or entire, red when young, veined and toothed. The flowers are tiny, star-shaped, and lack petals, but sometimes have colorful bracts, and are borne in panicles in mid and late summer.

✔ Architectural plants	✖ Flowers insignificant
✔ Handsome seed-heads	✖ Foliage poisonous
✔ Good for drying for winter	✖ Prone to slug damage

CULTIVATION
Grow in moist, deep, fertile soil in sun or part shade.

PROPAGATION
Seed should be sown in a cold frame in autumn. Division can be carried out in early spring.

Rheum
'Ace of Hearts'

Zone 7
Height and spread: 4ft. (1.2m)

Rheum palmatum
var. *tanguticum*

Zone 7
Height and spread: 6ft. (2m)

RHIPSALIDOPSIS *(Cactaceae)*
Common names: Easter cactus

A genus of perennial epiphytic cacti from Central and South America. The stem segments are three- or four-angled, or oblong, bristly, and flat. The flowers are borne on the segment ends in spring, and are bell-shaped.

 Evergreen

CULTIVATION
Under glass, grow in cactus compost or epiphytically on a tree branch in bright filtered light. Water freely during growth, very sparingly during dormancy.

Out of doors, grow on a tree branch in part shade.

PROPAGATION
Seed should be sown in heat in spring or summer. Stem cuttings may be taken in spring or summer.

Rhipsalidopsis rosea

Zone 10
Height and spread: 4in. (10cm)

RHODANTHEMUM *(Asteraceae)*
Common names: None

A genus of ten species of perennials and subshrubs from exposed rocky sites in North Africa, plus one species from Spain. Their three-lobed leaves are silvery in some species. The daisy-like flowers are solitary, have pronounced bracts, and are borne on tall, unbranched stems over long periods in spring and summer.

✔ Long-flowering ✖ Prone to aphid attack
✔ Drought-tolerant
✔ Handsome foliage
✔ Disease-free

CULTIVATION
Under glass, grow in loam-based potting compost in full light. Water freely during growth, but with moderation in winter.

Out of doors, grow in sharply-draining soil in sun.

PROPAGATION
Seed should be sown in a cold frame in spring.

Rhodanthemum
'African Eyes'

Zone 8
Height: 6in. (15cm) Spread: 4in. (10cm)

R

Rhodanthemum catananche

Zone 8
Height: 6in. (15cm) Spread: 1ft. (30cm)

Rhodanthemum gayanum

Zone 8
Height and spread: 1ft. (30cm)

Rhodanthemum hosmariense
A.G.M.

Zone 8
Height and spread: 1ft. (30cm)

R

RHODIOLA *(Crassulaceae)*

Common names: Roseroot

A genus of 50 species of rhizomatous perennials from sunny, stony habitats across the northern hemisphere. They have brown, scaly basal leaves and thick, stiff stems bearing oval, triangular or lance-shaped, fleshy, gray-green alternate leaves. The flowers are small stars and are borne in dense, round, terminal racemes or corymbs in early summer.

✔ Drought-tolerant ✘ Prone to aphid attack

✔ Handsome foliage

CULTIVATION

Grow in any fertile soil in sun.

PROPAGATION

Seed should be sown in a cold frame in spring or autumn. Divide in spring or early summer. Leaf cuttings may be taken in summer.

Rhodiola pachyclados

Zone 4
Height: 6in. (15cm) Spread: 1ft. (30cm)

Rhodiola rosea

Zone 1
Height: 1ft. (30cm) Spread: 8in. (20cm)

Rhodiola wallichiana

Zone 6
Height and spread: 1ft. (30cm)

RHODOCHITON *(Scrophulariaceae)*

Common names: None

A genus of only three species of herbaceous climbing perennials from Mexican woodland. The twining leaf stalks bear simple, alternate, toothed, heart-shaped leaves. The pendent, reddish-black flowers have five rounded segments, inflated calyces and prominent long-tubed corollas, borne over a long period from summer to autumn.

✔ Long-flowering

✔ Handsome foliage

CULTIVATION

Under glass, grow in loam-based potting compost in full light, but with shade from midday sun. Water freely during growth, but keep just moist in winter. Repot in spring when needed.

Out of doors, grow in moist, well-drained soil in sun.

PROPAGATION

Seed should be sown at 64°F (18°C) as soon as it is ripe, or in spring.

Rhodochiton atrosanguineus
A.G.M.

Zone 9
Height: 10ft. (3m) Spread: 2ft. (60cm)

R

RHODOHYPOXIS *(Hypoxidaceae)*

Common names: None

A genus of six species of cormous, herbaceous perennials from open meadows in regions of eastern South Africa and Swaziland that have heavy rainfall in summer. Their leaves are basal, hairy and lance-shaped. The flowers are flat, solitary, and have six-tepals deployed in two rows of three, inner and outer, fused at their bases to form a tube, and borne over long periods in summer.

Rhodohypoxis baurii
A.G.M.

Zone 8
Height and spread: 4in. (10cm)

✔ Long-flowering

✔ Handsome foliage

✔ Disease-free

CULTIVATION
Under glass, grow in a mix of equal parts ericaceous compost, sharp sand and leaf mould in full light. Water freely during growth, keep just moist in winter.

Out of doors, grow in acid, humus-rich well-drained soil in sun. Protect against winter wet.

PROPAGATION
Seed should be sown at 54°F (12°C) as soon as it is ripe, or in spring. Divide, or separate offsets, in spring.

RICINUS *(Euphorbiaceae)*

Common names: None

A genus of but a single species of evergreen monoecious, suckering subshrub, *R. communis*, from stony slopes, wasteland and roadsides in north-east Africa and western Asia. The leaves are large, shiny and palmately-lobed. The flowers are small, cup-shaped, and borne in spikes in summer. The stigma is red in both female and male plants. All parts, but the seeds especially, contain a deadly toxin, ricin.

Ricinus communis
'Impala'

Zone 9
Height: 4ft. (1.2m) Spread: 12ft. (4m)

✔ Handsome foliage   ✘ All parts very poisonous

✔ Disease-free   ✘ Foliage is skin-irritant

✘ Invasive

CULTIVATION
Under glass, grow in loam-based potting compost in full light. Water freely during growth, sparingly in winter.

Out of doors, grow in well-drained, humus-rich fertile soil in sun.

PROPAGATION
Seed should be soaked for 24 hours and sown at 70°F (21°C) in spring.

RODGERSIA *(Saxifragaceae)*

Common names: None

A genus of six species of rhizomatous perennials from stream sides, moist woodland and scrubland in the mountains of Japan, Korea, China and Burma. Their handsome leaves are large, pinnate or palmate, basal, and tinted brown or red in some species. The flowers are small, star-shaped, lack petals, and are borne in pyramidal panicles in summer. They are followed by brown fruits.

✔ Handsome foliage   ✘ Prone to slug damage

✔ Architectural plants

✔ Have berries after flowering

CULTIVATION
Grow in moist, humus-rich soil in a sheltered corner in sun or part shade.

PROPAGATION
Seed should be sown in a cold frame, or division carried out, in spring.

Rodgersia aeculifolia
A.G.M.

Zone 5
Height: 6ft. (2m) Spread: 3ft. (90cm)

Rodgersia pinnata
'Alba'

Zone 5
Height: 3ft. (90cm) Spread: 4ft. (1.2m)

Rodgersia pinnata
'Elegans'

Zone 5
Height: 3ft. (90cm) Spread: 4ft. (1.2m)

Rodgersia pinnata
'Rosea'

Zone 5
Height: 3ft. (90cm) Spread: 4ft. (1.2m)

Rodgersia pinnata
'Superba' A.G.M.

Zone 5
Height: 3ft. (90cm) Spread: 4ft. (1.2m)

Rodgersia podophylla
A.G.M.

Zone 5
Height: 5ft. (1.5m) Spread: 6ft. (2m)

ROHDEA *(Convallariaceae)*

Common names: None

A genus of a single species of rhizomatous perennial, *R. japonica*, from woodland in Japan and south-west China. The handsome leaves are in a basal rosette, fleshy, and inversely lance-shaped. The flowers are narrow bells, greenish-white, and borne in dense spikes in early spring.

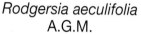 Handsome foliage ✗ Prone to slug damage

CULTIVATION
Grow in moist, deep soil in part or full shade.

PROPAGATION
Seed should be sown in a cold frame in autumn. Divide in spring.

R

Rohdea japonica 'Talbot Manor'

Zone 7
Height and spread: 8in. (20cm)
Foliage variegated

R

ROMNEYA *(Papaveraceae)*
Common names: Tree poppy; Maatilija poppy

A genus of two species of suckering, perennial subshrubs from scrubland and chaparral in south-eastern U.S.A., and northern Mexico. Their leaves are pinnatisect or pinnatifid, glaucous, and alternate. The poppy-like flowers are large, white, cup-shaped, with a central boss of yellow, and are solitary, and borne over a long period in summer. They can be difficult to establish, but are rampant when happy.

✔ Long-flowering ✗ Requires to be staked
✔ Handsome foliage ✗ Invasive
✔ Architectural plant ✗ Prone to slug damage
✗ Resents disturbance

CULTIVATION
Grow in well-drained, fertile soil in a sheltered corner in sun.

PROPAGATION
Seed should be sown in a cold frame in autumn, or divide in spring, but this is not tolerated well.

Romneya coulteri
A.G.M.

Zone 7
Height: 8ft. (2.5m) Spread: indefinite

ROMULEA *(Iridaceae)*
Common names: None

A genus of 80 species of cormous perennials from coastal cliff tops and mountainous regions of Europe, North Africa and South Africa. Their leaves are basal, linear, channeled and arching. Their crocus-like flowers are funnel-shaped, appear in spring. They may not open until mid-day, and close again in the evening.

✔ Trouble-free
✔ Pest-free

CULTIVATION
Under glass, grow in loam-based potting compost in full light; water moderately during growth and keep dry during their summer dormancy.

Out of doors, grow in well-drained fertile soil in sun.

PROPAGATION
Remove offsets whilst dormant, or sow seed at 54°F (12°C) in autumn.

Romulea bulbocodium

Zone 7
Height: 4in. (10cm) Spread: 2in. (5cm)

ROSCOEA *(Zingiberaceae)*
Common names: None

A genus of 18 species of tuberous perennials from slopes, thin forests and meadows in China and the Himalayas. Their leaves are stem, arching, and linear or obovate or ovate. Their orchid-like flowers are hooded, two-lipped, surrounded by bracts, and are produced from the leaf axils in summer or autumn—over a long period in the case of *R. purpurea*—it is very late to reappear (early summer). They prefer cool gardens.

✔ Disease-free ✗ Prone to slug damage

CULTIVATION
Plant tubers 6in. (15cm) deep in winter or early spring, in moist, humus-rich, well-drained soil in part shade.

PROPAGATION
Seed should be sown in a cold frame as soon as it is ripe. Divide tubers in spring.

R

Roscoea auriculata

Zone 6
Height: 2ft. (60cm) Spread: 8in. (20cm)

Roscoea
'Beesiana'

Zone 6
Height: 18in. (45cm) Spread: 1ft. (30cm)

Roscoea cautleoides
A.G.M. (yellow form)

Zone 6
Height: 2ft. (60cm) Spread: 8in. (20cm)

Roscoea cautleoides
A.G.M. (purple form)
Zone 6
Height: 1ft. (30cm) Spread: 8in. (20cm)
Handsome foliage

Roscoea purpurea

Zone 6
Height: 3ft. (90cm) Spread: 1ft. (30cm)

Roscoea wardii

Zone 6
Height and spread: 1ft. (30cm)

ROSULARIA *(Crassulaceae)*

Common names: None

A genus of 25 perennial succulents from the Iberian peninsula, and from Asia Minor to the Himalayas. They are rosette-forming, and the leaves are ovoid and hairy. The star-shaped flowers are saucer-shaped, and borne in trailing racemes in spring.

✔ Evergreen
✔ Long-flowering
✔ Drought-tolerant

✘ Prone to slug damage

CULTIVATION
Grow in sharply-drained, humus-rich soil in sun.

PROPAGATION
Separate offsets in spring.

Rosularia sedoides

Zone 7
Height: 2in. (5cm) Spread: 8in. (20cm)

RUDBECKIA *(Asteraceae)*

Common names: Coneflower; Black-eyed Susan

A genus of 20 species of annuals and rhizomatous perennials from thin woodland and moist meadowland in North America. Their leaves are simple or pinnatifid or pinnate, toothed, and veined. The daisy-like flowers have yellow ray florets and brown, black or green disc florets, and are solitary and borne over a long period from summer to autumn.

✔ Long-flowering   ✘ Highly allergenic

✔ Good cut flowers   ✘ Prone to slug damage

✔ Attracts bees

CULTIVATION
Grow in reliably moist but well-drained soil in sun or part shade.

PROPAGATION
Seed should be sown in a cold frame in early spring. Divide in spring or autumn.

Rudbeckia fulgida var. sullivantii 'Goldsturm' A.G.M.
(Showy coneflower)
Zone 4
Height: 2ft. (60cm) Spread: 18in. (45cm)

Rudbeckia 'Herbstonne'
Zone 3
Height: 6ft. (2m) Spread: 3ft. (90cm)

Rudbeckia hirta
Zone 4
Height: 3ft. (90cm) Spread: 18in. (45cm)
Short-lived

R

Rudbeckia laciniata 'Goldquelle' A.G.M.
Zone 3
Height: 3ft. (90cm) Spread: 18in. (45cm)

Rudbeckia maxima
(Great coneflower)
Zone 7
Height: 5ft. (1.5m) Spread: 1ft. (30cm)

Rudbeckia subtomentosa
(Sweet coneflower)
Zone 5
Height: 28in. (70cm) Spread: 2ft. (60cm)

R

RUELLIA *(Acanthaceae)*
Common names: Monkey plant; velvet plant

A genus of 150 species of evergreen perennials, subshrubs and shrubs from temperate and tropical America and Africa, and temperate Asia. Their leaves are entire, and opposite. The flowers are funnel-shaped, arise from the leaf axils, and may be solitary or in terminal panicles. They vary widely in hardiness.

✔ Evergreen   ✔ Disease-free

✔ Handsome foliage   ✔ Pest free

CULTIVATION
Under glass, grow tropical species in loam-free potting compost in high humidity and bright filtered light. Water freely during growth, but with moderation in winter.

Out of doors, grow hardy forms in moist, humus-rich, fertile soil in sun or part shade.

PROPAGATION
Seed should be sown at 75°F (24°C) in spring. Softwood cuttings may be taken in spring or early summer.

Ruellia graezicans

Zone 10
Height: 2ft. (60cm) Spread: 18in. (45cm)

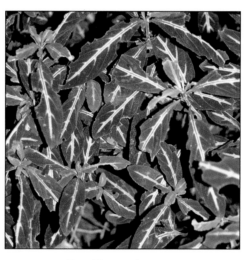

Ruellia makoyana
A.G.M.

Zone 10
Height: 2ft. (60cm) Spread: 18in. (45cm)

RUMEX *(Polygonaceae)*
Common names: Dock

A genus of 200 species of annuals, biennials and perennials from a variety of habitats such as stream sides, mountains, waste-land and cultivated ground in the temperate northern hemisphere. The perennials are usually tap-rooted. Their leaves are basal simple and of various shapes. The flowers are tiny, star-shaped, and are borne in whorls on dense terminal racemes or panicles in summer. They are followed by red-brown fruits. Some species are very invasive.

✔ Handsome foliage   ✘ All parts poisonous

✔ Handsome seed-heads   ✘ Foliage is skin-irritant

✔ Good for drying for winter   ✘ Self-seeds

                             ✘ Highly allergenic

CULTIVATION
Grow in any fertile well-drained soil in sun. Dead-head to prevent self-seeding.

PROPAGATION
Seed should be sown in situ in spring.

R

Rumex sanguineus
(Bloody dock; Red-veined dock)

Zone 6
Height: 32in. (80cm) Spread: 1ft. (30cm)

RUSSELIA *(Scrophulariaceae)*

Common names: Coral plant; Firecracker plant

A genus of 50 species of evergreen subshrubs and shrubs found at forest edges from Mexico, Cuba and Columbia. Their leaves are elliptic, scaly, and whorled or opposite. The flowers are tubular, and are solitary or borne in axillary cymes from spring to autumn.

✔ Long-flowering	✔ Free of pests
✔ Disease-free.	✔ Evergreen

CULTIVATION
Under glass, grow in loam-based potting compost in bright filtered or even full light. Water with moderation during growth and sparingly in winter.

Out of doors, grow in well-drained humus-rich soil in a sheltered corner in sun. Prune by dead-heading and for symmetry and size in spring.

PROPAGATION
Separate rooted layers in spring. Softwood cuttings may be taken at any time of year.

Russelia equisetiformis
A.G.M.

Zone 9
Height: 5ft. (1.5m) Spread: 8ft. (2.5m)

RUTA *(Rutaceae)*

Common names: Rue

A genus of eight specie of herbaceous perennials, subshrubs and shrubs from dry stony habitats in the Canary Islands, circum-Mediterranean regions and south-west Asia. Their leaves are alternate or opposite, aromatic, ovate or rounded, and pinnate or pinnatisect. The flowers are yellow, four- to five–petalled, fringed and borne in cymes an summer. The foliage may be used very sparingly as a culinary herb, but is poisonous in quantity and contact causes photo-dermatitis.

✔ Foliage aromatic	✘ Foliage poisonous
✔ Evergreen	✘ Foliage is skin-irritant
✔ Drought-tolerant	
✔ Handsome foliage	
✔ Culinary vegetable	

CULTIVATION
Grow in moderately fertile sharply-draining soil in sun.

PROPAGATION
Seed should be sown in a cold frame in spring. Semi-ripe cuttings may be rooted in summer.

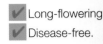

Ruta graveolens

Zone 5
Height: 3ft. (90cm) Spread: 32in. (80cm)

Ruta graveolens
'Jackman's Blue' A.G.M.

Zone 5
Height: 3ft. (90cm) Spread: 32in. (80cm)

Ruta graveolens
'Variegata'

Zone 5
Height: 3ft. (90cm) Spread: 32in. (80cm)

SAGITTARIA
SAINTPAULIA
SALVIA
SANDERSONIA
SANGUINARIA
SANGUISORBA
SANSEVIERIA
SANTOLINA
SAPONARIA
SARMIENTA
SARRACENIA
SASA
SAUROMATUM
SAURURUS
SAXIFRAGA
SCABIOSA
SCHIZOSTYLIS
SCHLUMBERGERA
SCHOENOPLECTUS
SCILLA
SCOLIOPUS
SCOPOLIA
SCROPHULARIA
SCUTELLARIA
SEDUM

SELAGINELLA
SELINUM
SEMIAQUILEGIA
SEMPERVIVUM
SENECIO
SERRATULA
SESELI
SESLERIA
SIDALCEA
SILENE
SILPHIUM
SINNINGIA
SISYRINCHIUM
SMILACINA
SOLANUM
SOLENOPSIS
SOLENOSTEMON
SOLIDAGO
x SOLIDASTER
SPARAXIS
SPHAERALCEA
SPIRANTHES

STACHYS
STERNBERGIA
STENOTAPHRUM
STIPA
STOKESIA
STRELITZIA
STREPTOCARPUS
STROBILANTHES
STROMANTHE
STYLOPHORUM
SUCCISA
SUTERA
SYMPHYANDRA
SYMPHYTUM

S

SAGITTARIA *(Alismataceae)*

Common names: Arrowhead

A genus of 20 species of submerged marginal and aquatic marginal annuals and tuberous perennials from muddy shores and shallow, still water in tropical and temperate Eurasia, and the Americas. Their leaves are arrow-shaped, or elliptic or linear or lance-shaped, submerged and aerial. The flowers are three-petalled saucers, and borne in whorls in panicles or racemes in summer.

✔ Disease-free

✖ Waterfowl eat tubers
✖ Self-seeds

CULTIVATION
Grow in water less than 1ft. (30cm) deep in sun. Cut back in late summer, and dead-head to prevent self-seeding.

PROPAGATION
Seed should be sown as soon as ripe in containers standing in shallow water. Separate runners, or collect tuber divisions in spring.

Sagittaria latifolia

Zone 7
Height: 4ft. (1.2m) Spread; 3ft. (90cm)

Sagittaria sagittifolia

Zone 7
Height: 3ft. (90cm) Spread: indefinite
Invasive

SAINTPAULIA *(Gesneriaceae)*

Common names: African violet

A genus of evergreen perennials from tropical East Africa where they are found on stream sides, banks and among rocks and even as epiphytes on trees. Their leaves are in rosettes, semi-succulent, elliptic or round. The flowers have five petals, two small upper and three large lower, and are solitary or in cymes throughout the year.

✔ Evergreen
✔ Long-flowering

✖ Prone to aphid attack
✖ Mildew prone

CULTIVATION
Under glass, grow at between 64-75°F (18-24°C) in loam-free potting compost in bright filtered light, with shade from mid-day sun, and high or moderate humidity—twelve hours of light (natural or artificial) and the above temperatures are necessary for continuous flowering. Water moderately during growth. Repot (but do not pot on), annually in similarly- sized pots and identical compost.

PROPAGATION
Seed should be sown at 75°F (24°C) as soon as it is ripe, or in early spring. Suckers or leaf cuttings a can be rooted in summer.

Saintpaulia ionantha

Zone 10
Height: 4in. (10cm) Spread: 6in. (15cm)

SALVIA *(Lamiaceae)*
Common names: Sage

A genus of 900 species of annuals, biennials and shrubs and perennials from all parts of the tropical and temperate world except, hot humid regions. They grow in sunny, dry sites such as rocky slopes, meadows, woodland and also in moist woodland. The perennials may be rhizomatous, fibrous-rooted or tuberous, herbaceous or evergreen. Their leaves may be basal or stem, and are entire, simple to pinnate, toothed, notched or scalloped, and opposite; they may be woolly, hairy, silvery, or aromatic. The flowers are two-lipped, the upper ones hooded and erect and the lower ones forked and spreading. They may be funnel- or bell-shaped or tubular, and have ovate or diamond-shaped colorful bracts; they are borne in terminal spikes or racemes, over long periods in summer, or are remontant. Some species attract bees, some are culinary herbs, some are short-lived. Taller species may require to be staked. They vary also in their degree of hardiness from tender to fully hardy.

 Long-flowering
 Low allergen
 Attracts bees

✗ Prone to slug damage
✗ Prone to aphid attack

Salvia aethiopis

Zone 7
Height and spread: 2ft. (60cm)

CULTIVATION

Under glass, grow tender species in any well-drained potting compost in full light with shade from hot sun. Water freely during growth, sparingly in winter except *SS. canariensis*, *leucantha* and *elegans*, all of which need moderate watering in winter. Humidity should be low to moderate.

Out of doors, grow in moist, humus-rich, well-drained soil (or sharply-drained in the case of species with woolly or hairy leaves) in sun or light shade. Protect tender and woolly-leaved species against cold drying winds and winter wet. *S. splendens* is usually grown as an annual in cold regions.

PROPAGATION

Sow seed of perennials in a cold frame, or divide in spring. Basal or softwood cuttings may be taken in spring or early summer, or semi-ripe cuttings may be rooted with bottom heat in late summer or autumn.

Salvia africana

Zone 9
Height and spread: 3ft. (90cm)

Salvia argentea A.G.M.

Zone 5
Height: 3ft. (90cm) Spread: 2ft. (60cm)
Handsome foliage/Short-lived

Salvia aurea
(africana-lutea)

Zone 9
Height and spread: 3ft. (90cm)

Salvia azurea

Zone 4
Height: 4ft. (1.2m) Spread: 3ft. (90cm)
Requires staking

Salvia buchananii A.G.M.

Zone 9
Height: 1ft. (30cm) Spread: indefinite
Invasive

S

Salvia cacaliifolia A.G.M.

Zone 9
Height: 4ft. (1.2m) Spread: 30 cm.(1 ft)
Requires staking

Salvia coccinea

Zone 8
Height: 30in. (75cm) Spread: 1ft. (30cm)

Salvia coccinea
'Coral Nymph'

Zone 8
Height: 30in. (75cm) Spread: 1ft. (30cm)

Salvia confertiflora

Zone 9
Height: 4ft. (1.2m) Spread: 2ft. (60cm)

Salvia darcyi

Zone 8
Height: 3ft. (90cm) Spread: 2ft. (60cm)

Salvia farinacea

Zone 9
Height: 2ft. (60cm) Spread: 1ft. (30cm)

Salvia farinacea
'Snowball'

Zone 9
Height: 2ft. (60cm) Spread: 1ft. (30cm)

Salvia farinacea
'Victoria' A.G.M.

Zone 9
Height: 2ft. (60cm) Spread: 1ft. (30cm)

Salvia forskaolii

Zone 7
Height: 3ft. (90cm) Spread: 18in. (45cm)

S

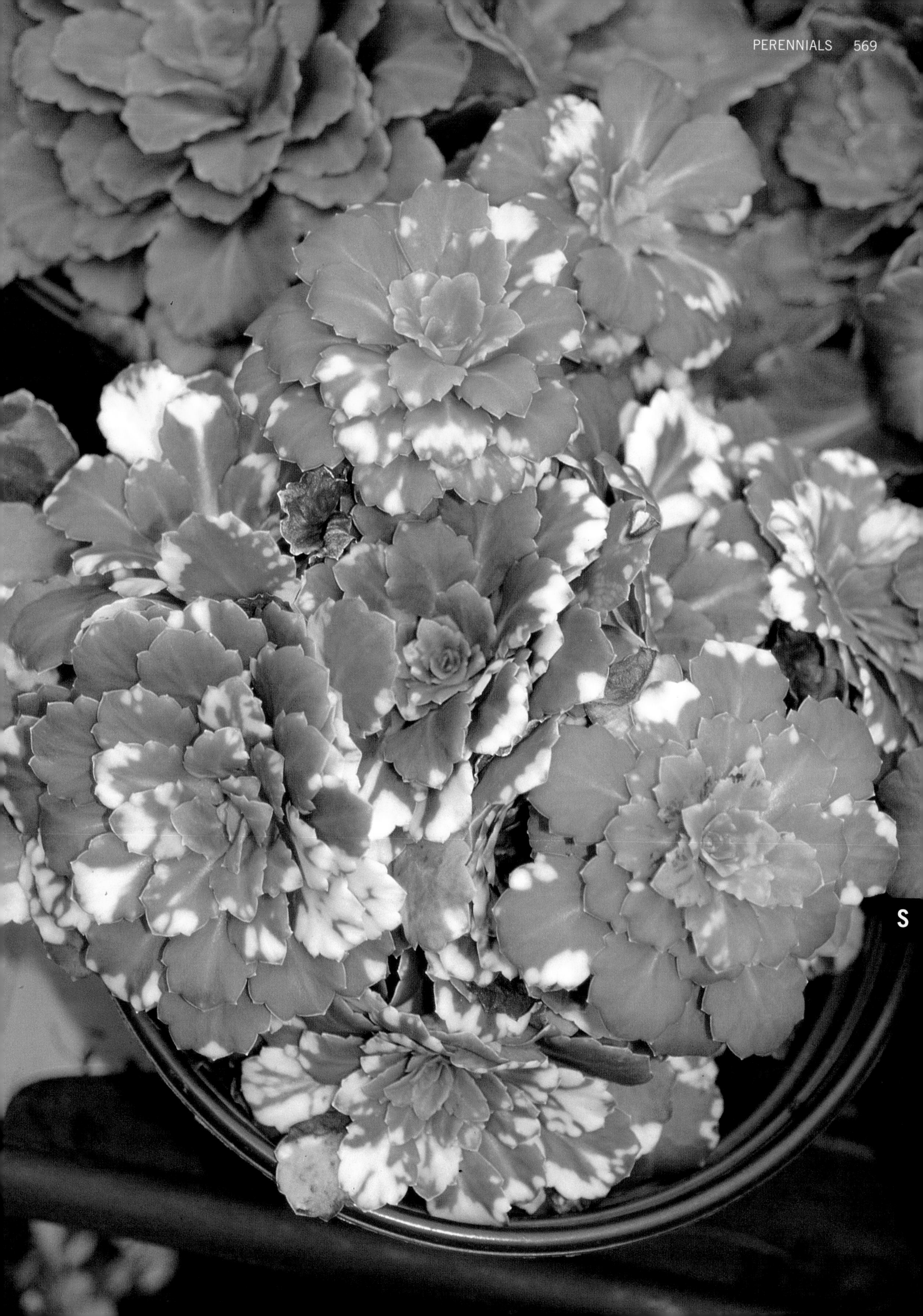

Salvia fulgens
A.G.M.

Zone 9
Height and spread: 1ft. (30cm)

Salvia glutinosa

Zone 5
Height: 3ft. (90cm) Spread: 2ft. (60cm)

Salvia greggii

Zone 9
Height and spread: 30in. (75cm)

Salvia greggii 'Desert Blaze'

Zone 9
Height and spread: 30in. (75cm)
Foliage variegated

Salvia greggii
'Peach' A.G.M.

Zone 9
Height and spread: 30in. (75cm)

Salvia involucrata 'Bethellii'

Zone 9
Height 5ft. (1.5m) Spread: 3ft. (90cm)
Requires staking

Salvia ionvolucrata 'Boutin' A.G.M.

Zone 9
Height: 5ft. (1.5m) Spread: 3ft. (90cm)
Requires staking

Salvia leucantha
A.G.M.

Zone 10
Height and spread: 3ft. (90cm)

Salvia microphylla
Zone 9
Height and spread: 4ft. (1.2m)

S

Salvia microphylla var. *neurepia*

Zone 9
Height and spread: 4ft. (1.2m)

Salvia nemorosa
'Ostfriedland' A.G.M.

Zone 5
Height: 3ft. (90cm) Spread: 2ft. (60cm)

Salvia nemorosa
'Pusztaflamme' A.G.M.

Zone 5
Height: 3ft. (90cm) Spread: 2ft. (60cm)

Salvia nipponica 'Fuji Snow'

Zone 5
Height and spread: 30in. (75cm)
Foliage variegated

Salvia officinalis

Zone 5
Height and spread: 18in. (45cm)
Culinary herb/Foliage aromatic/Evergreen

Salvia officinalis 'Icterina' A.G.M.
Zone 5
Height and spread: 18in. (45cm)
Handsome foliage/Foliage aromatic/
Evergreen/Culinary herb

Salvia officinalis 'Kew Gold' A.G.M.
Zone 5
Height and spread: 18in. (45cm)
Foliage aromatic/Culinary vegetable/
Evergreen/Handsome foliage

Salvia officinalis 'Tricolor' A.G.M.
Zone 5
Height and spread: 18in. (45cm)
Foliage aromatic/Culinary vegetable/
Evergreen/Handsome foliage

Salvia patens A.G.M.
Gentian salvia

Zone 8
Height: 2ft. (60cm) Spread: 18in. (45cm)

S

Salvia patens 'Cambridge Blue'
A.G.M. (Gentian salvia)

Zone 8
Height: 2ft. (60cm) Spread: 18in. (45cm)

Salvia patens
'White Trophy'

Zone 8
Height: 2ft. (60cm) Spread: 18in. (45cm)

Salvia pratensis
Haematodes Group A.G.M.

Zone 8
Height: 3ft. (90cm) Spread: 1ft. (30cm)

Salvia purpurea

Zone 9
Height: 6ft. (2m) Spread: 3ft. (90cm)
Requires staking

Salvia roemeriana
A.G.M.

Zone 8
Height and spread: 1ft. (30cm)

Salvia sclarea var. *turkestanica*
Hort.

Zone 5
Height: 3ft. (90cm) Spread: 1ft. (30cm)

Salvia spathacea
A.G.M.

Zone 8
Height: 1ft. (30cm) Spread: 3ft. (90cm)

Salvia splendens
'Scarlet King' A.G.M.

Zone 10
Height: 10in. (25cm) Spread: 1ft. (30cm)

Salvia uliginosa
A.G.M.

Zone 9
Height: 5ft. (1.5m) Spread: 3ft. (90cm)

S

Salvia verticillata

Zone 6
Height: 32in. (80cm) Spread: 20in. (50cm)

Salvia verticillata
'Alba'

Zone 6
Height: 32in. (80cm) Spread: 20in. (50cm)

SANDERSONIA *(Colchicaceae)*
Common names: None

A genus of but a single species of tuberous perennial climber, *S. aurantiaca*, from light woodland and rocky regions of South Africa. Its leaves are alternate, and tipped by tendrils. The flowers are pendent, urn-shaped, and solitary.

✔ Disease-free   ✘ Requires support
✔ Pest-free

CULTIVATION
Under glass, plant tubers 4in. (10cm) deep in late winter or early spring in grit-enriched loam-based compost in full light. Water freely during growth, but dry off in winter. Store tubers in a frost-free situation.

Out of doors, grow in humus-rich, well-drained soil in sun. Protect against winter wet.

PROPAGATION
Seed should be sown at 75°F (24°C) as soon as it is ripe. Divide tubers in autumn or winter.

Sandersonia aurantiaca

Zone 9
Height: 30in. (75cm) Spread: 4in. (10cm)

SANGUINARIA *(Papaveraceae)*
Common names: Bloodroot; Red pucoon

A genus of a single species of rhizomatous perennial, *S. canadensis*, from damp woodland in eastern North America. Its handsome leaves are heart- or kidney-shaped, scalloped, bluish-gray. The flowers are single or double, white, solitary cups borne over a brief period in spring—the double form lasts longer than the single.

✔ Handsome foliage   ✘ Prone to slug damage
✔ Disease-free   ✘ Brief-flowering
✔ Pest-free

CULTIVATION
Grow in moist, fertile, humus-rich, well-drained soil in part or full shade.

PROPAGATION
Seed should be sown in a cold frame in autumn. Divide after flowering.

Sanguinaria canadensis
'Plena' A.G.M.

Zone 3
Height: 6in. (15cm) Spread: 1ft. (30cm)

S

S

SANGUISORBA *(Rosaceae)*
Common names: Burnet

A genus of 18 species of rhizomatous perennials from either wet meadows or dry rocky or grassy sites in cool and temperate parts of the northern hemisphere. Their leaves are alternate, and pinnate, with elliptic, toothed, veined leaflets. The flowers are bottle-brush-like, small, fluffy, lack petals, and are borne in terminal spikes on tall wiry stems in summer or early autumn. Some are invasive, some short-lived, some need to be staked.

  Good cut flowers
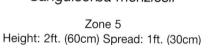 Handsome foliage

CULTIVATION
Grow in any reliably moist, well-drained soil in sun or part shade.

PROPAGATION
Seed should be sown in a cold frame, or division carried out, in autumn or spring.

Sanguisorba albiflora

Zone 5
Height and spread: 2ft. (60cm)
Short-lived

Sanguisorba canadensis

Zone 4
Height: 6ft. (2m) Spread: indefinite
Requires staking/Invasive

Sanguisorba menziesii

Zone 5
Height: 2ft. (60cm) Spread: 1ft. (30cm)

Sanguisorba obtusa

Zone 5
Height and spread: 2ft. (60cm)

Sanguisorba officinalis 'Tanna'

Zone 4
Height: 10in. (25cm) Spread: 2ft. (60cm)
Self-seeds

Sanguisorba tenuifolia 'Rosea'

Zone 4
Height: 4ft. (1.2m) Spread: 2ft. (60cm)

S

SANSEVIERIA *(Dracaenaceae)*

Common names: Bowstring hemp; Mother-in-law's tongue

A genus of 60 species of rhizomatous, suckering, evergreen perennials from dry stony habitats in subtropical and tropical India, Africa, Indonesia and Madagascar. Their leaves are stiff, fleshy, linear or ovate, upright or arching, and may be flat, cylindrical or concave. The flowers are produced intermittently by mature plants, and are fragrant, six-lobed tubes, borne in racemes or panicles.

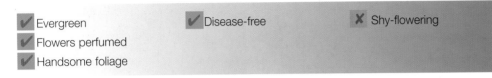

✔ Evergreen   ✔ Disease-free   ✘ Shy-flowering

✔ Flowers perfumed

✔ Handsome foliage

CULTIVATION

Under glass, grow in a mix of two parts potting compost and one part sharp sand in indirect or bright filtered light. Water with moderation during growth, sparingly in winter. Do not damage tips of leaves, or growth will cease.

Out of doors, grow in alkaline to neutral, poor, sharply-draining soil in sun.

PROPAGATION

Divide, or separate rooted suckers in spring. Leaf sections can be rooted with bottom heat in summer, but variegated types will be green.

Sansevieria trifasciata
'Mother-in-law's tongue'

Zone 10
Height: 4ft. (1.2m) Spread: indefinite

Sansevieria trifasciata
'Hahnii' A.G.M.

Zone 10
Height: 6in. (15cm) Spread: 7in. (18cm)

SANTOLINA *(Asteraceae)*

Common names: None

A genus of 18 species of evergreen subshrubs found in dry, stony habitats in the Mediterranean region. Their leaves are aromatic, pinnate or pinnatisect, and entire. The flowers are small, tubular, have only disc florets, and are surrounded by several rows of involucral bracts. They are borne in dense, button-like, heads in summer.

✔ Foliage aromatic   ✔ Handsome foliage   ✘ Highly allergenic

✔ Evergreen   ✔ Disease-free

✔ Drought-tolerant   ✔ Pest-free

CULTIVATION

Grow in well-drained, poor soil in sun. Cut flowered shoots back to within 1in. (2.5cm) of previous year's growth annually after flowering.

PROPAGATION

Seed should be sown in a cold frame in spring or autumn. Semi-ripe cuttings may be rooted with bottom heat in late summer.

Santolina chamaecyparissus
A.G.M.

Zone 7
Height: 18in. (45cm) Spread: 3ft. (90cm)

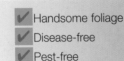

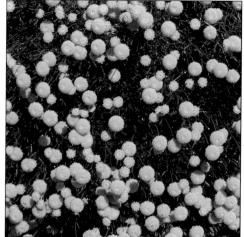

Santolina pinnata subsp.
neapolitana 'Edward Bowles'

Zone 7
Height: 30in. (75cm) Spread: 3ft. (90cm)

Santolina rosmarinifolia subsp.
rosmarinifolia

Zone 7
Height: 2ft. (60cm) Spread: 3ft. (90cm)

SAPONARIA *(Caryophyllaceae)*
Common names: Soapwort

A genus of 20 species of annuals and alpine and border perennials from the mountains of Europe and south-west Asia, where they inhabit meadows and rocky regions. Their leaves are entire, variously shaped, but narrow, and opposite. The flowers are flat, five-petalled, and borne in dense or loose cymes or panicles, in spring or summer.

✔ Disease-free   ✘ Prone to slug damage

CULTIVATION
Grow in fertile well-drained soil in sun. *S. ocymoides* needs sharply-drained soil and should be cut back hard after flowering to maintain compactness. *S. officinalis* should be dead-headed to prevent self-seeding.

PROPAGATION
Seed should be sown in an open frame in spring or autumn. Divide border perennials in spring or autumn. Softwood cuttings can be taken from border perennials in early summer.

Saponaria ocymoides

Zone 4
Height: 4in. (10cm) Spread: 18in. (45cm)
Evergreen

S

Saponaria officinalis
'Flore Pleno' (Bouncing Bet)
Zone 4
Height: 2ft. (60cm) Spread: 18in. (45cm)
Invasive/Self-seeds/Needs staking

Saponaria x olivana

Zone 4
Height: 2in. (5cm) Spread: 6in. (15cm)

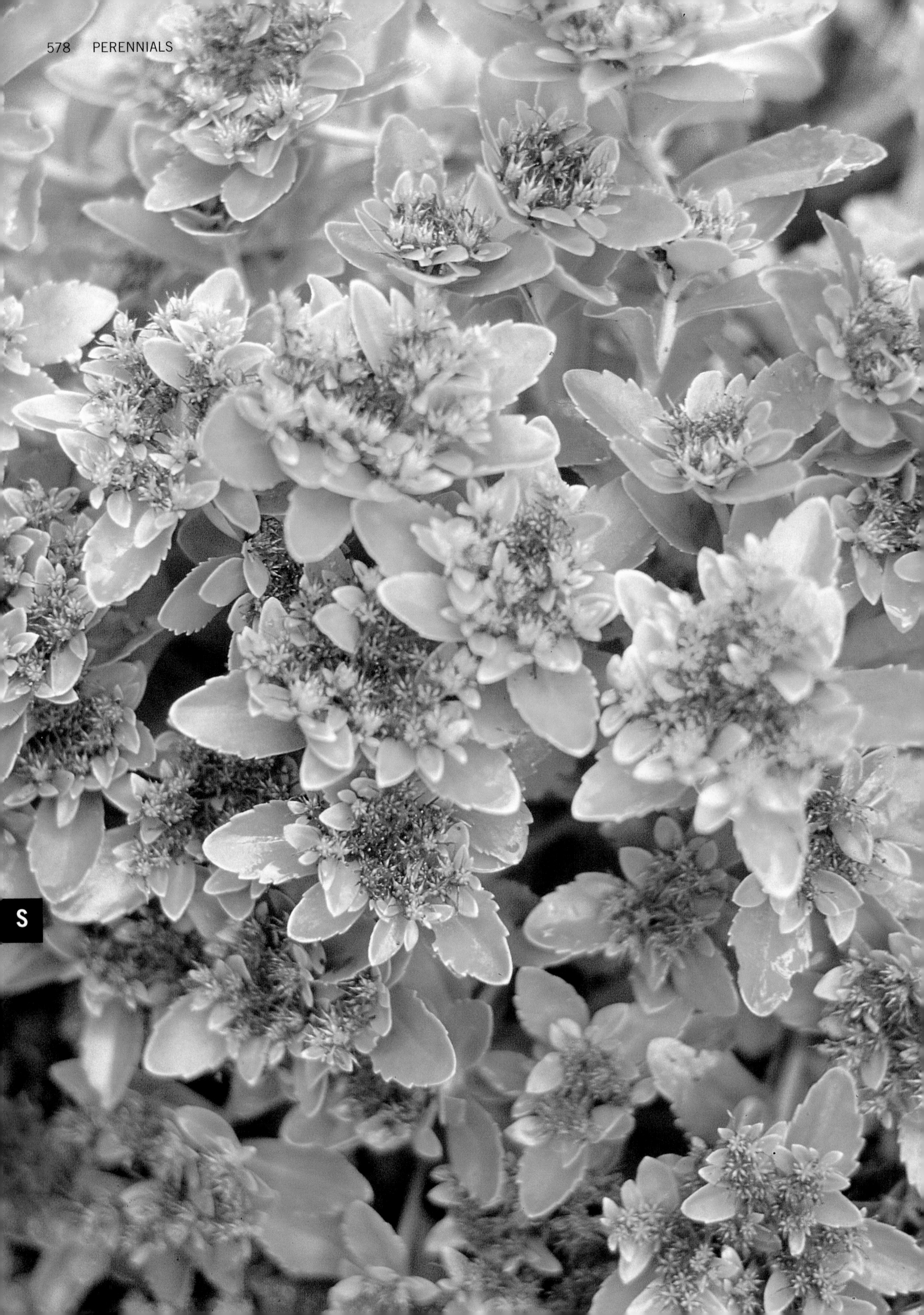

S

SARMIENTA *(Gesneriaceae)*
Common names: None

A genus of one species of evergreen, creeping perennial, *S. repens*, found growing epiphytically on trees in cool rainforest in temperate Chile. Its leaves are simple, elliptic to obovate, and opposite. The flowers are pendent, tubular and solitary, and borne in summer.

 Evergreen

CULTIVATION
Under glass, grow epiphytically or in a mix of two parts loam-free potting compost, one part leaf mould and one part granular bark, in indirect light. Water freely and mist daily in summer, and water sparingly in winter.

Out of doors, grow in a humus-rich soil and sphagnum moss mixture in part shade.

PROPAGATION
Seed should be sown at 70°F (21°C) in spring. Stem-tip cuttings may be rooted with bottom heat in late summer, or rooted stems may be separated in spring.

Sarmienta repens
A.G.M.

Zone 10
Height:1/2in. (1 cm) Spread: 1ft. (30cm)

SARRACENIA *(Sarraceniaceae)*
Common names: Pitcher plant

A genus of eight species of insectivorous rhizomatous perennials found in acid bogs from the Canadian Arctic to south-eastern U.S.A. They have rosettes that form handsome pitchers, which secrete nectar to trap insects. The flowers are cup-shaped, solitary, have five petals and five sepals, and appear in spring.

 Evergreen   ✗ Prone to aphids

CULTIVATION
Under glass, grow in a mix of one part lime-free compost, three parts sphagnum moss, and one part lime-free grit, in full light with shade from hot sun. Stand the pots in trays of lime-free water over summer. Keep cool, just moist, and well ventilated in winter.

Out of doors, grow in acid, moist, humus-rich, sharply-draining soil in sun. Use lime-free water to irrigate.

PROPAGATION
Seed should be kept cold for two weeks, then sown at 70°F (21°C) in spring in pots standing in trays of lime-free water. Pinch out seedlings when three tiny pitchers are seen.

Sarracenia catesbyi
A.G.M.

Zone 5
Height: 30in. (75cm) Spread: 3ft. (90cm)

Sarracenia flava
A.G.M.

Zone 7
Height and spread: 3ft. (90cm)

Sarracenia flava 'Cut Throat'

Zone 7
Height and spread: 3ft. (90cm)

Sarracenia purpurea subsp. *venosa*

Zone 6
Height: 6in. (15cm) Spread: 3ft. (90cm)

S

SASA *(Poaceae)*

Common names: None

A genus of some 50 species of rhizomatous, invasive, small bamboos from woodland and damp hollows in Korea, China and Japan. Their leaves are large, toothed, thick, tessellated and tend to wither round the edges in winter giving the impression of variegation. The leaves of *S. veitchii* are cream-margined in summer, but wither to yellow in winter (see photo). The canes are upright, cylindrical, smooth, and bristly, with a white bloom under the nodes.

✔ Handsome foliage   ✘ Prone to slug damage

✔ Disease-free   ✘ Invasive

CULTIVATION
Grow in moist, well-drained humus-rich soil in sun through to full shade. However, they must have root moisture when grown in sun.

PROPAGATION
Divide young rhizomes in spring.

Sasa veitchii

Zone 8
Height: 4ft. (1.2m) Spread: indefinite

SAUROMATUM *(Araceae)*

Common names: Monarch of the East

A genus of two species of spreading, tuberous perennials from shady cliff sides and woodland in East and West Africa and the Himalayas. The flowers are green, lance-shaped or oblong, black-spotted, foul-smelling spathes, with a greenish-purple spadix, borne in late spring and early summer, and followed by a single, handsome, pedate leaf with many lance-shaped segments, atop a tall stem.

✔ Handsome foliage   ✘ Foul-smelling flowers

✔ Disease-free   ✘ Invasive

CULTIVATION
Under glass, plant tubers 6in. (15cm) deep in late winter in loam-based potting compost in indirect or bright filtered light. Water moderately during growth, keep dry in winter.

Out of doors, grow in acid to neutral, humus-rich, well-drained soil in part shade.

PROPAGATION
Separate offsets during winter dormancy.

Sauromatum venosum

Zone 10
Height: 18in. (45cm) Spread: 8in. (20cm)

SAURURUS *(Saururaceae)*

Common names: Lizard's tail

A genus of two species of rhizomatous, perennials from bogland in North America and east Asia. Their leaves are large, entire, heart-shaped, and alternate. The flowers are small, white, numerous, have three or four basally-joined carpels, and are borne in terminal racemes in summer.

✔ Flowers perfumed

✔ Handsome foliage

CULTIVATION
Grow in shallow water or wet soil in sun.

PROPAGATION
Divide in spring or autumn.

Saururus cernuus

Zone 5
Height: 4ft. (1.2m) Spread: 8in. (20cm)

SAXIFRAGA *(Saxifragaceae)*
Common names: Rockfoil; Saxifrage

A genus of 440 species of annuals, biennials and perennials from the mountains of the northern hemisphere. The perennials are cushion-forming, but they vary greatly in habit, and may be evergreen, semi-evergreen or herbaceous. Leaves vary widely also. The flowers are cup- or star-shaped, and may be solitary or in panicles, cymes or racemes. The genus is classified into 15 sections, as according to Gornall (1987), but only some sections are of general horticultural interest, the remainder being for specialist growers only. Each entry has its classification noted:

1. Ciliatae	6. Heterisia	11. Gymnopera
2. Cymbalaria	7. Porphyrion	12. Cotylea
3. Merkianae	8. Ligulatae	13. Odontophyllae
4. Micranthes	9. Xanthizoon	14. Mesogyne
5. Irregulares	10. Trachyphyllum	15. Saxifraga

✔ Low allergen
✔ Handsome foliage
✔ Disease-free

✘ Prone to slug damage

CULTIVATION
Varies, and each plant is placed in a group for this purpose:

Group A: grow in moist, well-drained soil in part or deep shade.

Group B: grow in alkaline to neutral, moist, sharply-draining, soil in light shade.

Group C: grow in alkaline to neutral, reliably moist, but well-drained soil in sun—but not hot sun or the leaves will scorch.

Group D: grow in an alpine house in a mix of two parts loam and one of coarse grit, or outdoors in alkaline to neutral, very sharply-drained soil, or in a scree bed, in sun. Some in this group are totally intolerant of winter wet.

PROPAGATION
Seed should be sown in autumn in a cold frame. Detach rosettes and root in late spring or early summer. Herbaceous perennial types may be divided in spring.

Saxifraga 'Blackberry and Apple Pie' (5, Group A)

Zone 7
Height and spread: 1ft. (30cm)

Saxifraga 'Cheap Confections' (5, Group A)

Zone 7
Height and spread: 1ft. (30cm)

Saxifraga 'Correvoniana' (8, Group C or D)

Zone 6
Height: 2in. (5cm) Spread: 8in. (20cm)

Saxifraga 'Crystal Pink' (5, Group A)

Zone 7
Height and spread: 6in. (15cm)

Saxifraga fortunei A.G.M. (5, Group A)

Zone 7
Height and spread: 1ft. (30cm)

S

Saxifraga fortunei
'Mount Nachi' (5, Group A)

Zone 7
Height and spread: 1ft. (30cm)

Saxifraga fortunei
'Nigra' (5, Group A)

Zone 7
Height and spread: 1ft. (30cm)

Saxifraga granulata
'Flore Pleno' (15, Group B)

Zone 5
Height: 14in. (35cm) Spread: 1ft. (30cm)

Saxifraga hostii
(8, Group C or D)

Zone 6
Height: 20in. (50cm) Spread: 8in. (20cm)

Saxifraga
'Silver Cushion' (15, Group B)

Zone 5
Height and spread: 6in. (15cm)

Saxifraga 'Southside Seedling'
A.G.M. (8, Group C or D)

Zone 7
Height and spread: 1ft. (30cm)

S

Saxifraga stolonifera
A.G.M. (5, Group A)

Zone 5
Height: 1ft. (30cm) Spread: 18in. (45cm)

Saxifraga stolonifera
'Tricolor' (5, Group A)

Zone 5
Height: 1ft. (30cm) Spread: 18in. (45cm)

Saxifraga 'Tumbling Waters' A.G.M.
(8, Group D)

Zone 7
Height: 18in. (45cm) Spread: 1ft. (30cm)

Saxifarga x urbium
(London Pride) (11, Group A)
Zone 6
Height: 1ft. (30cm) Spread: indefinite
Invasive

Saxifraga x urbium
'Aureopunctata' (11, Group A)
Zone 6
Height: 1ft. (30cm) Spread: indefinite
Invasive

Saxifraga x urbium
'Variegata' (11, Group A)
Zone 6
Height: 1ft. (30cm) Spread: indefinite
Invasive

Saxifraga veitchiana (5, Group A)

Zone7
Height: 1ft. (30cm) Spread: indefinite
Invasive

Saxifraga
'Winston Churchill' (15, Group B)

Zone 5
Height and spread: 6in. (15cm)

SCABIOSA *(Dipsacaceae)*

Common names: Scabious; Pincushion flower

A genus of 80 species of annuals, biennials and perennials from sunny dry slopes and meadows in the Mediterranean area, Eurasia, Japan and Africa. Their leaves are basal, simple, lobed or entire, and pinnatisect or pinnatifid, The flowers are solitary, or in clusters, and have large ray florets and a pincushion-like central dome of disc florets, in summer, over long periods in some instances. Some are short-lived.

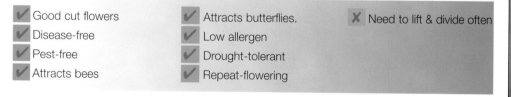

✔ Good cut flowers	✔ Attracts butterflies.	✘ Need to lift & divide often
✔ Disease-free	✔ Low allergen	
✔ Pest-free	✔ Drought-tolerant	
✔ Attracts bees	✔ Repeat-flowering	

CULTIVATION
Grow in alkaline to neutral, well-drained, fertile soil in sun. Protect against excessive winter wet. Dead-head to encourage repeat-flowering.

PROPAGATION
Seed should be sown in a cold frame as soon as it is ripe, or in spring. Take basal cuttings, or divide in spring.

Scabiosa atropurpurea

Zone 7
Height: 3ft. (90cm) Spread: 10in. (25cm)
Flowers perfumed/Short-lived

S

S

Scabiosa caucasica 'Clive Greaves'
A.G.M. (Caucasian scabious)
Zone 4
Height and spread: 2ft. (60cm)
Long-flowering

Scabiosa
'Butterfly Blue'

Zone 6
Height and spread: 16in. (40cm)

Scabiosa columbaria var.
ochroleuca (Dove scabious)
Zone 6
Height: 30in. (75cm) Spread: 3ft. (90cm)
Long-flowering

Scabiosa 'Irish Perpetual-flowering'

Zone 6
Height: and spread: 1ft. (30cm)
Long-flowering

Scabiosa
'Pink Mist' (PBR)

Zone 6
Height and spread: 16in. (40cm)

SCHIZOSTYLIS *(Iridaceae)*
Common names: Kaffir lily

A genus of but a single species of evergreen, rhizomatous perennial, *S. coccinea*, from watersides and damp meadows in Southern Africa. Their leaves are erect, linear or sword-shaped, and keeled. The gladiolus-like flower spikes are composed of open cup-shaped flowers, borne in late autumn to early winter, or longer in warm gardens.

✔ Long-flowering	✘ Need to lift & divide often
✔ Good cut flowers	
✔ Low allergen	
✔ Disease-free	
✔ Pest-free	
✔ Winter-flowering	

S

Schizostylis coccinea forma. *alba*

Zone 6
Height: 2ft. (60cm) Spread: 1ft. (30cm)

CULTIVATION
Grow in reliably moist, well-drained soil in a warm corner in sun.

PROPAGATION
Seed should be sown at 61°F (16°C) in spring.

Schizostylis coccinea
'Major' A.G.M.

Zone 6
Height: 2ft. (60cm) Spread: 1ft. (30cm)

Schizostylis coccinea
'Professor Barnard'

Zone 6
Height: 2ft. (60cm) Spread: 1ft. (30cm)

Schizostylis coccinea
'Sunrise' A.G.M.

Zone 6
Height: 2ft. (60cm) Spread: 1ft. (30cm)

SCHLUMBERGERA *(Cactaceae)*

Common names: Christmas Cactus

A genus of six species of epiphytic or terrestrial perennial cacti from tropical rainforest in south-east Brazil. The arching, brittle stems are subdivided into flat, obovate or oblong, leaf-like, truncate segments, with notched edges. The terminal segments bear solitary, open, trumpet-shaped flowers with narrow petals in winter/spring or in summer/autumn.

✔ Handsome foliage   ✔ Winter-flowering

✔ Disease-free   ✔ Evergreen

CULTIVATION
Under glass, grow in epiphytic cactus compost in indirect bright light, in moderate humidity. Water with moderation at all times. Repot in spring every few years.

Out of doors, grow in acid to neutral, moist, humus-rich, well-drained soil in light or part shade. Must have shelter from strong winds and heavy rain.

PROPAGATION
Seed should be sown at 70°F (21°C) in spring. Stem cuttings can be taken from spring to early summer.

Schlumbergera truncata

Zone 9
Height and spread: 1ft. (30cm)

SCHOENOPLECTUS *(Cyperaceae)*

Common names: None

A genus of 80 species of evergreen rhizomatous marginal aquatic perennials from lake margins and stream sides across the world. Their grassy leaves may be submerged or above the surface. The flowers are insignificant, and are borne on cylindrical stems in summer.

✔ Handsome foliage

✔ Disease-free

✔ Pest-free

CULTIVATION
Plant rhizomes 1ft. (30cm) deep in still or slow-moving water, or in wet soil, in sun. Cut back annually to restrict size in small pools. Reverting stems of *S. lacustris* 'Zebrinus' should be cut back to the rhizome.

PROPAGATION
Rhizome pieces should be rooted between mid-spring and summer.

Schoenoplectus lacustris subsp.
tabernaemontani 'Zebrinus'

Zone 7
Height: 3ft. (90cm) Spread: indefinite

S

SCILLA *(Hyacinthaceae)*
Common names: None

A genus of 90 species of bulbous perennials found in a range of habitat from sea shore to mountains, such as woodland, meadow, and rocky slopes. All have a dormant period, except *S. peruviana*. The leaves are basal, semi-erect, elliptic or linear, and are sometimes channeled. The flowers are flat or bell- or star-shaped, and are borne in corymbs or terminal racemes at all times of the year except winter. Some are evergreen.

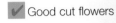 Good cut flowers

CULTIVATION
Under glass, plant bulbs 4in. (10cm) deep in late summer or early autumn in a mix of two parts loam-based potting compost, one part grit and one part leaf mould, in full light. Water freely during growth, keep dry during dormancy in summer.

Out of doors, plant bulbs 4in. (10cm) deep in late summer or early autumn in moist, well-drained, fertile soil in sun or part shade.

PROPAGATION
Seed should be sown in a cold frame as soon as it is ripe. Separate offsets when dormant.

Scilla hohenakeri

Zone 6
Height: 8in. (20cm) Spread: 2in. (5cm)

Scilla lilio-hyacinthus

Zone 6
Height: 10in. (25cm) Spread: 3in. (8cm)

Scilla natalensis

Zone 9
Height: 4ft. (1.2m) Spread: 4in. (10cm)

Scilla peruviana

Zone 8
Height: 18in. (45cm) Spread: 1ft. (30cm)

SCOLIOPUS *(Trilliaceae)*
Common names: Footed adder's tongue

A genus of but two species of herbaceous perennials from woodland in western U.S.A. Their leaves are basal, elliptic or oblong, nicely-veined, and paired. The flowers are have three upright inner tepals and three spreading outer ones, and arise from stemless buds in stalkless umbels from the roots in spring.

✔ Handsome foliage
✔ Disease-free

✘ Flowers malodorous
✘ Prone to slug damage

CULTIVATION
Under glass, grow in an alpine house in loam-free potting compost in filtered light.

Out of doors, grow in acid to neutral, moist, well-drained humus-rich soil in part or deep shade.

PROPAGATION
Seed should be sown in a cold frame as soon as it is ripe.

Scoliopus bigelovii

Zone 7
Height: 4in. (10cm) Spread: 6in. (15cm)

SCOPOLIA *(Solanaceae)*

Common names: None

A genus of five species of rhizomatous perennials from woodland in Eurasia, China, Japan and the Himalayas. Their leaves are simple, entire, boldly-veined and alternate. The flowers are solitary, pendent bells, which appear in spring.

- ✔ Disease-free
- ✔ Pest-free
- ✘ All parts poisonous

CULTIVATION
Grow in alkaline to neutral, moist, well-drained soil in part shade.

PROPAGATION
Seed should be sown *in situ* in spring or autumn, or in a cold frame in autumn. Division can be carried out in spring.

Scopolia carniolica

Zone 5
Height: 18in. (45cm) Spread: 2ft. (60cm)

SCROPHULARIA *(Scrophulariaceae)*

Common names: Figwort

A genus of 200 species of herbaceous perennials and subshrubs found in habitats ranging from dry wasteland and scrubland, to moist meadows and woodland and marshland in tropical Central and North America. They are coarse, sometimes malodorous, plants. Their leaves are simple, entire or toothed or scalloped or lobed, and opposite. The foxglove-like flowers are two-lipped, and borne in terminal cymes.

- ✔ Low allergen
- ✔ Handsome foliage
- ✔ Disease-free
- ✘ Prone to slug damage

CULTIVATION
Grow in moist, well-drained soil in light shade. *S. auriculata* can be grown 6in. (15cm) deep in water, and in its variegated form it should not be allowed to flower if it is to retain its foliage appeal.

PROPAGATION
Seed should be sown in situ in spring or autumn, or divide in spring. Basal cuttings can be taken in spring, and softwood cuttings in summer.

Scrophularia auriculata
'Variegata'

Zone 5
Height: 30in. (75cm) Spread: 2ft. (60cm)

S

SCUTELLARIA *(Lamiaceae)*

Common names: Skullcap; Helmet flower

A genus of 300 species of annuals, perennials and a few subshrubs found across the temperate regions and the mountains of tropical areas. The perennials may be rhizomatous or fibrous-rooted. Their leaves are entire or pinnatifid, hairy or sometimes toothed, and opposite. The flowers are two-lipped, tubular, with colored bracts in many cases, and are solitary or borne in pairs from the leaf axils, or in terminal racemes or spikes, in summer.

✔ Good cut flowers   ✘ Prone to aphid attack
✔ Disease-free

CULTIVATION
Grow in alkaline to neutral, well-drained, fertile, gritty, soil in sun or part shade.

PROPAGATION
Seed should be sown in a cold frame in autumn. Division can be carried out in spring or autumn. Softwood or basal cuttings can be taken in late spring or early summer.

Scutellaria incana

Zone 5
Height: 4ft. (1.2m) Spread: 2ft. (60cm)

Scutellaria integrifolia

Zone 5
Height: 2ft. (60cm) Spread: 1ft. (30cm)

Scutellaria scordiifolia

Zone 5
Height and spread: 1ft. (30cm)

SEDUM *(Crassulaceae)*

Common names: Stonecrop

A genus of 400 species of annuals, biennials, perennials, subshrubs and shrubs of wide distribution in divergent habitats, such as arid regions of South America and the mountains of the northern hemisphere. They are mostly succulent, and the perennials may be herbaceous, semi-evergreen or evergreen. They vary widely in form and hardiness. The leaves are fleshy, flat or cylindrical, and opposite, alternate or whorled. The flowers are five-petaled stars, borne in terminal panicles, racemes or cymes in summer and autumn.

✔ Attracts butterflies   ✘ All parts poisonous
✔ Drought-tolerant   ✘ Sap is skin-irritant
✔ Handsome foliage   ✘ Prone to slug damage
✔ Attracts bees   ✘ Prone to aphid attack

CULTIVATION
Under glass, grow tender species in a mix of three parts loam-based potting compost, one part leaf mould and two parts grit in full light, and with good ventilation. Water moderately during growth, sparingly in winter.

Sedum acre

Zone 5
Height: 2in. (5cm) Spread: 32in. (80cm)
Evergreen

Out of doors, grow in alkaline to neutral, well-drained soil in sun, or in light shade in the instance of vigorous species. The larger herbaceous species should be divided every few years to retain flowering, and spreading species should be trimmed back after flowering to maintain shape.

PROPAGATION

Seed of tender species should be sown at 64°F (18°C) in early spring. Seed of hardy species should be sown in a cold frame in autumn. Division of all species can be done in spring. Softwood cuttings may be taken in early summer.

Sedum acre 'Aureum'

Zone 5
Height: 2in. (5cm) Spread: 32in. (80cm)
Evergreen

Sedum aizoon
'Euphorbiodes'

Zone 7
Height and spread: 14in. (35cm)

Sedum
'Bertram Anderson' A.G.M.

Zone 4
Height: 6in. (15cm) Spread: 1ft. (30cm)

Sedum erythrostictum
'Frosty Morn'
Zone 4
Height: 18in. (45cm) Spread: 1ft. (30cm)
Needs to be staked

Sedum erythrostictum
'Mediovariegatum'
Zone 4
Height: 18in. (45cm) Spread: 1ft. (30cm)
Needs to be staked

Sedum hidakanum

Zone 6
Height: 4in. (10cm) Spread: 1ft. (30cm)

Sedum kamtschaticum
'Variegatum' A.G.M.

Zone 7
Height: 4in. (10cm) Spread: 10in. (25cm)

Sedum kamtshaticum var.
ellacombeanum A.G.M.

Zone 7
Height: 4in. (10cm) Spread: 10in. (25cm)

S

Sedum
'Lynda Windsor'

Zone 7
Height: 1ft. (30cm) Spread: 8in. (20cm)

Sedum lineare 'Variegatum'

Zone 7
Height: 10in. (25cm) Spread: 18in. (45cm)
Evergreen

Sedum morganianum A.G.M.

Zone 9
Height: 2in. (5cm) Spread: 1ft. (30cm)
Evergreen

Sedum populifolium

Zone 4
Height: 1ft. (30cm) Spread: 18in. (45cm)
Flowers perfumed

Sedum pulchellum

Zone 8
Height and spread: 6in. (15cm)

Sedum
'Purple Emperor'

Zone 6
Height: 6in. (15cm) Spread: 1ft. (30cm)

Sedum rubrotinctum

Zone 9
Height: 10in. (25cm) Spread: 8in. (20cm)
Evergreen

Sedum
'Ruby Glow' A.G.M.

Zone 7
Height: 1ft. (30cm) Spread: 18in. (45cm)

Sedum rupestre

Zone 4
Height: 6in. (15cm) Spread: 2ft. (60cm)
Evergreen

S

Sedum sieboldii
'Mediovariegatum' A.G.M.

Zone 6
Height: 4in. (10cm) Spread: 1ft. (30cm)

Sedum spathulifolium
'Cape Blanco' A.G.M.

Zone 7
Height: 4in. (10cm) Spread: 2ft. (60cm)

Sedum spathulifolium
'Purpureum' A.G.M.

Zone 7
Height: 4in. (10cm) Spread: 2ft. (60cm)

Sedum spectabile A.G.M.

Zone 4
Height and spread: 18in. (45cm)
Needs to be staked

Sedum spurium 'Fuldaglut'

Zone 7
Height: 4in. (10cm) Spread: 2ft. (60cm)
Evergreen

Sedum spurium
'Ruby Mantle'

Zone 7
Height: 4in. (10cm) Spread: 2ft. (60cm)

Sedum spurium 'Variegatum'

Zone 7
Height: 4in. (10cm) Spread: 2ft. (60cm)
Evergreen

Sedum telephium

Zone 4
Height: 2ft. (60cm) Spread: 1ft. (30cm)

Sedum telephium
'Abbey Dore'

Zone 4
Height: 2ft. (60cm) Spread: 1ft. (30cm)

S

Sedum telephium
'Arthur Branch'

Zone 4
Height: 2ft. (60cm) Spread: 1ft. (30cm)

Sedum telephium
'Matrona'

Zone 4
Height: 2ft. (60cm) Spread: 1ft. (30cm)

Sedum telephium
'Munstead Red'

Zone 4
Height: 2ft. (60cm) Spread: 1ft. (30cm)

Sedum telephium subsp. *maximum*
'Atropurpureum' A.G.M.

Zone 4
Height: 2ft. (60cm) Spread: 1ft. (30cm)

Sedum telephium subsp. *ruprechtii*

Zone 4
Height: 2ft. (60cm) Spread: 1ft. (30cm)

SELAGINELLA *(Selaginellaceae)*

Common names: None

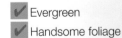

A genus of 700 species of evergreen rhizomatous perennials found in habitats ranging from rainforest to semi-desert, in tropical zones as well as parts of alpine and temperate regions. They are essentially foliage plants and vary from small, creeping moss-like plants which root as they go, to tall scramblers. The foliage is pinnatisect, and ferny or moss-like. They form spores in terminal leafy spikes.

✔ Evergreen   ✔ Disease-free   ✘ Flowers insignificant
✔ Handsome foliage   ✔ Pest-free

CULTIVATION
Under glass, grow in a mix of two parts loam-based potting compost and one of leaf mould, in indirect or bright filtered light, and with high humidity. Water freely during growth, and very sparingly in winter.

Out of doors, grow in acid to neutral, moist, humus-rich, fertile soil in a sheltered corner in part shade.

PROPAGATION
Spores should be sown at 70°F (21°C) as soon as they are ripe. Rhizomes can be divided in spring. Rooted stems can be detached in spring.

Selaginella kraussiana
A.G.M.

Zone 9
Height: 1in. (2.5cm) Spread: indefinite

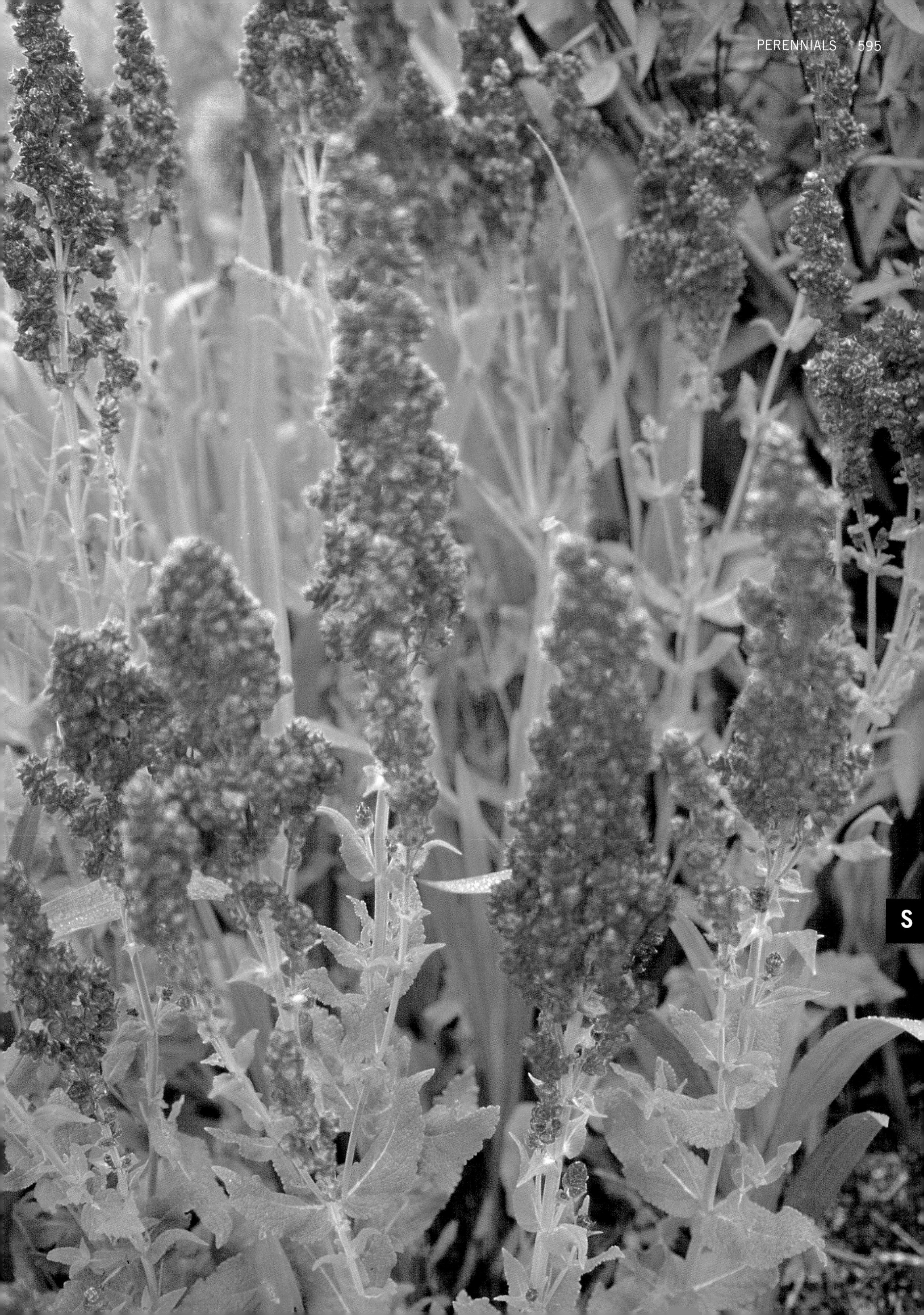

Selaginella martensii
'Albomarginata'

Zone 9
Height: 6in. (15cm) Spread: 8in. (20cm)

Selaginella rodriguesiana

Zone 9
Height: 2in. (5cm) Spread: 2ft. (60cm)

SELINUM *(Apiaceae)*

Common names: None

A genus of six species of tap-rooted perennials from scrubland, rocky slopes and mountain meadows in temperate Europe and the Himalayas. The finely-dissected triangular leaves are two- or three-pinnate, the lobes toothed and elliptic. The flowers are small white stars borne in large, flat umbels from midsummer to early autumn.

✔ Handsome foliage	✘ Prone to slug damage
✔ Architectural plants	✘ Mildew prone
	✘ Resents disturbance

CULTIVATION
Grow in moist, well-drained fertile soil in sun or part shade.

PROPAGATION
Seed should be sown in a cold frame as soon as it is ripe. Prick seedlings out into deep containers as soon as possible to circumvent root disturbance. Division can be carried out in spring, but is not advised.

Selinum wallichianum

Zone 8
Height: 6ft. (2m) Spread: 2ft. (60cm)

SEMIAQUILEGIA *(Ranunculaceae)*

Common names: None

A genus of seven species of perennials from the mountains of East Asia. Their leaves are biternate or ternate. The columbine-like flowers lack spurs, have swollen bases, and are borne in panicles in spring and summer.

✔ Disease-free	✘ Short-lived
	✘ Prone to slug damage

CULTIVATION
Grow in acid to neutral, moist, well-drained soil in a sheltered corner in sun, with shade at mid-day, or in part shade.

PROPAGATION
Seed should be sown in a cold frame as soon as it is ripe.

Semiaquilegia ecalcarata

Zone 6
Height: 1ft. (30cm) Spread: 8in. (20cm)

SEMPERVIVUM *(Crassulaceae)*
Common names: Houseleek

A genus of 40 species of evergreen succulent perennials found in the Eurasian mountains. Their leaves are in rosettes, thick, pointed, with bristle-fringed edges in many cases, and covered in a web of white hairs in some instances. The flowers are star-shaped, and borne in branching flat-topped terminal cymes on upright stems, in summer. Any rosette that flowers dies, but new rosettes are borne on runners.

✔ Evergreen   ✔ Handsome foliage
✔ Drought-tolerant   ✔ Pest-free

CULTIVATION
Under glass, soft, hairy species resent winter wet so are best grown in an alpine house in a mix of equal parts grit and loam-based potting compost.

Out of doors, grow in sharply-draining soil in sun.

PROPAGATION
Seed should be sown in a cold frame in spring. Offsets can be rooted in spring or early summer.

Sempervivum arachnoideum
A.G.M. (Cobweb houseleek)

Zone 5
Height: 4in. (10cm) Spread: 1ft. (30cm)

Sempervivum arachnoideum
'Rubrum'

Zone 5
Height: 4in. (10cm) Spread: 1ft. (30cm)

Sempervivum calcareum

Zone 5
Height: 4in. (10cm) Spread: 1ft. (30cm)

Sempervivum
'Commander Hay' A.G.M.

Zone 5
Height: 4in. (10cm) Spread: 1ft. (30cm)

Sempervivum
'Lipari'

Zone 5
Height: 4in. (10cm) Spread: 1ft. (30cm)

Sempervivum
'Oddity'

Zone 5
Height: 4in. (10cm) Spread: 1ft. (30cm)

S

S

SENECIO *(Asteraceae)*
Common names: None

A genus of over 1,000 species of annuals, biennials, perennials, shrubs and trees found worldwide both at sea level and in the mountains, and in wet and dry habitats—not surprisingly, their cultural needs vary widely. Their leaves are basal, and sometimes stem, and are entire or lobed, and commonly silver or gray. The daisy-like flowers are terminal and solitary or borne in corymbs, in summer.

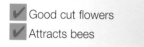

- ✔ Good cut flowers
- ✔ Attracts bees
- ✗ All parts poisonous
- ✗ Prone to aphid attack
- ✗ Highly allergenic

CULTIVATION
Under glass

Group 1: grow in a mix of two parts loam-based potting compost, one part grit and one part leaf mould, in full light and ample ventilation. Water with moderation during growth, and keep just moist in winter.

Out of doors

Group 2: grow in poor, sharply-drained soil in sun.

Group 3: grow in fertile, well-drained soil in sun.

Group 4: grow in moist or boggy soil in sun or part shade.

PROPAGATION
Seed of cultivation Groups 1 and 2 should be sown at 75°F (24°C), and for Groups 3 and 4 in a cold frame, in spring. Groups 2 and 4 can be divided in spring, or basal cuttings may be taken then. Group 1 may be divided as growth commences, softwood cuttings can be taken in early summer or semi-ripe cuttings taken in mid to late summer. Silver-foliaged forms in cultivation Group 3 should have semi-ripe cuttings taken between mid and late summer.

Senecio cineraria
(Group 3)

Zone 8
Height and spread: 2ft. (60cm)

Senecio cineraria
'Silver Dust' A.G.M. (Group 3)

Zone 8
Height and spread: 2ft. (60cm)

Senecio doronicum
(Group 2)

Zone 5
Height and spread: 10ft. (3.5m)

Senecio himalaya
(Group 2)

Zone 8
Height: 2ft. (60cm) Spread 18in. (45cm)

S

Senecio leucophyllus
(Group 3)

Zone 6
Height and spread: 8in. (20cm)

Senecio polyodon
(Group 2)

Zone 6
Height: 1ft. (30cm) Spread: 2ft. (60cm)

Senecio pulcher
(Group 4)

Zone 8
Height: 2ft. (60cm) Spread: 18in. (45cm)

Senecio smithii
(Group 3)

Zone 7
Height: 4ft. (1.2m) Spread: 1ft. (30cm)

Senecio viravira
A.G.M. (Group 2)

Zone 8
Height: 2ft. (60cm) Spread: 3ft. (90cm)

SERRATULA *(Asteraceae)*

Common names: None

A genus of 70 species of perennials from Europe, Japan and North Africa. Their leaves are pinnately deep-cut, toothed and alternate. The cornflower-like flowers are tubular, and perfect, and are solitary or in loose corymbs, in late autumn.

✔ Drought-tolerant
✔ Handsome foliage

CULTIVATION
Grow in any well-drained, fertile soil in sun. Divide in spring.

PROPAGATION
Seed should be sown in a cold frame in autumn or spring.

Serratula seoanei

Zone 7
Height and spread: 1ft. (30cm)

SESELI *(Apiaceae)*
Common names: None

A genus of 80 species of biennials and perennials from Eurasia, most of which have little garden value. Their leaves are hairy, glaucous, and pinnatisect with wedge-shaped segments. The flowers are small, and borne in compact umbels of up to 60, in summer.

 Handsome foliage

CULTIVATION
Grow in well-drained fertile soil in sun.

PROPAGATION
Seed should be sown in a cold frame in autumn or spring; division can also be carried out at these times.

Seseli gummiferum

Zone 6
Height: 3ft. (90cm) Spread: 2ft. (60cm)

SESLERIA *(Poaceae)*
Common names: None

A genus of 33 species of evergreen, perennial grasses from dry or damp grassland in the mountains and hills of Europe. Their narrowly-linear leaves are grass-like. The flowers are in spiky, cylindrical panicles in summer.

 Evergreen   Highly allergenic
Disease-free
Pest-free

CULTIVATION
Grow in alkaline to neutral, well-drained soil in sun or light shade.

PROPAGATION
Seed should be sown in a cold frame in spring or autumn. Divide in spring.

Sesleria glauca

Zone 6
Height 1ft. (30cm) Spread: 8in. (20cm)

SIDALCEA *(Malvaceae)*
Common names: False mallow; Prairie mallow; Checker mallow

A genus of 25 species of annuals and perennials found in woodland glades, mountain stream sides and grassland in Central and western North America. Their basal leaves are palmate or kidney-shaped or rounded, and toothed. The stem leaves are palmately-lobed. The hollyhock-like, five-petalled flowers are borne in dense terminal racemes atop tall stems in summer.

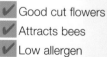 Good cut flowers   Require to be staked
Attracts bees   Prone to slug damage
Low allergen
Repeat-flowering

CULTIVATION
Grow in any soil that is not waterlogged, but preferably in acid to neutral, well-drained sandy soil in sun. Cut back after flowering to encourage repeat-flowering.

PROPAGATION
Sow seed in a cold frame, or divide, in spring or autumn.

Sidalcea candida
(White prairie mallow)

Zone 5
Height: 32in. (80cm) Spread: 18in. (45cm)

S

S

Sidalcea
'Croftway Red'

Zone 6
Height: 3ft. (90cm) Spread: 18in. (45cm)

Sidalcea
'Elsie Heugh'

Zone 6
Height: 3ft. (90cm) Spread: 45 cm.(18in.)

Sidalcea malviflora
(Foothills checker-mallow)

Zone 6
Height: 4ft. (1.2m) Spread: 18in. (45cm)

Sidalcea
'Party Girl'

Zone 6
Height: 3ft. (90cm) Spread: 18in. (45cm)

Sidalcea
'William Smith' A.G.M.

Zone 6
Height: 3ft. (90cm) Spread: 18in. (45cm)

SILENE *(Caryophyllaceae)*
Common names: Campion; Catchfly

A genus of 500 species of annuals, biennials, and perennials found in habitats such as meadowland, open woodland, and mountain screes of the northern hemisphere, and the circum-Mediterranean lands in particular. Others are from the mountains of South America and tropical Africa. The perennials may be herbaceous or evergreen. The high alpine species require alpine house treatment. Their leaves are varied, and may be linear, ovate or obovate, and are entire and opposite. The flowers are five-petalled, and the calyx is tubular and inflated in many species. The petals may be notched or split. They are solitary, or borne in clusters, sprays, cymes or panicles in spring, summer or autumn.

Silene dioica

Zone 6
Height: 30in. (75cm) Spread: 18in. (45cm)

✔ Drought-tolerant
✔ Attracts bees

✘ Prone to slug damage
✘ Self-seeds
✘ Short-lived

CULTIVATION
Grow in alkaline to neutral, well-drained, soil in sun or part shade. *S. hookeri* must have acid soil, and very good drainage. Dead-head to prevent self-seeding.

PROPAGATION
Seed should be sown in a cold frame in autumn. Basal cuttings can be taken in spring.

Silene dioica
'Rosea Plena'

Zone 6
Height: 32in. (80cm) Spread: 18in. (45cm)

Silene dioica
'Thelma Kaye'

Zone 6
Height: 32in. (80cm) Spread: 18in. (45cm)

Silene hookeri

Zone 5
Height: 2in. (5cm) Spread: 6in. (15cm)

Silene uniflora
'Druett's Variegated'

Zone 3
Height and spread: 8in. (20cm)

Silene uniflora
'Robin Whitebreast'

Zone 3
Height 20 cm.(8in.) Spread: 1ft. (30cm)

Silene uniflora
'Rosea'

Zone 3
Height and spread: 8in. (20cm)

SILPHIUM *(Asteraceae)*

Common names: Rosinweed; Prairie dock

A genus of 20 species of herbaceous perennials from scrubland, prairies, fields and open woodland in eastern and central U.S.A., and Canada. Their leaves are basal, coarse, lance-shaped, ovate or triangular, toothed or pinnatifid, and opposite or alternate. The daisy-like flowers are large, and borne in branching corymbs.

- ✔ Good cut flowers
- ✔ Architectural plants
- ✔ Disease-free
- ✔ Pest-free

- ✘ Highly allergenic

CULTIVATION
Grow in alkaline to neutral, moist, deep, fertile soil in sun or part shade. Likes heavy soil.

PROPAGATION
Seed should be sown in a cold frame as soon as it is ripe. Division can be done in spring.

Silphium laciniatum

Zone 4
Height: 10ft. (3.5m) Spread: 2ft. (60cm)

SINNINGIA *(Gesneriaceae)*

Common names: Gloxinia

A genus of 40 species of shrubs and tuberous perennials from tropical forest in South and Central America. Their leaves are fleshy, ovate, and in opposite pairs. The flowers are tubular or trumpet- or bell-shaped, solitary or clustered, and borne in summer.

 Handsome foliage

CULTIVATION

Under glass, grow in loamless potting compost in indirect or bright filtered light, and high humidity. Water with moderation during growth, and dry off in winter.

Out of doors, grow in acid to neutral, moist, well-drained soil in part or deep shade.

PROPAGATION

Seed should be surface-sown at 70°F (21°C) in spring. Divide in spring.

Sinningia speciosa

Zone 10
Height and spread: 1ft. (30cm)

SISYRINCHIUM *(Iridaceae)*

Common names: None

A genus of 90 species of annuals and rhizomatous perennials found in nature in the Americas, but some are widely naturalized in other regions. They occur in a range of habitats from sea level to mountains, and their leaves are in basal clumps, linear, or sword-shaped. The flowers are cup- or star- or trumpet-shaped, and are solitary or borne in clusters of up to eight enclosed in two spathe bracts, in spring and summer. Some species are short-lived, some are evergreen.

✔ Drought-tolerant   ✘ Self-seeds
✔ Low allergen   ✘ Need to lift & divide often
✔ Handsome foliage

CULTIVATION

Grow in alkaline to neutral, well-drained, poor soil in sun. Dead-head to prevent self-seeding. Protect against excessive winter wet.

PROPAGATION

Seed should be sown in a cold frame in spring or autumn. Divide in spring.

Sisyrinchium angustifolium

Zone 3
Height: 20in. (50cm) Spread: 6in. (15cm)

Sisyrichium californicum

Zone 9
Height and spread: 6in. (15cm)

Sisyrinchium 'Californian Skies'

Zone 9
Height: 6in. (15cm) Spread: 4in. (10cm)

Sisyrinchium californicum Brachpus Group

Zone 8
Height: 2ft. (60cm) Spread: 6in. (15cm)

S

Sisyrinchium idahoense
'Album'

Zone 3
Height and spread: 6in. (15cm)

Sisyrinchium
'Pole Star'

Zone 3
Height and spread: 8in. (20cm)

Sisyrinchium
'Quaint and Queer'

Zone 7
Height and spread: 8in. (20cm)

Sisyrinchium striatum

Zone 8
Height: 3ft. (90cm) Spread: 1ft. (30cm)
Evergreen

Sisyrinchium striatum 'Aunt May'

Zone 8
Height: 3ft. (90cm) Spread: 1ft. (30cm)
Evergreen/Variegated foliage

SMILACINA *(Convallariaceae)*

Common names: False Solomon's seal; Wild spikenard

A genus of 25 species of rhizomatous perennials found in woodland in Central and North America and Asia. Their leaves are ovate or lance-shaped, veined and alternate. The flowers are star-shaped, perfumed, white, and borne in terminal panicles or racemes in spring. They are followed by green berries, which turn red.

✔ Flowers perfumed
✔ Have berries after flowering
✔ Disease-free

✔ Pest-free
✔ Good for drying for winter

CULTIVATION
Grow in acid to neutral, moist, humus-rich, fertile soil in part or full shade.

PROPAGATION
Seed should be sown in a cold frame in autumn. Divide in spring.

Smilacina racemosa A.G.M.

Zone 4
Height: 3ft. (90cm) Spread: 2ft. (60cm)

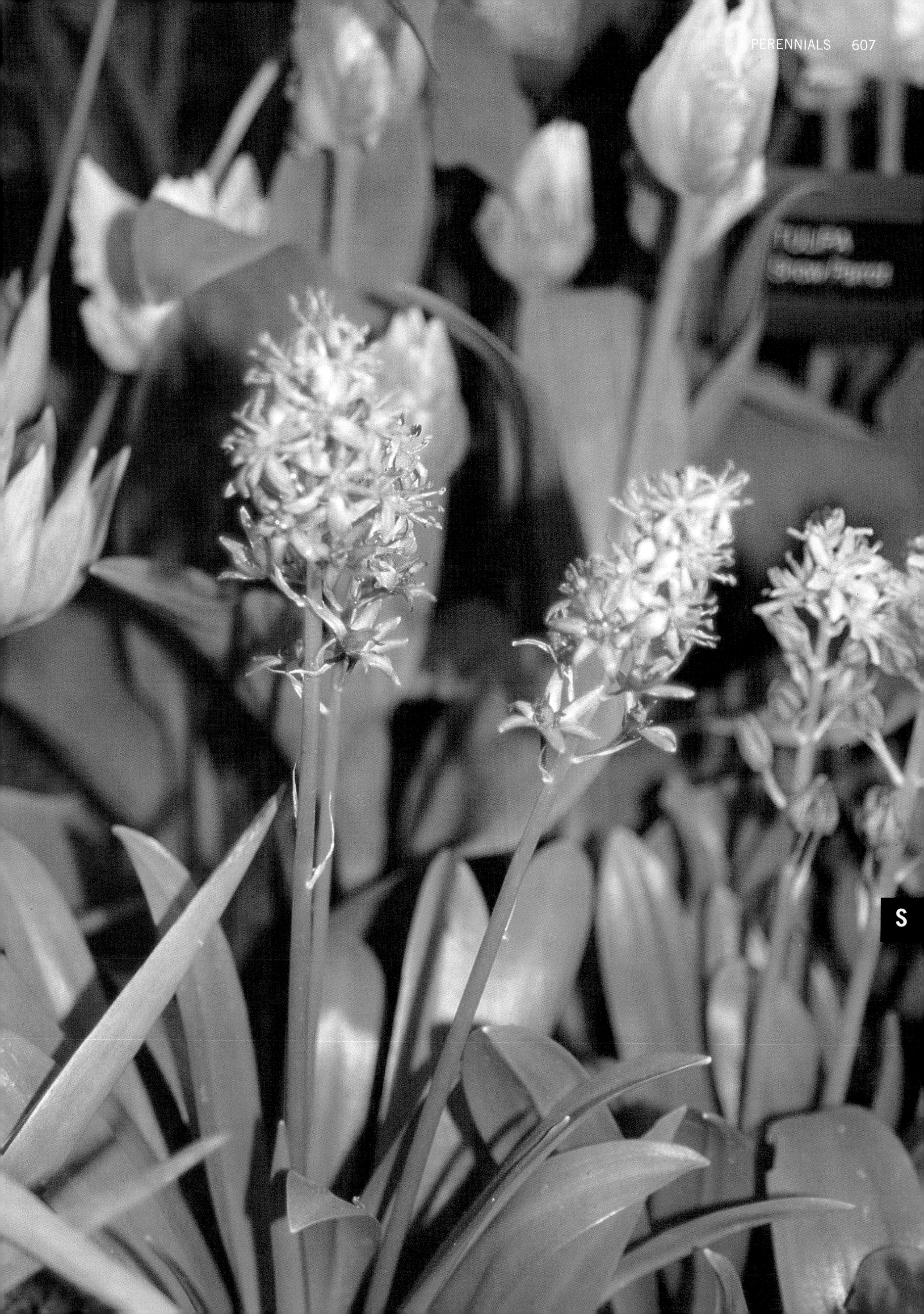

SOLANUM *(Solanaceae)*
Common names: None

A genus of 1,400 species of annuals, biennials, perennials (including the potato and the eggplant), climbers, subshrubs, shrubs and tree from a variety of habitats across the world. The perennials are herbaceous. Their leaves are entire or lobed or pinnate, and alternate. The flowers are small, star-, bell- or trumpet-shaped, and are borne singly or in cymes, panicles or umbels from spring to autumn. They are followed by fruits.

✔ Long-flowering
✔ Handsome foliage

✘ All parts poisonous
✘ Prone to aphid attack

CULTIVATION
Under glass, grow in loam-based potting compost in high humidity and full light, with shade at mid-day, or in bright filtered light. Water freely during growth, sparingly in winter.

Out of doors, grow in alkaline to neutral, moist, well-drained soil in sun. Prune climbers in late winter or early spring by cutting back to within three or four buds of permanent framework.

PROPAGATION
Seed should be sown at 68°F (20°C) in spring. Semi-ripe cuttings can be taken of climbers and rooted with bottom heat from summer to early autumn.

Solanum dulcamara
'Variegata' (Deadly nightshade)

Zone 4
Height: 12ft. (4m) Spread: 2ft. (60cm)

Solanum laxum
'Album' A.G.M.

Zone 9
Height: 20ft. (6m) Spread: 2ft. (60cm)

Solanum laxum
'Album Variegatum'

Zone 9
Height: 20ft. (6m) Spread: 2ft. (60cm)

Solanum laxum
'Aureovariegatum'

Zone 9
Height: 20ft. (6m) Spread: 2ft. (60cm)

Solanum pyracanthum

Zone 10
Height: 6ft. (2m) Spread: 1ft. (30cm)

Solanum tuberosum
'Golden Wonder' Potato

Zone 8
Height: 3ft. (90cm) Spread: 1ft. (30cm)

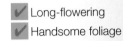

SOLENOPSIS *(Campanulaceae)*
Common names: None

A genus of 25 species of annuals and perennials found in exposed, dry areas in Central and South America, and Australia. Their leaves are ovate or linear or oblong, lobed or pinnatisect, and alternate. The flowers are solitary, salverform, long-tined, five-petalled stars, borne from spring to late autumn provided they are dead-headed.

✔ Long-flowering
✔ Disease-free
✔ Handsome foliage

✘ Prone to aphid attack

CULTIVATION
Under glass, grow in loam-based potting compost in full light. Water with moderation during growth, and sparingly in winter.

Out of doors, grow in well-drained, fertile soil in sun. Dead-head to prolong flowering.

PROPAGATION
Seed should be sown at 64°F (18°C) in spring. Softwood cuttings may be taken in summer.

Solenopsis axillaris

Zone 9
Height and spread: 1ft. (30cm)

SOLENOSTEMON *(Lamiaceae)*
Common names: Coleus; Flame nettle; Painted nettle

A genus of 60 species of evergreen perennials from tropical forests of Asia and Africa. They are grown for their foliage, the flowers being unspectacular. The leaves are ovate, toothed, hairy, opposite and colorful. The flowers are tiny, two-lipped, tubular, and borne in whorls at any time of year.

✔ Handsome foliage
✔ Long-flowering
✔ Disease-free

✘ Short-lived
✘ Flowers insignificant

CULTIVATION
Under glass, grow in loam-based potting compost in bright filtered or moderate light. Water freely during growth, but keep just moist in winter. Repot every spring.

Out of doors, grow in reliably moist, humus-rich soil in a sheltered corner in sun or part shade. Pinch out in early season to promote bushiness.

PROPAGATION
Seed should be surface-sown at 75°F (24°C) in spring. Softwood cuttings may be rooted with bottom heat in spring or summer.

S

Solenostemon
'Display'

Zone 10
Height and spread: 2ft. (60cm)

Solenostemon
'Juliet Quartermain'

Zone 10
Height and spread: 2ft. (60cm).

S

Solenostemon
'Mission Gem'

Zone 10
Height and spread: 2ft. (60cm)

Solenostemon
'Pineapplette' A.G.M.

Zone 10
Height and spread: 2ft. (60cm)

Solenostemon
'Red Velvet'

Zone 10
Height and spread: 2ft. (60cm)

Solenostemon
'Rose Blush'

Zone 10
Height and spread: 2ft. (60cm)

Solenostemon
'Walter Turner'

Zone 10
Height and spread: 2ft. (60cm)

SOLIDAGO *(Asteraceae)*

Common names: Golden Rod; Aaron's rod

A genus of 100 species of vigorous perennials from riversides, prairies and roadsides in North and South America and Asia. Their leaves are lance-shaped or elliptic, entire or toothed, veined, and alternate. The flowers are small daisies borne in one-sided panicles or racemes, in late summer and autumn.

✔ Good cut flowers	✘ Highly allergenic
✔ Attracts butterflies	✘ Self-seeds
	✘ Mildew prone

CULTIVATION
Grow in gritty, well-drained soil in sun. Dead-head to prevent self-seeding.

PROPAGATION
Divide in spring or autumn.

Solidago flexicaulis
'Variegatus'

Zone 4
Height: 30in. (75cm) Spread: 18in. (45cm)

Solidago
'Goldenmosa' A.G.M.

Zone 4
Height: 32in. (80cm) Spread: 18in. (45cm)

X SOLIDASTER *(Asteraceae)*

Common names: None

A genus of a single species of perennial, *x S. luteus*, of hybrid garden origin between *Aster ptarmicoides* and *Solidago canadensis*. Its leaves are lance-shaped or elliptic or linear, and alternate. The flowers are daisy-like, small, and borne in branched panicles from midsummer to early autumn.

✔ Good cut flowers   ✘ Highly allergenic
✔ Attracts butterflies   ✘ Self-seeds
                           ✘ Mildew prone

CULTIVATION
Grow in well-drained fertile soil in sun. Dead-head to prevent self-seeding.

PROPAGATION
Division in spring. Basal cuttings can be taken then also.

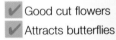

x Solidaster luteus

Zone 6
Height: 3ft. (90cm) Spread: 1ft. (30cm)

x Solidaster luteus
'Lemore' A.G.M.

Zone 6
Height: 32in. (80cm) Spread: 1ft. (30cm)

SPARAXIS *(Iridaceae)*
Common names: Harlequin flower

A genus of six species of cormous perennials found in wet, rocky habitats in South Africa. Their leaves are lance- or sword-shaped, ribbed and in a basal fan. The flowers are wide funnels, and borne in loose spikes of up to five in spring and summer.

- Disease-free
- Pest-free

CULTIVATION
Under glass, plant corms 4in. (10cm) deep in autumn in a mix of equal parts loam-based potting compost, grit and leaf mould, in full light, with shade at mid-day. Water sparingly, even during growth, and keep completely dry in winter.

Out of doors, grow in well-drained, fertile soil in a sheltered corner in sun. Protect against frost in winter.

PROPAGATION
Seed should be sown in a cold frame as soon as it is ripe. Separate offsets during dormancy.

Sparaxis elegans

Zone 9
Height: 18in. (45cm) Spread: 4in. (10cm)

SPHAERALCEA *(Malvaceae)*
Common names: Globe mallow; False mallow

A genus of 60 species of annuals, perennials, subshrubs and shrubs found in well-drained, warm regions such as scrubland, wasteland and mountainsides in North and South America, and southern Africa. Their downy leaves are round or linear or lance-shaped, simple or lobed or palmate, toothed and spirally-arranged. The mallow-like flowers are cup- or saucer-shaped, and solitary or in panicles or racemes over longish periods in summer.

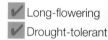
- Long-flowering
- Drought-tolerant
- Handsome foliage
- Pest-free

CULTIVATION
Under glass, grow in loam-based, grit-enriched potting compost, in full light; water sparingly whilst dormant. Repot in spring each year.

Out of doors, grow in sharply-draining, soil in a warm corner in sun. Protect against winter wet.

PROPAGATION
Seed should be sown at 55°F (13°C) in spring. Divide in spring. Strike softwood or basal cuttings with bottom heat in spring or early summer.

Sphaeralcea fendleri

Zone 8
Height: 32in. (80cm) Spread: 2ft. (60cm)

Sphaeralcea munroana

Zone 8
Height: 32in. (80cm) Spread: 3ft. (90cm)

S

SPIRANTHES *(Orchidaceae)*

Common names: None

A genus of 50 species of tuberous orchids found in woodland and grassland in North America in particular, with a few from Eurasia. They are mainly terrestrial, but some are epiphytic and are found in temperate or tropical regions, so can vary widely in degree of hardiness. Their leaves are in basal rosettes, ovate or round or lance-shaped, and fleshy or papery. The flowers are small, and borne in spiral racemes on tall stems.

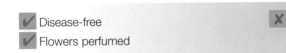

✔ Disease-free

✔ Flowers perfumed

✘ Prone to aphid attack

CULTIVATION

Under glass, grow in terrestrial orchid compost in bright filtered light. Water freely during growth, keep dry and frost-free in winter.

Out of doors, plant whilst dormant in moist, well-drained, leafy, humus-rich soil in a sheltered corner in part shade. Keep dry and protect tender species against frost in winter.

PROPAGATION

Divide when dormant.

Spiranthes gracilis

Zone 3
Height: 30in. (75cm) Spread: 4in. (10cm)

STACHYS *(Lamiaceae)*

Common names: Hedge nettle; Betony; Woundwort

A genus of 300 species of annuals, perennials and evergreen shrubs found in various habitats such as scrubland, wasteland, hillsides, mountainsides, forest clearings and stream sides in the temperate northern hemisphere. The perennials are rhizomatous and stoloniferous. Their leaves are large, stalked, basal, and small stalkless stem, and ovate or elliptic or lance-shaped, toothed or scalloped, wrinkled, veined and hairy. They may be pleasantly or unpleasantly aromatic. The flowers are two-lipped, tubular, hooded, and borne in spikes of axillary whorls, or racemes.

✔ Good cut flowers

✔ Drought-tolerant

✔ Attracts bees

✔ Attracts butterflies

✘ Prone to slug damage

✘ Mildew prone

✘ Need to be staked

CULTIVATION

Under glass, alpine species are best grown in an alpine house in gritty, loam-based potting compost in full light.

Out of doors, grow in fertile, well-drained soil in sun or part shade.

PROPAGATION

Seed should be sown in a cold frame in spring or autumn. Divide in spring.

Stachys byzantina
(Woolly betony)

Zone 5
Height: 18in. (45cm) Spread: 2ft. (60cm)

Stachys byzantina
'Big Ears'

Zone 5
Height: 18in. (45cm) Spread: 2ft. (60cm)

Stachys byzantina
'Striped Phantom'

Zone 5
Height: 18in. (45cm) Spread: 2ft. (60cm)

S

S

Stachys candida

Zone 5
Height: 6in. (15cm) Spread: 1ft. (30cm)

Stachys macrantha

Zone 5
Height: 2ft. (60cm) Spread: 1ft. (30cm)

Stachys macrantha
'Superba'

Zone5
Height: 2ft. (60cm) Spread: 1ft. (30cm)

Stachys monieri

Zone 5
Height: 20in. (50cm) Spread: 18in. (45cm)

Stachys officinalis
(Common betony)

Zone 5
Height: 2ft. (60cm) Spread: 1ft. (30cm)

STERNBERGIA *(Amaryllidaceae)*

Common names: Autumn daffodil

A genus of eight species of bulbous perennials found in fields, stony ground and scrubland from southern Europe across to Central Asia. Their leaves are basal, erect, and strap-shaped or linear or lance-shaped. The crocus-like flowers are solitary, goblets or funnels and are borne on leafless stems in autumn.

 Resent transplantation

CULTIVATION
Under glass, plant bulbs 6in. (15cm) deep in late summer in a mix of equal parts loam, grit and leaf mould in full light. Water sparingly during growth, sparingly after flowering, and keep completely dry during dormancy.

Out of doors, grow in sharply-draining, fertile soil in sun. Do not split and divide unless flowering is impaired.

PROPAGATION
Seed should be sown at 61°F (16°C) as soon as it is ripe. Separate offsets during dormancy.

Sternbergia sicula

Zone 7
Height: 3in. (8cm) Spread: 2in. (5cm)

STENOTAPHRUM *(Poaceae)*
Common names: None

A genus of six species of annual or perennial grasses from across the subtropical and tropical regions of the world, where they are found for the greater part at the seaside, and rarely inland. Their leaves are upright, linear or lance-shaped, and folded or flat. The flowering spikelets are greenish-brown, and borne in racemes in summer.

- ✔ Evergreen
- ✔ Handsome foliage
- ✔ Disease-free
- ✔ Pest-free
- ✘ Highly allergenic
- ✘ Invasive

CULTIVATION
Under glass, grow in loam-based potting compost in full light. Water freely whilst in growth, but sparingly in winter.

Out of doors, grow in moist, well-drained soil in sun. Protect against frost in winter.

PROPAGATION
Divide in spring, or take nodal cuttings in late spring or summer.

Stenotaphrum secundatum
'Variegataum' A.G.M.

Zone 9
Height: 6in. (15cm) Spread: indefinite

STIPA *(Poaceae)*
Common names: Feather grass; Spear grass; Needle grass

A genus of 300 species of annual and herbaceous or evergreen perennial grasses found on stony slopes and in woodland across the temperate parts of the world. Their leaves are linear, in-rolled or flat, and pleated. The flowers are in narrow panicles of flattened spikes, borne from early summer to autumn.

- ✔ Long-flowering
- ✔ Disease-free
- ✔ Pest-free
- ✔ Architectural plants
- ✘ Highly allergenic

CULTIVATION
Grow in fertile, well-drained soil in sun. Tidy up in spring by removing dead leaves.

PROPAGATION
Seed should be sown in a cold frame in spring. Divide in spring or early summer.

Stipa gigantea A.G.M.

Zone 8
Height: 5ft (1.5m) Spread: 4ft. (1.2m)
Evergreen

STOKESIA *(Asteraceae)*
Common names: Stokes' aster

A genus of but one species of evergreen perennial, *S. laevis*, from moist acid soil in south-eastern U.S.A. The leaves are simple, entire and smooth, and are in basal rosettes. The cornflower-like flowers are long-lasting, and are solitary or in flat corymbs from midsummer to autumn.

- ✔ Evergreen
- ✔ Good cut flowers
- ✔ Disease-free
- ✔ Pest-free
- ✘ Highly allergenic
- ✘ Needs to be staked

CULTIVATION
Grow in acid, moist, very well drained soil in sun—it damps off in heavy, wet soil. Dead-head to prolong flowering.

PROPAGATION
Seed should be sown in a cold frame in autumn. Division can be done in spring, or root cuttings taken in late winter.

Stokesia laevis

Zone 5
Height: 2ft. (60cm) Spread: 18in. (45cm)

S

Stokesia laevis 'Alba'

Zone 5
Height: 2ft. (60cm) Spread: 18in. (45cm)

STRELITZIA *(Strelitziaceae)*

Common names: Bird of paradise

A genus of five species of evergreen perennials from bushland and riverbanks in South Africa. Their leaves resemble those of the banana closely and are large, long-stalked, and lance-shaped or oblong. The flowers have horizontal green spathes, and the flowers arise from the top of the spathe in sequence. They vary in color, and are crested.

✔ Good cut flowers ✔ Repeat-flowering
✔ Evergreen ✔ Disease-free

Strelitzia reginae
A.G.M.

Zone 9
Height: 6ft. (2m) Spread: 3ft. (90cm)

CULTIVATION

Under glass, grow in loam-based potting compost in full light, but with mid-day shade, and good ventilation. Water freely during growth, but sparingly in winter. Repot every other year.

Out of doors, grow in moist, fertile, well-drained soil in a sheltered corner in sun or part shade.

PROPAGATION

Seed should be sown at 70°F (21°C) in spring. Rooted suckers can be separated in spring.

STREPTOCARPUS *(Gesneriaceae)*

Common names: Cape primrose

A genus of 130 species of annuals, perennials and subshrubs from rainforest, wet banks, damp rocks and grassland in southern Africa, Madagascar and China. Some are epiphytic, some are monocarpic. Their leaves are round or linear, wrinkled, hairy, and veined, and are in basal rosettes or in opposite pairs on the stems. The flowers are tubular, two-lipped, and are borne in axillary cymes, or from the leaf rosettes.

✔ Long-flowering
✔ Handsome foliage

Streptocarpus
'Crystal Ice' A.G.M (PBR)

Zone 10
Height and spread: 1ft. (30cm)

CULTIVATION

Under glass, grow in loam-free potting compost in bright filtered light with shade at mid-day. Water freely during growth, but allowing the compost to dry out between waterings. Keep just moist in winter. Repot every spring.

Out of doors, grow in moist, leafy, well-drained, humus-rich soil in part shade.

PROPAGATION

Seed should be surface-sown at 64°F (18°C) in early spring. Divide in spring. Leaf cuttings may be taken in spring or early summer.

Streptocarpus 'Cynthia'

Zone 10
Height and spread: 1ft. (30cm)

Streptocarpus 'Heidi'

Zone 10
Height and spread: 10in. (25cm)

Streptocarpus parviflorus

Zone 10
Height: 10in. (25cm) Spread: 8in. (20cm)

Streptocarpus saxorum

Zone 10
Height: 6in. (15cm) Spread: 2ft. (60cm)

Streptocarpus 'Tina'

Zone 10
Height and spread: 10in. (25cm)

STROBILANTHES *(Acanthaceae)*

Common names: None

A genus of 250 species of perennials or shrubs found in woodland edges in Madagascar and Asia. Their leaves are lance-shaped or elliptic or ovate, toothed or entire, and opposite. The flowers are funnel-shaped or tubular, five-lobed, two-lipped, and are borne in conical spikes or panicles in summer.

 Disease-free

CULTIVATION
Grow in sharply-draining fertile soil in sun or part shade.

PROPAGATION
Seed should be sown at 64°F (18°C) in spring. Softwood or basal cuttings can be taken in spring or early summer, and rooted with bottom heat.

Strobilanthes atropurpureus

Zone 5
Height: 4ft. (1.2m) Spread: 3ft. (90cm)

S

S

STROMANTHE *(Marantaceae)*

Common names: None

A genus of 13 species of perennials found in clearings and forest floors in South and Central America. Their handsome leaves are ovate, obovate, lance-shaped or elliptic, and borne at the bottom of the flowering stems. The cup-shaped flowers have colorful bracts and are borne in panicles or racemes in winter to spring and summer.

✔ Winter-flowering   ✔ Disease-free

✔ Handsome foliage

CULTIVATION

Under glass, grow in any potting compost in bright filtered light. Water freely during growth, and moderately in winter.

Out of doors, grow in moist, fertile soil in sun or part shade.

PROPAGATION

Seed should be sown at 64°F (18°C) in early spring. Divide carefully when dormant.

Stromanthe
'Multicolor'

Zone 10
Height and spread: 18in. (45cm)

Stromanthe
'Triostar'

Zone 10
Height and spread: 18in. (45cm)

STYLOPHORUM *(Papaveraceae)*

Common names: Celandine poppy

A genus of three species of herbaceous perennials from eastern North America and East Asia. Their leaves are in basal rosettes, and stem, and are pinnatisect. The poppy-like flowers are tallow saucers borne on terminal umbels in spring and summer.

✔ Long-flowering   ✖ Prone to slug damage

✔ Handsome foliage   ✖ Self-seeds

✔ Handsome seed-heads   ✖ Resents disturbance

CULTIVATION

Grow in moist, humus-rich soil in part or deep shade. Dead-head to prevent self-seeding.

PROPAGATION

Seed should be sown in a cold frame in autumn. Division can be done in spring, but is not well tolerated.

Stylophorum diphyllum
(Celandine poppy)

Zone 7
Height and spread: 1ft. (30cm)

S

Stylophorum lasiocarpum

Zone 7
Height: 18in. (45cm) Spread: 1ft. (30cm)

SUCCISA *(Dipsacaceae)*
Common names: Devil's bit scabious; Blue buttons

A genus of but a single species of rhizomatous perennial, *S. pratensis*, found in wet moorland and boggy meadows in Eurasia and north-west Africa. Its leaves are elliptic or obovate, and in basal rosettes. The flowers are solitary, pincushion-like, resemble scabious flowers, and are borne from midsummer to late autumn.

✔ Long-flowering
✔ Disease-free
✔ Pest-free

CULTIVATION
Grow in humus-rich, acid to neutral, reliably moist soil in sun or part shade.

PROPAGATION
Seed should be sown in a cold frame in spring or autumn. Basal cuttings may be taken in spring.

Succisa pratensis

Zone 5
Height and spread: 2ft. (60cm)

SUTERA *(Scrophulariaceae)*
Common names: None

A genus of annuals, perennials and evergreen shrubs found in wood edges in South Africa. Their leaves are elliptic, toothed, lobed or scalloped and opposite. The flowers are small, five-lobed, salverform, and produced singly from the leaf axils, or borne in terminal or axillary cymes, panicles, spikes or racemes in summer and autumn.

✔ Long-flowering   ✘ Prone to aphid attack

CULTIVATION
Under glass, grow in loam-based potting compost in full light. Water freely during growth, but sparingly in winter.

Out of doors, grow in fertile, well-drained soil in sun.

PROPAGATION
Seed should be sown at 64°F (18°C) in spring. Divide in spring or take stem-tip cuttings and root with bottom heat in summer.

Sutera cordata
'Snowflake'

Zone 9
Height and spread: 1ft. (30cm)

Sutera
'Olympic Gold'

Zone 9
Height 1ft. (30cm) Spread: 18in. (45cm)

SYMPHYANDRA *(Campanulaceae)*

Common names: None

A genus of a dozen species of rhizomatous perennials from the mountains of the eastern Mediterranean, the Caucasus, Central Asia and Korea. Their leaves are reniform, toothed, hairy and basal. The flowers are bell-shaped or tubular, and are borne in panicles, corymbs or racemes over long periods in summer.

✔ Long-flowering	✘ Self-seeds
✔ Handsome foliage	✘ Prone to slug damage
✔ Free-flowering	✘ Short-lived
✔ Disease-free	

Symphyandra armena

Zone 7
Height: 18in. (45cm) Spread: 1ft. (30cm)

CULTIVATION
Grow in fertile, light, well-drained soil in sun or part shade. Dead-head to prevent self-seeding.

PROPAGATION
Seed should be sown in a cold frame as soon as it is ripe.

SYMPHYTUM *(Boraginaceae)*

Common names: Comfrey

A genus of 35 species of perennials found in damp habitats such as stream sides, roadsides, woodland, scrubland and wasteland in Eurasia and North Africa. They are coarse, rhizomatous, hairy and bristly and can be invasive. Their leaves are ovate, or oblong, or lance-shaped, or elliptic, wrinkled, veined and basal. The flowers are tubular, and borne in terminal cymes, in spring or summer.

✔ Low allergen	✘ Leaves and roots poisonous
✔ Attracts bees	✘ Foliage is skin-irritant
✔ Handsome foliage	
✔ Disease-free	
✔ Pest-free	

S

Symphytum
'Goldsmith'

Zone 5
Height and spread: 1ft. (30cm)

CULTIVATION
Grow in moist, fertile soil in sun or part shade. Dead-head variegated forms to retain variegation.

PROPAGATION
Seed should be sown in a cold frame in spring or autumn. Divide in spring. Root cuttings may be taken in early winter.

Symphytum ibericum

Zone 5
Height: 16in. (40cm) Spread: indefinite
Invasive

Symphytum ibericum
'Landthorne's Pink'

Zone 5
Height and spread: 18in. (45cm)

Symphytum
'Lambrook Sunrise'

Zone 5
Height: 22in. (55cm) Spread: 18in. (45cm)

Symphytum orientale

Zone 5
Height: 28in. (70cm) Spread: indefinite
Invasive

Symphytum x uplandicum

Zone 5
Height: 6ft. (2m) Spread: indefinite
Invasive

Symphytum x uplandicum
'Axminster Gold'

Zone 5
Height: 6ft. (2m) Spread: 4ft. (1.2m)

S

Symphytum x uplandicum
'Variegatum' A.G.M.

Zone 5
Height: 6ft. (2m) Spread: 4ft. (1.2m)

S

TANACETUM
TARAXACUM
TELEKIA
TELLIMA
TEUCRIUM
THALICTRUM
THERMOPSIS
THUNBERGIA
THYMUS
TIARELLA
TIGRIDIA
TOLMEIA
TRACHELIUM
TRACHELOSPERMUM
TRADESCANTIA
TRICYRTIS
TRIFOLIUM
TRILLIUM
TRITELEIA
TRITONIA
TROLLIUS
TROPAEOLUM
TUBERARIA
TULBAGHIA
TULIPA
TWEEDIA

T

TANACETUM *(Asteraceae)*
Common names: Pyrethrum; Feverfew

A genus of 70 species of annuals, perennials and subshrubs from a range of habitats in the temperate northern hemisphere, such as meadows, dry slopes, cliffs and meadowland. Their leaves are simple or pinnate to tripinnate, toothed or scalloped, aromatic and mostly basal, but some have spirally-deployed stem leaves. The daisy-like flowers are solitary or in corymbs, and have yellow discs and yellow, white or red ray florets.

✔ Repeat-flowering	✘ Short-lived
✔ Good cut flowers	✘ Prone to slug damage
✔ Handsome foliage	✘ Foliage is skin-irritant

CULTIVATION
Grow in any well-drained soil in sun. Dead-head to encourage repeat-flowering.

PROPAGATION
Seed should be sown at 55°F (13°C) in late winter or early spring. Divide, or take basal cuttings, in spring.

Tanacetum coccineum
'Brenda' A.G.M.

Zone 5
Height: 30in. (75cm) Spread: 18in. (45cm)

Tanacetum coccineum
Eileen May Robinson' A.G.M.

Zone 5
Height: 30in. (75cm) Spread: 45 cm(18 in)

Tanacetum coccineum
'James Kelway' A.G.M.

Zone 5
Height: 30in. (75cm) Spread: 18in. (45cm)

Tanacetum coccineum
'Snow Cloud'

Zone 5
Height: 30in. (75cm) Spread: 18in. (45cm)

Tanacetum parthenium (Feverfew)

Zone 6
Height: 2ft. (60cm) Spread: 1ft. (30cm)
Self-seeds

Tanacetum parthenium 'Aureum'

Zone 6
Height: 2ft. (60cm) Spread: 1ft. (30cm)
Self-seeds

Tanacetum parthenium 'Rowallane'

Zone 6
Height: 2ft. (60cm) Spread: 1ft. (30cm)
Self-seeds.

T

Tanacetum ptarmiciflorum
'Silver Feather'

Zone 9
Height: 2ft. (60cm) Spread: 16in. (40cm)

Tanacetum vulgare

Zone 4
Height: 3ft. (90cm) Spread: 18in. (45cm)
Invasive

Tanacetum vulgare 'Silver Lace'

Zone 4
Height: 3ft. (90cm) Spread: 18in. (45cm)
Invasive

TARAXACUM *(Asteraceae)*
Common names: Dandelion

A large genus of tap-rooted perennials from arctic and temperate regions of the northern hemisphere in particular. Their leaves are simple or pinnate, and in basal rosettes. The flowers are yellow daisies, borne over long periods in spring and summer.

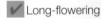 Long-flowering

✗ Self-seeds
✗ Resent disturbance

CULTIVATION
Grow in any well-drained, fertile soil in sun or part shade. Dead-head to prevent self-seeding.

PROPAGATION
Seed should be sown as soon as it is ripe.

Taraxicum faeroensis

Zone 5
Height and spread: 1ft. (30cm)

Taraxicum officinale

Zone 5
Height and spread: 1ft. (30cm)

TELEKIA *(Asteraceae)*
Common names: None

A genus of two species of herbaceous perennials found in stream sides and moist woodland across Eurasia. The leaves are basal, ovate, toothed, and alternate stem. The daisy-like flower-heads are solitary, have yellow disc and ray florets, and are borne in branching sprays from early summer to early autumn.

✔ Long-flowering	✘ Invasive	
✔ Architectural plants	✘ Self-seeds	
✔ Foliage aromatic	✘ Prone to slug damage	
	✘ Highly allergenic	

CULTIVATION
Grow in moist soil in a sheltered corner in shade.

PROPAGATION
Seed should be sown as soon as it is ripe. Divide in spring.

Telekia speciosa

Zone 6
Height: 6ft. (2m) Spread: 3ft. (90cm)

TELLIMA *(Saxifragaceae)*
Common names: Fringe cups

A genus of a single species of herbaceous perennial, *T. grandiflora*, from cool, moist woodland in western North America. The leaves are in basal rosettes, hairy, triangular, heart- or kidney-shaped, five to seven-lobed, toothed and scalloped. The flowers are tiny, bell-shaped, five-petalled, and are borne in tall terminal racemes from late spring to midsummer.

✔ Low allergen	✘ Flowers insignificant	
✔ Handsome foliage	✘ Prone to slug damage	
	✘ Self-seeds	

CULTIVATION
Grow in any humus-rich soil in sun or part shade.

PROPAGATION
Seed should be sown in a cold frame as soon as it is ripe, or in spring. Division may be done in spring.

Tellima grandiflora
(Alaskan fringe-cup)

Zone 6
Height: 30in. (75cm) Spread: 1ft. (30cm)

Tellima grandiflora
'Forest Frost'

Zone 6
Height: 30in. (75cm) Spread: 1ft. (30cm)

T

T

TEUCRIUM *(Lamiaceae)*
Common names: None

A genus of 300 species of perennials, subshrubs and shrubs from woodland, thickets, mountains and dry stony regions across the world. The aromatic leaves are lobed or simple, toothed or entire, and in opposite pairs. The flowers are bell-shaped or tubular, and are borne in whorled clusters or racemes in summer and autumn.

✔ Long-flowering
✔ Foliage aromatic
✔ Drought-tolerant
✔ Handsome foliage

CULTIVATION
Grow in alkaline to neutral, well-drained soil in sun.

PROPAGATION
Seed should be sown in a cold frame as soon as it is ripe. Softwood cuttings taken in early summer or semi-ripe cuttings in midsummer require bottom heat to root.

Teucrium hyrcanicum

Zone 6
Height: 30in. (75cm) Spread: 1ft. (30cm)

Teucrium x lucidrys

Zone 5
Height: 20in. (50cm) Spread: 1ft. (30cm)

Teucrium x lucidrys
'Variegatum'

Zone 5
Height: 20in. (50cm) Spread: 1ft. (30cm)

Teucrium polium

Zone 7
Height and spread: 1ft. (30cm)

Teucrium scorodonia
'Crispum Marginatum'

Zone 6
Height and spread: 3ft. (90cm)

T

THALICTRUM *(Ranunculaceae)*
Common names: Meadow rue

A genus of 130 species of perennials found in shady, moist, mountainous sites and on stream sides and meadows in the temperate northern hemisphere in particular, but all over the world except Australasia. They may be rhizomatous or tuberous. Their leaves are alternate, four-pinnate or four-ternate, with lobed and toothed leaflets. The flowers are tiny, lack petals, but the sepals are petal-like, and are borne in terminal racemes, corymbs or panicles in early summer. They thrive best where summers are cool and moist.

✔ Good cut flowers	✘ Mildew prone
✔ Drought-tolerant	✘ Prone to slug damage
✔ Handsome foliage	✘ Resent disturbance
✔ Low allergen	✘ Self-seeds

CULTIVATION
Grow in moist, humus-rich soil in part shade. *T. flavum* subsp. *glaucum* needs sun and drier soil. Taller varieties may require to be staked.

PROPAGATION
Seed should be sown as soon as it is ripe, or in spring. Divide in early spring as growth is starting, but divisions are slow to establish. *T. delavayi* 'Hewitt's Double' is sterile and may be propagated only by division.

Thalictrum aquilegifolium
'White Cloud'

Zone 6
Height: 3ft. (90cm) Spread: 45 cm.(18 in)

Thalictrum delavayi
A.G.M.

Zone 6
Height: 5ft. (1.5m) Spread: 2ft. (60cm)

Thalictrum delavayi
'Album'

Zone 6
Height: 5ft. (1.5m) Spread: 2ft. (60cm)

Thalictrum delavayi
'Hewitt's Double' A.G.M.
Zone 6
Height: 5ft. (1.5m) Spread: 2ft. (60cm)
Sterile cultivar

Thalictrum flavum

Zone 6
Height: 3ft. (90cm) Spread: 18in. (45cm)

Thalictrum flavum
subsp. *glaucum* A.G.M.

Zone 6
Height: 3ft. (90cm) Spread: 2ft. (60cm)

T

Thalictrum kiusianum

Zone 8
Height: 4in. (10cm) Spread: 1ft. (30cm)

Thalictrum minus adiantifolium

Zone6
Height: 80 cm.(32in.) Spread: 1ft. (30cm)

Thalictrum rochebrunianum

Zone 8
Height: 3ft. (90cm) Spread: 1ft. (30cm)

THERMOPSIS *(Papilionaceae)*
Common names: None

A genus of 20 species of rhizomatous perennials from stream sides, grassland and woodland in Russia, east Asia, northern India and North America. Their attractive leaves are basal and stem, alternate, and three-palmate. The lupin-like, pea flowers have round, standard petals and keel and wing petals, and are borne in axillary or terminal racemes in spring and summer.

✔ Good cut flowers	✘ Prone to slug damage
✔ Attracts bees	✘ Resent disturbance

CULTIVATION
They tolerate a wide range of conditions but do best in well-drained, loamy soil in sun or part shade.

PROPAGATION
Seed should be sown at 55°F (13°C) in spring; move seedlings into their flowering positions as soon as possible, as they resent transplantation.

Thermopsis lanceolata

Zone 3
Height: 32in. (80cm) Spread: 1ft. (30cm)

Thermopsis rhombifolia
var. *montana*

Zone 4
Height: 3ft. (90cm) Spread: 2ft. (60cm)

T

THUNBERGIA *(Acanthaceae)*

Common names: Black-eyed Susan

A genus of 100 species of annuals, evergreen perennial climbers and shrubs from forest floor, and rocky areas, in southern and tropical Africa, temperate and tropical Asia, and Madagascar. Their leaves are ovate or elliptic or rounded, opposite, and may be lobed or toothed. The flowers are tubular or salverform, five-lobed, and solitary borne from the leaf axils or in terminal racemes, in summer.

✔ Evergreen
✔ Disease-free

CULTIVATION
Under glass, grow in loam-based potting compost in full light with shade at mid-day. Water freely whilst in growth, sparingly in winter.

Out of doors, grow in moist, well-drained fertile soil in sun or part shade. Prune in early spring for size and shape.

PROPAGATION
Seed should be sown at 64°F (18°C) in spring. Layer in spring. Greenwood cuttings may be taken in early summer or semi-ripe cuttings in mid to late summer, but bottom heat is required to root.

Thunbergia alata
(Black-eyed Susan)

Zone 10
Height: 8ft. (2.5m) Spread: 2ft. (60cm)

THYMUS *(Lamiaceae)*

Common names: Thyme

A genus of 350 species of evergreen, aromatic perennials, subshrubs and shrubs from dry, limy grassland across Eurasia. Their leaves are small, oval or linear, and opposite. The flowers are small, two-lipped, tubular, have conspicuous bracts and are borne in terminal clusters or whorled racemes in summer. Several species (*TT. vulgaris, x citriodorus* and *herba-barona*) have culinary use. The status of many cultivars is uncertain.

✔ Attracts bees
✔ Disease-free
✔ Evergreen
✔ Pest-free
✔ Foliage aromatic

CULTIVATION
Grow in alkaline to neutral, well-drained soil in sun. Cut back vigorous forms after flowering to retain compactness.

PROPAGATION
Seed should be sown in a cold frame in spring. Divide in spring. Take softwood cuttings in early spring or semi-ripe cuttings in mid to late summer.

Thymus citriodorus
'Golden Queen'
Zone 7
Height: 1ft. (30cm) Spread: 18in. (45cm)
Foliage variegated

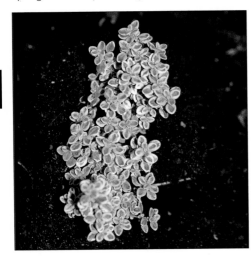

Thymus citriodorus
'Variegatus'

Zone 7
Height: 1ft. (30cm) Spread: 18in. (45cm)

Thymus 'Doone Valley'

Zone 7
Height: 5in. (12cm) Spread: 14in. (35cm)
Foliage variegated

Thymus 'Hartington Silver'

Zone 7
Height: 1ft. (30cm) Spread: 14in. (35cm)
Foliage variegated

T

T

Thymus
'Peter Davis'

Zone 7
Height ' 4in. (10cm) ' Spread: 8in. (20cm)

Thymus pulegioides
'Bertram Anderson' A.G.M.

Zone 7
Height: 5in. (12cm) Spread: 1ft. (30cm)

Thymus pulegioides 'Foxley'

Zone 7
Height: 1ft. (30cm) Spread: 2ft. (60cm)
Foliage variegated

Thymus serpyllum 'Goldstream'

Zone 7
Height: 5in. (12cm) Spread: 1ft. (30cm)
Foliage variegated

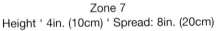

Thymus serpyllum
var. *coccineus* 'Minor'

Zone 7
Height: 4in. (10cm) Spread: 1ft. (30cm)

Thymus vulgaris
'Silver Posie'

Zone 7
Height: 1ft. (30cm) Spread: 16in. (40cm)

TIARELLA *(Saxifragaceae)*

Common names: Foam flower

A genus of seven species of herbaceous, rhizomatous perennials from stream sides and woodland in east Asia and North America. Their basal leaves are heart-shaped or round or ovate, toothed, simple, or palmately-lobed, hairy and veined. The flowers are tiny, fluffy stars, borne in terminal racemes or panicles over a long period in spring and summer.

✔ Long-flowering   ✘ Prone to slug damage
✔ Disease-free
✔ Low allergen
✔ Handsome foliage
✔ Drought-tolerant
✔ Good ground cover in shade

CULTIVATION
Grow in moist, cool, humus-rich soil in part or deep shade. Protect against winter wet.

PROPAGATION
Sow seed in a cold frame as soon as ripe, or in spring, when division can also be carried out.

Tiarella
'Black Snowflake'

Zone 3
Height: 10in. (25cm) Spread: 1ft. (30cm)

Tiarella cordifolia
A.G.M.

Zone 3
Height: 1ft. (30cm) Spread: 2ft. (60cm)

Tiarella cordifolia
'Cygnet'

Zone 3
Height: 8in. (20cm) Spread: 18in. (45cm)

Tiarella
'Mint Chocolate'

Zone 3
Height: 6in. (15cm) Spread: 18in. (45cm)

Tiarella polyphylla

Zone 7
Height: 16in. (40cm) Spread: 1ft. (30cm)

Tiarella
'Starfish'

Zone 3
Height: 8in. (20cm) Spread: 1ft. (30cm)

Tiarella wherryi
A.G.M.

Zone 6
Height and spread: 8in. (20cm)

Tiarella wherryi 'Heronswood'

Zone 6
Height and spread: 8in. (20cm)
Foliage variegated

T

T

TIGRIDIA *(Iridaceae)*
Common names: Peacock flower; Tiger flower

A genus of 23 species of bulbous perennials from dry sandy locations, and grassland in Guatemala and Mexico. Their basal leaves are narrow, and sword- or lance-shaped. The flowers may be upright and iris-like or tulip-shaped and pendent, and are short-lived, but appear in succession in summer. They have three large outer segments and three smaller inner ones. They may require to be staked in exposed areas.

✔ Pest-free
✔ Repeat-flowering

✘ Prone to virus attack

CULTIVATION
Under glass, plant bulbs 4in. (10cm) deep in loam-based potting compost with added grit. Water freely during growth, keep dry during dormancy. Repot in spring.

CULTIVATION
Out of doors, grow in well-drained, gritty, soil in sun. Lift bulbs in autumn in cold regions after flowering and store in a dry, frost-free situation.

PROPAGATION
Seed should be sown at 64°F (18°C) in spring. Offsets may be separated during dormancy.

Tigridia pavonia
(iris-form)

Zone 9
Height: 5ft. (1.5m) Spread: 4in. (10cm)

Tigridia pavonia
(tulip-form)

Zone 9
Height: 5ft. (1.5m) Spread: 4in. (10cm)

TOLMEIA *(Saxifragaceae)*
Common names: Pick-a-back plant; Youth-on-age

A genus of one species of herbaceous perennial, *T. menziesii*, from western North America. The basal leaves are kidney-shaped and shallowly-lobed, hairy, veined, toothed and produce young plants where the blade and the leaf-stalk join. The perfumed flowers are small, greenish-purple cups, and are borne on leafy stems in one-sided racemes in spring and early summer. Can be grown as a house plant.

✔ Flowers perfumed
✔ Handsome foliage
✔ Disease-free
✔ Pest-free
✔ Good ground cover in shade
✘ Invasive
✘ Flowers inconspicuous

Tolmeia menziesii

Zone 7
Height: 2ft. (60cm) Spread: 6ft. (2m)

CULTIVATION
Under glass, grow in loam-based potting compost in indirect or bright filtered light. Water freely during growth, but sparingly in winter.

Out of doors, grow in moist, humus-rich soil in a cool corner in part or deep shade.

PROPAGATION
Seed should be sown in a cold frame in autumn. Division in spring. Plantlets can be removed from the leaves in mid- to late summer, and potted up.

Tolmeia menziesii
'Taff's Gold' A.G.M.
Zone 7
Height: 2ft. (60cm) Spread: 6ft. (2m)
Foliage variegated.

TRACHELIUM *(Campanulaceae)*

Common names: Throatwort

A genus of seven species of perennials from limy soils in the Mediterranean area. Their leaves are tiny, oblong, lance-shaped, or round, alternate and simple. The flowers are five-petalled, tubular, and solitary or borne in corymbs, in summer.

✔ Good cut flowers   ✘ Prone to aphid attack
✔ Drought-tolerant

CULTIVATION
Under glass, grow in an alpine house in a mix of equal parts sharp sand, loam and leaf mould, with shade at midday.

Out of doors, grow in any well-drained soil in sun.

PROPAGATION
Seed should be sown at 61°F (16°C) in early spring. Softwood cuttings may be taken in early summer.

Trachelium caeruleum
A.G.M. (Blue throatwort)

Zone 9
Height: 1.2 m.(4 ft) Spread: 1ft. (30cm)

TRACHELOSPERMUM *(Apocynaceae)*

Common names: None

A genus of twenty species of evergreen climbing perennials from woodland in India across to Japan. Their leaves are ovate or lance-shaped, and opposite. The stems contain a milky latex. The white flowers are star-shaped, with five lobes and cylindrical tubes, and are borne in axillary or terminal cymes, in mid and late summer. They are followed by fruit pods in warm climates only.

✔ Disease-free
✔ Pest-free
✔ Have handsome seed pods

CULTIVATION
Under glass, grow in loam-based potting compost in full light, with shade at mid-day. Water freely during growth, sparingly in winter. Prune in early spring for size and shape.

Out of doors, grow against a warm wall in well-drained fertile soil in sun or part shade.

PROPAGATION
Layer in autumn, or take semi-ripe cuttings and root with bottom heat in summer.

Trachelospermum jasminoides
'Tricolor'

Zone 8
Height: 28ft. (9m) Spread: 6ft. (2m)

Trachelospermum jasminoides
'Variegata'

Zone 8
Height: 28ft. (9m) Spread: 6ft. (2m)

TRADESCANTIA *(Commelinaceae)*

Common names: Spiderwort; Wandering Jew

A genus of 65 species of evergreen perennials from scrubland, woodland or disturbed ground in all three Americas. They may be fibrous-rooted or tuberous, and tuft-forming or trailing. Their leaves are fleshy, ovate or lance-shaped, hairy in some, and alternate. The short-lived flowers are saucer-shaped, with three petals and three sepals and in terminal or axillary cymes. They vary widely in degree of hardiness, and some of the tender species are handsome foliage plants. The hardy forms are repeat-flowering.

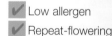

| ✔ Low allergen | ✘ Foliage is skin-irritant |
| ✔ Repeat-flowering | ✘ Need to lift & divide often |

CULTIVATION

Under glass, grow tender forms in loam-based potting compost in bright filtered light. Water with moderation during growth, and sparingly in winter. Remove shoots that revert to green from foliage plants as they appear.

Out of doors, hardy forms should be grown in moist, fertile soil in sun or part shade.

PROPAGATION

Take stem-tip cuttings of tender species at any time of year, and root in cutting compost or in water. Hardy species should be divided in spring or autumn.

Tradescantia x andersoniana
'Isis' A.G.M.

Zone 5.
Height and spread: 2ft. (60cm)

Tradescantia x andersoniana
'Karminglut'

Zone 5
Height and spread: 2ft. (60cm)

Tradescantia x andersoniana
'Osprey' A.G.M.

Zone 5
Height and spread: 2ft. (60cm)

Tradescantia x andersoniana
'Purewell Giant'

Zone 5
Height and spread: 2ft. (60cm)

T

Tradescantia x andersoniana
'Sweet Kate'

Zone 5
Height and spread: 2ft. (60cm)

Tradescantia x andersoniana
'Zwanenberg Blue'

Zone 5
Height and spread: 2ft. (60cm)

Tradescantia fluminensis
'Albovittata' (Wandering Jew)

Zone 9
Height: 6in. (15cm) Spread: 8in. (20cm)

Tradescantia fluminensis
'Quadricolor'

Zone 9
Height: 6in. (15cm) Spread: 8in. (20cm)

Tradescantia fluminensis
'Quicksilver' A.G.M.

Zone 9
Height: 6in. (15cm) Spread: 8in. (20cm)

Tradescantia ohiensis

Zone 7
Height: 3ft. (90cm) Spread: 2ft. (60cm)

Tradescantia pallida
'Purpurea' A.G.M.

Zone 8
Height: 8in. (20cm) Spread: 16in. (40cm)

Tradescantia zinnia
'Albomarginata'

Zone 9
Height: 7ft. (2.2m) Spread: 2ft. (60cm)

Tradescantia zebrine
A.G.M.

Zone 9
Height: 6in. (15cm) Spread: 8in. (20cm)

T

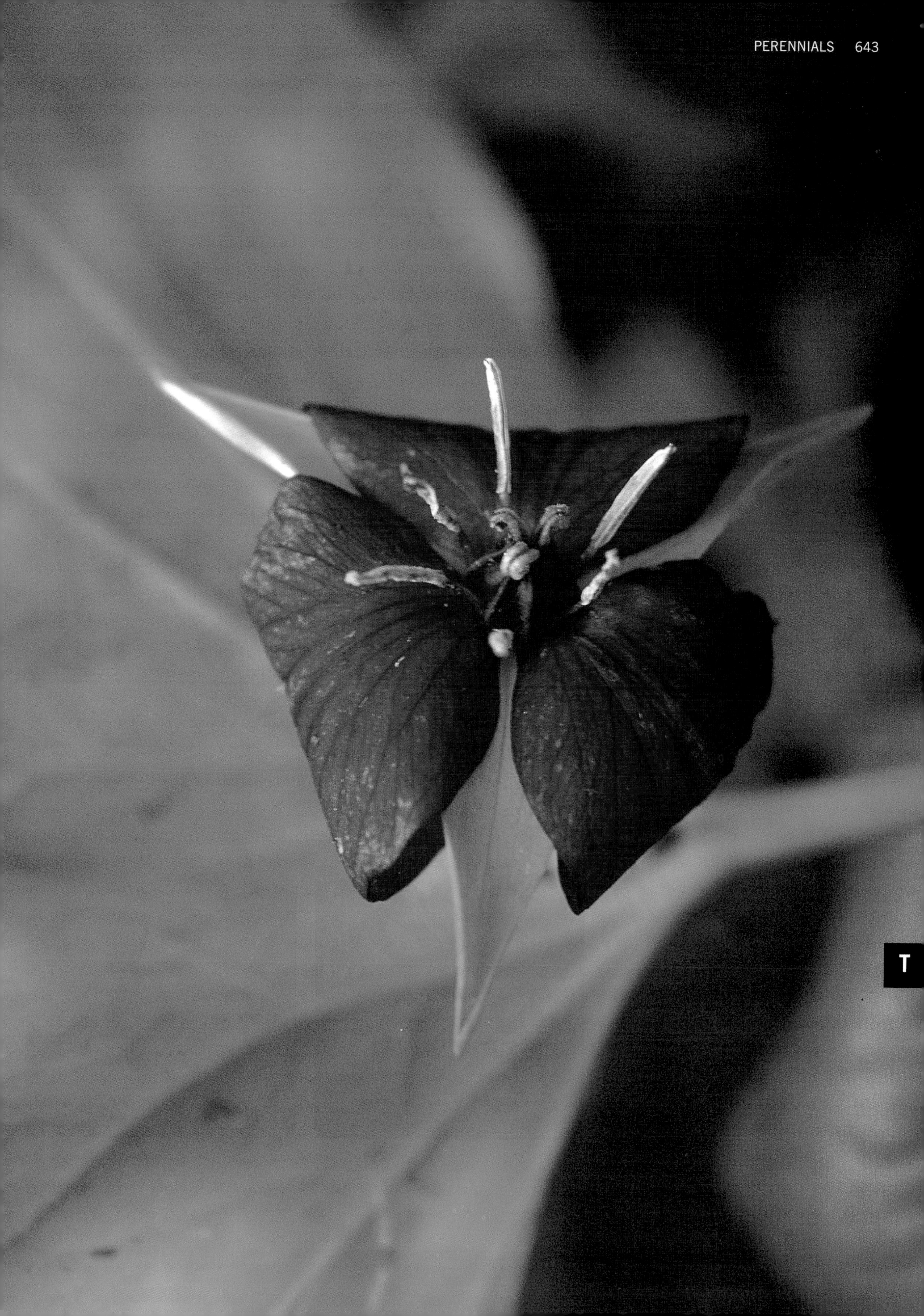

TRICYRTIS *(Convallariaceae)*
Common names: Toad lily

A genus of 16 species of herbaceous perennials found in moist woodland and on cliffs and mountains in the eastern Himalayas and the Philippines. They may be stoloniferous or rhizomatous. Their leaves are oblong or lance-shaped, pointed, alternate, veined prominently, and stem-clasping. The flowers are bell- or star- or funnel-shaped, six-tepalled, and are borne singly or in clusters from the leaf axils, but may be borne in cymes.

✔ Good cut flowers
✔ Disease-free

✗ Prone to slug damage

CULTIVATION
Grow in moist, humus-rich, well-drained soil in part or deep shade, except *T. latifolia*, which prefers drier soil.

PROPAGATION
Seed should be sown as soon as it is ripe in a cold frame. Divide in early spring whilst still dormant.

Tricyrtis formosana

Zone 7
Height: 30in. (75cm) Spread: 18in. (45cm)

Tricyrtis hirta

Zone 5
Height: 30in. (75cm) Spread: 2ft. (60cm)

Tricyrtis hirta 'Aureomarginata'

Zone 5
Height: 30in. (75cm) Spread: 2ft. (60cm)

Tricyrtis latifolia

Zone 5
Height: 30in. (75cm) Spread: indefinite
Invasive

Tricyrtis ohsumiensis

Zone 5
Height: 8in. (20cm) Spread: 1ft. (30cm)

Tricyrtis 'Tojen'

Zone 5
Height: 30in. (75cm) Spread: 18in. (45cm)

T

TRIFOLIUM *(Papilionaceae)*
Common names: Clover

A genus of 240 species of annuals, biennials and herbaceous perennials found in scree or grassy meadowland in the northern hemisphere in particular, but across the world except Australasia. Their leaves are usually tripalmate, but may be up to seven-palmate, and the leaflets may be entire or toothed. The pea-like flowers are small, and borne in heads or racemes, in spring and summer. They are perfumed in some species. Many are very highly invasive weeds.

✔ Attracts bees   ✘ Self-seeds
✔ Handsome foliage
✔ Disease-free
✔ Pest-free

CULTIVATION
Grow in moist, well-drained soil in sun.

PROPAGATION
Seed should be sown in a cold frame in spring. Detach rooted stems, or divide in spring

Trifolium ochroleucon

Zone 4
Height: 2ft. (60cm) Spread: 3ft. (90cm)

Trifolium pannonicum
(Hungarian clover)

Zone 5
Height and spread: 3ft. (90cm)

Trifolium repens

Zone 4
Height: 1ft. (30cm) Spread: 20in. (50cm)

Trifolium repens
'Purpurascens Quadrifolium'
Zone 4
Height: 4in. (10cm) Spread: indefinite
Invasive

TRILLIUM *(Trilliaceae)*
Common names: Wake robin; Wood lily; Trinity flower; Toadshade

A genus of 30 species of rhizomatous herbaceous perennials from woodlands and scrubland in North America in particular, with a few from the Himalayas and north-east Asia. Their leaves are arranged in an apical whorl of three atop short, erect stems, and are elliptic, lance-shaped, diamond-shaped or ovate, veined, and often marbled in bronze or purple. The flowers are terminal, solitary, nodding or upright, cup- or funnel-shaped, and have three leaf-like outer sepals and three inner petals.

✔ Handsome foliage   ✘ Prone to slug damage
✔ Disease-free   ✘ Resent transplantation

CULTIVATION
Grow in acid to neutral, moist, humus-rich, deep soil in part or deep shade. Mulch annually using leaf mould.

PROPAGATION
Seed should be sown as soon as it is ripe in a shaded cold frame. Leaves do not appear for two years, and flowering will not occur for between five and seven years. Division can be carried out after flowering—each division must have a growing point—but is not tolerated well.

Trillium chloropetalum
var. *giganteum* A.G.M.

Zone 6
Height: 16in. (40cm) Spread: 8in. (20cm)

T

Trillium cuneatum

Zone 6
Height: 2ft. (60cm) Spread: 1ft. (30cm)

Trillium erectum
A.G.M.

Zone 4
Height: 20in. (50cm) Spread: 1ft. (30cm)

Trillium flexipes

Zone 4
Height: 16in. (40cm) Spread: 1ft. (30cm)

Trillium grandiflorum

Zone 5
Height: 16in. (40cm) Spread: 18in. (45cm)

Trillium grandiflorum
'Snow Bunting'

Zone 5
Height: 16in. (40cm) Spread: 18in. (45cm)

Trillium luteum
A.G.M.

Zone 5
Height: 16in. (40cm) Spread: 1ft. (30cm)

Trillium ovatum

Zone 5
Height: 20in. (50cm) Spread: 8in. (20cm)

Trillium parviflorum

Zone 6
Height and spread: 1ft. (30cm)

Trillium pusillum

Zone 6
Height: 6in. (15cm) Spread: 4in. (10cm)

T

Trillium recurvatum

Zone 5
Height: 16in. (40cm) Spread: 1ft. (30cm)

Trillium sessile

Zone 4
Height: 1ft. (30cm) Spread: 20 cm.(8in.)

Trillium vaseyi

Zone 6
Height: 26in. (65cm) Spread: 1ft. (30cm)

TRITELEIA *(Alliaceae)*
Common names: None

A genus of 15 species of cormous perennials found in chaparral, grassland and pine woodland in western U.S.A. Their leaves are basal, and narrowly-linear. The flowers are funnel-shaped, and borne in umbels in early summer.

✔ Disease-free
✔ Pest-free

CULTIVATION
Under glass, grow in grit-enhanced, loam-based potting compost in full light. Water freely during growth, dry off and keep frost-free during dormancy.

Out of doors, grow in light, gritty, well-drained soil in sun.

PROPAGATION
Seed should be sown at 61°F (16°C) as soon as it is ripe, or in spring; seedlings take up to five years to reach flowering size. Separate corms during dormancy.

Triteleia ixiodes
'Starlight'

Zone 7
Height: 2ft. (60cm) Spread: 3in. (8cm)

TRITONIA *(Iridaceae)*
Common names: None

A genus of 28 species of cormous perennials found in stony or grassy hillsides in Swaziland and South Africa. Their leaves are linear or lance-shaped, and two-ranked. The flowers are cup- or funnel-shaped, and borne in slender spikes in spring.

✔ Good cut flowers
✔ Drought-tolerant
✔ Disease-free
✔ Pest-free

CULTIVATION
Under glass, plant corms 4in. (10cm) deep in spring, in loam-based potting compost with added grit, in full light. Water freely during growth, and reduce in winter until dry. Repot annually in spring.

Out of doors, grow in sharply-draining soil in sun. Mulch in winter to protect against winter wet.

PROPAGATION
Seed should be sown at 61°F (16°C) as soon as it is ripe. Separate offsets during dormancy.

T

Tritonia crocata
'Hyalina'

Zone 9
Height: 20in. (50cm) Spread: 3in. (8cm)

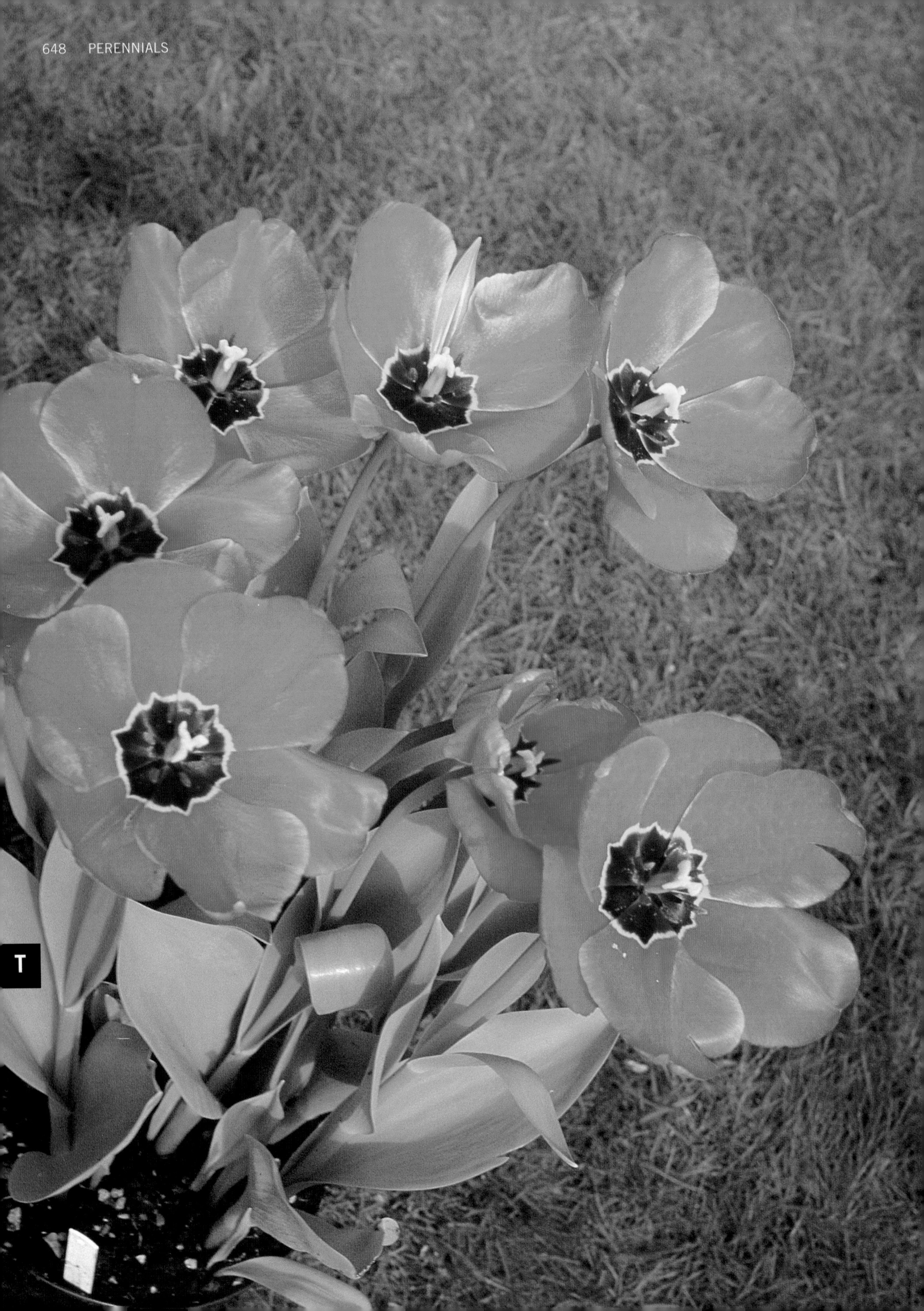

T

Tritonia disticha
subsp. *rubrolucens*

Zone 9
Height: 3ft. (90cm) Spread: 6in. (15cm)

Tritonia
'Konigin Fabiola'

Zone 9
Height: 1ft. (30cm) Spread: 4in. (10cm)

TROLLIUS *(Ranunculaceae)*
Common names: Globeflower

A genus of 24 species of herbaceous perennials from wet, or moist meadows in the cool, temperate regions of Eurasia and North America. Their leaves are in basal rosettes, palmately-lobed, and the lobes are toothed or divided. The buttercup-like flowers are solitary, terminal, bowl-shaped or spherical, with petal-like sepals, and are borne in spring or summer.

✔ Good cut flowers   ✘ Mildew prone
✔ Low allergen
✔ Handsome foliage

CULTIVATION
Grow in reliably moist, deep, fertile soil in sun or part shade.

PROPAGATION
Seed should be sown in a cold frame as soon as it is ripe. It may not germinate until the following year. Divide either as new growth is appearing, or after flowering.

Trollius acaulis

Zone 6
Height: 1ft. (30cm) Spread: 6in. (15cm)

Trollius chinensis
'Imperial Orange'

Zone 5
Height: 3ft. (90cm) Spread: 18in. (45cm)

Trollius x cultorum
'Lemon Queen'

Zone 5
Height: 3ft. (90cm) Spread: 18in. (45cm)

T

Trollius x cultorum
'Orange Princess' A.G.M.

Zone 5
Height: 3ft. (90cm) Spread: 18in. (45cm)

Trollius x cultorum
'Superbus' A.G.M.

Zone 5
Height: 3ft. (90cm) Spread: 18in. (45cm)

Trollius europaeus

Zone 5
Height: 3ft. (90cm) Spread: 18in. (45cm)

Trollius
'Pritchard's Giant'

Zone 5
Height: 3ft. (90cm) Spread: 2ft. (60cm)

Trollius yunnanensis

Zone 5
Height: 28in. (70cm) Spread: 1ft. (30cm)

TROPAEOLUM *(Tropaeolaceae)*

Common names: Nasturtium; Flame creeper

A genus of 90 species of annuals and herbaceous perennials, mainly climbers, from cool mountains of South and Central America. Many are tuberous. The leaves are peltate, round, palmately-lobed with five to seven leaflets, or entire, and alternate. The flowers are funnel-shaped, with five clawed petals, and five indifferent sepals, and are borne singly from the leaf axils in summer.

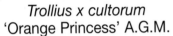

✔ Long-flowering

✔ Handsome foliage

✘ Prone to slug damage

✘ Resent disturbance

CULTIVATION
Grow in moist, well-drained soil in sun, but acid to neutral soil for *T. speciosum*.

PROPAGATION
Seed should be sown in a cold frame as soon as it is ripe. Germination can be erratic. Stem-tip cuttings can be taken in late summer and rooted with bottom heat. Divide *TT. speciosum* and *tuberosum* in early spring.

Tropaeolum pentaphyllum

Zone 8
Height: 18ft. (6m) Spread: 2ft. (60cm)

Tropaeolum polyphyllum
(Wreath nasturtium)

Zone 8
Height: 4in. (10cm) Spread: 4ft. (1.2m)

Tropaeolum speciosum A.G.M.
(Flame creeper; Flame nasturtium)

Zone 8
Height: 10ft. (3.5m) Spread: 3ft. (90cm)

Tropaeolum tricolor
A.G.M.

Zone 8
Height: 10ft. (3.5m) Spread: 3ft. (90cm)

Tropaeolum tuberosum 'Ken Aslet'
A.G.M. (Tuber nasturtium)

Zone 8
Height: 12ft. (4m) Spread: 3ft. (90cm)

TUBERARIA *(Cistaceae)*
Common names: None

A genus of a dozen species of annuals and perennials from woodland, heathland or scrubland in southern and Central Europe. The leaves are in basal rosettes, simple, and round or lance-shaped. The flowers are shallow cups and are borne in terminal cymes in late spring and summer.

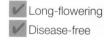 Long-flowering
✔ Disease-free

✘ Prone to slug damage

CULTIVATION
Grow in any soil that is well-drained, in sun.

PROPAGATION
Seed should be sown at 61°F (16°C) in early spring. Rosette cuttings may be taken in spring. Rooted rosettes should be removed in spring.

Tuberaria lignosa

Zone 8
Height: 1ft. (30cm) Spread: 3ft. (90cm)

TULBAGHIA *(Alliaceae)*
Common names: None

A genus of two dozen species of perennials from various habitats in temperate and tropical southern Africa. They may be bulbous or tuberous, herbaceous or semi-evergreen. Their leaves are simple, strap-shaped or linear, basal and smell of garlic. The tubular flowers have flared mouths, and are borne in umbels over a long period from late spring to autumn. They are perfumed in most species.

✔ Long-flowering   ✘ Prone to aphid attack
✔ Foliage aromatic
✔ Drought-tolerant

CULTIVATION
Under glass, grow in loam-based potting compost, with added grit, in full light. Water freely during growth, sparingly in autumn, and keep dry over winter.

Out of doors, grow in loamy, humus-rich, well-drained soil in sun.

PROPAGATION
Seed should be sown in a cold frame as soon as it is ripe, or in spring. Divide in spring.

Tulbaghia cepacea

Zone 8
Height: 2ft. (60cm) Spread: 8in. (20cm)

Tulbaghia cominsii

Zone 8
Height: 10in. (25cm) Spread: 4in. (10cm)

Tulbaghia violacea

Zone 7
Height: 2ft. (60cm) Spread: 1ft. (30cm)
Flowers perfumed

Tulbaghia violacea 'Silver Lace'

Zone 7
Height: 2ft. (60cm) Spread: 1ft. (30cm)
Flowers perfumed/Foliage variegated

T

TULIPA *(Liliaceae)*
Common names: Tulip

A genus of 100 species of bulbous perennials found in hot dry regions, from sea level to alpine levels in Central Asia in particular, but also the Middle East, Europe and other parts of Asia. Their leaves are mainly basal, with some on the stems decreasing in size from below upwards. They are ovate or broadly linear, channeled or wavy-edged, and hairy in some. The goblet- or bowl-shaped flowers have six tepals, are borne on upright stems, and are terminal and solitary or in clusters of up to a dozen. Tulips can be classified as per the list and International register of tulip names by K.A.V. Voor Bloembollenculture 1996. Each plant featured has its classification in brackets:

Group 1: Single Early

Group 2: Double Early

Group 3: Triumph

Group 4: Darwin hybrids

Group 5: Single late, incl. Cottage and Darwin

Group 6: Lily-flowered

Group 7: Fringed

Group 8: Viridiflora

Group 9: Rembrandt

Group 10: Parrot

Group 11: Double late

Group 12: Kaufmanniana

Group 13: Fosteriana

Group 14: Greigii

Group 15: Miscellaneous

✔ Handsome foliage

✔ Good cut flowers

✗ Prone to slug damage

✗ All parts poisonous

✗ Foliage skin-irritant

✗ Prone to aphid attack

✗ Mice love bulbs

✗ Prone to viruses

CULTIVATION
Plant at a depth of 4–6in. (10–15cm) in late summer or autumn in well-drained fertile soil in sun, and protected against wind. Protect against excessive wet. Bulbs of all groups except 12, 14, and species should be lifted when the foliage has died down and ripened in a cold greenhouse, safe from mice, and replanted in autumn.

PROPAGATION
Seed of species should be sown in a cold frame in autumn. Flowering size will not be attained for several years. Offsets of cultivars should be separated in summer, and replanted.

Tulipa
'Angelique' A.G.M. (Group 11)

Zone 5
Height: 1ft. (30cm) Spread: 2in. (5cm)

Tulipa
'Apeldoorn' (Group 4)

Zone 5
Height: 2ft. (60cm) Spread: 2in. (5cm)

Tulipa 'Apeldoorn's Elite' A.G.M.
(Group 4)

Zone 5
Height: 2ft. (60cm) Spread: 2in. (5cm)

Tulipa
'Artist' A.G.M. (Group 8)

Zone 5
Height: 18in. (45cm) Spread: 2in. (5cm)

Tulipa
'Bright Gem' (Group 15)

Zone 5
Height: 14in. (35cm) Spread: 2in. (5cm)

Tulipa
'Burning Heart' (Group 1)

Zone 5
Height: 18in. (45cm) Spread: 2in. (5cm)

Tulipa clusiana var. *chrysantha*
A.G.M. (Group 15)

Zone 6
Height: 1ft. (30cm) Spread: 2in. (5cm)

Tulipa
'Esperanto' A.G.M. (Group 8)
Zone 5
Height: 20in. (50cm) Spread: 2in. (5cm)
Foliage variegated

Tulipa
'Fantasy' A.G.M. (Group 10)

Zone 5
Height: 22in. (55cm) Spread: 2in. (5cm)

Tulipa
'Flaming Parrot' (Group 10)

Zone 5
Height: 22in. (55cm) Spread: 2in. (5cm)

Tulipa kaufmanniana
'Shakespeare' (Group 12)

Zone 5
Height: 10in. (25cm) Spread: 2in. (5cm)

Tulipa
'Keizerskroon' A.G.M. (Group 1)

Zone 5
Height: 1ft. (30cm) Spread: 2in. (5cm)

T

Tulipa linifolia
A.G.M. (Group 15)

Zone 5
Height: 8in. (20cm) Spread: 2in. (5cm)

Tulipa
'Marilyn' (Group 6)

Zone 5
Height: 1ft. (30cm) Spread: 2in. (5cm)

Tulipa
'Monte Carlo' (Group 2)

Zone 5
Height: 1ft. (30cm) Spread: 2in. (5cm)

Tulipa 'New Design' (Group 3)

Zone 5
Height: 18in. (45cm) Spread: 2in. (5cm)
Foliage variegated

Tulipa
'Oranje Nassau' A.G.M. (Group 2)

Zone 5
Height: 1ft. (30cm) Spread: 2in. (5cm)

Tulipa
'Pinocchio' (Group 14)

Zone 5
Height: 1ft. (30cm) Spread: 2in. (5cm)

Tulipa praestans
'Fusilier' A.G.M. (Group 15)

Zone 5
Height: 1ft. (30cm) Spread: 2in. (5cm)

Tulipa praestans
'Unicum' (Group 15)
Zone 5
Height: 1ft. (30cm) Spread: 2in. (5cm)
Foliage variegated

Tulipa
'Queen of Sheba'

Zone 6
Height: 2ft. (60cm) Spread: 2in. (5cm)

T

Tulipa 'Red Riding Hood' A.G.M.
(Group 14)
Zone 5
Height: 8in. (20cm) Spread: 2in. (5cm)
Foliage variegated

Tulipa saxatilis Bakeri Group
(Group 15)

Zone 6
Height: 14in. (35cm) Spread: 2in. (5cm)

Tulipa
'Stockholm' A.G.M. (Group 2)

Zone 5
Height: 1ft. (30cm) Spread: 2in. (5cm)

Tulipa tarda
A.G.M. (Group 15)

Zone 5
Height: 6in. (15cm) Spread: 2in. (5cm)

Tulipa
'Toronto' A.G.M. (Group 14)

Zone 5
Height: 8in. (20cm) Spread: 2in. (5cm)

Tulipa turkestanica
A.G.M. (Group 15)

Zone 5
Height: 1ft. (30cm) Spread: 2in. (5cm)

Tulipa urumiensis
A.G.M. (Group 15)

Zone 5
Height: 6in. (15cm) Spread: 2in. (5cm)

T

T

TWEEDIA *(Asclepiadaceae)*

Common names: None

A genus of but one species of evergreen scrambling subshrub, *T. caerulea*, from rocky areas and scrubland in Uruguay and Brazil. Its leaves are simple and opposite, lance-shaped or oblong, and downy. The flowers are five-petalled and tubular, with oblong petals, and are borne in few-flowered cymes from summer to early autumn.

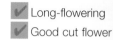

✔ Long-flowering

✔ Good cut flower

✘ Requires staking

CULTIVATION

Under glass, grow in loam-based potting compost in full light. Water freely during growth, sparingly in winter.

Out of doors, grow in moist, fertile well-drained soil in sun. Support must be provided.

PROPAGATION

Seed should be sown at 59°F (15°C) in spring. Softwood cuttings may be taken in summer, and rooted with bottom heat.

Tweedia caerulea
A.G.M.

Zone 10
Height: 4ft. (1.2m) Spread: 8in. (20cm)

T

UMBILICUS
UNCINIA
UROSPERMUM
UTRICULARIA
UVULARIA

U

UMBILICUS *(Crassulaceae)*
Common names: Navelwort; Pennywort

A genus of 18 succulent perennials from Eurasia. Their leaves are basal, long-stalked, round, peltate, with a central dimple resembling the umbilicus. The flowers are small, tubular, greenish-white and borne in spikes in summer. A wonderful wall plant.

✔ Drought-tolerant ✘ Self-seeds

✔ Handsome foliage

CULTIVATION
Grow in sharply-draining soil in sun or part shade.

PROPAGATION
Seed should be sown in a cold frame in spring or autumn.

Umbilicus rupestris

Zone 7
Height: 16in. (40cm) Spread: 6in. (15cm)

UNCINIA *(Cyperaceae)*
Common names: Hook sedge

A genus of 45 species of evergreen, monoecious, perennial grasses, found in damp tussocks, moist woodland or swampland across temperate zones of the southern hemisphere except southern Africa. The smooth leaves are three-angled or cylindrical, channeled, and grass-like. The flowers are in spikes, with the female flowers below and the male on top. The female flowers give rise to hooked fruits.

✔ Evergreen ✘ Highly allergenic

✔ Disease-free

✔ Pest-free

CULTIVATION
Grow in moist, humus-rich, well-drained soil in sun or part shade.

PROPAGATION
Seed should be sown at 55°F (13°C) in spring. Division can be carried out between late spring and midsummer.

Uncinia rubra

Zone 8
Height: 1ft. (30cm) Spread: 16in. (40cm)

UROSPERMUM *(Asteraceae)*
Common names: None

A genus of two annual or short-lived perennials from the Mediterranean region. Their leaves are oblanceolate to obovate, hairy, toothed, and gray-green. The dandelion-like flowers are large and solitary and borne on tall stems in summer.

✔ Drought-tolerant ✘ Highly allergenic

✔ Handsome foliage ✘ Self-seeds

✘ Short-lived

CULTIVATION
Grow in sharply-draining soil in sun.

PROPAGATION
Seed should be sown in spring, when division can also be carried out, and basal cuttings taken.

Urospermum delachampii

Zone 6
Height: 16in. (40cm) Spread: 2ft. (60cm)

U

U

UTRICULARIA *(Lentibulariaceae)*

Common names: Bladderwort

A genus of 180 species of aquatic or epiphytic, insectivorous, annuals and perennials found across the world in shallow, stagnant water (especially if it harbors mosquito larvae) or growing epiphytically on forest trees. Their floating leaves are thread-like or linear, spongy, and in a whorl, and have bladders designed to trap insects. The stems are submerged, and they lack roots. The pouched flowers are solitary or in racemes.

✔ Disease-free
✔ Pest-free

CULTIVATION

Indoors, grow in an aquarium in soft water free of algae, in sun.

Out of doors, grow in a pond of acid, shallow water.

PROPAGATION

Buds that have sunk to the bottom can be collected and replanted. Divide the mat of floating foliage in summer.

Utricularia blanchettii

Zone 10
Height: 4in. (10cm) Spread: 6in. (15cm)

Utricularia longifolia

Zone 10
Height: 2ft. (60cm) Spread: 6in. (15cm)

UVULARIA *(Convallariaceae)*

Common names: Merrybells

A genus of five species of rhizomatous perennials found in woodland of eastern North America. Their leaves are ovate or lance-shaped, and alternate. The flowers are six-tepalled, tubular, or bell-shaped, and are solitary or paired, and terminal.

✔ Good cut flowers   ✘ Prone to slug damage
✔ Handsome seed-heads
✔ Disease-free

CULTIVATION

Grow in moist, humus-rich, well-drained soil in part or full shade.

PROPAGATION

Seed should be sown in a cold frame as soon as it is ripe. Division can be carried out in early spring.

Uvularia grandiflora
A.G.M. (Large merrybells)

Zone 4
Height: 32in. (80cm) Spread: 2ft. (60cm)

U

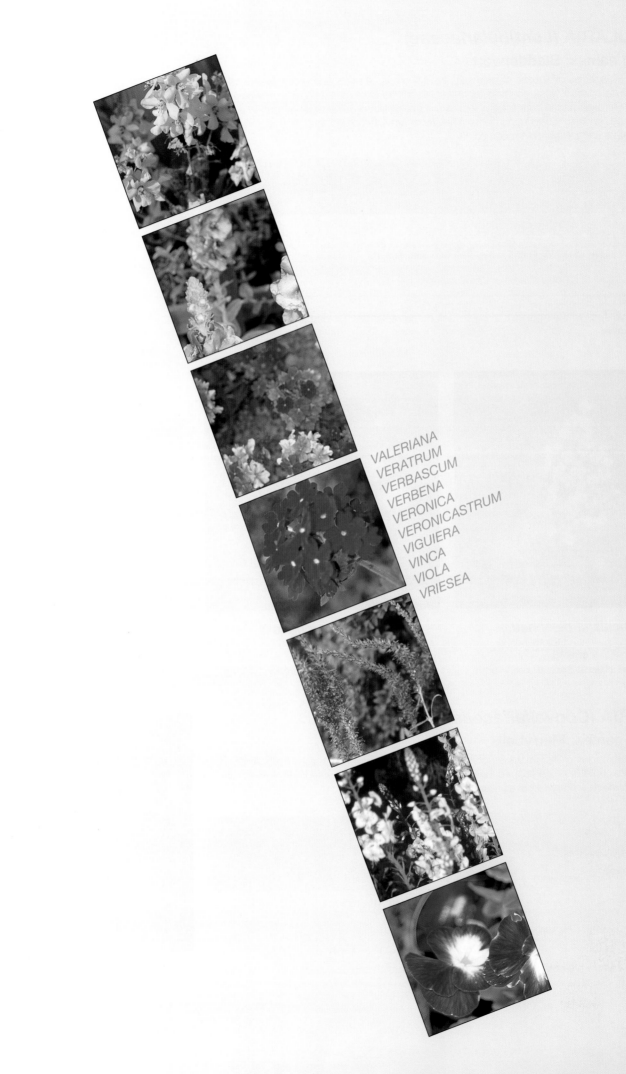

VALERIANA
VERATRUM
VERBASCUM
VERBENA
VERONICA
VERONICASTRUM
VIGUIERA
VINCA
VIOLA
VRIESEA

V

VALERIANA *(Valerianaceae)*
Common names: All heal

A genus of 200 species of annuals, rhizomatous perennials, subshrubs and shrubs from all parts of the world except Australasia. They are found in moist meadows, wet woodland or stream sides, in mountains for the greater part. Their leaves are usually simple, but may be pinnate or pinnatifid, and may consist of basal simple leaves and pinnate stem leaves. They may be aromatic—unpleasantly so in some cases. The flowers are small salvers, borne in terminal cymes in summer.

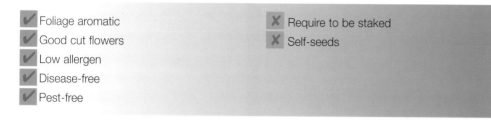

- ✔ Foliage aromatic
- ✔ Good cut flowers
- ✔ Low allergen
- ✔ Disease-free
- ✔ Pest-free
- ✘ Require to be staked
- ✘ Self-seeds

CULTIVATION
Grow in moist soil in sun or part shade. Dead-head to prevent self-seeding.

PROPAGATION
Seed should be sown in spring, or basal cuttings may be taken then.

Valeriana officinalis
subsp. *sambucifolia*

Zone 4
Height: 6ft. (2m) Spread: 30in. (75cm)

Valeriana phu
'Aurea'

Zone 6
Height: 5ft. (1.5m) Spread: 2ft. (60cm)

Valeriana montana

Zone 5
Height: 16in. (40cm) Spread: 8in. (20cm)

VERATRUM *(Melianthaceae)*
Common names: None

A genus of 45 species of rhizomatous perennials from damp meadows and woodland across the northern hemisphere. The leaves are alternate, pleated, veined, and broadly elliptic to ovate. The flowers are small, star-shaped, and are borne in terminal panicles in early and midsummer.

- ✔ Good cut flowers
- ✔ Handsome seed-heads
- ✔ Handsome foliage
- ✔ Disease-free
- ✘ Prone to slug damage
- ✘ Highly allergenic
- ✘ All parts poisonous
- ✘ Foliage skin-irritant

CULTIVATION
Grow in reliably moist, fertile, humus-rich, well-drained soil in a sheltered corner in sun or part shade.

PROPAGATION
Seed should be sown in a cold frame as soon as it is ripe. Division can be done in spring or autumn.

Veratrum album

Zone 5
Height: 6ft. (2m) Spread: 2ft. (60cm)

V

Veratrum nigrum
A.G.M.

Zone 6
Height: 4ft. (1.2m) Spread: 2ft. (60cm)

VERBASCUM *(Scrophulariaceae)*

Common names: Mullein

A genus of 360 species of many annuals, biennials, short-lived perennials and subshrubs from wasteland, dry hillsides and open woodland in Eurasia and North Africa. The perennials may be evergreen or semi-evergreen. Their soft-textured leaves are usually in basal rosettes, hairy, woolly sometimes, simple, entire or scalloped, lobed or toothed, and alternate. The outward-facing, saucer-shaped flowers may be clustered within the rosette, or borne in dense spikes on tall erect stems over a long period in summer.

✔ Drought-tolerant	✔ Handsome foliage	✘ Short-lived
✔ Attracts bees	✔ Architectural plants	✘ Self-seeds
✔ Long-flowering		✘ Mildew prone

CULTIVATION
Grow in poor, neutral to alkaline, well-drained soil in sun. *V.* 'Letitia' must have sharply-draining soil.

PROPAGATION
Seed should be sown in a cold frame in late spring/early summer. Take root cuttings in winter. Divide in spring.

Verbascum bombyciferum A.G.M.

Zone 6
Height: 5ft. (1.5m) Spread: 3ft. (90cm)
Evergreen

Verbascum chaixii
(Chaix mullein)

Zone 5
Height: 3ft. (90cm) Spread: 18in. (45cm)

Verbascum chaixii
'Album'

Zone 5
Height: 3ft. (90cm) Spread: 18in. (45cm)

Verbascum chaixii
'Gainsborough' A.G.M.
Zone 5
Height: 4ft. (1.2m) Spread: 1ft. (30cm)
Requires to be staked

Verbascum dumulosum
A.G.M.

Zone 8
Height: 10in. (25cm) Spread: 16in. (40cm)

Verbascum
'Helen Johnson' A.G.M.
Zone 7
Height: 3ft. (90cm) Spread: 1ft. (30cm)
Evergreen

Verbascum
'Jackie'

Zone 6
Height: 3ft. (90cm) Spread: 18in. (45cm)

Verbascum
'Letitia' A.G.M.

Zone 5
Height and spread: 10in. (25cm)

Verbascum nigrum
(Dark mullein)

Zone 5
Height: 3ft. (90cm) Spread: 2ft. (60cm)

Verbascum olympicum
(Olympic mullein)
Zone 6
Height: 6ft. (2m) Spread: 2ft. (60cm)
Requires to be staked.

Verbascum phoeniceum
(Purple mullein)
Zone 6
Height: 4ft. (1.2m) Spread: 18in. (45cm)
Requires to be staked

Verbascum phoeniceum
'Flush of White'

Zone 6
Height: 4ft. (1.2m) Spread: 18in. (45cm)

Verbascum phoeniceum
'Violetta'

Zone 6
Height: 4ft. (1.2m) Spread: 18in. (45cm)

V

V

VERBENA *(Verbenaceae)*
Common names: None

A genus of 250 species of annuals, perennials and subshrubs from open, sunny habitats in both temperate and tropical parts of all three Americas, with a few from southern Europe. Their leaves are pinnatifid or pinnate, toothed, and opposite. The small flowers are salverform, with two upper and three lower petals, and with a tubular corolla flared at the mouth. They are borne in panicles, spikes, corymbs or cymes, or singly, over a long period in summer to autumn.

✔ Long-flowering   ✘ Prone to slug damage
✔ Drought-tolerant   ✘ Self-seeds
✔ Handsome foliage   ✘ Mildew prone

CULTIVATION

Under glass, grow in loam-based potting compost, with extra grit, in full light. Water freely during growth, but sparingly in winter.

Out of doors, grow in moist, well-drained soil in sun.

PROPAGATION

Seed should be sown at 70°F (21°C) in autumn or spring. Divide in spring. Stem-tip cuttings may be taken in late summer.

Verbena bonariensis

Zone 8
Height: 6ft. (2m) Spread: 30in. (75cm)
A see-through plant

Verbena hastata

Zone 8
Height: 4ft. (1.2m) Spread: 2ft. (60cm)

Verbena hastata 'Alba'

Zone 3
Height: 4ft. (1.2m) Spread: 2ft. (60cm)

Verbena
'Homestead Purple'

Zone 8
Height: 18in. (45cm) Spread: 20in. (50cm)

Verbena x hybrida
'Loveliness'

Zone 9
Height: 18in. (45cm) Spread: 20in. (50cm)

Verbena x hybrida
'Quartz Burgundy'

Zone 9
Height: 18in. (45cm) Spread: 20in. (50cm)

V

Verbena x hybrida
'Red Cascade'

Zone 9
Height: 18in. (45cm) Spread: 20in. (50cm)

Verbena
'Sissinghurst' A.G.M.

Zone 8
Height: 18in. (45cm) Spread: 20in. (50cm)

VERONICA *(Scrophulariaceae)*

Common names: Speedwell

A genus of 250 species of annuals, perennials and subshrubs found in wet grassland, meadows and swampland, as well as in dry meadows, scree and grassland, in Europe for the greater part. Their leaves are linear, lance-shaped, oblong, or round, toothed or entire, and opposite or alternate. The flowers are small, outward-facing, tubular with four or five spreading petals, and are borne on tall terminal or axillary spikes or racemes from spring to autumn.

✔ Long-flowering
✔ Attracts bees
✔ Low allergen
✔ Handsome foliage

✘ Mildew prone

CULTIVATION
Grow in moist, loamy, fertile, well-drained soil in sun or part shade.

PROPAGATION
Seed should be sown in a cold frame in autumn. Divide in spring or autumn.

Veronica catarractae

Zone 4
Height: 3ft. (90cm) Spread: 1ft. (30cm)

Veronica gentianoides

Zone 4
Height and spread: 18in. (45cm)

Veronica gentianoides
'Tissington White'

Zone 4
Height and spread: 18in. (45cm)

V

V

Veronica gentianoides
'Variegata'

Zone 4
Height and spread: 18in. (45cm)

Veronica montana
'Corinne Tremaine'

Zone 4
Height: 1ft. (30cm) Spread: 2ft. (60cm)

Veronica
'Ray of Fire'

Zone 5
Height: 30in. (75cm) Spread: 2ft. (60cm)

Veronica spicata subsp. *incana*
A.G.M. (Spike speedwell)

Zone 3
Height and spread: 1ft. (30cm)

Veronica spicata 'Rotfuchs'
(Woolly speedwell)

Zone 3
Height and spread: 1ft. (30cm)

VERONICASTRUM *(Scrophulariaceae)*

Common names: Culver's root

A genus of three species of perennials from open woodland, scrubland, prairies, meadows and grassy mountain slopes in North America, Siberia and Japan. Their leaves are simple, toothed and in horizontal whorls. The flowers are salverform, and have short tubes and four to five short lobes, and are borne in tall, veronica-like racemes in midsummer and autumn.

✔ Good cut flowers
✔ Long-flowering
✔ Drought-tolerant
✔ Handsome foliage
✔ Handsome seed-heads
✔ Low allergen

✘ Resents disturbance
✘ Mildew prone
✘ Prone to slug damage

CULTIVATION
Grow in moist, fertile, humus-rich soil in sun or part shade.

PROPAGATION
Seed of species should be sown in a cold frame in autumn. Species and cultivars may be divided in spring.

Veronicastrum virginicum
forma. *album*

Zone 3
Height: 6ft. (2m) Spread: 18in. (45cm)

Veronicastrum virginicum
'Pink Glow'

Zone 3
Height: 6ft. (2m) Spread: 18in. (45cm)

VIGUIERA *(Compositae)*

Common names: None

A genus of 150 species of perennials and shrubs from hot, dry sandy areas in tropical North and South America. Their leaves are lanceolate or oblanceolate, or linear, entire or toothed. The daisy-like flowers are usually yellow, and are solitary or borne in long-stalked cymes in summer.

✔ Handsome foliage
✔ Long-flowering

✘ Highly allergenic

CULTIVATION
Grow in sharply-draining, humus-rich, soil in sun.

PROPAGATION
Seed should be sown in heat in spring. Divide in spring.

Viguiera multiflora

Zone 10
Height: 3ft. (90cm) Spread: 2ft. (60cm)

VINCA *(Apocynaceae)*

Common names: Periwinkle

A genus of seven species of herbaceous perennials and evergreen subshrubs found in woodland in Eurasia and North Africa. Their leaves are ovate or elliptic or lance-shaped, simple and opposite. The flowers are star-shaped, five-petalled, and are borne singly in the leaf axils over a long period from spring to autumn.

✔ Long-flowering
✔ Evergreen
✔ Pest-free

✘ Invasive
✘ All parts poisonous

CULTIVATION
Grow in any soil in sun or part shade; they flower best in sun. Do not allow to dry out. Cut back hard in spring.

PROPAGATION
Divide between autumn and spring. Semi-ripe cuttings may be taken in summer.

Vinca major

Zone 7
Height: 18in. (45cm) Spread: indefinite

V

Vinca major
'Variegata' A.G.M.

Zone 7
Height: 18in. (45cm) Spread: indefinite

Vinca minor

Zone 4
Height: 8in. (20cm) Spread: indefinite

Vinca minor
'Aureovariegata'

Zone 4
Height: 8in. (20cm) Spread: indefinite

Vinca minor
'Illumination'

Zone 4
Height: 8in. (20cm) Spread: indefinite

VIOLA *(Violaceae)*

Common names: Pansy; Violet; Violetta

A genus of 500 species of annuals, biennials and perennials and a few subshrubs from various habitats in the temperate world. The perennials may be herbaceous, semi-evergreen or evergreen. Their leaves are very varied; they range from entire to finely pinnatisect, with stipules. The flowers are solitary, occasionally paired, and borne in the leaf axils. They are five-petalled, arranged two upper, two lateral and one spurred lower. Many flower over long periods in summer. Pansies are cultivars of *V. wittrockiana,* and are biennial or short-lived perennials; they are not included here. Violas (Va) are also known as tufted pansies, are perennial, and usually scented. Violettas(Vtta) are very compact, perennial, scented and each flower has a central yellow mark.

V

✔ Long-flowering	✘ Prone to slug damage
✔ Flowers perfumed	✘ Mildew prone
✔ Good cut flowers	✘ Self-seeds

CULTIVATION
Grow in moist, fertile, humus-rich, well-drained soil in sun or part shade. Dead-head to prevent self-seeding. Cut vigorous forms back hard after flowering to maintain compactness.

PROPAGATION
Seed should be sown in a cold frame as soon as it is ripe, or in spring. *VV. biflora* and *cornuta* can be divided in spring or autumn.

Viola biflora (Va)

Zone 4
Height: 3in. (8cm) Spread: 8in. (20cm)

Viola
'Buttercup' (Vtta)

Zone 7
Height and spread: 8in. (20cm)

Viola
'Columbine' (Va)

Zone 7
Height: 8in. (20cm) Spread: 1ft. (30cm)

Viola cornuta
A.G.M. (Va)

Zone 7
Height: 6in. (15cm) Spread: 8in. (20cm)

Viola cornuta
Alba Group (Va)

Zone 7
Height: 6in. (15cm) Spread: 8in. (20cm)

Viola
'Etain' (Va)

Zone 7
Height and spread: 1ft. (30cm)

Viola
'Janet' (Va)

Zone 7
Height: 8in. (20cm) Spread: 1ft. (30cm)

Viola
'Jackanapes' A.G.M. (Va)

Zone 7
Height: 8in. (20cm) Spread: 18in. (45cm)

Viola
'Jeanne Bellew' (Va)

Zone 7
Height: 8in. (20cm) Spread: 18in. (45cm)

V

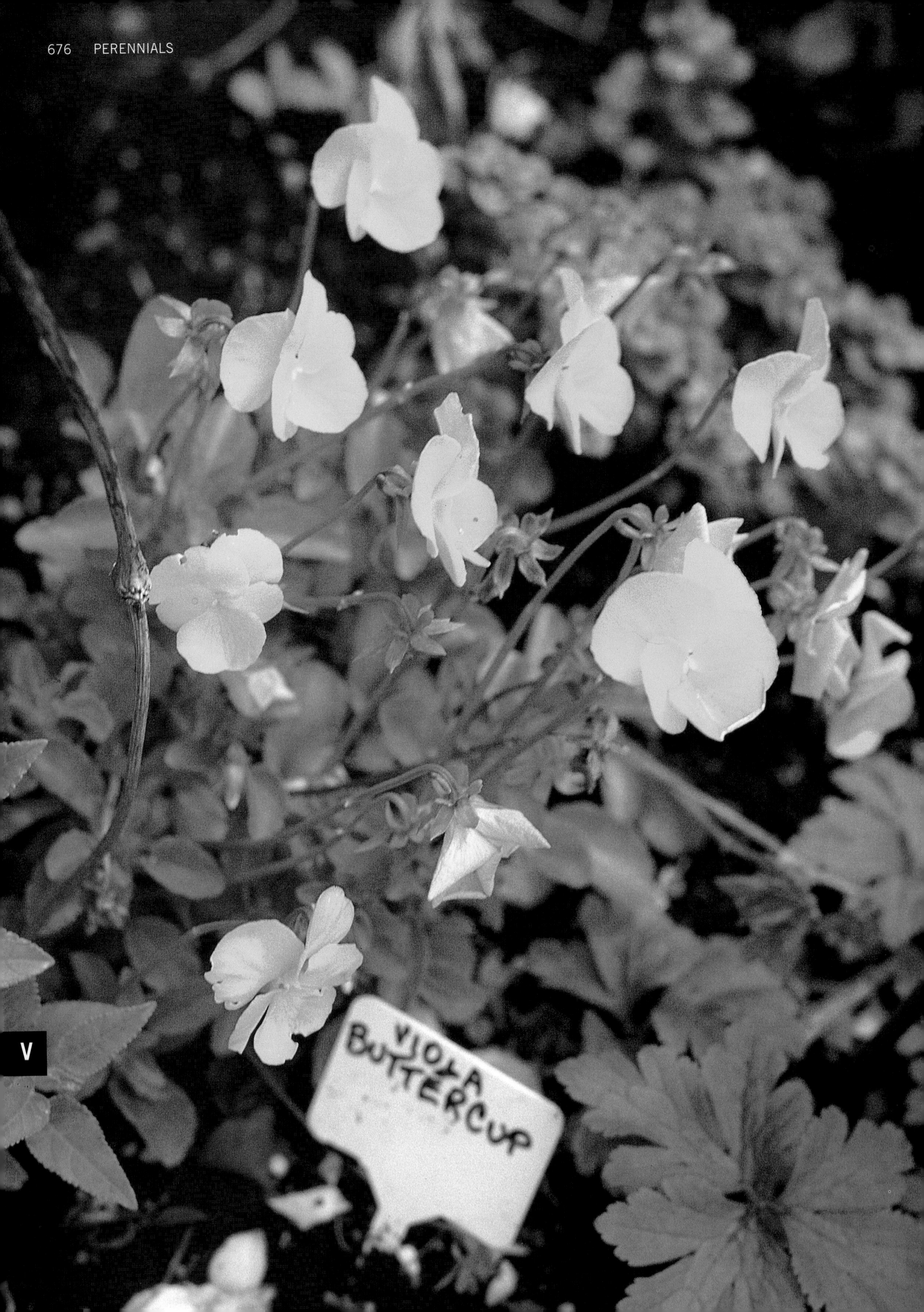
VIOLA
BUTTERCUP

Viola
'Maggie Mott' A.G.M. (Va)

Zone 7
Height and spread: 1ft. (30cm)

Viola odorata
(Va)

Zone 7
Height: 8in. (20cm) Spread: 1ft. (30cm)

Viola
'Rebecca' (Vtta)

Zone 7
Height: 6in. (15cm) Spread: 8in. (20cm)

Viola riviniana
'Ed's Variegated' (Va)

Zone 7
Height: 6in. (15cm) Spread: 8in. (20cm)

Viola sororia
'Freckles'

Zone 7
Height: 4in. (10cm) Spread: 8in. (20cm)

Viola
'Tony Venison' (Va)

Zone 7
Height: 4in. (10cm) Spread: 8in. (20cm)

Viola tricolor
(Va)

Zone 4
Height 5in. (12cm) Spread: 6in. (15cm)

Viola
'Victoria's Blush' (Va)

Zone 7
Height and spread: 1ft. (30cm)

Viola
'Zoe' (Vtta)

Zone 7
Height: 6in. (15cm) Spread: 8in. (20cm)

V

VRIESEA *(Bromeliaceae)*

Common names: None

A genus of 250 species of evergreen perennials from forests and rocky cliffs at altitude in Mexico, Central and South America, and the West Indies. They are epiphytic for the greater part, and form rosettes of linear-lance-shaped leaves, with smooth edges and often with cross-banding. The flowers are of varied shape, and are borne in two-ranked, spiky racemes or panicles from the rosette center in summer or autumn.

✔ Evergreen   ✗ Epiphytic
✔ Disease-free

CULTIVATION
Under glass, grow on a tree branch or bark or in standard bromeliad compost in moderate light. Keep the center of the rosette full of water during growth, but keep just moist in winter.

Out of doors, grow epiphytically as above in shade.

PROPAGATION
Seed should be sown at 75°F (24°C) when ripe. Separate offsets in spring.

Vriesea x poelmanii
'White Line'

Zone 10
Height: 18in. (45cm) Spread: 1ft. (30cm)

V

WACHENDORFIA
WATSONIA
WOODSIA
WOODWARDIA

W

WACHENDORFIA *(Haemodoraceae)*

Common names: None

A genus of 25 species of evergreen tuberous perennials from sloping grasslands in South Africa. Their basal leaves are linear, veined, pleated, erect, and deployed in two opposite rows. The flat flowers are star-shaped, six-tepalled, yellow, and borne in terminal panicles in early summer.

✔ Architectural plants   ✘ Prone to slug damage

✔ Good cut flowers

✔ Disease-free

CULTIVATION

Under glass, grow in a compost mix of equal parts loam, leaf mould and sharp sand in full light. Water freely during growth, and keep just moist in winter.

Out of doors, grow in reliably moist, fertile soil in sun.

PROPAGATION

Seed should be sown at 64°F (18°C) in autumn or spring. Divide tubers in spring.

Wachendorfia thyrsiflora

Zone 8
Height: 6ft. (2m) Spread: 18in. (45cm)

WATSONIA *(Iridaceae)*

Common names: None

A genus of 60 species of cormous perennials from plateaus and rocky slopes in South Africa and Madagascar. Their basal leaves are erect, and sword-shaped. The flowers are tubular, six-tepalled, have curved tubes and are held horizontally on tall spikes at various seasons.

✔ Good cut flowers   ✘ Need to be staked

✔ Drought-tolerant

✔ Disease-free

✔ Pest-free

CULTIVATION

Under glass, grow in a mix of equal parts loam, sharp sand and leaf mould in full light. Water freely during growth, and keep just moist in winter.

Out of doors, grow in well-drained, humus-rich soil in sun. In cold gardens, lift corms in autumn and store in a dry and frost-free plave over winter.

PROPAGATION

Seed should be sown at 64°F (18°C) in autumn. Separate corms in spring.

Watsonia borbonica

Zone 9
Height: 5ft. (1.5m) Spread: 4in. (10cm)

Watsonia borbonica
subsp. *borbonica*

Zone 9
Height: 5ft. (1.5m) Spread: 4in. (10cm)

Watsonia densiflora

Zone 9
Height: 5ft. (1.5m) Spread: 4in. (10cm)

W

Watsonia
Pink Hybrid

Zone 9
Height: 5ft. (1.5m) Spread: 4in. (10cm)

Watsonia marginata

Zone 9
Height: 6ft. (2m) Spread: 6in. (15cm)

WOODSIA *(Woodsiaceae)*
Common names: Holly-fern; Woodsia

A genus of 25 species of herbaceous, rhizomatous terrestrial ferns found in mountains and uplands of the northern hemisphere in particular. Their fronds are pinnate or bipinnate, with pinnatifid pinnae. The sporangia are in cup-shaped indusia.

- ✔ Handsome foliage
- ✔ Disease-free
- ✔ Pest-free

CULTIVATION
Grow in moist but sharply-draining soil in part shade. Surround rhizome with small stones.

PROPAGATION
Spores should be sown at 61°F (16°C) as soon as they are ripe. Divide during dormancy.

Woodsia polystichoides
A.G.M.

Zone 4
Height: 1ft. (30cm) Spread: 16in. (40cm)

WOODWARDIA *(Blechnaceae)*
Common names: Chain fern

A genus of ten species of terrestrial ferns from damp, sheltered parts or acid bogland of warm-temperate regions of North America and Eurasia. They may be herbaceous or evergreen. They are large plants with arching pinnate fronds, and pinnatifid pinnae. Bulbils may form on the frond tips or on their upper surface. The sori are deployed in a chain-like manner underneath the pinnae.

- ✔ Handsome foliage
- ✔ Disease-free
- ✔ Pest-free

CULTIVATION
Grow in damp, neutral soil in a sheltered corner in part shade.

PROPAGATION
Spores should be sown at 61°F (16°C) in late summer or early autumn. Division can be done in spring.

Woodwardia radicans A.G.M.

Zone 8
Height: 6ft. (2m) Spread: 10ft. (3.5m)
Evergreen

W

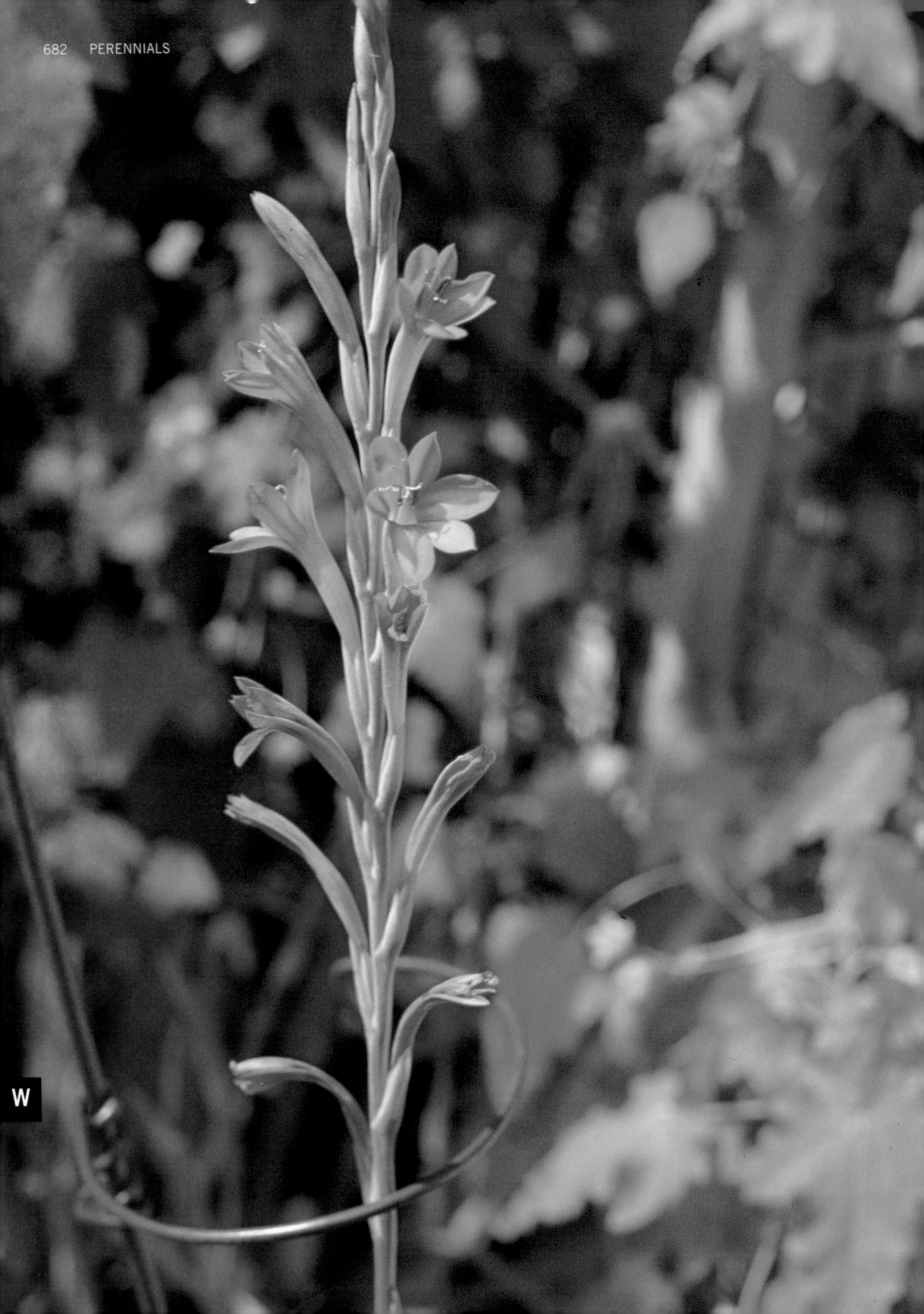

YUCCA

Y

YUCCA (Agavaceae)
Common names: Adam's needle

A genus of woody perennials, evergreen shrubs and erect trees found in deserts, sand dunes and hot dry plains of Central and North America and the West Indies. The perennials are rosette-forming. Their leaves are lance-shaped or linear. The flowers are hemispherical or bell-shaped, and are borne in erect or pendent racemes in mid- and late summer.

✔ Evergreen   ✘ Prone to aphid attack
✔ Good cut flowers
✔ Handsome foliage
✔ Handsome foliage

CULTIVATION
Under glass, grow in loam-based potting compost in full light. Water with moderation during growth, sparingly in winter.

Out of doors, grow in any well-drained soil in sun. Dead-head after flowering.

PROPAGATION
Seed of tender forms should be sown at 75°F (24°C), and of hardy types at 64°F (18°C) in spring. Root cuttings may be taken in winter.

Yucca baccata
(Blue yucca; Banana yucca)

Zone 9
Height: 5ft. (1.5m) Spread: 3ft. (90cm)

Yucca carnerosana

Zone 9
Height: 12ft. (4m) Spread: 6ft. (2m)

Yucca filamentosa
A.G.M.

Zone 7
Height: 30in. (75cm) Spread: 5ft. (1.5m)

Yucca filamentosa
'Bright Edge'

Zone 7
Height 30in. (75cm) Spread: 5ft. (1.5m)

Yucca filamentosa
'Colour Guard'

Zone 7
Height: 30in. (75cm) Spread: 5ft. (1.5m)

Yucca filamentosa
'Variegata'

Zone 7
Height: 30in. (75cm) Spread: 5ft. (1.5m)

Y

Yucca flaccida
'Golden Sword' A.G.M.

Zone 7
Height: 2ft. (60cm) Spread: 5ft. (1.5m)

Yucca flaccida
'Ivory' A.G.M.

Zone 7
Height: 2ft. (60cm) Spread: 5ft. (1.5m)

Yucca
'Garland's Gold'

Zone 7
Height: 2ft. (60cm) Spread: 4ft. (1.2m)

Yucca gloriosa
'Variegata' A.G.M.

Zone 7
Height and spread: 6ft. (2m)

Yucca rostrata

Zone 8
Height: 10ft. (3.5m) Spread: 6ft. (2m)

Yucca whipplei
(Our Lord's candle)

Zone 8
Height: 3ft. (90cm) Spread: 4ft. (1.2m)

ZALUZIANSKYA
ZANTEDESCHIA
ZAUSCHNERIA
ZEPHYRANTHES
ZIGADENUS

Z

ZALUZIANSKYA *(Scrophulariaceae)*

Common names: None

A genus of 35 species of annuals and short-lived, evergreen perennials from rocky slopes and grassland in southern Africa. Their leaves are varied in shape and size, toothed, sticky and opposite or alternate. The flowers are salverform or tubular, perfumed, and are borne in terminal spikes over a long period in summer.

- ✔ Evergreen
- ✔ Flowers perfumed
- ✔ Disease-free
- ✘ Short-lived

CULTIVATION
Under glass, grow in a mix of equal parts loam, leaf mould and grit. Water freely during growth but keep just moist in winter.

Out of doors, grow in moist, well-drained soil in sun. Shear over after flowering.

PROPAGATION
Seed, if available, should be sown at 55°F (13°C) as soon as it is ripe, or in spring. Stem-tip cuttings may be taken in summer.

Zaluzianskya ovata
ex Lesotho

Zone 9
Height: 25 cm.(10 in) Spread: 2ft. (60cm)

ZANTEDESCHIA *(Araceae)*

Common names: Arum lily; Calla lily

A genus of six species of perennials from moist areas, swampland, and lakesides in southern and East Africa. They have tuberous rhizomes. Their leaves are lance- or arrow- or heart-shaped. The flowers are spathes, which are brightly-colored and appear in late spring or early summer.

- ✔ Good cut flowers
- ✔ Handsome foliage
- ✔ Low allergen
- ✘ All parts poisonous
- ✘ Sap is skin irritant
- ✘ Highly allergenic
- ✘ Prone to aphid attack

CULTIVATION
Under glass, grow in loam-based potting compost in full light. Water freely during growth, but keep just moist in winter.

Out of doors, grow in moist, humus-rich soil in sun. *Z. aethiopica* can be grown as a marginal aquatic.

PROPAGATION
Seed should be sown at 81°F (27°C) when ripe. Divide rhizomes in spring.

Zantedeschia aethiopica
A.G.M. (Common calla)

Zone 8
Height: 3ft. (90cm) Spread: 2ft. (60cm)

Zantedeschia aethiopica
'Green Goddess' A.G.M.

Zone 8
Height: 3ft. (90cm) Spread: 2ft. (60cm)

Zantedeschia albomaculata
(Spotted calla)

Zone 9
Height: 16in. (40cm) Spread: 8in. (20cm)

Z

**Zantedeschia
'Black-eyed Beauty'**

Zone 9
Height: 16in. (40cm) Spread: 6in. (15cm)

**Zantedeschia elliottiana
A.G.M.**

Zone 9
Height: 3ft. (90cm) Spread: 10in. (25cm)

**Zantedeschia
'Florex Gold'**

Zone 9
Height: 22in. (55cm) Spread: 8in. (20cm)

**Zantedeschia
'Pot of Gold'**

Zone 9
Height: 2ft. (60cm) Spread: 1ft. (30cm)

**Zantedeschia rehmannii
A.G.M.**

Zone 9
Height: 16in. (40cm) Spread: 11in. (28cm)

ZAUSCHNERIA *(Onagraceae)*

Common names: Californian fuchsia

A genus of four species of subshrubs/perennials from dry slopes, and coastal sage and chaparral in western North America. They may be herbaceous or evergreen. The leaves are small, linear, ovate or lance-shaped, alternate or opposite, and stalkless. The flowers are funnel-shaped or tubular, and are borne in terminal racemes from late summer to autumn.

✔ Long-flowering
✔ Disease-free
✔ Drought-tolerant

✗ Prone to slug damage

CULTIVATION
Grow in well-drained, fertile soil in a sheltered corner in sun.

PROPAGATION
Seed should be sown in a cold frame in spring. Basal cuttings can be rooted with bottom heat in spring.

Z

Zauschneria californica
A.G.M.

Zone 8
Height and spread: 1ft. (30cm)

Zauschneria californica
subsp. *cana*

Zone 8
Height: 2ft. (60cm) Spread: 18in. (45cm)

ZEPHYRANTHES *(Amaryllidaceae)*
Common names: Rain flower; Windflower

A genus of 70 species of bulbous perennials found in grassland in both North and South America. They may be herbaceous or evergreen. Their leaves are basal and narrowly linear. The flowers are crocus-like, tubular or funnel-shaped, and are borne from spring to autumn.

✔ Long-flowering
✔ Disease-free
✔ Pest-free

CULTIVATION
Under glass, plant bulbs 4in. (10cm) deep in autumn in a mix of loam-based potting compost and sharp sand, in equal parts. Water freely during growth, keep just moist in winter.

Out of doors, grow in moist, well-drained soil in sun.

PROPAGATION
Seed should be sown at 64°F (18°C) as soon as it is ripe. Offsets may be separated in spring.

Zephyranthes candida

Zone 9
Height: 8in. (20cm) Spread: 3in. (8cm)

Zephyranthes flavissima

Zone 8
Height: 8in. (20cm) Spread: 3in. (8cm)

Z

ZIGADENUS *(Melianthiaceae)*

Common names: Death camas

A genus of 18 species of rhizomatous or bulbous perennials from open woodland and grassland in north-east Asia, Mexico and North America. Their basal leaves are linear, keeled or folded. The flowers are small, star-shaped, six-tepalled, and are borne in upright panicles or racemes in summer.

✔ Good cut flowers

✔ Disease-free

✔ Pest-free

✘ All parts poisonous

CULTIVATION
Grow in moist, well-drained fertile soil in sun or part shade.

PROPAGATION
Seed should be sown at 64°F (18°C) when ripe, or in spring. Division can be carried out in spring or autumn.

Zigadenus elegans

Zone 3
Height: 28in. (70cm) Spread: 8in. (20cm)

Z

GLOSSARY

FLOWERS

Spike

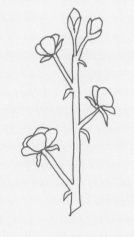

Spike

Helicoid cyme

Scorpoid cyme

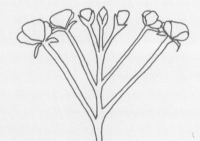

Corymb

Umbel

Cyme

LEAVES

Parrallel veined

Linear

Net veined

Oblong

Elliptical

Ovate

Obovate

Rhomboidal

Cordate

Palmate   Palmate compound

Lanceolate

A

A.G.M. – Award of Garden Merit, indicates that the plant has been under trial at its Wisley garden by the Royal Horticultural Society for garden worthiness, and has been decreed to be outstanding.

alternate leaf – leaves arranged alternately up the stem.

anemoniform – flower similar to an anemone

annual – a plant that flowers and dies in one season.

arrow-shaped leaf – a leaf with a pointed apex and two pointed lower lobes.

B

basal – forming or belonging to the bottom layer or base.

basal rosette – leaves arranged around the base of the stem, to form a rosette.

biennial – a plant that flowers and dies in its second year.

bipinnate leaf – a compound leaf made up of several pinnate units.

blade – expanded area on either side of the midrib of a leaf.

bracts – specialized leaves that are often brightly-colored and resemble a flower.

bulb – swollen underground stem, in which energy is stored to help survive the winter.

C

calyx – the set of sepals on the base of the flower that protect the flower bud.

carpel – the female reproductive organ of a flower.

compound leaf – leaf composed of several separate leaflets arising from the same petiole.

compound palmate leaf – leaf composed of several leaflets to create a palmate shape.

compound pinnate leaf – leaf composed of several leaflets to create a pinnate shape.

cordate leaf – a heart-shaped leaf, broadly ovate but with a pointed apex and the base turning in to form a notch for the petiole.

corm – a swollen underground stem, in which energy is stored to help survive the winter.

corymb – a cluster of florets in which the stalks are arranged at random along the peduncle, but the florets are at one level creating a flat, round top.

cyme – a cluster of florets in which the inner or top florets open first, blooming downwards along the peduncle.

D

dicotyledon – flowering plant in which the seedling has two leaflets.

dioecious – species in which the stamens and pistils are on separate plants, so plants of both sexes are required before fruit can form.

disc florets – a small, tubular floret, that combines with many others in a disc shape in a composite flower such as a tansy.

Oblanceolate

Spatulate

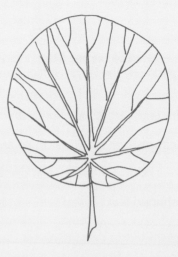

Orbicular

Opposite

Alternate

Pinnate

Whorled

Compound pinnate

Bipinnate

E

elliptical leaf – a leaf two or three times longer than wide, and tapering to an acute or rounded base.

entire leaf – leaf with smooth edges.

epiphyte – a plant that grows on another plant.

evergreen – a plant that retains its leaves all year round.

F

fibrous-rooted – root system made up of main roots branching off into smaller rootlets.

floret – small flower making up a composite flower head.

H

helicoid cyme – a cluster of florets, which are all on one side of the peduncle.

herbaceous – a plant that loses its leaves or dies back in the autumn.

hermaphroditic – a plant having stamens and pistils in the same flower.

I

indusium – a thin membranous covering.

inflorescence – a cluster of flowers on a floral stem.

involucre – a whorl or rosette of bracts surrounding an inflorescence or at the base of an umbel.

K

keel – a prow-shaped pair of petals.

L

lanceolate leaf – a leaf longer than wide, tapering towards the apex and rounded at the base.

lance-shaped leaf – a long, pointed leaf, slightly wider at the base but tapering sharply.

linear leaf – a narrow leaf, several times longer than wide and approximately the same width down its length.

M

monocarpic – a plant that dies after flowering.

monocotyledon – flowering plant in which the seedling has one leaflet.

monoecious – plants that have male and female flowers on one plant.

N

net-veined leaf – leaf in which the veins branch from the main midrib(s) and then subdivide into smaller veinlets.

O

oblanceolate leaf – a leaf longer than wide, tapering towards the apex and base.

oblong leaf – a leaf that is longer than it is wide, with a roughly even width along most of its length and rounded at both base and apex.

Basal rosette

Tripalmate

Arrow-shaped

Lanced-shaped

Entire

Serrated

Lobed

Toothed

obvate leaf – an egg-shaped leaf, wide at the apex and tapering towards the base.

opposite leaf – leaves arrange opposite each other along the stem.

orbicular leaf – a rounded, circular leaf.

ovate leaf – an egg-shaped leaf, wide at the base and tapering towards the apex.

P

palmate leaf – leaf with five or more lobes whose midribs all radiate from one point.

panicle – a loose, branching cluster of flowers.

parallel-veined leaf – leaf in which the veins run essentially parallel to each other, connected by minute, straight veinlets.

PBR – Plant Breeders' Rights, indicates a cultivar that has been patented by the raisers, and propagation for resale cannot be carried out without the permission of the breeder.

peduncle – an elongated flower stem.

pendent – hanging down.

perennials – a plant that lives and flowers for three or more years.

perfect flower – a flower that contains functional stamens and pistils.

petals – the highly colored portions of a flower.

petiole – stalk that supports the leaf blade.

pinna – primary division of a pinnate leaf, especially a fern (plural pinnae).

pinnate leaf – compound leaf with pairs of leaflets arranged alternately on either side of the stem.

pinnatifid – divided pinnately, but not all the way to the central axis.

pseudoumbels – looking like umbels.

R

raceme – flower cluster with separate flowers attached by short, equal stalks at equal distances along a central stem.

ray florets – a strap-shaped floret, that combines with many others in a ray formation in a composite flower such as a dandelion.

remontant – plant that will flower a second time if dead-headed.

reniform – kidney-shaped.

rhizomes – swollen underground stem, in which energy is stored to help survive the winter.

rhomboidal leaf – a leaf in a rhomboid shape, wide in the center and tapering sharply at apex and base.

S

scandent – having a climbing habit.

scorpioid cyme – a cluster of florets, which are alternate to each other along the peduncle.

semi-evergreen – a plant that retains a few leaves over the winter.

sepals – small, green, leaf-like structures on the base of the flower that protect the flower bud.

sessile – attached directly by its base, without a stalk or peduncle.

simple leaf – leaf in which the blade is a single continuous unit.

solitary flower – a single flower on a stem.

sorus – spore-producing receptacle on the underside of a fern frond (plural sori).

spadix – a spike of minute fowers closely arranged round a fleshy axis, and typically enclosed in a spathe.

spathe – large sheathing bract enclosing the flower cluster.

spatulate leaf – a rounded leaf, tapering towards the base.

spike – flower cluster with separate sessile flowers, at equal distances along a central stem.

sporangium – receptacle in which asexual spores are formed (plural sporangia).

spore – a reproductive cell.

spur – a slender, tubular projection from the base of a flower.

stipule – a small, leaf-like appendage to a leaf, typically in pairs at the base of the leaf stalk.

stolon – a creeping horizontal plant stem or runner, that takes root along its length to form new plants.

T

tepal – a segment of the outer whorl of a flower that has no difference between petals and sepals.

terrestrial – on the ground.

toothed – notched edges.

tripalmate leaf – leaf formed of three leaflets in a palmate shape.

tuber – swollen underground stem, in which energy is stored to help survive the winter.

twining – twisting around.

U

umbel – a cluster of florets in which the stalks arise from one point, but the florets are at one level creating a flat, round top.

W

whorled leaf – leaves arranged in circles along the stem.

APPENDICES A – POSITIVE ATTRIBUTES

1) Trouble-free perennials

Acaena	Celmisia	Grindelia	Perovskia
Acorus	Centranthus	Haberlea	Petasites
Actaea	Cephalaria	Hakenochloa	Phormium
Adiantum	Chamaemelum	Happlopappus	Phuopsis
Albuca	Chelidonum	Haworthia	Pilosella
Alopecurus	Chlorophytum	Hedychium	Plectranthus
Alpinia	Chrtsogonum	Hedysarum	Pleioblastus
Ampelopsis	Cimicifuga	Helianthemum	Polypodium
Amsonia	Claytonia	X Heucherella	Pontederia
Anagallis	Cymbopogon	Holcus	Potentilla
Ananas	Cypella	Homeria	Protea
Anaphalis	Cyrtanthus	Hordeum	Pterocephalus
Anemonopsis	Dactyorhiza	Hyacinthus	Ratibida
Anomatheca	Darmera	Imperata	Romulea
Antennaria	Davallia	Isatis	Roscoea
Arenaria	Deschampsia	Juncus	Ruellia
Arisarum	Desmodium	Lachenalia	Russelia
Aristea	Dianella	Ledebouria	Sandersonia
Armeria	Dicksonia	Leptinella	Sanguinaria
Arundo	Dierama	Leycesteria	Santolina
Asarina	Dietes	Libertia	Sauromatum
Asclepias	Dionaea	Lithodora	Scabiosa
Aspidistra	Diplaarhena	Lophospermum	Schizostylis
Asplenium	Dracunculus	Lysichiton	Scopolia
Astelia	Dryas	Malvastrum	Selaginella
Athyrium	Dryopteris	Mandevilla	Silphium
Azolla	Echinacea	Marrubium	Smilacina
Ballota	Elscholzia	Matteuccia	Sparaxis
Baptisia	Erinus	Melianthus	Stenotaphrum
Belamcanda	Eriogonum	Melica	Stokesia
Bellis	Erodium	Mellitis	Succisa
Bidens	Eucharis	Milium	Symphytum
Blechnum	Euryops	Miscanthus	Thymus
Boykinia	Felicia	Mitchella	Tolmeia
Brimeura	Festuca	Moraea	Trachelospermum
Buglossoides	Fittonia	Myrrhis	Trifolium
Bulbine	Francoa	Nectaroscordum	Triteleia
Bulbinella	Galium	Nymphoides	Tritonia
Buphthalmum	Galtonia	OlsyniumOnoclea	Uncinia
Bupleurum	Gaura	Ophiopogon	Valeriana
Caladium	Gazania	Ornithogalum	Watsonia
Calamagrostis	Glaucium	Osmunda	Woodsia
Callirhoe	Glottiphyllum	Pallenis	Woodwardia
Callisia	Glyceria	Partehocissus	Zephyranthes
Camassia	Glycyrrhiza	Peltoboykinia	Zigadenus
Catharanthus	Goniolimon	Pentaglottis	
Cedronella	Graptopetalum	Peperomia	

2)   Long-flowering perennials

Acanthus	Cerastium	Lilonium	Rehmannia
Achillea	Chrysogonum	Linum	Rhodanthemum
Achimenes	Cyrtanthus	Lithodora	Rhodochiton
Aechmea	Dactylis	Lophospermum	Rhodohypoxis
Aeonium	Dahlia	Lythrum	Romneya
Alcea	Diascia	Malva	Rudbeckia
Alchemilla	Eccremocarpus	Malvastrum	Russelia
Aloe	Episcia	Matthiola	Saintpaulia
Alstroemeria	Eriophyllum	Mertensia	Salvia
Althaea	Erodium	Mimulus	Schizostylis
Ananas	Erysimum	Mirabilis	Solanum
Anchusa	Eucomis	Molinia	Solenopsis
Anemone x hybrida	Felicia	Monarda	Sphaeralcea
Anemone multifida	Fuchsia	Nemesia	Stipa
Angelonia	Gaillardia	Nepeta	Streptocarpus
Anisodontea capensis	Gazania	Nerine	Stylophorum
Anthemis	Gerbera	Nicotiana	Succisa
Anthurium	Geum	Nierembergia	Sutera
Arctotis	Gillenia	Oenothera	Symphyandra
Argyranthemum	Gloriosa	Origanum	Taraxacum
Asarina procumbens	Glotiphyllum	Orostachys	Telekia
Aster x frikartii 'Monch'	Guzmania	Osteospermum	Teucrium
Astilbe	Gypsophila	Ourisia	Tiarella
Astrantia	Helianthemum	Pallenis	Tropaeolum
Begonia grandis	Helianthus	Pelargonium	Tuberaria
Begonia semperflorens	X Heuchella	Penstemon	Tulbaghia
Belamcanda chinensis	Hylomecon	Pentas	Tweedia
Bellis	Impatiens	Pericallis	Verbascum
Bidens	Ipomoea	Persicaria	Verbena
Borago pygmaea	Juncus	Petrorhagia	Veronica
Buphthalmum salicifolium	Kalanchoe	Petunia	Veronicasrtum
Calamintha	Lachenalia	Phuopsis	Viguiera
Calceolaria	Lampranthus	Phygelius	Viola
Catananche	Lavatera	Polygala	Zauschneria
Celosia	Leucanthemum	Potentilla	Zephyranthes
Centurium	Lewisia	Pratia	
Centranthus	Leymus	Ratibida	

3) Repeat-flowering perennials

Anchusa	Echinacea	Haworthia	Scabiosa
Astrantia	Epilobium	Isoplexis	Sidalcea
Brunnera	Erigeron	Leontodon	Strelitzia
Campanula lactiflora	Erinus	Lobularia	Tanacetum
Campanula takesimana	Fragaria	Lupinus	Tigridia
Coreopsis	Gaura	Lychnis	Tradescantia
Chaerophyllum	Gunnera	Omphalodes	

4) Evergreen perennials

Acaena	Callisia	Helleborus	Podranea
Aeonium	Campanula porschkiana	Heloniopsis	Polygala
Aeschynanthus	Carex morrowi	X Heucherella	Polystichium
Aethionema	Carex oshimensis	Hoya	Portulacaria
Agave	Carex testacea	Iberis	Pratia
Aglaonema	Catharanthus	Isoplexis	Protea
Aichryson	Celmisia	Jovibarba	Ramonda
Ajuga	Cerastium	Lampranthus	Raoulia
Alonsoa	Chiastophllum	Lavandula	Reineckea
Anchusa	Chirita	Ledebouria	Rhipsalidopsis
Angelonia	Chrysogonum	Libertia	Rosularia
Anigosanthos	Clivia	Liriope	Ruellia
Anisodontea	Cobaea	Lithodora	Russelia
Arenaria	Cymbopogon	Luzula	Ruta
Argyranthemum	Deschampsia	Matteuccia	Saintpaulia
Aristaea	Dianella	Melianthus	Salvia (some)
Artemisia	Dianthus	Mitchella	Sansevieria
Arundo	Dicksonia	Monstera	Santolina
Asarina	Dierama	Morina	Sarracenia
Asarum	Dietes	Myosotidium	Schumbergera
Asclepias	Diplarrhena	Neoregelia	Sedum (some)
Asparagus	Elymus	Nephrolepsis	Selaginella
Aspidistra	Epidendrum	Opiopogon	Sempervivum
Asplenium	Epigaea	Orostachys	Sesleria
Astelia	Epipremnum	Ourisia	Stenotaphrum
Atilbe glaberrima	Farfugium	Pandorea	Stokesia
Aubrieta	Felicia	Parahebe	Strelitzia
Aurinia	Festuca	Passiflora	Thunbergia
Ballota	Francoa	Pelargonium	Thymus
Bellis	Gazania	Pentas	Uncinia
Bergenia	Geum	Phalaris	Vinca
Billbergia	Hrindelia	Phormium	Vreisea
Blechnum	Haberlea	Plantago	Yucca
Calandrinia	Haworthia	Platycerium	Zaluzianskya
Calanthe	Helianthemum	Plectranthus	
Calceolaria	Helictotrichon	Pleioblastus	

5)   Drought-tolerant perennials

Acanthus	Echium	Lewisia	Rehmannia
Achillea	Edaraianthus	Limonium	Rhodanthemum
Agapanthus	Elscholzia	Linaria	Rhodiola
Agastache	Eremurus	Linum	Rosularia
Agave	Erigeron	Liripe	Ruta
Allium	Eriophyllum	Lotus	Santolina
Alyssum	Erodium	Lychnis	Scabiosa
Anemone nemorosa	Erysimum	Malvastrum	Sedum
Anisodontea capensis	Felicia	Marrubium	Sempervivum
Anomatheca	Fritillaria	Megacarpaea	Serratula
Anthericum	Gaillardia	Megacarpaea	Silene
Aristaea	Galanthus	Melianthus	Sisyrinchium
Artemisia	Gaura	Nepeta	Sphaeralcea
Arthropodium	Geranium	Nerine	Stachys
Asarina	Gladiolus	Oenothera	Teucrium
Asphodeline	Glaucium	Onosma	Thalictrum
Asphodelus	Grindelia	Orthrosanthus	Tiarella
Ballota	Gypsophila	Ostrowskia	Trachelium
Begonia grandis	Hedysarum	Othonna	Tritonia
Borago pygmaea	Helianthemum	Oxalis	Tulbaghia
Buglossoides	Hieracium	Pallenis	Umbilicus
Bulbine	Hordeum	Papaver	Urospermum
Bupleurum	Hyacinthus	Paraquilegia	Verbascum
Camassia	Hypericum	Pentas	Verbena
Catananche	Ipheion	Perovskia	Watsonia
Cedronella	Isoplexis	Phlomis	Zauschneria
Centranthus	Jasione	Physalis	
Claytonia	Jovibarba	Phyteuma	
Cynara	Knautia	Pilosella	
Dianthus	Lathrus	Plantago	
Dictamnus	Lavandula	Polystichium	
Dietes	Lavatera	Prunella	
Digitalis	Leonotis	Pulsatilla	
Dracunculus	Leptinella	Puschkinia	
Echinops	Leucanthemum	Ratibida	

6) Perennials for cut flowers

Acanthus	Chrysanthemum	Helenium	Osteospermum
Achillea	Cirsium	Helianthus	Paeonia
Aconitum	Clematis	Helichrysum	Papaver
Ajania	Codonopsis	Heliopsis	Paradisea
Agapanthus	Cynara	Helleborus	Persicaria
Alcea	Dahlia	Heuchera	Phlomis
Allium	Delphinium	X Heucherella	Phygelius
Alonsoa	Dianthus	Hieracium	Physostegia
Amaryllis	Dicentra	Hosta	Platycodon
Anaphalis	Dictamnus	Incarvillea	Pleione
Anchusa	Dierama	Inula	Polygonatum
Anemone x hybrida	Digitalis	Kirengeshoma	Pulsatilla
Anthericum	Disporum	Knautia	Ratibida
Anthurium	Dodecatheon	Kniphofia	Rudbeckia
Aquilegia	Doronicum	Lavatera	Sanguisorba
Arisaema	Dracunculus	Leontodon	Scilla
Artemisia	Echinacea	Leucanthemum	Scutellaria
Aruncus	Echinops	Leucojum	Senecio
Asclepias	Elscholzia	Liatris	Sidalcea
Asphodelus	Eremurus	Lilium	Silphium
Aster	Erigeron	Limonium	Smilacina
Astilbe	Eucomis	Linaria	Solidago
Astrantia	Foeniculum	Liriope	X Solidaster
Baptisia	Francoa	Lobelia	Stachys
Belamcanda	Gaillardia	Lunaria	Stokesia
Bergenia	Galanthus	Lupinus	Strelitzia
Bletilla	Galega	Lychnis	Tanacetum
Brunnera	Gazania	Lysimachia	Thalictrum
Buphthalmum	Gentiana	Lythrum	Thermopsis
Bupleurum	Gerbera	Macleaya	Trachelium
Calanthe	Geum	Mertensia	Tricyrtis
Caltha	Gillenia	Monarda	TritoniaTrollius
Camassia	Gladiolus	Morina	Tulipa
Campanula	Goniolimon	Muscari	Tweedia
Canna	Grindelia	Muosotidium	Uvularia
Catananche	Grindelia	Myosotis	Veratrum
Celosia	Gypsophila	Myrrhis	Veronicastrum
Centranthus	Haplopappus	Narcissus	Wachendorfia
Cephalaria	Haworthia	Nemesia	Watsonia
Chaerophyllum	Hedychium	Nerine	Yucca
Chelone	Hedysarum	Ornithogalum	Zigadenus

7) Low-allergen perennials

Acanthus	Cardasmine	Iris	Polemonium
Aegopodiun	Clematis	Kirengeshoma	Potentilla
Agapanthus	Dicentra	Kniphofia	Prunella
Ajuga	Dierama	Lamium	Pulmonaria
Alcea	Digitalis	Lavatera	Rosularia
Alchemilla	Dryas	Liriope	Salvia
Allium	Epilobium	Lysimachia	Saxifraga
Alyssum	Epimedium	Lythrum	Scabiosa
Anchusa	Eremurus	Macleaya	Schizostylis
Anemone x hybrida	Galtonia	Mertensia	Scrophularia
Aquilegia	Gentiana	Mimulus	Sidalcea
Armeria	Geranium	Monarda	Sisyrinchium
Aruncus	Geum	Omphalodes	Symphytum
Asphodeline	Gladiolus	Papaver	Tellima
Astilbe	Helianthemum	Passiflora	Tiarella
Astrantia	Hemerocallis	Penstemon	Tradescantia
Baptisia	Heuchera	Petunia	Trollius
Bergenia	X Heucherella	Phlox	Valeriana
Brunnera	Hosta	Phormium	Veronica
Camassia	Hyssopus	Physostegia	
Canpanula	Iberis	Platycodon	

8) Perennials which attract butterflies

Agastache	Calamintha	Eryngium	Mentha
Ajania	Centaurea	Eupatorium	Nepeta
Ajuga	Centranthus	Helenium	Phlox paniculata
Alcea	Cephalaria	Hesperis	Saponaria
Alyssum	Chrysanthemum	Hyssopus	ScabiosaSedum
Arabis	Coreopsis	Iberis	Solidago
Aster	Dahlia	Knautia	X Solidaster
Astrantia	Echinacea	Lavandula	Stachys
Aubrieta	Echinops	Lunaria	Thymus
Aurinia	Erigeron	Melissa	

9) Perennials which attract bees

Allium	Epilobium	Inula	Potentilla
Alstroemeria	Eranthis	Isatis	Prunella
Althaea	Erigeron	Knautia	Pulmonaria
Asclepias	Eryngium	Kniphofia	Rudbeckia
Anchusa	Eupatorium	Lavandula	Salvia
Anemone	Fuchsia	Liatris	Scabiosa
Asclepias	Galanthus	Ligularia	Sedum
Astrantia	Galega	Lilium	Senecio
Calamintha	Galium	Linum	Sidalcea
Camassia	Galtonia	Lupinus	Silene
Campanula	Geum	Lythrum	Stachys
Centaurea	Gypsophila	Malva	Symphytum
Clematis	Hedysarum	Melissa	Thermopsis
Colchicum	Helenium	Mentha	Thymus
Coreopsis	Helianthus	Monarda	Trifolium
Cosmos	Heliopsis	Nepeta	Verbascum
Dahlia	Heuchera	Oenothera	Veronica
Doronicum	Hyacinthus	Origanum	
Echinacea	Hyssopus	Petasites	
Echinops	Iberis	Polemonium	

10) Perennials with perfumed flowers

Alpinia	Diplarrhena	Hosta 'Sweet Susan'	Mitchella
Amaryllis	Erinus	Hyacinthoides	Narcissus
Arabis	Erysimum	Hyacinthus orientalis	Pandorea
Asphodeline	Eucharis	Hymenocallis	Paradisea
Begonia grandis	Filipendula	Ipheion	Phuopsis
Butomus	Galanthus	Lavandula	Reineckea
Cardiocrinum	Galium	Lilium monadelphum	Sansevieria
Clematis heracleifolia	Galtonia candicans	Lilium pumilum	Saururus
Convallaria majalis	Hedysarum	Lilium regale	Smilacina
Cosmos atrosanguineus	Helleboru odorus	Lilium speciosum	Spiranthes
Crambe	Hesperis	Lobularia	Tolmeia
Crinum x powellii	Homeria	Lunaria	Tulbaghia (some)
Dianthus	Hosta 'Honeybells'	Matthiola	Viola
Dictamnus	Hosta plantaginea'	Mirabilis	Zaluzianskya

11) Perennials with aromatic foliage

Achillea filipendula	Chrysanthemum	Lavandula	Pelargonium
Achillea millefolium	Cymbopogon	Leontopodium	Perovskia
Alyssum	Dictamnus albus	Leptinella	Ruta
Anthemis	Elscholzia stauntonii	Melissa	Salvia (some)
Artemisia	Filipendula ulmaria	Melittis	Telekia
Ballota pseudodictamnus	Foeniculumvulgare	Monarda	Teucrium
Calamintha	Geranium incanum	Myrrhis	Thymus
Cedronella canariensis	Helichrysum italicum	Nectaroscordum	Tulbaghia
Chaerophyllum hirsutum	Houttuynia cordata	Nepeta	Valeriana
Chamaemelum nobile	Hyssopus officinalis	Origanum	

12) Perennials which have berries after flowering

Arisaema (some)	Convallaria majalis	Fuchsia	Pachyphragma
Arisaema	Cornus	Iris foetidissima	Phytolacca
Ampelopsis	Dianella	Liriope	Podophyllum
Anthurium	Diphylleia	Maianthemum	Polygonatum
Arum italicum	Disporum	Mitchella	Reineckea
Clintonia umbellata	Dracunculus vulgaris	Myrrhis	Ridgersia
Coriaria	Fragaria	Ophiopogon	Smilacina

13) Perennials with attractive seed-heads

Acaena	Arisaema	Dierama	Iris (some)
Acanthus	Artemisia	Diplarrhena	Lathyrus vernus
Achillea	Asphodeline	Echinops	Levisticum
Aconitum	Asphodelus	Eremurus	Libertia
Agapanthus	Astilbe	Eryngium	Linaria
Alchemilla	Baptisia	Eupatorium	Morina
Allium	Belamcanda	Euphorbia (some)	Physalis
Alopecurus	Cardiocrinum	Galtonia	Pterocephalus
Alsroemeria	Catananche	Gillenia	Pulsatilla
Althaea	Centaurea	Glaucium	Rheum
Anaphalis	Cimicifuga simplex	Gypsophila	Rumex
Anthericum	Clematis (some)	Hyacinthoides	Styloporum
Anemone x hybrida	Crambe maritima	Incarvillea	Trachelospermum

APPENDICES B – NEGATIVE ATTRIBUTES

14) Perennials which self-seed

Acanthus (some)	Camapanula persicifolia	Lamium	Pimpinella
Achillea millefolium	Chelidonum	Leontodon	Polemonium
Alcea	Cicerbita	Linaria	Polygonatum
Alchemilla	Cirsium	Lunaria	Prunella
Alisma	Cynara	Lychnis	Pulmonaria
Allium christohii	Digitalis	Lythrum	Rumex
Angelica	Echinops	Malva	Sagittaria
Anthericum	Echium	Marrubium	Silene
Anthriscus	Epilobium	Melissa	Solidago
Antirrhinum	Erodium	Mertensia	Stylophorum
Aquilegia	Foeniculum	Milium	Symphyandra
Asphodeline	Galega	Mimulus	Taraxacum
Asphodelus	Galtonia	Mitella	Telekia
Asplenium	Glaucium	Muscari	Tellima
Astrantia	Hesperis	Myosotis	Thalictrum
Begonia grandis	Hieracium	Nectaroscordum	Trifolium
Bellis	Holcus	Oenothera	Umbilcus
Borago	Hyacinthoides	Papaver	Urospermum
Brunnera	Imperata	Parahebe	Valeriana
Bupleurum	Isatis	Pentaglottis	Verbascum
Campanula lactiflora	Juncus	Phytolaca	Verbena
Campanula latifolia	Kohleria	Pilosella	Viola

15) Highly allergenic perennials

Achillea	Cortaderia	Helictotrichon	Primula
Aconitum	Cymbopogon	Holcus	Ranunculus
Alstroemeria	Dactylis	Hordeum	Ratibida
Anaphalis	Deschampsia	Juncus	Rudbeckia
Anemone nemorosa	Dianthus	Lavandula	Rumex
Angelica	Dictamnus	Leontodon	Santolina
Arctotis	Echinacea	Leucanthemella	Senecio
Argyranthemum	Echinops	Leucanthemum	Sesleria
Armoracia	Elymus	Leymus	Silphium
Arnica	Erysimum	Ligularia	Solidago
Artemisia	Euphorbia	Lilium	X Solidaster
Arum	Festuca	Luzula	Stenotaphrum
Aster	Foeniculum	Melica	Stipa
Caltha	Gaillardia	Milium	Sokesia
Carex	Gazania	Miscanthus	Telekia
Catananche	Gerbera	Molinia	Uncinia
Centaurea	Glyceria	Osteospermum	Urospermum
Chamaemelum	Hakonechloa	Phalaris	Veratrum
Chelidonum	Helenium	Pilosella	Vigueira
Coreopsis	Helianthus	Plantago	Zantedeschia

16) Poisonous perennials (All parts are poisonous unless specified)

Aconitum
Actaea (berries)
Adonis
Alocasia
Amaryllis
Anemone blanda
Anemone nemorosa
Anemone ranunculoides
Anemone rivularis
Aquilegia
Arisaema
Arnica
Arum
Astrantia
Caladium
Calla
Catharanthus
Chaerophyllum hirsutum
Chelidonum

Chrysanthemum
Colchicum
Cyclamen persicum
Convallaria majalis
Coriaria terminalis (seeds)
Crinum x powellii
Delphinium
Dendranthema weyrichii
Dendranthema yesoense
Dianthus
Dicentra
Dictamnus
Dieffenbachia
Diigitalis
Echium
Epipremnum
Eranthis
Euphorbia
Galanthus

Gloriosa
Helenium
Helianthus
Helleborus
Hyacinthoides
Hyacinthus
Ipomoea (seeds)
Iris
Lathyrus (seeds)
Lupinus (seeds)
Mandevilla
Monstera (not fruits)
Nerine
Ornithogalum
Paeonia
Paris (seeds)
Parthenocissus (berries)
Persicaria (sap)
Physalis (except berries)

Phytolacca
Podophyllum
Polygonatum
Pulsatilla
Rheum (foliage)
Ricius
Rumex
Ruta (foliage)
Scopolia
Sedum
Senecio
Solanum
Symphytum (leaves and roots)
Tulipa
Veratrum
Vinca
Zantedeschia
Zigadenus

17) Perennials which are skin-irritant

Aconitum
Allium (bulbs)
Alocasia
Amsonia
Anemone
Aquilegia
Arisaema
Armoracia
Arum
Asclepias
Caladium
Calla
Chelidonum
Cichorium
Clematis

Cypripedium parviflorum
Delphinium
Dendranthema
Dicentra
Dictamnus
Dieffenbachia
Digitalis
Echium
Epipremnum
Eranthis
Euphorbia
Galanthus
Gloriosa
Helenium
Helianthus

Helleborus
Hyacinthoides
Hyacinthus
Iris
Lobelia
Mandevilla
Monstera (fruits)
Narcissus (sap)
Nicotiana
Onosma (foliage)
Ornithogalum
Pelargonium
Persicaria (sap)
Physalis (foliage)
Phytolacca (sap)

Primula (foliage)
Pulsatilla (sap)
Ranunculus (sap)
Ricinus (foliage)
Rumex (foliage)
Ruta (foliage)
Sedum (sap)
Tanacetum (foliage)
Tradescantia (foliage)
Tulipa (foliage)
Veratrum (foliage)
Zantedeschia (sap)

18) Invasive perennials

Acanthus hungaricus
Acanthus mollis
Acanthus spinosus
Achilles ptarmica
Aegopodium podagraria
Ajania pacifica
Arisarum proboscideum
Arum italicum
Aruncus dioicus
Asclepias syriaca
Athyrium nipponicum
Azolla filiculoides
Bacopa monieri
Blechnum chilense
Buglossoides
   purpureocaerulea
Campanula persicifolia
Campanula glomerata

Campanula pulla
Campanula rotundifolia
Cardamine pentaphyllos
Cardamine pratensis
Cardiocrinum giganteum
Cerastium tomentosum
Ceratostigma plumbaginoides
Chamaemelum nbile
Cimicifuga
Circaea lutetiana
Convallaria majalis
Cornus canadensis
Cryptanthus bromeliodides
Davallia mariesii
Dicentra 'Pearl Drops'
Eomecon chionanthum
Epilobium
Fittonia verschaffeltii

Fragaria
Galega
Galium
Glyceria
Houttuynia cordata
Hylomecon japonicum
Juncus effusus
Leonotis
Leymus
Lilium bulbiferum
Macleaya
Maianthemum
Malvastrum
Myriophyllum
Nectaroscordum
Nephrolepsis
Passiflora
Petasites

Phalaris
Phygelius
Physalis
Physostegia
Polypodium vulgare
Pratia
Prunella
Ricinus
Romneya
Sasa
Sauromatum
Stenotaphrum
Symphytum ibericum
Telekia
Tolmeia
Vinca

19) Short-lived perennials

Achillea ptarmica
Aethionema
Agastache
Alcea
Anagallis
Anchusa
Anthirrinum
Anthemis tinctoria
Anthemis sanci-johannes
Aquilegia
Arabis
Asarina procumbens
Baptisia australis
Belamcanda chinensis
Bupleurum falcatum
Borago pygmaea
Calandrinia

Calamintha nepeta
Campanula barbata
Campanula 'Burghaltii'
Campanula pulla
Campanula pyramidalis
Carlina acaulis
Catananche caerulea
Centaurium
Claytonia nivalis
Convolvulus tricolor
Coreopsis
Crepis
Cynoglossum nervosum
Dianthus
Diascia
Dicentra spectabilis
Dictamnus albus

Edraianthus
Erigeron
Erinus
Erysimum
Gaillardia
Gaura
Hedysarum
Hesperis
Iresine
Isatis
Lavatera
Leontopodium
Leucanthemopsis
Linum
Lobelia
Lobularia
Lotus

Lupinus
Malva
Matthiola
Meconopsis
Megacarpaea
Mimulus
Myosotis
Nicotiana Oenothera
Orthrosanthus
Rehmannia
Silene
Solenostemon
Symphyandra
Tanacetum
Urospermum
Verbascum

20) Perennials which need to be lifted and divided regularly

Achillea	Camassia	Erigeron	Muscari
Aconitum	Campanula persicifolia	Galanthus	Narcissus
Acorus	Campanula pulla	Geum	Ornithogalum
Aster amellus	Coreopsis	Helenium	Pulmonaria
Aster thomsonii	Crocosmia	Heliopsis	Schizostylis
Astilbe	Crocus	Hemerocallis	Sisyrinchium
Bergenia	Doronicum	Heuchera	
Butomus	Dracunculus	Liatris	

21) Perennials which resent transplantation

Acanthus	Chaerophyllum	Foeniculum	Miscanthus
Aciphylla	Cichorium	Gentiana	Oenothera (some)
Aconitum	Claytonia	Gerbera	Paeonia
Adenophora	Clivia	Glaucidium	Papaver
Adonis	Convolvulus tricolor	Glaucium	Pentaglottis
Agapanthus	Crambe	Glycyrrhiza	Pimpinella
Alstromeria	Crepis	Haberlea	Platycodon
Anemone x hybrida	Cynara	Hacquetia	Romneya
Angelica	Dictamnus	Hedysarum	Pulsatilla
Aristea	Dierama	Hepatica	Selinum
Arctotis	Dietes	Hesperis	Sternbergia
Asclepias	Echinops	Invarvillea	Stylophorum
Baptisia	Echeveria	Isatis	Taraxacum
Brunsvigia	Echium	Leontopodium	Thalictrum
Callirhoe	Eriogonum	Limonium	Thermopsis
Campanula lactiflora	Eryngium	Linum	Trillium
Catananche	Euphorbia	Lupinus	Tropaeolum
Centranthus	Farfugium	Megacarpaea	
Cephalaria	Ferula	Mertensia	

APPENDIX C – PERENNIALS FOR SPECIAL SITUATIONS

22) Perennials for acid soils

Adonis	Cornus canadensis	Hacquetia	Sarracenia
Agave	Cryptanthus	X Heucherella	Scoliopus
Anemonopsis macrophylla	Cypripedium	Hylomecon	Selaginella
Arisaema	Deschampsia	Kirengeshoma	Semiaquilegia
Asarum	Dianella	Lilium (some)	Sidalcea
Blechnum	Dicksonia	Liriope	Sinningia
Bulbinella	Dionaea	Lupinus	Smilacina
Caladium	Diplarrhena	Matteuccia	Stokesia
Calceolaria	Dodecatheon	Nemesia	Succisa
Celmisia	Epigaea	Onoclea	Trillim
Cicerbita	Erythronium	Orchis	Tropaelum speciosum
Clintonia	Gentiana asclepiadea	Osmunda	
	Haberlea	Protea	

23) Perennials for shade

Actaea	Bergenia	Davallia	Maianthemum
Adiantum	Bilbergia	Dicentra	Matteuccia
Adonis	Blechnum	Dicksonia	Melica
Aegopodium	Borago pygmaea	Digitalis	Mellitis
Aeonium	Boykinia	Diphtlleia	Mertensia
Alchemilla	Brunnera	Disporum	Mitchella
Alocasia	Calanthe	Doronicum	Mitella
Alpinia	Callisia	Drtopteris	Monstera
Anemone x hybrida	Campanula latifolia	Eomecon	Mukdenia
Anemone nemorosa	Cardamine	Epimedium	Myosotidium
Anemonella	Cardiocrinum	Epipactis	Myrrhis
Anemonopsis	Carex	Eucharis	Neoregelia
Angelica	Cautleya	Eupatorium	Nephrolepis
Anthurium	Ctenanthe	Euphorbia (some)	Olsynium
Arisaema	Chaerophyllum	Gentiana asclepiadea	Omphalodes
Arisarum	Chelidonum	Geranium (some)	Onoclea
Arum italicum	Chrysogonum	Guzmania	Oprys
Aruncus	Cicerbita	Haberlea	Orchis
Asarina	Cimicifuga	Heloniopsis	Osmunda
Asarum	Clintonia	Helleborus	Ourisia
Asparagus	Codonopsis	Heuchera	Pachyphragma
Aspidistra	Convallaria	X Heucherella	Paris
Asplenium	Cortusa	Hosta	Patrinia
Aster microphyllus	Corydalis	Hyacinthoides	Peltoboykinia
Astilbe	Cyclamen	Hylomecon	Pentaglottis
Athyrium	Cypripedium	Iris foetidissima	Peperomia
Begonia grandis	Dactylorhiza	Kohleria	Petasits

Peucedanum	Podophyllum	Pulmonaria	Selaginella
Pilea	Poltstichium	Rhipsalidopsis	Tiarella
Platycerium	Pratia	Rohdea	Trillium
Plectranthus	Pteris	Roscoea	Woodsia

24) Perennials for the bog garden or pond margin

Acorus	Chelone	Hemerocallis	Kirengeshoma
Alisma	Cimicifuga simplex	Hosta	Lysichiton
Aruncus dioicus	Cotula	Houttuynia	Mimulus luteus
Astilbe	Darmera	Inula magnifica	Parnassia
Bacopa	Eupatorium	Iris ensata	Pontederia
Butomus	Filipendula	Iris 'Holden Clough'	Sagittaria
Calamagrostis	Fritillaria meleagris	Iris laevigata	Schoenoplectus
Caltha	Geum rivale	Iris pseudacorus	Scrophularia
Cardamine	Glyceria	Iris laevigata	Senecio (some)
Cardiocrinum	Gunnera	Iris sibirica	

25) Aquatic perennials

Azolla	Houttuynia	Myriophyllum	Utricularia
Caltha	Juncus spiralis	Nymphaea	
Carex	Myosotis scorpiodes	Nymphoides	

26) Perennials for ground cover

Acaena	Astilbe	Dianthus	X Heucherella
Acanthus	Aubrieta	Dicentra	Hosta
Achillea	Ballota	Dryopteris	Houttuynia
Adiantum	Bergenia	Eomecon	Hypericum
Aegopodium	Blechnum	Epimedium	Iberis
Ajuga	Brunnera	Erigeron glaucus	Lamium
Alchemilla	Buphthalmum	Eriogonum umbellatum	Limonium
Alyssum	Calamintha	Eriophyllum lanatum	Maianthemum
Anaphalis	Campanula carpatica	Erodium carviflorum	Mazus
Anemone x hybrida	Campanula latiloba	Euphorbia polychroma	Mitchella
Antennaria	Centaurea	Filipendula	Patrinia
Anthericum	Cerastium	Fragaria	Peltoboykinia
Arabis	Chiastophyllum	Geranium	Pentaglottis
Arenaria	Claytonia sibirica	Geum	Petasites
Arisarum	Convallaria	Gypsophila	Phlaris
Armeria	Corydalis	Helianthemum	Pratia
Artemisia	Crambe	Helleborus	Tiarella
Aruncus	Cyclamen	Hemerocallis	
Aster microphyllus	Darmera	Heuchera	

27) Architectural perennials

Acanthus	Cynara cardunculus	Kniphofia	Myrrhis
Aciphylla	Darmera peltata	Leonotis	Rheum
Aeonium	Dierama	Levisicum	Rodgersia
Amicia	Echinops	Leycesteria	Romneya
Angelica archangelica	Echium	Leymus	Selinum
Calamagrostis	Eremurus	Ligularia	Silphium
Cephalaria	Eupatorium	Lilium (some)	Stipa
Chusquea	Ferula	Lupinus arboreus	Telekia
Cortaderia	Hedychium	Macleaya	Veronicastrum
Crambe	Helianthus	Megacarpaea	Wachendorfia
Crassula	Heliopsis	Melianthus	Yucca
Culeou	Inula magnifica	Miscanthus	

28) Perennials for dry gardens – see Appendix A

29) Perennials for seaside gardens

Achillea	Dianthus	Libertia	Physostegia
Acanthus	Dierama	Limonium	Potentilla
Alsroemeria	Echinacea	Linaria	Pulsatilla
Amaryllis	Echinops	Lupinus	Romneya coulteri
Anaphalis	Erigeron	Lychnis	Salvia
Anchusa	Erodium	Melissa	Scabiosa
Anemone	Eryngium	Mertensia	Schizostylis
Anthemis	Euphorbia	Mimulus	Scrophularia
Anthericum	Fascicularia	Morina	Sedum
Armeria	Filipendula	Myosotidium	Senecio
Artemisia	Geranium	Nerine	Sisyrinchium
Bergenia	Gypsophila	Oenothera	Stachys
Catananche	Heuchera	Origanum	Stokesia
Centaurea	Hieracium	Osteospermum	Tritoma
Centranthus	Iris	Penstemon	Veronica
Crambe	Kniphofia	Perovskia	Viscaria
Crocosmia	Lathyrus	Phormium	Yuca
Cynoglossum	Lavatera	Phygelius	Zantedeschia

30) Deer-resistant perennials

Acanthus	Crocosmia	Leucanthemum x superbum	Pulmonaria
Aconitum	Delphinium	Leucujum	Romneya
Agapanthus	Dicentra	Liriope	Rudbeckia
Agave	Digitalis	LupinusLychnis coronaria	Salvia
Allium	Epimedium	Melianthus	Satueja
Amaryllis	Euphorbia	Melissa	Scabiosa
Aquilegia	Festuca glauca	Mellittis	Sisyrinchium
Artemisia	Filipendula	Mentha	Tellima
Arum	Gaillardia	Mirabilis	Thalictrum
Astilba	Gerenium	Myosotis	Tiarella
Campanula	Helianthus	Narcissus	Trillium
Carex	Helichrysum	Nepeta	Veratrum
Centaurea	Helleborus	Origanum	Vinca
Ceratostigma	Hosta	Paeonia	Yucca
Clematis	Iris	Papaver	
Cortaderia	Kniphofia	Polygonatum	
Crinum	Lavandula	Potentilla	

31) Rabbit-resistant perennials

Acanthua	Cyclamen	Kniphofia	Pulmonaria
Aconitum	Cynara	Lamium	Rheum
Agapanthus	DahliaDelphinium	Lavatera	Romneya
Alchemilla	Digitalis	Leuojum	Rosmarinus
Anaphalis	Doronicum	Liriope	Ruta
Anemone	EpimediumEranthis	Lupinus	Saxigraga geum
Aquilegia	Eupatorium	Luzula	Saxifraga x umbrosa
Aster	Euphorbia	Lysimachia	Sedum
Astilbe	Fuchsia	Malva	Stachys olympica
Bergenia	Galanthus	Melissa	Tellima
Brunnera	Gentiana asclepiadea	Miscanthus	Tradescantia
Campanual lactiflora	Geranium	Narcissus	Trillium
Campanula latifolia	Hedychium	Nepeta	Trollius
Cardiocrinum	Helenium	Omphalodes	Tulipa
Clematis	Helianthus	Orchis	Verbena
Colchicum	Helleborus	Paeonia	Vinca
Convallaria	Hemerocallis	Papaver	Yucca
Cortaderia	Hosta	Phormium	Zantedeschia
Corydalis	Houttuynia	Phytolacca	
Crinum	Iris	Polygonatum	
Crocosmia	Kirengeshoma	Polygonum	

BIBLIOGRAPHY

GENERAL REFERENCE

Award of Garden Merit Plants. The Royal Horticultural Society, London 2003

Ajilvsgi, G. *Wildflowers of Texas.* Shearer Publishing, Bryan, 1984

Barr, C.A. *Jewels of the Plains, Grasslands and Hills.* University of Minnesota Press, Minneapolis, 1983

Beckett, K.A. *The A-Z of Garden Plants.* Orbis Publishing, London, 1985

Bell, C.R. and Taylor, B.J. *Florida Wild Flowers and Roadside Plants.* Laurel Hill Press, Chapel Hill, 1982

Bird, R. *The Cultivation of Hardy Perennials.* B.T.Batsford, London, 1994

Bird, R. *Woodland Gardening.* Souvenir Press, London, 1992

Blundell. M. Collins *Guide to the Wild Flowers of East Africa.* Collins, London, 1987

Bramwell, D and Bramwell Z. *Wild flowers of the Canary Islands.* Stanley Thornes, London, 1974

Brickell , C. Editor-in-chief. *The Royal Horticultural Society Gardeners' Encyclopaedia of Plants and Flowers.* Dorling Kindersley, London, 1997

Brickell , C. Editor-in-chief *The Royal Horticultural Society A-Z Encyclopaedia of Garden Plants and Flowers* Dorling Kindersley, London, 1997

Brown, C.A. *Wildflowers of Louisiana and Adjoining States* Louisiana State University Press, Baton Rouge, 1972

Chapman, P., Davidson, W. and Martin, M. *An Illustrated Guide to Popular Houseplants.* Salamander Books Ltd, London, 1987

Chatto, B. *The Dry Garden.* J.M. Dent, London, 1978

Clark, L.J. *Wild flowers of the Pacific Northwest.* Gray's Publishing Ltd, Sidney B.C., 1976

Cooke I. *The Plantfinder's Guide to Tender Perennials.* David & Charles, Newton Abbot, 1998

Craigmyle, M.B.L. *The Illustrated Encyclopaedia of Perennials.* Salamander Books Ltd, London, 1999

Craigmyle, M.B.L. *Long-flowering Garden Plants.* Salamander Books Ltd, London, 2001

Craigmyle ,M.B.L. *Popular Flowering Plants.* Chartwell Books Inc, New Jersey, 2003

Da Costa, A. and de O. Franquinho, L. *Madeira; Plants and Flowers.* Ribeiro and Filhos, Madeira, 1999

Duncan, W.H. and Foote, L.E. *Wildflowers of the Southeastern.* United States University of Georgia Press, Athens, 1975

Evans, A. *The Peat Garden and its Plants.* J.M. Dent, London, 1974

Franquinho, L.O. and Da Costa, A. *Madeira; Plants and Flowers.* Ribeiro and Filhas, Funchal, 1998

Frohne, D. and Pfander, H.J. *A Colour Atlas of Poisonous Plants.* Wolfe Publishing, London, 1983

Gabrielson, I.N. *Western American Alpines.* Theophrastus, Sakonnet, 1932

Genders, R. *The Scented Flora of the World.* Robert Hale, London,1994

Grey-Wilson, C. and Mathew, B. *Bulbs; The Bulbous Plants of Europe and their Allies.* Collins, London, 1981

Griffith, A.N. *Collins Guide to Alpines and Rock Garden Plants.* Collins, London, 1964

Griffiths, M. *Index of Garden Plants: Derived from The Royal Horticultural Society New Dictionary of Gardening.* Macmillan Press, London, 1994

Grimshaw, J. *The Gardener's Atlas: The origin, discovery and cultivation of the world's most popular flowering plants.* Little, Brown and Co, London, 2001

Grounds, R. *The Plantfinder's Guide to Ornamental Grasses.* David & Charles, Newton Abbot, 1998

Hessayon, D.G. *The House Plant Expert.* Transworld Publishers Ltd, London, 1998

Heywood, V.H. Consultant Editor. *Flowering Plants of the World.* Oxford University Press, Oxford, 1978

Howes, E.N. *Plants and Beekeeping.* Faber & Faber, London, 1979

Huntingdon, L. *Creating a Low-allergy Garden.* Mitchell Beasley, London, 1998

Huxley, A. and Taylor, W. *Flowers of Greece and the Aegean.* Chatto & Windus, London, 1977

Ingwersen, W. *Manual of Alpine Plants.* Will Ingwersen & Dunnsprint, East Grinstead, 1978

Jellito, L., Schacht, W. and Fessler, A. *Hardy Herbaceous Perennials* (two volumes). Timber Press, Portland, Oregon, U.S.A.

Jones, D. *Encyclopaedia of Ferns.* Thomas C. Lothian, Port Melbourne, 1987

Justice, W.S. and Bell, C.R. *Wild Flowers of North*

Carolina and Neighboring States. University of North Carolina Press, Chapel Hill, 1968

Kidd, M.M. *South African Wild Flower Guide, 3 Cape Peninsula.* Botanical Society of South Africa, Cape Town, 4th Edition, 1996

Kohlein, F. and Menzel, P. *The Encyclopaedia of Plants for Garden Situations.* B.T.Batsford, London, 1994

Lord, T. Principal Editor. *The R.H.S. Plant-finder 2003-2004.* Dorling Kindersley, London, 2003

Mathew, B. and Baytop, T. *The Bulbous Plants of Turkey.* B.T. Batsford in association with the Alpine Garden Society, London, 1984

Mathew, B. *The Larger Bulbs.* B.T. Batsford in association with the Royal Horticultural Society, London, 1978

Mathew, B. Growing Bulbs: *The Complete Practical Guide.* B.T. Batsford, London, 1997.

Mathew, B. and Swindells, P. *The Gardener's Guide to Bulbs.* Mitchell Beasley, London, 1994

Mierow, D. and Shrestha, T.B. *Himalayan Flowers and Trees.* Sahayogi Press, Kathmand, 1987

Molyneux, B. and Forrester, S. *The Austraflora A-Z of Australian Plants.* Reed New Holland, Sydney, 2002

Niehaus, T.F. *Sierra Wildflowers: California Natural History Guide 32.* University of California Press, Berkeley, 1974

Onderstall, J. *South African Wild Flower Guide 4. Transvaal Lowland and Escarpment, including the Kruger National Park* Botanical Society of South Africa, Cape Town, 1984

Parker, H. Editor. *Perennials: A Royal Horticultural Society Plant Guide.* Dorling Kindersley, London, 1996

Philipson, W.R. and Hearn, D. *Rock Garden Plants of the Southern Alps.* New Zealand The Caxton Press, Christchurch, 1967

Phillips, R. and Rix, M. Editor: Matthew, B. *Bulbs.* Pan Books, London, 1989

Phillips, R. and Rix, M. *Climbers for Walls and Arbours.* Pan Books, London, 1998

Phillips, R. and Rix, M. *Conservatory and Indoor Plants & Plants for Warm Gardens (two volumes).* Pan Books, London, 1998

Phillips, R. and Rix, M. *Perennials Early-flowering & Perennials Late-flowering (two volumes).* Pan Books, London, 1991

Phillips, R. and Rix, M. *Plants for Shade.* Pan Books, London, 1998

Polunin, O. *Flowers of Greece and the Balkans: A Field Guide.* Oxford University Press, Oxford, 1980

Polunin, O. *Plants and Flowers of Malaysia.* Times Editions Pte Ltd, Singapore, 1988

Polunin, O. *Plants and Flowers of Singapore.* Times Editions Pte Ltd, Singapore, 1987

Polunin. O. and Huxley, A. *Flowers of the Mediterranean.* Chatto & Windus, London, 1970

Polunin, O. and Smythies, B.E. *Flowers of South-west Europe: A Field Guide.* Oxford University Press, Oxford, 1973

Reader's Digest New Encyclopaedia of Garden Plants and Flowers. The Readers Digest Association, London, 2001

Redgrove, H. Editor. *An Illustrated Handbook of Bulbs and Perennials.* Cassell, London, 1991

Rickett, H.W. *Wild Flowers of the United States Vol. 2: The South-Eastern States.* McGraw-Hill, New York, 1967

Richards, B.W. and Kaneko, A. *Japanese Plants.* Shufunomoto Co Ltd, Tokyo, 1988

Rodgers, B.R. *The Dried Flower Encyclopaedia.* Simon & Shuster, London, 1988

Robinson, P. *Drought-resistant Gardening: A Royal Horticultural Society Practical Guide.* Dorling Kindersley, London, 1999

Royal Horticultural Society Plant Guide: Perennials. Dorling Kindersley, London, 1996

Royal Horticultural Society Plant Guide: Shrubs and Climbers. Dorling Kindersley, London, 1996

Sajeva, M. and Costanzo, M. *Succulents II: The New Illustrated Dictionary.* Timber Press, Portland Oregon, 2002

Segall, B. Consultant. *Botanica: The illustrated A-Z of over 10, 000 garden plants, and how to grow them.* Mynah, N.S.W. Australia, 1997

Stary, F. and Berger, Z. *Poisonous Plants.* Magna Books, Leicester, 1995

Thomas, G.S. *Perennial Garden Plants, or the modern florilegium.* J.M.Dent, London, 1990

Thomas, G.S. *Plants for Ground Cover.* J.M.Dent, London, 1990

Trehane, P. et al. *International Code of Nomenclature for Cultivated Plants.* Quarterjack Publishing, Wimborne , 1995

Vance, F.R., Jowsey, J.R. and Mclean, J.S. *Wildflowers across the Prairies Western.* Producer Prairie Books, Saskatoon, 1977

Vance, F.R., Jowsey, J.R. and Mc Lean, J.S. *Wildflowers of the Northern Great Plains.* University of Minnesota Press, Minneapolis, 1984

Walters et al. *The European Garden Flora* (five volumes). Cambridge University Press, Cambridge, 1984-1988

Ward, G.B., and Ward, O.M. *Colorful Desert Wildflowers of California and Arizona Living Desert Association.* Palm Desert, No date

Williams, J.G. and Williams A.E. *Field Guide to the Orchids of North America.* Universe Books, New York, 1983

Winegar, D. Desert *Wildflowers: Drylands of North America.* Beautiful America Publishing Company, Beaverton, 1982

SPECIFIC GROUPINGS

Anderson, E, and Park, R. *Growing Gladioli.* Christopher Helm, London, 1989

Barker, D.G. *Epimediums and other Herbaceous Berberidaceae.* The Hardy Plant Society, 1996

Bartlett, M. *Gentians.* Blandford Press, 1975

Bath, T. and Jones, J. *The Gardener's Guide to Growing Hardy Geraniums.* David & Charles, Newton Abbot, 1994

Bell, M. *The Gardener's Guide to Growing Temperate Bamboos.* David & Charles, Newton Abbot, 2000

Bird, R. *Border Pinks.* The Crowood Press, Marlborough, 1997

Bird, R. Lilies: *An illustrated identifier and guide to cultivation.* Apple Press, London, 1997

Blanchard, J.W. *Narcissus: A guide to Wild Daffodils.* The Alpine Garden Society, Pershore, 1990

Bond, S. *Hostas.* Ward Lock, London, 1994

Case, F.W. and Case, R.B. *Trilliums.* Timber Press, Portland, 1997

Clark, D. *The Hardy Fuchsia Guide.* Oakleigh Publications, Monkswood, 1992

Cooke, I. *The Gardener's Guide to Growing Cannas.* David & Charles, Newton Abbot, 2001

Cobb, J.L.S. *Meconopsis.* Christopher Helm, London, 1989

Cohen V.A. *A Guide to the Pacific Coast Irises.* British Iris Society, 1967

Cooper, A. *Penstemons.* Power Publications, Ferndown, 1996

Cribb, P. and Bailes, C. *Hardy Orchids.* Christopher Helm, London, 1989

Crook, H.C. *Campanulas and Bellflowers in Cultivation.* Blandford Press, London, 1959

Davies, D. *Alliums: The Ornamental Onions.* B.T.Batsford, London, 1992

Erhardt, W. *Hemerocallis: Day Lilies.* B.T.Batsford, London, 1992

Fuller, R. Pansies, *Violas and Violettas: The Complete Guide.* The Crowood Press, Marlborough, 1990

Goldblatt, P. *The Genus Watsonia.* National Botanic Gardens, South Africa, 1989

Green, R. *Asiatic Primulas: A Gardener's Guide.* Alpine Garden Society, Pershore, 1976

Grenfell, D. *The Gardener's Guide to Growing Daylilies.* David & Charles, Newton Abbot, 1998

Grenfell, D. *The Gardener's Guide to Growing Hostas.* David & Charles, Newton Abbot, 1996

Grey-Wilson, C. *Poppies: The Poppy family in the wild and cultivation.* B.T.Batsford, London, 1993

Harmer, J. and Elliott, J. *Phlox.* The Hardy Plant Society, Pershore, 2001

Hewitt, J. *Pulmonarias.* The Hardy Plant Society, Pershore, 1994

Ingwersen, W. *The Dianthus.* Collins, London, 1949

Ingram, T. *Umbellifers.* The Hardy Plant Society, Pershore, 1993

Innes, M. *The World of Iridaceae-A Comprehensive Record.* Holly Gate International Ltd, Ashington, 1985

Jacobs, D.L. and Jacobs, R.L. *Trilliums in Woodland and Garden: American Treasures Ecogardens.* Decatur, Georgia, 1997

Jefferson-Brown M. and Howland, H *The Gardener's Guide to Growing Lilies.* David & Charles, Newton Abbot, 1995

Jones, J. et al. *Hardy Geraniums.* The Hardy Plant Society, Pershore, 1993

Kellaway, D. *Clematis and the Ranunculaceae: A family of flowers.* Pavilion Books Ltd, London, 1994

Key, H. *Pelargoniums.* Cassell in association with The Royal Horticultural Society, London, 1993

Kohlein, F. *Iris.* Christopher Helm, London, 1981

Kohlein, F. *Saxifrages and Related Genera.* B.T.Batsford, London, 1984

Lewis, P. *Campanulas in the Garden.* The Hardy Plant Society, Pershore, 2002

Lewis, P. and Lynch, M. *Campanulas.* Christopher Helm, London, 1989

Liden, M. and Zetterlund, H. *Corydalis.* Alpine Garden Society, Pershore, 1997

Linnegar, S. and Hewitt, *J. Irises: A Wisley Handbook.* Cassell, London, 1990

Lloyd, C. *Clematis.* Collins, London, 1980

Mann-Taylor, J. *Phlomis.* N.C.C.P.G., Wisley, 1998

Mathew, B. *The Iris.* B.T.Batsford, London, 1981

Page, M. *The Gardener's Guide to Growing Peonies.* David & Charles, Newton Abbot, 1997

Picton, P. *The Gardener's Guide to Growing Asters.* David & Charles, Newton Abbot, 1999

Pradhan, U.C. *Himalayan Cobra Lilies: Their Botany and Culture.* Primulàceae Books, Darjeeling, 1990

Pratt, K. and Jefferson-Brown, M. *The Gardener's Guide to Growing Fritillaries.* David & Charles, Newton Abbot, 1997

Reed, D. Editor. *Lilies and Related Plants: Fritillaria Number.* The Royal Horticultural Society Lily Group, 1988-9

Rice, G. and Strangman, E. *The Gardener's Guide to Growing Hellebores*. David & Charles, Newton Abbot, 1994

Robinson, M. Primulas: *The Complete Guide.* The Crowood Press, Marlborough, 1996

Stebbings, G. *The Gardener's Guide to Growing Irises.* David & Charles, Newton Abbot, 1997.

Stocks, A. *Some Herbaceous Members of the Saxifragaceae Family.* The Hardy Plant Society, Pershore, 1995

Sutton, J. *The Gardener's Guide to Growing Salvias.* David & Charles, Newton Abbot, 1999

Swindells, P. A *Plantsman's Guide to Primulas.* Ward Lock, London, 1989

Taylor, J.M. *Phlomis: The Neglected Genus*. N.C.C.P.G., Wisley, 1998

Turner, R. *Euphorbias: A Gardener's Guide.* B.T.Batsford, London, 1995

Wall, B. *Begonias: A Wisley Handbook.* Cassell, London, 1988

Way, D. *Penstemons.* The Hardy Plant Society, Pershore, 1996

Way, D. and James, P. *The Gardener's Guide to Growing Penstemons.* David & Charles, Newton Abbot, 1998

Wendelbo, P. and Mathew, B. *Iridaceae in: Flora des Iranischen hochlands und der umrahmenden gebirge.* Academische Druck-u, Graz, 1975

White, S. *Origanum.* N.C.C.P.G., Wisley, 1998

Witton, D. *Euphorbias.* The Hardy Plant Society, Pershore, 2000

Yeo, C. *Salvias* (two parts). Pleasant View Nursery, Newton Abbot, 1995 & 1997

Yeo, P.F. *Hardy Geraniums*. Croom Helm, London & Sydney, 1983

INDEX

INDEX OF LATIN NAMES

INDEX OF COMMON NAMES